The Politics Of American Economic Policy Making

Second Edition

The Politics Of American Economic Policy Making

Second Edition

Edited by

Paul Peretz

M.E. Sharpe
Armonk, New York
London, England

Library of Congress Cataloging-in-Publication Data

The politics of American economic policy making / edited by Paul Peretz. — 2nd ed.
p.   cm.
Includes bibliographical references.
ISBN 1-56324-566-3 (alk. paper). — ISBN 1-56324-567-1 (pbk.)
1. Finance, Public—United States.
2. Industrial policy—United States.
3. Fiscal policy—United States.
4. United States—Economic policy.
5. United States—Politics and government.
HJ257.P59   1996
338.973—dc20
95-41956
CIP

Printed in the United States of America

The paper used in this publication meets the minimum requirements of
American National Standard for Information Sciences—
Permanence of Paper for Printed Library Materials,
ANSI Z 39.48-1984.

BM (c)   10   9   8   7   6   5   4   3   2   1
BM (p)   10   9   8   7   6   5   4   3   2   1

Contents

Introduction

The Importance of Economic Policy

Anyone who has turned on the evening news cannot help but be struck by the degree to which foreign affairs and foreign policy, economic conditions and economic policy, dominate national reporting. In a way, it is easy to understand why foreign affairs should receive such extensive coverage. Whether we go to war or not is obviously a matter of concern to every citizen, and the possibility of nuclear war means that what happens in remote flashpoints may affect all of us.

By contrast, what is reported about our own economy—about indexes and indicators, rising rates, falling rates, seasonal fluctuations, the size of the money supply, and the value of the dollar—is often obscure, even for reasonably well-informed viewers. Yet, economic policy has unmistakable direct and indirect impacts on our daily lives. The single most important effect is on employment. Psychologists say that becoming unemployed is one of life's major traumas, on a par with divorce or severe illness. In good times, such as 1989, when unemployment is low, over six million people are unemployed in the United States. In bad times, such as 1992, the number rises to over nine million.

National economic policy plays a critical role in determining the levels of employment and unemployment. It also helps determine food and clothing prices, salaries and wages, mortgage and tax rates; it affects the safety of the goods we buy and the cost of a hospital stay. In the long run, it determines the prosperity of the United States in comparison with other countries, and the standard of living of the average citizen.

Economic policy has a myriad of indirect effects as well. It helps determine the amounts available to be spent (if we so decide) on public goods. It is the arena in which we decide what resources to allocate to national defense, medical research, crime control, pensions for the elderly, and the cleanup of toxic waste dumps. Regulation of the economy helps determine all sorts of things, from

1

whether we have local train service and pollution-free air and water, to whether minorities are hired in the construction industry.

During the 1980s and 1990s the United States has seen an increased level of economic policy activism on the part of the federal government, sparked by low growth, stagnant wages, and high unemployment. There has been extensive deregulation in some industries, accompanied by increasing regulation in others. There have been three major tax bills and four lesser ones. There have been two major revisions of Social Security financing, together with several minor ones. There have been large increases in defense spending followed by steady decreases. There have been cuts in domestic programs, followed by increases, with new decreases on the horizon. Power over the health of the economy has increasingly shifted from elected officials to the unelected Federal Reserve, which has tried to maintain a tight monetary policy. These policies have brought reduced inflation, increased long-term unemployment, slightly below-average growth, a huge trade deficit, and large federal deficits.

The Purpose of This Book

The recent intensity of economic policy activity, together with the somewhat lackluster economic performance that has accompanied it, has greatly increased interest among economists and political scientists in the relationship between government and the economy. The essays collected in this volume are some of the best efforts to explore this question. In making the selections, my intention was to cover most of the central areas of concern and to maintain a balance between older, classic pieces and newer articles that represent the latest research in each area. My focus is on the major competing theories in each area and the better articles that have tried to test those theories. I have tried to find pieces that outline the author's major theory but are accessible to readers without an extensive background in economics. Nonetheless the readings are not always easy. I have therefore written introductions to each section and each article to give those new to this area some help. I have also written brief summary articles at the end of each of the three empirical sections, to update the reader on recent activity in each area and to show how the readings relate to these current events.

I have divided the readings into four major sections, dealing with broad theories, government regulation of the private sector, economic policy formation, and effects of economic policies on economic outcomes. The reader should note that these divisions are rough and that some articles in one section could reasonably have been put in another.

The first section of the book presents some broad theories about the relationship between government and the economy. We start by looking at the standard view of that relationship held by most American economists, which is that government has an important role to play in the economy. We then look at a conservative challenge to this view, which holds that government should play a minimal role in economic affairs. Finally we look at a neo-Marxist view, which holds that government has no choice but to play an active role in the economy, to preserve the capitalist system.

The second section of the book looks at government regulation of private business. We first consider the view that regulation is the result of periodic attempts by consumers to curb the excesses of business. We then look at an opposing view that regulation is an attempt by business to use the power of the state to exploit consumers. Finally we look at the topic of deregulation in order to sort out when it is justified and when it is not.

In the third section of the book we look at policies that determine the state of the economy. These are generally referred to as macroeconomic policies—as distinguished from microeconomic policies, which seek to influence individual business decisions. The three chief instruments that can be used to affect the overall health of the economy are changes in government spending, changes in taxes, and changes in the quantity of money created.

In part A of this section we investigate three theories about factors influencing government expenditures in the short term—that is, the federal budget. We will look at arguments that policies are largely determined by the difficulty of getting information, that they are determined through political struggle, and that they are determined by the bureaucracy.

In part B we look at some causes of changes in taxes. After looking at the most important forces determining tax policy, we will look at supply-side arguments for lowering income taxes and a counterargument that sees this as a hidden attempt to redistribute to the rich.

In part C we look the federal deficit. One view, which sees excessive democracy as the basic cause of deficits, argues that it might be reasonable to embed a balanced-budget provision in the Constitution. Another view argues that even if one accepts that the deficit is a major problem, this might have more costs than benefits.

Taken together, changes in expenditures and taxes, or fiscal policy, constitute one of the major means of affecting the health of the economy. The other macroeconomic tool is monetary policy. In part D of the third section we look at the question of control of monetary policy. One article argues that monetary policy should be in the hands of bureaucrats directly responsible to elected officials. The second argues that control should remain with the appointed Federal Reserve Board. The last argues that elected officials have much more control over monetary policy than they appear to.

The fourth section of the book looks at the impact of politics on some important economic outcomes. We begin by looking at the effects of changes in tariff policies and exchange-rate policies. These are seen as increasing business power, driving down blue-collar wages, and leading to increases in government size. We then turn to the effects of the electoral cycle and changes in party control. These are seen as leading to an economy with political business cycles, partisan redistribution, and lower unemployment under the Democrats.

I would like to note that, while I made a conscious effort to avoid selecting especially difficult pieces for inclusion in this collection, this is a highly technical literature and it is inevitable that some readers will have difficulty with some of the articles. For this reason I have provided head notes, to help readers new to the terrain to proceed through the articles with more confidence. I need hardly add (which of course is why I am adding it) that these summaries are, at best, aids to understanding and not substitutes for the material in the articles.

Changes in the Second Edition

This book has been changed substantially from the first edition published in 1987. I have deleted the section on industrial policy, reasoning that if an administration that contains Robert Reich is not doing it, it is unlikely to be implemented in this country. The increasing importance of international factors prompted me to include new readings in this area. The decade-long battles over the deficit led me to include a new section on the deficit. I have increased the readings in the public choice tradition. I have put summaries of current events at the end of each of the three empirical sections. These changes are intended to make the book more relevant and to focus on more important topics.

* * *

No book is complete without thanks to those who helped make it possible. My primary thanks must go to Patricia Kolb and Michael Weber, my editors at M.E. Sharpe, Inc. Pat first suggested that I put together a book of this type and bullied me into abandoning my normally obscure writing style for the somewhat more comprehensible one in this book. Michael Weber talked me into doing a second edition and prodded me where necessary to get this done. Esther Clark and Eileen Gaffney were also very helpful in seeking permissions and handling final editing.

I would also like to thank my wife, Jean Schroedel, who read the drafts of my essays in this volume and made valuable suggestions (as well as putting up with my crankiness). I thank Don McCrone, Dennis Quinn, Neil Berch, Chris Heaphy, Steven Rose, and Alexander Hicks for help with the first edition of this book. Neil Berch, John Mikesel, Jeff Frieden, and an anonymous reviewer (who I think was John Woolley) made suggestions that helped shape the second edition. Scott Frisch and Amy Watson provided me with invaluable research assistance. A course I taught jointly with Tom Anton first got me to look seriously at economic policy.

Last I would like to thank my students at California State University–Fullerton, at Brown University, and at the University of Washington, for pretesting much of the material in this book and—most important—turning thumbs down on some of the material not in this book.

1. Broad Theories

Few questions are more central to the way a society is organized than the relation between government and the economy. Indeed the most important conflict of the postwar era, the competition between capitalism and communism, was primarily an argument over the role of government in controlling the economy.

While over the course of time there have been a very wide range of positions about the form the political economy should take, ranging from anarchy to theocracy to communism, the range of dispute in the United States today is much narrower. Among American *public finance* economists there is general agreement that most goods and services can be provided most efficiently through free competition in the private sector. There is also considerable agreement that some types of goods, generally dubbed *public goods*, cannot be easily provided through the private sector and must be provided by government. There is also accord that government should play some part in redistributing society's goods, and should pursue policies aimed at increasing the efficiency of the private sector and stabilizing the economy. Most American economists think that governments that seek to do more than this run the risks of making the economy less efficient and lowering long-term growth. The recent collapse of the Soviet Union and the Communist regimes of Eastern Europe is seen as confirming evidence for this idea of limited government intervention.

Within these boundaries, however, considerable disagreement remains. The reading by Musgrave and Musgrave is representative of the traditional position taken by public finance economists who generally hold that a moderate amount of government intervention in the economy is desirable. It maintains that government should provide a wide range of public goods, including services like education and health care. It feels that inequities in society argue for a generous redistribution from the better-off to the poorer elements in society. It argues that government needs to actively intervene in the management of the economy to avoid frequent recessions and occasional depressions. It holds that private markets are less competitive than is desirable and that there is a need for government regulation to prevent business from abusing the public.

Milton Friedman, the author of our second reading, is generally seen as reviving an older view which holds that government should play a lesser role in the economy. This increasingly influential view sees the major role of government as one of providing the defense and law and order that make contracts and private markets possible. It feels that government provision of other goods tends to be inefficient, and that where government does provide them, it should do so through contracts with private producers. It holds that strong efforts to redistribute income lead to reduced work effort and savings, cutting economic growth. It says that government attempts to manage the economy are often misconceived, ill-timed, or rendered impotent by expectations, and that government should concentrate on providing a stable money supply and a balanced budget and avoid fine-tuning the economy. It maintains that the extent of monopoly in the private sector is often exaggerated, and its evils overstated. It fears that attempts by government to solve admitted problems like pollution and poor information can easily result in doing more harm than good.

These two schools of thought have had considerable influence on the political scene in the United States. The views of the traditional school have been very influential in the thinking of members of the Democratic Party and moderate Republicans. Most Democratic presidents have actively tried to influence the health of the economy. Successive Democratic Congresses have widened the range of public goods provision and have enacted new redistributive policies. Republicans and conservative Democrats have in turn been heavily influenced by the second school. Republican presidents have been somewhat less willing to intervene to ensure growth. Republican members of Congress have generally opposed policies that redistribute income, and have obstructed attempts to widen the number of goods provided by government.

The last reading in the section is included primarily because it shows how the meaning of economic terms is influenced by our underlying assumptions about the way the world works. O'Connor sees the state as torn between the need to maintain investment and the need to maintain political support from the people. He sees these as contradictory and tries to show how the efforts of capitalist states to deal with this contradiction pushes them from one crisis to another. What is most interesting about this article is that while it uses many of the same categories as the Musgrave and Friedman articles, their meaning changes dramatically when put into the context of a theory that sees the state as a malevolent organization serving the capitalist class rather than as a beneficial organization serving the interests of the general public.

As well as the theoretical articles in this section, there are other articles in this book that represent important theoretical positions. Two articles, those by Robert Reich and Jude Wanniski, are important in this context because they advocate economic approaches currently being used to justify major changes in economic policy. The article by Reich, currently Labor secretary in the Clinton administration, serves as the justification for the Clinton administration's emphasis on worker training, education, public investment, and competitive trade policy. The article by Wanniski on supply-side economics was used to justify the Reagan administration's mix of defense-spending increases and tax cuts and is currently being cited by many Republicans in the House of Representatives as justification for combining deficit reduction with tax cuts.

Finally five articles, those by Musgrave, Downs, Stigler, Niskanen, and Buchanan, contain elements of public choice theory, an approach that tries to show that much political behavior can be viewed as the result of self-interested behavior by individuals. Musgrave shows the importance of the free-rider problem. Downs shows how the interests of the median voter control policy. Stigler shows how a few people to whom an issue is important can seize control of that policy. Niskanen shows that rational bureaucrats have an interest in producing budgets that are too large, and Buchanan shows that democracy may be incompatible with balanced budgets. The public choice approach has become an increasingly important explanation of political behavior and the five authors in this book are responsible for some of the major advances in this area.

For Further Reading

Good public finance textbooks representing the mainstream view in this area are Richard Musgrave and Peggy Musgrave's *Public Finance in Theory and Practice,* and Joseph Stiglitz's *Economics of the Public Sector.* A good exposition of the more conservative view is Edgar and Jacqueline Browning's *Public Finance and the Price System.* A good source for the development of economic theory over the last two hundred years is Mark Blaug's *Economic Theory in Retrospect.* E. K. Hunt and Howard Sherman's *Economics: An Introduction to Traditional and Radical Views* gives a good introduction to leftist economic theory. Lester Thurow's *Dangerous Currents: The State of Economics* has good sections on supply-side and expectations theory. The best review of public choice theory is Dennis C. Mueller's *Public Choice II.* Two accessible journals that frequently feature articles in this area are *Challenge: The Magazine of Economic Affairs* and *The Journal of Economic Literature.*

References

Blaug, Mark. 1985. *Economic Theory in Retrospect.* 4th ed. New York: Cambridge University Press.

Browning, Edgar, and Jacqueline Browning. 1994. *Public Finance and the Price System.* 4th ed. New York: Macmillan.

Hunt, E. K., and Howard J. Sherman. 1985. *Economics: An Introduction to Traditional and Radical Views.* 5th ed. New York: Harper and Row.

Mueller, Dennis C. *Public Choice II.* 1989. New York: Cambridge University Press.

Musgrave, Richard, and Peggy Musgrave. 1989. *Public Finance in Theory and Practice.* 5th ed. New York: McGraw Hill.

Stiglitz, Joseph. 1989. *Economics of the Public Sector.* 2d ed. New York: Norton.

Thurow, Lester. 1983. *Dangerous Currents: The State of Economics.* New York: Random House.

1.1 Fiscal Functions: An Overview

RICHARD A. MUSGRAVE and PEGGY B. MUSGRAVE

The branch of economics that deals with the relation between government and the economy is called public finance. *In this chapter from their book* Public Finance, *Peggy B. Musgrave and Richard A. Musgrave outline what most regard as the central theoretical framework in public finance.*

The authors argue that the most useful way of looking at the role of government is to see it as having three primary tasks—distribution, stabilization, and allocation. A government performs its distributive *function when it alters the income shares that result from the operation of free-market forces, in order to better approximate society's judgment as to what is fair. For example, society may tax an employed executive and then provide support payments to an elderly blind person.* Stabilization *is the task of maintaining a reasonable growth rate and keeping unemployment as low as possible, without setting off inflation or incurring large debts to other countries.* Allocation *is decision-making on how much society should spend on "public goods" such as defense and sewage treatment, which are more efficiently provided by government, as opposed to private goods such as food and clothing, which are most efficiently provided by the free market.*

The reader should keep in mind that while almost all economists agree that most governments perform these three functions in some measure, they tend to disagree over the proper scope of the government role in each area. Disagreement is especially strong over the extent to which government should redistribute income.

A. Introduction

In the United States economy of today, over 20 percent of GNP is purchased by government; total government expenditures including transfers equal 35 percent thereof and tax revenue absorbs over 30 percent of GNP. Though sizable, this government participation falls short of that in other developed economies, especially those in Western Europe, where the governmental share of economic activity is frequently over 50 percent. Beyond the budgetary function, public policy influences the course of economic activity through monetary, regulatory, and other devices. Public enterprise also plays a major role in most European countries, though it is of limited importance in the United States. The modern "capitalist" economy is thus a thoroughly mixed system in which public and private sector forces interact in an integral fashion. The economic system, in fact, is neither public nor private, but involves a mix of both sectors.

Subject of Study

This book deals with the economics of the public sector as that sector operates in a mixed system. Its operation includes not only financing but has broad bearing on the level and allocation of resource use, the distribution of income, and the level of economic activity. Although our subject matter is traditionally referred to as public finance, the book thus deals with the real as well as the financial aspects of the problem. Moreover, we cannot deal with "public" economics only. Since the public sector operates in interaction with the private, both sectors enter the analysis. Not only do the effects of expenditure and tax policies depend upon the reaction of the private sector, but the need for fiscal measures is determined by how the private sector would perform in their absence.

Notwithstanding this broad view, we will not deal with the entire range of economic policy but limit ourselves to that part which operates through the *revenue* and *expenditure* measures of the public budget. Other aspects, such as the regulation of competition through the courts, the operation of public enterprise, and the conduct of monetary policy, are only minor budget items, but of great importance as instruments of economic policy. Yet, we will deal with them only where they are associated with the economics of budget policy. The term "public sector" as used here thus refers to the budgetary sector of public policy only.

Modes of Analysis

In an analysis of the public sector, various types of questions may be asked. They include the following:

1. What criteria should be applied when one is judging the merit of various budget policies?

2. What are the responses of the private sector to various fiscal measures, such as tax and expenditure changes?

3. What are the social, political, and historical forces which have shaped the present fiscal institutions and which have determined the formulation of contemporary fiscal policy?

Question 1 requires a "normative" perspective—i.e., a type of economic analysis that deals with how things *should* be done—and asks how the quality of fiscal institutions and policies can be evaluated and how their performance can be improved. The answer requires setting standards of "good" performance. Corresponding to the analysis of efficient behavior of households and firms in the private sector, defining such standards calls for a type of economics which is referred to as "welfare economics" in professional jargon. Its application to the public sector is more difficult, however, because the objectives of fiscal policy are not given but must be determined through the political process. Moreover, objectives of efficiency in resource use must be supplemented by considerations of equity and distributional justice, thus enlarging the sphere of normative analysis.

Question 2 must be asked if the outcome of alternative policies is to be traced. If the merits of a corporation profits tax or of a sales tax are to be judged, one must know who will bear the final burden, the answer to which in turn depends on how the private sector responds to the imposition of such taxes. Or if aggregate demand is to be increased, one must know what the effects of the reduction in taxes or increase in public expenditures will be, effects which once more depend upon the magnitude and speed of responses by consumers and firms in the private sector. Analyzing the effects of fiscal measures thus involves what has been referred to as "positive" economics—i.e., the type of economic analysis which deals with predicting, on the basis of empirical analysis, how firms and consumers will respond to economic changes and with testing such predictions empirically.

Question 3 likewise involves a "positive" approach, asking in this case why the fiscal behavior of governments is what it is. This is not only a matter of economics but also includes a wide range of historical, political, and social factors. How do interest groups try to affect the fiscal process, and how do legislators respond to interest-group pressures? How are the fiscal preferences of voters determined by their income and their social and demographic characteristics, and how does the political process, in fact, serve to reflect their preferences?

Need for Public Sector

From the normative view, why is it that a public sector is required? If one starts with the premises generally accepted in our society that (1) the composition of output should be in line with the preferences of individual consumers and that (2) there is a preference for decentralized decision making, why may not the entire economy be left to the private sector? Or, putting it differently, why is it that in a supposedly private enterprise economy, a substantial part of the economy is subject to some form of government direction rather than left to the "invisible hand" of market forces?

In part, the prevalence of government may reflect the presence of political and social ideologies which depart from the premises of consumer choice and decentralized decision making. But this is only a minor part of the story. More important, there is the fact that the market mechanism alone cannot perform all economic functions. Public policy is needed to guide, correct, and supplement it in certain respects. It is important to realize this fact, since it implies that the proper size of the public sector is, to a significant degree, a technical rather than an ideological issue. A variety of reasons explain why such is the case, including the following:

1. The claim that the market mechanism leads to efficient resource use (i.e., produces what consumers want most and does so in the cheapest way) is based on the condition of competitive factor and product markets. Thus, there must be no obstacles to free entry and consumers and producers must have full market knowledge. Government regulation or other measures may be needed to secure these conditions.

2. They may also be needed where competition is inefficient due to decreasing cost.

3. More generally, the contractual arrangements and exchanges needed for market operation cannot exist without the protection and enforcement of a governmentally provided legal structure.

4. Even if the legal structure is provided and barriers to competition are removed, the production or consumption characteristics of certain goods are such that they cannot be provided for through the market. Problems of "externalities" arise which lead to "market failure" and require correction by the public sector, either by way of budgetary provisions, subsidy, or tax penalty.

5. Social values may require adjustments in the distribution of income and wealth which results from the market system and from the transmission of property rights through inheritance.

6. The market system, especially in a highly developed financial economy, does not necessarily bring high employment, price level stability, and the socially desired rate of economic growth. Public policy is needed to secure these objectives. As the events of the eighties have shown, this is the case especially in an open economy subject to international repercussions.

7. Public and private points of view on the rate of discount used in the valuation of future (relative to present) consumption may differ.

As we will see later, items 4 through 6 are of particular importance in evaluating budget policy.

To argue that these limitations of the market mechanism call for corrective or compensating measures of public policy does not prove, of course, that any policy measure which is undertaken will in fact improve the performance of the economic system. Public policy, no less than private policy, can err and be inefficient, and the basic purpose of our study of public finance is precisely that of exploring how the effectiveness of policy formulation and application can be improved.

Major Functions

Although particular tax or expenditure measures affect the economy in many ways and may be designed to serve a variety of purposes, several more or less distinct policy objectives may be set forth. They include:

1. The provision for social goods, or the process by which total resource use is divided between private and social goods and by which the mix of social goods is chosen. This provision may be termed the *allocation function* of budget policy. Regulatory policies, which may also be considered a part of the allocation function, are not included here because they are not primarily a problem of budget policy.

2. Adjustment of the distribution of income and wealth to ensure conformance with what society considers a "fair" or "just" state of distribution, here referred to as the *distribution function.*

3. The use of budget policy as a means of maintaining high employment, a reasonable degree of price level stability, and an appropriate rate of economic growth, with allowances for effects on trade and on the balance of payments. We refer to all these objectives as the *stabilization function.*

While these policy objectives differ, any one tax or expenditure measure is likely to affect more than one objective. As will be noted presently, the problem, therefore, is how to design budget policy so that the pursuit of one goal does not void that of another.

B. The Allocation Function

We begin with the allocation function and the proposition that certain goods— referred to here as *social,* or public, as distinct from *private* goods—cannot be provided for through the market system, i.e., by transactions between individual consumers and producers. In some cases the market fails entirely, while in others it can function only in an inefficient way. Why is this the case?

Social Goods and Market Failure

The basic reason for market failure in the provision of social goods is not that the need for such goods is felt collectively whereas that for private goods is felt individually. While people's preferences are influenced by their social environment, in the last resort wants and preferences are experienced by individuals and not by society as a whole. Moreover, both social and private goods are included in their preference maps. Just as I can rank my preferences among housing and backyard facilities, so I may also rank my preferences among my private yard and my use of public parks. Rather, the difference arises because the benefits to which social goods give rise are not limited to one particular consumer who purchases the goods, as is the case for private goods, but become available to others as well.

If I consume a hamburger or wear a pair of shoes, these particular products will not be available to other individuals. My and their consumption stand in a rival relationship. But now consider measures to reduce air pollution. If a given improvement in air quality is obtained, the resulting gain will be available to all who breathe. In other words, consumption of such products by various individuals is "nonrival" in the sense that one person's partaking of benefits does not reduce the benefits available to others. This has important implications for how consumers behave and how the two types of goods are to be provided.

The market mechanism is well suited for the provision of private goods. It is based on exchange, and exchange can occur only where there is an exclusive title to the property which is to be exchanged. In fact, the market system may be viewed as a giant auction where consumers bid for products and producers sell to the highest bidders. Thus the market furnishes a signaling system whereby producers are guided by consumer demands. For goods such as hamburgers or pairs of shoes this is an efficient mechanism. Nothing is lost and much is gained when consumers are excluded unless they pay. Application of the exclusion principle tends to be an efficient solution.

But such is not the case with respect to social goods. Here it would be inefficient to exclude any one consumer from partaking in the benefits, since such participation does not reduce consumption by anyone else. The application of exclusion would thus be undesirable even if it were readily feasible. Given such conditions, the benefits from social goods are not vested in the property rights of particular individuals, and the market cannot function. With benefits available to all, consumers will not voluntarily offer payments to the suppliers of such goods. I will benefit as much from the consumption of others as from my own, and with thousands or millions of other consumers present, my payment will be only an insignificant part of the total. Hence, no voluntary payment is made, especially where many consumers are involved. The linkage between producer and consumer is broken and the government must step in to provide for such goods.

A need for public provision may arise even in situations where consumption is rival, so that exclusion would be appropriate. Such is the case because exclusion may be impossible or prohibitively expensive. Thus, space on a crowded city intersection is scarce, but a mechanism of charging each passing car is hardly feasible. Once more, government must step in when the market cannot deal with the situation.

Public Provision for Social Goods

The problem, then, is how the government should determine how much of such goods is to be provided. Refusal of voluntary payment by consumers is not the basic difficulty. The problem could be solved readily if the task were merely one of sending the tax collector to consumers to whom the benefits of social goods accrue. But matters are not this simple. The difficulty lies in deciding the type and quality of a social good that should be supplied to begin with and how much a particular consumer should be asked to pay. It may be reasonable to rule that the individual should pay for the benefits received, as in the case of private goods, but this does not solve the problem; the difficulty lies in finding out how these benefits are valued by the recipient.

Just as individual consumers have no reason to offer voluntary payments to the private producer, so they have no reason to reveal to the government how highly they value the public service. If I am only one member in a large group of consumers, the total supply available to me is not affected significantly by my own contribution. Consumers have no reason to step forward and declare what the service is truly worth to them individually unless they are assured that others will do the same. Placing tax contributions on a voluntary basis would therefore be to no avail. People will prefer to enjoy as free riders what is provided by others. A different technique is needed by which the supply of social goods and the cost allocation thereof can be determined.

This is where the political process must enter the picture as a substitute for the market mechanism. Voting by ballot must be resorted to in place of voting by dollar bids. Since voters know that they will be subject to the voting decision (whether by simple majority or some other voting rule), they will find it in their interest to vote such that the outcome will fall closer to their own preferences. Decision making by voting becomes a substitute for preference revelation through the market, and the collection of cost shares thus decided upon must be implemented via the tax system. As shown later, taxation generates efficiency costs or deadweight losses which do not arise in a market for private goods. The result of the vote, moreover, will not please everyone but it can only hope to approximate an efficient solution. It will do so more or less perfectly, depending on the efficiency of the voting process and the homogeneity of the community's preferences in the matter.

National and Local Social Goods

Although social goods are available equally to those concerned, their benefits may be spatially limited. Thus, the benefits from national defense accrue nationwide while those from streetlights are of concern only to local residents. This suggests that the nature of social goods has some interesting bearing on the issue of fiscal federalism—centralization or decentralization. As we will see later, a good case can be made for letting national public services be provided by national government and local public services by local government.[1]

Public Provision Versus Public Production

Before considering how such public provision is to be arranged, we must draw a clear distinction between public *provision* for social goods, as the term is used here, and public *production*. These are two distinct and indeed unrelated concepts which should not be confused with one another.

Private goods may be produced and sold to private buyers either by private firms, as is normally done, or by public enterprises, such as public power and transportation authorities or the nationalized British coal industry. Social goods, such as spaceships or military hardware, similarly may be produced by private firms and sold to government; or they may be produced directly under public management, as are services rendered by civil servants or municipal enterprises. If we say that social goods are *provided* publicly, we mean that they are financed through the budget and made available free of direct charge. How they are *produced* does not matter. When looking at the public sector in the national accounts, we will see that the cost of such provision is divided about equally between compensation paid to public employees (whose output may be viewed as public production) and outputs purchased from private firms.[2] Public production of private goods which are then sold in the market plays only a very limited role in the U.S. system.

C. The Distribution Function

The allocation function, concerned with the provision of social goods, inevitably departs from the market process but nevertheless poses the type of problem with which economic analysis has traditionally been concerned, i.e., the efficient use of resources given a prevailing distribution of income and pattern of consumer preferences. The issue of distribution is more difficult to handle. Yet, distribution issues are a major (frequently *the* major) point of controversy in the budget debate. In particular, they play a key role in determining tax and transfer policies.

Determinants of Distribution

In the absence of policy adjustments, the distribution of income and wealth depends first of all on the distribution of factor endowments, including personal earnings abilities and the ownership of accumulated and inherited wealth. The distribution of income, based on this distribution of factor endowments, is then determined by the process of factor pricing, which in a competitive market sets factor returns equal to the value of the marginal product. The distribution of income among individuals thus depends on their factor endowments and the prices which they fetch in the market.

This distribution of income may or may not be in line with what society considers fair or just. A distinction must be drawn between (1) the principle that efficient factor use requires factor inputs to be valued in line with competitive factor pricing and (2) the proposition that the distribution of income among families should be fixed by the market process. Principle I is an economic rule that must be observed if there is to be efficient use of resources, whether in a market economy or in a planned economy. Proposition 2 is a different matter. For one thing, factor prices as determined in the market may not correspond with the competitive norm. But even if all factor prices, including wages and other returns to personal services, were determined competitively, the resulting pattern of distribution might not be acceptable. It typically involves a substantial degree of inequality, especially in the distribution of capital income; and though views on distributive justice differ, most would agree that some adjustments are required, if only to provide an adequate floor at the bottom of the scale. Such adjustments, however, may involve efficiency costs, and the costs must be allowed for in designing distribution policies.

How Income Should Be Distributed

Economics helps to determine what constitutes an efficient use of resources, based on a given pattern of distribution and effective demand. But there is the further question of what constitutes a fair or just state of distribution. Modern economic analysis has steered shy of this problem. The essence of modern welfare economics has been to define economic efficiency in terms which exclude distributional considerations. A change in economic conditions is said to be efficient (i.e., to improve welfare) if and only if the position of some person, say A, is improved without that of anyone else, including B and C, being worsened. This criterion, which may be qualified and amended in various ways, cannot be applied to a redistributional measure which by definition improves A's position at the expense of B's and C's. While the "someone gains, no one loses" rule has served well in assessing the efficiency of markets and of certain aspects of public policy, it contributes little to solving the basic social issues of fair distribution.

The answer to the question of fair distribution involves considerations of social philosophy and value judgment. Philosophers have come up with a variety of answers, including the view that persons have the right to the fruits derived from their particular endowments, that distribution should be arranged so as to maximize total happiness or satisfaction, and that distribution should meet certain standards of equity, which, in a limiting case, may be egalitarian. The choice among these criteria is not simple, nor is it easy to translate any one criterion into the corresponding "correct" pattern of distribution. We will encounter these difficulties when dealing with redistribution policy again in interpreting the widely accepted proposition that people should be taxed in line with their "ability to pay."

There are two major problems involved in the translation of a justice rule into an actual state of income distribution. First, it is difficult or impossible to compare the levels of utility which various individuals derive from their income. There is no simple way of adding up utilities, so that criteria based on such comparisons are not operational. This limitation has led people to think in terms of social evaluation rather than subjective utility measurement. The other difficulty arises from the fact that the size of the pie which is available for distribution is not unrelated to how it is to be distributed. As noted before, redistribution policies may involve an efficiency cost which must be taken into account when one is deciding on the extent to which equity objectives should be pursued.

Notwithstanding these difficulties, however, distributional considerations remain an important issue of public policy. Attention appears to be shifting from the traditional concern with relative income positions, with the overall state of equality, and with excessive income at the top of the scale, to adequacy of income at the lower end. Thus the current discussion emphasizes prevention of poverty, setting what is considered a tolerable cutoff line or floor at the lower end rather than putting a ceiling at the top, as was once a major concern. This, as we will see, has important bearing on the design of the tax structure.

Fiscal Instruments of Distribution Policy

Among various fiscal devices, redistribution is implemented most directly by (1) a tax-transfer scheme, combining progressive taxation of high-income with a subsidy to low-income households.[3] Alternatively, redistribution may be implemented by (2) progressive taxes used to finance public services, especially those such as public housing, which particularly benefit low-income households. Finally, redistribution may be achieved by (3) a combination of taxes on goods purchased largely by high-income consumers with subsidies to other goods which are used chiefly by low-income consumers.

In choosing among alternative policy instruments, allowance must be made for resulting deadweight losses or efficiency costs, i.e., costs which arise as consumer or producer choices are interfered with. Redistribution via an income tax transfer mechanism has the advantage that it does not interfere with particular consumption or production choices. However, even this mechanism is not without its "efficiency cost," since the choice between income and leisure will be distorted. As we will see later, an optimal solution might call for a complex mix of taxes and subsidies. However, we will disregard this for the time being and think of the function of the distribution branch as being met by a set of direct income taxes and transfers.

While redistribution inevitably involves an efficiency cost, this conse-quence by itself establishes no conclusive case against such policies. It merely tells us that (1) any given distributional change should be accom-plished at the least efficiency cost and (2) a need exists for balancing con-flicting equity and efficiency objectives. An optimally conducted policy must allow for both concerns.

D. The Stabilization Function

Having dealt with the role of budget policy in matters of allocation and distribu-tion, we must now note its bearing on the macro performance of the economy, i.e., on targets such as high employment, a reasonable degree of price level stability, soundness of foreign accounts, and an acceptable rate of economic growth.

Need for Stabilization Policy

Achievement of these targets does not come about automatically but requires policy guidance. Without it, the economy tends to be subject to substantial fluctuations and may suffer from sustained periods of unemployment or infla-tion. To make matters worse, unemployment and inflation—as we have painfully learned in the 1970s—may exist at the same time. With growing international interdependence, forces of instability may be transmitted from one country to another, which further complicates the problem.

The overall level of employment and prices in the economy depends upon the level of aggregate demand, relative to potential or capacity output valued at prevailing prices. The level of demand is a function of the spending decisions of millions of consumers, corporate managers, financial investors, and unincorpo-rated operators. These decisions in turn depend upon many factors, such as past and present income, wealth position, credit availability, and expectations. In any one period, the level of expenditures may be insufficient to secure full employ-ment of labor and other resources. For various reasons, including the fact that wages and prices tend to be downwardly rigid, there is no ready mechanism by which such employment will restore itself automatically. Expansionary measures to raise aggregate demand are then needed. At other times, expenditures may exceed the available output under conditions of high employment and thus may cause inflation. In such situations, restrictive measures are needed to reduce demand. Furthermore, just as deficient demand may generate further deficiency, so may an increase in prices generate a further price rise, leading to renewed inflation. In neither case is there an automatic adjustment process which ensures that the economy is promptly returned to high employment and stability. Chang-ing expectations introduce a dynamic force which may prove a source of growth as well as of system instability and decline.

Instruments of Stabilization Policy

Policy instruments available to deal with these problems involve both monetary and fiscal measures, and their interaction is of great importance.

Monetary Instruments

While the market mechanism, if it functions well, may be relied upon to determine the allocation of resources among private goods, it cannot by itself regulate the proper money supply. As Walter Bagehot pointed out a century ago, "Money does not control itself." If left to its own devices, the banking system will not generate precisely that money supply which is compatible with economic stability, but will—in response to the credit demands of the market—accentuate prevailing tendencies to fluctuation. Therefore, the money supply must be controlled by the central banking system and be adjusted to the needs of the economy in terms of both short-run stability and longer-run growth. Monetary policy—including the devices of reserve requirements, discount rates, and open market policy—is thus an indispensable component of stabilization policy. Expanding the money supply will tend to increase liquidity, reduce interest rates, and thereby increase the level of demand, with monetary restriction working in the opposite direction.

Fiscal Instruments

Fiscal policy as well has a direct bearing on the level of demand. Raising public expenditures will be expansionary as demand is increased, initially in the public sector and then transmitted to the private market. Tax reduction, similarly, may be expansionary as taxpayers are left with a higher level of income and may be expected to spend more. Changes in the level of deficit thus play an important role. At the same time, much will depend on how the deficit is financed. If accompanied by an easy monetary policy, the expansionary effects of deficit finance will be greater as the deficit can be met by increased credit. If matched by tight money, placing the additional debt will call for an increase in the rate of interest and thus have a restrictive effect on market transactions. Moreover, effects upon international capital flows, as the American economy has seen in the 1980s, are again of major importance.

E. Coordination of Budget Functions

As noted before, budget policy involves a number of distinct objectives, but these overlap in practice, thereby complicating an efficient policy design, i.e., a design which does justice to its diverse goals.

Suppose first that the public wishes an increased supply of public services.

Increased taxes are needed to pay for these, which leads in turn to the question of how they should be distributed. Depending on what taxes are used, taxation may well change the distribution of income that remains available for private use. Hence some voters may favor (reject) the proposed change in public services because they like (dislike) the associated change in distribution rather than because they like (or dislike) the public service. Ideally, the two issues would be separated: Society would provide for what is considered a fair state of distribution and then adjust the financing of public services in line with the benefits which taxpayers derive therefrom. Because this two-step procedure is difficult to accomplish, decisions on the provision of public services tend to be mixed with and distorted by distributional considerations. Similar reasoning also applies in the reverse direction, when the supply of public services and hence taxes are to be reduced.

Next suppose that society wishes to shift distribution in the direction of greater (lesser) equality. Such a shift may be accomplished by using progressive (regressive) taxes to finance transfers to lower (higher) incomes. But it may also be done by increasing (reducing) the supply of public services of particular value to low (high) income groups. This, however, interferes with the pattern of public services which consumers want to obtain at a given distribution of income. Once more, one policy objective may be implemented such that it interferes with another.

Finally, consider the role of fiscal policy in stabilization. Suppose that a more (less) expansionary policy is needed. This may be accomplished by raising (lowering) outlays on public services or by reducing (raising) the level of taxation. In the former case the allocation objective of fiscal policy is interfered with, whereas in the latter it is not. However, in the latter case there is the further question of how changes in the level of taxation are to be implemented. For stabilization measures to be neutral regarding both allocation and distribution goals, proportional changes in the level of tax rates might offer the appropriate solution.

There are many exceptions which call for qualification of the simple rules just given. Nevertheless, it is important to keep in mind that there are distinct policy objectives and policy should try to minimize conflicts among them.

F. Summary

This chapter, being itself in the form of a summary, can hardly be summarized further. However, the main ideas presented are these:

1. Modern so-called capitalist economies are in fact mixed economies, with one-third or more of economic activity occurring in the public sector.
2. For purposes of this book, the term public sector is used to refer to the parts of governmental economic policy which find their expression in budgetary (expenditure and revenue) measures.

3. Three major types of budgetary activity are distinguished: namely, (a) the public provision of certain goods and services, referred to as "social goods"; (b) adjustment in the state of distribution of income and wealth; and (c) measures to deal with unemployment, inflation, and inadequate economic growth.

4. In discussing the provision of social goods (the allocation function), reference is made to goods and services which must be paid for through budgetary finance. Whether the production of these goods is by a public agency or whether the goods and services are purchased from private firms is a different matter.

5. Provision for social goods poses problems which differ from those which arise in connection with private goods. Since social goods are nonrival in consumption, consumer preferences are not revealed by consumer bidding in the market. Therefore a political process and budgetary finance are required.

6. The pattern of distribution which results from the existing pattern of factor endowments and their sale in the market is not necessarily one which society considers as fair. Distributional adjustments may be called for, and tax and transfer policies offer an effective means of implementing them, thus calling for a distribution function in budget policy.

7. Tax and expenditure policies affect aggregate demand and the level of economic activity. Their conduct has important bearing on maintaining economic stability, including high employment and control of inflation. Hence, the stabilization function enters as the third budgetary concern.

8. A major problem is how to conduct fiscal policy so that its major objects—including allocation, distribution, and stabilization aspects—can be met at the same time.

Notes

1. For reasons see Richard and Peggy Musgrave, *Public Finance in Theory and Practice,* 5th ed. (New York: McGraw Hill, 1989), p. 446.

2. See ibid, p. 17.

3. A *progressive* tax is defined as one in which the ratio of tax to income rises with income.

1.2. The Role of Government in a Free Society

MILTON FRIEDMAN

In this reading, Nobel Prize winner Milton Friedman presents a somewhat more restrictive view of the proper role of government than that offered by Musgrave and Musgrave. Arguing that it is imperative to maintain the maximum freedom for individuals, he maintains that the government's role should be limited primarily to three tasks: establishing the conditions for the functioning of free markets, providing law and order, and dealing with what Friedman terms "neighborhood effects." All of these are forms of what are called "public goods" (the Musgraves refer to them as "social goods"). Friedman also argues that many of the services currently performed by government could be better provided by the private market.

Many of the policy changes introduced by the Reagan administration can be considered applications of Friedman's views. The reader should note that Friedman places less stress on redistribution than the Musgraves do, that he thinks fewer things can properly be called public goods, and that he thinks stabilization is best assured if government sets unchanging policy goals rather than trying to fine-tune the economy.

The reader should also note that the author tends to see freedom as freedom from state interference rather than as freedom from coercion by powerful private actors such as large businesses. In the nineteenth century this view was referred to as liberalism, and so Friedman refers to himself as a liberal, although he is generally now characterized as a conservative.

A common objection to totalitarian societies is that they regard the end as justifying the means. Taken literally, this objection is clearly illogical. If the end does not justify the means, what does? But this easy answer does not dispose of the objection; it simply shows that the objection is not well put. To deny that the end justifies the means is indirectly to assert that the end in question is not the ultimate end, that the ultimate end is itself the use of the proper means. Desirable or not, any end that can be attained only by the use of bad means must give way to the more basic end of the use of acceptable means.

To the liberal, the appropriate means are free discussion and voluntary cooperation, which implies that any form of coercion is inappropriate. The ideal is unanimity among responsible individuals achieved on the basis of free and full discussion. This is another way of expressing the goal of freedom. . . .

From this standpoint, the role of the market . . . is that it permits unanimity without conformity; that it is a system of effectively proportional representation. On the other hand, the characteristic feature of action through explicitly political channels is that it tends to require or to enforce substantial conformity. The typical issue must be decided "yes" or "no"; at most, provision can be made for a fairly limited number of alternatives. Even the use of proportional representation in its explicitly political form does not alter this conclusion. The number of separate groups that can in fact be represented is narrowly limited, enormously so by comparison with the proportional representation of the market. More important, the fact that the final outcome generally must be a law applicable to all groups, rather than separate legislative enactments for each "party" represented, means that proportional representation in its political version, far from permitting unanimity without conformity, tends toward ineffectiveness and fragmentation. It thereby operates to destroy any consensus on which unanimity with conformity can rest.

There are clearly some matters with respect to which effective proportional representation is impossible. I cannot get the amount of national defense I want, and you, a different amount. With respect to such indivisible matters we can discuss, and argue, and vote. But having decided, we must conform. It is precisely the existence of such indivisible matters—protection of the individual and the nation from coercion are clearly the most basic—that prevents exclusive reliance on individual action through the market. If we are to use some of our resources for such indivisible items, we must employ political channels to reconcile differences.

The use of political channels, while inevitable, tends to strain the social cohesion essential for a stable society. The strain is least if agreement for joint action need be reached only on a limited range of issues on which people in any event have common views. Every extension of the range of issues for which explicit agreement is sought strains further the delicate threads that hold society together. If it goes so far as to touch an issue on which men feel deeply yet differently, it may well disrupt the society. Fundamental differences in basic values can seldom if ever be resolved at the ballot box; ultimately they can only be decided, though not resolved, by conflict. The religious and civil wars of history are a bloody testament to this judgment.

The widespread use of the market reduces the strain on the social fabric by rendering conformity unnecessary with respect to any activities it encompasses. The wider the range of activities covered by the market, the fewer are the issues on which explicitly political decisions are required and hence on which it is necessary to achieve agreement. In turn, the fewer the issues on which agreement is necessary, the greater is the likelihood of getting agreement while maintaining a free society.

Unanimity is, of course, an ideal. In practice, we can afford neither the time nor the effort that would be required to achieve complete unanimity on every issue. We must perforce accept something less. We are thus led to accept majority rule in one form or another as an expedient. That majority rule is an expedient rather than itself a basic principle is clearly shown by the fact that our willingness to resort to majority rule, and the size of the majority we require, themselves depend on the seriousness of the issue involved. If the matter is of little moment and the minority has no strong feelings about being overruled, a bare plurality will suffice. On the other hand, if the minority feels strongly about the issue involved, even a bare majority will not do. Few of us would be willing to have issues of free speech, for example, decided by a bare majority. Our legal structure is full of such distinctions among kinds of issues that require different kinds of majorities. At the extreme are those issues embodied in the Constitution. These are the principles that are so important that we are willing to make minimal concessions to expediency. Something like essential consensus was achieved initially in accepting them, and we require something like essential consensus for a change in them.

The self-denying ordinance to refrain from majority rule on certain kinds of issues that is embodied in our Constitution and in similar written or unwritten constitutions elsewhere, and the specific provisions in these constitutions or their equivalents prohibiting coercion of individuals, are themselves to be regarded as reached by free discussion and as reflecting essential unanimity about means.

I turn now to consider more specifically, though still in very broad terms, what the areas are that cannot be handled through the market at all, or can be handled only at so great a cost that the use of political channels may be preferable.

Government as Rule-Maker and Umpire

It is important to distinguish the day-to-day activities of people from the general customary and legal framework within which these take place. The day-to-day activities are like the actions of the participants in a game when they are playing it; the framework, like the rules of the game they play. And just as a good game requires acceptance by the players both of the rules and of the umpire to interpret and enforce them, so a good society requires that its members agree on the general conditions that will govern relations among them, on some means of arbitrating different interpretations of these conditions, and on some device for enforcing compliance with the generally accepted rules. As in games, so also in society, most of the general conditions are the unintended outcome of custom, accepted unthinkingly. At most, we consider explicitly only minor modifications in them, though the cumulative effect of a series of minor modifications may be a drastic alteration in the character of the game or of the society. In both games and society also, no set of rules can prevail unless most participants most of the time conform to them without external sanctions; unless, that is, there is a broad underlying social consensus. But we cannot rely on custom or on this consensus alone to interpret and to enforce the rules; we need an umpire. These then are the basic roles of government in a free society: to provide a means whereby we can modify the rules, to mediate differences among us on the meaning of the rules, and to enforce compliance with the rules on the part of those few who would otherwise not play the game.

The need for government in these respects arises because absolute freedom is impossible. However attractive anarchy may be as a philosophy, it is not feasible in a world of imperfect men. Men's freedoms can conflict, and when they do, one man's freedom must be limited to preserve another's—as a Supreme Court Justice once put it, "My freedom to move my fist must be limited by the proximity of your chin."

The major problem in deciding the appropriate activities of government is how to resolve such conflicts among the freedoms of different individuals. In some cases, the answer is easy. There is little difficulty in attaining near unanimity to the proposition that one man's freedom to murder his neighbor must be sacrificed to preserve the freedom of the other man to live. In other cases, the answer is difficult. In the economic area, a major problem arises in respect of the conflict between freedom to combine and freedom to compete. What meaning is to be attributed to "free" as modifying "enterprise"? In the United States, "free" has been understood to mean that anyone is free to set up an enterprise, which means that existing enterprises are not free to keep out competitors except by selling a better product at the same price or the same product at a lower price. In the continental tradition, on the other hand, the meaning has generally been that enterprises are free to do what they want, including the fixing of prices, division of markets, and the adoption of other techniques to keep out potential competitors. Perhaps the most difficult specific problem in this area arises with respect to combinations among laborers, where the problem of freedom to combine and freedom to compete is particularly acute.

A still more basic economic area in which the answer is both difficult and important is the definition of property rights. The notion of property, as it has developed over centuries and as it is embodied in our legal codes, has become so much a part of us that we tend to take it for granted, and fail to recognize the extent to which just what constitutes property and what rights the ownership of property confers are complex social creations rather than self-evident propositions. Does my having title to land, for example, and my freedom to use my property as I wish, permit me to deny to someone else the right to fly over my land in his airplane? Or does his right to use his airplane take precedence? Or does this depend on how high he flies? Or how much noise he makes? Does voluntary exchange require that he pay me for the privilege of flying over my land? Or that I must pay him to refrain from flying over it? The mere mention of royalties, copyrights, patents; shares of stock in corporations; riparian rights, and the like, may perhaps emphasize the role of generally accepted social rules in the very definition of property. It may suggest also that, in many cases, the existence of a well specified and generally accepted definition of property is far more important than just what the definition is.

Another economic area that raises particularly difficult problems is the monetary system. Government responsibility for the monetary system has long been recognized. It is explicitly provided for in the constitutional provision which gives Congress the power "to coin money, regulate the value thereof, and of foreign coin." There is probably no other area of economic activity with respect to which government action has been so uniformly accepted. This habitual and by now almost unthinking acceptance of governmental responsibility makes thorough understanding of the grounds for such responsibility all the more necessary, since it enhances the danger that the scope of government will spread from activities that are, to those that are not, appropriate in a free society, from providing a monetary framework to determining the allocation of resources among individuals. . . .

In summary, the organization of economic activity through voluntary exchange presumes that we have provided, through government, for the maintenance of law and order to prevent coercion of one individual by another, the enforcement of contracts voluntarily entered into, the definition of the meaning of property rights, the interpretation and enforcement of such rights, and the provision of a monetary framework.

Action Through Government on Grounds of Technical Monopoly and Neighborhood Effects

The role of government just considered is to do something that the market cannot do for itself, namely, to determine, arbitrate, and enforce the rules of the game. We may also want to do through government some things that might conceivably be done through the market but that technical or similar conditions render it difficult to do in that way. These all reduce to cases in which strictly voluntary exchange is either exceedingly costly or practically impossible. There are two general classes of such cases: monopoly and similar market imperfections, and neighborhood effects.

Exchange is truly voluntary only when nearly equivalent alternatives exist. Monopoly implies the absence of alternatives and thereby inhibits effective freedom of exchange. In practice, monopoly frequently, if not generally, arises from government support or from collusive agreements among individuals. With respect to these, the problem is either to avoid governmental fostering of monopoly or to stimulate the effective enforcement of rules such as those embodied in our anti-trust laws. However, monopoly may also arise because it is technically efficient to have a single producer or enterprise. I venture to suggest that such cases are more limited than is supposed but they unquestionably do arise. A simple example is perhaps the provision of telephone services within a community. I shall refer to such cases as "technical" monopoly.

When technical conditions make a monopoly the natural outcome of competitive market forces, there are only three alternatives that seem available: private monopoly, public monopoly, or public regulation. All three are bad so we must choose among evils. Henry Simons, observing public regulation of monopoly in the United States, found the results so distasteful that he concluded public monopoly would be a lesser evil. Walter Eucken, a noted German liberal, observing public monopoly in German railroads, found the results so distasteful that he concluded public regulation would be a lesser evil. Having learned from both, I reluctantly conclude that, if tolerable, private monopoly may be the least of the evils.

If society were static so that the conditions which give rise to a technical monopoly were sure to remain, I would have little confidence in this solution. In a rapidly changing society, however, the conditions making for technical monopoly frequently change and I suspect that both public regulation and public monopoly are likely to be less responsive to such changes in conditions, to be less readily capable of elimination, than private monopoly.

Railroads in the United States are an excellent example. A large degree of monopoly in railroads was perhaps inevitable on technical grounds in the nineteenth century. This was the justification for the Interstate Commerce Commission. But conditions have changed. The emergence of road and air transport has reduced the monopoly element in railroads to negligible proportions. Yet we have not eliminated the ICC. On the contrary, the ICC, which started out as an agency to protect the public from exploitation by the railroads, has become an agency to protect railroads from competition by trucks and other means of transport, and more recently even to protect existing truck companies from competition by new entrants. Similarly, in England, when the railroads were nationalized, trucking was at first brought into the state monopoly. If railroads had never been subjected to regulation in the United States, it is nearly certain that by now transportation, including railroads, would be a highly competitive industry with little or no remaining monopoly elements.

The choice between the evils of private monopoly, public monopoly, and public regulation cannot, however, be made once and for all, independently of the factual circumstances. If the technical monopoly is of a service or commodity that is regarded as essential and if its monopoly power is sizable, even the short-run effects of private unregulated monopoly may not be tolerable, and either public regulation or ownership may be a lesser evil.

Technical monopoly may on occasion justify a *de facto* public monopoly. It cannot by itself justify a public monopoly achieved by making it illegal for anyone else to compete. For example, there is no way to justify our present public monopoly of the post office. It may be argued that the carrying of mail is a technical monopoly and that a government monopoly is the least of evils. Along these lines, one could perhaps justify a government post office but not the present law, which makes it illegal for anybody else to carry mail. If the delivery of mail is a technical monopoly, no one will be able to succeed in competition with the government. If it is not, there is no reason why the government should be engaged in it. The only way to find out is to leave other people free to enter.

The historical reason why we have a post office monopoly is because the Pony Express did such a good job of carrying the mail across the continent that, when the government introduced transcontinental service, it couldn't compete effectively and lost money. The result was a law making it illegal for anybody else to carry the mail. That is why the Adams Express Company is an investment trust today instead of an operating company. I conjecture that if entry into the mail-carrying business were open to all, there would be a large number of firms entering it and this archaic industry would become revolutionized in short order.

A second general class of cases in which strictly voluntary exchange is impossible arises when actions of individuals have effects on other individuals for which it is not feasible to charge or recompense them. This is the problem of "neighborhood effects." An obvious example is the pollution of a stream. The man who pollutes a stream is in effect forcing others to exchange good water for bad. These others might be willing to make the exchange at a price. But it is not feasible for them, acting individually, to avoid the exchange or to enforce appropriate compensation.

A less obvious example is the provision of highways. In this case, it is technically possible to identify and hence charge individuals for their use of the roads and so to have private operation. However, for general access roads, involving many points of entry and exit, the costs of collection would be extremely high if a charge were to be made for the specific services received by each individual, because of the necessity of establishing toll booths or the equivalent at all entrances. The gasoline tax is a much cheaper method of charging individuals roughly in proportion to their use of the roads. This method, however, is one in which the particular payment cannot be identified closely with the particular use. Hence, it is hardly feasible to have private enterprise provide the service and collect the charge without establishing extensive private monopoly.

These considerations do not apply to long-distance turnpikes with high density of traffic and limited access. For these, the costs of collection are small and in many cases are now being paid, and there are often numerous alternatives, so that there is no serious monopoly problem. Hence, there is every reason why these should be privately owned and operated. If so owned and operated, the enterprise running the highway should receive the gasoline taxes paid on account of travel on it.

Parks are an interesting example because they illustrate the difference between cases that can and cases that cannot be justified by neighborhood effects, and because almost everyone at first sight regards the conduct of National Parks as obviously a valid function of government. In fact, however, neighborhood effects may justify a city park; they do not justify a national park, like Yellowstone National Park or the Grand Canyon. What is the fundamental difference between the two? For the city park, it is extremely difficult to identify the people who benefit from it and to charge them for the benefits which they receive. If there is a park in the middle of the city, the houses on all sides get the benefit of the open space, and people who walk through it or by it also benefit. To maintain toll collectors at the gates or to impose annual charges per window overlooking the park would be very expensive and difficult. The entrances to a national park like Yellowstone, on the other hand, are few; most of the people who come stay for a considerable period of time and it is perfectly feasible to set up toll gates and collect admission charges. This is indeed now done, though the charges do not cover the whole costs. If the public wants this kind of an activity enough to pay for it, private enterprises will have every incentive to provide such parks. And, of course, there are many private enterprises of this nature now in existence. I cannot myself conjure up any neighborhood effects or important monopoly effects that would justify governmental activity in this area.

Considerations like those I have treated under the heading of neighborhood effects have been used to rationalize almost every conceivable intervention. In many instances, however, this rationalization is special pleading rather than a legitimate application of the concept of neighborhood effects. Neighborhood effects cut both ways. They can be a reason for limiting the activities of government as well as for expanding them. Neighborhood effects impede voluntary exchange because it is difficult to identify the effects on third parties and to measure their magnitude; but this difficulty is present in governmental activity as well. It is hard to know when neighborhood effects are sufficiently large to justify particular costs in overcoming them and even harder to distribute the costs in an appropriate fashion. Consequently, when government engages in activities to overcome neighborhood effects, it will in part introduce an additional set of neighborhood effects by failing to charge or to compensate individuals properly. Whether the original or the new neighborhood effects are the more serious can only be judged by the facts of the individual case, and even then, only very approximately. Furthermore, the use of government to overcome neighborhood effects itself has an extremely important neighborhood effect which is unrelated to the particular occasion for government action. Every act of government intervention limits the area of individual freedom directly and threatens the preservation of freedom indirectly. . . .

Our principles offer no hard and fast line [on] how far it is appropriate to use government to accomplish jointly what it is difficult or impossible for us to accomplish separately through strictly voluntary exchange. In any particular case of proposed intervention, we must make up a balance sheet, listing separately the advantages and disadvantages. Our principles tell us what items to put on the one side and what items on the other and they give us some basis for attaching importance to the different items. In particular, we shall always want to enter on the liability side of any proposed government intervention, its neighborhood effect in threatening freedom, and give this effect considerable weight. Just how much weight to give to it, as to other items, depends upon the circumstances. If, for example, existing government intervention is minor, we shall attach a smaller weight to the negative effects of additional government intervention. This is an important reason why many earlier liberals, like Henry Simons, writing at a time when government was small by today's standards, were willing to have government undertake activities that today's liberals would not accept now that government has become so overgrown.

Action Through Government on Paternalistic Grounds

Freedom is a tenable objective only for responsible individuals. We do not believe in freedom for madmen or children. The necessity of drawing a line between responsible individuals and others is inescapable, yet it means that there is an essential ambiguity in our ultimate objective of freedom. Paternalism is inescapable for those whom we designate as not responsible.

The clearest case, perhaps, is that of madmen. We are willing neither to permit them freedom nor to shoot them. It would be nice if we could rely on voluntary activities of individuals to house and care for the madmen. But I think we cannot rule out the possibility that such charitable activities will be inadequate, if only because of the neighborhood effect involved in the fact that I benefit if another man contributes to the care of the insane. For this reason, we may be willing to arrange for their care through government.

Children offer a more difficult case. The ultimate operative unit in our society is the family, not the individual. Yet the acceptance of the family as the unit rests in considerable part on expediency rather than principle. We believe that parents are generally best able to protect their children and to provide for their development into responsible individuals for whom freedom is appropriate. But we do not believe in the freedom of parents to do what they will with other people. The children are responsible individuals in embryo, and a believer in freedom believes in protecting their ultimate rights.

To put this in a different and what may seem a more callous way, children are at one and the same time consumer goods and potentially responsible members of society. The freedom of individuals to use their economic resources as they want includes the freedom to use them to have children—to buy, as it were, the services of children as a particular form of consumption. But once this choice is exercised, the children have a value in and of themselves and have a freedom of their own that is not simply an extension of the freedom of the parents.

The paternalistic ground for governmental activity is in many ways the most troublesome to a liberal; for it involves the acceptance of a principle—that some shall decide for others—which he finds objectionable in most applications and which he rightly regards as a hallmark of his chief intellectual opponents, the proponents of collectivism in one or another of its guises, whether it be communism, socialism, or a welfare state. Yet there is no use pretending that problems are simpler than in fact they are. There is no avoiding the need for some measure of paternalism. As Dicey wrote in 1914 about an act for the protection of mental defectives, "The Mental Deficiency Act is the first step along a path on which no sane man can decline to enter, but which, if too far pursued, will bring statesmen across difficulties hard to meet without considerable interference with individual liberty."[1] There is no formula that can tell us where to stop. We must rely on our fallible judgment and, having reached a judgment, on our ability to persuade our fellow men that it is a correct judgment, or their ability to persuade us to modify our views. We must put our faith, here as elsewhere, in a consensus reached by imperfect and biased men through free discussion and trial and error.

Conclusion

A government which maintained law and order, defined property rights, served as a means whereby we could modify property rights and other rules of the economic game, adjudicated disputes about the interpretation of the rules, enforced contracts, promoted competition, provided a monetary framework, engaged in activities to counter technical monopolies and to overcome neighborhood effects widely regarded as sufficiently important to justify government intervention, and which supplemented private charity and the private family in protecting the irresponsible, whether madman or child—such a government would clearly have important functions to perform. The consistent liberal is not an anarchist.

Yet it is also true that such a government would have clearly limited functions and would refrain from a host of activities that are now undertaken by federal and state governments in the United States, and their counterparts in other Western countries. . . . [I]t may help to give a sense of proportion about the role that a liberal would assign government simply to list, in closing this chapter, some activities currently undertaken by government in the U.S., that cannot, so far as I can see, validly be justified in terms of the principles outlined above:

1. Parity price support programs for agriculture.

2. Tariffs on imports or restrictions on exports, such as current oil import quotas, sugar quotas, etc.

3. Governmental control of output, such as through the farm program, or through pro-rationing of oil as is done by the Texas Railroad Commission.

4. Rent control, such as is still practiced in New York, or more general

price and wage controls such as were imposed during and just after World War II.

5. Legal minimum wage rates, or legal maximum prices, such as the legal maximum of zero on the rate of interest that can be paid on demand deposits by commercial banks, or the legally fixed maximum rates that can be paid on savings and time deposits.

6. Detailed regulation of industries, such as the regulation of transportation by the Interstate Commerce Commission. This had some justification on technical monopoly grounds when initially introduced for railroads; it has none now for any means of transport. Another example is detailed regulation of banking.

7. A similar example, but one which deserves special mention because of its implicit censorship and violation of free speech, is the control of radio and television by the Federal Communications Commission.

8. Present social security programs, especially the old-age and retirement programs compelling people in effect (a) to spend a specified fraction of their income on the purchase of retirement annuity, (b) to buy the annuity from a publicly operated enterprise.

9. Licensure provisions in various cities and states which restrict particular enterprises or occupations or professions to people who have a license, where the license is more than a receipt for a tax which anyone who wishes to enter the activity may pay.

10. So-called "public housing" and the host of other subsidy programs directed at fostering residential construction such as F.H.A. and V.A. guarantee of mortgage, and the like.

11. Conscription to man the military services in peacetime. The appropriate free market arrangement is volunteer military forces; which is to say, hiring men to serve. There is no justification for not paying whatever price is necessary to attract the required number of men. Present arrangements are inequitable and arbitrary, seriously interfere with the freedom of young men to shape their lives, and probably are even more costly than the market alternative. (Universal military training to provide a reserve for war time is a different problem and may be justified on liberal grounds.)

12. National parks, as noted above.

13. The legal prohibition on the carrying of mail for profit.

14. Publicly owned and operated toll roads, as noted above.

This list is far from comprehensive.

Note

1. A. V. Dicey, *Lectures on the Relation between Law and Public Opinion in England during the Nineteenth Century* (2d. ed.; London: MacMillan & Co., 1914), p. li.

1.3. The Fiscal Crisis of the State

JAMES O'CONNOR

In this introduction to his fascinating but controversial book, The Fiscal Crisis of the State, *James O'Connor outlines a very different model for looking at the role of government in the economy. He starts by claiming that governments have two basic functions. One is to maintain the process of investment, which keeps the capitalist system running. O'Connor calls this the* capital accumulation function. *The second is to maintain the support of the people for the current unequal distribution of economic, social, and political power. He calls this the* legitimacy function.

O'Connor's central argument is that these two functions necessarily conflict. The state is subject to pressure simultaneously from large firms, which want the government to cover an ever increasing share of their real costs, and from taxpayers, who resent having to pay higher and higher taxes to support these subsidies. Governments attempt makeshift solutions, but these rapidly degenerate, giving rise to new crises. It will be interesting for the reader to ask how well this reading from 1973 predicts the large federal deficits and other economic problems of the 1980s and 1990s.

"Lockheed Gets Loan Guarantees," "President Says, 'No Vietnam Dividend,' " "New $50 Million BART Issue," "Medicare Spending up 20%," "30% City Budget Increase," "Teachers' Strike Begins Third Week," "Violence Mars Welfare Rights Demonstration"—these were some of the typical headlines of the 1960s and early 1970s. Each is a variation on the same theme: Corporations want government to build more freeways; bankers and investors want government to underwrite more loans and investments; small businessmen and farmers want more subsidies; organized labor wants more social insurance; welfare rights groups want higher income allowances, more housing, and better public health services; government employees want higher wages and salaries; and government agencies want more appropriations.

Other familiar headlines—"School Bond Issue Voted Down," "Gallup Poll: Tax Relief Top Worry," "Unified School District Referendum Defeated," "Commuter Tax Declared Unconstitutional," "Homeowners Vote to Shift Tax to Downtown Business," "Reagan Supports State Withholding Tax"—tell a similar story. Large corporations and wealthy investors want working people and small businessmen to foot the bill for airport modernization, freeway expansion, rapid transit, water investment projects, and pollution control. Small businessmen and homeowners want property tax relief. Middle-income wage and salary earners want income tax relief. Poor people want tax relief, period. Suburbanites don't want to pay taxes in the central city where they work, and they don't want central-city residents to get any of the taxes that they pay in the suburbs.

Every economic and social class and group wants government to spend more and more money on more and more things. But no one wants to pay new taxes or higher rates on old taxes. Indeed, nearly everyone wants lower taxes, and many groups have agitated successfully for tax relief. Society's demands on local and state budgets seemingly are unlimited, but people's willingness and capacity to pay for these demands appear to be narrowly limited. And at the federal level expenditures have increased significantly faster than the growth of total production. In the words of the head of the Federal Reserve System,

> We stand at a crossroads in our fiscal arrangements. Many of our citizens are alarmed by the increasing share of their incomes that is taken away by Federal, State, and local taxes. . . . The propensity to spend more than we are prepared to finance through taxes is becoming deep-seated and ominous. An early end to Federal deficits is not now in sight. Numerous Federal programs have a huge growth of expenditures built into them, and there are proposals presently before the Congress that would raise expenditures by vast amounts in coming years.[1]

We have termed this tendency for government expenditures to outrace revenues the "fiscal crisis of the state." There is no iron law that expenditures must always rise more rapidly than revenues, but it is a fact that growing needs which only the state can meet create ever greater claims on the state budget. Several factors, singly or in combination, may offset the crisis. People who need government-provided services may be ignored and their need neglected, as happened in New York's welfare cutback during the 1970–1971 recession. Corporations that want loans and subsidies from the government may not get them, as happened in the Congressional defeat of proposed subsidies for the development of the SST. Government-employee income may fall behind private sector income or below the cost of living, but this does not mean that these workers get automatic pay increases. In fact, the government may even freeze wages and salaries in an attempt to ameliorate the fiscal crisis. Furthermore, people can be forced to pay higher taxes. Should they be unwilling to pay taxes directly because large numbers oppose particular spending programs, the government can force them to pay taxes indirectly by financing increased expenditures via inflation or credit expansion—as the Johnson Administration did during the peak years of American aggression in Southeast Asia.

A combination of some of these countertendencies resulted in budgetary surpluses in many state and local governments in 1972. According to one "optimistic" estimate, state and local governments will be able to meet their normal needs through 1975 by increasing tax rates by not more than 5 percent.[2]

The volume and composition of government expenditures and the distribution of the tax burden are not determined by the laws of the market but rather reflect and are structurally determined by social and economic conflicts between classes and groups. The English Prime Minister Gladstone once said that "budgets are not merely matters of arithmetic, but in a thousand ways go to the root of prosperity of individuals, and relations of classes, and the strength of Kingdoms." The "relations of classes" were then expressed in many ways that today are of only historical interest. In modern America individual well-being, class relationships, and national wealth and power are bound up in the agony of the cities, poverty and racism, profits of big and small business, inflation, unemployment, the balance-of-payments problem, imperialism and war, and other crises that seem a permanent part of daily life. No one is exempt from the fiscal crisis and the underlying social crisis which it aggravates. We need a way to think about and ultimately act on this fiscal crisis that clarifies the contradictory processes which find both their reflection and cause in the government budget. We need a theory of government budget and a method for discovering the meaning for the political economy and society as a whole.

Perhaps then we will be able to answer such questions as: Who will pay for rising government expenditures? Will some kinds of spending rise while others are cut back? Can the government deliver more services for less taxes? Why don't Americans want to pay for services that presumably benefit the "people"? Can the fiscal system survive in its present form? Political-economic analysis is needed to answer these and dozens of other equally important related questions.

The Theoretical Bankruptcy of Traditional Economics

The theory of government budget put forth in this work is based on the study of fiscal politics, an investigation of the sociological foundations of government or state finances.[3] The main concerns of fiscal politics are to discover the principles governing the volume and allocation of state finances and expenditures and the distribution of the tax burden among various economic classes. The major work of the German Marxist Rudolph Goldscheid, founder of the contemporary science of fiscal politics, appeared in the second decade of this century.[4] A few years thereafter Joseph Schumpeter wrote glowingly of the promise of fiscal politics:

> The public finances are one of the best starting points for an investigation of society, especially though not exclusively of its political life. The full fruit-fulness of this approach is seen particularly at those turning points, or better epochs, during which existing forms begin to die off and to change into some-thing new. This is true both of the causal significance of fiscal policy (insofar as fiscal events are an important element in the causation of all change) and of the symptomatic significance (insofar as everything that happens has its fiscal reflection). Notwithstanding all the qualifications which always have to be made . . . we may surely speak of . . . a special field: fiscal sociology, of which much may be expected.[5]

Schumpeter's optimism proved to be premature. The budget remains, in his words, a "collection of hard, naked facts" not yet "drawn into the realm of sociology." "Unfortunately," one scholar confesses, "there exists no integrated theory of the economics and politics of public finance which would serve as a framework for analyzing [state] finances."[6] No blunter admission of theoretical bankruptcy can be found than the declaration that within the mainstream of Western economic thought,

> public finance, traditionally, has neither contained a theory of demand nor one of supply. . . . The scholar from outer space, coming to earth in the post-Marshallian era, might have concluded on perusing the English language liter-ature that governments exist wholly apart from their citizens, that these units impose taxes on individuals and firms primarily to nourish the state; and he might have thought that positive public finance consists in predicting the ef-fects of these taxes.[7]

The "scholar from outer space" would have been only partly right. Orthodox public finance theorists are concerned not only with the economic effects of taxation (and expenditures), but also with the problem of what the government should take away in taxes (and provide in expenditures). For example, in his study of state enterprise Ralph Turvey writes that "because it is public, what interests us about public enterprise is how it ought to behave. . . . [W]e are not so much concerned with understanding its behavior and making predictions as with criticizing and making recommendations."[8] Turvey's interest lies in how the behavior of state enterprise can be made to conform to a preconceived notion of economic optimum. This is the focus of the best known treatise on public fi-nance, Richard Musgrave's *The Theory of Public Finance*. Musgrave tries to synthesize the entire modern literature on government finance and, in particular, "to state the rules and principles that make for an efficient conduct of the public economy." Musgrave devises an "optimal budget plan on the basis of initially defined conditions" and then tries to "see how it can be achieved." He calls it "a normative or optimal theory of the public household."[9]

The effect of this emphasis on normative theory has been to ignore the application of the theory of economic growth. The absence of an "integrated theory of the economics and politics of public finance" (or "a theory of demand and supply of public goods and services") has compelled economists to adopt an almost metaphysical attitude toward government spending. For example, the Keynesian Evsey Domar theorized that government expenditures can be dealt with (1) by assuming that they are exogenous, or determined by forces outside the economic system; (2) by merging them with consumption expenditures; or (3) by assuming them away altogether. The last alternative is obviously completely unsatisfactory and to assume that government spending is determined by undefinable outside forces is to beg the question. And merging all government spending with private consumption is merely a convenient fiction. Methods of analysis such as this have led two public finance specialists to write that "growth models in their present form cannot be treated as anything more than exercises in a technique of arrangement."[10]

As government expenditures come to constitute a larger and larger share of total spending in advanced capitalist countries, economic theorists who ignore the impact of the state budget do so at their own (and capitalism's) peril. Currently, economists do not consider actual determinants in their theoretical models but rather restrict themselves to estimates of the volume of state spending necessary to effect desired changes such as high employment or more rapid accumulation and growth. Their premise is that the government budget should and can be increased or lowered to compensate for reduced or increased private spending. Many orthodox economists believe that the volume of federal spending (if not its composition) is determined by and inversely related to the volume of private spending.

As will be seen in the course of this study, the orthodox approach is at best simplistic. Although changes in tax rates and tax structure have been increasingly used to regulate private economic activity, the growth of federal spending over the past two or three decades has not resulted from the government's adopting compensatory fiscal policies, "except perhaps to a very limited degree."[11] Particular expenditures and programs and the budget as a whole are explicable only in terms of power relationships within the private economy.

Summation of the Theory of the Fiscal Crisis

To avoid "exercises in a technique of arrangement," we have attempted to develop a theory of economic growth that is rooted in the basic economic and political facts of late capitalist society. We hope to elucidate the relationship between the private and state sectors and between private and state spending. Although we believe that many of the ideas presented can be adapted to the experience of other advanced capitalist countries, the focus is on the post–World War II United States. Basically an interpretation of the period's economic development and crisis tendencies, this study does not offer a comprehensive analysis of state budgetary planning and policy or a comprehensive guide to state finance. Many of the data presented have been chosen more to illustrate a line of theoretical argument than to verify a set of hypotheses.

The categories that make up this theoretical framework are drawn from Marxist economics and adapted to the problem of budgetary analysis. Our first premise is that the capitalistic state must try to fulfill two basic and often mutually contradictory functions—*accumulation* and *legitimization.* This means that the state must try to maintain or create the conditions in which profitable capital accumulation is possible. However, the state also must try to maintain or create the conditions for social harmony. A capitalist state that openly uses its coercive forces to help one class accumulate capital at the expense of other classes loses its legitimacy and hence undermines the basis of its loyalty and support. But a state that ignores the necessity of assisting the process of capital accumulation risks drying up the source of its own power, the economy's surplus production capacity and the taxes drawn from this surplus (and other forms of capital). This contradiction explains why President Nixon calls a legislated increase in profit rates a "job development credit," why the government announces that new fiscal policies are aimed at "stability and growth" when in fact their purpose is to keep profits high and growing, why the tax system is nominally progressive and theoretically based on "ability to pay" when in fact the system is regressive. The state must involve itself in the accumulation process, but it must either mystify its policies by calling them something that they are not, or it must try to conceal them (e.g., by making them into administrative, not political, issues).

Our second premise is that the fiscal crisis can be understood only in terms of the basic Marxist economic categories (adapted to the problems taken up here). State expenditures have a twofold character corresponding to the capitalist state's two basic functions: social capital and social expenses. *Social capital* is expenditures required for profitable private accumulation; it is indirectly productive (in Marxist terms, social capital indirectly expands surplus value). There are two kinds of social capital: social investment and social consumption (in Marxist terms, social constant capital and social variable capital). *Social investment* consists of projects and services that increase the productivity of a given amount of labor power and, other factors being equal, increase the rate of profit. A good example is state-financed industrial-development parks. *Social consumption* consists of projects and services that lower the reproduction costs of labor and, other factors being equal, increase the rate of profit. An example of this is social insurance, which expands the reproductive powers of the work force while simultaneously lowering labor costs. The second category, *social expenses,* consists of projects and services which are required to maintain social harmony—to fulfill the state's "legitimization" function. They are not even indirectly productive. The best example is the welfare system, which is designed chiefly to keep social peace among unemployed workers. (The costs of politically repressed populations in revolt would also constitute a part of social expenses.)

Because of the dual and contradictory character of the capitalist state, nearly every state agency is involved in the accumulation and legitimization functions, and nearly every state expenditure has this twofold character. For example, some education spending constitutes social capital (e.g., teachers and equipment needed to reproduce and expand work-force technical and skill levels), whereas other outlays constitute social expenses (e.g., salaries of campus policemen). To take another example, the main purpose of some transfer payments (e.g., social insurance) is to reproduce the work force, whereas the purpose of others (e.g., income subsidies to the poor) is to pacify and control the surplus population. The national income accounts lump the various categories of state spending together. (The state does not analyze its budget in class terms.) Clearly, the different categories cannot be separated if each budget item is not examined.

Furthermore precisely because of the social character of social capital and social expenses, nearly every state expenditure serves these two (or more) purposes simultaneously, so that few state outlays can be classified unambiguously. For example, freeways move workers to and from work and are therefore items of social consumption, but they also transport commercial freight and are therefore a form of social investment. And, when used for either purpose, they may be considered forms of social capital. However, the Pentagon also needs freeways; therefore they in part constitute social expenses. Despite this complex social character of state outlays we can determine the political-economic forces served by any budgetary decision, and thus the main purpose (or purposes) of each budgetary item.

The first basic thesis presented here is that the growth of the state sector and state spending is functioning increasingly as the basis for the growth of the monopoly sector and total production. Conversely, it is argued that the growth of state spending and state programs is the result of the growth of the monopoly industries. In other words, the growth of the state is both a cause and effect of the expansion of monopoly capital.

More specifically, the socialization of the cost of social investment and social consumption capital increases over time and increasingly is needed for profitable accumulation by monopoly capital. The general reason is that the increase in the social character of production (specialization, division of labor, interdependency, the growth of new social forms of capital such as education, etc.) either prohibits or renders unprofitable the private accumulation of constant and variable capital. The growth of the monopoly sector is irrational in the sense that it is accompanied by unemployment, poverty, economic stagnation, and so on. To insure mass loyalty and maintain its legitimacy, the state must meet various demands of those who suffer the "costs" of economic growth.

It might help to compare our approach with traditional economic theory.

Bourgeois economists have shown that increases in private consumption beget increases in private investment via the accelerator effect. In turn, increases in private investment beget increases in private consumption via the multiplier effect. Similarly, we argue that greater social investment and social consumption spending generate greater private investment and private consumption spending, which in turn generate surplus capital (surplus productive capacity and a surplus population) and a larger volume of social expenses. Briefly, the supply of social capital creates the demand for social expenses. In effect, we work with a model of expanded reproduction (or a model of the economy as a whole) which is generalized to take into account the socialization of constant and variable capital costs and the costs of social expenses.[12] The impact of the budget depends on the volume and indirect productivity of social capital and the volume of social expenses. On the one hand, social capital outlays indirectly increase productive capacity and simultaneously increase aggregate demand. On the other hand, social expense outlays do not increase productive capacity, although they do expand aggregate demand. Whether the growth of productive capacity runs ahead [of] or behind the growth of demand thus depends on the composition of the state budget. In this way, we can see that the theory of economic growth depends on class and political analyses of the determinants of the budget.

This view contrasts sharply with modern conservative thought, which asserts that the state sector grows at the expense of private industry. We argue that the growth of the state sector is indispensable to the expansion of private industry, particularly monopoly industries. Our thesis also contrasts sharply with a basic tenet of modern liberal thought—that the expansion of monopoly industries inhibits the growth of the state sectors.[13] The fact of the matter is that the growth of monopoly capital generates increased expansion of social expenses. In sum, the greater the growth of social capital, the greater the growth of the monopoly sector. And the greater the growth of the monopoly sector, the greater the state's expenditures on social expenses of production.

The second basic thesis in this study is that the accumulation of social capital and social expenses is a contradictory process which creates tendencies toward economic, social, and political crises. Two separate but related lines of analysis are explored.

First, we argue that although the state has socialized more and more capital costs, the social surplus (including profits) continues to be appropriated privately. The socialization of costs and the private appropriation of profits creates a fiscal crisis, or "structural gap," between state expenditures and state revenues. The result is a tendency for state expenditures to increase more rapidly than the means of financing them.[14] While the accumulation of social capital indirectly increases total production and society's surplus and thus in principle appears to underwrite the expansion of social expenses, large monopoly-sector corporations and unions strongly resist the appropriation of this surplus for new social capital or social expense outlays.

Second, we argue that the fiscal crisis is exacerbated by the private appropriation of state power for particularistic ends. A host of "special interests"— corporations, industries, regional and other business interests—make claims on the budget for various kinds of social investment. (These claims are politically processed in ways that must either be legitimated or obscured from public view.) Organized labor and workers generally make various claims for different kinds of social consumption, and the unemployed and poor (together with businessmen in financial trouble) stake their claims for expanded social expenses. Few if any claims are coordinated by the market. Most are processed by the political system and are won or lost as a result of political struggle. Precisely because the accumulation of social capital and social expenses occurs within a political framework, there is a great deal of waste, duplication, and overlapping of state projects and services. Some claims conflict and cancel one another out. Others are mutually contradictory in a variety of ways. The accumulation of social capital and social expenses is a highly irrational process from the standpoint of administrative coherence, fiscal stability, and potentially profitable private capital accumulation. We discuss the ways in which struggles around the control of the budget have developed in recent years and the ways in which these struggles impair the fiscal capacity of the system and potentially threaten the capacity of the system to produce surplus.

Notes

1. Arthur F. Burns, statement to the Joint Economic Committee, July 26, 1972, *Federal Reserve Bulletin,* August 1972, p. 699. Burns concludes that "the fundamental problem . . . is how to regain control over Federal expenditures." As this study will attempt to show, the lack of control of federal expenditures is merely a symptom of a much more deep-rooted problem.

2. Richard Musgrave and A. Mitchell Polinsky: cited by Edward C. Banfield, "Revenue Sharing in Theory and Practice," *The Public Interest,* 33 (Spring 1971), 35.

3. The conventional phrase "public finance" reveals the ideological content of orthodox economic thought by prejudging the question of the real purposes of the budget. The phrase "state finance" is preferable to "public finance" (and "state sector" to "public sector," etc.) precisely because it remains to be investigated how "public" are the real and financial transactions that take place in the state sector. For example, many so-called public investments are merely special forms of private investments.

4. Rudolf Goldscheid, "A Sociological Approach to the Problem of Public Finance," reprinted in translation in Richard Musgrave and Alan T. Peacock, eds., *Classics in the Theory of Public Finance* (New York: 1958); *Staatssozialismus oder Staatskapitalismus* (Wien-Leipzig, 1917); *Sozialisierung der Wirtschaft oder Staatsbankerott* (Leipzig-Wien, 1919).

5. Joseph Schumpeter, "The Crisis of the Tax State," reprinted in *International Economic Papers,* No. 4 (1954), p.7. Schumpeter was expecting much of the mainstream of economic thought (the orthodox or bourgeois economists). Fiscal sociology has always been central to the Marxist tradition. Marx himself wrote extensively on the subject. For example, compare Marx's conclusion that "tax struggle is the oldest form of class struggle" with the contemporary English Marxist John Eaton's statement that "state expenditure is . . . unceasingly the battleground of class interests."

6. Glenn W. Fisher, *Taxes and Politics, A Study of Illinois Public Finance* (Urbana, Ill.: 1969), p. 3.

7. James M. Buchanan, *The Demand and Supply of Public Goods* (Chicago: 1968), p. v. Political scientists also have tended to take the state and political order for granted in their analyses of politics and administration as natural phenomena. See Theodore Lowi, "Decision Making vs. Policy Making: Toward an Antidote for Technocracy," *Public Administration Review,* 30:3 (May/June 1970).

8. Ralph Turvey, *Public Enterprise* (Baltimore: 1968).

9. Richard A. Musgrave, *The Theory of Public Finance* (New York: 1959), p. 4. Musgrave's treatise is a perfect example of what Paul Baran was talking about years ago when he wrote that "in our time . . . faith in the manipulative omnipotence of the State has all but displaced analysis of its social structure and understanding of its political and economic functions." Paul A. Baran, *The Longer View* (New York: 1969), p. 262.

10. Evsey Domar, *Essays in the Theory of Economic Growth* (New York: 1957), p. 6; Alan T. Peacock and Jack Wiseman, *The Growth of Public Expenditures in the United Kingdom* (Princeton, N.J.: 1961), p. 10.

11. Herbert Stein, *The Fiscal Revolution in America* (Chicago: 1969), p. 69. Stein is an establishment economist who participated in many crucial corporate and government decisions in the 1950s and 1960s. He was associated for a long time with the corporate-dominated Committee for Economic Development and was chief economic advisor to President Nixon in 1971–1972. "[A] very limited degree" means that Congress is more receptive to new spending bills during periods of recession. Three other exceptions to the general rule should be noted: (1) In 1958, the federal government began extending unemployment insurance programs to give workers additional purchasing power and thus offset expected declines in private spending (the policy has been applied fitfully since 1958). (2) Federal highway expenditures have been adjusted to smooth out fluctuations in the economy. However, fiscal policy probably has affected the timing of government outlays much more than the total volume of highway spending. (3) The President has tried to regulate spending by impounding funds (impounded funds rose from about 3.5 percent of total appropriations in 1964 to roughly 5.5 percent in 1971).

12. We have not presented a theory of the relationship between private investment and private consumption in either the short run or long run. Nor have we worked out in detail the dialectical movements between the different kinds of state expenditures. Consider, briefly, education expenditures. Education spending does double-duty as both constant and variable capital. The education system also temporarily takes surplus population off the labor market. In other words, the growth of education simultaneously absorbs surplus labor and expands productivity (and thus creates more surplus labor). In short, education spending creates and eliminates surplus capital simultaneously. Any detailed study of the education system would have to take this basic contradiction into account. A further complication arises to the degree that the growth of the education establishment and the growth of militarism are inseparable processes (as they seem to have been in the United States). It is probably true that one of the reasons that state-financed higher education in Europe is relatively undeveloped is that military and related spending is comparatively small.

Finally, it might be added that both Marx's notion of realization crises and Keynesian notions of crises of effective demand require emendation. The reason is that "supply creates its own demand" in ways that neoclassical economics never dreamed of.

13. The standard conservative work is Milton Friedman's *Capitalism and Freedom* (Chicago: 1962). The standard liberal work is John Kenneth Galbraith's *The Affluent Society* (Boston: 1958).

14. The socialization of profits consists of the redistribution of productive wealth from capital to labor, or the confiscation of the owning classes by the working class. Although

wealth and profits as a whole have not been socialized, a portion of surplus value is appropriated by the state and used to finance expanded social capital and social expense outlays. Instead of private capital "plowing back" a portion of surplus value into expanded reproduction (net capital formation) in a particular corporation or industry, the state "plows back" that part of the pool of surplus value that it appropriated into expanded social reproduction (new social capital formation) in industry as a whole. However, the state also appropriates part of constant and variable capital. Because capital's and labor's claims on budgetary resources are processed by the political mechanism, there is rarely a one-to-one correspondence between sources of financing and the uses of tax monies. On the one hand, taxes must appear to conform to bourgeois democratic norms of "equity" and "ability to pay." On the other hand, the mixed character of social capital and social expense outlays makes it difficult to develop clearly defined criteria for identifying state expenditures empirically. Perhaps the closest correspondence between private and social forms of capital is the tax on payrolls (levied on private variable capital or wages) which is used to finance social insurance (a form of social variable capital).

2. Regulation of the Private Sector

Government can affect economic outcomes by influencing the total demand for goods, by choosing to produce certain goods itself, or by enacting rules that prescribe how private industry can operate. The most common way in which government sets rules for private industry is through the regulation of business activity.

Business regulation can be instituted to control business for the benefit of the consumer or to enable business to exploit consumers. There are a number of ways in which regulation can help consumers. *Natural monopoly regulation* prevents industries that are natural monopolies, such as the gas or electric industries, from charging the high prices that their market position would otherwise allow them to do. *Information regulation* takes place when the government investigates and tries to correct potentially harmful business practices such as building with asbestos, putting unsafe drugs on the market, or failing to properly cook hamburger. *Negative externality regulation* is government control of air pollution, excessive noise, toxic waste, and other problems that occur as a by-product of industrial or commercial activity. *Positive externality regulation* such as the patent laws or setback regulations for houses encourage people to undertake activities that have side-benefits for others.

But regulation is not just instituted to benefit consumers. *Producer regulation* (a form of what economists term *rent seeking*) occurs when competitive businesses use the power of government to raise the prices of their products and restrict entry into the industry. Many considered airline regulation to be of this kind, and groups as diverse as doctors, cabbies, and beauty parlor operators use licensing to restrict entry into their profession. *Public property regulation* takes place when the government allocates the use of natural resources, such as the airwaves and national parks, between competing interests wishing to use those resources. As McConnell (1966) has shown, this generally results in the expropriation of public assets by business. *Moral regulation* such as banning prostitution or forcing people to wear motorcycle helmets is used to force consumers to do what government and/or the majority think is right for them.

Cross-subsidization benefits neither business nor most consumers. It occurs when regulation is undertaken to subsidize one set of consumers at the expense of another. For example, requiring hospitals to admit all sick people whether they can pay or not leads to solvent patients being charged higher fees to cover the losses. Another example is the lower utility rates sometimes given to the poor, elderly, and veterans, which raise everyone else's rates.

The articles in this section by Downs and Stigler take different positions on the underlying dynamic of regulation. Downs sees government as continually striving to do what the average voter wants it to do. Thus he thinks that the extent of regulation depends primarily on what the general public thinks is in its interest. Stigler feels that most business activity is invisible to the general public and that government is captured by informed and powerful business groups who use government to extract as much as they can from the public. The reader should note that it is quite possible that they are both partially right, with regulation occurring for a variety of reasons.

The other two readings in this section look at the topic of deregulation. The reader should note that just as regulation may serve or harm the consumer, deregulation can aid consumers or harm them. Those who argue for deregulation use three sets of arguments. One is that some regulation was never in the interest of consumers in the first place and hence deregulation would benefit them. The second is that changes in technology or capture by industry have made regulation that was once in the interest of consumers no longer in their interest. The last is that even when a theoretical case can be made for regulation on behalf of consumers, the costs of regulating may be so great as to outweigh the benefits. In the reading in this volume Weidenbaum concentrates on the third of these arguments.

Those who oppose deregulation say that the costs of regulation are often exaggerated by industry in order to remove rules that benefit the consumer. These proponents of regulation say that regulation often has hidden benefits, like increased safety or quality of service, that are lost when one deregulates. And they say that the benefits are often undercounted by those who wish to abuse the public. Arrow represents what might be thought of as the moderate rebuttal to deregulation arguments, arguing that deregulation is useful in some cases but should not be overdone.

For Further Reading

Two good general introductions to the politics of regulation are Kenneth Meier's *Regulation: Politics, Bureaucracy and Economics* and Alan Stone's *Regulation and Its Alternatives*. A sound introduction to the economic considerations involved in regulation is Douglas Needham's *The Economics and Politics of Regulation: A Behavioral Approach*. James Q. Wilson's *The Politics of Regulation* contains a number of interesting case studies of different regulatory agencies.

Samuel Huntington's "The Marasmus of the ICC" and Marver Bernstein's *Regulating Business by Independent Commission* show how regulatory agencies can be co-opted by the businesses they are regulating. Richard Posner's "Taxation by Regulation" expounds the notion that taxation is a motive for regulation. Barry Mitnick's *The Political Economy of Regulation* and Paul Quirk's *Industry Influence in Regulatory Agencies* outline and analyze most of the major political theories about regulation. *The Federal Regulatory Directory,* published by The Congressional Quarterly, gives up-to-date facts about regulatory agencies. Murray Weidenbaum's *The Future of Business Regulation: Private Action and Public Demand* outlines a regulatory reform program which served as a guide for the Reagan administration's efforts at deregulation. Leonard Weiss and Michael Klass's *Regulatory Reform: What Actually Happened* examines the effects of deregulation under the Carter and Reagan administrations.

References

Bernstein, Marver H. 1955. *Regulating Business by Independent Commission.* Princeton N.J.: Princeton University Press.

Congressional Quarterly Press. 1986. *Federal Regulatory Directory.* 5th ed. Washington D.C.: Congressional Quarterly Press.

Gilligan, Thomas W., William J. Marsall, and Barry R. Weingast. 1987. "Regulation and the Theory of Legislative Choice: The Interstate Commerce Act of 1887." *Journal of Law and Economics* 32: 35–62.

Huntington, Samuel. 1952. "The Marasmus of the ICC." *Yale Law Journal* 61 (April): 467–509.

McConnell, Grant. 1966. *Private Power and American Democracy.* New York: Knopf.

Meier, Kenneth J. 1985. *Regulation: Politics, Bureaucracy and Economics.* New York: St. Martin's Press.

Mitnick, Barry. 1980. *The Political Economy of Regulation.* New York: Columbia University Press.

Needham, Douglas. 1983. *The Economics and Politics of Regulation: A Behavioral Approach.* Boston: Little Brown.

Posner, Richard A. 1971. "Taxation by Regulation." *Bell Journal of Economics and Management Science* 3:1 (spring): 22–50.

Quirk, Paul J. 1981. *Industry Influence in Regulatory Agencies.* Princeton, N.J.: Princeton University Press.

Stone, Alan. 1982. *Regulation and Its Alternatives.* Washington D.C.: Congressional Quarterly Press.

Weidenbaum, Murray. 1979. *The Future of Business Regulation: Private Action and Public Demand.* New York: AMACOM.

Weiss, Leonard W., and Michael W. Klass, eds. 1986. *Regulatory Reform: What Actually Happened.* Boston: Little Brown.

Wilson, James Q., ed. 1980. *The Politics of Regulation.* New York: Basic Books.

2.1. Up and Down with Ecology: The "Issue-Attention Cycle"

ANTHONY DOWNS

We typically think of business regulation as an attempt by the public, or consumers, to curb the excesses of private business. Such regulation becomes necessary when businesses, in their effort to reduce costs and increase profits in the face of competition, undertake practices that could harm their customers or the surrounding community. In this essay Anthony Downs tries to show the circumstances under which such excesses will be curbed in a democracy.

Downs outlines a five-part "issue-attention cycle," which he applies to the great wave of environmental regulation that took place in the 1960s and early 1970s. In the first stage, a problem exists but the general public is not aware of it. In the second stage, the public discovers the problem and there is public outrage, followed by demands for regulation. In the third stage, attempts to solve the problem make the public aware of the (generally high) costs of solving the problem. In the fourth stage, the issue becomes less popular and is replaced in the public consciousness by new problems whose solution costs are not yet publicly perceived. In the fifth and final stage, the original issue sinks into the background at a higher level of public consciousness than before the issue was raised, but at a far lower level than before the costs of solving the problem became apparent.

It is important to note that Downs views regulation as taking place for the benefit of the general public. He also sees the degree of public support as the crucial variable both in establishing and in maintaining regulation. Thus Downs implicitly assumes that regulatory policy is produced through an open demo-

Reprinted with permission of the author and *The Public Interest*, No. 28 (Summer 1972): 38–50. Copyright © 1972 by National Affairs, Inc.

cratic process aimed at satisfying the needs of the average consumer. He spells these assumptions out in more detail in the early chapters of An Economic Theory of Democracy (1957).

American public attention rarely remains sharply focused upon any one domestic issue for very long—even if it involves a continuing problem of crucial importance to society. Instead, a systematic "issue-attention cycle" seems strongly to influence public attitudes and behavior concerning most key domestic problems. Each of these problems suddenly leaps into prominence, remains there for a short time, and then—though still largely unresolved—gradually fades from the center of public attention. A study of the way this cycle operates provides insights into how long public attention is likely to remain sufficiently focused upon any given issue to generate enough political pressure to cause effective change.

The shaping of American attitudes toward improving the quality of our environment provides both an example and a potential test of this "issue-attention cycle." In the past few years, there has been a remarkably widespread upsurge of interest in the quality of our environment. This change in public attitudes has been much faster than any changes in the environment itself. What has caused this shift in public attention? Why did this issue suddenly assume so high a priority among our domestic concerns? And how long will the American public sustain high-intensity interest in ecological matters? I believe that answers to these questions can be derived from analyzing the "issue-attention cycle."

The Dynamics of the "Issue-Attention Cycle"

Public perception of most "crises" in American domestic life does not reflect changes in real conditions as much as it reflects the operation of a systematic cycle of heightening public interest and then increasing boredom with major issues. This "issue-attention cycle" is rooted both in the nature of certain domestic problems and in the way major communications media interact with the public. The cycle itself has five stages, which may vary in duration depending upon the particular issue involved, but which almost always occur in the following sequence:

1. The Pre-problem Stage

This prevails when some highly undesirable social condition exists but has not yet captured much public attention, even though some experts or interest groups may already be alarmed by it. *Usually, objective conditions regarding the problem are far worse during the pre-problem stage than they are by the time the public becomes interested in it.* For example, this was true of racism, poverty, and malnutrition in the United States.

2. Alarmed Discovery and Euphoric Enthusiasm

As a result of some dramatic series of events (like the ghetto riots in 1965 to 1967), or for other reasons, the public suddenly becomes both aware of and alarmed about the evils of a particular problem. This alarmed discovery is invariably accompanied by euphoric enthusiasm about society's ability to "solve this problem" or "do something effective" within a relatively short time. The combination of alarm and confidence results in part from the strong public pressure in America for political leaders to claim that every problem can be "solved." This outlook is rooted in the great American tradition of optimistically viewing most obstacles to social progress as *external* to the structure of society itself. The implication is that every obstacle can be eliminated and every problem solved *without any fundamental reordering of society itself,* if only we devote sufficient effort to it. In older and perhaps wiser cultures, there is an underlying sense of irony or even pessimism which springs from a widespread and often confirmed belief that many problems cannot be "solved" *at all* in any complete sense. Only recently has this more pessimistic view begun to develop in our culture.

3. Realizing the Cost of Significant Progress

The third stage consists of a gradually spreading realization that the cost of "solving" the problem is very high indeed. Really doing so would not only take a great deal of money but would also require major sacrifices by large groups in the population. The public thus begins to realize that part of the problem results from arrangements that are providing significant benefits to someone—often to millions. For example, traffic congestion and a great deal of smog are caused by increasing automobile usage. Yet this also enhances the mobility of millions of Americans who continue to purchase more vehicles to obtain these advantages.

In certain cases, technological progress can eliminate some of the undesirable results of a problem without causing any major restructuring of society or any loss of present benefits by others (except for higher money costs). In the optimistic American tradition, such a technological solution is initially assumed to be possible in the case of nearly every problem. Our most pressing social problems, however, usually involve either deliberate or unconscious exploitation of one group in society by another, or the prevention of one group from enjoying something that others want to keep for themselves. For example, most upper-middle-class whites value geographic separation from poor people and blacks. Hence any equality of access to the advantages of suburban living for the poor and for blacks cannot be achieved without some sacrifice by middle-class whites of the "benefits" of separation. The increasing recognition that there is this type of relationship between the problem and its "solution" constitutes a key part of the third stage.

4. Gradual Decline of Intense Public Interest

The previous stage becomes almost imperceptibly transformed into the fourth stage: a gradual decline in the intensity of public interest in the problem. As more and more people realize how difficult, and how costly to themselves, a solution to the problem would be, three reactions set in. Some people just get discouraged. Others feel positively threatened by thinking about the problem; so they suppress such thoughts. Still others become bored by the issue. Most people experience some combination of these feelings. Consequently, public desire to keep attention focused on the issue wanes. And by this time, some other issue is usually entering Stage Two; so it exerts a more novel and thus more powerful claim upon public attention.

5. The Post-problem Stage

In the final stage, an issue that has been replaced at the center of public concern moves into a prolonged limbo—a twilight realm of lesser attention or spasmodic recurrences of interest. However, the issue now has a different relation to public attention than that which prevailed in the "pre-problem" stage. For one thing, during the time that interest was sharply focused on this problem, new institutions, programs, and policies may have been created to help solve it. These entities almost always persist and often have some impact even after public attention has shifted elsewhere. For example, during the early stages of the "War on Poverty," the Office of Economic Opportunity (OEO) was established, and it initiated many new programs. Although poverty has now faded as a central public issue, OEO still exists. Moreover, many of its programs have experienced significant success, even though funded at a far lower level than would be necessary to reduce poverty decisively.

Any major problem that once was elevated to national prominence may sporadically recapture public interest; or important aspects of it may become attached to some other problem that subsequently dominates center stage. Therefore, problems that have gone through the cycle almost always receive a higher average level of attention, public effort, and general concern than those still in the pre-discovery stage.

Which Problems Are Likely to Go Through the Cycle?

Not all major social problems go through this "issue-attention cycle." Those that do generally possess to some degree three specific characteristics. First, the majority of persons in society are not suffering from the problem nearly as much as some minority (a *numerical* minority, not necessarily an *ethnic* one). This is true of many pressing social problems in America today—poverty, racism, poor public transportation, low-quality education, crime, drug addiction, and unemployment, among others. The number of persons suffering from each of these ills is very large *absolutely*—in the millions. But the numbers are small *relatively*—usually less than 15 percent of the entire population. Therefore, most people do not suffer directly enough from such problems to keep their attention riveted on them.

Second, the sufferings caused by the problem are generated by social arrangements that provide significant benefits to a majority or a powerful minority of the population. For example, Americans who own cars—plus the powerful automobile and highway lobbies—receive short-run benefits from the prohibition of using motor-fuel tax revenues for financing public transportation systems, even though such systems are desperately needed by the urban poor.

Third, the problem has no intrinsically exciting qualities—or no longer has them. When big-city racial riots were being shown nightly on the nation's television screens, public attention naturally focused upon their causes and consequences. But when they ceased (or at least the media stopped reporting them so intensively), public interest in the problems related to them declined sharply. Similarly, as long as the National Aeronautics and Space Administration (NASA) was able to stage a series of ever more thrilling space shots, culminating in the worldwide television spectacular of Americans walking on the moon, it generated sufficient public support to sustain high-level Congressional appropriations. But NASA had nothing half so dramatic for an encore, and repetition of the same feat proved less and less exciting (though a near disaster on the third try did revive audience interest). So NASA's Congressional appropriations plummeted.

A problem must be dramatic and exciting to maintain public interest because news is "consumed" by much of the American public (and by publics everywhere) largely as a form of entertainment. As such, it competes with other types of entertainment for a share of each person's time. Every day, there is a fierce struggle for space in the highly limited universe of newsprint and television viewing time. Each issue vies not only with all other social problems and public events, but also with a multitude of "non-news" items that are often far more pleasant to contemplate. These include sporting news, weather reports, crossword puzzles, fashion accounts, comics, and daily horoscopes. In fact, the amount of television time and newspaper space devoted to sports coverage, as compared to international events, is a striking commentary on the relative value that the public places on knowing about these two subjects.

When all three of the above conditions exist concerning a given problem that has somehow captured public attention, the odds are great that it will soon move through the entire "issue-attention cycle"—and therefore will gradually fade from the center of the stage. The first condition means that most people will not be continually reminded of the problem by their own suffering from it. The second condition means that solving the problem requires sustained attention and effort, plus fundamental changes in social institutions or behavior. This in turn means that significant attempts to solve it are threatening to important groups in society. The third condition means that the media's sustained focus on this problem soon bores a majority of the public. As soon as the media realize that their emphasis on this problem is threatening many people and boring even more, they will shift their focus to some "new" problem. This is particularly likely in America because nearly all the media are run for profit, and they make the most money by appealing to the largest possible audiences. Thus, as Marshall McLuhan has pointed out, it is largely the audience itself—the American public—that "manages the news" by maintaining or losing interest in a given subject. As long as this pattern persists, we will continue to be confronted by a stream of "crises" involving particular social problems. Each will rise into public view, capture center stage for a while, and then gradually fade away as it is replaced by more fashionable issues moving into their "crisis" phases.

The Rise of Environmental Concern

Public interest in the quality of the environment now appears to be about midway through the "issue-attention cycle." Gradually, more and more people are beginning to realize the immensity of the social and financial costs of cleaning up our air and water and of preserving and restoring open spaces. Hence much of the enthusiasm about prompt, dramatic improvement in the environment is fading. There is still a great deal of public interest, however, so it cannot be said that the "post-problem stage" has been reached. In fact, as will be discussed later, the environmental issue may well retain more attention than social problems that affect smaller proportions of the population. Before evaluating the prospects of long-term interest in the environment, though, it is helpful to analyze how environmental concern passed through the earlier stages in the "issue-attention cycle."

The most obvious reason for the initial rise in concern about the environment is the recent deterioration of certain easily perceived environmental conditions. A whole catalogue of symptoms can be arrayed, including ubiquitous urban smog, greater proliferation of solid waste, oceanic oil spills, greater pollution of water supplies by DDT and other poisons, the threatened disappearance of many wildlife species, and the overcrowding of a variety of facilities from commuter expressways to National Parks. Millions of citizens observing these worsening conditions became convinced that *someone* ought to "do something" about them. But "doing something" to reduce environmental deterioration is not easy. For many of our environmental problems have been caused by developments that are highly valued by most Americans.

The very abundance of our production and consumption of material goods is responsible for an immense amount of environmental pollution. For example, electric power generation, if based on fossil fuels, creates smoke and air pollution or, if based on nuclear fuels, causes rising water temperatures. Yet a key foundation for rising living standards in the United States during this century has been the doubling of electric power consumption every 10 years. So more pollution is the price we have paid for the tremendous advantages of being able to use more and more electricity. Similarly, much of the litter blighting even our remotest landscapes stems from the convenience of using "throwaway packages." Thus, to regard environmental pollution as a purely external negative factor would be to ignore its direct linkage with material advantages most citizens enjoy.

Another otherwise favorable development that has led to rising environmental pollution is what I would call the democratization of privilege. Many more Americans are now able to participate in certain activities that were formerly available only to a small, wealthy minority. Some members of that minority are incensed by the consequences of having their formerly esoteric advantages spread to "the common man." The most frequent irritant caused by the democratization of privilege is congestion. Rising highway congestion, for example, is denounced almost everywhere. Yet its main cause is the rapid spread of automobile ownership and usage. In 1950, about 59 percent of all families had at least one automobile, and seven percent owned two or more. By 1968, the proportion of families owning at least one automobile had climbed to 79 percent, and 26 percent had two or more cars. In the 10 years from 1960 to 1970, the total number of registered automotive vehicles rose by 35 million (or 47 percent), as compared to a rise in human population of 23 million (or only 13 percent). Moreover, it has been estimated that motor vehicles cause approximately 60 percent of all air pollution. So the tremendous increase in smog does not result primarily from larger population, but rather from the democratization of automobile ownership.

The democratization of privilege also causes crowding in National Parks, rising suburban housing density, the expansion of new subdivisions into formerly picturesque farms and orchards, and the transformation of once tranquil resort areas like Waikiki Beach into forests of high-rise buildings. It is now difficult for the wealthy to flee from busy urban areas to places of quiet seclusion, because so many more people can afford to go with them. The elite's environmental deterioration is often the common man's improved standard of living.

Our Soaring Aspirations

A somewhat different factor which has contributed to greater concern with environmental quality is a marked increase in our aspirations and standards concerning what our environment ought to be like. In my opinion, rising dissatisfaction with the "system" in the United States does not result primarily from poorer performance by that system. Rather, it stems mainly from a rapid escalation of our aspirations as to what the system's performance ought to be. Nowhere is this phenomenon more striking than in regard to the quality of the environment. One hundred years ago, white Americans were eliminating whole Indian tribes without a qualm. Today, many serious-minded citizens seek to make important issues out of the potential disappearance of the whooping crane, the timber wolf, and other exotic creatures. Meanwhile, thousands of Indians in Brazil are still being murdered each year—but American conservationists are not focusing on that human massacre. Similarly, some aesthetes decry "galloping sprawl" in metropolitan fringe areas, while they ignore acres of rat-infested housing a few miles away. Hence, the escalation of our environmental aspirations is more selective than might at first appear.

Yet regarding many forms of pollution, we are now rightly upset over practices and conditions that have largely been ignored for decades. An example is our alarm about the dumping of industrial wastes and sewage into rivers and lakes. This increase in our environmental aspirations is part of a general cultural phenomenon stimulated both by our success in raising living standards and by the recent emphases of the communications media. Another cause of the rapid rise in interest in environmental pollution is the "explosion" of alarmist rhetoric on this subject. According to some well publicized experts, all life on earth is threatened by an "environmental crisis." Some claim human life will end within three decades or less if we do not do something drastic about current behavior patterns.

Are things really that bad? Frankly, I am not enough of an ecological expert to know. But I am skeptical concerning all highly alarmist views because so many previous prophets of doom and disaster have been so wrong concerning many other so-called "crises" in our society.

There are two reasonable definitions of "crisis." One kind of crisis consists of a rapidly deteriorating situation moving towards a single disastrous event at some future moment. The second kind consists of a more gradually deteriorating situation that will eventually pass some subtle "point of no return." At present, I do not believe either of these definitions applies to most American domestic problems. Although many social critics hate to admit it, the American "system" actually serves the majority of citizens rather well in terms of most indicators of well-being. Concerning such things as real income, personal mobility, variety and choice of consumption patterns, longevity, health, leisure time, and quality of housing, most Americans are better off today than they have ever been and extraordinarily better off than most of mankind. What is *not* improving is the gap between society's performance and what most people—or at least highly vocal minorities—believe society *ought* to be doing to solve these problems. Our aspirations and standards have risen far faster than the beneficial outputs of our social system. Therefore, although most Americans, including most of the poor, are receiving more now, they are enjoying it less.

This conclusion should not be confused with the complacency of some superpatriots. It would be unrealistic to deny certain important negative trends in American life. Some conditions are indeed getting worse for nearly everyone. Examples are air quality and freedom from thievery. Moreover, congestion and environmental deterioration might forever destroy certain valuable national amenities if they are not checked. Finally, there has probably been a general rise in personal and social anxiety in recent years. I believe this is due to increased tensions caused by our rapid rate of technical and social change, plus the increase in worldwide communication through the media. These developments rightly cause serious and genuine concern among millions of Americans.

The Future of the Environmental Issue

Concern about the environment has passed through the first two stages of the "issue-attention cycle" and is by now well into the third. In fact, we have already begun to move toward the fourth stage, in which the intensity of public interest in environmental improvement must inexorably decline. And this raises an interesting question: Will the issue of environmental quality then move on into the "post-problem" stage of the cycle?

My answer to this question is: Yes, but not soon, because certain characteristics of this issue will protect it from the rapid decline in public interest typical of many other recent issues. First of all, many kinds of environmental pollution are much more visible and more clearly threatening than most other social problems. This is particularly true of air pollution. The greater the apparent threat from visible forms of pollution and the more vividly this can be dramatized, the more public support environmental improvement will receive and the longer it will sustain public interest. Ironically, the cause of ecologists would therefore benefit from an environmental disaster like a "killer smog" that would choke thousands to death in a few days. Actually, this is nothing new; every cause from early Christianity to the Black Panthers has benefited from martyrs. Yet even the most powerful symbols lose their impact if they are constantly repeated. The piteous sight of an oil-soaked seagull or a dead soldier pales after it has been viewed even a dozen times. Moreover, some of the worst environmental threats come from forms of pollution that are invisible. Thus, our propensity to focus attention on what is most visible may cause us to clean up the pollution we can easily perceive while ignoring even more dangerous but hidden threats.

Pollution is also likely to be kept in the public eye because it is an issue that threatens almost everyone, not just a small percentage of the population. Since it is not politically divisive, politicians can safely pursue it without fearing adverse repercussions. Attacking environmental pollution is therefore much safer than attacking racism or poverty. For an attack upon the latter antagonizes important blocs of voters who benefit from the sufferings of others or at least are not threatened enough by such suffering to favor spending substantial amounts of their money to reduce it.

A third strength of the environmental issue is that much of the "blame" for pollution can be attributed to a small group of "villains" whose wealth and power make them excellent scapegoats. Environmental defenders can therefore "courageously" attack these scapegoats without antagonizing most citizens.

Moreover, at least in regard to air pollution, that small group actually has enough power greatly to reduce pollution if it really tries. If leaders of the nation's top auto-producing, power-generating, and fuel-supplying firms would change their behavior significantly, a drastic decline in air pollution could be achieved very quickly. This has been demonstrated at many locations already.

Gathering support for attacking any problem is always easier if its ills can be blamed on a small number of "public enemies"—as is shown by the success of Ralph Nader. This tactic is especially effective if the "enemies" exhibit extreme wealth and power, eccentric dress and manners, obscene language, or some other uncommon traits. Then society can aim its outrage at a small, alien group without having to face up to the need to alter its own behavior. It is easier to find such scapegoats for almost all forms of pollution than for other major problems like poverty, poor housing, or racism. Solutions to those problems would require millions of Americans to change their own behavior patterns, accept higher taxes, or both.

The possibility that technological solutions can be devised for most pollution problems may also lengthen the public prominence of this issue. To the extent that pollution can be reduced through technological change, most people's basic attitudes, expectations, and behavior patterns will not have to be altered. The traumatic difficulties of achieving major institutional change could thus be escaped through the "magic" of purely technical improvements in automobile engines, water purification devices, fuel composition, and sewage treatment facilities.

Financing the Fight Against Pollution

Another aspect of anti-pollution efforts that will strengthen their political support is that most of the costs can be passed on to the public through higher product prices rather than higher taxes. Therefore, politicians can demand enforcement of costly environmental quality standards without paying the high political price of raising the required funds through taxes. True, water pollution is caused mainly by the actions of public bodies, especially municipal sewer systems, and effective remedies for this form of pollution require higher taxes or at least higher prices for public services. But the major costs of reducing most kinds of pollution can be added to product prices and thereby quietly shifted to the ultimate consumers of the outputs concerned. This is a politically painless way to pay for attacking a major social problem. In contrast, effectively combatting most social problems requires large-scale income redistribution attainable only through both higher taxes and higher transfer payments or subsidies. Examples of such politically costly problems are poverty, slum housing, low-quality health care for the poor, and inadequate public transportation.

Many ecologists oppose paying for a cleaner environment through higher product prices. They would rather force the polluting firms to bear the required costs through lower profits. In a few oligopolistic industries, like petroleum and automobile production, this might work. But in the long run, not much of the total cost could be paid this way without driving capital out of the industries concerned and thereby eventually forcing product prices upwards. Furthermore, it is just that those who use any given product should pay the full cost of making it—including the cost of avoiding excessive pollution in its production. Such payment is best made through higher product prices. In my opinion, it would be unwise in most cases to try to pay these costs by means of government subsidies in order to avoid shifting the load onto consumers. We need to conserve our politically limited taxing capabilities to attack those problems that cannot be dealt with in any other way.

Still another reason why the cleaner-environment issue may last a long time is that it could generate a large private industry with strong vested interests in continued spending against pollution. Already dozens of firms with "eco-" or "environ-" in their names have sprung up to exploit supposedly burgeoning anti-pollution markets. In time, we might even generate an "environmental-in-dustrial complex" about which some future President could vainly warn us in his retirement speech! Any issue gains longevity if its sources of political support and the programs related to it can be institutionalized in large bureaucracies. Such organizations have a powerful desire to keep public attention focused on the problems that support them. However, it is doubtful that the anti-pollution industry will ever come close to the defense industry in size and power. Effective anti-pollution activities cannot be carried out separately from society as a whole because they require changes in behavior by millions of people. In contrast, weapons are produced by an industry that imposes no behavioral changes (other than higher taxes) on the average citizen.

Finally, environmental issues may remain at center stage longer than most domestic issues because of their very ambiguity. "Improving the environment" is a tremendously broad and all-encompassing objective. Almost everyone can plausibly claim that his or her particular cause is another way to upgrade the quality of our life. This ambiguity will make it easier to form a majority-sized coalition favoring a variety of social changes associated with improving the environment. The inability to form such a coalition regarding problems that adversely affect only minority-sized groups usually hastens the exit of such problems from the center of public attention.

All the factors set forth above indicate that circumstances are unusually favor-able for launching and sustaining major efforts to improve the quality of our environment. Yet we should not underestimate the American public's capacity to become bored—especially with something that does not immediately threaten them, or promise huge benefits for a majority, or strongly appeal to their sense of injustice. In the present mood of the nation, I believe most citizens do not want to confront the need for major social changes on any issues except those that seem directly to threaten them—such as crime and other urban violence. And even in regard to crime, the public does not yet wish to support really effective changes in our basic system of justice. The present Administration has apparently concluded that a relatively "low-profile" government—one that does not try to lead the public into accepting truly significant institutional changes—will most please the majority of Americans at this point. Regardless of the accuracy of this view, if it remains dominant within the federal government, then no major environmental programs are likely to receive long-sustained public attention or support.

Some proponents of improving the environment are relying on the support of students and other young people to keep this issue at the center of public attention. Such support, however, is not adequate as a long-term foundation. Young people form a highly unstable base for the support of any policy because they have such short-lived "staying power." For one thing, they do not long enjoy the large amount of free time they possess while in college. Also, as new individuals enter the category of "young people" and older ones leave it, different issues are stressed and accumulated skills in marshaling opinion are dissipated. Moreover, the radicalism of the young has been immensely exaggerated by the media's tendency to focus attention upon those with extremist views. In their attitudes toward political issues, most young people are not very different from their parents.

There is good reason, then, to believe that the bundle of issues called "improving the environment" will also suffer the gradual loss of public attention characteristic of the later stages of the "issue-attention cycle." However, it will be eclipsed at a much slower rate than other recent domestic issues. So it may be possible to accomplish some significant improvements in environmental quality—if those seeking them work fast.

2.2. The Theory of Economic Regulation

GEORGE STIGLER

Anthony Downs sees regulation as being driven by the demands of the electorate. In this reading, Nobel Prize winner George Stigler argues that regulation is not instituted to help consumers but to help the industry being regulated.

He argues that even though industry pays lip service to the idea of free competition, competition is not something that the heads of most individual firms want for themselves. In a competitive market, firms are frequently forced to charge a lower price than they would like, can be driven out of business if they make mistakes, and will often lose money during recessions. In a competitive market, raising the price of your product will lead to current competitors' under-cutting you and/or new competitors entering the market. Stigler thinks businesses use government regulation as a way of solving these problems. Government can set prices in an industry, force all current firms to charge those prices, and prevent potential competitors from entering the market. It is therefore in the interests of competitive firms to seek government regulation in order to realize these benefits.

Stigler argues that firms have been very successful in obtaining such regula-tion to benefit themselves, but disguise this with arguments that the regulation is in the public interest. It follows that much regulation that appears to have been instituted to benefit the public has actually been instituted to benefit business at the expense of the public.

The state—the machinery and power of the state—is a potential resource or threat to every industry in the society. With its power to prohibit or compel, to take or give money, the state can and does selectively help or hurt a vast number

Reprinted with permission from *Bell Journal of Law and Economics and Management Science* 2, *1*, pp. 243–261.

of industries. That political juggernaut, the petroleum industry, is an immense consumer of political benefits, and simultaneously the underwriters of marine insurance have their more modest repast. The central tasks of the theory of economic regulation are to explain who will receive the benefits or burdens of regulation, what form regulation will take, and the effects of regulation upon the allocation of resources.

Regulation may be actively sought by an industry, or it may be thrust upon it. A central thesis of this paper is that, as a rule, regulation is acquired by the industry and is designed and operated primarily for its benefit. There are regulations whose net effects upon the regulated industry are undeniably onerous; a simple example is the differentially heavy taxation of the industry's product (whiskey, playing cards). These onerous regulations, however, are exceptional and can be explained by the same theory that explains beneficial (we may call it "acquired") regulation.

Two main alternative views of the regulation of industry are widely held. The first is that regulation is instituted primarily for the protection and benefit of the public at large or some large subclass of the public. In this view, the regulations which injure the public—as when the oil import quotas increase the cost of petroleum products to America by $5 billion or more a year—are costs of some social goal (here, national defense) or, occasionally, perversions of the regulatory philosophy. The second view is essentially that the political process defies rational explanation: "politics" is an imponderable, a constantly and unpredictably shifting mixture of forces of the most diverse nature, comprehending acts of great moral virtue (the emancipation of slaves) and of the most vulgar venality (the congressman feathering his own nest).

Let us consider a problem posed by the oil import quota system: why does not the powerful industry which obtained this expensive program instead choose direct cash subsidies from the public treasury? The "protection of the public" theory of regulation must say that the choice of import quotas is dictated by the concern of the federal government for an adequate domestic supply of petroleum in the event of war—a remark calculated to elicit uproarious laughter at the Petroleum Club. Such laughter aside, if national defense were the goal of the quotas, a tariff would be a more economical instrument of policy: it would retain the profits of exclusion for the treasury. The nonrationalist view would explain the policy by the inability of consumers to measure the cost to them of the import quotas, and hence their willingness to pay $5 billion in higher prices rather than the $2.5 billion in cash that would be equally attractive to the industry. Our profit-maximizing theory says that the explanation lies in a different direction: the present members of the refining industries would have to share a cash subsidy with all new entrants into the refining industry.[1] Only when the elasticity of supply of an industry is small will the industry prefer cash to controls over entry or output.

This question, why does an industry solicit the coercive powers of the state rather than its cash, is offered only to illustrate the approach of the present paper. We assume that political systems are rationally devised and rationally employed, which is to say that they are appropriate instruments for the fulfillment of desires of members of the society. This is not to say that the state will serve any person's concept of the public interest: indeed the problem of regulation is the problem of discovering when and why an industry (or other group of likeminded people) is able to use the state for its purposes, or is singled out by the state to be used for alien purposes.

I. What Benefits Can a State Provide to an Industry?

The state has one basic resource which in pure principle is not shared with even the mightiest of its citizens: the power to coerce. The state can seize money by the only method which is permitted by the laws of a civilized society, by taxation. The state can ordain the physical movements of resources and the economic decisions of households and firms without their consent. These powers provide the possibilities for the utilization of the state by an industry to increase its profitability. The main policies which an industry (or occupation) may seek of the state are four.

The most obvious contribution that a group may seek of the government is a direct subsidy of money. The domestic airlines received "air mail" subsidies (even if they did not carry mail) of $1.5 billion through 1968. The merchant marine has received construction and operation subsidies reaching almost $3 billion since World War II. The education industry has long shown a masterful skill in obtaining public funds: for example, universities and colleges have received federal funds exceeding $3 billion annually in recent years, as well as subsidized loans for dormitories and other construction. The veterans of wars have often received direct cash bonuses.

We have already sketched the main explanation for the fact that an industry with power to obtain governmental favors usually does not use this power to get money: unless the list of beneficiaries can be limited by an acceptable device, whatever amount of subsidies the industry can obtain will be dissipated among a growing number of rivals. The airlines quickly moved away from competitive bidding for air mail contracts to avoid this problem.[2] On the other hand, the premier universities have not devised a method of excluding other claimants for research funds, and in the long run they will receive much-reduced shares of federal research monies.

The second major public resource commonly sought by an industry is control over entry by new rivals. There is considerable, not to say excessive, discussion in economic literature of the rise of peculiar price policies (limit prices), vertical integration, and similar devices to retard the rate of entry of new firms into oligopolistic industries. Such devices are vastly less efficacious (economical) than the certificate of convenience and necessity (which includes, of course, the import and production quotas of the oil and tobacco industries).

Figure 1. **Certificates for Interstate Motor Carriers**

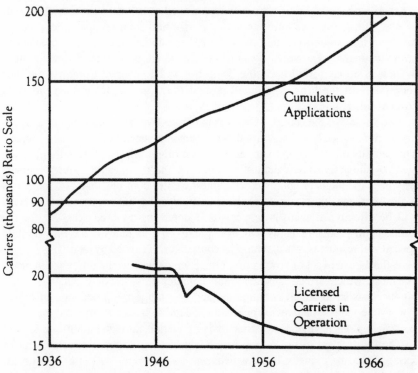

Source: George Stigler, "The Theory of Economic Regulation," *Bell Journal of Economics and Management Science* 2, no. 1 (Spring 1971): Table 15.5.

The diligence with which the power of control over entry will be exercised by a regulatory body is already well known. The Civil Aeronautics Board has not allowed a single new trunk line to be launched since it was created in 1938. The power to insure new banks has been used by the Federal Deposit Insurance Corporation to reduce the rate of entry into commercial banking by 60 percent.[3] The interstate motor carrier history is in some respects even more striking, because no even ostensibly respectable case for restriction on entry can be developed on grounds of scale economies (which are in turn adduced to limit entry for safety or economy of operation). The number of federally licensed common carriers is shown in Figure 1: the immense growth of the freight hauled by trucking common carriers has been associated with a steady secular decline of numbers of such carriers. The number of applications for new certificates has been in excess of 5,000 annually in recent years: a rigorous proof that hope springs eternal in an aspiring trucker's breast.

We propose the general hypothesis: every industry or occupation that has enough political power to utilize the state will seek to control entry. In addition, the regulatory policy will often be so fashioned as to retard the rate of growth of new firms. For example, no new savings and loan company may pay a dividend rate higher than that prevailing in the community in its endeavors to attract deposits.[4] The power to limit selling expenses of mutual funds, which is soon to be conferred upon the Securities and Exchange Commission, will serve to limit the growth of small mutual funds and hence reduce the sales costs of large funds.

One variant of the control of entry is the protective tariff (and the corresponding barriers which have been raised to interstate movement of goods and people). The benefits of protection to an industry, one might think, will usually be dissipated by the entry of new domestic producers, and the question naturally arises: why does the industry not also seek domestic entry controls? In a few industries (petroleum) the domestic controls have been obtained, but not in most. The tariff will be effective if there is a specialized domestic resource necessary to the industry; oil-producing lands is an example. Even if an industry has only durable specialized resources, it will gain if its contraction is slowed by a tariff.

A third general set of powers of the state which will be sought by the industry are those which affect substitutes and complements. Crudely put, the butter producers wish to suppress margarine and encourage the production of bread. The airline industry actively supports the federal subsidies to airports; the building trade unions have opposed labor-saving materials through building codes. . . .

The fourth class of public policies sought by an industry is directed to price fixing. Even the industry that has achieved entry control will often want price controls administered by a body with coercive powers. If the number of firms in the regulated industry is even moderately large, price discrimination will be difficult to maintain in the absence of public support. The prohibition of interest on demand deposits, which is probably effective in preventing interest payments to most nonbusiness depositors, is a case in point. Where there are no diseconomies of large scale for the individual firm (e.g., a motor trucking firm can add trucks under a given license as common carrier), price control is essential to achieve more than competitive rates of return.

Limitations Upon Political Benefits

These various political boons are not obtained by the industry in a pure profit-maximizing form. The political process erects certain limitations upon the exercise of cartel policies by an industry. These limitations are of three sorts.

First, the distribution of control of the industry among the firms in the industry is changed. In an unregulated industry each firm's influence upon price and output is proportional to its share of industry output (at least in a simple arithmetic sense of direct capacity to change output). The political decisions take account also of the political strength of the various firms, so small ones have a

Table 1

Import Quotas of Refineries as Percent of Daily Input of Petroleum (Districts I–IV, July 1, 1959–Dec. 31, 1959)

Size of Refinery (thousands of barrels)	Percent Quota
0–10	11.4
10–20	10.4
20–30	9.5
30–60	8.5
60–100	7.6
100–150	6.6
150–200	5.7
200–300	4.7
300 and over	3.8

Source: Hearing, Select Committee on Small Business, U.S. Congress, 88th Cong., 2nd Sess., Aug. 10 and 11, 1964, p. 121.

larger influence than they would possess in an unregulated industry. Thus, when quotas are given to firms, the small firms will almost always receive larger quotas than cost-minimizing practices would allow. The original quotas under the oil import quota system will illustrate this practice (Table 1). The smallest refiners were given a quota of 11.4 percent of their daily consumption of oil, and the percentage dropped as refinery size rose.[5] The pattern of regressive benefits is characteristic of public controls in industries with numerous firms.

Second, the procedural safeguards required of public processes are costly. The delays which are dictated by both law and bureaucratic thoughts of self-survival can be large: Robert Gerwig found the price of gas sold in interstate commerce to be 5 to 6 percent higher than in intrastate commerce because of the administrative costs (including delay) of Federal Power Commission reviews.[6]

Finally, the political process automatically admits powerful outsiders to the industry's councils. It is well known that the allocation of television channels among communities does not maximize industry revenue but reflects pressures to serve many smaller communities. The abandonment of an unprofitable rail line is an even more notorious area of outsider participation.

These limitations are predictable, and they must all enter into the calculus of the profitability of regulation of an industry. . . .

II. The Costs of Obtaining Legislation

When an industry receives a grant of power from the state, the benefit to the industry will fall short of the damage to the rest of the community. Even if there were no deadweight losses from acquired regulation, however, one might expect a democratic society to reject such industry requests unless the industry controlled a majority of the votes.[7] A direct and informed vote on oil import quotas would reject the scheme. (If it did not, our theory of rational political processes would be contradicted.) To explain why many industries are able to employ political machinery to their own ends, we must examine the nature of the political process in a democracy.

A consumer chooses between rail and air travel, for example, by voting with his pocketbook: he patronizes on a given day that mode of transportation he prefers. A similar form of economic voting occurs with decisions on where to work or where to invest one's capital. The market accumulates these economic votes, predicts their future course, and invests accordingly.

Because the political decision is coercive, the decision process is fundamentally different from that of the market. If the public is asked to make a decision between two transportation media comparable to the individual's decision on how to travel—say, whether airlines or railroads should receive a federal subsidy—the decision must be abided by everyone, travelers and nontravelers, travelers this year and travelers next year. This compelled universality of political decisions makes for two differences between democratic political decision processes and market processes.

1. The decisions must be made simultaneously by a large number of persons (or their representatives): the political process demands simultaneity of decision. If A were to vote on the referendum today, B tomorrow, C the day after, and so on, the accumulation of a majority decision would be both expensive and suspect. (A might wish to cast a different vote now than last month.)

The condition of simultaneity imposes a major burden upon the political decision process. It makes voting on specific issues prohibitively expensive: it is a significant cost even to engage in the transaction of buying a plane ticket when I wish to travel; it would be stupendously expensive to me to engage in the physically similar transaction of voting (i.e., patronizing a polling place) whenever a number of my fellow citizens desired to register their views on railroads versus airplanes. To cope with this condition of simultaneity, the voters must employ representatives with wide discretion and must eschew direct expressions of marginal changes in preferences. This characteristic also implies that the political decision does not predict voter desires and make preparations to fulfill them in advance of their realization.

2. The democratic decision process must involve "all" the community, not simply those who are directly concerned with a decision. In a private market, the nontraveler never votes in rail versus plane travel, while the huge shipper casts many votes each day. The political decision process cannot exclude the uninterested voter: the abuses of any exclusion except self-exclusion are obvious. Hence, the political process does not allow participation in proportion to interest and knowledge. In a measure, this difficulty is moderated by other political activities besides voting which do allow a more effective vote to interested

parties: persuasion, employment of skilled legislative representatives, etc. Nevertheless, the political system does not offer good incentives like those in private markets to the acquisition of knowledge. If I consume ten times as much of public service A (streets) as of B (schools), I do not have incentives to acquire corresponding amounts of knowledge about the public provision of these services.[8]

These characteristics of the political process can be modified by having numerous levels of government (so I have somewhat more incentive to learn about local schools than about the whole state school system) and by selective use of direct decision (bond referenda). The chief method of coping with the characteristics, however, is to employ more or less full-time representatives organized in (disciplined by) firms which are called political parties or machines.

The representative and his party are rewarded for their discovery and fulfillment of the political desires of their constituency by success in election and the perquisites of office. If the representative could confidently await reelection whenever he voted against an economic policy that injured the society, he would assuredly do so. Unfortunately virtue does not always command so high a price. If the representative denies ten large industries their special subsidies of money or governmental power, they will fixate themselves to the election of a more complaisant successor: the stakes are that important. This does not mean that every large industry can get what it wants or all that it wants: it does mean that the representative and his party must find a coalition of voter interests more durable than the anti-industry side of every industry policy proposal. A representative cannot win or keep office with the support of the sum of those who are opposed to: oil import quotas, farm subsidies, airport subsidies, hospital subsidies, unnecessary navy shipyards, an inequitable public housing program, and rural electrification subsidies.

The political decision process has as its dominant characteristic infrequent, universal (in principle) participation, as we have noted: political decisions must be infrequent and they must be global. The voter's expenditure to learn the merits of individual policy proposals and to express his preferences (by individual and group representation as well as by voting) are determined by expected costs and returns, just as they are in the private marketplace. The costs of comprehensive information are higher in the political arena because information must be sought on many issues of little or no direct concern to the individual, and accordingly he will know little about most matters before the legislature. The expression of preferences in voting will be less precise than the expressions of preferences in the marketplace because many uninformed people will be voting and affecting the decision.[9]

The channels of political decision-making can thus be described as gross or filtered or noisy. If everyone has a negligible preference for policy A over B, the preference will not be discovered or acted upon. If voter group X wants a policy that injures non-X by a small amount, it will not pay non-X to discover this and act against the policy. The system is calculated to implement all strongly felt preferences of majorities and many strongly felt preferences of minorities but to disregard the lesser preferences of majorities and minorities. The filtering or grossness will be reduced by any reduction in the cost to the citizen of acquiring information and expressing desires and by any increase in the probability that his vote will influence policy.

The industry which seeks political power must go to the appropriate seller, the political party. The political party has costs of operation, costs of maintaining an organization and competing in elections. These costs of the political process are viewed excessively narrowly in the literature on the financing of elections: elections are to the political process what merchandising is to the process of producing a commodity, only an essential final step. The party maintains its organization and electoral appeal by the performance of costly services to the voter at all times, not just before elections. Part of the costs of services and organization are borne by putting a part of the party's workers on the public payroll. An opposition party, however, is usually essential insurance for the voters to discipline the party in power, and the opposition party's costs are not fully met by public funds.

The industry which seeks regulation must be prepared to pay with the two things a party needs: votes and resources. The resources may be provided by campaign contributions, contributed services (the businessman heads a fundraising committee), and more indirect methods such as the employment of party workers. The votes in support of the measure are rallied, and the votes in opposition are dispersed, by expensive programs to educate (or uneducate) members of the industry and of other concerned industries.

These costs of legislation probably increase with the size of the industry seeking the legislation. Larger industries seek programs which cost the society more and arouse more opposition from substantially affected groups. The tasks of persuasion, both within and without the industry, also increase with its size. The fixed size of the political "market," however, probably makes the cost of obtaining legislation increase less rapidly than industry size. The smallest industries are therefore effectively precluded from the political process unless they have some special advantage such as geographical concentration in a sparsely settled political subdivision.

If a political party has in effect a monopoly control over the governmental machine, one might expect that it could collect most of the benefits of regulation for itself. Political parties, however, are perhaps an ideal illustration of Demsetz's theory of natural monopoly.[10] If one party becomes extortionate (or badly mistaken in its reading of effective desires), it is possible to elect another party which will provide the governmental services at a price more closely proportioned to the costs of the party. If entry into politics is effectively controlled, we should expect one-party dominance to lead that party to solicit requests for protective legislation but to exact a higher price for the legislation.

The internal structure of the political party, and the manner in which the perquisites of office are distributed among its members, offer fascinating areas for study in this context. The elective officials are at the pinnacle of the political system—there is no substitute for the ability to hold the public offices. I conjecture that much of the compensation to the legislative leaders takes the form of extrapolitical payments. Why are so many politicians lawyers? Because everyone employs lawyers, so the congressman's firm is a suitable avenue of compensation, whereas a physician would have to be given bribes rather than patronage. Most enterprises patronize insurance companies and banks, so we may expect that legislators commonly have financial affiliations with such enterprises.

The financing of industry-wide activities such as the pursuit of legislation raises the usual problem of the free rider.[11] We do not possess a satisfactory theory of group behavior—indeed this theory is the theory of oligopoly with one addition: in the very large number industry (e.g., agriculture) the political party itself will undertake the entrepreneurial role in providing favorable legislation. We can go no further than the infirmities of oligopoly theory allow, which is to say, we can make only plausible conjectures such as that the more concentrated the industry, the more resources it can invest in the campaign for legislation.

Occupational Licensing

The licensing of occupations is a possible use of the political process to improve the economic circumstances of a group. The license is an effective barrier to entry because occupational practice without the license is a criminal offense. Since much occupational licensing is performed at the state level, the area provides an opportunity to search for the characteristics of an occupation which give it political power.

Although there are serious data limitations, we may investigate several characteristics of an occupation which should influence its ability to secure political power:

1. *The size of the occupation.* Quite simply, the larger the occupation, the more votes it has. (Under some circumstances, therefore, one would wish to exclude noncitizens from the measure of size.)

2. *The per capita income of the occupation.* The income of the occupation is the product of its numbers and average income, so this variable and the preceding will reflect the total income of the occupation. The income of the occupation is presumably an index of the probable rewards of successful political action: in the absence of specific knowledge of supply and demand functions, we expect licensing to increase each occupation's equilibrium income by roughly the same proportion. In a more sophisticated version, one would predict that the less the elasticity of demand for the occupation's services, the more profitable licensing would be. One could also view the in-

come of the occupation as a source of funds for political action, but if we view political action as an investment this is relevant only with capital-market imperfections.[12]

The average income of occupational members is an appropriate variable in comparisons among occupations, but it is inappropriate to comparisons of one occupation in various states because real income will be approximately equal (in the absence of regulation) in each state.

3. *The concentration of the occupation in large cities.* When the occupation organizes a campaign to obtain favorable legislation, it incurs expenses in the solicitation of support, and these are higher for a diffused occupation than a concentrated one. The solicitation of support is complicated by the free-rider problem in that individual members cannot be excluded from the benefits of legislation even if they have not shared the costs of receiving it. If most of the occupation is concentrated in a few large centers, these problems (we suspect) are much reduced in intensity: regulation may even begin at the local governmental level. We shall use an orthodox geographical concentration measure: the share of the occupation in the state in cities over 100,000 (or 50,000 in 1900 and earlier).

4. *The presence of a cohesive opposition to licensing.* If an occupation deals with the public at large, the costs which licensing imposes upon any one customer or industry will be small and it will not be economic for that customer or industry to combat the drive for licensure. If the injured group finds it feasible and profitable to act jointly, however, it will oppose the effort to get licensure, and (by increasing its cost) weaken, delay, or prevent the legislation. The same attributes—number of voters, wealth, and ease of organization—which favor an occupation in the political arena, of course, favor also any adversary group. Thus, a small occupation employed by only one industry which has few employers will have difficulty in getting licensure; whereas a large occupation serving everyone will encounter no organized opposition.

An introductory statistical analysis of the licensing of select occupations by states is summarized in Table 2. In each occupation the dependent variable for each state is the year of first regulation of entry into the occupation. The two independent variables are: (1) the ratio of the occupation to the total labor force of the state in the census year nearest to the median year of regulation; (2) the fraction of the occupation found in cities over 100,000 (over 50,000 in 1890 and 1900) in that same year. We expect these variables to be negatively associated with year of licensure, and each of the nine statistically significant regression coefficients is of the expected sign.

The results are not robust, however: the multiple correlation coefficients are small, and over half of the regression coefficients are not significant (and in these cases often of inappropriate sign). Urbanization is more strongly associated

Table 2

Initial Year of Regulation as a Function of Relative Size of Occupation and Degree of Urbanization

Occupation	Number of States Licensing	Median Census Year of Licensing	Regression Coefficients (and T-Values)		R²
			Size of Occupation (relative to labor force)	Urbanization (share of occupation in cities over 100,000)ᵃ	
Beauticians	48	1930	−4.03 (2.50)	5.90 (1.24)	0.125
Architects	47	1930	−24.06 (2.15)	−6.29 (0.84)	0.184
Barbers	46	1930	−1.31 (0.51)	−26.10 (2.37)	0.146
Lawyers	29	1890	−0.26 (0.08)	−65.78 (1.70)	0.102
Physicians	43	1890	0.64 (0.65)	−23.80 (2.69)	0.165
Embalmers	37	1910	3.32 (0.36)	−4.24 (0.44)	0.007
Registered Nurses	48	1910	−2.08 (2.28)	−3.36 (1.06)	0.176
Dentists	48	1900	2.51 (0.44)	−22.94 (2.19)	0.103
Veterinarians	40	1910	−10.69 (1.94)	−37.16 (4.20)	0.329
Chiropractors	48	1930	−17.70 (1.54)	11.69 (1.25)	0.079
Pharmacists	48	1900	−4.19 (1.50)	−6.84 (0.80)	0.082

Sources: The Council of State Governments, "Occupational Licensing Legislation in the States," 1952, and U.S. Census of Population, various years.
ᵃ50,000 in 1890 and 1900.

than size of occupation with licensure.[13] The crudity of the data may be a large source of these disappointments: we measure, for example, the characteristics of the barbers in each state in 1930, but fourteen states were licensing barbers by 1910. If the states which licensed barbering before 1910 had relatively more barbers, or more highly urbanized barbers, the predictions would be improved. The absence of data for years between censuses and before 1890 led us to make only the cruder analysis.[14]

In general, the larger occupations were licensed in earlier years.[15] Veterinarians are the only occupation in this sample who have a well defined set of customers, namely livestock farmers, and licensing was later in those states with large numbers of livestock relative to rural population. The within-occupation analyses offer some support for the economic theory of the supply of legislation.

A comparison of different occupations allows us to examine several other variables. The first is income, already discussed above. The second is the size of the market. Just as it is impossible to organize an effective labor union in only one part of an integrated market, so it is impossible to regulate only one part of the market. Consider an occupation—junior business executives will do—which has a national market with high mobility of labor and significant mobility of employers. If the executives of one state were to organize, their scope for effective influence would be very small. If salaries were raised above the competitive level, employers would often recruit elsewhere so the demand elasticity would be very high.[16] The third variable is stability of occupational membership: the longer the members are in the occupation, the greater their financial gain from control of entry. Our regrettably crude measure of this variable is based upon the number of members aged 35–44 in 1950 and aged 45–54 in 1960: the closer these numbers are, the more stable the membership of the occupation. The data for the various occupations are given in Table 3.

The comparison of licensed and unlicensed occupations is consistently in keeping with our expectations: (1) the licensed occupations have higher incomes (also before licensing, one may assume); (2) the membership of the licensed occupations is more stable (but the difference is negligible in our crude measure); (3) the licensed occupations are less often employed by business enterprises (who have incentives to oppose licensing); (4) all occupations in national markets (college teachers, engineers, scientists, accountants) are unlicensed or only partially licensed. The size and urbanization of the three groups, however, are unrelated to licensing. The interoccupational comparison therefore provides a modicum of additional support for our theory of regulation.

III. Conclusion

The idealistic view of public regulation is deeply imbedded in professional economic thought. So many economists, for example, have denounced the ICC for its prorailroad policies that this has become a cliche of the literature. This criticism seems to me exactly as appropriate as a criticism of the Great Atlantic and Pacific Tea Company for selling groceries, or as a criticism of a politician for currying popular support. The fundamental vice of such criticism is that it misdirects attention: it suggests that the way to get an ICC which is not subservient to the carriers is to preach to the commissioners or to the people who appoint the commissioners. The only way to get a different commission would be to change the political support for the Commission, and reward commissioners on a basis unrelated to their services to the carriers.

Table 2.3

Characteristics of Licensed and Unlicensed Professional Occupations, 1960

Occupation	Median Age (years)	Median Education (years)	Median Earnings (50–52 wks.)	Instability of membership[a]	Percent Not Self-Employed	Percent in Cities over 50,000	Percent of Labor Force
Licensed:							
Architects	41.7	16.8	$9,090	0.012	57.8%	44.1%	0.045%
Chiropractors	46.5	16.4	6,360	0.053	5.8	30.8	0.020
Dentists	45.9	17.3	12,200	0.016	9.43	4.5	0.128
Embalmers	43.5	13.4	5,990	0.130	52.8	30.2	0.055
Lawyers	45.3	17.4	10,800	0.041	35.8	43.1	0.308
Prof. Nurses	39.1	13.2	3,850	0.291	91.0	40.6	0.868
Optometrists	41.6	17.0	8,480	0.249	17.5	34.5	0.024
Pharmacists	44.9	16.2	7,230	0.119	62.3	40.0	0.136
Physicians	42.8	17.5	14,200	0.015	35.0	44.7	0.339
Veterinarians	39.2	17.4	9,210	0.169	29.5	14.4	0.023
Average	43.0	16.3	8,741	0.109	39.7	35.7	0.195
Partially Licensed:							
Accountants	40.4	14.9	6,450	0.052	88.1	43.5	0.698
Engineers	38.3	16.2	8,490	0.023[b]	96.8	31.6	1.279
Elem. School Teachers	43.1	16.5	4,710		99.1	18.8	1.482
Average	40.6	15.9	6,550	0.117[c]	94.7	34.6	1.153
Unlicensed:							
Artists	38.0	14.2	5,920	0.103	77.3	45.7	0.154
Clergymen	43.3	17.0	4,120	0.039	89.0	27.2	0.295
College Teachers	40.3	17.4	7,500	0.085	99.2	36.0	0.261
Draftsmen	31.2	12.9	5,990	0.098	98.6	40.8	0.322
Reporters and Editors	39.4	15.5	6,120	0.138	93.9	43.3	0.151
Musicians	40.2	14.8	3,240	0.081	65.5	37.7	0.289
Natural Scientists	35.9	16.8	7,490	0.264	96.3	32.7	0.221
Average	38.3	15.5	5,768	0.115	88.5	37.6	0.242

Source: U.S. Census of Population, 1960.

[a] $1 - R$ where R = ratio: 1960 age 45–54 to 1950 age 35–44.

[b] Not available separately; Teachers N.E.C. (incl. secondary school and other) = 0.276.

[c] Includes figure for Teachers N.E.C. in note b.

Until the basic logic of political life is developed, reformers will be ill equipped to use the state for their reforms, and victims of the pervasive use of the state's support of special groups will be helpless to protect themselves. Economists should quickly establish the license to practice on the rational theory of political behavior.

Notes

1. The domestic producers of petroleum, who also benefit from the import quota, would find a tariff or cash payment to domestic producers equally attractive. If their interests alone were consulted, import quotas would be auctioned off instead of being given away.

2. See Keyes, L.S., *Federal Control of Entry into Air Transportation* (Cambridge, Mass.: Harvard University Press, 1951), pp. 60ff.

3. See Peltzman, S., "Entry in Commercial Banking," *Journal of Law and Economics* (October 1965).

4. The Federal Home Loan Bank Board is the regulatory body. It also controls the amount of advertising and other areas of competition.

5. The largest refineries were restricted to 75.7 percent of their historical quota under the earlier voluntary import quota plan.

6. Gerwig, R.W., "Natural Gas Production: A Study of Costs of Regulation," *Journal of Law and Economics* (October 1962): 69–92.

7. If the deadweight loss (of consumer and producer surplus) is taken into account, even if the oil industry were in the majority it would not obtain the legislation if there were available some method of compensation (such as sale of votes) by which the larger damage of the minority could be expressed effectively against the lesser gains of the majority.

8. See Becker, G.S., "Competition and Democracy," *Journal of Law and Economics* (October 1958).

9. There is an organizational problem in any decision in which more than one vote is cast. If because of economies of scale it requires a thousand customers to buy a product before it can be produced, this thousand votes has to be assembled by some entrepreneur. Unlike the political scene, however, there is no need to obtain the consent of the remainder of the community, because they will bear no part of the cost.

10. Demsetz, H., "Why Regulate Utilities?," *Journal of Law and Economics* (April 1968).

11. The theory that the lobbying organization avoids the "free rider" problem by selling useful services was proposed by Thomas G. Moore ("The Purpose of Licensing," *Journal of Law and Economics* [October 1961]) and elaborated by Mancur Olson *(The Logic of Collective Action* [Cambridge, Mass.: Harvard University Press, 1965]). The theory has not been tested empirically.

12. Let n = the number of members of the profession and y = average income. We expect political capacity to be in proportion to (ny) so far as benefits go, but to reflect also the direct value of votes, so the capacity becomes proportional to ($n^a y$) with $a > 1$.

13. We may pool the occupations and assign dummy variables for each occupation; the regression coefficients then are:

  size of occupant relative to labor force: -0.450 ($t = 0.59$)
  urbanization: -12.133 ($t = 4.00$).

Thus urbanization is highly significant, while size of occupation is not significant.

14. A more precise analysis might take the form of a regression analysis such as:

Year of licensure = constant

+ b_1 (year of critical size of occupation)

+ b_2 (year of critical urbanization of occupation),

where the critical size and urbanization were defined as the mean size and mean urbanization in the year of licensure.

15. Lawyers, physicians, and pharmacists were all relatively large occupations by 1900, and nurses also by 1910. The only large occupation to be licensed later was barbers; the only small occupation to be licensed earlier was embalmers.

16. The regulation of business in a partial market will also generally produce very high supply elasticities within a market: if the price of the product (or service) is raised, the pressure of excluded supply is very difficult to resist. Some occupations are forced to reciprocity in licensing, and the geographical dispersion of earnings in licensed occupations, one would predict, is not appreciably different than in unlicensed occupations with equal employer mobility. Many puzzles are posed by the interesting analysis of Arlene S. Holen in "Effects of Professional Licensing Arrangements on Interstate Labor Mobility and Resource Allocation," *Journal of Political Economy* 73 (1915): 492–98.

2.3. The Consumer's Stake in Deregulation: The Benefit/Cost Test

MURRAY WEIDENBAUM

In recent years many people have come to feel that there is too much government regulation, and that it needs to be reduced. Murray Weidenbaum, who was chair of the Council of Economic Advisors under President Reagan, has been in the forefront of this movement. In his many books and articles on the subject he has argued that some regulation was never justified in the first place, that technological changes often remove the original reasons for regulation, and that even where it has a theoretical justification, it often causes more problems than it solves.

In this reading Weidenbaum primarily deals with the last of these justifications for deregulation. He shows that the process of regulating imposes a series of direct costs on government (e.g., hiring inspectors) and industry (e.g., installing scrubbers in smokestacks), and some less obvious indirect costs, such as higher wages for regulated workers. He argues that it is therefore necessary to systematically weigh the benefits and costs involved in regulating, to sort out justifiable from unjustifiable regulation. He then puts forward some specific areas where he thinks further deregulation can be justified.

The reader should note that the Office of Management and Budget now routinely subjects new regulatory proposals to cost/benefit tests and that every president from Ford to Clinton has helped refine cost/benefit analysis of regulation.

At first glance, the government imposition of socially desirable requirements on business appears to be an inexpensive way of achieving national objectives.

Previously published in *Vital Speeches of the Day* (November 1990), pp. 186–89. Reprinted by permission of the author.

Regulation seems to cost the government very little and therefore is not considered to be much of a burden on the taxpayer.

But the public does not escape paying the full cost. Every time an agency—in its attempt to safeguard the environment or foster occupational health or promote product safety—imposes on business a more expensive method of production, the cost of the resultant product will necessarily rise.

If consumers knew how much they were paying for regulation, they probably would be very upset. The high cost generated by rulemaking results in large part because government agencies do not feel great pressure to worry about it. Compliance costs do not show up in their budgets, but in the budgets of the private sector.

More important than the amount of money involved is the increasing intervention by government in the daily lives of its citizens. Decisions by government agencies alter, influence, or even determine what we can buy, how we can use the goods and services we own, and how we earn our daily living. Government decisions increasingly affect what we wear, what we eat, and how we play. There are few items of business or consumer expenditures that escape regulation by one or more national, state, or local governments.

The pervasive expansion in regulation of business is also altering fundamentally the relation between business and government. The concept of a regulated industry has become archaic. We now live in an economy in which every company feels the power of government in its day-to-day operations.

It is hard to overestimate the great variety of government involvement in business which has been occurring in the United States. No business today, large or small, can operate without obeying a myriad of government restrictions and directives.

Entrepreneurial decisions fundamental to the business enterprise have become subject to government influence, review, or control—decisions such as: What lines of business to go into? What products and services to produce? Which investments to finance? How to produce goods and services? Where to make them? How to market them? What prices to charge? What profit to keep?

Every major department of the American corporation has one or more counterparts in government that controls or influences its internal decision making. There is almost a "shadow" organization chart of public officials matching the organizational structure of each private company. The scientists in corporate research laboratories now do much of their work to ensure that the products they develop are not rejected by lawyers in regulatory agencies.

The engineers in manufacturing departments must make sure the equipment they specify meets the standards promulgated by Labor Department authorities. Marketing staffs must follow procedures established by government administrators in product safety agencies. The location of business facilities must conform with a variety of environmental statutes. Many activities of personnel staffs are geared to meeting the standards of the various agencies concerned with employment conditions. Finance departments bear the brunt of the rising government paperwork burden imposed on business.

Few aspects of business escape government review or influence. As a result, each major business function has undergone an important internal transformation. These changes have increased the overhead costs of doing business and often deflected management and employee attention from the basic tasks of designing, producing, and distributing new and better or cheaper goods and services. The cost of complying with domestic regulation is a handicap in competing against foreign firms who produce under less burdensome regulatory regimes.

Impetus for most of the expansion in government power over business does not come from the industries being regulated; generally they have shown minimum enthusiasm for EPA, OSHA, and EEOC. If anything, they claim that the "benefits" to them of these regulations are negative. Pressures for the new style of regulation come, rather, from a variety of citizen groups concerned primarily with non-economic aspects of national life—environmentalists, consumer groups, labor unions, and civil rights organizations.

To talk or write about the regulated industry "capturing" its regulators is, to put it kindly, a quaint way of viewing the fundamental shift in business decision making taking place, the shift of power from private managers to public officials. Yet, the core of the economist's version of the "capture" theory still holds—public policy is dominated by the organized pressure groups who attain their benefits at the expense of the more diffused and larger body of consumers.

Rather than the railroad baron (a relatively easy target for attack), the villains of the piece often have become self-styled representatives of the public interest who have succeeded in identifying their personal prejudices with the national well-being.

Consider the extent to which business firms, in performing the traditional middleman function, serve the unappreciated and involuntary role of proxy for the consumer interest. That is most apparent in the case of retailers opposing restrictions on imports that would raise the prices of the goods they buy—and sell.

At this point, let me issue a disclaimer. I do not represent the public interest either. I have spent many years in government helping to make public policy, but I have never met a mortal man or woman who truly represented the public interest. Good government policy, if we ever get it, reconciles a variety of bona fide, legitimate interests. Is clean air a legitimate interest? How about high levels of unemployment? And bringing down inflation? Is producing safer products a legitimate concern? The answer to each of these questions is, "Yes, they are all important interests."

We need a mechanism for balancing these interests—rather than taking the simple-minded approach of automatically labeling one set of interests "public interests," which are supposedly good, and labeling the other set "special or business interests," which are presumably bad. This is precisely why we need an approach that considers costs *and* benefits.

Examining the Benefits of Regulation

The benefits of regulation are fundamental. To the extent that government rules result in healthier workplaces, safer products, and a cleaner environment, these benefits are very real. I have chosen these words carefully. The mere presence of a government agency does not automatically guarantee that its worthy objectives will be achieved. Nor are we justified in jumping to the opposite conclusion that no government agencies can achieve any good.

The serious—and difficult—question is how much benefit the regulation does produce and whether it is worth the cost. Society's bottom line is not the impact of regulatory actions on government or on business, but the effect on consumers and on citizens generally.

The relevant issue therefore is not, "Are you for or against government intervention?" Rather, it involves a very practical question: "Does this specific type of government activity work?" The sad reality is that it often does not—or it works against the interest of the consumer. This reality has been recognized in some areas. Deregulation of the airlines has reduced the cost to the traveling public. Cutting back the regulation of railroads and trucking likewise has benefited consumers, albeit indirectly, by curbing the cost of shipping commodities.

Deregulation Is Working

Progress has been made during the last decade in cutting back some of the older forms of economic regulations—where competition in the marketplace can do a better job of protecting the consumer than the imposition of bureaucratic judgments on private enterprise.

The movement to deregulate transportation, telecommunications, and energy markets over the past 10 years has been a triumph of ideas over entrenched political interests.

It was not a realignment of political forces that caused the shift toward deregulation. The most significant developments were supported by a bipartisan coalition in both the legislative and executive branches of the federal government. Consumer activists offered support at vital points, as did leaders of both political parties. But the most important role was played by a very unusual set of actors in the public policy arena: economists, political scientists, legal scholars, and similar purveyors of ideas.

Our Center for the Study of American Business played a modest role in all this. By focusing on the high costs to consumers, we helped move the subject of regulation from the academic journals and the business pages to the front pages and the nightly news. The issue hit a responsive chord with the media, influential policy groups, and finally Congress. A few simple concepts made the issue attractive. First, in a period of escalating inflation, a strategy of reducing regulation presents policymakers with an opportunity to deal with that critical issue in a way that does not involve a tradeoff with jobs. Indeed, curbing the proliferation of rules cuts both costs and barriers to production and employment.

Secondly, the burdens of regulation are a hidden tax on the consumer. This cost increase is buried in the form of higher prices but it is very real and often regressive.

Thirdly, a variety of carefully researched examples of regulatory silliness have reached the public consciousness. The first was the dead haul—the ICC requirement that resulted in trucks returning empty even though there was ample opportunity to fill them up with cargo. You need no great expertise in transportation to resent this waste.

This unusual form of applied research focused increasingly on the Occupational Safety and Health Administration. OSHA jokes (based on that research) became a staple of business conversation. Did you hear the one about the OSHA rule that spittoons have to be cleaned daily? Is it true that OSHA made one little company build separate his and her toilets even though the only two employees of the firm were married to each other? Did OSHA really issue a bulletin to farmers telling them to be careful around cows and not to step into manure pits?

Progress on deregulation built up slowly until dramatic momentum developed in the 1970s and 1980s. With airline deregulation, fares fell drastically and planes filled up. The airline experience provides a striking example of how regulation had been hurting the consumer (the traveling public).

In several areas, substantial backsliding has occurred. In the 1980s, restrictions have been extended on the import of automobiles, meat, motorcycles, sugar, steel, and textiles. In the early 1990s, we are seeing expansion in a variety of costly social regulation, with little effort to seek out more efficient approaches.

All in all, however, the general impact of deregulation on the American economy has been positive. The lessened governmental intervention has expanded the role of competition and market forces. Virtually every study of the effects of deregulation has concluded that the results have been lower costs, thus raising demand, and creating new opportunities for both producers and consumers of the previously regulated activities.

Opportunities have been created for new enterprises and for their employees in the deregulated industries. The position of American industry in an increasingly competitive global economy has been strengthened.

In any event, a decade of substantial reform of regulation has drawn to a close. How do we rebuild that earlier momentum? The sensible goal is not to reduce the burden on business by easing the enforcement of existing regulation, but to ensure that the regulations that are enforced benefit the consumer. The objective should be to determine which regulations make sense, which should be modified, and which lack sufficient justification. Let us try to develop such an approach.

Another Wave of Regulatory Reform

The very first step is educational. The public must come to understand that it is paying very substantially for all those supposedly good things that government regulators are doing for it.

Economists are prone to take measurements of economic phenomena. Data on the costs and benefits that flow from government regulation can be used to show the public and the government the large amounts of resources that are devoted to meet federal mandates.

Such analysis helps to shift the public dialogue onto higher ground. The pertinent policy questions are no longer, "Are you for or against clean air or safe products?" or other such absolutes. Increasingly, the public discussions are in terms of such less emotional and long-neglected questions as, "How well is the regulatory process working?" and, "Are there better ways of achieving the public's desires?"

Congress should endorse the kind of common sense embodied in the federal appeals court decision which stopped OSHA from issuing new benzene regulations. The court's language is instructive: "Although the agency does not have to conduct an elaborate cost/benefit analysis . . . it does have to determine whether the benefits expected from the standards bear a reasonable relationship to the costs imposed by the standard."

The second step is to recognize that creating a government bureau and giving it large amounts of money and power does not necessarily mean that the air will be any cleaner or the water any purer. The results may be the reverse. The environmental label has been used to justify subsidies to politically powerful regions of the country. In a misguided effort to keep medicines that may generate any adverse side-effects off the market, the regulatory authorities often deprive patients of newer, more effective products.

In fact, the regulatory activity often generates unexpected negative effects, such as stifling innovation. I am not sure whether Henry Ford's original model T could have survived today's environmental challenges. "Darn thing was dangerous; why you could break your arm cranking it."

The third step is to sort out those regulatory programs that are worth the costs they impose, from those that fail a benefit/cost test. The regulation of entry and pricing in the airline market by the now defunct Civil Aeronautics Board (CAB) was an example of regulatory activities not worthwhile. The elimination of the CAB has lowered the real cost of air travel and increased the travel choices available to most passengers.

On the other hand, despite their many shortcomings, the social regulatory agencies such as the Occupational Safety and Health Administration and the Food and Drug Administration conduct a variety of activities that contribute to the public welfare. That does not necessarily mean that every OSHA or FDA rule and requirement is optimally conceived or even necessary.

Environmental protection, product safety, and other regulatory efforts should be related to their costs to the consumer, availability of new products, and employment. A parallel can be drawn to macro-economic matters, where important and conflicting objectives are recognized and where attempts are made to trade off among these goals (for example, as between rapid growth and inflation).

In structuring regulatory programs, emphasis should be placed on developing basic principles (such as economic incentives) to guide the companies subject to regulation. This approach is far more efficient than the traditional case-by-case adjudication so beloved by attorneys.

Requiring all regulatory agencies to perform benefit/cost analysis of proposed regulations is a useful check on counterproductive government activity.

No analytical approach is totally value free, but benefit/cost analysis has less ideological baggage than most other alternatives. To an economist, "overregulation" is not an emotional term. It is merely shorthand for regulation for which the costs to the public are greater than the benefits.

Critics who are offended by the notion of subjecting regulation to a benefit/cost test unwittingly expose the weakness of their position. They must fear that their pet rules would flunk the test. After all, showing that a regulatory activity generates an excess of benefits is a strong justification for continuing it.

Benefit/cost analysis is a neutral concept, giving equal weight to a dollar of benefits and to a dollar of costs. The painful knowledge that resources available to safeguard human lives are limited causes economists to become concerned when they see wasteful use of those resources because of regulation.

Regulatory reform is not a matter of technical measurements or administrative procedures. Government decision makers need to view the regulatory mechanism differently than they do now. Rather than relying on regulation to control every facet of private behavior, the regulatory device needs to be seen as a powerful tool to be used with great care and discretion. Basically, it is attitudes that need to be changed.

Experience with the job safety program provides a cogent example. Although the government's safety rules have resulted in billions of dollars in public and private outlays, the goal of a substantially safer work environment has not been achieved.

A more satisfying answer to improving the effectiveness of government regulation of private activities requires a major change in the approach to regulation, and one not limited to the job safety program. If the objective of public policy is to reduce accidents, then public policy should focus directly on the reduction of accidents. Excessively detailed regulations are often merely a substitute—the normal bureaucratic substitute—for hard policy decisions.

Rather than placing emphasis on issuing citations to employers who fail to fill forms out correctly or who do not post the required notices, stress should be placed on regulating those employers with high and rising accident rates. Perhaps fines should be levied on those establishments with the worst safety records. As the accident rates decline toward some sensible standard, the fines could be reduced or eliminated.

But the government should not be much concerned with the way a specific organization achieves a safer working environment. Some companies may find it more efficient to change work rules, others to buy equipment, and still others to retrain workers. Making this choice is precisely the kind of operational business decision making that government should avoid, but that now dominates regulatory programs.

Reforming federal regulations should emphasize changing or repealing the basic statutes which gave birth to regulatory programs. For starters, here is a modest agenda for revising the basic laws that govern the regulation of business in the United States:

1. *Environmental regulation should make much more use of market-based approaches.* The legislation on water pollution control should be overhauled. Rather than requiring specific control technologies to be used to reduce pollution, government authorities should charge effluent fees. The primary objective of this approach is to provide an incentive for reducing pollution in the first place. The idea is to allow the polluter the choice of methods to be used, reducing compliance costs while simultaneously accelerating cleanup. Furthermore, by increasing prices of high-polluting products, consumers would be motivated to purchase cheaper, less polluting competitive products. Anti-pollution efforts would not stem from idealism, but rather from a straightforward desire to maintain competitive positions. This would be more cost-effective than the present reliance on standards, which almost invariably are postponed because of court battles or lack of sufficient technology.

2. *Progress on deregulation of transportation should be accelerated.* The agencies that still regulate prices, entry and exit of firms in the transportation industry—the Interstate Commerce Commission and the Federal Maritime Commission—should be eliminated. Their interment would end the CAB's monopoly of the federal graveyard for regulatory commissions.

3. *Outmoded regulation of financial institutions should be reduced.* Statutes that unduly restrict competition in the banking system should be repealed, especially the McFadden Act which limits the geographic expansion of commercial banks and the Glass-Steagall Act which inhibits their entry into other types of financial services. Enforcement could then focus on serious cases of fraud and similar lawbreaking.

4. *The regulation of exports should be cut back drastically.* While export controls on highly-classified military equipment are likely to remain and they should, such restrictions should not be imposed merely as an effort to achieve foreign or domestic policy objectives. The embargoes on grain exports were exercises in futility. Restricting exports of items readily obtainable in world markets does not hurt the foreign buyer, yet it punishes domestic producers and their employees.

5. *The regulation of imports through quotas should be determined.* Quotas and other quantitative restrictions on imports hurt the economy more than they benefit the specific industry they are designed to protect—and even more than tariffs. At least tariffs work through the price system and, unlike quotas, some of the benefits accrue to the Treasury and ultimately to American taxpayers.

Under all forms of trade restriction, consumers wind up paying higher prices. Those other domestic industries which purchase the higher-priced products become less competitive and they often then join the chorus for government intervention. Moreover, the incentive of the "protected" companies to become more efficient is reduced in the process.

6. *A fundamental rewrite of the statutory framework for social regulation should be undertaken.* Unrealistic goals and objectives should be eliminated. Their continued presence undermines confidence in the overall effectiveness of government activities. For example, in giving EPA the task of overseeing the cleansing of the nation's water, the Congress established the goal of "zero discharge" of untreated waste by 1984. In retrospect, the task was impossible and Congress realized that at the time.

The most fundamental need is to help the public understand the limits of government rulemaking. Even if the EPA were staffed entirely with Newtons and Einsteins, it could not meet the present statutory expectations of cleaning all of the water, air, and land in and around the United States nor could the Consumer Product Safety Commission effectively regulate the 2 million companies producing the 10,000 products within its jurisdiction.

The need is not for greater compassion, commitment, or technological expertise—those we have in abundance. What is required now is the willingness and the courage to make difficult choices among the many alternative demands for government regulation of private activity.

2.4. Two Cheers for Government Regulation

KENNETH ARROW

The previous readings in this section all refer to regulation narrowly defined. In this reading, Nobel Prize winner Kenneth Arrow looks at all government intervention in the economy as a form of regulation. Writing in 1982, during the peak of the Reagan revolution, he assesses the arguments of people like Friedman and Weidenbaum for significantly weakened government intervention.

Arrow argues that government has always played a substantial part in regulating the economy, and that in a complex modern society such intervention is more necessary than it used to be. He thinks that while there are excesses in government intervention, most intervention meets the needs of citizens and will not and should not be significantly curtailed. His broader view of regulation also reminds us that the government can indirectly tax and spend through regulations on business and can regulate business through its taxing and spending.

The reader should note the two quotes that introduce this piece—one from Karl Marx praising capitalism and the other from Milton Friedman praising government—if only as evidence that economists can have a sense of humor.

[The bourgeoisie] has been the first to show what man's activity can bring about. It has accomplished wonders far surpassing Egyptian pyramids, Roman aqueducts, and Gothic cathedrals; it has conducted expeditions that put in the shade all former Exoduses of nations and crusades.

—Karl Marx and Friedrich Engels, *The Communist Manifesto*

The expressways crisscrossing the country, magnificent dams spanning great rivers, orbiting satellites are all tributes to the capacity of government to command great resources. The school system, with all its defects and problems . . .

has widened the opportunities available to American youth and contributed to the extension of freedom.

—Milton Friedman, *Capitalism and Freedom*

The state has never been absent from the conduct of economic life. Its division was a revolutionary idea of the unknown eighteenth-century French statesman who first advised his king, "Laissez-faire. Let us do." But of course neither the French physiocratic school nor Adam Smith denied the state a role in governing the economy. They were concerned, as we are today, with determining the boundaries between public and private control. Smith saw clearly enough that there were functions that the state alone could perform. What is more, he believed that it was not merely private enterprise as such but competitive private enterprise that was the source of economic growth. He discoursed eloquently on the sloth and inefficiencies of monopoly, whether private or governmental. Indeed, he was decidedly negative about the efficiency of large economic organizations, and his excoriations of the joint-stock company or corporation will come as a surprise to those who think that the private sector of today bears a close resemblance to Smith's envisaged competitive order.

Indeed, pure laissez-faire economics has never been tried, although nineteenth-century Great Britain came the closest. Apart from state action, there are other forms of collective action to disturb the competitive ideal. There are the rings, pools, cartels, and trusts of the business community; and there are trade unions. The competitive order breeds insecurity; its ideal of efficiency depends precisely on fear of failure. Indeed, Adam Smith saw a perpetual threat to competition from the entrepreneurs themselves:

> People of the same trade seldom meet together, for merriment and diversion, but the conversation ends in a conspiracy against the public.

Smith was much less condemnatory of "combinations of workmen"; they were bound to be weaker than the "combinations of masters" who opposed them.

Despite the words of Smith, the unregulated conflict of private, organized groups has been avoided. To deal with industrial relations issues, the capitalist world has developed varying kinds of regulation of collective bargaining, which is a form of state power. To meet the need for security among the workers and the poor generally, forms of social insurance have evolved and grown in importance, starting with Germany in 1883 (though the United States did not develop a national system such as social security until 1935). Antitrust and similar legislation, on the one hand, and regulation of natural monopolies, railroads, and utilities, on the other, have met the degradation of competition by collusion and monopoly.

Nor have other forms of state intervention been wanting. A constant theme of all governments, regardless of the presiding party, has been the provision or subsidization of mass transportation (canals, railroads, and highways, in that order) as well as bridges and harbors. Capital-intensive aid to agriculture, and for irrigation and flood control, has also been a special province of the American polity. Nor can one neglect education, which could, in principle, be carried out in the private sector but that has everywhere been predominantly a governmental concern.

Though the state's role has never been small, it has increased in the postwar period. By now, one third of the U.S. gross national product passes through federal, state, and local government coffers. In addition, there is considerable regulation of private economic activity, not only the familiar regulation of prices of utilities and railroads but also that controlling environmental hazards. The age-old role of government in regulating the money supply has evolved into a general responsibility for achieving economic stability. Typical of this was the reaction to a severe economic crisis, the result of OPEC's sudden raising of petroleum prices in 1973. A professed anti-statist Republican administration immediately slapped controls on the price of oil.

The growth of government activity has necessarily created injuries to many, some real, some merely perceived. Taxes, particularly at the local level, have evoked the most immediate protest, as have the costs of regulation. The government has clearly not satisfied all the needs it has claimed to. Inflation is seen as the most conspicuous failure of the system, with economic stagnation and unemployment a close second.

The Reagan victory is the latest expression of the resulting demand for sharp reductions in the role of the state. It represents a new peak of a generalized opposition to increased government expenditures and regulations, which was seen earlier in the campaigns for limits on taxes or expenditures and, indeed, in many policies of the Carter administration. The more extreme views of libertarians and anarchists, who aim to restrict the state to minimal functions, have attracted little support, though they are not without the intellectual and aesthetic appeal of strong logical consistency. (Libertarians would turn the air force over to private enterprise.) But a great deal of rhetoric has been spoken about drastically reducing the role of the government in its budget, in its regulatory scope, and in its ambitions to stabilize the economy.

I do not agree that there is any reason to reduce the scope of government activity within the foreseeable future if our aim is a better economic, social, and physical life. Nor do I believe that there will be any significant reduction in this scope, regardless of change of administration or the elections of coming years. These two statements—about what should be and what is politically possible— are not completely unrelated. In a democratic system, what is politically possible represents, though in a crude and sometimes distorted way, what people want. I do not assert that it is a universal truth that right is measured by desires or votes. But when it comes to economic rather than moral good, there is no legitimate criterion of policy other than giving people what they want, or should want if they are properly informed.

The current mixed economy, with its high but not dominant proportion of government activity, did not emerge by accident or by the willful design of corrupt politicians. It arose as a series of responses to felt needs. This condition does not mean that the specifics of the mixed economy must be regarded as ideal. On the contrary, just as in the private sector, particular commodities may always be found wanting or be replaced by superior alternatives. But the needs met by the government sector must be recognized. To argue for drastic reduction is to say that their desirability is illusory or that the private sector will rush in with alternatives.

An economist, of whatever school, necessarily recognizes limits. Whether he defends the present mixture of private and public controls or argues for a closer approximation to laissez-faire, the economist should never claim to advocate a utopia. In a world of limited resources and imperfect understanding, all that can be asked for is the reduction of flaws. Like political democracy, to which it is so linked, the mixed economy has much to answer for; it is merely less bad than its alternatives.

The private competitive order is best at increasing private income as much as possible, though even in this it is not without problems. This is an important aim and is a precondition of achieving other goals of individuals; I am not a believer in stopping economic growth. But private income and consumption are only part of what men and women live for; they are only means to achieving the real goals of life. Keynes once gave a toast to economists: "The trustees, not of civilization, but of the possibility of civilization."

The endurance of the social order, the sense that we are all members of one another, is vital to the meaning of civilization. Such a notion is essential to the free enterprise system itself, which cannot flourish without a social structure. These links among individuals at a more concrete level have been dramatized in concerns about the environment. I have already mentioned the demand for security, exemplified not only by the welfare system but also by the Chrysler Corporation. The vast inequalities of income generated by the private economic system weaken a society's sense of mutual concern.

These few examples illustrate the range of goals that our economic system is striving to achieve. It stands to reason that the more goals there are to be achieved, the greater the variety of means needed to achieve them. The economist Jan Tinbergen has stated as a general principle of policy that in trying to achieve economic goals, the number of instruments has to equal the number of goals. These instruments do indeed include private decisions to buy and sell and to set prices, but they also include the instruments in the hands of government: tax rates, expenditures, the legal framework within which private economic decisions are made, and regulation of all kinds.

Complexity is not comfortable, and the normal desire is to avoid it, to find the simple solution. The nineteenth-century historian Jakob Burckhardt predicted the rise of the "terrible simplifiers," and indeed they emerged in lockstep with totalitarianism. The Nazis, the Fascists, and the communists all offer simple solutions to complex issues, which was a major part of their appeal in the past and to some still is even today. But for the next decade, in this country at least, they are not likely to form a serious part of political discourse. It is the other simplification— that of Ronald Reagan's, for instance—the drastic reduction in government's role, which has more immediate appeal.

I find in most people's thinking a surprising incongruity between the demand for reduced government and the specifics that are needed to realize that aim. Milton Friedman's television series, "Free to Choose" and the best-selling book by Milton and Rose Friedman based on it, have reached a large audience and evidently an appreciative one. Yet I wonder how many listeners and readers have fully understood their proposals, admirably explicit though they are. The social security system should be dismantled. All government support of higher education should be ended. The government should cease all support of research and development. Elementary and secondary education should be turned over to free enterprise. All licensing of professions, including physicians and lawyers, should be ended. All restrictions on prescription drugs based on their lack of efficacy should be ended. This is far from an exhaustive list.

Over the years, a body of economic theory has grown up that has sought to explain the criteria by which the boundary of government intervention in the economy is to be judged. Richard Musgrave has formulated a convenient three-fold classification of the government's functions, and I follow it here: *allocation, distribution,* and *stabilization.*

The private sector, left to its own devices, allocates resources to different uses and different individuals. For various reasons, it has long been a staple argument among economists that the resulting allocation, while efficient in many areas, will fail in some. The most obvious are the goods that serve society as a whole— defense, justice, police, most roads. Why would any one person want to maintain a road? The expenditures must therefore be public ones. (Most people would add at least primary and secondary education to the list.) Public expenditures mean public taxes.

More broadly, there are other cases in which public intervention, not necessarily expenditure, is necessary to change the way in which resources are used. Take the example of environmental hazards, particularly air- and waterborne pollution. Dumping wastes in a stream may ruin fisheries; this loss should, in a proper economic accounting, be charged against the dumper, but it is impractical to do so. Thus the public must intervene in some way, either by charging the dumper for the costs imposed on others or by regulations. The effects of pollution fall not merely on production but also on comfort, health, and life.

It is easy to see the costs of environmental regulation of business in terms of enforcement costs and of additional capital equipment needed to contain wastes. But it is equally easy to see the benefits of cleaner air and cleaner water. I think that while regulation has gone too far or been misdirected in some areas—such as occupational safety—it has probably not gone far enough in those of chemical handling and waste disposal.

A second classic ground for intervention is that of natural monopoly, as in the case of utilities, where competition must inevitably fail. Here I agree with the critics who say that too much is regulated. Many industries that are basically competitive, such as railroads, have been regulated, largely in the interest of that particular industry. But what would be the consequences of permitting electricity to be produced by companies with no regulation of prices or service?

The second, much less articulated, purpose of government intervention is to redistribute income. The private sector produces enormous disparities in income received. To be fair about it, so does every other economic system. In communist countries, the very high incomes are indeed largely cut off, but they are replaced by concentrations of power. One virtue of a mixed economy in a democracy is precisely that the productivity of a free enterprise system can be joined to a greater equalization of consumption. Other countries, even highly productive ones such as Sweden, West Germany, and Japan, have achieved greater degrees of income equality than has the United States.

Nevertheless, a fundamental change in income distribution through taxation is not on the current political agenda. What I do think is strongly desired, however, is a commitment to the relief of poverty. Redistribution of income to the very poor in the form of welfare programs, food stamps, subsidized medical care, and now subsidized energy for house heating, is a fundamental part of our economic commitment. It is true that complaints are rampant about the abuses of the system (or, more precisely, the unsystematic conglomeration of programs) and the incentives the system provides for laziness and withdrawal from the labor force. But all polls show that a majority of the people still favor retention of the welfare system.

Actually, the largest redistribution of income under our present government programs is not from the well-off to the poor but from the workers to the retired: the social security program. Its financing may indeed create serious (though by no mean insurmountable) problems in the future, as the percentage of retired workers rises. A modest raising of the retirement age, fully justified by the American people's improved health, would solve them.

Martin Anderson, now assistant to the president, and other conservative economists have argued recently that there is no need for further action to help the poor or the old, because in fact they are not so badly off. What these studies really show is that the anti-poverty programs of the 1960s and the social security programs as they have evolved have in fact been very successful, and repudiation of them does not seem called for.

Finally, the third major service the government can offer the economy is its stabilization. The business cycle has been a recurring and fundamental property of the capitalist system almost since its inception. Recurrent periods of underemployment of men and capital were observed as early as the first half of the nineteenth century. We still do not have a systematic theory, but we do have a general understanding: the economic system is decentralized, so little information about the whole system is available to any one participant; wages and prices not only allocate resources and contribute to efficiency but are also the sources of individuals' incomes and are, therefore, vigorously protected and promoted. In textbook theories of the smoothly working economy, prices and wages fall whenever supply exceeds demand, and rise in the opposite case. In fact, they are rigid or only slowly moving, so that unemployment, for example, is not immediately followed by sharp drops in wages. There is too much pressure to maintain them.

For this reason, Keynes and others before and after him have urged a more active role for the government. It is better to stimulate an insufficient demand by government intervention than to let valuable resources remain idle. The measures might include government spending, or tax cuts to stimulate private spending, or increases in the supply of money to make it easier for industry to invest. All of these have been used increasingly in the postwar period. I note that, both here and in countries following similar policies, the period of active government intervention was the most stable ever. In particular, the years from 1961 to 1967 saw the longest sustained prosperity in our history. This was the period when the recommendations of Keynesian policy were most carefully followed.

Indeed, despite the current disillusionment of supply-side economists, for whom Keynes is anathema, the policies of alteration of effective demand have served their economy well. The problem today is not that we do not know how to eliminate unemployment; it is that the wage and price rigidities I mentioned before—together with a policy of sustained full employment, accompanied by the irruptions of the Vietnam war and the oil price increases—have set off an inflationary spiral. It is the dilemma foreseen when Keynesian policy was first being urged— that a stable full-employment economy has a built-in inflationary bias.

This is a dilemma for policy, but does not imply that government stabilization policy is a mistake. Inflation is an evil, but not comparable to the wastage and cruelty of repeated unemployment.

These, then, are the functions the government can perform and is performing in the operation of the economy. I think the principle that the government can make a contribution is clear. But there is another objection raised by Reagan, Friedman, and other critics of government intervention: that the government by its nature is bound to do its jobs badly. The idea is that decisions made on behalf of others are apt to be made with less care and awareness of what the beneficiaries really want. Examples of this principle are bureaucratic inertia, political pressures on policy-making, and close connections between interest groups and the particular agencies charged with their regulation. The market makes delicate adjustments between desire and scarcity, because each individual makes his or her own decision; political decisions, made by voting, are necessarily cruder, of a "yes or no" variety.

There is no denying that these criticisms have some truth in them. The market, when it works, creates more pressure for efficiency, for innovation, and for the best use of technology for the desires of users. But most of what the government does is beyond the province of private business. One can easily speak of the capture of regulatory commissions by the regulated industry; but one can easily find many examples where regulation has protected consumers without hampering technological innovation. The statistical services, which I know best, have a record for accuracy, scrupulousness, and sophistication that is the envy of the world.

Nor is the efficiency of private enterprise quite so ideal. I have already referred to its overall inefficiencies in allocation and instability. Industry today is dominated by large firms; bureaucracy is no longer a monopoly of the government. The automobile and steel industries have shown less than perfect agility in responding to changing technology and changing demands, a melancholy fact recorded in both the companies' profit-and-loss statements and the nation's balance-of-trade figures. Routine operation and spending other people's money are as characteristic of business as they are of the government. Perhaps, in the distant future, there may be a confluence of the two.

Let me take the example of the energy sector to illustrate the considerable role the government has always played, for good or ill. Let me repeat: I favor decontrolling oil prices. It would nevertheless be falsifying history to pretend that the imposition of oil price controls was a sudden aberration from a free-market policy. The U.S. government and others have helped oil companies obtain concessions in foreign countries, sometimes by none too gentle means. Not long ago, by historical standards, the Texas Railroad Commission was an earlier and more efficient OPEC that carefully restricted production to keep prices up. As cheaper foreign oil became available, the federal government intervened by setting import quotas to keep up domestic oil prices. Natural-gas prices have been regulated; oil and natural-gas drilling have been given special tax treatment. Finally, dwarfing all previous interventions, OPEC itself is a massive participation by governments.

This story is designed to be even-handed, but it shows that the government's role has never been negligible, although it has probably been bad more often than good. On present policy issues, to what extent should the United States rely on the market? For allocation of oil itself, certainly. Dismantling the regulatory apparatus and refusing to use rationing are all to the good. But how should the country anticipate and respond to sudden interruptions of supply? How about synthetic fuel development? Encouragement of solar energy in its various forms? Support of research and development of photovoltaic cells or the breeder reactor or fusion? For most of these issues there is hardly any politically significant difference of opinion, as congressional votes show; the government is firmly in the picture, in some cases more firmly than I would judge desirable.

Many of the problems of government intervention stem from its inflexible form. As I have repeatedly noted, allocation through prices is more efficient, and takes better account of individual circumstances, than does regulation. When the government does intervene, it can use pricelike mechanisms. For example, in the synthetic fuels program, the government could announce a price, somewhat but not excessively above the current world price of oil, at which it will purchase synthetic fuel in the future. If private companies choose to build the plants with this guaranteed market, well and good. If they do not, it is a sign that we are not yet ready for synthetic fuels. Similarly, as regards pollution, it would be better to tax effluents from smokestacks, at a rate reflecting costs imposed on others, than to set regulated limits plant by plant.

The way the government intervenes in the economy has changed and should continue to change. Old functions become useless and pernicious, new needs emerge. But the general level of government intervention is likely to remain basically unchanged for the next decade, and it is in the general interest that it should do so.

Recent Developments
in Business Regulation

Recent History

Regulation of private industry in the United States has not been a continuous
process but one of periodic increases followed by periods of quiescence. After a
very active period in the 1930s when a number of new regulatory agencies were
formed, the period from about 1940 to 1965 was one of little new activity on the
regulatory front. During the late 1960s and the 1970s there was a new wave of
primarily social legislation almost unprecedented in its scope. In this period, over
100 new regulatory agencies were created, and previously lightly regulated areas
such as equal employment, workplace safety, and the environment became quite
heavily regulated.

Whenever there is a major change in the way that society does things, it is
normal for a reaction to set in after the first flush of enthusiasm is past. Starting
in the mid-1970s, an increasing amount of attention has been paid to the benefits
of deregulation. Four broad changes have taken place under the aegis of deregulation. One, begun under the Ford administration, has been a continuing effort to
assess both the benefits and the costs of proposed new regulations put forward by
the regulatory agencies. This bipartisan effort, which reached its height during
the Reagan administration, sought to prevent regulation from making American
industry inefficient by loading it with unjustifiable costs. Because agencies were
thought unlikely to restrain themselves, responsibility for performing cost/benefit
analyses of regulations was transferred to the Office of Management and Budget,
a body with the expertise necessary to perform the often difficult calculations
and with a bias towards cutting spending. While for a few years under the
Reagan administration there was a tendency to politicize these cost/benefit anal-

yses, over time they have become a useful restraint on the system.

The second major thrust has been toward deregulation in the area of producer regulation. Many of the industries that were regulated during the Roosevelt administration in the 1930s to stop predatory pricing and economic collapse had increasingly used that regulation to prevent new entrants and charge higher prices to consumers. Moreover, the effort to maintain this artificial system led to many inefficient rules, such as the one forbidding some long-distance trucks from picking up return freight. The Carter administration began the process of deregulating many of these industries and the Reagan administration continued it. Airlines, trucking, railroads, and oil all had their prices deregulated and lesser efforts were made in other cases of producer regulation. Most studies of this kind of deregulation show high net benefits, and there has been little enthusiasm for reregulation in this area.

The third major thrust was to cut back on much information-based and natural-monopoly regulation. Unlike the other two changes which took place under presidents of both parties, this type of deregulation primarily occurred in the Reagan and Bush administrations. There was partial deregulation in the banking and savings and loan industry, cable television, the telephone industry, and the power industry. This type of deregulation was generally viewed as less successful than that in the producer-monopoly area. The changes in the savings and loan industry were particularly costly to the country.

Finally the Reagan administration made a number of administrative efforts to reverse or halt some of the negative-externality and workplace-safety regulations put in place in the preceding decade. Faced with an unsympathetic Democratic Congress, the Reagan administration used budget cuts, personnel changes and changes in administrative rules to slow down many of the adjustments mandated in the recently passed regulatory laws. While these changes did have the desired effect in the short term, few of them lasted past the end of Reagan's first term. The fact that Reagan's handpicked successor chose to run as the "environmental president" shows how little these changes were in tune with prevailing sentiment in the country as a whole.

One might expect that with all this emphasis on deregulation, the federal government would be spending less on regulation and reducing the number of regulations. In some areas this is true. As we can see in figure 1, industry-specific regulation, most of which falls into the category of producer regulation, has decreased 14 percent in the 1980-to-1994 period. Energy regulation, also generally a form of producer regulation, has fallen by 70 percent in the same period. The decline of union power has also led to some erosion in the regulation of job safety and working conditions, with spending in that area falling by 17 percent in the period.

But these declines have more than been made up for by increased regulation in other areas. How can this be explained, given the generally deregulatory stance of both Republican and Democratic presidents? Three factors stand out as

Figure 1. **Real Spending by Regulatory Agencies, 1970–1994**

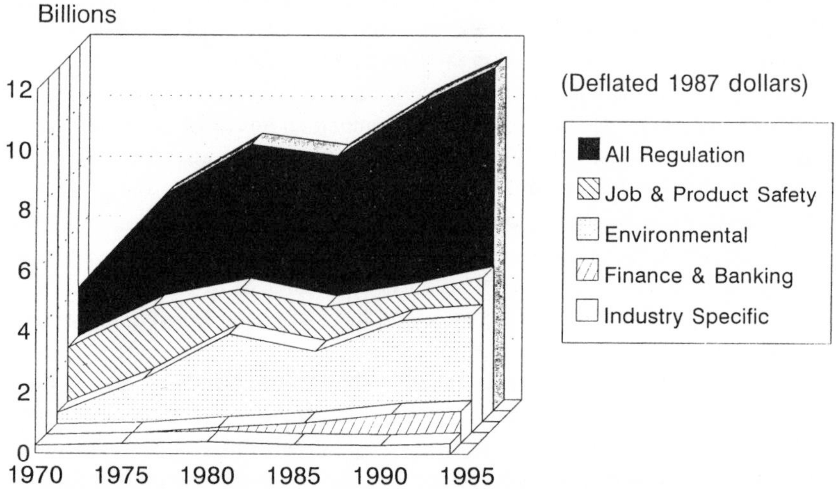

Source: Congressional Quarterly Press, *Federal Regulatory Directory 1994,* p. 14.

explanations. The most ironic is deregulation itself. While deregulation has generally been successful and has led to decreased regulatory spending, the costs to taxpayers from savings and loan deregulation easily outweigh all the benefits from the other areas of deregulation. The attempts to partially deregulate the savings and loan and banking industries led to so many savings and loan failures that a huge staff had to be hired to work out rescue attempts and to liquidate the huge number of federally insured loans of bankrupt savings and loans. Between 1975 and 1994 the number of regulators in the finance and banking area increased from 6,400 to 16,100. Estimates of the total cost of savings and loan deregulation to the federal government alone currently hover in the $120 billion range.

A second factor leading to increased regulation has been the lagged effects of earlier legislation. In general it takes quite a while for any agency to gear up to do its job fully, and typically there is a long period in which additional rules and legislation are seen to be necessary to complete the job originally envisaged. For example, in the early 1970s the Environmental Protection Agency was given the responsibility of cleaning up toxic waste dumps. After more than twenty years, less than 10 percent of the dumps have been cleaned up and the estimated costs of the cleanup continue to soar.

The third major factor has been the lack of change in Congress. The Democratic Party controlled the House of Representatives for the entire 1970-to-1994 period, and it controlled the Senate for all except the 1980-to-1986 period. Most types of regulation seek to regulate business in the interests of consumers or workers. Thus one might reasonably expect that when the party in power places more weight on the interests of business, such regulation would decrease. Most see the Republican Party as the party of business, and hence one would expect that Democrats would be more willing to burden business and Republicans to ease those burdens. Interestingly the only period when real regulatory costs decreased was during the early 1980s, when Republicans controlled both the presidency and the Senate.

This factor has obviously changed considerably in the wake of the 1994 elections. With Republicans newly ascendent in both chambers of Congress, attempts are already being made to reduce the amount of regulation. If a Republican wins the White House in 1996, we will probably see a reversal in the upward trend to regulatory spending.

To what degree do the recent changes in the regulatory area support the points of view put forward in the readings in this section? The first reading by Anthony Downs is a partial theory of regulation applying only to regulation that gives benefits to a minority at the long-term expense of the majority. Where these conditions are met, Downs postulates a five-part process where early regulatory enthusiasm declines as the cost of solving the problems becomes apparent. The theory was designed with environmental legislation in mind, and so it is best tested here. Looking at the course of environmental legislation, it is clear that much of the Downs model accurately describes what has happened. There was indeed a period of alarmed discovery followed by attempts to deal with the problem. The costs to the public did indeed escalate, and opposition has indeed developed to existing regulation. But the key part of the model, in which the increasing costs to the public lead to general opposition to environmental action followed by its reduction, has not yet occurred. As costs have increased, public support for the environment has remained generally high. Opposition has come instead from interests such as West Coast logging workers and businesses that bear a disproportionate share of the costs. Environmental policy has been reined in only where the costs to one segment of the population are particularly high, as with the spotted owl controversy, or when the Republicans have taken action on behalf of business.

What does recent history have to say about the Stigler thesis that regulation is instituted to benefit business? Again the thesis is only partly borne out. There is little doubt that producer monopoly, the use of government to obtain monopolistic prices in what should be a competitive or oligopolistic market, has indeed been common in the United States. There is also little doubt that the reasons Stigler gives for this are valid ones, and that pockets of this kind of regulation remain in areas such as the maritime industry. However, one should note two trends that reduce the general applicability of Stigler's insight. One is that, somewhat ironically, the attention drawn to producer regulation by people such as Stigler, Huntington, Bernstein, and Kahn has led to deregulation in precisely this area. This in turn means that what economists term *rent seeking* is harder to find in the regulatory area. The other is that most regulation is no longer of this type.

The recent upsurge in safety, information-based, and negative-externality–based types of regulation have left producer regulation a much smaller slice of the regulatory pie. Moreover, if most regulation was done to benefit business, one might expect it to increase under Republicans and decrease under Democrats, something which does not seem to fit recent events.

The articles by Weidenbaum and Arrow are largely about the extent to which government regulation of private economic activity was justified. Much of the deregulatory activity of the past two decades was influenced by the arguments of Weidenbaum and his Democratic counterpart, Alfred Kahn. Both strongly advocated deregulation and both played a part in implementing it, Kahn as chair of the Civil Aeronautics Board in the Carter administration and Weidenbaum as chair of the Council of Economic Advisors in the Reagan administration. It is clear that there has been considerable change in the area of producer regulation due in large part to a stream of arguments from these two gentlemen. This deregulation has generally been as successful as was claimed. In areas such as airlines, long-distance trucking, oil, and railroads, wages have fallen, new competitors have driven down prices, and consumers have generally paid less. The use of cost/benefit analysis also owes much to Weidenbaum.

However, when it comes to regulation in other areas, over which Arrow and Weidenbaum disagree, the record to date has been one of caution, with periodic changes often followed by retreats. Attempts to cut environmental regulation in the early part of the Reagan administration met with public disapproval and were followed by increases. There have been cycles over regulation of advertising and marketing of consumer products, with Republicans generally being more inclined to deregulation and Democrats often pushing for increases in regulation. Cable television has been deregulated, reregulated, and deregulated once again in the last fifteen years. In general, Congress and successive presidents have followed the advice of Arrow somewhat more closely than that of Weidenbaum and have sought to regulate in the interests of the consumer while getting rid of many of the worst abuses.

3. Fiscal and Monetary Policy

There are many policy tools that can be used to change economic behavior. Trade policies and exchange-rate policies can be used to change the balance between imports and exports. Labor-market policies can be used to influence underlying unemployment. Immigration policies can affect the supply of labor. Research and development spending can affect productivity. Wage-price policies can affect short-run inflation.

But of all the policy tools available to government, the most powerful by far are fiscal and monetary policies. Traditionally these are studied together, as the policies pursued in one area act to constrain what is possible or desirable in the other. The standard macroeconomics course is largely an examination of how these policies interact and how they affect the economy.

However, when we examine the politics of economic policy making, it is advisable to look at monetary policy, tax policy, and expenditure policy separately. In part this is because there are few, if any, overarching theories in political science to explain interaction among the different policies, and in part it is because the political systems surrounding the three areas are much more distinctly separate than the economic systems.

There are exceptions to this generalization. Both Bach (1971) and Pierce (1971) have written books that make some attempt at integration. Much of the writing about applied policy looks at how outcomes in one area constrain the others. Some analysts have tried to apply incrementalist theory to the three types of policy (Wildavsky 1964, Sharkansky 1969, Knott 1983). The political business-cycle theory has been tested against both monetary- and fiscal-policy outcomes (Tufte 1978, Beck 1987). But on the whole, the literature tends to concentrate on one area at a time.

The plan of this book generally follows this tendency, and looks at the three policies separately. However, I thought it would be useful to begin part three with an essay that discusses the three types of policy and their relation to one another. Therefore, I include a brief piece by myself that introduces readers to the different policy areas and points out the similarities and differences between them.

For Further Reading

A good economics test in this area is Robert Gordon's *Macroeconomics*. A brief introduction to policy making in this area is Carl Lieberman's *Making Economic Policy*. For other readings, see the comments in this section in parts 3A, 3B, 3C, and 3D.

References

Bach, George L. 1971. *Making Monetary and Fiscal Policy*. Washington D.C.: The Brookings Institution.

Beck, Nathaniel. 1987. "Elections and the Fed: Is There a Political Monetary Cycle?" *American Journal of Political Science* 3:1 (February): 194–216.

Gordon, Robert J. 1991. *Macroeconomics*. 5th ed. Glenview, Ill.: Scott Foresman.

Knott, Jack. 1983. "Uncertainty and Federal Reserve Decision Making." Paper presented at the annual meeting of the American Political Science Association, Chicago, Ill., September 1–4.

Lieberman, Carl. 1991. *Making Economic Policy*. Englewood Cliffs, N.J.: Prentice Hall.

Pierce, Lawrence C. 1971. *The Politics of Fiscal Policy Formation*. Pacific Palisades, Calif.: Goodyear.

Sharkansky, Ira. 1969. *The Politics of Taxing and Spending*. Indianapolis, Ind.: University of Indiana.

Tufte, Edward. 1978. *Political Control of the Economy*. Princeton, N.J.: Princeton University Press.

Wildavsky, Aaron. 1964. *The Politics of the Budgetary Process*, 1st ed. Boston: Little Brown.

3.1. The Politics of Fiscal and Monetary Policy

PAUL PERETZ

This essay is intended as a brief introduction to macroeconomic policy-making in the United States. It attempts to identify the most important actors in the determination of policy outcomes and the degree to which the different kinds of macroeconomic policy are coordinated. Three general points are developed. The first is that the three major types of economic policy—that is, expenditure policy, tax policy, and monetary policy—are less coordinated than most economists would recommend, because different "subgovernments" with different policy processes control these policy areas. The second is that each type of policy tends to specialize in different economic tasks, with monetary policy concentrating on stabilizing the economy, tax policy concentrating on determining the allocation between public and private goods, and expenditure policy concentrating on re-distribution and allocating between different public goods. The third is that political participation is greatest in expenditure policy and least in tax and monetary policy, with the result that expenditure policies are more redistributive and more in accord with the interests of the majority. While there are important exceptions to these statements, the existence of the tendencies does to some degree explain economic outcomes.

The Economic Policy Process

There are three primary methods for affecting the overall shape of the economy: changing the supply of money, changing the level of taxation, and changing the level of government spending. When we alter the amount of money in circulation with the aim of raising or lowering interest rates, we call this *monetary policy;* tax and expenditure policies together are called *fiscal policy.*

All three means can be used to expand the economy. Raising government expenditures creates work in the government sector or gives money to those who receive government payments, such as the aged. In turn, the newly hired workers or recipients of transfer payments spend much of their money in the private sector. This raises the demand for goods such as clothing and automobiles, which means that new workers will be hired in these industries and business will have good reason to invest in new plants and machinery.

We can achieve much the same effect by lowering taxes. This leaves more money in people's pockets, money they can then spend on consumer goods. This again causes more people to be employed in consumer industries and gives business a reason to invest in new capital.

Finally, monetary policy achieves similar results through somewhat different means. When the government increases the supply of money, those who need to borrow money find it easier to obtain and hence can borrow at lower interest rates. When interest rates go down, consumers borrow more money to buy goods such as automobiles and houses. This increases employment in those sectors. At the same time businesses are more likely to invest, because the cost of the money they borrow to finance their investments has gone down. This leads to new hiring in the investment sector of the economy.

As we have seen, changes in both monetary and fiscal policy can be used to expand or contract the economy. Some administrations place more weight on one type of policy than another. Typically, Republican administrations place more weight on monetary policy, Democratic administrations on fiscal policy (Peretz 1983). Which policy should be relied on to carry most of the burden is a function of the administration's other aims, the length of time it takes for the policies to affect the economy, and the economic beliefs of the political actors.

The point about the other aims is fairly straightforward. If, for example, one wishes to stimulate the economy while aiding the poor at the same time, one might, like President Johnson, increase transfer payments to the elderly and those on welfare or, like President Clinton, expand the earned income tax credit, a subsidy to lower income taxpayers. If, on the other hand, one wished to help the well-off, one might, like President Reagan, cut the taxes of those with the highest rates or, like President Bush or Newt Gingrich, seek to reduce capital gains tax rates.

The point about the length of time it takes for a policy to have impact is somewhat more complex. In general, one would like one's policy to affect the economy in the shortest possible time. This is because it is difficult to forecast very far in advance where the economy is going; hence, the longer the lag time, the more likely it is that the stimulus will be too late. Much depends, of course, on the time it takes for the policy to work its way through the political process (the inside lag); then comes the time it takes to affect the economy once it goes into operation (the outside lag) (Pierce 1971). In general, monetary policy has the shortest inside lag but the longest outside lag. Expenditure changes have the longest inside lag but the shortest outside lag. Tax policy is intermediate for both types of lag.

The point about the beliefs of actors should be fairly clear. Economists do not all agree on the relative usefulness of the different policy tools. Monetarists, for example, tend to believe that the quantity of money is the most important tool, especially for controlling inflation. Keynesians place more weight on the independent effect of fiscal policy. Expectations theorists believe that economic policy has less effect than we suppose, because the market successfully anticipates what will be done. Over the last thirty years, different administrations have been dominated by those with one or another set of beliefs. In general, monetarists have been more influential during Republican administrations and Keynesians during Democratic ones, although there has been an overall trend toward monetarist beliefs.

The Interdependence of Monetary and Fiscal Policy

It is generally agreed by economists that it is best to coordinate tax and expenditure policies to move the economy in one and the same direction. It is also generally agreed that the economy performs better when monetary policy is coordinated with both types of fiscal policy.

When policy makers fail to coordinate the three policy tools, two negative effects occur. One is that the policies tend to cancel one another out, failing to produce the intended effects. The other is that when different policy tools pull in different directions, distortions are introduced which serve to make the economy less efficient or to produce new problems for the future. For example, it was the combination of a stimulative fiscal policy and a restrictive monetary policy that placed disproportionate burdens on the housing and automotive industries in the early part of the Reagan administration.

But the other side of this coin is that when one policy tool is mishandled, the other tool can compensate to some degree for this. Over the last fifteen years, large structural deficits have made it much harder to use fiscal policy to manage the economy. In response, the Federal Reserve has kept real interest rates high to prevent overstimulation of the economy. And when progress has been made toward reducing the deficit, as it was in 1993, the Federal Reserve has eased off somewhat on the monetary brake.

The Political Separation of Monetary, Tax, and Expenditure Policy

We have seen that there are good reasons to coordinate the two kinds of fiscal policy as well as fiscal and monetary policy. What is most notable about the way that these policies are made in the United States, however, is the degree to which different players and different institutions have political control over the different policy tools. While there are some actors who have influence in all three areas, and while the the fiscal policy process has become marginally more unified over the last twenty years, what is most notable is that the policies are made separately and that the mechanisms set up to coordinate the three policies are weak.

The greatest coordination occurs between the two types of fiscal policy; the least between monetary policy and fiscal policy. But the overall separation is sufficiently great to make it productive to look at expenditure, tax, and monetary policy making in terms of little subgovernments arrayed around each policy area.

Expenditure Policy

The Process

Government expenditures are determined in a long and complex budgetary process that stretches over two and a half years. In March to June of the first year, agencies review current operations and receive estimates from their subunits. In the same general period, the Office of Management and Budget (OMB), working with the president and his economic advisers, produces rough guidelines for agency spending totals and gives them to the agencies. Over the succeeding summer, the agencies decide on their spending priorities in consultation with those in the OMB who have responsibility for their programs. This generally results in cuts in the amounts that their subunits had requested.

Around October the agencies submit their budgets to the OMB. In the period between October and January, the OMB, the Treasury, and the Council of Economic Advisers prepare economic forecasts as well as forecasts of revenues for the financial year beginning in October of the second year. Generally these revenue forecasts are lower than the amount requested by the agencies, and, as a consequence, the budgets requested by most of them are cut. However, some favored programs that are high on the president's agenda are cut only minimally or may even be enhanced.

By the first Monday in February of the second year, the OMB submits the president's budget to Congress, while the Council of Economic Advisers submits a report outlining the economic assumptions behind the budget. The budget is then referred to the budget committees in the House of Representatives and the Senate. Their responsibility is to look at the broad revenue and expenditure totals proposed and then to decide whether the totals are in line with current deficit-reduction targets and how the money will be divided between the twenty major spending functions. At the same time, the appropriations committees in the House and the Senate examine the details of the proposed expenditures. If tax changes are proposed, these are studied by the Ways and Means Committee in the House and the Finance Committee in the Senate.

The budget committees, after consulting with one another, are meant to produce a concurrent resolution putting limits on the amount that can be appropriated in each category and spelling out any changes in the law that are necessary to reach their targets; and have the resolution approved by April 15. The budget is then broken down into thirteen separate bills and examined by the appropriations committees. These bills are reconciled with the overall limits set by the budget committees and are all supposed to be passed by the beginning of the budget year on October 1. In practice, the deadlines for both the budget resolution and the passing of the appropriations bills are almost never met, and it is normal for current spending to be extended into the next fiscal year until the process finally disgorges the relevant spending bill.

This normally complex process has been further complicated since 1985 by attempts to make the budget totals fit under arbitrarily chosen spending caps laid out in the Gramm-Rudman-Hollings bills of 1985 and 1987 and the Bush budget compromise of 1990. Elaborate provisions requiring the president to enforce draconian cuts on about half the budget if Congress fails to come in under the targets have resulted in complex and often counterproductive attempts to meet those targets by the beginning of the budget year. The usefulness of these provisions is open to question. While the targets have always been formally met, "unexpected" increases in spending have usually ensured that by the end of the budget year, more had been spent than was laid out in the targets. Further the targets themselves have usually been relaxed when they really began to threaten favored spending programs.

During the fiscal year, supplemental spending bills are sometimes passed in order to deal with unanticipated spending needs. At the end of the fiscal year (that is, in October of the third year), there is an audit of expenditures by the General Accounting Office, to ensure that appropriated funds were spent as intended and not misappropriated or spent on other programs.

The Major Players

The expenditure process involves a large number of actors and engenders considerable political conflict. As a process, it is almost a model for what political scientists call *pluralism,* with large numbers of players joining together in groups and coalitions in order to realize their political ends.

We saw above that many different groups in both the executive branch and the legislative branch have an influence on the budget. To these must be added the vast number of interest groups representing those who are the beneficiaries of government spending or who will pay the bill. These interest groups lobby at all stages of the budgetary process. They pressure the White House to give priority to their concerns, they urge the agencies to request more money to benefit their constituents, and they pressure congressional committees to authorize the spending.

Interest groups are most likely to apply political pressure when benefits that they previously received are threatened; for example, when cuts in Social Security or Medicare are proposed, organizations representing the elderly mobilize in opposition. Thousands of groups have permanent offices in Washington, so that their representatives can participate on a more routine basis, often in alliance with bureaucrats in the spending agencies. In most cases the groups concentrate on the particular category of spending of most concern to their constituents. But some of the larger "peak" organizations representing broader groups, such as labor and business, also attempt to influence the total amount to be spent on defense and domestic programs.

Despite the multitude of participants in the process, one should not infer that all actors are of equal importance. Within the executive branch the White House and the Office of Management and Budget are the central actors—increasingly so in recent years (Heclo 1984; Greider 1985). The White House is important in setting the general priorities within which the executive branch operates. President Reagan, for example, was quite successful in shifting spending from domestic programs to defense. The OMB is extremely important in deciding which agencies and programs are to receive more funding and which will receive less. Traditionally, the OMB has tried to apply professional criteria while working within the president's priorities. But, although this is still largely true, there has been some politicization of the agency.

Within Congress, the two budget committees, the two appropriation committees, and the House and Senate leadership are most important. The budget committees, first established in 1974, are primarily important in setting total spending levels. Their record in terms of ability to make their divisions of those totals stick is somewhat mixed. The budget committees are important—but less powerful than their central role in the process makes them appear to be. "Both committees," it has been observed, "are in truth adding machine committees that take the demands of spending committees and impose as much constraint on them as the current Congressional mood allows" (Ippolito 1981, 104). The appropriations committees are still the most important center of power over expenditures in the legislative branch. That power, however, lies not in the full committees, but in their subcommittees. It is here that the budget proposed by the executive is closely scrutinized and detailed allocations are made. As many observers have noted, this results in considerable fragmentation and makes detailed trade-offs between different areas virtually impossible (Shepsle and Weingast 1984). Finally, the House and Senate leaderships are important primarily in managing the budget, making sure that deadlines are met, and resolving impasses over such things as the deficit.

Why So Many Players?

Despite recent attempts to centralize it, decision making on expenditure policy remains quite fragmented. Indeed, much of the conflict in our political system revolves around the making of the budget, with vast numbers of groups both inside and outside the government struggling to influence the result. As we shall see, this is much less true of tax and monetary policy making.

Why does expenditure policy involve so many players and so much effort? The primary reason is that expenditure policy is far more than simply a means of controlling the economy. Large numbers of people, ranging from defense contractors to residents of nursing homes, are directly or indirectly dependent on government payments and have good reason to favor expansion of "their" programs. But, since all spending programs compete for a limited total of funds, the beneficiaries of a program often have to battle other, similarly motivated people. Moreover, much of the battle over redistribution (from the rich to the poor, or vice versa) occurs over budget expenditures. Because spending programs are biased toward those who are less well off, there are continual attempts by those representing the better off to cut expenditures, and by those representing the less well off to maintain or increase them.

For both these reasons, the struggle over the budget is one of the central struggles in our society.

Tax Policy

Tax policy would seem logically to connect with expenditure policy as part of the budgetary process described above. But, despite recent reforms aimed at integrating tax and expenditure policy, the two processes remain largely separate. This has changed somewhat in recent years as the combination of divided party control of government and major deficit reduction packages has led to explicit negotiated tradeoffs between tax and expenditure changes. Sometimes, when the deficit appears frighteningly large, Congress will legislate small tax increases or user fees as part of the budgetary process. But in general, tax changes, though sometimes sparked by projected revenue shortfalls, take place through a rather different process.

In the executive branch, the primary responsibility for tax policy lies with the Treasury. Within the Treasury, the Internal Revenue Service is responsible for tax collection and produces rules applying the general laws passed by Congress to particular cases. But the primary responsibility for tax changes lies with the economists in the Office of Tax Analysis and the lawyers on the Tax Legislative Council (Reese 1979). The Treasury, and especially the Office of Tax Analysis, tends to have what might be termed a conservative, pro-revenue orientation. While often loath to embark on major changes in taxes, the Treasury continually seeks to close the loopholes in existing tax laws.

Under most presidents the Treasury shares the responsibility for major tax changes with the Office of Management and Budget and the Council of Economic Advisers. The latter has in the past been important in recommending major tax increases or decreases, with the Kennedy tax cut of 1964 being especially notable.

Presidents and their major policy advisers also have some tax ideas of their own. Generally these are distributional in character, as in the case of President Reagan's successful effort to lower income tax rates for higher-income earners and President Clinton's equally successful attempt to raise those rates again. The pattern has been that Democrats seek to redistribute resources to the working class and lower middle class and Republicans to the upper middle class and the wealthy, but sometimes one will see partial exceptions such as the $500 income tax credit per child proposed by Republican Speaker of the House Newt Gingrich in 1995. Presidential interest in changing the tax system used to be unusual, but in recent years presidents and party leaders have seen tax reductions as a way to gain votes for their parties. The deficits that followed these decreases have in turn put tax increases on the agenda. Thus even presidents like George Bush, with little personal interest in changing the tax system, have found themselves proposing substantial tax changes.

In Congress, the major responsibility for taxes lies with the Ways and Means Committee in the House and the Finance Committee in the Senate, with the former being generally regarded as slightly more important. Tax changes that are proposed in the budget are referred to these committees after little or no "preprocessing" in the budget committees. Many major tax-change proposals bypass the budgetary route altogether and are referred directly to the committees. Although the increased power of Speaker Gingrich has weakened both bodies, they still are the crucial gatekeepers for any tax change, as the conflict over the 1986 income tax reform and the 1995 flat tax versus sales tax debate demonstrates (*Congressional Quarterly* 1985; 1986; 1995).

Interest-group participation in tax policy, while considerable, is far less than it is in expenditure policy. This is for two primary reasons. One is the sheer complexity of tax policy. It takes a considerable investment in learning to be able to participate in any but the most peripheral way, and many people who might participate simply do not understand the effects of current or proposed taxes on them. The other is the "free rider" phenomenon. People may be completely dependent on government spending, but taxes represent only a portion of their income. Given the high costs of participation, and the low likelihood that it will pay off, most people leave it to others to participate.

The result is that interest-group participation in tax policy making has a distinctly upper-income bias. Because they earn a lot, and because the income tax is progressive, corporations and wealthy individuals consider it worth their while to pay the high costs of participation. Few other groups do, except for academics, some public-interest tax groups of both the left and the right, and the major "peak" organizations. Consequently, most of the interest-group participation in tax policy making at the federal level centers around an endless search for tax breaks and exemptions of certain kinds of income (Reese 1979).

Outcomes

The differences between the tax and expenditure policy processes lead to some important differences in the outcomes of the two policies. The most marked is the effect of the two types of policy on the distribution of income. In terms of pure economics, there is no reason why redistribution cannot be accomplished equally well through expenditures or taxes. However, in the United States, as in most other developed nations, most redistribution from the better off to the less well off is achieved through government expenditures (Musgrave and Musgrave 1980).

People often assume that taxes redistribute from the rich to the poor. However, if one takes into consideration the combined effect of federal, state, and local taxes in the United States, taxes have little net impact on the distribution of income, as regressive Social Security and sales taxes offset the mildly progressive federal income tax. There is reason to think that the recent changes in the federal tax code, by increasing the taxation of wage and salary income, have shifted more of the tax burden to the middle classes.

Expenditures, on the other hand, are strongly progressive. This is for two reasons, one obvious and one not so obvious. The obvious one is that over half of the federal budget and a significant part of every state budget is spent on transfer payments—such as Social Security, Medicaid, and food stamps—which are biased toward those with low incomes. The less obvious reason is that the benefits of federal expenditures constitute a relatively larger percent of the income of the poor. For example, if a person who earns $10,000 a year and has one car, and another person who earns $100,000 a year and has one car, each pays 10 percent of their income to fund the building of a road, the rich person will pay ten times as much but will get roughly the same benefit.

While the reasons for expenditures' being so much more progressive than taxes are open to conjecture, the observer cannot help but be struck by the fact that expenditure policy, with a relatively wide base of political participation, redistributes to the less well off, while tax policy, dominated by more affluent participants, redistributes far less. An implication of this is that the well-off have an incentive to reduce government spending. However, because they are more powerful in the tax area, and because taxes are always unpopular, it is easier for these groups to seek to lower taxes, in an effort to constrain the growth in government revenue. If taxes are reduced, but spending continues to increase, the result is likely to be a growing federal deficit. This may help explain why deficits in the last forty years have been generally higher under Republican than under Democratic presidents.

Monetary Policy

The Formal Process

Monetary policy is even more insulated from democratic participation than is tax policy. Formally, the process through which monetary policy is determined is far removed from the hurly-burly of the political arena. The Federal Reserve system, a complex web of bodies with appointed members, has major responsibility for determining policy. The web consists of twelve regional banks, the Open Market Committee, and the Federal Reserve Board, together with a number of advisory bodies. The key players in this web are the chairman and six additional governors of the Federal Reserve Board. They are responsible for determining the money supply, thus influencing interest rates and, through these, the operation of the economy (Bach 1971).

Members of the board are appointed by the president for fourteen-year terms. Federal Reserve Board chairmen are appointed to four-year terms, but two and a half years after the presidential election. This means that the members of the board, more than any other economic agency, are independent of the president and Congress. Formally, the only real limit on what the board does is the possibility that Congress could restrict its powers, but this is not likely to happen (Weintraub 1978).

The governors of the Federal Reserve conduct a process of economic forecasting and targeting, having in mind a number of important goals. These are the achievement of a reasonably low rate of unemployment, moderate and steady growth, low inflation, and an even balance of payments. The goal of low inflation is usually given priority. If their forecasts indicate that the economy is moving in an undesired direction, the governors take corrective action—usually by buying or selling government bonds. This has the effect of increasing or decreasing the amount of money, and hence expanding or contracting the economy.

About once a year the governors announce economic targets based on their forecasts, giving private actors some indication of the sorts of decisions the board is likely to be making. Usually these targets are bands within which the board intends monetary growth to occur. They might, for example, announce that Ml (money, narrowly defined) will grow between 6 and 9 percent in the coming year. They then try to stay within that band, making adjustments on the basis of their forecasts. But it is not unusual for monetary growth to exceed the board's self-imposed targets.

The Federal Reserve Board's power to influence the economy is differently valued by different observers. On the good side, it has been argued that the governors are experts; that they are freer of political pressures than the president and Congress; that they are needed to keep inflation from getting out of hand; and that they can act more expeditiously than the president and Congress.

On the bad side, it has been argued that economic policy in a democracy should be decided by elected officials; that the governors represent a very narrow range of interests, preeminently in banking; that the conservative bent of the governors inclines them to tolerate and even cause unacceptably—and unnecessarily—high unemployment rates; and finally, that the board's policies often are very often wrong and ill-timed (Reagan 1961).

The Informal Process

Thus far, our discussion has assumed that the Federal Reserve system does in fact control monetary policy. Yet, most observers agree that the president, despite his limited formal power in this area, has influence over the Fed, whether or not he can limit its independence (Woolley 1984). Some argue that Congress, too, has more power than one would initially expect, but others maintain that Congress is essentially powerless to alter Federal Reserve policy.

The claim of presidential influence over the Fed is usually based on the memoirs of Federal Reserve governors or other evidence that on some occasions monetary policy changed in accord with a president's priorities, with the reasons for this usually being left obscure. What is perhaps the most plausible explanation of congruence between Federal Reserve policy and a president's policies is the board's recognition of a practical need to coordinate its policies with the fiscal policies pursued by the president and Congress. It is also possible that the board, conscious that it lacks legitimating electoral support, is reluctant to oppose the will of elected officials too strongly.

To the degree that Congress has power to influence economic policy, it generally acts to promote economic expansion. During recessions Congress attempts to influence the Fed to refloat the economy. Presidents also tend to favor expansion. Even conservative presidents like Reagan and Nixon have pushed for looser monetary policies, especially during periods of economic downturn. And it is not unknown for presidents to try to generate economic expansion near election time (Rose 1974)

There is no substantial interest-group pressure on monetary policy, unlike spending and tax policy. But bankers, monetarist economists, and the conglomerate of financial interests usually described as "Wall Street" have privileged access to the Federal Reserve system and do exert influence on it.

The Obscurity of Monetary Policy and Its Consequences

Monetary policy is much more insulated from the political process than is fiscal policy, even if not as insulated as a formal account of the policy process would lead one to expect. This independence springs from three sources. One is the sheer difficulty of understanding monetary policy. Its effects are only dimly understood by the general public, few of whom are able to connect changes in monetary policy with their own lives. The second is that monetary policy has less immediate effects on the distribution of income and the allocation of public and private goods than tax and expenditure policy. Because taxing and spending have clear, immediate effects and are conflictual issues for most political players, they feel impelled to participate in fiscal policy making. Finally, the structure of governance in monetary policy is designed to restrict participation, and those who attempt it open themselves to the charge that they are interfering in matters where they have no place.

This insulation has two major effects. One is that it is easier to use the monetary policy tool. The time between deciding on a policy and implementing it can be as little as a day, versus the months or years it can take to change expenditure and tax policy. An ironic result of this is that presidents often rely on monetary policy for short-term manipulation of the economy, and it is their own relative lack of control over the policy that enables them to do so.

The other major effect is that monetary policy is generally more deflationary than fiscal policy. Many think that this is because Federal Reserve governors—unlike presidents and members of Congress, who need to win elections—have little incentive to expand the economy. Reinforcing factors here may be the predominantly conservative, upper-income background of the members of the board and the influence of bankers on their decisions.

Conclusions

Despite surface similarities, the three major economic policy tools involve political processes that differ in important respects. While each policy area has participation from the executive branch, the legislative branch, and interest groups, different groups within those broad categories are important for each type of policy. The political processes are sufficiently dissimilar that outcomes in the three areas diverge substantially, making policy coordination all the more difficult.

These differences are not accidental. They stem from three basic factors. One is the degree to which the ends sought in each policy area involve conflict. The health of the economy is a non-zero-sum game, in which all players can win, even if some may win more than others. Issues of distribution and allocation are more zero-sum in character. Wins for one side tend to spell losses for the other side, and this draws many highly motivated participants into the fray.

The second factor is the effect of policy changes on individuals. While expenditure policy involves decisions that can determine someone's livelihood, the effects of tax and monetary policy on individual well-being are usually more indirect and partial.

The third factor is the complexity of the issues. Issues of spending are easy to grasp and their implications are relatively straightforward. Tax issues are more complex and their consequences are less obvious. Monetary policy is opaque to the average citizen and the impact of changes in monetary policy on an individual's welfare is usually a mystery.

These three factors all work in the same direction. Each tends to increase participation in expenditure policy, reduce participation in monetary policy, and produce intermediate participation in tax policy.

I would argue that these differences have implications for democracy in the United States. While economic policies are usually the most significant of all public policies for the welfare of individuals, participation in economic policy making is on balance not very extensive. While this may make it easier to reach policy decisions, it should be seen as problematic by those who believe that the American people should control the policies that most affect their lives.

References

Bach, George L. 1971. *Making Monetary and Fiscal Policy.* Washington D.C.: The Brookings Institution.

Congressional Quarterly Weekly Report. 1985. July 6: 1315–22. 1986. June 14: 1377–79; June 14: 1311–13. 1995. August 12: 2430.

Greider, William. 1985. *The Education of David Stockman and Other Americans.* New York: E.P. Dutton.

Heclo, Hugh. 1984. "Executive Budget Making" in Gregory B. Mills and John L. Palmer, *Federal Budget Policy in the 1980s.* Washington D.C.: The Urban Institute Press.

Ippolito, Dennis S. 1981. *Congressional Spending.* Ithaca, N.Y.: Cornell University Press.

LeLoup, Lance T. 1986. *Budgetary Politics.* 3d ed. Brunswick, Ohio: Kings Court.

Musgrave, Richard A., and Peggy Musgrave. 1980. *Public Finance in Theory and Practice.* 3d ed. New York: McGraw Hill.

Peretz, Paul. 1983. *The Political Economy of Inflation in the United States.* Chicago: University of Chicago Press.

Pierce, Lawrence C. 1971. *The Politics of Fiscal Policy Formation.* Pacific Palisades, Calif.: Goodyear.

Reagan, Michael D. 1961. The Political Structure of the Federal Reserve System. *American Political Science Review* 55 (March).

Reese, T. J. 1979. *The Politics of Taxation.* Westport, Conn.: Quorum.

Rose, Sanford. 1974. The Agony of the Federal Reserve. *Fortune* (January).

Senate Budget Committee. 1985. *The Congressional Budget Process: How it Works.* Washington, D.C.: U.S. Government Printing Office.

Shepsle, Kenneth A., and Barry R. Weingast. 1984. "Legislative Politics and Budget Outcomes" in Gregory B. Mills and John L. Palmer, *Federal Budget Policy in the 1980s.* Washington, D.C.: The Urban Institute Press.

Weintraub, Robert. 1978. Congressional Supervision of Monetary Policy. *Journal of Monetary Economics* 4 (April).

Woolley, John T. 1984. *Monetary Politics: The Federal Reserve and the Politics of Monetary Policy.* New York: Cambridge University Press.

3A. Budgetary Policy

Most studies of the budget are concerned with the political processes through which government expenditures are determined, and the reasons why governments spend more on some things than on others. In the United States the three major types of expenditure are *defense* expenditures, the provision of *services* such as education and police, which cannot efficiently be provided by the free market, and *transfer payments* such as Social Security, which take money from one group of people and give it to a different group. In terms of the categories developed in the article by Musgrave in part 1, most of the expenditures on defense and services are on public goods, while most transfers are intended to redistribute to those perceived to be particularly deserving of public aid.

Until the late 1950s political scientists viewed the budgetary process as a complex struggle between actors in the legislative and executive branches—with considerable prompting from interest groups (see Smithies 1955 or Burkhead 1956 for a review of the early literature). Economists, on the other hand, tended to believe that public expenditures were a rough-and-ready approximation to the desires of the public, and that their job was to show how one could change expenditures to increase the benefits to the public and reduce the costs. In the late 1950s a new model, initially expounded by Wildavsky and Lindblom and elaborated by people such as Barber (1966) and Sharkansky (1969), challenged the conventional wisdom, and in a few years became the conventional wisdom itself.

This model, termed *incrementalism,* held that because of the immense complexity of the budgetary process, it was necessary for legislators to adopt simple rules to allow speedy decisions while minimizing political conflict. They did this, it was argued, by accepting the expenditures made in the preceding period (the base) without reexamining them closely and by concentrating their attention on the generally small increases (the increment) proposed by the departments responsible for the policies. This, it was argued, led to a slow but steady increase in government expenditures. The theory was backed up with evidence showing that government expenditures for each department did in fact increase at a slow but steady rate.

In the 1970s this model ran into two major types of objection. One group held that while incrementalists were correct in thinking that expenditures in each policy area increased slowly but steadily, they were wrong about the reason for this. These increases, they pointed out, could be the result of slow changes in need, locked-in spending on interest, multiyear contracts and entitlement programs, overall limits on what was available to be spent, a stable balance of power between contending forces, or the tendency of programs to build their own constituencies (Crecine 1969; Wanat 1978; Le Loup 1978). The other group held that the incrementalists were wrong in asserting that expenditures in each category all grew slowly, and argued that if one looked at more detailed policies, examined changes made within the executive branch, included defense agencies, or looked at agency budgets over longer periods, other than year-to-year changes, one would find much more variability in the budgets than incrementalists allowed for (Bailey and O'Connor 1975; Gist 1976; Le Loup 1978; Wanat 1978).

While much of the more recent quantitative work in this field has continued to accept the idea of incrementalism, there has been a tendency to break up expenditures into different types and argue that some of the variability in growth can be explained by other factors (Fischer and Kamlet 1984). In the nonquantitative work there has been a renewed interest in the institutional structure within which budgets are made in Congress, and in the role of party ideology in determining budget outcomes. Some hold that these are important in explaining some of the distinctly nonincremental character of expenditure change under the Reagan administration (Penner 1979; Wander et al. 1984).

The readings in this section look at three general explanations of the budgetary process. The article by Davis, Dempster, and Wildavsky seeks to show that the United States budget is in fact made using incrementalist methods. The essay by Natchez and Bupp challenges this view and argues that, looked at correctly, the budget process is more pluralist than incrementalist. The article by Pitsava and Draper argues that Natchez and Bupp are wrong and that recent developments support an incrementalist interpretation of the budget process. The selection by Niskanen argues that expenditures are determined by the bureaucracy, which has an incentive to overspend.

For Further Reading

Good introductions to American budgeting at the federal level are Lance Le Loup's *Budgetary Politics* and Aaron Wildavsky's *The New Politics of the Budgetary Process*. The classic books on state and local budgeting are Ira Sharkansky's *The Politics of Taxing and Spending* and Thomas Anton's *The Politics of State Expenditure in Illinois,* though both are now a little out of date.

Irene Rubin's *The Politics of Public Budgeting* and Richard Aronson and John Hilley's *Financing State and Local Governments* provide a more recent view of the state and local budgeting. Most public finance books contain chapters on budgeting. Thomas Lynch's *Public Budgeting in America* and Donald Axelrod's *Budgeting for Modern Government* are good general books on how to construct a public budget. Haveman and Margolis's *Public Expenditure and Policy Analysis* contains useful articles on cost/benefit analysis. Howard Schuman's *Politics and the Budget* gives a good feel for the nitty gritty of federal budget politics. Wander et al.'s *Congressional Budgeting* and Albert Hyde's *Government Budgeting* are useful collections of articles.

Bibliography

Anton, Thomas. 1966. *The Politics of State Expenditures in Illinois.* Urbana, Ill.: University of Illinois Press.

Aronson, J. Richard, and John L. Hilley. 1986. *Financing State and Local Governments.* 4th ed. Washington, D.C.: The Brookings Institution.

Axelrod, Donald. 1994. *Budgeting for Modern Government.* 2d ed. New York: St. Martin's Press.

Barber, James D. 1966. *Power in Committees: An Experiment in Governmental Process.* Chicago: Rand McNally.

Bailey, John J., and Robert J. O'Connor. 1975. Operationalizing Incrementalism: Measuring the Muddles. *Public Administration Review* (January/February).

Burkhead, Jesse. 1956. *Governmental Budgeting.* New York: John Wiley.

Crecine, John P. 1969. Defense Budgeting: Constraints and Organizational Adaptation. Discussion Paper No. 6, University of Michigan, Institute of Public Policy Studies.

Fischer, Gregory W., and Mark S. Kamlet. 1984. Explaining Presidential Priorities: The Competing Aspiration Levels Model of Macrobudgetary Decision Making. *American Political Science Review* 78 (June).

Gist, John R. 1976. "Increment" and "Base" in the Congressional Appropriations Process. Paper presented at the Midwest Political Science Association Meetings, May 1, Chicago, Ill.

Haveman, Robert H., and Julius Margolis. 1983. *Public Expenditure and Policy Analysis.* 3d ed. Boston: Houghton Mifflin.

Hyde, Albert C. 1992. *Government Budgeting: Theory, Process, Politics.* 2d ed. Pacific Grove, Calif.: Brooks Cole.

Le Loup, Lance. 1978. The Myth of Incrementalism: Analytical Choices in Budgetary Theory. *Polity* 10:4 (Summer).

Le Loup, Lance. 1986. *Budgetary Politics.* 3d ed. Brunswick, Ohio: Kings Court Press.

Lynch, Thomas D. 1995. *Public Budgeting in America.* 4th ed. Englewood Cliffs, N.J.: Prentice Hall.

Penner, Rudolph G., ed. 1979. *The Congressional Budget Process After Five Years.* Washington, D.C.: American Enterprise Institute.

Rubin, Irene. 1993. *The Politics of Public Budgeting.* 2d ed. Chatham, N.J.: Chatham House.

Sharkansky, Ira. 1969. *The Politics of Taxing and Spending.* Indianapolis, Ind.: University of Indiana.

Shuman, Howard E. 1992. *Politics and the Budget: The Struggle Between the President and Congress.* 3d ed. Englewood Cliffs, N.J.: Prentice Hall.

Smithies, Arthur. 1955. *The Budgeting Process in the United States.* New York: McGraw Hill.

Wanat, John. 1978. *Introduction to Budgeting.* North Scituate, Mass.: Duxbury Press.

Wander, W. Thomas, F. Ted Herbert, and Gary W. Copeland. 1984. *Congressional Budgeting: Politics, Process and Power.* Baltimore: The Johns Hopkins University Press.

Wildavsky, Aaron. 1988. *The New Politics of the Budgetary Process.* Boston: Little Brown.

3A.1. A Theory of the Budgetary Process

OTTO A. DAVIS, M. A. H. DEMPTSTER, and AARON WILDAVSKY

*In their pathbreaking but difficult article, Davis, Dempster, and Wildavsky exam-
ine the way budgets are actually made in the United States. The authors provide
evidence that the incrementalist method best describes the budgetary process.
They reach this conclusion in four steps.*

*In the first section Wildavsky makes a qualitative argument that incremental-
ism makes considerable sense in the American political system, and that the
incremental pattern of slow change over time fits what we know about how the
system works.*

*The authors then argue that if their theory is correct, there should be small,
slow increases over time in the funding each agency receives. They test this in
two ways. First, they look to see how the amounts requested by the Bureau of the
Budget on behalf of each agency vary from the amounts each agency was given
by Congress the previous year (equation 1). Second, they determine how much
Congress changes these requests (equation 4).*

*In their results, shown in Table 1, they find that Congress makes little change
in most of the agency budgets submitted by the Bureau of the Budget, and that
most of these budgets are similar in size to those approved by Congress in the
previous year. However, the latter result is less strong than the former. In general, receiving a correlation coefficient greater than .90 is taken as strong evidence that the factors the researcher thinks might be important are, in fact,
important. Because the correlations for each agency generally exceed this figure, the results have been seen as strong evidence of an incremental process.*

Finally, in a fourth step the authors look at the cases where their theory does not appear to hold well and show that most of them are associated with something they expected to have an independent effect—a new president taking office.

The material in this essay, especially in parts II–IV, is technically quite difficult, but it has been included here because it is the seminal article on incrementalism, and permits comparison with the next essay (by Natchez and Bupp).

There are striking regularities in the budgetary process. The evidence from over half of the non-defense agencies indicates that the behavior of the budgetary process of the United States government results in aggregate decisions similar to those produced by a set of simple decision rules that are linear and temporally stable. For the agencies considered, certain equations are specified and compared with data composed of agency requests (through the Bureau of the Budget) and Congressional appropriations from 1947 through 1963. The comparison indicates that these equations summarize accurately aggregate outcomes of the budgetary process for each agency.

In the first section of the paper we present an analytic summary of the federal budgetary process, and we explain why basic features of the process lead us to believe that it can be represented by simple models which are stable over periods of time, linear, and stochastic.[1] In the second section we propose and discuss the alternative specifications for the agency–Budget Bureau and Congressional decision equations. The empirical results are presented in section three. In section four we provide evidence on deviant cases, discuss predictions, and [outline] future work to explore some of the problems indicated by this kind of analysis.

I. The Budgetary Process

Decisions depend upon calculation of which alternatives to consider and to choose.[2] A major clue toward understanding budgeting is the extraordinary complexity of the calculations involved. There are a huge number of items to be considered, many of which are of considerable technical difficulty. There is, however, little or no theory in most areas of policy which would enable practitioners to predict the consequences of alternative moves and the probability of their occurring. Nor has anyone solved the imposing problem of the interpersonal comparison of utilities. Outside of the political process, there is no agreed upon way of comparing and evaluating the merits of different programs for different people whose preferences vary in kind and in intensity.

Participants in budgeting deal with their overwhelming burdens by adopting aids to calculation. By far the most important aid to calculation is the incremental method. Budgets are almost never actively reviewed as a whole in the sense of considering at once the value of all existing programs as compared to all possible alternatives. Instead, this year's budget is based on last year's budget, with special attention given to a narrow range of increases or decreases.

Incremental calculations proceed from an existing base. (By "base" we refer to commonly held expectations among participants in budgeting that programs will be carried out at close to the going level of expenditures.) The widespread sharing of deeply held expectations concerning the organization's base provides a powerful (although informal) means of securing stability.

The most effective coordinating mechanisms in budgeting undoubtedly stem from the roles adopted by the major participants. Roles (the expectations of behavior attached to institutional positions) are parts of the division of labor. They are calculating mechanisms. In American national government, the administrative agencies act as advocates of increased expenditure, the Bureau of the Budget acts as Presidential servant with a cutting bias, the House Appropriations Committee functions as a guardian of the Treasury, and the Senate Appropriations Committee as an appeals court to which agencies carry their disagreements with House action. The roles fit in with one another and set up patterns of mutual expectations which markedly reduce the burden of calculation for the participants. Since the agencies can be depended upon to advance all the programs for which there is prospect of support, the Budget Bureau and the Appropriations Committees respectively can concentrate on fitting them into the President's program or paring them down.

Possessing the greatest expertise and the largest numbers, working in the closest proximity to their policy problems and clientele groups, and desiring to expand their horizons, administrative agencies generate action through advocacy. But if they ask for amounts much larger than the appropriating bodies believe reasonable, the agencies' credibility will suffer a drastic decline. In such circumstances, the reviewing organs are likely to cut deeply, with the result that the agency gets much less than it might have with a more moderate request. So the first guide for decision is: do not come in *too* high. Yet the agencies must also not come in too low, for the reviewing bodies assume that if agency advocates do not ask for funds they do not need them. Thus, the agency decision rule might read: come in a little too high (padding), but not too high (loss of confidence).

Agencies engage in strategic planning to secure these budgetary goals. Strategies are the links between the goals of the agencies and their perceptions of the kinds of actions which will be effective in their political environment. Budget officers in American national government uniformly believe that being a good politician—cultivation of an active clientele, development of confidence by other officials (particularly the appropriations subcommittees), and skill in following strategies which exploit opportunities—is more important in obtaining funds than demonstration of agency efficiency.

In deciding how much money to recommend for specific purposes, the House Appropriations Committee breaks down into largely autonomous subcommittees in which the norm of reciprocity is carefully followed. Specialization is carried further as subcommittee members develop limited areas of competence and jurisdiction. Budgeting is both incremental and fragmented as the subcommittees deal with adjustments to the historical base of each agency. Fragmentation and specialization are increased through the appeals functions of the Senate Appropriations Committee, which deals with what has become (through House action) a fragment of a fragment. With so many participants continually engaged in taking others into account, a great many adjustments are made in the light of what others are likely to do.

This qualitative account of the budgetary process contains clear indications of the kind of quantitative models we wish to develop. It is evident, for example, that decision-makers in the budgetary process think in terms of percentages. Agencies talk of expanding their base by a certain percentage. The Bureau of the Budget is concerned about the growth rates for certain agencies and programs. The House Appropriations Committee deals with percentage cuts, and the Senate Appropriations Committee with the question of whether or not to restore percentage cuts. These considerations suggest that the quantitative relationships among the decisions of the participants in the budget process are linear in form.

The attitudes and calculations of participants in budgeting seem stable over time. The prominence of the agency's "base" is a sign of stability. The roles of the major participants are powerful, persistent, and strongly grounded in the expectations of others as well as in the internal requirements of the positions. Stability is also suggested by the specialization that occurs among the participants, the long service of committee members, the adoption of incremental practices such as comparisons with the previous year, the fragmentation of appropriations by program and item, the treatments of appropriations as continuously variable sums of money rather than as perpetual reconsiderations of the worth of programs, and the practice of allowing past decisions to stand while coordinating decision-making only if difficulties arise. Since the budgetary process appears to be stable over periods of time, it is reasonable to estimate the relationships in budgeting on the basis of time series data.

Special events that upset the apparent stability of the budgetary process can and do occur. Occasionally, world events take an unexpected turn, a new President occupies the White House, some agencies act with exceptional zeal, others suffer drastic losses of confidence on the part of the appropriations subcommittees, and so on. It seems plausible to represent such transient events as random shocks to an otherwise deterministic system. Therefore, our model is stochastic rather than deterministic.

The Politics of the Budgetary Process contains a description of strategies which various participants in budgeting use to further their aims. Some of these strategies are quite complicated. However, a large part of the process can be explained by some of the simpler strategies which are based on the relationship between agency requests for funds (through the Budget bureau) and Congressional appropriations. Because these figures are made public and are known to all participants, because they are directly perceived and communicated without fear of information loss or bias, and because the participants react to these figures, they are ideal for feedback purposes. It is true that there are other indicators—special events, crises, technological developments, actions of clientele groups which are attended to by participants in the budgetary process. But if these indicators have impact, they must quickly be reflected in the formal feedback mechanisms—the actions of departments, the Bureau of the Budget, and Congress—to which they are directed. Some of these indicators (see section four) are represented by the stochastic disturbances. Furthermore, the formal indicators are more precise, more simple, more available, more easily interpreted than the others. They are, therefore, likely to be used by participants in the budgetary process year in and year out. Present decisions are based largely on past experience, and this lore is encapsulated in the amounts which the agencies receive as they go through the steps in the budgetary cycle.

For all the reasons discussed in this section, our models of the budgetary process are linear, stable over periods of time, stochastic, and strategic in character. They are "as if" models: an excellent fit for a given model means only that the actual behavior of the participants has an effect equivalent to the equations of the model. The models, taken as a whole, represent a set of decision rules for Congress and the agencies.

II. The Models

In our models we aggregate elements of the decision-making structure. The Budget Bureau submissions for the agency are used instead of separate figures for the two kinds of organizations. Similarly, at this stage in our analysis, we use final Congressional appropriations instead of separating out committee action, floor action, conference committee recommendations, and so on. We wish to emphasize that although there may be some aggregation bias in the estimation of the postulated structure of decision, this does not affect the linearity of the aggregate relationships. If the decisions of an agency and the Bureau of the Budget with regard to that agency depend linearly upon the same variable (as we hypothesize), then the aggregated decision rule of the two, treated as a single entity, will depend linearly upon that variable. By a similar argument, the various Congressional participants can be grouped together so that Congress can be regarded as a single decision-making entity. While the aggregating procedure may result in grouping positive and negative influences together, this manifestly does not affect the legitimacy of the procedure; linearity is maintained.[3]

Our models concern only the requests presented in the President's budget for an individual agency and the behavior of Congress as a whole with regard to the agency's appropriation. The models do not attempt to estimate the complete decision-making structure for each agency from bureau requests to departments to submission through the Budget Bureau to possible final action in the Senate and House. There are several reasons for remaining content with the aggregated figures we use. First, the number of possible decision rules which must be considered grows rapidly as each new participant is added. We would soon be overwhelmed by the sheer number of rules invoked. Second, there are genuine restrictions placed on the number of structural parameters we can estimate because (a) some data, such as bureau requests to departments, are unavailable, and (b) only short time series are meaningful for most agencies. It would make no sense, for example, to go back in time beyond the end of World War II when most domestic activity was disrupted.[4]

Since the agencies use various strategies and Congress may respond to them in various ways, we propose several alternative systems of equations. These equations represent alternative decision rules which may be followed by Congressional and agency–Budget Bureau participants in the budgetary process. One important piece of data for agency–Budget Bureau personnel who are formulating appropriations requests is the most recent Congressional appropriation. Thus, we make considerable use of the concept "base," operationally defined as the previous Congressional appropriation for an agency, in formulating our decision rules. Since the immediate past exercises such a heavy influence on budgetary outcomes, Markov (simultaneous, difference) equations are particularly useful. In these Markov processes, the value of certain variables at one point in time is dependent on their value at one or more immediately previous periods as well as on the particular circumstances of the time.

We postulate several decision rules for both the agency–Budget Bureau requests and for Congressional action on these requests. For each series of requests or appropriations, we select from the postulated decision rules that rule which most closely represents the behavior of the aggregated entities. We use the variables

- y_t the appropriation passed by Congress for any given agency in the year t. Supplemental appropriations are not included in the y_t.
- x_t the appropriation requested by the Bureau of the Budget for any given agency for the year t. The x_t constitutes the President's budget request for an agency.

We will also introduce certain symbols representing random disturbances of each of the postulated relationships. These symbols are explained as they are introduced.

A. Equations for Agency–Budget Bureau Decision Rules

The possibility that different agencies use different strategies makes it necessary to construct alternative equations representing these various strategies. Then, for each agency in our sample, we use time series data to select that equation which seems to describe best the budgetary decisions of that agency. In this section we present three simple models of agency requests. The first states agency requests as a function of the previous year's appropriation. The second states requests as a function of the previous appropriation as well as a function of the differences between the agency request and appropriation in the previous year. The third states requests as a function of the previous year's request. In all three linear models provision is made for a random variable to take into account the special circumstances of the time.

An agency, while convinced of the worth of its programs, tends to be aware that extraordinarily large or small requests are likely to be viewed with suspicion by Congress; an agency does not consider it desirable to make extraordinary requests which might precipitate unfavorable Congressional reaction. Therefore, the agency usually requests a percentage (generally greater than one hundred percent) of its previous year's appropriation. This percentage is not fixed; in the event of favorable circumstances, the request is a larger percentage of the previous year's appropriation than would otherwise be the case; similarly, the percentage might be reduced in the event of unfavorable circumstances.

Decisions made in the manner described above may be represented by a simple equation. If we take the average of the percentages that are implicitly or explicitly used by budget officers, then any request can be represented by the sum of this average percentage of the previous year's appropriation plus the increment or decrement due to the favorable or unfavorable circumstances. Thus

$$x_t = \beta_0 y_{t-1} + \varepsilon_t \tag{1}$$

The agency request (through the Budget Bureau) for a certain year is a fixed mean percentage of the Congressional appropriation for that agency in the previous year plus a random variable (normally distributed with mean zero and unknown but finite variance) for that year.

is an equation representing this type of behavior. The average or mean percentage is represented by β_0. The increment or decrement due to circumstances is represented by ε_t, a variable which requires some special explanation. It is difficult to predict what circumstances will occur at what time to put an agency in a favorable or unfavorable position. Numerous events could influence Congress's (and the public's) perception of an agency and its programs—the occurrence of a destructive hurricane in the case of the Weather Bureau, the death by cancer of a friend of an influential congressman, in the case of the National Institutes of Health, the hiring (or losing) of an especially effective lobbyist by some interest group, the President's becoming especially interested in a program of some agency as Kennedy was in mental health, and so on. (Of course, some of them may be more or less "predictable" at certain times to an experienced observer, but this fact causes no difficulty here.) Following common statistical practice we may represent the sum of the effects of all such events by a random variable that is an increment or decrement to the usual percentage of the previous year's appropriation. In equation (1), then, ε_t represents the value which this random variable assumes in year t.

We have chosen to view the special events of each year for each agency as random phenomena that are capable of being described by a probability density or distribution. We assume here that the random variable is normally distributed with mean zero and an unknown but finite variance. Given this specification of the random variable, the agency makes its budgeting decisions as if it were operating by the postulated decision rule given by equation (1).

An agency, although operating somewhat like the organizations described by equation (1), may wish to take into account an additional strategic consideration: while this agency makes a request which is roughly a fixed percentage of the previous year's appropriation, it also desires to smooth out its stream of appropriations by taking into account the difference between its request and appropriation for the previous year. If there were an unusually large cut in the previous year's request, the agency submits a "padded" estimate to make up for the loss in expected funds; an unusual increase is followed by a reduced estimate to avoid unspent appropriations. This behavior may be represented by equation or decision rule where

$$x_t = \beta_1 y_{t-1} + \beta_2(y_{t-1} - x_{t-1}) + \chi_t \tag{2}$$

The agency request (through the Budget Bureau) for a certain year is a fixed mean percentage of the Congressional appropriation for that agency in the previous year plus a fixed mean percentage of the difference between the Congressional appropriation and the agency request for the previous year plus a stochastic disturbance.

χ_t is a stochastic disturbance, which plays the role described for the random variable in equation (1), the β's are variables reflecting the aspects of the previous year's request and appropriation that an agency takes into account: β_1 represents the mean percentage of the previous year's request which is taken into account, and β_2 represents the mean percentage of the difference between the previous year's appropriation and request $(y_{t-1} - x_{t-1})$ which is taken into account. Note that $\beta_2 < 0$ is anticipated so that a large cut will (in the absence of the events represented by the stochastic disturbance) be followed by a padded estimate and vice versa.[5]

Finally, an agency (or the President through the Bureau of the Budget), convinced of the worth of its programs, may decide to make requests without regard to previous Congressional action. This strategy appeals especially when Congress has so much confidence in the agency that it tends to give an appropriation which is almost identical to the request. Aside from special circumstances represented by stochastic disturbances, the agency's request in any given year tends to be approximately a fixed percentage of its request for the previous year. This behavior may be represented by

$$x_t = \beta_3 x_{t-1} + \rho_t \tag{3}$$

The agency request (through the Budget Bureau) for a certain year is a fixed mean percentage of the agency's request for the previous year plus a random variable (stochastic disturbance).

where ρ_t is a stochastic disturbance and β_3 is the average percentage. Note that if the agency believes its programs to be worthy, $\beta_3 > 1$ is expected.[6]

These three equations are not the only ones which may be capable of representing the actual behavior of the combined budgeting decisions of the agencies and the Bureau of the Budget. However, they represent the agency–Budget Bureau budgeting behavior better than all other decision rules we tried.[7]

B. Equations for Congressional Decision Rules

In considering Congressional behaviors we again postulate three decision equations from which a selection must be made that best represents the behavior of Congress in regard to an agency's appropriations. Since Congress may use various strategies in determining appropriations for different agencies, different Congressional decision equations may be selected as best representing Congressional appropriations for each agency in our sample. Our first model states Congressional appropriations as a function of the agency's request (through the Budget Bureau) to Congress. The second states appropriations as a function of the agency's request as well as a function of the deviation from the usual relationship between Congress and the agency in the previous year. The third model states appropriations as a function of that segment of the agency's request that is not part of its appropriation or request for the previous year. Random variables are included to take account of special circumstances.

If Congress believes that an agency's request, after passing through the hands of the Budget Bureau, is a relatively stable index of the funds needed by the agency to carry out its programs, Congress responds by appropriating a relatively fixed percentage of the agency's request. The term "relatively fixed" is used because Congress is likely to alter this percentage somewhat from year to year because of special events and circumstances relevant to particular years. As in the case of agency requests, these special circumstances may be viewed as random phenomena. One can view this behavior as if it were the result of Congress' appropriating a fixed mean percentage of the agency requests; adding to the amount so derived a sum represented by a random variable. One may represent this behavior as if Congress were following the decision rule

$$y_t = a_0 x_t + \eta_t \tag{4}$$

The Congressional appropriation for an agency in a certain year is a fixed mean percentage of the agency's request in that year plus a stochastic disturbance.

where a_0 represents the fixed average percentage and η_t represents the stochastic disturbance.

Although Congress usually grants an agency a fixed percentage of its request, this request sometimes represents an extension of the agency's programs above (or below) the size desired by Congress. This can occur when the agency and the Bureau of the Budget follow Presidential aims differing from those of Congress, or when Congress suspects that the agency is padding the current year's request. In such a situation Congress usually appropriates a sum different from the usual percentage. If a_1 represents the mean of the usual percentages, this behavior can be represented by equation or decision rule

$$y_t = a_1 x_t + v_t \qquad (5)$$

where v_t is a stochastic disturbance representing that part of the appropriations attributable to the special circumstances that cause Congress to deviate from a relatively fixed percentage. Therefore, when agency aims and Congressional desires markedly differ from usual (so that Congress may be said to depart from its usual rule) the stochastic disturbance takes on an unusually large positive or negative value. In order to distinguish this case from the previous one, more must be specified about the stochastic disturbance v_t. In a year following one in which agency aims and Congressional desires markedly differed, the agency makes a request closer to Congressional desires, and/or Congress shifts its desires closer to those of the agency (or the President). In the year after a deviation, then, assume that Congress will tend to make allowances to normalize the situation. Such behavior can be represented by having the stochastic disturbance v_t generated in accordance with a first order Markov scheme. The stochastic component in v_t is itself determined by a relation

$$v_t = a_2 v_{t-1} + \varepsilon_t \qquad (6)$$

where ε_t is a random variable. The symbol v_t therefore stands for the stochastic disturbance in the previous year (v_{t-1}) as well as the new stochastic disturbance for the year involved (ε_t). Substituting (6) into (5) gives

$$y_t = a_1 x_t + a_2 v_{t-1} + \varepsilon_t \qquad (7)$$

The Congressional appropriation for an agency is a fixed mean percentage of the agency's request for that year plus a stochastic disturbance representing a deviation from the usual relationship between Congress and the agency in the previous year plus a random variable for the current year.

as a complete description of a second Congressional decision rule. If Congress never makes complete allowance for an initial "deviation," then $-1 < a_2 < 1$ is to be expected.

To complete the description of this second Congressional decision rule, we will suppose $0 < a_2 < 1$. Then, granted a deviation from its usual percentage, Congress tends to decrease subsequent deviations by moving steadily back toward its usual percentage (except for the unforeseeable events or special circumstances whose effects are represented by the random variable ε_t). For example, if in a particular year $v_{t-1} > 0$, and if in the following year there are no special circumstances so that $\xi_t = 0$, then $v_t = a_2 v_{t-1} < v_{t-1}$. The deviation in year t is smaller than the deviation in year $t - 1$. However, if $-1 < a_2 < 0$ after an initial deviation, Congress tends to move back to its usual rule (apart from the disturbances represented by the random variable ε_t) by making successively smaller deviations which differ in sign. For example, if $v_{t-1} > 0$, then apart from the disturbance ε_t it is clear that $v_t = a_2 v_{t-1} < 0$, since $a_2 < 0$. Finally, if $a_2 = 0$, decision rule (7) is the same as the previous rule (4).

The specialization inherent in the appropriation process allows some members of Congress to have an intimate knowledge of the budgetary processes of the agencies and the Budget Bureau. Thus, Congress might consider that part of the agency's request (x_t) which is not based on the previous year's appropriation or request. This occurs when Congress believes that this positive or negative remainder represents padding or when it desires to smooth out the agency's rate of growth. If Congress knows the decision rule that an agency uses to formulate its budgetary request, we can let λ_t represent a dummy variable defined as $\lambda_t = \xi_t$ if the agency uses decision rule (1); $\lambda_t = \beta_2(y_{t-1} - x_{t-1}) + \chi_t$ if the agency uses decision rule (2); and $\lambda_t = \rho_t$ if the agency uses decision rule (3). Suppose that Congress appropriates, on the average, an amount which is a relatively fixed percentage of the agency's request plus a percentage of this (positive or negative) remainder λ_t. This behavior can be represented by the "as if" decision rule

$$y_t = a_3 x_t + a_4 \lambda_t + v_t \tag{8}$$

The Congressional appropriation for an agency is a fixed mean percentage of the agency's request for a certain year plus a fixed mean percentage of a dummy variable which represents that part of the agency's request for the year at issue which is not part of the appropriation or request of the previous year plus a random variable representing the part of the appropriation attributable to the special circumstances of the year.

where v_t is a stochastic disturbance whose value in any particular year represents the part of the appropriation attributable to the agency's special circumstances of the year. One might expect that Congress takes only "partial" account of the remainder represented by λ_t, so $0 < a_4 < 1$.

III. Empirical Results

Times series data for the period 1947–1963 were studied for fifty-six non-defense agencies of the United States Government. The requests (x_t) of these agencies were taken to be the amounts presented to Congress in the President's budget. For eight sub-agencies from the National Institutes of Health, data for a shorter period of time were considered, and the requests (x_t) of these eight sub-agencies were taken to be their proposals to the Bureau of the Budget.[8] In all instances the Congressional decision variable (y_t) was taken to be the final appropriation before any supplemental additions. The total appropriations (without supplements) of the agencies studied amounted to approximately twenty-seven percent of the non-defense budget in 1963. Over one-half of all non-defense agencies were investigated; the major omissions being the Post Office and many independent agencies. A minimum of three agencies was examined from each of the Treasury, Justice, Interior, Agriculture, Commerce, Labor, and Health, Education and Welfare Departments.[9]

If the agency–Budget Bureau disturbance is independent of Congressional disturbance,[10] the use of ordinary least squares (OLS) to estimate most of the possible combinations of the proposed decision equations is justified. OLS is identical to the simultaneous full information maximum likelihood (FIML) technique for most of the present systems. This is not so, however, for some systems of equations because of the presence of an auto-correlated disturbance in one equation of the two and the consequent non-linearity of the estimating equations. In equation (6) the stochastic disturbance for year t is a function of the value of the disturbance in the previous year. In a system of equations in which auto-correlation occurs in the first equation, an appropriate procedure is to use OLS to estimate the alternative proposals for the other equation, decide by the selection criteria which best specifies the data, use the knowledge of this structure to estimate the first equation, and then decide, through use of appropriate criteria, which version of the first equation best specifies the data.

The principal selection criterion we used is that of maximum (adjusted) correlation coefficient (R). For a given dependent variable this criterion leads one to select from alternative specifications of the explanatory variables, that specification which leads to the highest sample correlation coefficient. The estimations of the alternative specifications must, of course, be made from the same data.[11] The second criterion involves the use of the d-statistic test for serial correlation of the estimated residuals of a single equation.[12] This statistic tests the null hypothesis of residual independence against the alternative of serial correlation. We used the significance points for the d-statistic of Theil and Nagar.[13] When the d-statistic was found to be significant in fitting the Congressional decision equation (4) to an agency's data, it was always found that equation (7) best specified Congressional behavior with respect to the appropriations of that agency in the sense of yielding the maximum correlation coefficient. A third criterion is based on a test of the significance of the sample correlation between the residuals of (4) and the estimated λ_t of the equation selected previously for a given agency. David's significance points for this statistic were used to make a two-tailed test at the five percent level of the null hypothesis that the residuals are uncorrelated.[14] When

Table 1

Best Specifications for Each Agency Are High

Frequencies of correlation coefficients

	1 —	.995 —	.99 —	.98 —	.97 —	.96 —	.95 —	.94 —	93 —	.90 —	.85 — 0
Congres-sional	21	8	15	4	5	2	2	1	5	2	2
Agency–Bureau	9	2	2	8	5	2	4	3	5	11	10

significant correlation occurred, it was always found that Congressional decision equation (8), in which a function of the deviation from the usual relationship between request and the previous year's appropriation enters explicitly, best specified appropriation behavior with respect to the agency in question.

The statistical procedures were programmed for the Carnegie Institute of Technology's Control Data G-21 electronic computer in the 20-Gate algebraic compiling language. The selection among alternate specifications according to the criteria established was not done automatically; otherwise all computations were performed by machine. Since the results for each agency are described in detail elsewhere,[15] and a full rendition would double the length of the paper, we must restrict ourselves to summary statements. The empirical results support the hypothesis that, up to a random error of reasonable magnitude, the budgetary process of the United States government is equivalent to a set of temporally stable linear decision rules. Estimated correlation coefficients for the best specification of each agency are generally high. Although the calculated values of the multiple correlation coefficients (R's) tend to run higher in time series than in cross-sectional analysis, the results are good. We leave little of the variance statistically unexplained. Moreover the estimated standard deviations of the coefficients are usually much smaller than one-half of the size of the estimated coefficients, a related indication of good results. Table 1 presents the frequencies of the correlation coefficients.

The fits between the decision rules and the time series data for the Congressional decision equations are, in general, better than those for the agency–Bureau of the Budget equations. Of the 64 agencies and sub-agencies studied, there are only 14 instances in which the correlation coefficient for the agency (or sub-agency) equation was higher than the one for the corresponding Congressional equation. We speculate that the estimated variances of the disturbances of the agency–Budget Bureau decision rules are usually larger because the agencies are closer than Congress to the actual sources that seek to add new programs or expand old ones.

Table 2 presents a summary of the combinations of the agency–Bureau of the

Table 2

Number of Agencies Explained by Simple and Complex Budget Equations

		Agency–Budget Bureau Equations		
		1 (simple)	2 (sophisticated)	3 (sophisticated)
	4 (simple)	44*	1	8
Congress Equations	7 (sophisticated)	1	0	0
	8 (sophisticated)	12	0	0

*Including eight sub-agencies from the National Institutes of Health.

Budget and Congressional decision equations. For those agencies studied, the most popular combinations of behavior are the simple ones represented by equations (4) and (1) respectively. When Congress uses a sophisticated "gaming" strategy such as (7) or (8), the corresponding agency–Bureau of the Budget decision equation is the relatively simple (1). And, when Congress grants exactly or almost exactly the amount requested by an agency, the agency tends to use decision equation (3).

Our discussion thus far has assumed fixed values for the coefficients (parameters) of the equations we are using to explain the behavior underlying the budgetary process. In the light of many important events occurring in the period from 1946 to 1963, however, it seems reasonable to suppose that the appropriations structure of many government agencies was altered. If this is correct, the coefficients of the equations—literally, in this context, the values represented by the on-the-average percentages requested by the agencies and granted by Congress—should change from one period of time to the next. The equations would then be temporally stable for a period, but not forever. The year when the coefficient of an equation changes from one value to another is termed the "shift point." The time series we are using are so short that it is possible to find only one meaningful shift point in each of the two equations that describe the budget request and appropriation best fitting an agency. We, therefore, broke each time series into two parts and used Chow's F-statistic[16] to determine temporal stability by testing the null hypothesis that the underlying coefficients did not shift (against all alternatives) for the individual equations. We used four categories for the coefficients of a decision equation defined as follows:

> *Temporally very stable:* The F-statistic is small and the coefficients estimated from the first and last part of the series are virtually the same.
> *Temporally stable:* The F-statistic is small, but the coefficients estimated from the first and last parts of the series appear to be different.

Table 3

Congressional Behavior Tends to Become More Sophisticated

	First period decision equations		
	1 (simple)	2 (sophisticated)	3 (sophisticated)
4 (simple)	45	0	10
7 (sophisticated)	1	0	0
8 (sophisticated)	2	0	0

	Second period decision equations		
	1 (simple)	2 (sophisticated)	3 (sophisticated)
4 (simple)	35	1	9
7 (sophisticated)	1	0	0
8 (sophisticated)	12	0	0

Not temporally stable: The F-statistic is large but not significant at the ten percent level and the coefficients estimated from the first and last parts of series appear to be different.

Temporally unstable: The F-statistic is significant at the ten percent level.

Of the Congressional decision equations, six were temporally very stable, 12 were temporally stable, 12 were not temporally stable, and 28 were temporally unstable. Of the agency–Bureau of the Budget decision equations, four were temporally very stable, 18 were temporally stable, 18 were not temporally stable, and 18 were temporally unstable.[17] Since a substantial majority of cases fall into the not temporally stable and temporally unstable categories, it is evident that while the process is temporally stable for short periods, it may not be stable for the whole period.

Table 3 presents a summary of the combinations of the agency–Bureau of the Budget and Congressional decision equations when each series is broken into two parts. These specifications are referred to as "first period" and "second period" for all agencies even though the years at which the time series were broken vary. While the most frequent combinations of behavior are the simple ones represented by equations (4) and (1) respectively, there is a marked tendency for Congressional behavior to become more sophisticated: the incidence of the gaming behavior represented by equation (8) increases over time.[18]

The budgetary process seems to become more linear over time in the sense that the importance of the "special circumstances" appears to diminish. Table 4 presents frequencies of the correlation coefficients for the first and second periods. Although there is a different number of correlation coefficients in each

Table 4

The Budgetary Process Is Becoming More Linear

	Frequencies of correlation coefficients										
	1 —	.995 —	.99 —	.98 —	.97 —	.96 —	.95 —	.94 —	93 —	.90 —	.85 — 0
First Period	9	5	8	5	3	6	8	4	18	24	21
Second Period	27	5	13	8	8	15	7	5	12	8	6

period (111 in the first period and 114 in the second),[19] Table 4 shows clearly that D fits are better for the second period, which is sufficient evidence of increasing linear tendencies. To us it seems reasonable to expect an increasing use of simplifying rules of thumb as the budget grows in size and the pressure of time on key decision makers increases. Yet this is only one of a number of possible explanations. For example, the data are not deflated for changes in the price level during the early years. Since there were larger increases in the price level during the early years, this might help explain why the fits are better during the second period.

When only one shift point is presumed, most shifts are discovered during the first two budgets of the Eisenhower Administration (1954–1955). Table 5 presents, for both Congressional and agency–Budget Bureau decision equations, frequencies of the shift points for (a) those equations whose coefficients are in the not temporally stable or temporally unstable categories and (b) those agencies for which the decision rules of the participants appeared to change. While it is certainly possible that shift points do not occur as dramatically and as sharply as shown here, and that it may take several years for actual behavior to change noticeably, Table 5 nevertheless makes it clear that likely shifts are concentrated in the first period of the Eisenhower administration.

We said, in Section II, that we expected $\beta_0, \beta_1, \beta_3$, to be greater than one, and β_2 to be negative. In 56 instances this expectation is satisfied, but eight exceptions were noted. In the two cases where the estimated $\beta_3 < 1$, explanations are immediately available. First, the fit for the Bureau of Employment Security is not good. Second, the Office of Territories evidences most un-Parkinsonian behavior: its activities decline with a decrease in the number of territories. In the six other exceptions, the estimated coefficient is $\beta_0 < 1$. For three of these, Congress tends to appropriate an amount greater than the request, and two of the three represent an interesting phenomenon. When those parts of requests and appropriations directly related to loans are omitted from the data for both the Rural Electrification Administration and the Federal Housing Administration, the estimated coefficients are of the magnitudes expected with $\beta_0 > 1$ and $a_0 < 1$.

Table 5

Likely Shift Points Are Concentrated in the First Years of the Eisenhower Administration

	Frequencies of shift points																
	48	49	50	51	52	53	54	55	56	57	58	59	60	61	62	T	
Congres-sional	0	2	3	1	0	1	17	16	1	1	3	0	0	1	0	46	(40)
Agency–Bureau	0	2	4	0	2	3	15	13	3	0	2	1	0	2	1	37	(36)

However, when the data relating to loans are included, then $\beta_0 < 1$ and $a_0 > 1$. Apparently, Congress favors the loan programs more than do the agencies or the Budget Bureau.

As a rule, the d-statistics resulting from fitting the best specifications were not significant. It would thus appear that all major underlying trended variables (with the possible exception of variables with the same trend) have been accounted for by these specifications. When an exception to this rule did exist, the authors made a careful examination of the residuals in an effort to determine the reason for such a situation. It appeared that in most of these instances the cause was either (a) that the coefficients shifted slowly over several years and not abruptly at one point in time, or (b) that restricting the search to only one shift point left undetected an additional shift either very early or very late in the series.

In an attempt to unmask the trended variable most likely (in our opinion) to have been ignored, and to cast some light upon the notion of "fair share," final appropriations y_t for each agency were regressed on total non-defense appropriations z_t. This time series was taken from the *Statistical Abstract of the United States*. The results were poor. Indeed, the sample correlations between y_t and z_t are usually worse than those between y_t and x_t. Moreover, the d-statistics are usually highly significant and the residual patterns for the regression show the agency's proportion of the non-defense budget to be either increasing or decreasing over time. However, it should be noted that even those exceptional cases where the agency trend is close to that of the total non-defense appropriation do not invalidate the explicit decision structure fitted here. A similar study, with similar results, was conducted at the departmental level by regressing y_t for the eight National Institutes of Health on y_t for the Public Health Service, the agency of which they are a part. Finally, the y_t for selected pairs of agencies with "similar" interests were regressed on each other with uniformly poor results.

Although empirical evidence indicates that our models describe the budgetary process of the United States government, we are well aware of certain deficiencies in our work. One deficiency, omission of certain agencies from the study, is not serious because over one-half of all non-defense agencies were investigated.

Nevertheless, the omission of certain agencies may have left undiscovered examples of additional decision rules. We will shortly study all agencies whose organizational structure can be traced. We will also include supplemental appropriations.

A more serious deficiency may lie in the fact that the sample sizes, of necessity, are small. The selection criterion of maximum sample correlation, therefore, lacks proper justification, and is only acceptable because of the lack of a better criterion. Further, full-information maximum likelihood estimators, and especially biased ones, even when they are known to be consistent, are not fully satisfactory in such a situation, although they may be the best available. However, the remedy for these deficiencies must await the results of future theoretical research on explosive or evolutionary processes.

IV. The Deviant Cases and Prediction: Interpretation of the Stochastic Disturbances

The intent of this section is to clarify further the interpretation of the stochastic disturbances as special or unusual circumstances represented by random variables. While those influences present at a constant level during the period serve only to affect the magnitude of the coefficients, the special circumstances have an important, if subsidiary, place in these models. We have indicated that although outside observers can view the effects of special circumstances as a random variable, anyone familiar with all the facts available to the decision-makers at the time would be able to explain the special circumstances. It seems reasonable therefore to examine instances where, in estimating the coefficients, we find that the estimated values of the stochastic disturbances assume a large positive or negative value. Such instances appear as deviant cases in the sense that Congress or the agency–Budget Bureau actors affected by special circumstances (large positive or negative values of the random variable) do not appear to be closely following their usual decision rule at that time but base their decisions mostly on these circumstances. The use of case studies for the analyses of deviant phenomena, of course, presupposes our ability to explain most budgeting decisions by our original formulations. Deviant cases, then, are those instances in which particular decisions do not follow our equations. It is possible to determine these deviant instances simply by examining the residuals of the fitted equations: one observes a plot of the residuals, selects those which appear as extreme positive or negative values, determines the year to which these extreme residuals refer, and then examines evidence in the form of testimony at the Appropriations Committees, newspaper accounts and other sources. In this way it is possible to determine at least some of the circumstances of a budgetary decision and to investigate whether or not the use of the random variables is appropriate.[20]

Finally, it should be pointed out that in our model the occurrence of extreme

Table 6

Deviant Cases Cluster in Years of Political Change

	'48	'49	'50	'51	'52	'53	'54	'55	'56	'57	'58	'59	'60	'61	'62	'63
Agency–Bureau	8	2	1	1	1	4	6	4	1	1	2	3	4	2	8	7

disturbances represents deviant cases, or the temporary setting aside of their usual decision rules by the decision-makers in the process, while coefficient shifts represent a change (not necessarily in form) of these rules.

From the residuals of one-half of the estimated Congressional decision equations, a selection of 55 instances (approximately 14 percent of the 395 Congressional decisions under consideration) were identified as deviant.[21] Table 6 shows the yearly frequency of the occurrence of deviant cases. It is apparent that deviancy grows in years of political change; in 1948 the Republican 80th Congress made a determined effort to reduce appropriations submitted by the Democratic President; the years 1953 through 1955 mark the beginning of Eisenhower's Presidency; the large number of deviant cases in 1962 and 1963 are related to the accession to office of Kennedy and Johnson. The latter category of deviant cases, we will explain later, may be misclassifications in the sense that the passage of time and the corresponding accumulation of additional evidence may reveal shift points, i.e., changes in the "average percentages" of the decision processes, rather than "exceptional circumstances." Nevertheless, this fact causes no particular problem in light of our purposes here, and the cases may be viewed as if they are appropriately classified.

Table 7 categorizes the cases according to estimates of why deviance occurred. It should be noted that the largest category, significant policy change, involves the lack of a budgetary base for the agency in question. In order to highlight the meaning we give to random phenomena, an illustration of each category follows. This analysis explains why, although the deviant cases are understandable to an experienced observer or participant, an outsider would have to regard them as essentially random disturbances to an otherwise deterministic system. Indeed, no two events in the categories of Table 7 are likely, *a priori*, either to be the same or to occur in any particular year.

Significant policy change

The Southwestern Power Administration is typical of agencies whose appropriations fluctuate unduly because basic policy is being negotiated. Deviance was evident in 1948, 1949, 1954, and 1955. The SPA continually requested funds for the building of transmission lines, and Congress repeatedly eliminated the request from their appropriations, insisting that private enterprise would supply the necessary facilities. In 1948 the Bureau of the Budget

Table 7

Deviant Cases May Be Viewed as Random Events

Categories of deviance	Number of cases
Significant policy change	20
Fiscal policy change	8
Felt need of Congressional supervision	6
Amended estimate due to a time factor	6
Single event	5
Large new legislative program	4
Reorganization of agency	1
Non-identifiable	5
Total N =	55

recommended $7,600,000 of which only $125,000 was appropriated, with stringent and explicit instructions that printing and mailing of materials calculated to increase clientele among rural and municipal electrical cooperatives cease.

The Korean War increased demands for electric power. Deviance occurred in 1955 not because of appropriations cuts but because of House floor amendments and Senate Appropriations Committee increases. Public policy then became stabilized as Congress established a budgetary base. The following years fit our equations.

Fiscal policy changes
The Foreign Agricultural Service's 1963 appropriation is deviant in appropriation figures, but, because $3,117,000 was provided by transferring funds from Sec. 32, the total budget for FAS is close to the Budget Bureau's initial request.

Felt need of Congressional supervision
The House Committee reports on Office of Territories for 1953 show a lack of confidence in the agency. The tenor can be judged by House Report 1622: "The Department was advised last year that the Committee did not intend to provide appropriations for an endless chain of capital investment in the Alaska Railroads. Army testimony was conflicting as to the need for a road and railways. There is need for a coordinated plan before the Committee can act intelligently with regard to the railroad."

Amended estimate due to time factor
Typical of this type of deviance is the Commodity Stabilization Service's appropriation for 1958. On the basis of figures from County Agricultural Agents, Secretary Ezra Taft Benson scaled down his request from $465 million to $298 million. A more accurate estimate was made possible because of added time.

Large new legislative program
This is especially apt to affect an agency if it is required to implement several new programs simultaneously. The Commissioner of Education said in refer-

ence to the student loan program, "We have no way of knowing because we never had such a program, and many of the institutions never had them." The NDEA Act alone had ten new entitlements.

Reorganization of an agency
The only example is the Agricultural Marketing Service's appropriation for 1962. Funds were reduced because of a consolidation of diverse activities by the Secretary of Agriculture and not through reorganization as a result of Congressional demands.

Non-identifiable
This applies, for example, to the Public Health Service where a combination of lesser factors converge to make the agency extremely deviant for 1959, 1960, 1961, and 1962. Among the apparent causes of deviance are publicity factors, the roles of committee chairmen in both House and Senate, a high percentage of professionals in the agency, and the excellent press coverage of health research programs. No one factor appears primarily responsible for the deviance.

Our models are not predictive but explanatory. The alternate decision equations can be tried and the most appropriate one used when data on requests and appropriations are available. The appropriate equation explains the data in that, given a good fit, the process behaves "as if" the data were generated according to the equation. Thus, our explanatory models are backward looking; given a history of requests and appropriations, the data appear as if they were produced by the proposed and appropriately selected scheme.

The models are not predictive because the process is only temporally stable for short periods. We have found cases in which the coefficients of the equations change, i.e., cases in which there are alterations in the realized behavior of the processes. We have no *a priori* theory to predict the occurrence of these changes, but merely our *ad hoc* observation that most occurred during Eisenhower's first term. Predictions are necessarily based upon the estimated values of the coefficients and on the statistical properties of the stochastic disturbance (sometimes called the error term). Without a scientific method of predicting the shift points in our model, we cannot scientifically say that a request or an appropriation for some future year will fall within a prescribed range with a given level of confidence. We can predict only when the process remains stable in time. If the decision rules of the participants have changed, our predictions may be worthless: in our models, either the coefficients have shifted or, more seriously, the scheme has changed. Moreover, it is extremely difficult to determine whether or not the observation latest in time represents a shift point. A sudden change may be the result either of a change in the underlying process or a temporary setting aside of the usual decision rules in light of special circumstances. The data for several subsequent years are necessary to determine with any accuracy whether a change in decision rules indeed occurred.

It is possible, of course, to make conditional predictions by taking the estimated coefficients from the last shift point and assuming that no shift will occur.
Limited predictions as to the next year's requests and appropriations could be
made and might turn out to be reasonably accurate. However, scholarly efforts
would be better directed toward knowledge of why, where, and when changes in
the process occur so that accurate predictions might be made.

The usual interpretation of stochastic (in lieu of deterministic) models may, of
course, be made for the models of this paper, i.e., not all factors influencing the
budgetary process have been included in the equations. Indeed, many factors
often deemed most important, such as pressure from interest groups, are ignored.
Part of the reason for this lies in the nature of the models: they describe the
decision process in skeleton form. Further, since the estimations are made, of
necessity, on the basis of time series data, it is apparent that any influences that
were present at a constant level during the period are not susceptible to discovery
by these methods. However, these influences do affect the budgetary process by
determining the size of the estimated coefficients. Thus, this paper, in making a
comparative study of the estimated coefficients for the various agencies, suggests
a new way of approaching constant influences.

No theory can take every possible unexpected circumstance into account, but
our theory can be enlarged to include several classes of events. The concentration of shift points in the first years of the Eisenhower administration implies that
an empirical theory should take account of changes in the political party controlling the White House and Congress.

We also intend to determine indices of clientele and confidence so that their
effects, when stable over time, can be gauged.[22] Presidents sometimes attempt to
gear their budgetary requests to fit their desired notion of the rate of expenditures
appropriate for the economic level they wish the country to achieve. By checking
the Budget Message, contemporary accounts, and memoirs, we hope to include a
term (as a dummy variable) which would enable us to predict high and low
appropriations rates depending on the President's intentions.

V. Significance of the Findings

We wish to consider the significance of (a) the fact that it is possible to find
equations which explain major facets of the federal budgetary process and (b) the
particular equations fitted to the time series. We will take up each point in order.

A. It Is Possible to Find Equations for the Budgetary Process

There has been controversy for some time over whether it is possible to find
laws, even of a probabilistic character, which explain important aspects of the
political process. The greatest skepticism is reserved for laws which would explain how policy is made or account for the outcomes of the political process.

Without engaging in further abstract speculation, it is apparent that the best kind of proof would be a demonstration of the existence of some such laws. This, we believe, we have done.

Everyone agrees that the federal budget is terribly complex. Yet, as we have shown, the budgetary process can be described by very simple decision rules. Work done by Simon, Newell, Reitman, Clarkson, Cyert and March, and others on simulating the solution of complex problems, has demonstrated that in complicated situations human beings are likely to use heuristic rules or rules of thumb to enable them to find satisfactory solutions.[23] Braybrooke and Lindblom have provided convincing arguments on this score for the political process.[24] Wildavsky's interviews with budget officers indicate that they, too, rely extensively on aids to calculation.[25] It is not surprising, therefore, as our work clearly shows, that a set of simple decision rules can explain or represent the behavior of participants in the federal budgetary process in their efforts to reach decisions in complex situations.

The most striking fact about the equations is their simplicity. This is perhaps partly because of the possibility that more complicated decision procedures are reserved for special circumstances represented by extreme values of the random variable. However, the fact that the decision rules generally fit the data very well is an indication that these simple equations have considerable explanatory power. Little of the variance is left unexplained.

What is the significance of the fact that the budgetary process follows rather simple laws for the general study of public policy? Perhaps the significance is limited; perhaps other policy processes are far more complex and cannot be reduced to simple laws. However, there is no reason to believe that this is the case. On the contrary, when one considers the central importance of budgeting the political process—few activities can be carried on without funds—and the extraordinary problems of calculation which budgeting presents, a case might better be made for its comparative complexity than for its simplicity. At present it is undoubtedly easier to demonstrate that laws, whether simple or complex, do underlie the budgetary process than to account for other classes of policy outcomes, because budgeting provides units of analysis (appropriations requests and grants) that are readily amenable to formulating and testing propositions statistically. The dollar figures are uniform, precise, numerous, comparable with others, and, most important, represent an important class of policy outcomes. Outside of matters involving voting or attitudes, however, it is difficult to think of general statements about public policy that can be said to have been verified. The problem is not that political science lacks propositions which might be tested. Works of genuine distinction like Herring's *The Politics of Democracy,* Truman's *The Governmental Process,* Hyneman's *Bureaucracy in a Democracy,* Neustadt's *Presidential Power,* Buchanan and Tullock's *The Calculus of Consent,* contain implicit or explicit propositions which appear to be at least as interesting as (and potentially more interesting than) the ones tested in this paper. The real difficulty is that political scientists have been unable to develop a unit of analysis (there is little agreement on what constitutes a decision) that would permit them to test the many propositions they have at their command. By taking one step toward demonstrating what can be done when a useful unit of analysis has been developed, we hope to highlight the tremendous importance that the development of units of analysis would have for the study of public policy.

B. The Significance of the Particular Equations

Let us examine the concepts that have been built into the particular equations. First, the importance of the previous year's appropriation is an indication that the notion of the base is a very significant explanatory concept for the behavior of the agencies and the Budget Bureau. Similarly, the agency–Budget Bureau requests are important variables in the decisions of Congress. Second, some of the equations, notably (7) and (8) for Congress, and (2) for the agency–Budget Bureau, incorporate strategic concepts. On some occasions, then, budgeting on the federal level does involve an element of gaming. Neither the Congress nor the agencies can be depended upon to "take it lying down." Both attempt to achieve their own aims and goals. Finally, the budgetary process is only temporally stable. The occurrence of most changes of decision rules at a change in administration indicates that alterations in political party and personnel occupying high offices can exert some (but not total) influence upon the budgetary process.

Our decision rules may serve to cast some light on the problem of "power" in political analysis. The political scientist's dilemma is that it is hardly possible to think about politics without some concept of power, but that it is extremely difficult to create and then to use an operational definition in empirical work. Hence, James March makes the pessimistic conclusion that "The Power of Power" as a political variable may be rather low.[26] The problem is particularly acute when dealing with processes in which there is a high degree of mutual dependence among the participants. In budgeting, for example, the agency–Budget Bureau and Congressional relationships hardly permit a strict differentiation of the relative influence of the participants. Indeed, our equations are built on the observation of mutual dependence; and the empirical results show that how the agency–Budget Bureau participants behave depends on what Congress does (or has done) and that how Congress behaves depends on what the agency–Budget Bureau side is doing (or has done). Yet the concept of power does enter the analysis in calculations of the importance that each participant has for the other; it appears in the relative magnitude of the estimated coefficients. "Power" is saved because it is not required to carry too great a burden. It may be that theories which take power into account as part of the participants' calculations will prove of more use to social science research than attempts to measure the direct exercise of influence. At least we can say that theories of calculation, which animate the analysis of *The Politics of the Budgetary Process* and of this paper, do permit us to state and test propositions about the outcomes of a political process. Theories of power do not yet appear to have gone this far.

In the field of economics, work has long been done on organizational units called industrial firms. In political science, however, despite the flurry of excitement over organization theory, there has been no empirical demonstration of the value of dealing with various public organizations as comparable entities. By viewing governmental bodies not as distinctly different agencies but as having certain common properties (here, in budgetary calculations and strategies), we hope to have shown the utility to empirical theory of treating organizations *qua* organizations. Despite the differences among the organizations studied—some follow different decision rules and are affected by different random disturbances—it is analytically significant to explain their behavior by virtue of features they share as organizations.

It should be clear that we are dealing with general models of organizations and not with individual policies. One cannot say anything directly about water, land, health, or other transportation policies, from inspection of our models of a given agency. But this limit is not inherent in our approach. It is possible, for example, to calculate from our data present and future estimated rates of growth for virtually all domestic agencies since World War II. Agencies with similar growth rates may be segregated and examined for common features. The growth rates of agencies in similar areas of policy, such as public health and natural resources, may be compared, and the fortunes of policies in those areas deduced. Individual agencies may be broken down into sub-units or the courses of certain policy programs charted to explain the differential treatment they receive. While pursuing this type of analysis, we hope to have one advantage. We shall be working from a general model of the budgetary process. It will, therefore, be possible for us to locate our efforts within this larger scheme. To know whether one is dealing with a normal or deviant case, to know one's position in this larger universe is to be able to give more general meaning to the individual and particular circumstances with which one must be involved in handling small parts of the total process.

The general mode of analysis we have developed here may be pursued in many different contexts. Similar studies could be undertaken in state and local governments as well as foreign countries.[27] Private firms and public agencies may be conceptualized in parallel terms through their budgetary mechanisms.[28] By comparing the processes underlying budgeting in a variety of political and economic systems, it may be possible to state more elegantly and precisely the conditions under which different forms of behavior would prevail. . . .

Notes

1. [As originally published, this article included a technical appendix which defined terms. Readers interested in the methodology should look there for additional guidance.]

2. The description which follows is taken from Aaron Wildavsky, *The Politics of the Budgetary Process* (Boston, 1964). Portions of the comments on the House Appropriations Committee are from Richard Fenno, "The House Appropriations Committee as a Political System: The Problem of Integration," *[American Political Science] Review,* 56 (1962), 310–324.

3. See H. Thiel, *Linear Aggregation of Economic Relations* (Amsterdam, 1954).

4. Our subsequent discussion of "shift" or "break" points should also make clear that it is not realistic to expect meaningful time series of great length to be accumulated for most agencies in the United States government.

5. Since some readers may not be familiar with the notation we are using, a brief explanation may be in order. As a coefficient of the equation, β_2 is an unknown number that must be estimated from the data, and this coefficient multiplies another number (y_{t-1} $-x_{t-1}$) that may be computed by subtracting last year's request from last year's appropriation. We want the equation to say that the agency will try to counteract large changes in their appropriations by changing their normal requests in the next year. If the agency asks for much more than it thinks it will get and its request is cut, for example, the expression $(y_{t-1} - x_{t-1})$ will be a negative number written in symbolic form as $(y_{t-1} - x_{t-1}) < 0$. A rule of multiplication says that a negative number multiplied by another negative number gives a positive number. If an agency pads its requests, however, it presumably follows a cut with a new request which incorporates an additional amount to make allowance for future cuts. In order to represent this behavior, that is to come out with a positive result incorporating the concept of padding, the unknown coefficient β_2 must be negative ($\beta_2 < 0$).

6. The agency that favors its own programs should increase its requests over time. In the absence of the stochastic disturbance (when the random variable is 0), the request in a given year should be larger than the request in the previous year so that $x_t >_{t-1}$. Therefore, the unknown coefficient β_2 must be larger than one ($\beta_3 > 1$) since it multiplies last year's request.

7. Other gaming strategies are easily proposed. Suppose, for example, that a given agency believes that it knows the decision rule that Congress uses in dealing with it, and that this decision rule can be represented by one of (4), (7), or (8), above. Presume, for reasons analogous to those outlined for (8), that this agency desires to take into account that positive or negative portion of the previous year's appropriation y_{t-1}, that was not based on the previous year's request x_{t-1} This consideration suggests

$$x_t = \beta_4 y_{t-1} + \beta_5 \Delta_{t-1} + \delta_t$$

as an agency decision rule where Δ_{t-1} is a dummy variable representing in year $t-1$ the term not involving x_{t-1}, in one of (4), (7) or (8) above. If one believes that agency and Bureau of the Budget personnel are sufficiently well acquainted with the senators and congressmen to be able to predict the value of the current stochastic disturbance, then it becomes reasonable to examine a decision rule of the form

$$x_t = \beta_6 y_{t-1} + \beta_7 \Delta_t + \sigma_t$$

where σ_t is defined as above. No evidence of either form of behavior was found, however, among the agencies that were investigated. We also estimated the parameters of the third order auto-regressive scheme for the requests of an individual agency

$$x_t + \beta_8 x_{t-1} + \beta_9 t_{-2} + \beta_{10} t_{-3} + \gamma_t$$

in an attempt to discover if naive models would fit as well as those above. In no case did this occur and generally the fits for this model were very poor. A similar scheme was estimated for the appropriations y_t of an individual agency with similar results with respect to equations (4), (7) and (8) above. Since the "d" statistic suggests that no higher order Markov process would be successful, no other rules for agency behavior were tried.

8. Agency proposals to the Bureau of the Budget are not reported to the public and could be obtained only for these eight sub-agencies.

9. Three interrelated difficulties arise in the analysis of the time series data x_t, y_t for an agency. The first problem is the choice of a technique for estimating the parameters of the alternative schemes in some optimal fashion. Given these estimates and their associated statistics, the second problem is the choice of criteria for selecting the model best specifying the system underlying the data. Finally, one is faced with the problem of examining the variability of the underlying parameters of the best specification. We believe that our solution to these problems, while far from optimal, is satisfactory given the present state of econometric knowledge. See our presentation in "On the Process of Budgeting: An Empirical Study of Congressional Appropriations," by Otto Davis, M.A.H. Dempster, and Aaron Wildavsky, to appear in Gordon Tullock (ed.), *Papers on Non-Market Decision Making,* Thomas Jefferson Center, University of Virginia. See especially section 4 and the appendix by Dempster, which contains discussions and derivations of estimation procedures, selection criteria and test statistics for the processes in section II of this paper.

10. We make the assumption that these two disturbances are independent throughout the paper. Notice, however, that dependence between the disturbances explicitly enters decision equation (8) of section II and those of footnote 7. For these equations, the assumption refers to the disturbance of the current year. That is, we allow the possibility that special circumstances may affect a single participant (Bureau of the Budget or Congress) as well as both. When the latter case occurred, our selection criteria resulted in the choice of equation (8) as best specifying Congressional behavior.

11. We are estimating the unknown values of the coefficients (or parameters) of regression equations for each agency. All of our estimators are biased. We use biased estimators for the simple reason that no unbiased estimators are known. The property of consistency is at least a small comfort. All of our estimators are consistent. It might be noted that all unbiased estimators are consistent, but not all consistent estimators are unbiased.

12. This statistic is known as the Durbin-Watson ratio. A description of the test may be found in J. Johnston, *Econometric Methods* (New York, 1963), p. 92.

13. H. Theil and A.L. Nagar, "Testing the Independence of Regressional Disturbances," *Journal of the American Statistical Association,* 56 (1961), 793–806. These significance points were used to construct further significance points when necessary. See Davis, Dempster, and Wildavsky, *op. cit.*

14. The test is described in T.W. Anderson, *An Introduction to Multivariate Analysis* (New York, 1958), pp. 69–71. See Dempster's appendix to Davis, Dempster, and Wildavsky, *op. cit.,* for some justification of the use of the test.

15. See Davis, Dempster, and Wildavsky, *op. cit.*

16. G.C. Chow, "Tests of Equality Between Sets of Coefficients in Two Linear Regressions," *Econometrica,* 28 (1960), 591–605, and the appendix to Davis, Dempster, and Wildavsky, *op. cit.*

17. In a few instances an inspection of the residuals indicated that a shift point occurred so early or so late in the series that it was not possible to compute a meaningful stationary F-Statistic. In these few cases the deviant observations were dropped and the usual analysis performed on the shortened time series. Thus we "forced" a break in every case in order to perform subsequent operations.

18. The apparent discrepancy between the latter part of Table 3 and Table 1 is caused by the fact that for two agencies, the Bureau of the Census and the Office of Education, although the agency–Bureau of the Budget decision equations are temporally stable and best specified as (1), when a shift point is forced, the criteria indicate (3) for the latter period.

19. Some of the shift points appeared to occur so early in the series that it was not possible to calculate a correlation coefficient.

20. The importance of analyzing deviant cases is suggested in: Milton M. Gordon, "Sociological Law and the Deviant Case," *Sociometry,* 10 (1947); Patricia Kendall and Katharine Wolf, "The Two Purposes of Deviant Case Analysis," in Paul F. Lazarsfeld and Morris Rosenberg (eds.), *The Language of Social Research,* (Glencoe, 1962), pp. 103–137; Paul Horst, *The Prediction of Personal Adjustment: A Survey of the Logical Problems and Research Techniques* (New York, 1941); and Seymour Lipset, Martin Trow, and James Coleman, *Union Democracy* (New York, 1960).

21. We are indebted to Rose M. Kelly, a graduate student in the Department of Political Science, University of California, Berkeley, who did the research on the deviant cases and provided the data for Tables 6 and 7.

22. See Wildavsky, *op. cit.,* pp. 64–68, for a discussion of clientele and confidence. In his forthcoming book, *The Power of the Purse* (Boston, 1966), Richard Fenno provides further evidence of the usefulness of these categories.

23. Geoffrey P.E. Clarkson, *Portfolio Selection: A Simulation of Trust Investment* (Englewood Cliffs, N.J., 1962); G.P.E. Clarkson and H.A. Simon, "Simulation of Individual and Group Behavior," *American Economic Review,* 50 (1960), 920–932; Richard Cyert and James March (eds.), *Behavioral Theory of the Firm* (Englewood Cliffs, N.J., 1963); Allen Newell, "The Chess Machine: An Example of Dealing with a Complex Task by Adaptation," *Proceedings of the Western Joint Computer Conference* (1955), pp. 101–108; Allen Newell, J.C. Shaw, and H.A. Simon, "Elements of a Theory of Human Problem Solving," *Psychological Review,* 65 (1958), 151–166; Allen Newell and H.A. Simon, "The Logic Theory Machine: A Complex Information Processing System," *Transactions on Information Theory* (1956), 61–79; W.R. Reitman, "Programming Intelligent Problem Solvers," *Transactions on Human Factors in Electronics,* HFE–2 (1961), pp. 26–33; H.A. Simon, "A Behavioral Model of Rational Choice," *Quarterly Journal of Economics,* 60 (1955), 99–118; and H.A. Simon, "Theories of Decision Making in Economics and Behavioral Science," *American Economic Review,* 49 (1959), 253–283.

24. David Braybrooke and Charles Lindblom, *A Strategy of Decision* (New York, 1964).

25. Wildavsky, *op. cit.,* pp. 8–63.

26. James March, "The Power of Power," in David Easton, ed., *Varieties of Political Theory* (Englewood Cliffs, N.J., 1966), pp. 39–70.

27. See the forthcoming studies by John P. Crecine on budgeting in Pittsburgh, Detroit, and Cleveland, and by Donald Gerwin on the Pittsburgh School District. . . .

28. Aaron Wildavsky, "Private Markets and Public Arenas," *The American Behavioral Scientist,* vol. 9 no. 7. (Sept. 1965), pp. 33–39.

3A.2. Policy and Priority in the Budgetary Process

PETER B. NATCHEZ and IRVIN C. BUPP

The incrementalist thesis challenged an extensive political science literature which held that budgets were formed through political conflict, and that they change with shifts in the power and influence of competing groups. In this reading, Natchez and Bupp argue that the incrementalist thesis is overstated and that the strong results achieved by Dempster, Davis, and Wildavsky are due to the particular data and methods they used.

While not denying that there is some truth to the concept of incrementalism, the authors attempt to show that budgets are also determined by the sort of political struggles that political scientists have always thought important. They argue that incrementalists miss this struggle because of the type of evidence they use and the way they analyze it. Especially important is the fact that incrementalists focus on agencies *rather than on* programs. *Thus they miss the fact that programs within an agency may have very different fates, even when the amount received by the agency as a whole varies little over time. They also show that the fate of a program is affected by the direction of even small changes—upward or downward—and whether growth is steady or intermittent. They also demonstrate that rather small year-to-year changes can amount to very large changes over time.*

The authors seek to prove their point by examining programs within the Atomic Energy Commission. They first demonstrate that the change in the Commission's budget over time fits the pattern identified by Davis, Dempster, and Wildavsky. Then they devise prosperity scores to measure the relative success of different programs within the agency and show that in the 1958–1972 period the different programs had markedly different budget histories. They

Reprinted with permission from *The American Political Science Review* 67, 3 (September 1973), pp. 951–63. Copyright © 1973 by the American Political Science Association.

attribute this to the importance of entrepreneurial political activity by both agency leaders and outside political actors.

Politics and the Budgetary Process

By an impressive margin the federal government spends more money, does more things, and affects more people than it did twenty-five, or even ten, years ago. But the record of innovation and expansion has not been uniform; rather the prosperity of individual programs has varied widely during this period. Some programs have continuously prospered, grown, and evidently become permanent fixtures in the governmental system: farm commodity supports, highway construction, Social Security, and, most recently, health care. Others seem to have thrived only temporarily: aircraft nuclear propulsion, manned space flight, and the "Green Berets"; while still others have an uneven history of success and failure and are constantly involved in political turmoil: AID, Model Cities, and the Atomic Energy Commission's "Plowshare" program.

What is responsible for the success or failure of governmental programs? Who (or what) determines our national priorities? Political scientists have long regarded the budgetary process as the richest source of evidence on these matters. The assumption has been that the budgetary process, the most important "action forcing" mechanism in government, reflects the aspirations and controversies which cause some programs to be favored over others. Within the budgetary process clashes of interest and priority should be expressed in real dollar terms. Evidence concerning the goals of program directors and clients, the support of agency heads, the surveillance of the Office of Management and Budget (formerly the Bureau of the Budget), the strategic choices of the president, and the influence of Congress should all be contained in the data generated annually by the federal budget cycle.[1]

More recent quantitative analyses of the federal budgetary process do not, however, support these assumptions. Instead, a younger generation of political scientists has discovered "striking regularities" indicating that what happens in any given year closely resembles what had happened in the previous year.[2] Implicit in this approach is the view that the strategic and tactical choices, the interagency disputes and alliances, the battles with the Office of Management and Budget (OMB), and the appeals for presidential support, all make very little difference. In the end what happens during any given period pretty much determines what will happen in subsequent periods.

There is, of course, an important element of truth in these findings. Administrative budgets are not rewritten from scratch every year; and it is a little silly to judge the consequences of policy innovations as if they were. Further, it is undoubtedly true that political historians (and public administrators) often exaggerate the importance of particular policies, choices, and competing personalities. After all, they find the business of public administration interesting precisely because it embodies great controversies between powerful forces—conflicts which seem both to be inherent in and to shed light upon the process of popular government.

Still, the gap between traditional and quantitative approaches to the budget remains. It is not enough to dismiss the conclusions of the older school out of hand, as the product of too much enthusiasm for public administration and the inevitable result of unsystematic research. Much of the traditional literature comes from men who in fact have served in government—participant observers, if you will—and their description of the central role of the budgetary process as a policy vehicle is important if only because that is what they saw happening. The challenge of the quantitative budget studies is precisely over the question of how much public policy is embedded in the budgetary process. Their argument is that administrators rarely depart significantly from what they are already doing. They "muddle through" as best they can, making only marginal changes in the established operations of government. Consequently, agency budgets are massively stable from one year to the next.[3] Bureaucratic behavior and the budgets that result from it seem to reduce to a simple set of operating principles that, at the same time, leave no room for other explanations.

> The most striking fact about the equations [which describe the budgetary process] is their simplicity. This is perhaps partly because of the possibility that more complicated decision procedures are reserved for special circumstances represented by extreme values of the random variable. However, the fact that the decision rules generally fit the data very well is an indication that these simple questions have considerable explanatory power. Little of the variance is left unexplained.[4]

In the end, this line of reasoning may yet provide a new and strong foundation for the study of public administration. However, it may be also that the relationship between public policy and the budgetary process has been obscured by the way the problem has been quantified.

The theme of this essay is that the political choices and conflicts inherent in the administration of government have been unnecessary casualties of the quantitative revolution. The problem is essentially one of theory. After reviewing the theoretical underpinnings of the quantitative budget studies we will suggest an alternative approach to the manipulation of budgetary data, developing along the way a methodology that will uncover controversies over policy and priorities.

The Incremental Model of Budgeting

The budgets of federal agencies are developed over a period which begins as much as eighteen months before appropriations requests are acted upon by the Congress. During this period agency budgets are typically formulated to meet the guidelines established by the OMB speaking for the president and his administration. The initial budgets normally undergo a sequence of successive reductions and appeals often culminating in a presidential review.

The budgetary process itself is composed of six stages, though the precise pattern that is followed may vary slightly by agency and department, particularly in the final stages of appeal and presidential review. The process begins with the budget guidelines that are sent down by the OMB. These are deliberately varied from year to year so as to communicate to the bureaucracy a sense of limited resources and to direct attention to items that happen to be of particular concern to the administration. Usually agencies will respond to the OMB by preparing "flash estimates" or "preview budgets." These budgets serve to begin the process of negotiation, and, in the weeks that follow, a series of informal estimates are established indicating how much expansion is likely to be considered reasonable in light of the administration's priorities.

On the basis of this information, the agency's comptroller begins to aggregate budget requests from the operating divisions within the department or agency. Of course, division requests regularly exceed the amount of money that, according to the OMB, will be available. Hence these estimates are worked over by the comptroller with an eye towards bringing them in line with administration expectations.

The comptroller's recommendations along with each division's request constitute the material from which an agency budget is produced. It is during this part of the process that competition *within* the agency (or department) reaches its greatest intensity. Each division struggles for funds against the budgetary interest of the other operating divisions, each trying to avoid the heavy hand of the comptroller by shifting the burden of budgetary cuts to some other division's programs.

The easiest way for a division to protect itself is, of course, to gain the support of the department secretary or agency chairman. But the competition for funds often extends beyond the administrative framework in which the operating divisions are located. Thus, it is not unusual to find program directors drawing in other elements of government—congressmen, other bureaus and departments, consultants, lobbyists, etc.—in order to gain some vital budgetary advantage. (Admiral Rickover, for one, was so skilled at managing his congressional support that he operated virtually outside the normal review procedures of the AEC.) The department or agency must now produce a series of budgetary settlements that compromise the demands of its working parts along with the push and pull of external political forces while, of course, trying to hold to OMB guidelines.

The budgetary outcomes at this stage of the process become formal requests to the president for funding and are sent to the OMB for review. Acting "in accordance with the President's program,"[5] the OMB "marks up" each budget, item by item, program by program—cutting away wherever it can, accepting other requests as submitted, and occasionally, adding money to some project that the administration looks upon with special favor. For the managers of the federal bureaucracy this is the most difficult part of the process, because it threatens to unbalance the blend of policies and priorities that has been arranged among a department's working parts. Yet the entire thrust of the OMB at this point is to attack budget requests that have produced unnecessary and expensive settlements. Budgets then are normally marked up with a heavy hand and returned to those who wrote them for reconsideration.

Here the agency or department has a choice: it can accept the OMB's actions as they stand or it can appeal to the OMB for some measure of restoration. It is important to note here that any further budgetary action by either the president or the OMB occurs only over contested items in the budget. Those items not disputed by the OMB or subsequently returned to the OMB by appeal are regarded as a settled part of the administration's budget. Thus, the budget is now agreed upon for the most part with only a small number of controversies remaining.

The OMB reconsiders those matters that are still disputed and again leaves the agency or department with a choice. Again the decision of the OMB can be accepted, thus settling the matter. There is, however, also the alternative of appealing the OMB's final action directly to the president. It is understood that each agency chairman or department secretary can argue for restorations directly before the president, much like a knight pleading before his king for special favor. The president's decision, of course, ends the process and the results are printed up and sent along to Congress (where specific issues can be reopened). Several things ought to be noted about the presidential budgetary reviews. The first is that this stage is centered on specific budgetary items and does not usually include a general review of the agency's or department's budget. Second, it is in these last stages of appeals that the budgetary process varies most widely. These variations usually reflect the relative stature of particular branches of government. (Thus military budgets, for example, have a preferred status in the appeal process.) Also, it is at this point that the standing of the department's chief administrator is determined. It is he who must go before the president and argue for funds that are presumably vital to his department's functions. Consequently, the degree of success that he has with the president is widely regarded as an evaluation of his administrative worth and, at the same time, a measure of the importance that agency or department has in the administration.

By design, then, the budgetary process produces a climate of scarcity in which the success of those who participate is measured by the number of dollars they are able to win. Indeed, the entire process of formulating budgets within agencies plays upon the institutional interests of bureaucrats so as to produce the explicit competition between alternative "policies."[6]

This competition among alternative programs seems to have been all but lost in the work of Davis, Dempster, and Wildavsky. These scholars have argued that budgets are produced by relatively straightforward incremental strategies and hence are not often an especially interesting source of conflict, not to mention change and innovation.[7] Specifically, they have examined the variations in fifty-six non-defense federal agencies from 1947 to 1963 and discovered that they can be explained very simply by a "set of simple decision rules that are linear and temporally stable."[8] In their most sophisticated equation (decision rule), Davis, Dempster, and Wildavsky argue that the congressional appropriation of any agency is

> . . . a fixed mean percentage of the agency's request for a certain year plus a fixed mean percentage of a dummy variable which represents that part of the agency's request for the year at issue which is not part of the appropriation or request of the previous year plus a random variable representing the part of the appropriation or request of the previous year plus a random variable representing the part of the appropriation attributable to the special circumstances of the year.[9]

This is to say that appropriations subcommittees normally give an agency some proportion of what it asked for, adjusted by things in dispute and special considerations peculiar to a particular year.

The point that Davis, Dempster, and Wildavsky most emphasize is that their decision rules fit the data: ". . . the results are very good. We leave very little of the variance statistically unexplained."[10] In fact, for the majority of congressional decisions (appropriations) their equations yield R^2s exceeding 99 per cent, and for all but two show R^2s above 90 per cent. Further, these decision rules seem to square neatly with other research which suggests that the budgetary process in appropriations subcommittees has become an institutionalized series of actions sanctioned by an elaborate set of norms and behaviors.[11]

The creative insights upon which Wildavsky and others have built are contained in the writings of Herbert Simon and his colleagues.[12] The theme of this work is that people are quite limited in their ability to process new information, generate alternatives, anticipate consequences, and weigh values. The Simon-Lindblom administrator faces a highly complicated world, a world of multiple values and goals related to each other in unknown ways. He has no very reliable way of predicting the consequences of alternative courses of action and little information pertinent to assessing these consequences even if he had an acceptable theory. As Crecine has put it,

> [He] is a man with limited knowledge, limited information, and limited cognitive ability, making a policy choice in an uncertain world by "drastically" simplifying the problem and making marginal adjustments in past "successful" policies to formulate current policies.[13]

The phrase that captures the essence of the administrative situation is "organized complexity."[14] And nowhere are its consequences more apparent than in the making of budgets. The budgetary process is, after all, a complicated procedure in which officials are usually under the intense pressure of time and circumstance. One expects that whatever decision rules have worked in the past will be used again in the solving of current disputes. Indeed, one does not expect the level of disagreement to be very high, because individual administrators can be expected to request funds for what they are already doing, give or take a little bit.

These observations are all quite true as far as they go. Across aggregations of decision-making units (federal agencies, municipal administrations or individual budget-makers), behavior at time "T" can be shown to be a robust function of comparable behavior at "T–1." What is striking is that administrative behavior is so very similar in all sorts of diverse organizations. State governments, business organizations, labor unions, organizations of every sort seem to promote the same sort of responses from those who administer them, responses that are rationalized in budgetary processes that do not seem to vary widely in effect from organization to organization.[15]

The trouble is that in politics the budgetary process, while certainly responding to the requirements of administrative life, is also a battlefield for conflicting priorities and alternative policies. The categories of analysis established by Wildavsky, Crecine, and others help us to understand the behavior of the pertinent decision maker as he attempts to resolve the problems that he faces. But this line of reasoning does not shed much light upon the sort of things which over time cause some activities to become the continuing policies of government while others fade and are discarded. It is this variation in the *competitive* success of alternative *programs,* rather than the cognitive processes of decision makers, which is central to the politics of public administration. It is this aspect of government that the "problem solving" perspective is inherently unable to explain.

Let us stress again that we are not quarreling with descriptions of administrative behavior. Quite to the contrary, our argument is premised on the findings of Simon, Lindblom, Cyert and March, and Wildavsky. Administrators in complex organizations *behave similarly.* However, accounting for these patterns of administrative behavior—itself vital to the science of public administration—is not the focus of our problem. We want to explain why some programs are repeatedly funded while others are considerably less successful, *given* that the behavior of their administrators is likely to be quite similar. This is to say that we are looking at a different level of public administration. Our focus is not on the behavior of administrators, per se, but on administrators as they are organized in terms of policy output, programs as they compete for dollars.

In a sense budget data present us with a measurement problem: *How are yearly government budgetary figures reordered so that they indicate policy choices and public priorities?* This is by no means an easy question to answer. For the budget reflects simultaneously a yearly *process of administration* and decisions among *alternative political priorities.* That is, budgets are at once measures of the way government is organized and of the policy decisions that the organization implements. Obviously, these are not the same things although they are nested within the very same data.

The fact that political choices and the budgetary process are so completely intertwined accounts for much of the confusion among approaches to public administration. What has happened is that the traditional scholars have spoken of public administration without placing it within the context of an annual, stable budgetary process. Thus, they have tended to write about policy as if that were the only thing that government was producing. In discovering that there is, in fact, a budgetary process in administration, younger and more quantitatively trained researchers assumed that the process of government, in addition to producing budgets, produced settlements on questions of public policy. Here the quantitative approach was a victim of its own theoretical and statistical precision. The budgetary process models worked so well that there simply did not seem to be anything left to explain.

The reason for the great statistical success of the quantitative budget studies lies in the fact that *agencies* were taken as the unit of analysis, yearly budget cycles being nothing more than replications of the same event over time. These data yielded to Wildavsky and his associates a simple set of equations (decision rules) that, by and large, seemed to describe how public policy is formulated while reserving more complex and sophisticated political strategies for a small number of "deviant cases." What has been captured—quite accurately—by this formulation is the great stability of the administrative structure of government. But because administrative categories have formed the basis of budgetary analysis, the entire process in which public policy is produced has been obscured.[16]

The first step, then, in untangling information on policy choices from data on the administration of government is to shift the level of analysis for agencies and departments to programs. This is to say that in the context of the budgetary process, programs are the operating units of public policy, that they provide "categories that are closer to being true outputs [of government] than the older categories."[17]

It should be noted, however, that it is difficult to make explicit comparisons *between* program budgets (although even with the data in this form a great deal can be done).[18] Programs vary widely in their scope, size, and content, and these differences are unfortunately reflected in their budgets. The amount of money necessary to fund a strong cancer research program differs substantially from the funding necessary to lift the incomes of the elderly above the "poverty line." Similarly, reducing the army's manpower budget by 100 million dollars has a markedly different effect from taking the same number of dollars away from OEO. In a fundamental way, then, all budgetary dollars are not equal; and while all policy outcomes are expressed in terms of dollars, some care must be taken to make this information commensurate across programs. This is to argue that merely shifting to programs as the basis of policy analysis is not in itself sufficient, that budgetary data organized by programs must themselves be transformed so that the relative prosperity of programs in the policy process can be measured and compared.

It should be added, finally, that programs have histories of support and opposition, and focusing explicitly on them returns this dimension to budgetary analyses. Agencies (or departments) usually do not have such histories associated with them (except in their first years of operation). They are normally accepted as part of the fixed institutional landscape, terrain that seems to change dramatically only during periods of great crisis and political turmoil. An important lesson of the Eisenhower and Nixon Administrations is that changing the party in power does not open up already established agencies to direct attack. However, the relative priorities for programs within an agency (and even the relative standing of the agency as a whole) do vary quite widely from administration to administration, even though the agency continues as an established part of government.

Thus, the salient characteristic of established agencies and departments is their stability—both organizational and budgetary. And again, it is this aspect of government that Wildavsky and others have captured so well. Yet within departmental and agency boundaries (and occasionally between them, e.g., the case of OEO) there is a constant struggle by program directors, lobbyists, congressmen, state and local politicians, and White House personnel to fund new ideas and to continue the funding of old ones. It is a competition that draws to it people and institutions with radically different ideas and purposes, and that decides, in the end, what public policies we are to have.

From this perspective the struggle to establish new public policies looks very much like the competitive ideal in nineteenth century capitalism. Entrepreneurs—"policy entrepreneurs," if you will—seek scarce resources for their programs. In their quest for funding and political authority, they use every available weapon: pressure from various constituencies and groups, aggressive selling inside government, attracting congressmen as innovators or as protectors (congressmen who in turn often lobby other congressmen), pressuring the White House as well as receiving pressure from the White House, and so on through a diverse range of opportunities and strategies. The fact that political strategies vary widely as a result of the peculiar combination of resources that happens to be available probably explains why "the case study method" of public administration was never able to produce a cogent set of generalizations. But this should not be taken as evidence that there is no struggle, that the process is one of slow, incremental change. Rather it suggests that the policy process in the United States is an open one where all sorts of influences are at play, and where—because the process is a long and complex one (six stages plus congressional action over more than eighteen months)—the competition between policies is reinforced and accentuated.

The Case of the AEC

To make these thoughts more concrete, let us turn to the activities of a particular federal agency: the Atomic Energy Commission. Though now a mature agency with established purposes and programs, the AEC was created and in many ways

Table 1

Correlations Between Budgetary Stages for 23 AEC Programs Pooled Across FY 1958–FY 1962

	Division	General Manager	AEC	OMB	Appeal	Presidential
Division	1.000					
General manager	.996	1.000				
AEC	.997	.999	1.000			
OMB	.995	.998	.997	1.000		
Appeal	.996	.997	.997	.998	1.000	
Final	.995	.996	.997	.998	.999	1.000

has continued to exist in an atmosphere of uncertainty and conflict about the appropriate applications of a new and poorly understood technology.[19] Was nuclear technology to be applied exclusively to the development of weapons? Or were its applications ultimately to be essentially civilian and peaceful? Could peaceful applications be carried out with economy and safety? By whom, and under whose supervision? These and other questions have defined areas of sharp conflict among philosophies of government and among programs and personalities. The early history of these disputes has been compiled and is presently being published as a multi-volume study of the Atomic Energy Commission.[20] A definitive account of the programs and controversies that developed over the years within the AEC, this material provides a rich historical context against which we can examine the AEC's activities as they are reflected in the agency's budgetary records. Perhaps more important, however, are the specific characteristics of the actual budgetary records upon which we have been able to draw. First, we have been able to identify and trace the histories in whole or in part of twenty-three distinct AEC programs during the period of 1958–1972. While these programs do not represent an exhaustive categorization of all AEC activities, they are all "real" programs as distinct from mere projects on the one hand or "accounting categories" on the other. The twenty-three identified programs are mutually exclusive but are not exhaustive of all Commission activities, comprising on the average about 90 per cent of any given year's total AEC operating budget.[21]

Second, within each of the fifteen "budget cycles," FY 1958–FY 1972, we have isolated six discrete stages beginning with the program divisions' requests to the Commission's general manager and ending with the official presidential budget for a given year. The intermediate stages represent the general manager's recommendation to the Commission; the Commission's "September" submission to the Administration; the OMB's "mark-up" of the submission, and the "appeal" of the "mark-up," either to the Office of Management and Budget or the president.[22] Consider now the data reflected in Table 1.

In Table 1 we have ignored the programmatic breakdown of the fifteen AEC budgets and have simply correlated the requests for allocations for each stage across the fiscal cycles for which we have data. For these fifteen observations, the funds requested at a given stage correlate almost perfectly with that requested at a previous stage and that granted at a subsequent stage. The perfection of these correlations is powerful support for Wildavsky's basic argument about the regularities of the budgetary process, but it suggests very little about the political conflicts which we *know* were taking place during the period spanned by this data. For, within this apparently stable framework, five substantial AEC programs were cancelled altogether, two major activities experienced a sharp monotonic decline in their fortunes, three grew impressively, and most others fluctuated widely. Moreover, the picture is not very much different at the program than at the agency level.

When requests and allocations are correlated at the program level there is on the whole less close association across stages but the average magnitude of the correlation coefficients is still quite high. Most are in the .80–.90 range, and out of twenty-three programs only four show associations of less than .70 between pairs of stages. So, even at places where conflict is *known* to have occurred, the budgetary process perspective merely uncovers "striking regularities." Simply changing the units of analysis, that is to say, does not uncover the underlying political competition that structures the process of policy formulation; a more profound change is required.

It is at this point that we come to manipulating budgetary data themselves, to transforming dollars so that they will better reflect the competitive struggle for growth, for continued (or renewed) prosperity. The elements that we have to work with are: the agency in which programs operate (i.e., the administrative context), the past success or failure of a program in obtaining funds, and the action that is taken on program requests as they pass through the budgetary cycle (i.e., a program budget from initial request to final presidential decision).[23] The raw data, of course, come in the form of absolute dollar levels of programs from year to year. And it is by transforming and recombining these data that we hope to create an "index of prosperity" which will reflect the relative political success or failure of programs as they compete for scarce resources. Such an index has to meet two different problems of comparability.[24]

The first has to do with the variation in the total AEC operating budget between FY 1958 and FY 1972, which was, of course, by no means constant over that period. In Table 2, we have computed the sum at each stage of the twenty-three programs on which we have calculated data. It varies from year to year, ranging from a low of $2006.3 million in FY 1967 to a high of $2568.5 million in FY 1963.[25]

It seems reasonable to argue that programs are equally prosperous only if each preserves its proportion of the total even as the total changes both from year to year *and* across the stages of budgetary process. A first step, then, toward operationalizing the notion of "prosperity" is to divide all program allocations at

Table 2

Total at Each Budget Stage for 23 AEC Programs (In $ Millions)

Fiscal Year	Division Request	General Manager	Commission	OMB	Appeal	Final
1958	2170.9	2059.1	2199.1	2081.2	2083.2	2076.6
1959	2414.9	2235.4	2267.9	2253.9	2253.9	2252.3
1960	2575.7	2501.7	2510.9	2447.5	2472.7	2451.0
1961	2494.3	2409.6	2368.8	2206.6	2310.3	2296.4
1962	2538.7	2499.2	2491.1	2285.3	2306.5	2343.0
1963	2586.2	2428.7	2447.5	2389.8	2592.3	2568.5
1964	2781.2	2468.5	2586.6	2366.7	2548.3	2381.4
1965	2505.1	2428.1	2447.0	2294.5	2283.1	2239.6
1966	2323.8	2251.4	2257.4	2104.0	2195.3	2129.1
1967	2213.6	2098.1	2118.2	1986.0	2034.4	2006.3
1968	2399.9	1999.1	2110.1	2005.8	2053.6	2026.4
1969	2438.2	2272.8	2269.8	2151.7	2225.3	2180.5
1970	2376.0	2238.9	2274.4	2104.8	2169.9	2037.4
1971	2469.4	2285.1	2303.9	2024.4	2121.0	2013.7
1972	2420.7	2179.5	2150.7	1962.6	1990.2	1980.5

all stages by the total for that stage. This procedure, however, leads to a second problem of comparability.

There is great variation in the absolute magnitude of program budgets. Among the twenty-three AEC programs for which we have data, several have budgets in the $5–10 million range, and a few have budgets that were greater than $400 million. The obvious consequence is that each of the smaller programs is a tiny proportion of the total agency budget and is thus "lost" for analytical purposes. For example, one of the most politically controversial AEC programs is "Plow-share," a project to develop non-weapons applications for nuclear explosives. This program has never commanded more than one per cent of the total Commission budget.

We need to normalize the percentages obtained by dividing each program budget by the appropriate total so that these small programs are not made to seem insignificant out of sheer tininess. To adjust for this problem we have first calculated for each budget stage a program's *mean* proportion of the total for that stage across either (a) all the years spanned by our data, or (b) when a program began or was cancelled within that period, the years during which the program existed. We have then divided a program proportion of the total for each stage/year by this mean and multiplied the quotient by 100, converting to a percentage. The effect is to normalize these percentages so that they average 100 for the period FY 1958–FY 1972, or, when appropriate, for the years a program existed. We believe that the characteristics of this index and its behavior over time are highly suggestive of the process of competitive growth, i.e., "prosperity" in which we are interested. Eventually we shall want to use "prosperity change scores." This is the numerical difference of the prosperity scores across years for a given stage and will be zero when a program's proportion of the stage total does not change over the years.

At this point, it is useful to state these arguments more formally. For a full array of budget observations for programs over a number of years across each budget stage, $D_{(i,j,k)}$, where

$i =$ programs (1–23 in the case of the AEC),
$j =$ a specified budget stage (1–6),
$k =$ years,
$T =$ Total agency budget for the sum of all programs

the corresponding array of prosperity scores, $P_{(i,j,k)}$ is defined as:

$$P_{(i,j,k)} = (Pr_{(i,j,k)}/\text{mean } p_{(i,j)})*100$$

where

$$\text{(a) } Pr_{(i,j,k)} = D_{(i,j,k)}/T_{(j,k)}$$

for

$$T_{(j,k)} = \sum_{i-1}^{23} D_{(i,j,k)}',$$

and where

$$\text{(b) mean } p_{(i,k)} = Tp_{(i,j)}/Ic_{(i,j)}'$$

for

$$Tp_{(i,j)} = \sum_{k-1}^{15} Pr_{(i,j,k)}',$$

and

$Ic_{(i,j)} =$ the number of years for which the ith program in the jth stage > 0.

In Table 3 we present the scores for four programs within the AEC, all of which show striking variance in prosperity. In fact, all twenty-three programs exhibited a lively and theoretically interesting variance, but limitations of space preclude discussing them all.[26]

We see quite vividly the growth, decay, and fluctuation of which we have spoken—all within the context of a roughly constant total budget. These variations were caused by political events, not the operation of a budgetary process. The sudden reversals in the fortunes of "Rover" were caused by various officials of three administrations having attached sharply different priorities to the undertaking. The competitive success of high energy physics resulted in part from the

Table 3

Four AEC Program Histories Expressed as "Prosperity Scores"

Fiscal Year	Rover (Nuclear Space Rocket)	High Energy Physics	Sherwood (Controlled Thermonuclear Research)	Nuclear Weapons (Research
1958	25	20	87	69
1959	19	25	95	75
1960	28	34	130	67
1961	34	36	95	68
1962	56	51	88	80
1963	128	82	86	94
1964	187	118	83	92
1965	165	107	80	109
1966	174	122	92	105
1967	173	144	103	104
1968	131	149	108	110
1969	145	147	109	122
1970	103	156	114	129
1971	94	154	123	133
1972	33	150	97	136

constant attention of the Atomic Energy Commission Chairman with a strong interest in pure research. High energy physics did not grow "accidentally" or "naturally"—indeed none of these curves represents any sort of "natural process." On the contrary, each is the record of a sequence of priority settings made within a political system. Programs do not naturally grow, decline, or remain constant, or anything else. They are caused to do all of these by politicians and administrators making often difficult choices among competing claims upon scarce resources.

This "authoritative allocation of values" is the essence of the political process, that is vividly portrayed in these prosperity scores. The relative stability of "Sherwood" (controlled thermonuclear research) is not an illustration of organizational process in Lindblom's terms.[27] Sherwood has remained constant, has *resisted* competing claims upon its share of the Commission budget, only because it has been supported by the Commission, the Office of Management and Budget, and the president. Its constant level of prosperity is an indicator of stable political support, not of the operation of some "budgetary constant." Its support could have evaporated completely much like the nuclear rocket program's (Rover)—a program which received high priority in the early years of the Kennedy administration only to be completely abandoned.

Alternatively, consider the history of weapons. This has been a truly prosperous enterprise and one with an especially suggestive administrative history. The circumstances surrounding the 1950 presidential decision to build thermonuclear bombs left the Atomic Energy Commission with little influence over the future of this program.[28] The function of the Commission came to be one of merely fulfilling requirements for nuclear explosives in the establishment of which it played no role. The AEC, that is, played no role in setting the priority of weapons relative to other nuclear activities or among types of weapons. The competition for resources among the latter took place with the relative priority of weapons already set by forces external to the Commission. The weapons program record of continuous prosperity is largely the story of the consequences of the actions taken in 1950. The program emerged from the "great thermonuclear debate" with a very real competitive advantage over other AEC programs. Weapons was a "stronger" program.[29]

These measures of prosperity permit us to summarize AEC program activities since 1956. We could, of course, just subtract a given program's prosperity in FY 1958 from its score in the FY 1972 and rank the program according to the numerical value of the result. The "net prosperity change" is not, however, an especially helpful number. Now, we can recover exactly the same rank ordering by working instead with "prosperity change scores." For any program, the mean of the distribution of these change scores across all fifteen yearly intervals is also an indicator of how that program has prospered during the period for which we have data. The numerical value of these indicators, moreover, has an instantly appealing interpretation. A glance at Table 4 shows that since FY 1958 fifteen programs have prospered and eight have not.

What does all this have to tell us about how priorities are established within government? There is growing interest in examining federal budgets to determine how the nation is allocating its resources and exercising its spending priorities. The authors of one of the best and most recent of such studies correctly point out that in order to understand what the federal budget for any one year says about the national priorities, one must pay attention to past trends.

> In determining priorities and formulating the federal budget, the President and his advisors do not start with a clean slate, deciding *de novo* how ... the expenditures for fiscal 1972 should be allocated in meeting national goals. Recent history, prior commitments, current political realities, relations with Congress, economic and social events beyond the control of budget makers— all play a major role in limiting their ability to change radically the current shape of the budget. What they consider desirable must be tempered by what they consider feasible.... The margin of truly free choice is surprisingly small.[30]

Still, patterns of obligation and expenditure do change even at the aggregated federal level. Schultze and his colleagues, too, have found impressive variation in the objects of government expenditures over time. They proceed to infer changing priorities from changing absolute outlays.[31] But we also know that programs are in explicit competition with each other as they move jointly

Table 4

Arithmetic Mean of Prosperity Change Scores, FY 1958–FY 1972, 23 AEC Programs (Presidential Budget)

Rank	Program	Mean
1	High Energy Physics	9.0
2	Nuclear Safety	8.1
3	Program Direction and Administration	7.1
4	General Reactor	6.1
5	Biology and Medicine	5.4
6	Cooperative Power	5.1
7	Weapons	4.5
8	Naval Reactors	4.5
9	Civilian Power	4.3
10	SNAP	4.1
11	Plowshare	3.5
12	Isotopes	3.3
13	Sherwood	0.57
14	Rover	.43
15	Euratom	.08
16	Training, Education, and Information	−2.2
17	Advanced Systems	−2.8
18	Special Nuclear Materials	−3.5
19	Pluto	−4.0
20	Army Reactors	−7.0
21	Merchant Ship	−7.7
22	Raw Materials	−13.6
23	Aircraft Nuclear Propulsion	−25.6

through the budget formulation process. A measure of relative priority levels must take account of this competition.

The prosperity index developed in the preceding pages does so; it extracts from each individual budgetary observation *a meaning determined by its context.* The essential idea here is that the individual budgetary figures must be seen as the product of two quite different processes. One is the *budgetary process,* the public accounting that organizations give for the dollars that they receive. The stress here is on organization, the continuing complex hierarchy of government—bureaus, divisions, agencies, and departments. And the key to understanding administrative behavior in these terms is in the incremental nature of the process. The other is the *policy process.* Here emphasis is on the competition among programs for scarce resources which are needed to expand, or to continue, or even to begin. The central problem in analyzing political competition between programs is to make the information about each comparable. Dollars are the operational unit of administration. Political competition is something else again. The great difficulty in untangling these two aspects of the budgetary process is that they occur simultaneously.

The methodological problem this poses can be handled by a series of transfor-

Table 5

**Product-Moment Correlations Prosperity Change Scores,
Presidential Budgets FY 1958–FY 1972 with Weapons Program**

Raw Materials	−0.47
Special Nuclear Materials	−.25
Civilian Power Reactors	−.13
Cooperative Power Reactors	−.32
Euratom	−.19
Merchant Ship Reactors	−.28
Army Reactors	ns*
Naval Reactors	ns
American Nuclear Propulsion	ns
Pluto	ns
Rover	ns
SNAP	−.26
General Reactor Technology	−.44
Advanced Systems	−.10
High Energy Physics	−.29
Sherwood	−.37
Biology and Medicine	−.24
Training, Education, and Information	ns
Isotopes	−.17
Plowshare	−.25
Program Direction	−.23

   *ns = not significant

mations which in general affect different observations in different numerical ways but whose result is a set of numbers which now may be compared freely among themselves. Inspection of these numbers confirms the fundamental proposition of this preliminary analysis: in the context of the "massively stable" processes cited by other scholars, there is considerable variation in the fortunes of federal activities *at the program level.* We believe that the explanation of this variance constitutes the real challenge for further empirical analysis of budgetary data.

Analyzing Federal Budgets

What has been the nature of the competition among programs? Has it been a "war of all against all" or are certain activities capable of causing other less strong programs to "pay" for their prosperity either by exercising first claim upon newly available resources or by actually growing at the expense of lower priority activities?

Professor Russett has suggested that we may be able to recover some evidence about the extent of such "benefits" or "payments" by examining the patterns of co-variation among yearly changes in program levels.[32] Since we now have strong *a priori* reason to believe the Atomic Energy Commission's weapons program to have been independent of other Commission activities for the past twenty years, the intercorrelation of changes in weapons prosperity with those in the other twenty-two programs seems especially pertinent. They are reported in Table 5.

It is clear that everyone pays for defense. With the exception of the Commission's various military reactor enterprises (the largest group among those with insignificant correlations) all AEC programs change scores are negatively associated with changes in the weapons program. As anticipated, the relationship between prosperity changes in raw materials and weapons is high and negative. Decay in the prosperity of the former has been strongly associated with the growth of weapons. But the latter has evidently not only benefited from the decline of this program, it has also in Russett's sense been able to make other programs, notably general reactor technology and controlled thermonuclear research, "pay" for its prosperity.

The difficulty with such patterns of co-variation is that, though fascinating, they may also be *wholly spurious*. Certainly they do not in themselves illuminate the real causal processes which produce variation in the prosperity of programs. At most, the *sign* of the associational measure, particularly when it is negative, may provide some clue about the right questions to be asked. Thus in the case of the AEC weapons program one could plausibly accept the overall pattern of inverse association as empirical confirmation of what we suspect on independent grounds. But positive correlations among prosperity change scores have no obvious causal interpretation and the meaning of differences in magnitude between any pair of negative coefficients is totally obscure. More important, the co-variation patterns cannot tell us why some programs are stronger than others. Assuming the competitive struggle for limited funds is not exactly a war of all against all, what is it that makes some more equal than others? Is it strong directors who make for strong programs by "running a tight ship" and by "effectively generating support at the agency and congressional levels?"[33] Directors generating such support are able to neutralize opposition by the most potent natural enemy, the Office of Management and Budget. Programs which are supported at the Commission, the Office of Management and Budget, presidential and congressional levels are prosperous; programs which are not supported soon fall victim to the exigencies of the budgetary process.[34]

This widely accepted professional wisdom, then, contains a clear theory of the governmental process. National priorities are not set by administrators with national constituencies; they are set at the operating levels of federal bureaus—by program directors sensitive to their own clienteles. National priorities are established by bureaucratic entrepreneurship in a process which settles priorities without anyone being aware of them. In this regard, Davis, Dempster, and Wildavsky's stochastic models perpetuate a fundamental error about the way government operates. The whole metaphor of an inert bureaucratic machine doing the same thing this year that it did last year misses the basic point. Priority setting in the federal bureaucracy resembles nineteenth century capitalism: Priorities are established by aggressive entrepreneurs at the operating levels of government. Programs prosper because energetic division directors successfully build political support to withstand continuous attacks upon a program's resource base by competing claims. As a consequence, the only matters which reach the president are those already in dispute. At the presidential level the administrative process is less one of "policy-making" than "dispute-settling." It is at this level that things are accepted simply because they have been accepted, that the desirable has to be adjusted to the feasible. On the whole, the differences which count, the actions which produce the patterns of relative prosperity and strength we have discussed occur at lower levels of the administrative process.

All of this is missed by taking the Wildavsky and Lindblom perspective. By concentrating on the underlying regularities of the administrative process, these scholars are obliged to argue (in effect) that except for learning adjustments, no changes of any significance occur. We have seen that real change does occur within this "massive stability," reflecting real conflicts over purpose and priority. The more telling point about the process is that the program director, the operating-level bureaucrat, is a central figure in the determination of public policy. The history of the Atomic Energy Commission's weapons program is far more typical of the way public values are allocated than is the dramatic termination of the aircraft nuclear propulsion program.[35]

This is a strong theory, and we must be careful to stress that our discussion is limited to the single agency on which we have data. But if this fact makes us somewhat cautious, we also feel that the concepts we have specified and the theory which underlies them are probably more—not less—applicable to other areas of government. The Atomic Energy Commission has been a fairly stable agency both in administrative organization and actual spending levels for the last ten years. That we find such great variation in the relative prosperity of programs here seems to suggest that we can expect greater fluctuations elsewhere, particularly in the controversial areas of social policy.[36] Do program directors occupy the same crucial position throughout the government? Is there more or less presidential leadership in other policy areas? For what programs is congressional intervention truly a significant factor?

These are the type of questions that need to be asked. By translating budgetary data into actual operating units of government programs, students of public administration should be able to provide more than speculative answers. Prosperity scores are themselves an important step in this direction, for they establish a measure of program prosperity and decay.

Notes

1. The "traditional" literature on the budgetary process is immense. The text and references in either Arthur Smithies, *The Budgetary Process in the United States* (New

York: McGraw-Hill Book Company, 1955), or Jesse Burkhead, *Governmental Budgeting* (New York: John Wiley and Sons, 1956), provide convenient guides. Of particular interest are: Richard E. Neustadt, "The Presidency and Legislation: The Growth of Central Clearance," *American Political Science Review,* 48 (September, 1954), 641–671; Arthur Maass, "In Accord with the President's Program," in C. J. Friedrich and K. Galbraith, eds., *Public Policy,* 4 (Harvard University Press, Cambridge, Mass., 1954), 77–93; Fritz Morstein Marx, "The Bureau of the Budget: Its Evolution and Present Role," I and II, *American Political Science Review,* 39 (August and October, 1945), 653–684 and 869–898; and Lucius Wilmerding, Jr., *The Spending Power* (New Haven: Yale University Press, 1943). The notion of an "action forcing" mechanism is, of course, Richard E. Neustadt's.

2. Aaron Wildavsky's highly influential *The Politics of the Budgetary Process* (Boston: Little, Brown and Co., 1964) is the watershed. The ideas embodied in this analysis were more precisely formulated in Otto A. Davis, M. A. H. Dempster, and Aaron Wildavsky, "A Theory of the Budgetary Process," *American Political Science Review,* 60 (September 1966), 529–547. See also, by the same authors, "On the Process of Budgeting: An Empirical Study of Congressional Appropriations," in *Papers on Non-Market Decision Making,* ed. Gordon Tullock (Charlottesville: Thomas Jefferson Center for Political Economy, 1966), pp. 63–133. This general analytic approach has been importantly extended by John P. Crecine. See his "A Computer Simulation Model of Municipal Resource Allocation" (paper delivered at the Midwest Conference of Political Science, April, 1966), as well as *Governmental Problem Solving* (Chicago, Ill.: Markham Pub. Co., 1969). See also Ira Sharkansky, *The Routines of Politics* (New York: Van Nostrand, 1969)

3. See in this regard Charles Lindblom, "The Science of 'Muddling Through,' " *Public Administration Review,* 29 (Spring, 1959), 79–88; and Charles Lindblom, *The Intelligence of Democracy: Decision Making Through Mutual Adjustment* (New York: The Free Press, 1965).

4. Davis, Dempster, and Wildavsky, p. 543.

5. See Arthur Maass, "In Accord with the President's Program," for an excellent discussion of the great subtlety and variation with which this phrase is used.

6. For a thorough review of one such cycle, see Irvin C. Bupp, "Priorities in Nuclear Technology: Program Prosperity and Decay in the USAEC, 1956–1971" (Ph.D. dissertation, Harvard University, 1971), chap. 1.

7. Davis, Dempster, and Wildavsky, pp. 540–543, do make explicit provision for deviant cases in their analysis. These are cases that lie beyond the normal rules of budgeting that they describe; they are also cases that presumably involve controversy, change, and innovation in the budgetary process. This line of thought is further developed in their subsequent article: "On the Process of Budgeting II: An Empirical Study of Congressional Appropriations," *Studies in Budgeting,* eds. R. F. Byrne, A. Charnes, W. W. Cooper, and D. Gilfords (North Holland, Amsterdam, 1971), pp. 292–375.

8. Davis, Dempster, and Wildavsky, p. 529.

9. Davis, Dempster, and Wildavsky, p. 534.

10. Davis, Dempster, and Wildavsky, p. 537.

11. Richard Fenno, "The House Appropriations Committee as a Political System: The Problem of Integration," *American Political Science Review,* 56 (1962), 310–324. See also Richard Fenno, *The Power of the Purse: Appropriations Politics in Congress* (Boston: Little, Brown and Co., 1966).

12. Herbert A. Simon, *Administrative Behavior,* 2nd ed. (New York: Macmillan, 1957); Herbert A. Simon, *Models of Man* (New York: Wiley, 1957); Herbert A. Simon, Donald Smithburg, and Victor Thompson, *Public Administration* (New York: Knopf, 1950); David Braybrooke and Charles Lindblom, *A Strategy of Decision* (New York: The Free Press of Glencoe, 1963); Richard Cyert and James March, eds., *A Behavioral Theory*

of the Firm (Englewood Cliffs: Prentice-Hall, 1963); H. A. Simon, "Theories of Decision Making in Economics and Behavioral Science," *American Economic Review,* 59 (June, 1959), 253–283; G. P. E. Clarkson and H.A. Simon, "Simulation of Individual Group Behavior," *American Economic Review,* 60 (Dec., 1960), 920–932.

13. Crecine, *Governmental Problem Solving,* p. 11.

14. Herbert Simon, "The Architecture of Complexity," Reprint No. 113 of the Graduate School of Industrial Administration, Carnegie Institute of Technology.

15. Compare: Thomas Dye, *Politics, Economics, and the Public: Policy Outcomes in the American States* (Chicago: Rand McNally and Co., 1966) with Cyert and March, and William Leiserson, *American Trade Union Democracy* (New York: Columbia University Press, 1959) with Crecine.

16. In policy terms the entire metaphor of normal and deviant cases is vastly misleading. With it, Davis, Dempster, and Wildavsky promote the idea that bureaucracy is largely inert, proceeding to do today essentially what it did yesterday, all without competition and controversy. The exceptions, by this logic, are reserved for a small number of deviant cases which involve "more complicated decision procedures."

The entire thrust of our argument is that the logic of the budgetary process involves public policies in a continuous struggle for scarce resources; that, if there is any "normal state of affairs" in the policy process, it is one of intense competition between programs for public funds. Further, this logic holds equally for policies that desire nothing more than to continue to do what they were doing last year. There is nothing simple or automatic about continuing. Again we must stress that we are speaking of policies and programs here, not the administrative framework in which they are managed. Thus when Davis, Dempster, and Wildavsky (pp. 544–545) suggest that the analysis of individual programs follow from the broad outlines established in their own work, we must respond that their emphasis on normal and deviant cases has started such research off in the wrong direction.

17. Roland N. McKean and Melvin Awshen, "Limitations, Risks and Problems," in *Program Budgeting: Program Analysis and the Federal Budget,* ed. David Novick (Cambridge, Mass.: Harvard University Press, 1965), p. 286.

18. For a thoughtful discussion which complements many of these points, see Charles L. Schultze, *The Politics and Economics of Public Spending* (Washington, D.C.: The Brookings Institution, 1968). Indirect, but vivid, support for many of the same arguments can be found in Charles L. Schultze, Edward R. Fried, Alice M. Rivlin, and Nancy H. Teeters, *Setting National Priorities: The 1972 Budget* (Washington, D.C.: The Brookings Institution, 1971). And at the municipal level see John E. Jackson's perceptive essay, "Politics and the Budgetary Process," *Social Science Research,* 1 (April, 1972), 35–60.

19. James R. Newman and Byron S. Miller, *The Control of Atomic Energy* (New-York: McGraw-Hill Book Co., 1948). See also David E. Lilienthal, *The Atomic Energy Years, 1945–1950* (New York: Harper and Row, 1964).

20. Richard G. Hewlett and Oscar E. Anderson, Jr., *The New World, 1939–1946, A History of the USAEC,* Vol. 1 (University Park, Pennsylvania; Pennsylvania State University Press, 1962); Richard G. Hewlett and Francis Duncan, *Atomic Shield, 1947–1953, A History of the USAEC,* Vol. 2 (University Park, Pennsylvania: Pennsylvania State University Press, 1969). . . .

21. One of the authors (Irvin Bupp) was for several years on the staff of the secretariat of the AEC and hence had access to the agency's internal financial records. This association led to AEC support under the auspices of the Office of the Historian for the research reported here.

It is perhaps also worth noting that the AEC is one of the very few executive agencies to have followed a generally consistent "output" format in its budgetary practices since its creation. This fortunate circumstance considerably simplified the problem of isolating and tracing distinct programs.

22. This fifth "appeal" stage is the only one not strictly comparable across all fifteen years. Records of this process were often difficult to locate, and for FY 1959 and FY 1960 there is no evidence that an "appeal" as such was allowed at all.

23. Congressional action is not included in our calculations, although a good case could be made for doing so. Congress is, after all, quite active in the budgetary process through its committee and subcommittee system; see Fenno, *Power of the Purse*. We are concerned, however, with the formulation of program budgets, not with their review. Congressional review of the budget really moves on to a different level of analysis. Of course, much of congressional influence is informal. As such, it should be entered into any explanation of why some programs prosper and others fail. This is again a different analytical problem from developing an index of program prosperity—the results of which can then be searched for appropriate causes.

24. For a somewhat different, but also highly imaginative, approach to this problem, see John Jackson, "Politics and the Budgetary Process."

25. For any given year or stage, the totals reflected in Table 2 are equal to about 90 per cent of the comparable total operating budget, the remaining 10 per cent being that portion of the AEC budget which we were unable to allocate to meaningful output categories. Since we are explicitly interested in competition among programs, the aggregated totals shown have been used as the basis for the transformation described in the text.

26. For a full discussion of all twenty-three programs, see Bupp, chapters 1–3.

27. Cf. Lindblom, "The Science of 'Muddling Through.' "

28. Hewlett and Duncan, pp. 362–409.

29. For a more careful definition of "program strength," see Bupp, chapter 2.

30. Schultze et al. (1971), *Setting National Priorities*.

31. Schultze et al., *Setting National Priorities*, pp. 19–21.

32. Bruce Russett, "Who Pays for Defense?" *American Political Science Review*, 63 (June, 1969), 412–426. See also, Bruce Russett, *What Price Vigilance: The Burdens of National Defense* (New Haven: Yale University Press, 1970), especially chapters 5 and 6.

33. These observations are based on a series of interviews with officials in AEC and the Office of Management and Budget.

34. Russett's substantive conclusions have recently been challenged. See Jerry Hollenhorst and Gary Ault, "An Alternative Answer to: Who Pays for Defense," *American Political Science Review*, 65 (Sept., 1971), 760–764.

By respecifying Russett's regression model to include several dummy variables, Hollenhorst and Ault claim to detect important "subperiod effects." This more methodologically sophisticated approach, however, seems to us merely to compound the original theoretical error. The posited relationshps are spurious.

35. See W. Henry Lambright, "Shooting Down the Nuclear Plane," Inter-University Case Program, ICP Case Series No. 104 (Indianapolis: Bobbs-Merrill, 1967).

36. Congress appears to be much more active in the area of social policy. An excellent account of administrative policy in this area refers again and again to congressional intervention in specific programs. See Gilbert Y. Steiner, *The State of Welfare* (Washington, D.C.: The Brookings Institution, 1971), or in a different area, Arthur Maass, *Muddy Waters: The Army Engineers and the Nation's Rivers* (Cambridge, Mass.: Harvard University Press, 1951).

3A.3. Making Sense of the Federal Budget the Old-Fashioned Way: Incrementally

BERNARD T. PITSVADA and FRANK D. DRAPER

Incrementalism came under heavy attack in the 1970s and 1980s. The massive and uneven budget cuts of the early Reagan years, the various deficit-driven plans for spending reductions, and the increasingly partisan structure of the budgetary process led many to conclude that incrementalism was either wrong or a less useful explanation than it once was. Even Wildavsky retreated somewhat, arguing that changes in Congress made incrementalism less applicable.

Pitsvada and Draper stand in the wind of this gathering consensus. Echoing much of the quantitative analysis of budgets, they argue that despite indications to the contrary, incrementalism remains the best single explanation of the budgetary process. They argue that there are just as many recent developments that are favorable to incrementalism as there are opposed to it. In particular, they cite the trend toward indexing budgets to inflation, projecting current budgets into the future, presenting budgets in terms of their departure from existing spending, and the heightened use of continuing resolutions that carry over the previous year's budget into the current year.

The reader should note that their arguments all justify the likelihood that there will be slow change from one year to the next. But even if this were true, it

*remains an open question whether slow change occurs because of incremental-
ism or for other reasons.*

Since Wildavsky and Fenno applied Lindblom's concept of pluralistically-based
incrementalism to the budgetary process during the 1960s, incrementalism has become the dominant analytical model for describing how budgeting in the federal
government really works.[1] The caricature of incrementalism that has arisen is that of
a decision-making process taken up for the most part with negotiations over increases and decreases to an existing "base," and not with a review of the budget in its
entirety. Over the years others have successfully elaborated and built upon what
remains the dominant paradigm in the field of budgetary research.[2]

The theory has not been without its many critics, however. One challenge that
was voiced almost immediately by Natchez and Bupp focused more on specific
programs within agencies rather than the "totals."[3] Thus, just because budgets
appear to be incremental (or decremental) in absolute dollar amounts, does not
always mean that base programs are being ignored, or that great changes in the
programs are not taking place. Others have accurately pointed out that when
annual changes in certain budget requests approach 20 to 30 percent, this strains
the traditional definition of incrementalism.[4] Then again, some critics have noted
that the "base" has different meanings.[5] For example, where the "base" is primarily a sum of transfer payments to individuals and organizations, agencies are probably less protective than when the "base" supports ongoing discretionary programs or
operating costs of agencies. There were, also, other voices of concern.[6]

Recent changes in the scope and nature of federal budgeting have brought the
status of incrementalism as an explanatory tool of how resources are allocated
into even more serious question. One recent article in the *Public Administration
Review,* for example, noted that changes in the budget process brought about by
the Budget and Impoundment Control Act of 1974, as well as Reagan administration attempts to dictate changes from the "top-down," diminish "the explanatory power of incrementalism" in periods of "budget shrinkage."[7]

We do not necessarily disagree with all the observations of the critics of
incrementalism. We do believe though that, on balance, incrementalism still
remains the best method of explaining and understanding budgets. We see five
basic factors of growing importance in federal budgeting that have added to,
rather than reduced the tendency toward incrementalism in budget analysis, and
thus have increased the utility of this approach. An examination of these factors
can bring into clearer focus the realities, as distinct from the rhetoric, surrounding budget decisions facing the federal establishment in mid-decade.

Indexing and Inflation

There are eight major federal programs that are indexed to the rate of inflation,
usually the Consumer Price Index (CPI). The programs range from the Social

Security System (by far the largest), to civil service and military retirement, to food stamps and child nutrition. These programs accounted for more than $195 billion of outlays in Fiscal Year 1982 (with Social Security payments accounting for about 70 percent of this amount), or more than one-quarter of all federal outlays that year. The Congressional Budget Office (CBO) Baseline Projections for Fiscal Year 1984–89 estimate that almost one-third of federal spending for that period is directly indexed. It is difficult to make a case that anything other than incrementalism directs these programs upward, since the rates of outlays are primarily increased by the incremental adjustment made for indices such as the CPI. While all these indexed programs are "entitlements," i.e., any person who meets the criteria stated in the enabling statutes is entitled to payments, it is hardly the number of new claimants that caused these programs to increase so greatly in the past few years. Without indexing or congressional action to increase payments there would probably not have been the Social Security "problem." We recognize that it is possible that Congress may have enacted legislation to increase these programs even more than the CPI (as it did in 1972 when Social Security benefits were increased by 20 percent), but Congress did not have to take such action because of indexing. Nevertheless, even if Congress had been required to pass periodic increases, Congress would probably have used some measure of the price level as a basis for protecting these programs from inflation.

The observation that may be made from this is that the more a budget contains indexed programs, the more it is likely to become incremental in nature. It will be incremental because indexing is an annual adjustment along a steady glide path related primarily to the CPI, and not a sporadic or periodic adjustment made by Congress every few years to "catch up" with past inflation. Such a situation holds true if the increase is, say, two percent or 12 percent because of the nature of how the added budgetary costs are calculated and applied. They simply are a net change, to an existing amount, that is established impersonally by rules based on previous legislation. The same situation theoretically would hold true if the CPI went down for a full year and entitlements were reduced to each eligible beneficiary.

When Wildavsky and Fenno wrote, they paid little attention to indexed programs or transfer payments such as Social Security. The combination of the two as we now know them did not even exist until the 1970s. Nevertheless, as transfer payments, indexed or not, become such a large part of the federal budget—the FY 1984 budget claims that 42 percent of outlays are transfer payments—the budget will likely become more incremental. Indexing merely ensures that a major part of it will.

Indexing represents just one method for coping with inflation. Another method, which is widely used for non-entitlement programs by the Department of Defense (DOD), is actually to budget for anticipated "cost growth," i.e., inflation. Since FY 1978, the DOD has been authorized by legislation (Public Law 94–361) to request additional obligational authority in the budget to cover the projected increased cost of purchasing defense-related goods. The budget justification material submitted to Congress by the DOD clearly differentiates increases from year to year for "program growth" and "cost growth." In fact, the DOD FY 1984 budget "reductions" proposed by Secretary Weinberger were, in part, the result of changing budgetary assumptions that projected a lower rate of inflation for that year than was originally expected. As a result the inflationary impact of these items purchased represents an incremental change to the budget.

Another long-standing method of budgeting for inflation is used by all federal agencies. The annual October pay raise for government employees is simply an inflation-based adjustment to existing federal pay levels. While the next October pay raise does not get included in the annual January budget submission, the impact of the previous year's pay raise is included in the budget as part of the existing agency base. The net result of this procedure is to cause a slow but steady creep upward in the budget as a mandatory cost of doing business.

Multiyear Budgeting

In his budget message that accompanied the FY 1980 budget, Jimmy Carter announced a relatively little-noticed budget reform that has also contributed to increasing the influence of incremental analysis in the federal budget. According to Carter, "For the first time, the budget reflects the 3-year budget planning system I have initiated to gain better control of the longer-range effects and direction of government policies."[8] By way of further explanation it was noted that while budgets since 1970 had displayed five-year projections of total outlays and receipts, agencies were now required to prepare budget requests by appropriation that extended two years beyond the budget year. This change was designed, among other things, to expand the government's planning horizon and identify long-term consequences of programmatic changes to the budget.[9] By displaying three-year costs it became necessary for agencies to project the future changes that current year programs would entail. Since such an approach does not call for analyzing prospective changes in resource levels resulting from additional *program changes* in future years, the basic approach must be limited to consider incremental adjustments to the *status quo* policy from the budget year. This change also has the effect of giving the first succeeding year a budgetary base accepted by all parties, including the OMB and Congress, from which to begin the next budget cycle. The focus of the next year's effort becomes the incremental change above the prior year base. This is almost a perfect description of Wildavsky's "aids to calculation."[10]

To confirm that this is in fact how budgeting proceeds we need only to examine the longest continuing multiyear budgeting effort in the federal government. When Robert McNamara, as secretary of defense, introduced his much-heralded Planning, Programming and Budgeting System (PPBS) into the DOD in 1961, a component part of that system was the Five Year Defense Plan (FYDP).

This so-called FYDP, which in reality is a seven-year display of resources (current year, budget year, and five program or "outyears"), is used as a basis of planning multiyear budgetary decisions and integrating various different appropriations into a single programmatic effort, such as building and fielding a Minuteman missile or Polaris submarine. Projecting budgetary outlays in a single year, such as the budget year, is a relatively imprecise science; projecting four years farther out is even more speculative. Nevertheless, the DOD usefully applied and still continues using the FYDP because outyears tend to be viewed as relatively minor extensions of the preceding year or years. The FYDP totals serve as a base from which the next annual cycle begins. Changes brought about by congressional action, cost growth, or strategic decisions are then implemented as incremental adjustments to the five-year program totals already in place. Thus, while some decisions made by the DOD hierarchy may be major and result in sizeable changes in future budgets, the *process* of making such changes within the DOD is viewed as incremental in that changes are applied to a given and accepted base that all participants use in program development. The use of this aid to calculation was never more apparent than when the Carter administration introduced Zero-Base Budgeting (ZBB) to the federal government in 1977. The Defense Department merely grafted ZBB onto its existing resource allocation mechanism, the PPB System. The DOD did not examine all resources from a zero base as the name implies but limited its analysis to 9 percent of the resources at the margin of its existing FY 1979–83 FYDP.[11]

While Wildavsky and Fenno both excluded DOD budgets from their studies, there is little reason to believe that other federal agencies do not follow a course similar to the DOD. It is simply easier and more realistic for agencies to operate this way. Once Congress sees outyear projections for a given program, adjustments to that program are likely to draw questions in terms of why projections changed incrementally as they come closer to reality. Multiyear budgets provide all actors in the process with a better basis for performing comparative analysis. If this were not the case budgets would not be structured to display prior-year, current-year, and budget-year totals side by side. Projecting two years beyond the budget-year merely provides more data upon which to focus in order to identify marginal changes from year to year. This is the stuff of which incrementalism is made.

Continuing Resolutions

Continuing resolutions are the authority Congress grants to agencies to continue obligating funds in the absence of an annual appropriations act. Such resolutions also act to further budgetary decision making by incremental steps.

Initially, the federal fiscal year was the same as the calendar year. But ever since the second appropriations act, in March 1790, Congress has had difficulty in passing appropriations before the beginning of the fiscal year.[12] It was this difficulty that caused Congress, in 1842, to change the date of the beginning of

Table 1

Enactment of Appropriation Acts, FY 1977–83

Fiscal Year	Passed House by Oct. 1	Enacted by Oct. 1	Enacted after Oct. 1	Not Enacted Separately
1977	13	10	3	60
1978	13	9	4	0
1979	13	5	7	1
1980	12	3	7	3
1981	12	0	8	5
1982	9	0	10	3
1983	5	1	5	7

the fiscal year from January 1 to July 1, and in the Budget and Impoundment and Control Act of 1974 from July 1 to October 1. Since the president is still required to submit the budget to Congress 15 days after Congress convenes in January of each year, moving the fiscal year to October 1 was designed to give Congress three more months to review the budget and pass the appropriate legislation. It has not worked out that way despite the best of intentions.

Table 1 reflects that over the last seven years late enactment of appropriations, and thus reliance on continuing resolutions, has become a fact of life for much of the federal government. (Of course, many federal programs operating on the basis of trust funds and/or permanent appropriations are not affected by the absence of annual appropriations acts. Such programs have standing legislative authority.) Even the House, which during Fiscal Years 1977 and 1978 had a reasonably good record in passing appropriations on time, has slipped in the last five years and especially the last two. One reason for the most recent difficulty in the House rests with the budget reductions proposed by the Reagan administration budget requests. As a means of resolving the heightened budgetary conflict brought about by these requests, Congress has employed a decision-making technique that attempts to cushion most of the areas of disagreement; that is, to resort to continuing resolutions. In this sense, a continuing resolution is the most incremental approach possible since it permits funding levels for agencies to be set based upon either or both houses' adjustment to the prior year totals or budget request.

The traditional approach in continuing resolutions places obligational authority at the lower figure of either house if both have passed separate bills but have not reconciled the differences; or if only one house has passed the appropriation, obligations may continue at the lesser amount appropriated or the current rate, which generally means the rate of the previous year.[13] The FY 1983 continuing resolution was somewhat different in that it set different rates of spending for various agencies by including much of the original appropriations act language in the resolution, thereby making it a sizeable piece of legislation. Nevertheless, Congress seemed intent on using the continuing resolutions as a means of putting its stamp on an incremental control of the budget. The one thing the Congress wanted to avoid throughout the entire review of the FY 1983 budget was the use of the reconciliation process as had been done the year before. The reconciliation process of the FY 1982 budget simply did too much violence to the legislative process. To allow budgetary decisions to be made on a once-and-for-all, "thumbs up" or "thumbs down" vote on a reconciliation bill flies in the face of Congress' conception of decentralized power. It would appear that as budgetary conflict increases, Congress uses continuing resolutions to restore order to the budget process by restoring the traditional grounds of negotiation, bargaining, and incrementalism. "Partisan mutual adjustment," "satisficing," "muddling through"—all part of the lexicon of the incrementalist approach to decision making—are what continuing resolutions seem to be all about.

Baseline Reviews

Section 605 (a) of the Budget and Impoundment Control Act of 1974 requires the president to submit a "current services" budget to the Congress each year. The law requires the submission "on or before November 10" but it has become customary to submit it along with the president's budget the following January. This current services estimate displays budget authority and outlays for the fiscal year ". . . if all programs and activities were carried on during such ensuing fiscal year at the same level as the fiscal year in progress and without policy changes in such programs and activities." Schick correctly points out that while the current services budget could be viewed as a neutral document, Congress has used it as a vehicle for achieving "incremental stability." According to Schick, "Congress institutionalized incrementalism in the form of the current services budget."[14] Congress has relied on the current services totals to represent the *status quo* and as a protection vehicle for agency "bases" and ongoing programs. The vehicle has also enabled certain non-indexed programs a degree of protection from inflation because what are displayed are totals designed to maintain a level of "services" rather than the current level of funding. Higher costs of doing the same work can be accommodated in a current services budget.

In addition, the same legislation (Section 202 (f)) also requires the Congressional Budget Office to submit by April 1 of each year a report to the Budget Committees which reflects budgetary options, which means alternative levels of revenues, outlays and budget authority. For the FY 1984 budget this report took the form of three separate reports. The key report was called *Baseline Budget Projections for Fiscal Years 1984–1988*. This document provided the CBO alternative to the executive branch estimates and projections. Considerable confusion resulted in the review of the budgets for Fiscal Years 1982 and 1983 because both branches insisted upon using their own baselines, which were different because of differing economic assumptions. Regardless of the differences, the key point is that established baselines were used by both the Congress and the administration. In some ways these baselines have substituted for the president's budget request as the point of departure for decision making.

Budgetary baselines, even though they represent multiyear projections which are not forecasts of future outcomes, tend to have the same incremental effect as the Defense Department's Five Year Defense Plan or multiyear budgets. They provide what the CBO calls "a useful starting point," which is given a great deal of credibility in the budgetary process. It is possible to view these multiyear projections as extending the concept of the single year budget base into a multiyear budget base. This has been how agencies that did not operate off a multiyear planning process, such as the Five Year Defense Plan, have tended to interpret the figures. Certainly these multiyear estimates were designed for other reasons: they were primarily intended to give Congress a multiyear view of its past actions and to preclude seeing just the "nose of the camel." Nevertheless, since the practice started in the mid-1970s (at about the same time that it became widely recognized that we were entering a period of fiscal constraint), Congress was quick to recognize that such documents had a strategic as well as informational use. A strong point in favor of budgetary baselines is that they can be used in the alliance between the participants in the "Iron Triangle" (i.e., congressional committees, agencies, and constituency groups) against an administration that attempts major budgetary changes. Baselines are sacred for these participants and incrementalism preserves baselines.

Incremental (Decremental) Budget Displays

There remains one other major force supporting incrementalism. Agencies prepare their respective budgets from a basically incrementalist perspective. How else can we explain how budgets resisted change when faced with major reforms imposed by presidents in terms of the way budgets were to be prepared? Neither the PPB System nor ZBB caused major changes to agency budgets. These two, so-called "rational-comprehensive" models of budget preparation were supposed to change how agencies looked at, prepared and justified their budgets. If this had really happened why was this not reflected in budgetary outcomes? While "top-down" perspectives may have expected programs to be evaluated against one another in the PPB System, or alternative levels of funding among existing programs to be "ranked" in ZBB, neither really came to pass. Congress rejected the PPB system and Wildavsky recounts the tale of how the House Appropriations Committee even threatened to abolish funds for an agency's office that had prepared the PPB documents.[15] The assessment of congressional use of ZBB was generally along similar lines.[16] In the end, agencies eventually presented their budgets to Congress in much the same way they had always done: reflecting incremental changes.

Just a cursory look at any agency's budget request document to Congress (as well as to the OMB) reflects how incrementally-oriented the display of budget material is, and how the display is designed to draw out incremental decisions. This display is a part of all agencies' "justification books." These books are submitted to Congress in conjunction with the president's budget request. They provide a more detailed explanation of the budget, primarily in terms of where and why this budget makes changes to agency activities and programs. The format and size of these justification books differ from agency to agency. They do, however, have one common thread: just like the president's budget they tend to focus on a three-year period—past year, current year, and budget request year. "Trails" are provided showing increases and decreases over these years. Congressional review of these budgets proceeds along similar lines. Thus, while the books display an agency's total budget request, the book is really an incremental adjustment. Appropriately,

> ... programs that continue at about the same level of funding from year to year are generally not highlighted for the simple reason that they show no change.... On the other hand, new programs or activities are displayed in greater detail for scrutiny because they represent changes from the preceding year. This structure, when coupled with the display of past year totals for comparison purposes, is at the heart of the Congressional incremental budget review.[17]

Conclusion

Probably the most compelling reason that supports an incremental view of the federal budget is the common sense one. We accept the fact that the budget is a reflection of societal needs as embodied in programs enacted by Congress as representatives of the majority will of "the people." If Congress is a reasonable reflection of popular will, then Congress simply enacts programs that people want. If it can be assumed that popular wants do not change drastically from year to year, neither should the budget, if one is a reasonably accurate reflection of the other. Thus, for example, permanent entitlement programs, protected from inflation, represent a baseline of stability that is reflected in how budgets are prepared and what they contain. Only drastic social upheaval (war), major depression, or revolution are likely to change this. (The first Castro budget was probably a lot different from the last Batista budget.) Changes in political philosophy do obviously change budgets; budget "systems" do not. As one official who actively participated in his state's implementation of ZBB said: "One's political philosophy [and the acceptance of such a philosophy] is far more important than one's budgeting technique in determining the size of government."[18] Political philosophies do not change all that often. Nor do budgets. To expect budgets to vary significantly from year-to-year, while at the same time expecting social needs and wants to remain relatively stable from year-to-year defies logic in a democratic society.

Also, if one introduces a time perspective to the stability surrounding budgets, it is easy to understand why some participants in the budget process, such as those in the "Iron Triangle," still cling essentially to incremental analysis. At any given point in time a federal agency is executing one budget, probably defending another budget before Congress, preparing a third budget to submit to the OMB, and planning subsequent year budgets. These various budgets, by definition, must relate to one another since that is how agencies perceive them.

Further, in any process that results in increases or decreases to programs, compromises weigh heavily on budgetary outcomes. But the great bulk of resource allocation decisions occur below the threshold of outside observation. What results is a relatively stable pattern of bureaucratic decision making that considers bureaucratic expectations, routines and arrangements—all factors that tend toward stability and incrementalism. Ironically, the "problem" with stability (i.e., increments or decrements to an existing base) is that it is not very visible. "Top down" budget making, which might be called the "big bang" approach, makes headlines; the "long whimper" mode (decremental budgeting) usually does not.[19] Any president can immediately attract attention by the threat of the "big bang," or a radical change in a program. Let the OMB issue annual guidance, however, to agencies to prepare their budget requests for the coming fiscal year at alternative levels of funding only slightly above or below last year's funding and the event goes unrecorded. Yet, the latter is often of more significance to an agency. Proposed severe reductions, for example, are easier for an agency to defend against; it is the drops of water over time that really cause the damage. As one observer of how the "big bang" approach is used in killing programs has noted,

> Because the conflict generated by big-bang termination efforts is more public and intense, examples of this process (both successful and unsuccessful) are easier to identify and more interesting to study. Indeed, how do you even distinguish a serious but unsuccessful attempt to achieve termination through decremental budgeting from the normal fluctuations in the policy budget? *There is no empirical evidence to suggest that termination occurs more frequently or more successfully as a result of sudden and vigorous efforts than as a result of a prolonged and subtle one. The big-bang mode is simply easier to identify and study.*[20] (Emphasis added)

Others have noted similar typology in killing programs by decremental budgeting.[21]

In summary, the federal establishment uses incrementalism because over the years incrementalism and all its trappings—indexing, multiyear budgeting, continuing resolutions, baseline reviews, and budget displays—provide a useful tool in avoiding and sometimes solving budgetary conflict. Incrementalism is reflective of stability, something that lawmakers and administration officials like to project more often than not. At the same time incrementalism is a two-edge sword: with stability has also come a steady and inexorable growth in federal expenditures. But here again incrementalism has something to say for itself. For just as incrementalism provided the vehicle for growth in the 1970s, so decrementalism (or at least a slower incremental path) may be the only realistic way of curbing growth in the remaining years of the 1980s. The radical paring of programs that occurred beginning in 1981 would appear to be going nowhere in the environment of mid-1980s. Considering the vested interests that are entrenched behind current programs, i.e., the "Iron Triangle" participants, the use of decremental budgeting may well be the only viable alternative in reducing such growth. The fact that this may occur from the "top-down," by either the OMB, the president, or by congressional budget resolution, is immaterial. Whoever said that incrementalism (or decrementalism) had to be exclusively a "bottom-up" approach?

Notes

1. Charles Lindblom, "The Science of 'Muddling Through,'" *Public Administration Review* 29 (Spring 1959), 79–88, and Lindblom and Robert Dahl, *Politics, Economics and Welfare* (New York: Harper & Row, 1953); Aaron Wildavsky, *The Politics of the Budgetary Process* (Boston: Little, Brown and Company, 1964); and Richard Fenno, *The Power of the Purse* (Boston: Little, Brown and Company, 1966).

2. For example, O.A. Davis, M.A.H. Dempster, and Aaron Wildavsky, "A Theory of the Budgetary Process," *American Political Science Review* 60 (September 1966); Peter B. Natchez and Irwin C. Bupp, "Policy and Priority in the Budgeting Process," *American Political Science Review* 67 (September 1973); and Ira Sharkansky, "Agency Requests Gubernational Support and Budget Success in State Legislatures," *American Political Science Review* 62 (December 1968).

3. Natchez and Bupp, *op. cit.*

4. See, for example, Charles Schultze, *The Politics and Economics of Public Spending* (Washington, D.C.: The Brookings Institution, 1968), p. 77ff.

5. John R. Gest, " 'Increment' and 'Base' in the Congressional Appropriations Process," *American Journal of Political Science* 21, No. 2 (May 1977), 242; and Mark S. Kamlet and David C. Mowery, "The Budgeting Base in Federal Resource Allocation," *American Journal of Political Science* 24, No. 4 (November 1980), 808–810.

6. See, for example, Lance T. Le Loup, "The Myth of Incrementalism: Analytical Choices in Budgetary Theory," *Polity* (Summer 1978), 488–509; and John J. Bailey and Robert J. O'Connor, "Operationalizing Incrementalism: Measuring the Muddles," *Public Administration Review* 35 (January/February 1975), 60–66.

7. Barry Bozeman and Jeffrey D. Straussman, "Shrinking Budgets and the Shrinkage of Budget Theory," *Public Administration Review* 42 (November/December 1982), 509–515.

8. *The Budget of the U.S. Government, Fiscal Year 1980,* Budget Message (Washington, D.C.: U.S. Government Printing Office, 1979), p. 7.

9. *Ibid.,* p. 31.

10. Wildavsky, *The Politics of the Budgetary Process, op. cit.,* p. 15.

11. Frank D. Draper and Bernard T. Pitsvada, *A First Year Assessment of Zero-Base Budgeting in the Federal Government—Another View* (Arlington, Va.: Association of Government Accountants, 1978), p. 3.

12. See Stanley Katz, "The Federal Fiscal Year: Its Origin and Prospects," *National Tax Journal* 13, No. 4 (December 1959), 346–366.

13. Robert W. Hartman, "Congress and Budget-Making," *Political Science Quarterly* 97, No. 3 (Fall 1982), 392.

14. Allen Schick, *Congress and Money* (Washington, D.C.: The Urban Institute, 1980), p. 217.

15. Aaron Wildavsky, *Budgeting* (Boston: Little, Brown and Company, 1975), p. 313.

16. Frank D. Draper and Bernard T. Pitsvada, "Congress and Executive Branch Budget Reform: The House Appropriations Committee and Zero-Base Budgeting," *International Journal of Public Administration* 2, No. 3 (1980), 331–374.

17. Frank D. Draper and Bernard T. Pitsvada, "Limitations in Federal Budget Execution," *Government Accountants Journal* 30, No. 3 (Fall 1981), 22.

18. Quoted in Allen Schick and Harry Hatry, "Zero-Base Budgeting: The Manager's Budget," *Public Budgeting and Finance* 2, No. 1 (Spring 1982), 85.

19. The terminology is that of Robert D. Behn, "How to Terminate a Public Policy: A Dozen Hints for the Would-Be Terminator," in Charles H. Levine, ed., *Managing Fiscal Stress* (Chatham, N.J.: Chatham House Publishers, 1980), 327–342.

20. *Ibid.*, p. 338. Since Behn's article was written—it first appeared in *Policy Analysis* in 1977—there has been, however, one "big bang" event: the demise of the Community Services Administration (CSA). After attempting in the early 1970s to abolish the Office of Economic Opportunity (OEO) by the "big bang" approach (requesting no appropriations for it in the second year of its authorization), and after finding its path blocked by Congress and the courts, the Nixon administration chose the decremental route: Using his executive authority, Nixon scattered OEO's responsibilities and its organizational units throughout the federal government. OEO's successor, the Community Services Administration, picked up what budget pieces were left and was then subjected to a decremental budget attack over the next several years. The agency had a mild comeback in FY 1977, only to see its budget slip away from it once again in the Carter years. By that time, after nearly a decade of the "long whimper," President Reagan administered the "big bang" (though some might call it the coup de grace). No new obligational authority was requested for it in FY 1982 and the last of its outlays were due to be expended in FY 1983.

21. See, for example, W. Henry Lambright and Harvey M. Sapolsky, "Terminating Federal Research and Development Programs," *Policy Sciences* 7 (June 1976), 199–213. Of particular relevance for today's decision makers is Lambright and Sapolsky's examination of the successful attempt during the 1970s to abolish NASA's Sustaining University Program (SUP), a program designed to aid students who were training in doctoral fields relevant to aerospace. A series of decremental budgets, ranging from $46 million to $9 million over four years, finally resulted in the program's abolishment in FY 1970. As the authors noted, "Rather than confronting the students and universities with a stark decision that would have affected their interests immediately, the decremental approach gave them time to adjust, to seek new support, or to learn to live with less" (p. 203).

3A.4. Bureaucracy: Servant or Master? Lessons from America

WILLIAM A. NISKANEN

Pluralist explanations of budgeting see spending as determined by political con-flict between beneficiaries and providers of different public goods. Incremental-ism sees budgeting as determined by the limited capacity of politicians and bureaucrats to analyze and process information. Niskanen, a former official in the Office of Management and Budget, sees budgets as determined by a bureau-cracy that is out of control.

Niskanen argues that just as managers in private firms have interests that do not always match those of stockholders, bureaucrats have interests that may be different from those of the public they serve. He thinks that the most important of these contrary interests is the desire to expand the size of the bureaucracy. He also feels that bureaucrats also have much better information about the value of their program than the politicians they serve, enabling them to pull the wool over the eyes of their nominal masters. Taken together, these two elements give bureaucrats both the desire to spend more than is socially justifiable and the ability to achieve their ends. He proposes a variety of structural changes in the bureaucracy, such as privatization and bureaucratic competition, to reduce the severity of this problem.

The reader should note that Niskanen's ideas have been extremely influential during the last fifteen years, most obviously within the Republican Party, but also with some Democrats and nonpartisan city managers.

Reprinted with permission from *Bureaucracy: Servant or Master? Lessons from Amer-ica* by William Niskanen (London: Institute of Economic Affairs, 1973), pp. 7–27.

I. An Economic Model of Bureaucracy

... This Paper outlines an alternative model of the behaviour of bureaus, both to explain a larger set of our contemporary perceptions about bureaucracy and to suggest changes in the nature and use of the bureaucracy to make it more responsive to the public interest. ...

The three elements of a theory of supply by bureaus are the following: (a) the distinguishing characteristic of bureaus, (b) the nature of the relations between bureaus and their environment, and (c) the maximand[1] of bureaucrats. The *critical* elements are the smallest set of characteristics, types of relations, and elements in the maximand that are necessary to develop hypotheses concerning that part of the behaviour of bureaus that is the subject of study.[2]

A. Concept and Functions

Main Characteristics of Bureaus

Bureaus are defined as those organizations that have *both* of the following characteristics:

1. Their owners and employees do not appropriate any part of the difference between revenues and costs as personal income.

2. Some part of the recurring revenues derive from other than the sale of output at a per-unit rate.

In a single sentence: *Bureaus are non-profit organizations that are financed, at least in part, from a periodic appropriation or grant.*

The first characteristic includes all non-profit organizations, such as all government agencies and enterprises, most educational institutions and hospitals, and the many forms of social, charitable, and religious organizations. It clearly excludes corporate businesses, partnerships, and sole proprietorships.[3,4]

The second characteristic includes all non-profit organizations that receive a periodic appropriation or grant. They include most non-profit organizations. Some government enterprises (such as power and transportation authorities) and private non-profit organizations are excluded by this characteristic, as their recurrent operations are financed entirely by the *sale* of output at a per-unit rate (even though they may have been established initially by an appropriation or grant).

The Product

What goods and services do bureaus specialize in providing? A clue to the answer is the second characteristic. Bureaus specialize in providing goods and services that some people prefer in larger amounts than would be supplied by their sale at a per-unit rate, e.g. defense. People with such preferences form or join collective organizations and contribute resources to them. In various ways, either through political processes or by moving, people choose their government and thus 'agree' to be taxed to provide resources to augment the supply of these goods and services. . . .[5]

Some other characteristics of the goods and services supplied by bureaus can be derived from the primary characteristic. Many goods and services supplied by bureaus are characterized by (i) high fixed costs of production or (ii) by difficulties in collecting fees, caused either by the definition of property rights or by the technology of marketing. It is incorrect, however, to interpret these secondary characteristics as rigidly defining the role of bureaus. They provide many goods and services that can be marketed quite adequately. . . .

Why Supply by Bureaucracy?

In the contemporary environment, when most goods and services that are augmented by collective action are supplied by bureaus, it is often difficult to understand the functional and historical bases for choosing bureaus, rather than profit-seeking organizations, to supply these services. The primary functional reason is the difficulty of defining their characteristics sufficiently to contract for their supply. This difficulty leads collective organizations to organize directly the supply themselves, hoping to substitute loyalty to the collective organization for the motivation of profits. The early bureaucracies were largely staffed by slaves, clerics, and sons of the nobility—individuals with a relatively low pecuniary motivation or those whose loyalty was more fully assured; the civil servant and the professional military officer are their modern counterparts. Around this functional basis there has developed a surprisingly pervasive ethical attitude (usually reinforced by the bureaucracy) that it is somehow wrong for an individual to profit by the supply of educational services, hospital services, and military forces.

The very problem which leads to the supply of some services by bureaus (the difficulty of defining output) creates one of the more important problems of controlling bureaus in any condition for which the objectives of the bureaucrats are not completely consistent with those of the collective organization. The difficulty of defining the desired characteristics also makes it difficult to give appropriate instructions to the bureaucrat. . . .

A more complete definition of the role of bureaus would be the following: bureaus specialize in the supply of those services that some collective organization wishes to augment beyond that supplied by the market and for which it is not prepared to contract with a profit-seeking organization. This is the most general possible definition, consistent with the recognition that the role of bureaus differs among environments, depending on the preferences of individuals and on specific institutional conditions.

'Bureaucrat'

The term 'bureaucrat' will sometimes be used in the more general sense to define any full-time employee of a bureau; in this sense the term is nearly synonymous with 'civil servant', although the latter term also often implies a full-time career employee. For the most part, however, the term will be used to define the senior official of any bureau with a separate identifiable budget. (Most large bureaus will include component bureaus, so there will usually be more than one bureaucrat, in this sense, in large bureaus.) These bureaucrats may be either career officials or directly appointed by the elected executive. . . .

Any form of organization, including bureaus, will differentially reward those whose capabilities and attitudes best serve the organization, and people will sort themselves out among forms of organization depending on their perceived reward. Bureaus reward a different type of personal behaviour from other forms and, as a group, bureaucrats will be individuals who are most adept at this type of behaviour. If bureaus differentially reward behaviour that other people consider undesirable, the pejorative connotation of the term 'bureaucrat' is neither surprising nor inaccurate. Bureaucrats are not 'just folks' any more than ball players, businessmen, and bishops are 'just folks'. They have different latent or developed characteristics, just as individuals in other professions have different characteristics. As individuals, bureaucrats are neither inherently superior nor inferior, but it is unwise not to recognise that they have some differentiating characteristics. . . .

B. Bureaus and Their Environment: The 'Marriage'

A bureau's environment is defined by its relations with three groups: first, the collective organization which provides the bureau's recurring appropriation or grant; second, the suppliers of labor and material factors of production; and third, in some cases, the customers for services sold at a per-unit rate. Of the three, a bureau's relations with its sponsor most strongly distinguishes its environment from that of other forms of organization.

The Sponsor

Most bureaus are financed by a single or dominant collective organization, usually a government department, which in turn is financed by tax revenues or by more or less compulsory contributions.[6] The officers of the collective organization are usually elected by a larger constituency but are often effectively self-perpetuating. These officers review the bureau's proposed activities and budget, approve the budget, monitor the methods and performance of the bureau and, usually, approve the appointment of the bureau head. As a consequence, the activities of the bureau head are largely dominated by his relations with the officers of the sponsoring organization. The sponsoring organization is usually dependent on a specific bureau to supply a given service, and the bureau usually does not have a comparable alternative source of financing. In the jargon of economics, the relation between the bureau and its sponsor is that of a 'bilateral monopoly'. As with all such relations (including conventional marriage), this relation is awkward and personal—characterized by both threats and deference, by both gaming and appeals to a common objective. No other type of relation combines threat, exchange, and integrative relations in such equal proportions. Such is the nature of the relation between a U.S. federal bureaucrat and Congress, between a university president and the state legislature (or the trustees of the university endowment), between a hospital director and the community fund, and between a research manager and the sponsoring agency. These relations could hardly be more unlike the rational-legal, impersonal relations which Max Weber finds characteristic of bureaucracy.

The Exchange Activity of Bureaus

What does a bureau exchange with its sponsor? *A bureau offers a promised set of activities and the expected output(s) of these activities for a budget.* The primary difference between the exchange relation of a bureau and that of a market organization is that a bureau offers a *total* output in exchange for a *budget,* whereas a market organization offers *units* of output at a *price.* The bureau's characteristic 'package' offer of a promised output for a budget has important implications for the behaviour of bureaus. Under many conditions it gives a bureau the same type of bargaining power as a profit-seeking monopoly that discriminates among customers or that presents the market with an all-or-nothing choice. The primary reason for the differential bargaining power of a monopoly bureau is the sponsor's lack of a significant alternative and its unwillingness to forego the services supplied by the bureau. Also, the interests of those officers of the collective organization responsible for reviewing the bureau are often best served by allowing the bureau to exploit this monopoly power. . . .

Characteristics of the Sponsor

The incentives, knowledge, and behaviour of the officers of collective organizations are probably more heterogeneous than those of the bureau. Nevertheless, some generalizations appear valid.

(a) Most important, the collective organizations are not profit-seeking. There is seldom any way for their officers to appropriate as personal income part of the difference between the budget they would be willing to grant and the budget they do grant to the bureau. On the contrary, some officers are more likely to be able to appropriate part of the bureau's expenditures as personal income or as a contribution to political party campaign expenses. The behaviour of elected officers can probably be best explained by the assumption that they wish to be re-elected or, at least, to be well regarded for the period of their elected service, and these incentives are only weakly related to the total net benefits generated by the services financed by the organization. The sponsors of many private bureaus are either other private bureaus (for example, foundations) or government bureaus.

(b) Also—possibly as important—there is usually a wide disparity in the relative information available to the sponsor and to the bureau. A bureaucrat can usually estimate his sponsor's demand quite accurately from previous budget reviews, recent changes in the composition of the sponsor organization, and recent constituent influences on their officers. As a rule, however, a bureaucrat will know much more about the costs and production processes of the bureau's services than will the officers of the sponsor. Previous budget-output offers by the bureau sometimes reveal little to the sponsor about the minimum budget that would be sufficient to supply a given output. A bureaucrat needs relatively little information, most of which can be estimated by revealed behaviour, to exploit his position as a monopoly supplier. The officers of the sponsoring organization, in contrast, need a lot of information, little of which can be estimated from revealed behaviour, to exploit their position as a monopoly buyer.

(c) Moreover, a bureaucrat has a stronger relative incentive and can work full-time to obtain the information relevant to his position (and to obscure information relevant to the sponsor). Most officers of private collective organizations and of state and local governments, however, serve only part-time. Even when nominally full-time, the officer usually has little incentive or opportunity to review the activities of the sponsored bureaus in competition with personal services for his constituents and other activities to assure his re-election. Although the nominal relation of a bureau and its sponsor is that of a bilateral monopoly, the relative incentives and available information, under most conditions, give the bureau the overwhelmingly dominant monopoly power.

Passive Role of Sponsor

For this reason, the theory developed here initially assumes a passive sponsor which knows the budget it is prepared to grant for a given quantity of services but does not have the incentive or the opportunity to obtain information on the minimum budget necessary to supply it. This assumption most accurately describes larger collective organizations (such as central governments) which finance a number of services and are faced by monopoly suppliers. It is less accurate for small functionally specialized collective organizations, where the officers have a personal relation with the constituents, the production processes are simple, and there are potential alternative sources of supply. The assumption of a passive sponsor and monopoly bureaus is probably most applicable to central governments, less applicable to local governments, and least applicable to private collective organizations like churches and country clubs.

Wage and Cost Discrimination

Most bureaus hire most labor and materials in competitive markets. Although the supply price to a single bureau or a set of bureaus may increase with the quantity hired, most bureaus must pay the same price for all similar labor or material. Under these conditions, a bureau's employment and procurement practices will be similar to those of a comparably sized profit-seeking firm.

Labor legislation, the automobile, and unions have destroyed most wage discrimination (among employees with comparable skills in a given firm) in the private labor market, and most similar material factors are traded at a common price. For several reasons, however, the bureaucracy is the last stronghold of wage and factor price discrimination. First, although such 'monopsony'[7] discrimination is not general among bureaus, it is more widely practiced than among profit-seeking firms. The first basis for wage and factor price discrimination is that bureaus are often monopoly suppliers of some services. These bureaus are thus also monopoly buyers of those labor skills and material factors that are specialized in the production of the monopolized services. Infantry officers are paid less than pilots in the same staff or management position, for example, because they have few alternative employments where they can market their specialized skills. . . .

The second basis for 'monopsony' discrimination is that bureaus often have a prior claim on resources considered to be in the public domain: healthy and intelligent young men, nuclear materials, land, the electronic frequency spectrum, the air space, etc. First-term soldiers are paid less than career soldiers in the same position because the military can often draft[8] more first-term manpower. The military pays less (zero) for nuclear materials and public land than for non-nuclear weapons and other land performing the same function, because it can usually command more of them from another bureau. . . .

Such opportunities for 'monopsonistic' discrimination are exploited by bureaus because it increases their budget and output. In addition, the transfer of resources from another bureau or regulatory commission at less than their opportunity cost (the wages, etc., they could command elsewhere) also increases the latter's budget or regulatory power. The exercise of wage and factor price discrimination is primarily limited to *national* bureaus (particularly the military) because of their stronger monopoly power, use of specialized resources, and command of the public domain. It should not be considered a general characteristic of bureaus.

Customers

Some bureaus, in addition to a recurrent grant from a collective organization, receive revenues from the sale of output to individuals at a per-unit rate (price).

This condition is characteristic of universities, hospitals, country clubs, cultural organizations, government printing offices, and postal services. These bureaus, in effect, face two groups of customers with different demands for the same service—one is represented by a collective organization financing the supply of services by a grant, the other directly buys them at a price. Mostly the group of customers includes, but is not limited to, the constituents of the collective organization.

When a bureau is strongly dependent on the revenues from the per-unit sale of services, its relations with customers will be similar to those of a profit-seeking business. It is interesting to contrast the general connotations of the terms 'bureaucratic methods' and 'business-like methods'. In bureaus, the attention to customer interests depends on the addition to the total financing (revenue) that originates in the sale of a service; in profit-seeking firms, this attention depends on the addition to total profits. A bureau whose sponsor is willing to compensate for any loss of revenues from sales, or that is a monopoly supplier of a service with a nearly fixed demand, will usually be quite indifferent to the interests of its customers, even if a large proportion of the total financing is from sales revenues. The indifferent treatment of the customers in state-financed schools and hospitals, under these conditions, should be expected. . . .

C. The Bureaucrat's Maximand

What, if anything, do bureaucrats maximize? . . . An economist's initial response will be that a bureaucrat, like anyone else, maximizes his personal utility. By itself this is not very helpful, but it does suggest that he will engage in *purposive* behaviour and that there are probably some elements in his utility other than the general welfare and the interests of the state.

The Theory of the Firm

The economist's theory of the firm provides suggestions on how to look for a less abstract proxy for a bureaucrat's utility. The businessman is represented as being unambiguously selfish. There may be elements in his utility other than personal income, but there are no prior assumptions that he has any personal interest in either efficiency or the general welfare; for some conditions these may be *consequences* of his purposive behaviour, but they are not the *objectives*. The central motivational assumption of this theory is that a businessman maximizes the profits (or, more precisely, the present value) of the firm.

Two types of arguments are advanced to support the plausibility of this assumption: rationality and survival. First, profit maximization by a competitive firm is demonstrated to be a property of rational behaviour (that is, consistent with utility maximization) if the labor which the businessman contributes to the firm is independent of his income.[9] This condition is determined culturally, but appears to be a more or less accurate representation of real life. Second, profit maximization by a competitive firm is demonstrated to be a property of organizational survival; some businessmen, for a time, may choose to maximize something other than profits, but if entry costs are low they are likely to be replaced by profit-maximizing businessmen. . . .[10]

Why a Bureaucrat Maximizes His Budget

What objective proxy for a bureaucrat's motive is suggested by the two corresponding rationality and survival arguments? These arguments are necessary to establish the plausibility of the central motivational assumption sufficiently for the theory to be seriously considered and tested. The 'proof' of the theory, of course, will depend on whether the hypotheses developed are generally consistent with observed behaviour.

(i) The Rational Bureaucrat on the Treadmill. First, the rationality argument. Among the several variables that may enter the bureaucrat's motives are: salary, perquisites of the office, public reputation, power, patronage, output of the bureau, ease of making changes, and ease of managing the bureau. All except the last two are a positive function of the total *budget* of the bureau during the bureaucrat's tenure.

The problems of making changes and the personal burdens of managing a bureau are often higher at higher budget levels, but both are reduced by *increases* in the budget. This effect creates a treadmill phenomenon, inducing bureaucrats to strive for increased budgets until they can turn over the management burdens of a stable higher budget to a new bureaucrat. Hence an interesting cyclical pattern emerges: bureaucrats interested in making changes resign when budgets are stabilized; their replacements will be satisfied with the other rewards of high budgets, or strive for further increases or, possibly, cut the budget in order to provide a basis for further increases.

A bureaucrat's utility need not be strongly dependent on every one of the variables which increase with the budget, but it must be positively and continuously associated with its size.[11] For these reasons, budget maximization should be an adequate proxy even for bureaucrats with a relatively low pecuniary motivation and a relatively high motivation for making changes 'in the public interest'. This conclusion is supported by the observation that the most distinguished U.S. public servants of recent years substantially increased their budgets.

The budget maximization assumption is not necessarily based on a cynical interpretation of the personal motivations of bureaucrats. Some bureaucrats, by either predisposition or indoctrination, undoubtedly try to serve (their perception of) 'the public interest'. A bureaucrat, however, is neither omniscient nor sovereign. He cannot acquire all the information on individual preferences and production opportunities that would be necessary to divine 'the public interest', and he does not have the authority to order an action that is contrary to either the personal interests or the different perceptions of 'the public interest' by other bureaucrats or officers of the collective organization. In a competitive industry, one profit-maximizer is often sufficient to induce all other firms to be profit-maximizers. In contrast, in a bureaucratic environment, one person who serves his personal interests or a different perception of public interest is often sufficient to *prevent* others from serving their perception of 'the public interest'. It is *impossible* for a single bureaucrat to act in 'the public interest', because of the limits on his information and the conflicting interests of others, regardless of his personal motivations. This leads even the most selfless bureaucrats to choose some feasible lower-level goal, and this usually leads to developing expertise in some narrow field. The development of expertise usually generates a sense of dedication, and it is understandable that many bureaucrats identify this dedication with the public interest. Moreover, as discussed below, a bureaucrat who may not be personally motivated to maximize the budget of his bureau is usually driven by internal and external conditions to the bureau to do just that. One should not be surprised, therefore, to hear the most dedicated bureaucrats describe their objective as increasing the budget for the service(s) (defense, education, housing) they provide. . . .

(ii) The Will to Survive. The survival argument reinforces the budget maximization assumption. Two groups of people significantly influence a bureaucrat's tenure in office: the employees of the bureau and the officers of the collective organization. The reasons for their interest in budget maximization by the bureaucrat are different but reinforcing.

A bureau's employees (the suppliers of other factors should also be included in this group) indirectly influence a bureaucrat's tenure both through the bureaucrat's personal rewards and through the real and perceived performance of the bureau. They can be co-operative, responsive, and efficient. Or they can deny information to the bureaucrat, undermine his directives, and embarrass him before the constituency and officers of the collective organization. Their behaviour depends on their perceived rewards of employment in the bureau. The employees' interests in larger budgets are obvious and similar to that of the bureaucrat: more opportunities for promotion, more job security, etc., and more profits to the contract suppliers of factors. A bureaucrat's life is not a happy one (tra la!), unless he can provide increasing budgets for his subordinate bureaucrats to disburse in salaries and contracts.

The powers of the collective organization over the bureaucrat's tenure are more obvious, but their interests in his budget maximization are not. They nominate and confirm the appointment of the bureaucrat and can force him to resign; so they have direct control of his tenure. One point, however, is not generally understood: both the executive and legislative officers reviewing the bureau fully expect the bureaucrat to propose aggressively more activities and higher budgets.

Indeed, they would not otherwise know how to perform their review role.[12] They lack the time, the information, and the staff necessary to formulate new programs. They depend on the bureau to seek out and propose these and to make a case for larger expenditures in old programs. The total activities and budget of most bureaus are beyond comprehensive understanding so the executive and legislative officers focus most of their review on the proposed *increments* and reveal their priorities by approving different proportions of them. At every stage of a multistage review process, the review officers are dependent on the bureaucrat to make a forceful case for his proposed budget, in part to determine whether a previous review has made too large a reduction. Any other behaviour by the bureaucrat would reduce the information on which such reviews are made. . . .

For some bureaucrats, for some time, budget maximization may not be rational behaviour (that is, consistent with the maximization of their utility); but the nature of their relations with both the bureau's employees and sponsor are such that bureaucrats who do not maximize their budget will have an unusually short tenure. . . .

(iii) The Constraint on Budget Maximization. Budget maximization is a necessary but not sufficient statement of the central motivational assumption of this theory of supply by bureaus. What limits the size of bureaus? More specifically, what ultimately relates the available budget to the necessary costs? . . .

The constraint that ultimately limits the size of bureaus is that, on the average, they must supply that output expected by the sponsor on its approval of the budget. A bureau that consistently promises more than it can deliver will be penalized by the discounting of future promises and therefore lower budgets. Conversely, a bureau that performs better than expected is likely to be rewarded by higher future budgets. As the output of most bureaus (even, sometimes, the *concept* of output) cannot be precisely determined, there will be substantial *variance around the expected output.* . . .

A complete statement of the central motivational assumption of this theory is thus: bureaucrats maximize the total budget of their bureau during their tenure, subject to the constraint that the budget must be equal to or larger than the minimum total costs of supplying the output expected by the sponsor. Added to the earlier definition of bureaus and a description of their environment, this motivational assumption about the maximand is the third critical element from which a theory of supply by bureaus is developed. . . .

II. General Conclusions on the Behaviour of Bureaus

Bureaus Are Too Large

The one most important general conclusion of my model of elementary bureaus is that they are too large. For given demand and cost conditions, they supply a quantity of services larger than would maximize the net benefits of the service. Most of the other conclusions about the behaviour of bureaus derive from this conclusion. At this point, it is valuable to identify those conditions in the government and legislature for which this general conclusion is relevant. Why cannot legislatures exercise their monopoly power as the single buyer of a bureau's services to confine the bureau to a lower, more nearly optimal output level? The two, rather general, conditions in a representative government that lead to acceptance of the bureaucratic equilibrium are:

1. A large national legislature, as a body, essentially serves as a representative referendum, either approving or failing to approve the proposed budget without the opportunity for significant amendment. Sometimes this is due to the rules and procedures necessary to conduct business in a large legislature, such as formal limitations on debate and amendments. More importantly, the legislature *does not usually have an alternative source* of supply of the service that is available at a *price*. This gives the bureau the opportunity to pursue proposed expenditure programs on an either-or, all-or-nothing, take-it-or-leave-it basis. The proposed expenditure program may generate net benefits only to those with high relative demands and who supply factors to the bureau and still be approved by the majority of the legislature.

2. The detailed review of a bureau's proposed budget is usually performed by a specialized committee within the government and/or legislature that is dominated by representatives of groups in the population with relatively high demands for the bureau's service (e.g. high-risk patients) or who own factors used by the bureau (e.g. a trade union of teachers). This general condition, in turn, results (1) from conditions that make the political *benefits* of spending proposals accrue primarily to their advocates while the political *costs* of the necessary taxes accrue to the entire body of elected officials, and (2) from the nature of the selection process for these review groups. As a consequence, advocacy of spending programs tends to be concentrated and the opposition is diffused. The incentives of the review group are not identical with those of the bureau, but they are usually consistent. As a rule, the interests of the review group are served by forwarding the bureau's proposal, with minor modifications, for approval by the legislature. The primary activity of these review groups is to make minimum changes in the proposed budget necessary to gain its approval.

These two conditions are characteristic of representative government, particularly national, but they are not inevitable. And changes in them, discussed below in Section III, provide promising opportunities for reducing the grossest bureaucratic abuses of the public interest.

The model has been extended to other aspects of bureaucratic behaviour, to more complex bureaus, and to different conditions in the sponsoring government. The general conclusions are summarized in the following section.

Production Behaviour

Most bureaus have an incentive to seek out and implement the most efficient combination of factors and production processes for a given quantity of output. This suggests that the general concern about the productive efficiency of bureaus is often misplaced, but there are three qualifications:

1. The *strength* of the incentive for productive efficiency is not as large as in a profit-seeking firm. In a business operating on a 5 per cent profit margin on sales, for example, a 5 per cent reduction in costs leads to a nearly 100 per cent increase in profits. In a bureau, however, a 5 per cent reduction in costs would lead to a somewhat smaller than 5 per cent increase in its budget. This difference in impact leads a bureaucrat to opt for an easier life at a somewhat lower level of efficiency than the same man would in a profit-seeking firm.

2. Many bureaus face factor costs (wages, fringe benefits, fees, rents, etc.) that are lower than their full value, due to the exemption from many forms of taxes and the reservation of some factors for government use. This will lead bureaus to over-use factors that are relatively underpriced to the bureau.

3. Some bureaus, most importantly those for which the demand has grown rapidly, have *no* marginal incentive for productive efficiency. This condition is limited and usually temporary, but probably explains most of the observed inefficiency of production by the bureaucracy. . . .

Distribution of Net Benefits

The bureaucratic supply of services generates disproportionately large gross benefits to people with the highest demands and to those who own the factors used by the bureaucracy. In the unconstrained bureaucratic equilibrium, all the net benefits accrue to people with high demands *relative to their share of taxes* and to owners of factors the bureaucratic supply of services generates *negative* net benefits to people with low demands relative to their share of taxes. The income distribution of their net gains and losses (other than the net gains to owners of factors) depends on a comparison of the income elasticity of demand[13] for these services and the progressivity of the tax schedule. If the income elasticity of demand is higher than the income elasticity of tax payments, most of the net benefits accrue to high-income groups; if lower, they accrue to low-income groups.

III. An Agenda of Alternatives

This final section summarizes three general types of alternatives to the bureaucratic supply of public services. The first set involves changes to or within the bureaucracy. The second involves changes in the sources of supply of public services, primarily involving market alternatives. The third involves changes in political institutions and processes.

In the aggregate, these alternatives are not a package deal. Some of the proposed changes would be valuable whether or not other changes are made. The national governments of large nations and the bureaucracies that supply services financed through them are now serving their citizens rather badly. In these conditions, an experiment with any portion of these changes should improve their performance.

A. Bureaucratic Alternatives

The major changes suggested by this evaluation are in the structure of the bureaucracy and changes in the incentives of bureaucrats. The value of the proposed structural changes is independent of the proposed incentive changes but is dependent, in part, on changes in the review process. The value of the proposed incentive changes, however, is largely dependent on the proposed structural changes.

1. Competitive Bureaucracy

The most important change would be to increase the competition among bureaus. . . . Competition among bureaus operates to reduce the inefficiency characteristic of a monopoly bureau in several ways. First, the reduction in demand and the increase in the elasticity of demand for the service supplied by any one bureau makes it likely that any bureau, other than one with a substantially superior production process, will have a budget-maximizing incentive to seek out and use efficient production processes. Second, budget proposals from the several bureaus give the review committee a better basis for identifying an inefficient budget proposal from a single bureau. These conditions increase the probability that the review committee will identify and approve a lower total budget for a given quantity of output than if the service were supplied by a monopoly bureau. One other effect of the competition among bureaus is likely to be a wider diversity of production processes, and this can be very important for services like national defense to insure against the catastrophic failure of any one process.

Competition among bureaus reviewed by a department secretary or legislative committee representing the high-demand group does not directly reduce the more general problem of the over-supply of the service, because the review committee is likely to choose the same quantity of output as would be chosen by a monopoly bureau—specifically, the largest output that would be approved by representatives of the middle-demand group. The competition among bureaus, however, increases the probability that one bureau will be strongly dissatisfied by the results of the review process. On occasion a dissatisfied bureaucrat may end-run the department or review committee and force the selection from among the several budget output proposals to be made by the President, or by the aggregate body of representatives where the representatives of the middle demand group have the decisive vote. Competition among bureaus thus tends to reduce the monopoly power of review groups dominated by representatives of the high demanders by providing a known alternative to the proposal and forcing the selection from alternatives outside. . . .

2. Incentives to Maximize Bureaus' 'Profit'

A second major change, which maintains the bureaucratic supply of services but changes the incentives of bureaucrats, should be considered. The general feature would be some form of reward to senior bureaucrats to induce them to maximize, not the total budget, but the difference between the obtainable budget and the minimum total costs of the service. A change with this general feature would create, in effect, a modified profit system within the bureaucracy. The primary value of changing the incentives of senior bureaucrats in this way is that it reduces both the problem of inefficiency and the problem of over-supply characteristic of the conventional monopoly bureau. Such a change in the incentives of bureaucrats would be desirable only in a competitive bureaucracy, because the maximization of the difference between total budget and total cost would lead to the under-supply of a service by a monopoly bureau. So this second bureaucratic alternative should be considered only in the context of the first.

Reward Systems

A system of rewarding senior bureaucrats to induce them to maximize the difference between total budget and total cost could take one of three forms. These reward systems are ranked in order of declining effectiveness but, probably, in order of increasing probability of being acceptable to our political institutions in the near future.

(i) *Personal rewards.* The first system would allow the senior bureaucrats to appropriate as personal income some proportion of the difference between the approved budget and the costs of supplying the approved quantity of output. The 'property right' in this income augmentation should probably be limited to bureaucrats whose appointment is subject to political confirmation. This reward system, of course, would work well only in bureaus supplying services for which the output is relatively easy to measure. . . .

(ii) *Deferred prizes.* The second type of reward system would pay senior bureaucrats large deferred 'prizes' for unusually efficient management. It would be less effective than the first system but probably more acceptable.

Senior bureaucrats would be paid only a salary during their tenure in office. Some period after they left office, say, after five years, they would be eligible to be considered for a set of large monetary prizes. The prize committee would consist of respected citizens, representing the major parties, with long overlapping tenures; new members of the prize committee would be nominated by the current executive and confirmed by the legislature. The prizes would be awarded on the consistency of the output of the bureau during the bureaucrat's tenure with the output promised in the budget-output proposals and the amount of funds the bureau returns to the general fund during this period. Individual prizes may be awarded to single former bureaucrats or to a group of senior former bureaucrats from a single bureau. The prizes should be quite large relative to annual salary and possible income after leaving the bureau. . . .

(iii) Increased freedom of action—'allowed activities'. The third type of reward system would permit bureaucrats to spend a proportion of the difference between the approved budget and the cost of approved programs on a restricted set of allowed activities, but would not permit them to appropriate any part of it as a direct augmentation of personal income. This system would be less effective than either of the first two, but it is substantially more acceptable. Indeed, a reward system of this general type is implicit in the practice of giving the best bureaucrats somewhat more management discretion and amenities. . . .

Summary

Better analysis and accounts, in some conditions, can improve the performance of the bureaucracy, but more generally the marginal value of analysis in support of the bureaucracy is either ambiguous or zero. In any event, better analysis and information are not a general solution to the problems of bureaucracy. The superior performance of market institutions is not due to their use of better or more analysis. Indeed, most of the formal, 'sophisticated' resource allocation analysis now serves the bureaucracy. The primary differences in the performance of different organizations are due, rather, to differences in their structure and the incentives of their managers. Some part of the analytical resources now serving the bureaucracy would clearly be better invested in further developing the understanding of our political institutions and the organizations which supply public services.

B. Market Alternatives

If the structure and incentives in a bureaucracy have to be changed so much to improve its performance, why not rely more on private markets, where this structure and incentive system now exist? A partial use of private sources of supply of public services from either profit-seeking or non-profit firms can be valuable (whether or not significant changes are made in the bureaucracy and the review committees) by providing the service at a price known to the representatives of the average voter from a source that is not administratively dependent on the bureaucracy and review committees. A private source of supply can significantly reduce the monopoly power of the bureaucracy and the review committee, even if its costs are higher than the minimum possible costs of bureaucratic supply and even if the private source of supply is not used.

A wide range of services financed by government are also marketed, or are potentially marketable, in the private sector. These services have the characteristic that there are direct private benefits to their consumers and presumed benefits to a more general public from their consumption by, at least, some groups; the available marketing technology must also permit the exclusion of non-paying potential consumers motivated by the private benefits.

The government's interest, in this case, is to augment the total supply on the presumption (seldom precisely defined, and almost never measured) that there are public, non-marketable marginal benefits. Where the government's primary interest is the income of certain groups, of course, a direct unrestricted income transfer or, if this created adverse effects on work behaviour, a wage subsidy, would be the most efficient form of government activity. Where the government's interest is dependent on the consumption of specific services, a direct per-unit subsidy is entirely appropriate and is usually the most efficient form.

Per-Unit Output Subsidies

If the public benefits are independent of the groups that consume the service, the most efficient form of subsidy is usually a per-unit output subsidy to producers, which leads to an expansion of general consumption by reducing the price to all consumers. The government subsidy goes directly to the producers, but the government makes no prior determination of the distribution of the subsidy among producers and does not intervene in the production process. Such a subsidy could take the form of paying a fixed amount per unit for the entire output (or, more efficiently, the additional output above some base-period output) to farmers, universities, hospitals, etc., for specific goods or services supplied by these organizations. Where the government's interest is to increase the general consumption, it is usually more efficient to subsidise output at a per-unit rate, but only because the administrative costs of dealing with producers are lower than the costs of channeling the subsidy through consumers. The consequences of a general output subsidy and a general consumption subsidy would be the same. . . .

Group Consumer Subsidies (Vouchers)

If the public benefits of a service are dependent on which group consumes a service, the most efficient form of subsidy is generally a voucher for a specified amount or value of the service granted directly to members of the restricted group.[14] Vouchers could take the form of food stamps, rent vouchers, tuition vouchers, travel vouchers, etc., that may be restricted to members of families with low incomes, students, or some other identified group. Restricted output subsidies granted to the producers could take the form of scholarships, lower medical charges, or lower-price tickets available only on identification as a member of the target group. There is not much difference in the economic effects of these two approaches. . . .

Private Supply of 'Pure' Public Services

Many services financed through government are 'pure' public services for which the same output is supplied to everyone, and non-paying beneficiaries cannot be (efficiently) excluded. The traditional functions of government—defense, law and order, etc.—are the characteristic examples. In some cases, these services would not be supplied at all in the absence of government financing. And at the present time most of them are supplied through bureaus.

Some parts of the inputs to the production of these services, however, are usually supplied under contract by profit-seeking firms. In the U.S., for example, most buildings used by bureaus are constructed by private firms; most military weapons, equipment, and supplies are developed and produced by private firms; the food services in government buildings and military bases are usually supplied by private firms.

For these services, the primary market alternatives to provision by bureaucracy involve the use of private firms to organize a 'higher' stage of the production. At the next 'higher' stage than the supply of buildings and equipment, private firms could bid to maintain buildings and even some weapons systems. At a next 'higher' level, private firms could bid to supply instrumental services, like many of the training activities now provided by the military services or the operation of computer facilities. At a still 'higher' level, private firms could bid on management contracts to operate the full spectrum of services necessary to supply some amount of a specific public service.

Private firms could bid to manage the postal services, the fire protection services, the terminal air traffic control system or, possibly, even the police services in a local community. A profit-seeking firm now provides fire protection services to some communities in the south-west U.S. on this basis. Some types of military forces should even be considered eligible for operation by private firms. A management contract is probably preferable to one which includes the supply of the major assets, in order to retain government ownership of the major assets and to assure the necessary standardization. . . .

C. Political Alternatives

The political alternatives involve major changes in the structure and procedures of the legislature and the executive branch that would improve the performance of national governments in supplying public services. A whole set of problems, caused primarily by the procedures for electing public officials that affect the degree to which they know and represent the interests of the population, are excluded from this discussion, which deals primarily with changes in (i) the structure of the review process, (ii) the size of the vote necessary for approval, and (iii) the system of tax charges.

1. Reducing the Monopoly Power of Committees

The first set of measures would maintain the specialized review committees and executive departments but reduce the dominant role of representatives of the high-demand group in the review process. In the legislature this would probably best be accomplished by a random assignment and periodic random re-assignment of legislators to the various review committees. The randomization of committee assignments would make each committee, with some small sampling error, representative of the distribution of interests in the entire legislature; and the decisive vote in each committee would be representative of the middle-demand group. A periodic random re-assignment would be necessary, primarily because review agents tend to become advocates over time. This is not due to any special venality, but to the subtle and almost unavoidable effects on one's own views of having to defend the results of the review process before a larger group. For the same reason, for example, teachers of the prevailing orthodoxy in any field tend to become its advocates. . . .

A second set of measures would maintain the procedures for selecting the review committees but would reduce their monopoly power. In the legislature, this could be done by a random assignment of review responsibilities among committees. . . .

2. A Two-Thirds Voting Rule?

One other measure should be considered as an alternative to these reforms. It is based on the recognition that the combination of the bureaucratic supply of services, a review process dominated by representatives of the high-demand group, and majority rule leads to the over-supply of public services with consequent losses to the low-demand group, indifference by the average voter, and net benefits accruing only to the high-demand group. This alternative would maintain both the bureaucratic supply and the present review process but would increase the vote of the legislature required for approval from a simple majority to some higher proportion. A two-thirds approval rule would significantly increase the total net benefits of the services. . . .

A common objection to a two-thirds rule, usually raised by political scientists, is that it would lead to an increasing deadlock on legislation. This objection has merit only if it is assumed that most legislation that would be approved by a majority is desirable. . . .

3. Progressive Tax System—Good and Bad

For public services for which the differences in demand are primarily dependent on differences in income, a progressive tax system could improve both the allocation of resources to the public sector and the distribution of tax charges. Compared to a proportional tax system, a progressive tax system would substantially lower the tax share of the low-demand group, slightly lower the tax share of the average voter, and increase the tax share of the high-demand group.

For public services for which the differences in demand are primarily due to conditions other than differences in income, a progressive tax system can significantly distort both the allocation of resources to the public sector and the distribution of tax charges. In our present political system, services for which there is likely to be the most controversy among different groups are those reviewed by committees dominated by representatives of high-demand, low-income constituencies. One protection against this problem would be to change the nature of selection to committees, possibly by the random assignment procedure described above. Another protection provided by the US federal system is to delegate the provision of services for which the differences in demands are strongly dependent on regional conditions to lower levels of government, maintaining provision through the national government of only those services for which the population demands are homogeneous except for differences in income. In this latter case, a progressive tax system can be an instrument of both allocative efficiency and distributional equity.

Conclusions

Bureaucracy and representative government are the creations of men. They should be the instruments of men. The parallel growth of bureaucracy and national government has made these institutions less responsive, to the point of confusions about whether the people or the institutions are effectively sovereign. . . . A wider understanding of the effects of bureaucracy and representative government and a recognition of the potential benefits accompanying specific identifiable changes, based on something like the theory outlined in this paper, may be required to realize these ideals.

Notes

1. The quantity they try to maximize (profits, sales, capital, turnover, budget, etc.).
2. My nominalist preference for the smallest set of assumptions reflects an aesthetic preference for an economy of constructs. Some people may prefer a larger set of assumptions as being more 'realistic', even though the additional assumptions are not necessary to address the subject of the Paper. I have no argument with these people if they recognize they have no argument with me. Our differences would be only in the specification of the subject of study or, possibly, in aesthetic preferences.

3. Some component units in profit-seeking organizations, however, may be bureaus. Any identifiable profit center, such as a product division, cannot be considered a bureau, but some staff units providing such services as advertising, public relations, and research have both of the critical characteristics of bureaus.

4. This first characteristic of bureaus also excludes mutual financial institutions, co-operatives, and families; although these institutions are normally classified as non-profit organizations, the identity of the owners and consumers permits the appropriation of residual revenues either in the form of personal income or in lower prices for certain goods and services.

5. Similarly people form or join private collective organizations. Both churches and country clubs, in effect, 'tax' their regular members. Charitable organizations and alumni associations in similar ways 'tax' those people who most strongly identify themselves with a community, activity, or university.

6. In Britain mainly 'national insurance'.

7. 'Monopsony': sole buyer; the opposite of monopoly: sole seller.

8. Could: the American draft was replaced by voluntary recruitment in early 1973.

9. Tibor Scitovsky, 'A Note on Profit Maximization and its Implications', *Review of Economic Studies XI* (1943), p. 57–60.

10. Armen A. Alchian, 'Uncertainty, Evolution, and Economic Theory', *Journal of Political Economy,* June 1950, pp. 211–221.

11. The rationality of budget maximization by bureaucrats may best be illustrated by considering the consequences of contrary behaviour. Consider the probable consequences for a subordinate manager who proves without question that the same output could be produced at, say, one-half the present expenditures. In a profit-seeking firm this manager would probably receive a bonus, a promotion, and an opportunity to find another such economy; if such rewards are not forthcoming in a specific firm, this manager usually has the opportunity to market his skills in another firm. In a bureau, at best, this manager might receive a citation and a savings bond, a lateral transfer, the enmity of his former colleagues, and the suspicion of his new colleagues. Those bureaucrats who doubt this proposition and who have good private employment alternatives should test it . . . once.

12. Aaron Wildavsky, *The Politics of the Budgetary Process* (Boston: Little, Brown & Co., 1964), pp. 160–165.

13. The income elasticity of demand for a commodity or service is the degree (measured as percentage) to which it responds to a change in income.

14. A major contribution to understanding of the economics of voucher systems has recently been made by Edgar Olsen, *Some Theorems in the Theory of Efficient Transfers,* p. 4081-1, The RAND Corporation, 1969.

3B. Tax Policy

Tax policy is just as important as expenditure policy and some think that it can be explained in much the same way. Thus economists conduct cost/benefit studies of different taxes and some political scientists think that tax policy can be explained by incrementalism (Witte 1985). There are, however, important differences between the two areas, and many think that these differences affect the process by which policy is made and the outcomes of that policy.

One important difference lies in the way that taxes and expenditures affect the general public. Expenditures confer large benefits on favored groups, which gives them a strong incentive to press for the establishment and maintenance of such benefits. Taxes impose smaller costs on the general public taken as a whole, giving almost everyone a reason to oppose taxes but only large taxpayers sufficient incentive to lobby (Buchanan 1967; Buchanan and Wagner 1977).

The other major difference arises from the complexity of taxes. Whereas everyone can understand that spending more on education benefits those with children more than those without, many fail to understand that taxes on business are largely paid for by consumers and that property taxes fall on renters and bondholders as well as on those who own houses. This complexity makes it more likely that people will support a tax structure that hurts them (Peretz 1983). It also means that many citizens lack the knowledge to get involved effectively in the political process.

Taken together these differences lead to a tax-policy process in which small interest groups serving the wealthy and business have more power over tax policy than they do over expenditure policy, and where the major political parties feel less constrained by the public in working out the form of tax changes. Complexity and ignorance also lead to blanket opposition to taxation whether it is good or bad for the average member of the public. The result is a tax structure that is more favorable to the better-off than the structure of expenditures.

Given all this, recent tax changes have generally been made for one of four reasons. The most obvious is that tax changes are often forced by increases in expenditures. While currently couched in terms of reducing the deficit, the bottom line is that when expenditures increase, there are strong pressures to increase revenues to pay for them. A second reason is party ideology. It is not by accident that recent tax changes under Democratic presidents generally redistribute downward, while tax changes under Republicans generally redistribute upward. The third major factor is the competition for votes. Given the public's antitax stance, tax reductions are always popular and the party may try to frame them in a way that appeals to a lot of voters. For example, this explains why Republicans in 1994 and 1995 pushed for an income tax *credit* for those with children, a change that does not fit the general pattern of Republican tax changes. Finally, many less obvious changes are made to benefit small but powerful groups who seek special treatment in the tax code. Oil depletion allowances are the classic example.

In the longer term other forces are sometimes important. Much of the most recent literature focusses on the role of the state. Changes in the Constitution or its interpretation have had an effect. The general balance of power between different social groups matters. And periodically the public gets sufficiently aroused to play an independent part in the tax struggle. These forces lead to larger but less frequent changes than the ones outlined in the preceding paragraph.

The readings in this section are primarily concerned with outlining the basic features of tax politics and providing two opposing criteria for evaluating proposed changes in the income tax system. The article by Peters outlines the major players in tax politics and shows how they interact. The article by Wanniski is a relatively sophisticated version of supply-side economics, a theory that claims that tax reductions, especially those on the wealthy, spark savings and work effort, leading to improved economic growth. The article by King, on the other hand, suggests that such arguments are often used to disguise redistribution from the poor and middle classes to the rich.

For Further Reading

A good introduction to the economic principles underlying taxation is Richard and Peggy Musgrave's *Public Finance in Theory and Practice*. A more conservative view is Edgar and Jacqueline Browning's *Public Finance and the Price System*. An interesting, but long, history of taxation is Caroline Webber and Aaron Wildavsky's *A History of Taxation and Expenditure in the Western World*. John Witte's *The Politics and Development of the Federal Income Tax* is a good history. Susan Hansen's *The Politics of Taxation: Revenue Without Representation* outlines some of the older theories on the politics of taxation. James Alt's article "The Evolution of Tax Structures" outlines some of the more recent political theories in the area. Ron King's excellent, but long, *Money, Time and Politics,* uses tax changes during the last century to show that tax politics is heavily shaped by the need to maintain economic growth and social consensus.

Two good books on how tax policy was made before 1980 are Lawrence Pierce's *The Politics of Fiscal Policy Formation* and Thomas Reese's *The Politics of Taxation*. Interesting recent case studies are Jeffery Birnbaum and Alan Murray's *Showdown at Gucci Gulch* and Bob Woodward's *The Agenda*. An interesting account of business influence over recent tax changes is Cathie Martin's *Shifting the Burden*. Guy Peters's *The Politics of Taxation* and Sven Steimo's *Taxation and Democracy* give a comparative view of the politics of taxation. Hibbs and Masden's article "Public Reaction to the Growth of Taxation and Government Expenditure" looks at public opinion on taxes. David Sears and Jack Citrin's *Tax Revolt: Something for Nothing in California* is a careful case study of the interaction between public opinion and tax reduction.

References

Alt, James. 1983. "The Evolution of Tax Structures," *Public Choice* 41, 1: 181–222.

Browning, Edgar K., and Jacqueline M. Browning. 1994. *Public Finance and the Price System*. 4th ed. New York: Macmillan.

Birnbaum, Jeffery, and Alan Murray. 1987. *Showdown at Gucci Gulch: Lawmakers, Lobbyists and the Unlikely Triumph of Tax Reform*. New York: Basic Books.

Buchanan, J. M. 1967. *Public Finance in Democratic Process: Fiscal Institutions and Democratic Choice*. Chapel Hill: University of North Carolina Press.

Buchanan, J. M., and R. Wagner. 1977. *Democracy in Deficit*. New York: Academic Press.

Hansen, Susan. 1983. *The Politics of Taxation: Revenue Without Representation*. New York: Praeger.

Hibbs, Douglas, and H. Masden. 1981. "Public Reaction to the Growth of Taxation and Government Expenditure." *World Politics* 33 (April): 413–35.

King, Ronald F. 1993. *Money, Time and Politics: Investment Tax Subsidies and American Democracy*. New Haven: Yale University Press.

Martin, Cathie J. 1991. *Shifting the Burden: The Struggle over Growth and Corporate Taxation*. Chicago: University of Chicago Press.

Musgrave, Richard, and Peggy Musgrave. 1989. *Public Finance in Theory and Practice*. 5th ed. New York: McGraw Hill.

Pierce, Lawrence. 1971. *The Politics of Fiscal Policy Formation*. Pacific Palisades, Calif.: Goodyear.

Peretz, Paul. 1983. *The Political Economy of Inflation*. Chicago: University of Chicago Press.

Peters, B. Guy. 1991. *The Politics of Taxation: A Comparative Perspective*. Cambridge, Mass.: Basil Blackwell.

Reese, T. J. 1979. *The Politics of Taxation*. Westport, Conn.: Quorum Books.

Sears, David O., and Jack Citrin. 1985. *Tax Revolt: Something for Nothing in California*. Enlarged ed. Cambridge, Mass.: Harvard University Press.

Steimo, Sven. 1993. *Taxation and Democracy: Swedish, British and American Approaches to Financing the Modern State*. New Haven: Yale University Press.

Webber, Carolyn, and Aaron Wildavsky. 1986. *A History of Taxation and Expenditure in the Western World*. New York: Simon and Schuster.

Witte, John F. 1985. *The Politics and Development of the Federal Income Tax*. Madison: University of Wisconsin Press.

Woodward, Bob. 1995. *The Agenda: Inside the Clinton White House*. New York: Pocket Books.

3B.1. Understanding Tax Policy

B. GUY PETERS

This reading by Guy Peters provides an excellent introduction to tax policy. He shows who is generally most influential in tax policy in developed Western nations and shows some of the ways in which that influence is exercised. He sees tax policy as primarily a political process influenced by such variables as which party is in power, the interests of different groups, political culture in different countries, and the shape of political institutions. He sees this political process as having its own internal logic which conflicts with the needs for simplicity, equity, and openness often cited as desirable by economists.

. . . Any government must find the means to pay for its own existence and for the services it provides to citizens. Taxation, therefore, is an essential activity if there is to be a government, but their necessity does not make the taxes any more popular. Citizens generally dislike paying taxes, and therefore politicians dislike passing laws calling for new or increased taxes. George Bush made a great deal of political mileage in the 1988 presidential campaign in the United States by telling people to "Read my lips—No new taxes." His reneging on that promise in 1990 may present several political difficulties for him in a try for reelection. The trick for government is to find ways to pay for themselves and their services while escaping the wrath, or perhaps even the notice, of their citizens.

Achieving the political balance between needed revenue and popular reactions involves not only decisions about the amount of tax money being extracted from citizens, but also how that money is raised. Some taxes (especially the income tax) are very visible to citizens and are more likely to produce political repercussions than are less visible taxes such as the value-added tax. Also, a

Reprinted with permission from *The Politics of Taxation: A Comparative Perspective* by Guy Peters (Cambridge, Mass.: Blackwell, 1991), pp. 1–15.

large number of taxes charged at lower rates usually will generate less political opposition for a government than will a few less charged at higher rates, although the administrative costs for government will be much greater with the number of smaller taxes. Thus, governments have a number of important and delicate decisions to make when they choose their tax policies.

I will concentrate my attention on the political issues involved in tax policy, but there are a number of other issues involved as well. Many of these are economic, and the discipline of economics has tended to dominate the study of taxation. The principal question which economics raises is what effect will the tax policies have on economic growth, and on the efficient use of resources in the national economy (Musgrave and Musgrave, 1984). The economics literature tends to place substantial emphasis on the distortions which taxation may create within economies, and therefore attempts to develop optimal systems of taxation that can generate needed public revenues without any serious distortions. This approach generally argues for low levels of taxation, and for broadly-based tax systems that collect some revenues from a variety of sources. It also tends to argue for granting very few special treatments for different types of income or expenditures—tax loopholes.

These desires by economists for simplicity and uniformity are often in conflict with political pressures, which tend to create numerous specialized benefits for groups, and even individuals, through the tax system. For example, governments have found it more convenient to subsidize middle-class housing by offering tax relief on mortgage payments than to provide a direct subsidy. Because tax policy is perceived to be extremely political by politicians and citizens, it is often safer for political entrepreneurs to create benefits by taxation than through expenditures (Manley, 1970; Witte, 1985). The same amount of benefit that would be obvious in an expenditure bill can be easily hidden in tax legislation.

Another of the concerns expressed by economists over tax policy is its potential effects on the distribution of wealth and income in a society. This again is often motivated by a concern with economic efficiency, and with the continuing maximum participation of citizens in the labor market (Hausman, 1981; Blomquist and Hansson-Brusewitz, 1990). The practical concern can, however, coincide with a more deeply ethical and social policy concern with the effects of tax policy on people and especially on the poor (Page, 1983, 22–41). The more wealthy and powerful in a society generally have greater political influence than do the poor, and have been able to shape most tax systems to suit themselves. This influence may have produced perceived (and real) inequities, and yet another set of criteria comes into play when we consider tax policy. These are the criteria of justice and fairness, and the possibilities of achieving those goals through the tax system—and through the expenditures funded by that taxation. These more philosophical criteria may be interpreted very differently by different people (Rawls, 1972; Nozick, 1974) but still constitute important factors in evaluating the impacts of tax policies on society.

Taxes are enacted by law, but the money they attempt to raise does not roll in automatically. Taxes must be administered, and people in government must devise means to collect the money that government is owed. Some taxes are easier to collect than are others. Sales tax in American states and cities, for example, is collected for government by merchants and is a simple percentage of their sales. On the other hand, income tax in most countries may be charged at a number of different rates with a number of possible exemptions and deductions; deciding who owes how much income tax can be a very difficult task. Not only are different taxes more or less difficult to administer, but governments can make choices that can minimize those difficulties. For example, in the United States, Canada, Sweden, and several other countries citizens are required to assess themselves for the income tax, while in most countries government itself does the assessment. The Internal Revenue Service in the United States, and its counterparts elsewhere, must still check to be sure that citizens have been honest and accurate when they have computed their taxes, but the amount of work and personnel required by government itself is still much less. . . . Therefore, another set of criteria to consider when making tax policy choices is how difficult the tax is to implement, and what revenue yield can be had at what cost.

We now have at least four sets of criteria to utilize when talking about tax policy—politics, economics, ethics, and administration. In this policymaking game, however, politics is trumps. None of the other criteria will carry much weight unless government is willing to accept it and enact it into law through the political process. Therefore, this chapter will concentrate on possible political explanations for tax policy choices, and it will be a review of the existing literature in the field. Although tax policy has become somewhat neglected by political scientists relative to other policy fields, there is still a substantial and interesting literature upon which to draw (Hansen, 1983; Steinmo, 1989; Robinson and Sandford, 1983; Hadenius, 1986; Good, 1980; Wilkes, 1980). . . .

The Political Roots of Tax Policy

Although often made to appear very technical and difficult to understand, tax policy is in many ways just another type of public policy.

It is made in approximately the same manner and the process of adoption can be conceptualized through much the same process model as used for other types of policy (Jones, 1986). In addition tax policy has the same types of effects on citizens as do other policies; it advantages some and disadvantages others. Tax policies, however, provoke stronger reactions from citizens than do many other policies, and may have to be adjusted frequently to meet changing political and economic circumstances (Hogwood and Peters, 1983). With these similarities to other types of policies, tax policy should be explicable through many of the same models and concepts.

At the same time, however, tax policy is also somewhat different. All policies have their own peculiarities, but tax policy is somewhat more distinctive than are others. First, although all citizens must pay taxes, few claim to understand tax policy (unlike policy domains such as education or transportation). It is perceived as sufficiently technical and complex that most citizens simply grumble and pay their taxes. Second, more than most other policies, the formulation of tax policy tends to be dominated by economists and lawyers. Lawyers are concerned with writing tax laws that are sufficiently watertight for government to collect the revenue it should. Economists are concerned with the potential negative economic effects of taxes and ways to prevent them (Aaron and Pechman, 1981). Again, both groups must accede to political concerns if there are conflicts but these experts are heavily involved in giving advice during the formulation stage of tax policy. Politics in this arena may involve mustering experts as well as mustering interest groups.

A third distinctive feature of taxation is that politicians can rarely use this policy area for their advantage in electoral politics. They are able to gain a great deal of power within the institutions of government by a thorough knowledge of tax policy, but citizens may not really appreciate the politicians responsible for tax laws. Even tax legislation which benefits many people, such as the tax reforms of the 1980s, may have harmful consequences politically. Those who are harmed by the legislation are more likely to remember who was involved than those who benefit, and any tax legislation simply places the issue of taxation before an unappreciative public. Only a relatively few politicians, such as Russell Long of Louisiana, have been able to achieve political popularity through their control of tax policy.

Finally, a great deal of tax policy is made while it is being implemented. Try as they might, the lawyers and politicians drafting tax legislation can think of only a small portion of the individual circumstances that can arise, and therefore a great deal of tax policy must be made as the collecting agencies confront individual taxpayers and the complex cases they present. Implementation is important in defining the real meaning of any policy (Pressman and Wildavsky, 1973), but appears to have an even greater impact in taxation than in other policy areas. Even more than most other policy areas, citizens have an interest in finding ways to circumvent the laws, and the implementors must determine which ways out of paying more tax are legal. Further, most citizens often are afraid of the tax authorities and may not contest the tax bureaucracies' rulings, thus giving greater latitude and authority to those bureaucracies.

With both the similarities and dissimilarities of tax policy to other types of public policy in mind, a number of possible political explanations for the policy choices made by governments will now be considered. These explanations will range across the various subfields of political science and policy studies, but all must take into account the pronounced difficulties that governments encounter in formulating and implementing a set of policies that are so essential to their survival, but which are almost never popular among the public. Further, an attempt will be made to take into account the different political circumstances of the OECD countries, and the consequences those political differences have for tax policy.

Political Culture

Perhaps the most general possible explanation for the differences in tax policies found among countries is that there are national styles of taxation, or that the political culture of a country tends to drive government toward formulating one type of solution rather than another for its tax problems. For example, it is often argued that the anti-statist values of many French and Italian citizens, and the consequent high levels of evasion of direct personal taxes, produce tax systems highly dependent upon indirect taxation (Haycraft, 1985, 107–8). Similarly, the tradition of property taxes as a means of financing local government (at least until Mrs Thatcher and the community charge) in the Anglo-American democracies generated much greater dependence upon that form of taxation in those countries than in others. In the United States the social security tax, justified as an insurance "contribution" rather than a real tax, has been more acceptable than other means of funding social programs. My own earlier research (Peters, 1980 . . .) found stable clusterings of taxation patterns among groups of industrialized democracies that persisted even with economic and political change. Thus, there does appear to be some justification for a cultural explanation of tax choices. These findings about tax policy are but a few manifestations of the argument King (1975) advanced that the best way to understand public policies is to understand the ideas and values which undergird them.

There may be good political reasons for a government to accept the political culture argument, in the form of the status quo, as its tax policy. This is, if a system for raising revenue exists already, and the taxes in operation are generating revenue at a reasonably acceptable rate, then that structure is probably at least minimally acceptable to the population. It therefore makes sense for the government simply to permit that system to continue to function and to generate such revenue as it will. Marginal adjustments to the tax system may be made for ideological or practical reasons, but the status quo ante may be a good guide to current policy (Rose and Karran, 1986). This argument assumes, as do other incremental arguments, that the past has been functional and has produced an array of policies which the public finds congenial and which corresponds to the basic political values of that public (March and Olsen, 1989). This is a very conservative proposition but one which may be substantially safer politically than are adventurous forays which require altering the existing tax policies to suit a new government's ideological or economic precepts.

Further, it is important to note the extent to which tax reform has proceeded differently in different political systems. Although there has been a sense of worldwide tax reform, the major action has been in the Anglo-American democracies rather than in the continental systems—with the exception of the Federal Republic of Germany (pre-reunification) (Hagemann, Jones, and Montador, 1988)—although some important reforms have occurred in these countries. Some nations, such as France, have resisted reform even though their tax systems are extremely complex and seemingly inefficient (Graham, 1990). Further, tax reforms have had a number of similarities in both the logic behind them and the details of the policy changes. While this may have occurred because the Anglo-American systems of taxation were the most in need of change, there also appears to be a cultural element involved. If nothing else, a general cultural belief about the meaning of "fairness" appeared to have informed these tax reform packages.

On the other hand, the direct linkage between taxes and the cultural environment of politics is difficult to make. If indeed tax-policy reflects some very difficult and potentially dangerous political decisions for politicians in power, it appears more likely that they would want to make more calculated choices (Alt, 1983). Culture may exert some influence over political choices, but it appears that more proximate values may offer a superior approach. In particular, the politicians may want to implement the values that they believe won the election for them. Further, in most societies "culture" is not a unitary concept, and there may be a number of different political cultures (sometimes parading as ideologies) attempting to exert their influence over policy choices. For example, Mogens Glistrup was able to find a strong anti-government subculture within Denmark, presumably a model Scandinavian Welfare State. This subcultural route may be, in fact, the way in which the ethical values mentioned above enter into the political foray; as noted there, values must be incorporated through the political process before they can be expected to have any significant influence over policies.

Public Opinion

Somewhat related to the above idea that political culture will determine or at least influence tax policy is the argument that public opinion should have a direct and determinate impact on policy. This influence typically works, if it works at all, through the mediating role of political parties and interest groups discussed below. On the other hand, there are ways in which public opinion can have a more direct impact on tax policy. The most obvious method is through initiatives and referenda on tax issues. Some states in the United States and the cantons in Switzerland permit citizens to propose changes in the law directly, and then to vote on the issue (Rhinow, 1984; Delley, 1978). The most famous example of direct lawmaking in tax policy is Proposition 13 in California, but some states in the United States require popular votes on all changes in state or local property tax and these votes can occur frequently (Ranney, 1985; 1987). In the case of referenda, voters are given an opportunity to approve or disapprove a tax proposal put to them by elected officials, while in the case of an initiative they are given the opportunity even to frame the proposal to be considered. These opportunities exist in relatively few countries, and then primarily at the subnational level, but are important instances in which public opinion can determine tax policy directly.

At a more general level, advocates of the public choice approach to political questions have argued in favor of a "median voter model" to explain tax and expenditure policy (Romer and Rosenthal, 1979; 1982; Chicoine, Walzer, and Deller, 1989). The argument of the public choice school is that in a functioning democracy tax and expenditure levels that go above the level desired by the average (median) voter will ultimately produce political retribution against the officials responsible for adopting them. This model of political behavior makes a number of assumptions about the ability of complex political systems to transmit discontent about taxes directly into policy changes. In reality, these assumptions come close to working only when there is an option for referendum (Pommerehne, 1978; Santerre, 1986). The public choice approach also makes the assumption that voters respond only, or perhaps primarily, to aggregate levels of taxing and spending, rather than to the quality of the services being provided, the personal characteristics of political leaders, or any of a number of other possible influences on their behavior. Although some assumptions underlying the public choice approach do appear suspect, it constitutes yet another theoretical point at which to begin the exploration of the politics, especially the mass politics, of tax policy.

There may be even more direct manifestations of public opinion about tax policy. Americans still remember that public opinion (of a sort) concerning tax policy in 1775 helped to spawn the separation of the United States from Britain, and have seen the power of more recent tax revolts (Beito, 1989; Sears and Citrin, 1985). Less dramatically, the manifest public dislike of the community charge, or "poll tax" in Britain helped to produce some modifications in the government's proposals (Evans, 1990). The riots that occurred in London may have hardened Mrs Thatcher's resolve to implement the policy; there was, however, a substantial softening of the proposals, and the introduction of a much larger social "safety net" to assist the poor, after numerous large-scale and peaceful protests took place throughout the United Kingdom (including in some Tory strongholds in the suburbs). Moreover, Conservative defeats in safe by-elections in 1990 and 1991, and the resignation of Mrs Thatcher made it possible to consider a major overhaul, if not complete abolition, of this extremely unpopular tax. The public rarely speaks loudly or with one voice on tax policy, but when it does there appears to be some chance that it will be heard.

Parties and Ideologies

Culture begins to have more clearly political and policy manifestations once it is converted into party programs and their associated ideologies. Everything else being equal, we would expect parties of the political left in office to adopt more progressive (personal and corporate income with high marginal rates) taxes, and parties of the political right to adopt more regressive (sales, insurance contributions) taxes. Some quantitative analyses have demonstrated this effect for tax policy in some time periods and some countries (Castles, 1982; Peters, 1974; 1980). Other more qualitative research has demonstrated significant influence of political portico on tax policy (Elvander, 1972a; Hadenius, 1981; Morrissey and Steinmo, 1987; Steinmo 1989) in some settings. Neither the quantitative or qualitative evidence, however, is overwhelming in its support for the point that parties have a major influence over tax policies.

Although there are some observed effects of party ideologies on tax policy, there is by no means an overwhelming tendency for differences in political parties to be manifested directly through differences in tax structures. The failure of Socialist Party in France to implement a more progressive tax structure and the increased reliance of Sweden under the Social Democrats on indirect taxes in the late 1980s are but two recent and obvious examples of the slippage between ideology and policy. There appears to be a large number of barriers standing between the promulgation of an ideology by a political party in an electoral campaign, and the implementation of that ideology through a new tax program once the party is in government.

In the first place, a party must win an election in order to implement its program. This is rather basic, but it is important to remember that in most industrialized democracies coalitions, rather than single parties, form the government of the day; of the 22 OECD countries only six had single party governments in 1990. Therefore, even if a political party is successful in getting into government, it generally will not be there alone and may have to compromise with its partners to make tax and other policies. Any one party may be able to get some of its program adopted by the coalition, but by no means all, and the resultant tax program may be a hash of many ideas rather than a clear statement of any single ideology. Even in the United States, which does not have coalition governments in the usual sense, tax reform appears more likely (at both the state and federal levels) when the legislature and executive are from the same political party (Portney, 1980).

The existence of a coalition government can be argued to influence the shape of the tax policies adopted, and it may affect the amount of revenue which a government is likely to be able to extract. Beginning with the basic assumption that taxes are not popular public policies, coalitions often attempt to minimize taxes, and especially to minimize the taxes paid by their constituent groups. That is, political parties with agrarian bases will attempt to minimize the amount of tax paid by farmers, while labor parties will attempt to minimize the amount of tax paid by the working class, and so on. Needing agreement among a number of parties will mean that it will be difficult to get agreement on enough taxation to pay for all the services the government must offer, and hence coalition governments may tend to run larger deficits than single party governments. Further, coalition governments may have to spend more, to be able to "pay off" all the members of the ruling coalition (Robertson, 1989) and that will only increase the deficit.

In the second place, once in office any government will find that any number of factors will impinge upon its ideological purity. Not the least of these factors will be the desire to be reelected. As noted above, changing the tax system is often not the best way to win the hearts and minds of the voters. Even if the changes in the tax system introduced are beneficial to most citizens, they may still create uncertainty and simply direct media attention to the amount of money which citizens are already paying in taxes and which they will continue to pay after the reform. Therefore, the best strategy (politically) is often to ignore the tax system and allow it to continue pretty much as it has been—perhaps with a few changes around the margin (Rose and Karran, 1986).

There are, of course, some good examples of political leaders who have been able to introduce large-scale tax policy measures and retain their popularity (President Reagan in 1981 and Helmut Kohl in 1986 are among the most obvious), but these successes appear to be the exceptions rather than the rule. Following from that statement it appears that most politicians have been attempting to hide the true costs of taxes from citizens rather than to make bold ideological statements about their tax policies. Even if a public statement is more bold than ideological, any statement about more taxes is likely to be political suicide, as Walter Mondale found out in 1984. There has been a tendency among the industrialized countries of the OECD world for tax systems to become increasingly similar over time. Countries such as France and Italy which have relied on indirect taxes have been increasing their direct tax burdens, while countries such as Sweden and Australia with very high direct tax burdens have shifted somewhat more toward indirect taxes. Ideology implies clear statements and placing most of a government's tax eggs in a few baskets, but tax politics appears to call for hiding the total burden in as many baskets as possible. The introduction of the "community charge" or poll tax to finance local government in Britain was a clear ideological move on the part of the Thatcher government, and one which met initially with severe political discontent (Game, 1988).

The final point which should be raised about the mass political considerations involved its tax policy arises from the literature on the "political business cycle" (Tufte, 1978; Schneider, 1984). The argument here is that the action of governments in taxing and spending will constitute a major portion of their attempts to be reelected. Further, a government's actions may not be the same throughout their term of office, but rather will be timed to coincide with the electoral cycle. If a government believes that it must increase taxes, or change the distribution of the tax burden, it will tend to do so early in its term of office so that any negative repercussion of the change (they hope) will have been forgotten by the time of the next election. Likewise, governments will attempt to increase public expenditure, especially for programs that benefit a number of individuals directly, late in their terms of office so that citizens would more likely remember the good deeds of the government and return them to office. Thus, as we examine the politics of tax policy, politicians must be cognizant of the temporal as well as the ideological dimension of political actions. Thus, Mrs Thatcher may have erred seriously in not introducing the poll tax until rather late in her third term of office, while President Reagan made a safer choice, and perhaps his only available choice, by pushing for his major tax change early in his first term. In both cases, there may have been little real choice for the leaders, but it does appear that timing does make a real difference in the political effects of a decision.

The reverse side of the above argument is that governments may be able to make any changes in the tax system early in their terms, but that opportunity will vanish later. Governments appear to enjoy "honeymoon periods" after their election in which they have greater influence with the rest of the political system (Bunce, 1981). A new government can claim a mandate from the people, and although that mandate is often very indistinct, the claim is a powerful political weapon. Unless the government acts promptly that window of opportunity will vanish, and other actors in the political system will begin to wonder by whom the next government will be composed. This closing of windows of opportunity may be especially evident for tax policies, given their general unpopularity. Again, timing counts for a great deal in politics, and making tax policy is little different than are other policies in that regard.

Group Politics

Another possible explanation for the shaping of the tax system in democratic political systems is that the universe of pressure groups plays a significant role in the process. This should not be surprising given that a general finding is that interest groups have significant political influence in all these systems—whether pluralist (Dahl, 1973) or corporatist (Schmitter and Lehmbruch, 1979). In the case of interest groups we would not, however, expect highly visible impacts on broad issues of tax policy—the amount of total taxes extracted or perhaps even the general distribution among different types of taxes. Rather, we would expect greater influence by those interest groups on the fine detail of tax policy, and in particular the pattern of deductions and exemptions—"loopholes"—made available to special interests through the tax system. Interest groups are sometimes argued to be more successful in tax policy than in other policy areas because its complex, technical character makes it easier for them to disguise their real influence in legal and economic jargon. Further, the relative secrecy in which tax policy is made in most countries provides interest groups with an arena in which their impact may not be as evident as in other policy areas (McQuaig, 1987).

The literature recounting the influence of interest groups on taxes is rather extensive, although most of it tends to be condemnations of the influence of special interests, and the consequent inequities written into the tax system. One of the most interesting of the analytical essays on the role of special interests in tax policy concerns their role in Canada. Good (1980) argues for an anticipatory model of tax policymaking in which the principal interest groups do not have to make overt representations of their positions to government. Morrissey (1990) argues much the same for Ireland, when he notes the importance of scanning alternatives, and the political coalitions around them, before making a policy choice. The positions of interest groups on tax policy changes are well known, or are readily predictable, and the decisionmakers in government will act so as to avoid conflict with any powerful groups. In this approach, if there is much overt political activity on the part of interest groups, both they and the policymakers have not done their jobs well.

If we look at the relationship of interest groups to tax policy from the perspective of James Q. Wilson's analysis of policymaking in the United States (1980; 1989), we would expect tax policymakers to have a great deal of influence over the final outcome of the process. Wilson argued that in a decisionmaking situation such as tax policy where there are a large number of interests involved with none being dominant—what he called an "interest group" situation—then the political institution involved has more opportunity for making the final policy decision based on its own values. Certainly tax policy is the target of any number of interests, and the decisionmakers therefore may have the opportunity to pick and choose among those groups. This opportunity is available especially in pluralist settings which do not require conflicting interests to work out compromise arrangements (Pen, 1987, 331–2) as might be required in corporatist interest group settings.

We should, however, expect somewhat different relationships between interest groups and government concerning tax policy, depending upon how those political relationships are structured. In pluralist systems, for example, the competitive involvement of interest groups in policymaking will tend to produce differential influence by groups over policy, and the creation of perhaps more specific deductions and exemptions, most favoring powerful producer groups (Freeman, 1965; Jordan, 1981). If policymakers have the ability to pick and choose, those are the types of interests picked most often to be rewarded. On the other hand, more corporatist systems with the legitimate involvement of a range of interest groups in policymaking should produce more balanced policy outcomes. The same total number of "loopholes" may be created, but they can be hypothesized to be more widely distributed among social groups. Likewise, corporatist structures tend to generate equal shares of many sorts of taxes, rather than greater reliance on only one or two major sources of revenue (Peters, 1981).

Given the conventional wisdom about the power of interest groups over policy, and particularly tax policy, the spate of tax reforms that occurred during the late 1980s and early 1990s is extremely surprising. A general characteristic of these reforms has been to eliminate many of the special privileges granted to special interests through the tax law. This has broadened the tax base and permitted decreased average and marginal tax rates for many taxpayers. Although many interest groups lobbied long and hard to protect their privileges, the reforms were adopted and implemented (Birnbaum and Murray 1987; Pechman, 1988; Gretschmann and Kenis, 1990). Also, some interest groups appeared to avoid the fray, sensing perhaps the limits of their power and legitimacy in democratic political systems bent on reform (Mucciaroni, 1990)

The successes of tax reform legislation . . . point to the development of a new type of interest group in tax politics, and to some degree in other types of politics as well. The conventional wisdom (Olson, 1965) has been that it is impossible to organize taxpayers qua taxpayers effectively. Their interests in any one tax are too diffuse, and their individual tax situations sufficiently different, that they will not organize in the same way as will more specific interests to gain special treatment. In contrast to this conventional wisdom, however, a number of public interest and taxpayer groups were involved in the tax reform process, generally pressing for fewer loopholes and a simpler tax system (Mucciaroni, 1990). This was especially true in the United States, but analogous groups have been seen in other countries as well. It does appear, therefore, that the policy community (Freeman and Stevens, 1987) surrounding tax policy has become much broader, and that broader citizen interests cannot now be excluded.

Policy Reasons

All tax decisions are policy decisions, but at times governments choose to make tax policies in order to produce other policy outcomes, rather than just to raise revenue. Taxes are but one among many instruments at the disposal of government (Linder and Peters, 1989). We have been discussing the preferences built into tax policy using the pejorative term "loopholes," but such preferences can produce positive benefits for the society as a whole. Not only may having the policies adopted be easier as a part of a tax bill than as an expenditure program, but they may be easier and less expensive to administer in the form of taxes as well. The subsidies given homeownership in most countries through tax benefits are widely distributed, generally beneficial, and much easier to administer than would be a direct housing subsidy to that large a segment of the population (Comeau, 1979). Thus, not all tax preferences are merely special preferences for the wealthy and powerful; some are more generally beneficial to the population. The difficulty, politically and socially, is determining which tax expenditures are which.

In addition to the above examples, earmarked (hypothecated) taxes may also be a positive means of reaching certain policy goals when other methods might generate large-scale conflict. Citizens may resist any new general taxes, but may be willing to accept a tax if its revenues go for a specified and popular purpose.

For example, widespread concern about the rather poor state of the National Health Service in Britain has prompted some to suggest a new tax just for that single purpose. This proposal certainly would not fit well with the general policies of the conservative government against taxation and public expenditure, but earmarking may make the proposal more acceptable even to that administration. Earmarking is doubly acceptable when it taxes "sin" (alcohol, tobacco, gambling) for "good" purposes (health or education).

Finally, taxes can be used as a mechanism for social control, and to produce general goods as well as a means of conferring special benefits. For example, there is concern in many countries about global warming and the "greenhouse effect" resulting in large part from emissions of carbon dioxide. A number of countries have advanced proposals for a carbon tax, on the use of carbon in the form of coal or petroleum, as a means of reducing consumption of fossil fuels (Johnson, 1990; Samuelson, 1990). Similarly, taxes on alcohol and tobacco, in addition to their revenue effects, are also intended to reduce consumption of those potentially harmful substances. There is some question about how effective any of these taxes intended to be control devices are (Cook, 1989; Baker and McKay, 1990), but they do constitute yet another policy option available to government in attempting to reach its goals.

Bibliography

Aaron, H. J., and J. A. Pechman (1981). *How Taxes Affect Economic Behavior.* Washington, DC: The Brookings Institution.

Alt, J. E. (1983). The evolution of tax structures. *Public Choice,* 41, 181–222.

Baker, P., and S. McKay (1990). *The Structure of Alcohol Taxes: A Hangover from the Past.* London: Institute for Fiscal Studies.

Beito, D. T. (1989). *Taxpayers in Revolt.* Chapel Hill, NC: University of North Carolina Press.

Birnbaum, J. H., and A. S. Murray (1987). *Showdown at Gucci Gulch.* New York: Random House.

Blomquist, N. S., and U. Hansson-Brusewitz (1990). The effects of taxes on male and female labor supply in Sweden. *Journal of Human Resources,* 25, 317–57.

Bunce, V. (1981). *Do New Leaders Make a Difference?* Princeton, NJ: Princeton University Press.

Castles, F. G. (1982). The impact of parties on public expenditure. In F. G. Castles (ed.), *The Impact of Parties.* London: Sage.

Chicoine, D. L., N. Walzer, and S. C. Deller (1989). Representative vs. direct democracy and government spending in the median voter model. *Public Finance,* 44, 225–36.

Comeau, R. L. (1979). Comparing direct spending and tax spending. *Canadian Taxation,* 1, 42–5.

Cook, D. (1989). *Poor Law, Rich Law.* Milton Keynes: Open University.

Dahl, R. (1973). *Polyarchy: Participation and Opposition.* New Haven, CT: Yale University Press.

Delley, J.-D. (1978). *L'initiative populaire en Suisse: Mythe et reality de la de'mocratie directe.* Lausanne: Edition l'age de l'homme.

Elvander, N. (1972). *Svensk skattpolitik 1945–70.* Stockholm: Rabén & Sjogren.

Evans, R. (1990). Limiting the poll tax damage. *Financial Times*, April 20.

Freeman, J. L. (1965). *The Political Process: Executive Bureau–Legislative Committee Relations*. Garden City, NY: Doubleday.

Freeman, J. L., and J. Stevens (1987). A theoretical and conceptual reexamination of sub-system politics. *Public Policy and Administration*, 2, 137–55.

Game, C. (1988). The underwhelming demand for the poll tax. *Public Money and Management*, 8 (winter), 55–8.

Good, D. (1980). *The Politics of Anticipation: Making Canadian Federal Tax Policy*. Ottawa: School of Public Administration Carleton University.

Graham, G. (1990). An Old Tax Is a Good Tax. *Financial Times*. Insert on France, June 28.

Gretschmann, K., and P. Kenis (1990). Political exchange: A theoretical reconsideration and some epirical evidence from taxation. In B. Marm (ed.), *Governance and Generalized Exchange: Self Organizing Policy Networks in Action*. Amsterdam: NorthHolland.

Hadenius, A. (1981). *Spelet om Skatten*. Stockholm: Norstedts.

Hadenius, A. (1986). *A Crisis of the Welfare State?* Stockholm: Almqvist & Wiksell.

Hagemann, R. P., B. R. Jones, and R. B. Montador (1988). Tax reform in OECD countries: Motives, constraints and practice. *OECD Economic Studies*, 10, 185–226.

Hansen, S. B. (1983). *The Politics of Taxation: Revenue Without Representation*. New York: Praeger.

Hausman, J. A. (1981). Labor supply. In H. J. Aaron and J. A. Pechman (eds.), *How Taxes Affect Economic Behavior*. Washington, DC: The Brookings Institution.

Haycraft, J. (1985). *Italian Labyrinth*. Harmondswoth: Penguin.

Hogwood, B. W., and B. G. Peters (1983). *Policy Dynamics*. Brighton: Wheatsheaf.

Johnson, R. (1990). Report urges 'Green' taxes in budget. *Financial Times*, January 26.

Jones, C. O. (1986). *An Introduction to the Study of Public Policy*. 3rd. ed. Monterey, CA: Brooks/Cole.

Jordan, A. G. (1981). Iron triangles, woolly corporatism and elastic nets: Images of the policy process. *Journal of Public Policy*, 1.

King, A. (1975). Ideas, institutions and the policies of governments: A comparative analysis. *British Journal of Political Science*, 5, 409–24.

Linder, S. H., and B. G. Peters (1989). Instruments of government: Perceptions and contexts. *Journal of Public Policy*, 9, 35–58.

McQuaig, L. (1987). *Behind Closed Doors*. Markham, Ont.: Viking.

Manley, I. F. (1970). *The Politics of Finance: The House Ways and Means Committee*. Boston, MA: Little, Brown.

March, J. G., and J. P. Olsen (1989). *Rediscovering Institutions*. New York: The Free Press.

Morrissey, O. (1990). Scanning the alternatives before taxing with consensus: Lessons for policymaking from the Irish wealth tax. *Administration* (Dublin), 38, 24–40.

Morrissey, O., and S. Steinmo (1987). The influence of party competition on post-war UK tax rates. *Policy and Politics*, 15, 195–206.

Mucciaroni, G. (1990). Public choice and the politics of comprehensive tax reform. *Governnance*, 3, 1–32.

Musgrave, R. A., and P. B. Musgrave. (1984). *Public Finance in Theory and Practice*. New York: McGraw-Hill.

Nozick, R. (1974). *Anarchy, the State and Utopia*. New York: Basic Books.

Olson, M. (1965). *The Logic of Collective Action*. Cambridge, MA: Harvard University Press.

Page, B. I. (1983). *Who Gets What From Government?* Berkeley, CA: University of California Press.

Pechman, J. A. (1988). *World Tax Reform: A Progress Report*. Washington, DC: The Brookings Institution.

Pen, J. (1987). Expanding budgets in a stagnating economy: The experience of the 1970s. In C. S. Maier (ed.), *Changing Boundaries of the Political.* Cambridge: Cambridge University Press.

Peters, B. G. (1974). Income Redistribution in France, Sweden and the United Kingdom. *Political Studies, 22,* 311–23.

Peters, B. G. (1980). Choices in taxation policy. In T. R. Dye and V. Gray (eds.), *The Determinants of Public Policy.* Lexington, MA: Lexington Books.

Peters, B. G. (1981). The problem of bureaucratic government. *Journal of Politics, 43,* 56–82.

Pommerehne, W. W. (1978). Institutional approaches to public expenditure. *Journal of Public Economics, 9,* 255-80.

Portney, K. E. (1980). State tax preference-orderings and partisan control of government. In L. Wade and W. Samuels (eds.), *Taxing and Spending Policy.* Lexington, MA: D. C. Heath.

Pressman, J. L., and A. Wildavsky. (1973). *Implementation.* Berkeley: University of California Press.

Ranney, A. (1985). Referendums and initiatives 1984. *Public Opinion, 7* (December/January), 15–17.

Ranney, A. (1987). Referendums and initiatives 1986. *Public Opinion, 9* (January/February), 44–6.

Rawls, J. A. (1972). *Theory of Justice.* Cambridge, MA: Harvard University Press.

Rhinow, R. A. (1984). Grundprobleme der schweizerischen Demokratie. *Zeitschrift fur Schweizerishes Recht, 103,* 117–271.

Robertson, J. D. (1989). Coalition leadership, government stability and macroeconomic policy in European democracies. In B. D. Jones (ed.), *Leadership and Politics.* Lawrence, KS: University of Kansas Press.

Robinson, A., and C. Sandford (1983). *Tax Policy-making in the United Kingdom.* London: Heinemann.

Romer, T. and H. Rosenthal (1979). The elusive median voter. *Journal of Public Economics, 12,* 143–70.

Romer, T., and H. Rosenthal (1982). Median voters or budget maximizers: Evidence from school expenditure referenda. *Economic Inquiry, 26,* 536–78.

Rose, R., and Karran, T. (1986). *Taxation by Political Inertia.* London: Macmillan.

Samuelson, M. (1990). Carbon tax urged to cut pollution. *Financial Times,* February 1.

Santerre, R. (1986). Representative versus direct democracy: A Tiebout test of relative performance. *Public Choice, 48,* 55–63.

Schmitter, P. C., and G. Lehmbruch. (1979). *Trends Toward Corporatist Intermediation.* London: Sage.

Schneider, F. (1984). Public attitudes toward economic conditions and their impact on government behavior. *Political Behavior, 6,* 211–27.

Sears, D. O., and J. Citrin. (1985). *Tax revolt: Something for nothing in California.* Enlarged ed. Cambridge, MA: Harvard University Press.

Steinmo, S. (1989). Political institutions and tax policy in the United States, Sweden and Britain. *World Politics, 61,* 500–35.

Tufte, E. R. (1978). *Political Control of the Economy.* Princeton, NJ: Princeton University Press.

Wilkes, J. (1980). *The Politics of Taxation.* Sydney: Hodder and Stoughton.

Wilson, J. Q. (1980). The politics of regulation. In J. Q. Wilson (ed.), *The Politics of Regulation.* New York: Basic Books.

Wilson, J. Q. (1989). *Bureaucracy.* New York: Basic Books.

Witte, J. F. (1985). *The Politics and Development of the Federal Income Tax.* Madison, WI: University of Wisconsin Press.

3B.2. Taxes, Revenues, and the "Laffer Curve"

JUDE WANNISKI

In the last decade, supply-side economics, once regarded as a foolish notion espoused only by radical right-wingers, has exerted considerable influence on government policy making. This influence has been especially pronounced in the area of tax policy. Much of the attractiveness of this theory comes from its promise that it is possible to stimulate the economy and raise total revenues by cutting taxes. This is a proposition with obvious attractions for politicians, who are normally under pressure from voters to increase expenditures while at the same time reducing taxes. This reading by Jude Wanniski explains why supply-siders think this feat is possible.

The central argument is that progressive taxes, which take an increasing percentage of one's income as that income rises, act to discourage people from working and saving. This is because people think they will keep less of what they earn if they work harder or more efficiently, as government takes a larger and larger bite of each increment of extra income. If this is true, it follows that lowering tax rates would encourage people to work harder and longer and to save more. This would lead to increases in employment and the amount of goods produced, which in turn would increase the revenue government gets through taxes on employment and sales of products.

The reader should note that most economists, while conceding that this effect is real, believe that it is partially offset by what they term the "income effect." This holds that if individuals require a certain amount of income to meet their needs, their response to higher taxes may be to work more, not less, in order to meet their income target. In the following essay, Wanniski, seeking to deal with this objection, expounds a more sophisticated version of supply-side theory. He

Reprinted with permission of the author and *The Public Interest*, No. 50 (Winter 1978), pp. 3–16. Copyright © 1978 by National Affairs, Inc.

claims that even if increasing taxes has the effect of increasing work effort, higher taxes may drive people into the untaxed underground economy, with the result that revenues are reduced.

As Arthur Laffer has noted, "there are always two tax rates that yield the same revenues." When an aide to President Gerald Ford asked him once to elaborate, Laffer (who is Professor of Business Economics at the University of Southern California) drew a simple curve, shown on the next page, to illustrate his point. The point, too, is simple enough—though, like so many simple points, it is also powerful in its implications.

When the tax rate is 100 percent, all production ceases in the money economy (as distinct from the barter economy, which exists largely to escape taxation). People will not work in the money economy if all the fruits of their labors are confiscated by the government. And because production ceases, there is nothing for the 100-percent rate to confiscate, so government revenues are zero.

On the other hand, if the tax rate is zero, people can keep 100 percent of what they produce in the money economy. There is no governmental "wedge" between earnings and after-tax income, and thus no governmental barrier to production. Production is therefore maximized, and the output of the money economy is limited only by the desire of workers for leisure. But because the tax rate is zero, government revenues are again zero, and there can be no government. So at a 0-percent tax rate the economy is in a state of anarchy, and at a 100-percent tax rate the economy is functioning entirely through barter.

In between lies the curve. If the government reduces its rate to something less than 100 percent, say to point A, some segment of the barter economy will be able to gain so many efficiencies by being in the money economy that, even with near confiscatory tax rates, after-tax production would still exceed that of the barter economy. Production will start up, and revenues will flow into the government treasury. By lowering the tax rate, we find an increase in revenues.

On the bottom end of the curve, the same thing is happening. If people feel that they need a minimal government and thus institute a low tax rate, some segment of the economy, finding that the marginal loss of income exceeds the efficiencies gained in the money economy, is shifted into either barter or leisure. But with that tax rate, revenues do flow into the government treasury. This is the situation at point B. Point A represents a very high tax rate and very low production. Point B represents a very low tax rate and very high production. Yet they both yield the same revenue to the government.

The same is true of points C and D. The government finds that by a further lowering of the tax rate, say from point A to point C, revenues increase with the further expansion of output. And by raising the tax rate, say from point B to point D, revenues also increase, by the same amount.

Revenues and production are maximized at point E. If, at point E, the government lowers the tax rate again, output will increase, but revenues will fall. And

Figure 1. **The Laffer Curve**

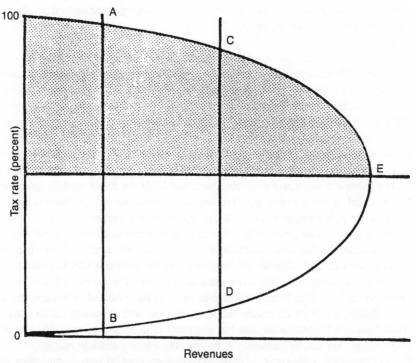

if, at point E, the tax rate is raised, both output and revenue will decline. The shaded area is *the prohibitive range for government,* where rates are unnecessarily high and can be reduced with gains in *both* output and revenue.

Tax Rates and Tax Revenues

The next important thing to observe is that, except for the 0-percent and 100-percent rates, there are no numbers along the "Laffer curve." Point E is not 50 percent, although it may be, but rather a variable number: *it is the point at which the electorate desires to be taxed.* At points B and D, the electorate desires more government goods and services and is willing—without reducing its productivity—to pay the higher rates consistent with the revenues at point E. And at points A and C, the electorate desires more private goods and services in the money economy, and wishes to pay the lower rates consistent with the revenues at point E. It is the task of the statesman to determine the location of point E, and follow its variations as closely as possible.

This is true whether the political leader heads a nation or a family. The father who disciplines his son at point A, imposing harsh penalties for violating both major and minor rules, only invites sullen rebellion, stealth, and lying (tax evasions on the national level). The permissive father who disciplines casually at point B invites open, reckless rebellion: His son's independence and relatively unfettered growth comes at the expense of the rest of the family. The wise parent seeks point E, which will probably vary from one child to another, from son to daughter.

For the political leader on the national level, point E can represent a very low or a very high number. When the nation is at war, point E can approach 100 percent. At the siege of Leningrad in World War II, for example, the people of the city produced for 900 days at tax rates approaching 100 percent. Russian soldiers and civilians worked to their physical limits, receiving as "pay" only the barest of rations. Had the citizens of Leningrad not wished to be taxed at that high rate, which was required to hold off the Nazi army, the city would have fallen.

The number represented by point E will change abruptly if the nation is at war one day and at peace the next. The electorate's demand for military goods and services from the government will fall sharply; the electorate will therefore desire to be taxed at a lower rate. If rates are not lowered consistent with this new lower level of demand, output will fall to some level consistent with a point along the prohibitive side of the "Laffer curve." Following World War I, for example, the wartime tax rates were left in place and greatly contributed to the recession of 1919–20. Warren G. Harding ran for President in 1920 on a slogan promising a "return to normalcy" regarding tax rates; he was elected in a landslide. The subsequent rolling back of the rates ushered in the economic expansion of the "Roaring Twenties." After World War II, wartime tax rates were quickly reduced, and the American economy enjoyed a smooth transition to peacetime. In Japan and West Germany, however, there was no adjustment of the rates; as a result, postwar economic recovery was delayed. Germany's recovery began in 1948, when personal income tax rates were reduced under Finance Minister Ludwig Erhard, and much of the government regulation of commerce came to an end. Japan's recovery did not begin until 1950, when wartime tax rates were finally rolled back. In each case, reduced *rates* produced increased *revenues* for the government. The political leader must fully appreciate the distinction between tax rates and tax revenues to discern the desires of the electorate.

The easiest way for a political leader to determine whether an increase in rates will produce more rather than less revenues is to put the proposition to the electorate. It is not enough for the politician to propose an increase from, say, point B to point D on the curve. He must also specify how the anticipated revenues will be spent. When voters approve a bond issue for schools, highways, or bridges, they are explicitly telling the politician that they are willing to pay the high tax rates required to finance the bonds. In rejecting a bond issue, however, the electorate is not necessarily telling the politician that taxes are already high enough, or that point E (or beyond) has been reached. The only message is that the proposed tax rates are too high a price to pay for the specific goods and services offered by the government.

Only a tiny fraction of all government expenditures are determined in this fashion, to be sure. Most judgments regarding tax rates and expenditures are made by individual politicians. Andrew Mellon became a national hero for engineering the rate reductions of the 1920s and was called "the greatest Treasury Secretary since Alexander Hamilton." The financial policies of Ludwig Erhard were responsible for what was hailed as "an economic miracle"—the postwar recovery of Germany. Throughout history, however, it has been the exception rather than the rule that politicians, by accident or design, have sought to increase revenues by lowering rates.

Work vs. Productivity

The idea behind the "Laffer curve" is no doubt as old as civilization, but unfortunately politicians have always had trouble grasping it. In his essay, *Of Taxes,* written in 1756, David Hume pondered the problem:

> Exorbitant taxes, like extreme necessity, destroy industry by producing despair; and even before they reach this pitch, they raise the wages of the labourer and manufacturer, and heighten the price of all commodities. An attentive disinterested legislature will observe the point when the emolument ceases, and the prejudice begins. But as the contrary character is much more common, 'tis to be feared that taxes all over Europe are multiplying to such a degree as will entirely crush all art and industry; tho' perhaps, their first increase, together with other circumstances, might have contributed to the growth of these advantages.

The chief reason politicians and economists throughout history have failed to grasp the idea behind the "Laffer curve" is their confusion of work and productivity. Through both introspection and observation, the politician understands that when tax rates are raised, there is a tendency to work harder and longer to maintain after-tax income. What is not so apparent, because it requires analysis *at the margin,* is this: As taxes are raised, individuals in the system may indeed work harder, but their productivity declines. Hume himself had some trouble with this point:

> There is a prevailing maxim, among some reasoners, that every new tax creates a new ability in the subject to bear it, and that each increase of public burdens increases proportionably the industry of the people. This maxim is of such a nature as is most likely to be abused; and is so much the more dangerous as its truth cannot be altogether denied: But it must be owned, when kept within certain bounds, to have some foundation in reason and experience.

Twenty years later, in *The Wealth of Nations,* Adam Smith had no such problem: In his hypothetical pin factory, what is important to a nation is not the effort of individuals but the productivity of *individuals working together.* When the tax rates are raised, the workers themselves may work harder in an effort to maintain their income level. But if the pin-making entrepreneur is a marginal manufacturer, the increased tax rate will cause him to shift into the leisure sphere or into a lower level of economic activity, and the *system* will lose *all* the production of the pin factory. The politician who stands in the midst of this situation may correctly conclude that the increase in tax rates causes people to work harder. But it is not so easy for him to realize that they are now less efficient in their work and are producing less.

To see this in another way, imagine that there are three men who are skilled at building houses. If they work together, one works on the foundation, one on the frame, and the third on the roof. Together they can build three houses in three months. If they work separately, each building his own home, they need six months to build the three houses. If the tax rate on homebuilding is 49 percent, they will work together, since the government leaves them a small gain from their division of labor. But if the tax rate goes to 51 percent, they suffer a net loss because of their teamwork, and so they will work separately. When they were pooling their efforts, since they could produce six houses in the same time it would take them to build three houses working alone, the government was collecting revenues almost equivalent to the value of three completed homes. At the 51-percent tax rate, however, the government loses all the revenue, and the economy loses the production of the three extra homes that could have been built by their joint effort.

The worst mistakes in history are made by political leaders who, instead of realizing that revenues could be gained by lowering tax rates, become alarmed at the fall in revenues that results when citizens seek to escape high tax rates through barter and do-it-yourself labor. Their impulse is to impose taxes that cannot be escaped, the most onerous of which is a poll tax or head tax, which must be paid annually for the mere privilege of living. Hume had no difficulty in pointing out the fallacy of that line of thinking:

> Historians inform us that one of the chief causes of the destruction of the Roman state was the alteration which Constantine introduced into the finances, by substituting a universal poll tax in lieu of almost all the tithes, customs, and excises which formerly composed the revenue of the empire. The people, in all the provinces, were so grinded and oppressed by the publicans [tax collectors] that they were glad to take refuge under the conquering arms of the barbarians, whose dominion, as they had fewer necessities and less art, was found preferable to the refined tyranny of the Romans.

The trouble with a poll tax, as Hume noted, is that it *can* be escaped—one method being not to defend your country against an aggressor who promises to remove the tax as soon as he has gained power. Montesquieu made a similar observation in Book XIII of *The Spirit of the Laws:*

Because a moderate government has been productive of admirable effects, this moderation has been laid aside; because great taxes have been raised, they wanted to carry them to excess; and ungrateful to the hand of liberty, of whom they received this present, they addressed themselves to slavery, who never grants the least favor.

Liberty produces excessive taxes; the effect of excessive taxes is slavery; and slavery produces diminution of tribute. . . .

It was this excess of taxes that occasioned the prodigious facility with which the Mahommedans carried on their conquests. Instead of a continual series of extortions devised by the subtle avarices of the Greek emperors, the people were subjected to a simple tribute which was paid and collected with ease. Thus they were far happier in obeying a barbarous nation than a corrupt government, in which they suffered every inconvenience of lost liberty, with all the horror of present slavery.

Modern governments have at least abandoned the notion of using a poll tax to generate revenues. Instead, they often go directly to the barter economy in search of revenues. Activities previously not admitted to the money economy and public marketplace because of public disapproval—e.g., gambling and pornography—are welcomed because of the promise of revenues. But this process tends to lower the quality of the marketplace itself, hastening the exodus or discouraging the entry of enterprises that have earned public approbation.

"Cracking Down"

Another timeless remedy of governments that find revenues falling on the face of rising tax rates is to increase the numbers and power of the tax collectors. Invariably, this method further reduces the flow of revenues to the treasury. Yet even with a thousand-year history of failure, the policy of "cracking down" on tax evasion remains a favorite of modern governments. Here is Adam Smith, in *The Wealth of Nations,* on why such policies are doomed from the start:

Every tax ought to be so contrived as both to take out and to keep out of the pockets of the people as little as possible, over and above what it brings into the public treasury of the state. A tax may either take out or keep out of the pockets of the people a great deal more than it brings into the public treasury in the four following ways.

First, the levying of it may require a great number of fixers, whose salaries may eat up the greater part of the produce of the tax, and whose perquisites may impose another additional tax upon the people.

Secondly, it may obstruct the industry of the people, and discourage them from applying to certain branches of business which might give maintenance and employment to great multitudes. While it obliges the people to pay, it may thus diminish, or perhaps destroy, some of the funds which might enable them to do so.

Thirdly, by the forfeitures and other penalties which these unfortunate individuals incur who attempt unsuccessfully to evade the tax, it may frequently ruin them, and thereby put an end to the benefit which the community might have received from the employment of their capitals. An injudicious tax offers a great temptation to smuggling. But the penalties of smuggling must rise in proportion to the temptation. The law, contrary to all the ordinary principles of justice, first creates the temptation, and then punishes those who yield to it; and it commonly enhances the punishment too in proportion to the very circumstances which ought certainly to alleviate it, the temptation to commit the crime.

Fourthly, by subjecting the people to the frequent visits and odious examination of the tax-gatherers, it may expose them to much unnecessary trouble, vexation, and oppression; and though vexation is not, strictly speaking, expense, it is certainly equivalent to the expense at which every man would be willing to redeem himself from it.

Adam Smith's point about smuggling may now seem obscure. After all, smuggling was something that went on in the 18th century, wasn't it? Consider the following excerpts from a recent editorial in *The Wall Street Journal,* which urged New York State and New York City to reduce their combined cigarette tax from 26¢ to 10¢ a pack:

Through our browsings in the *United States Tobacco Journal* we have learned of estimates that half the cigarettes smoked in New York City are smuggled in from North Carolina, where the tax is 2¢ a pack. State Senator Roy M. Goodman, a Manhattan Republican, says the state and city are losing $93 million a year in this fashion. The smugglers load 40-foot trailers with 60,000 cartons purchased legally at $2.40 each and peddle them in the city via the organized crime network for $3.75, which is $1.25 or more below legitimate retail.

Mr. Goodman recommends a one-year suspension of the city's 8¢-a-pack tax in order to break up the smuggling, plus an increase in the state enforcement field staff to 250 from the current 50, plus five years in jail for anyone caught smuggling 20,000 cartons or more. Last year only nine smugglers were jailed, each for a few months, with the common penalty $10 or $15.

If Mr. Goodman's solution were adopted, at the end of the year the smugglers would be back, and the state would have a bigger bureaucracy. More smugglers would be caught, more judges and bailiffs and clerks would have to be hired, more jails would have to be built and more jailers hired. The wives and children of the jailed smugglers would go on welfare.

Cutting the tax to 10¢ avoids all that. It immediately becomes uneconomic to smuggle. The enforcement staff of 50 can be assigned to more useful work, the state saving $1 million on that count alone. The courts would be less clogged with agents and smugglers, and the taxpayers would save court costs, as well as the costs of confining convicted smugglers and caring for their families.

The state and city would *appear* to face a loss of $50 million or $60 million in revenues, but of course smokers would now buy their cigarettes through legitimate channels and the 10¢ a pack would yield about as much in revenues as 26¢ a pack yields now. But that's not all. Legitimate dealers would double their cigarette sales, earning higher business profits and personal income that the city and state then taxes.

And don't forget the impact on the millions of cigarette smokers who would save 16¢ a pack. At a pack a day, that's $58.40 per year. At average marginal tax rates, a smoker has to earn more than $80 before Federal, state, and city taxes are deducted to get that amount. He can thus maintain his or her standard of living on $80 less in gross wage demands per year, which means it becomes economic for the marginal employer to do business in New York, increasing the number of jobs of all varieties and reducing cost and tax pressure on social services.

Among other benefits, the industrious smugglers would have to find legitimate employment. It might be argued that they would be thrown on the welfare rolls. But if we know New York City, they are already on the welfare rolls, and would be forced to get off once they have visible jobs.

The Finance Office of New York City, unwilling to take the advice of either Adam Smith or *The Wall Street Journal*, simply rejected the idea that lowering rates would produce expanded revenues. But Adam Smith's advice was not even taken in England at the time he tendered it. The theory was not tested until 1827, and then only by accident, by an Act of Parliament. Oddly enough, the incident in question involved tobacco smuggling. Stephen Dowell gives the following account in *A History of Taxation and Taxes in England:*

> The consumption of tobacco had failed to increase in proportion to the increase in the population. A curious circumstance had happened as regards the duty on tobacco. In effecting the statutory rearrangement of the duties in the previous year, the draughtsman of the Bill, in error, allowed one fourth of the duty to lapse in July. Unconsciously he had accomplished a master stroke, for his reduction in the duty was followed by a decrease in smuggling so considerable as to induce [Chancellor of the Exchequer] Robinson to allow his [budget] surplus, estimated at about £700,000, to go to continue the reduction thus unconsciously effected.

The Politburo of the Soviet Union has the same problem as the Finance Office of New York City: It also rejects the idea behind the "Laffer curve." The greatest burden to Soviet economic development is Soviet agriculture. Roughly 34.3 million Soviet citizens, out of a total population of 250 million, are engaged in producing food for the nation—and there is never enough. The United States, by contrast, employs only 4.3 million workers in food production, out of a total population of 200 million, generating an annual surplus for export equivalent to one-fourth the entire Soviet output. The drain on the Soviet economy is not only the low productivity of the farm sector. Because there are always shortages, and the state puts farm goods on the market at regulated prices rather than using the market system to allocate what is available, Soviet citizens spend billions of hours annually waiting in lines. If food were produced in plentiful quantities, it could still be allocated through regulated prices in conformance with Soviet ideology, but most of the lines would disappear, and the talents and energies of the urban work force would not be wasted in long lines.

The real source of this problem is the high marginal tax rates exacted on the state's collective farms. The state provides land, capital, housing, and other necessities on its collectives. It also permits the workers to keep 10 percent of the value of their production. The marginal tax rate is thus 90 percent. In agriculture, a small expenditure of effort might yield, say, 100 units of production; but twice the effort might be required for 150 units, and four times the effort for 200 units. The worker on the collective thus faces a progressive tax schedule so withering that any incentive to expend anything beyond a minimal effort is lost. With minimum work, he gets land, capital, housing, and other necessities, as well as 10 units of output. By quadrupling his effort (not necessarily physical effort, but perhaps increased attentiveness to details), he gets the same services and only 10 more units of output.

Meanwhile, however, the peasants on the collective farms are also permitted to tend private plots, the entire output of which is theirs to keep. The tax rate on these private plots is zero. Here is the result, as detailed by Hedrick Smith in *The Russians:*

> Twenty-seven percent of the total value of Soviet farm output—about $32.5 billion worth a year—comes from private plots that occupy less than 1 percent of the nation's agricultural lands (about 26 million acres). At that rate, private plots are roughly 40 times as efficient as the land worked collectively. . . . Peasants farm their own plots much more intensively than they do collective land.
>
> Ultimately, the Communist ideal is to have this last embarrassing but necessary vestige of private enterprise wither away as industrialized state farming grows in scale and output. Nikita Khrushchev, in spite of rural roots, pursued that end vigorously and earned the enmity of the peasantry. He cut the size of private plots to a maximum of half an acre and made life difficult for the farm market trade. I was told by Russian friends that Ukrainian peasants became so irate that they stopped selling eggs as food and made paint out of them.
>
> Under Brezhnev things have improved. The maximum plot went back up to an acre and measures were taken to improve farm market operations. Soviet figures show the private farm output grew nearly 15 percent from 1966 to 1973.

In terms of the "Laffer curve," what Khrushchev did by reducing the size of the private plots from one acre to one-half acre was to increase the marginal tax rate of the *system* from point C to point A. This was undoubtedly a major cause of his political downfall. On the other hand, Brezhnev moved the marginal tax rate of the system back to point C, increasing output and revenues to the previous levels. This was an "economic miracle" of minor dimensions, but it has undoubtedly contributed heavily to Brezhnev's durability as a political leader.

The Politics of the "Laffer Curve"

The "Laffer curve" is a simple but exceedingly powerful analytical tool. In one way or another, all transactions, even the simplest, take place along it. The homely adage, "You can catch more flies with molasses than with vinegar," expresses the essence of the curve. But empires are built on the bottom of this simple curve and crushed against the top of it. The Caesars understood this, and so did Napoleon (up to a point) and the greatest of the Chinese emperors. The Founding Fathers of the United States knew it well; the arguments for union (in *The Federalist Papers*) made by Hamilton, Madison, and Jay reveal an understanding of the notion. Until World War I—when progressive taxation was sharply increased to help finance it—the United States successfully remained out of the "prohibitive range."

In the 20th century, especially since World War I, there has been a constant struggle by all the nations of the world to get down the curve. The United States managed to do so in the 1920s, because Andrew Mellon understood the lessons of the "Laffer curve" for the domestic economy. Mellon argued that there are always two prices in the private market that will produce the same revenues. Henry Ford, for example, could get the same revenue by selling a few cars for $100,000 each, or a great number for $1,000 each. (Of course, Ford was forced by the threat of competition to sell at the low price.) The tax rate, said Mellon, is the "price of government." But the nature of government is monopolistic; government itself must find the lowest rate that yields the desired revenue.

Because Mellon was successful in persuading Republican Presidents—first Warren G. Harding and then Calvin Coolidge—of the truth of his ideas the high wartime tax rates were steadily cut back. The excess-profits tax on industry was repealed, and the 77-percent rate on the highest bracket of personal income was rolled back in stages, so that by 1925 it stood at 25 percent. As a result, the period 1921–29 was one of phenomenal economic expansion: GNP grew from $69.6 billion to $103.1 billion. And because prices fell during this period, GNP grew even faster in real terms, by 54 percent. At the lower rates, revenues grew sufficiently to enable Mellon to reduce the national debt from $24.3 billion to $16.9 billion.

The stock market crash of 1929 and the subsequent global depression occurred because Herbert Hoover unwittingly contracted the world economy with his high-tariff policies, which pushed the West, as an economic unit, up the "Laffer curve." Hoover compounded the problem in 1932 by raising personal tax rates almost up to the levels of 1920.

The most important economic event following World War II was also the work of a finance minister who implicitly understood the importance of the "Laffer curve." Germany had been pinned to the uppermost ranges of the curve since World War I. It took a financial panic in the spring of 1948 to shake

Germany loose. At that point, German citizens were still paying a 50-percent marginal tax rate on incomes of $600 and a 95-percent rate on incomes above $15,000. On June 22, 1948, Finance Minister Ludwig Erhard announced cuts that raised the 50-percent bracket to $2,200 and the 95-percent bracket to $63,000. The financial panic ended, and economic expansion began. It was Erhard, not the Marshall Plan, who saved Europe from Communist encroachment. In the decade that followed, Erhard again and again slashed the tax rates, bringing the German economy farther down the curve and into a higher level of prosperity. In 1951 the 50-percent bracket was pushed up to $5,000 and in 1953 to $9,000, while at the same time the rate for the top bracket was reduced to 82 percent. In 1954, the rate for the top bracket was reduced again, to 80 percent, and in 1955 it was pulled down sharply, to 63 percent on incomes above $250,000; the 50-percent bracket was pushed up to $42,000. Yet another tax reform took place in 1958: The government exempted the first $400 of income and brought the rate for the top bracket down to 53 percent. It was this systematic lowering of unnecessarily high tax rates that produced the German "economic miracle." As national income rose in Germany throughout the 1950s, so did revenues, enabling the government to construct its "welfare state" as well as its powerful national defense system.

The British empire was built on the lower end of the "Laffer curve" and dismantled on the upper end. The high wartime rates imposed to finance the Napoleonic wars were cut back sharply in 1816, despite warnings from "fiscal experts" that the high rates were needed to reduce the enormous public debt of £900 million. For the following 60 years, the British economy grew at an unprecedented pace, as a series of finance ministers used ever-expanding revenues to lower steadily the tax rates and tariffs.

In Britain, though, unlike the United States, there was no Mellon to risk lowering the extremely high tax rates imposed to finance World War I. As a result, the British economy struggled through the 1920s and 1930s. After World War II, the British government again made the mistake of not sufficiently lowering tax rates to spur individual initiative. Instead, the postwar Labour government concentrated on using tax policy for Keynesian objectives—i.e., increasing consumer demand to expand output. On October 23, 1945, tax rates were cut on lower income brackets and surtaxes were added to the already high rates on the upper-income brackets. Taxes on higher incomes were increased, according to Chancellor of the Exchequer Hugh Dalton, in order to "continue that steady advance toward economic and social equality which we have made during the war and which the Government firmly intends to continue in peace."

From that day in 1945, there has been no concerted political voice in Britain arguing for a reduction of the high tax rates. Conservatives have supported and won tax reductions for business, especially investment-tax income credits. But while arguing for a reduction of the 83-percent rate on incomes above £20,000 (roughly $35,000 at current exchange rates) of earned income and the 98-percent rate on "unearned income" from investments, they have insisted that government first lower its spending, in order to permit the rate reductions. Somehow, the spending levels never can be cut. Only in the last several months of 1977 has Margaret Thatcher, the leader of the opposition Conservative Party, spoken of reducing the high tax rates as a way of expanding revenues.

In the United States, in September 1977, the Republican National Committee unanimously endorsed the plan of Representative Jack Kemp of New York for cutting tax rates as a way of expanding revenues through increased business activity. This was the first time since 1953 that the GOP had embraced the concept of tax cuts! In contrast, the Democrats under President Kennedy sharply cut tax rates in 1962–64 (though making their case in Keynesian terms). The reductions successfully moved the United States economy down the "Laffer curve," expanding the economy and revenues.

It is crucial to Western economic expansion, peace, and prosperity that "conservative" parties move in this direction. They are, after all, traditionally in favor of income growth, with "liberals" providing the necessary political push for income redistribution. A welfare state is perfectly consistent with the "Laffer curve," and can function successfully along its lower range. But there must be income before there can be income redistribution. Most of the economic failures of the century can rightly be charged to the failure of conservatives to press for tax rates along the lower range of the "Laffer curve." Presidents Eisenhower, Nixon, and Ford were timid in this crucial area of public policy. The Goldwater Republicans of 1963–64, in fact, emphatically opposed the Kennedy tax-rate cuts!

If, during the remainder of this decade, the United States and Great Britain demonstrate the power of the "Laffer curve" as an analytical tool, its use will spread, in the developing countries as well as the developed world. Politicians who understand the curve will find that they can defeat politicians who do not, other things being equal. Electorates all over the world always know when they are unnecessarily perched along the upper edge of the "Laffer curve," and will support political leaders who can bring them back down.

3B.3. From Redistributive to Hegemonic Logic: The Transformation of American Tax Politics, 1894–1963

RONALD FREDERICK KING

While we think of supply-side economics as a recent invention, most of its elements have been around since the early part of this century. In this reading Ronald King looks at the key point underpinning supply-side economics, the assertion that high taxes on the wealthy will reduce economic growth. He sees this assertion as a convenient way to attack progressive taxes by converting what would otherwise be an argument between rich and poor to an argument about the requirements for economic growth (which benefits everyone).

He argues that when the income tax was first imposed, its burden fell heavily on the rich, arousing expectations that it would become a major means of income redistribution. This, King claims, led capitalist elites to search for a means to prevent this effect. In order to do so, they had to persuade politicians that it was not in the interests of the majority to use the income tax as a major redistributive weapon against the wealthy minority.

The key event for King is the general acceptance by both Republican and Democratic policy makers of an argument made in the 1920s by Treasury Secretary Andrew Mellon, a forerunner of the supply-side economists of the 1980s. Mellon argued that it was important to consider the effects of taxation on economic growth, and that heavy taxation of capital, by reducing savings, would reduce investment and growth. This, in King's view, converted a zero-sum argument over the distribution of the economic pie to a non-zero-sum argument about how the growth of the economic pie could be secured.

In assessing the significance of King's theory, it clearly matters a great deal whether Mellon's argument is true or false. If false, then acceptance of the view reduces redistribution without increasing growth. If true, then the majority faces a trade-off between current and future benefits. The reader should note that while in this article King seems to lean toward saying it is false, in his recent book Money, Time and Politics *he is more ambiguous.*

"The present assault upon capital is but the beginning." Thus wrote Justice Stephen J. Field in a concurring opinion to the 1895 Supreme Court decision declaring unconstitutional a 2 percent income tax on corporate profits and individual earnings over $4,000. "It will be but the stepping-stone to others, larger and more sweeping, till our political contests will become a war of the poor against the rich; a war constantly growing in intensity and bitterness."[1] Now, over eighty-five years later, federal income taxes appropriate considerably more than 2 percent of receipts and raise hundreds of billions of dollars annually. Yet the politics of fiscal policy formation can hardly be said to correspond to the early prognostications. There has been no "communistic march" to "confiscate wealth," "spoliate private property," and "ultimately wreck the American republic."[2] Tax politics has become routinized. It displays little of the divisive fervor that characterized the redistributive struggles of an earlier era. Allocational equity, much less equality, now constitutes just one among several ends of taxation and, indeed, is often compromised in the pursuit of objectives promising social benefits for all. Effective burdens are far less progressive than one might infer from the nominal rate schedules, and the notion of ability to pay, although an accepted part of American political ideology, does not operate as an absolute standard, serving instead to put the onus of proof on those wishing to introduce special exemptions and dispensations into the revenue code.

This essay seeks to explain why Justice Field's dire prediction did not come to pass, why contemporary American tax politics has not, after all, taken the form of a bitter class conflict over the apportionment of short-run liabilities. I base my explanation on two alternative perspectives on fiscal controversies that have been derived, by loose analogy, from mathematical models of distributional games. The first perspective corresponds to a strict zero-sum opposition, in which the total payoff is fixed and fungible: any benefit received by one player reduces the amount available to others. The second corresponds to an asymmetric and non-zero-sum game model, in which a marginal shift of resources to one sort of player potentially but with risk offers enhanced net discounted payoffs to all players over time.

Although further game analogies are possible, these two perspectives hold special importance for understanding tax struggles in the U.S., especially when viewed from a temporal, and not merely analytical, standpoint. Federal income taxation did once seriously threaten to promote zero-sum redistribution. Such tax redistribution was considered by many the only way to protect the people against undemocratic accumulations of wealth and power and to compel the rich to contribute their just share to the support of the government. However, the introduction of an investment-dependent logic stressing market consequences, represented by the second of our game models, effectively ended any redistributive hopes. It gradually altered the purposes attached to taxation policy and thus modified the way groups calculated their interest when revenue matters reached the political agenda. Grounded in the structural asymmetries of modern capitalism, this revised fiscal outlook was neither necessary to nor inherent in the taxation arena per se. Instead, it became established only after much struggle and as the result of a series of strategic choices. By the end of the Second World War, fiscal policy had become almost synonymous with macroeconomic policy. Prosperity subordinated apportionment, and the federal government fully accepted its role as indirect stimulator, regularly awarding incentives to both demand and supply yet possessing scant control over the private economic institutions expected to respond. The story to follow, therefore, chronicles certain major transformations in the game of U.S. federal taxation politics and the effects these have had on the range of predictable distributional outcomes. . . .

The Emergence of Hegemonic* Tax Logic

The political struggles over the passage of the initial federal income tax in the United States reflected fundamental conflict regarding the distribution of immediate government fiscal burdens. To income tax proponents, existing consumption taxes, which bore primarily upon the mass of citizens, were seen as being the product of undemocratic elite domination of the political process and as relieving avaricious wealth of its just obligations. To income tax opponents, by contrast, the subjection of a single class of taxpayers to discriminatory penalties simply because of their higher earnings demonstrated the dangers that an aroused populace could pose when the precept of equal treatment before the law was contradicted by short-run advantage. The conflict over taxation was certainly symbolic of a wider struggle over the development of the American society. Yet taxes, in themselves, were featured merely as representative of the perceived bias of public policy and the abuses of class legislation. The issue was defined on both sides in terms of distributional equity versus myopic greed. The principles of proper allocation were determined solely by the arrangement of current liabilities, and all wider, economic implications of tax impositions were explicitly denied.

Hegemony is a term derived from the work of Antonio Gramsci. It refers to the process through which the working class internalizes the values of the ruling class and comes to think that what is good for the rich is good for them.—Ed.

Some initial supporters of the tax did start to express reservations, even though the original income levy was quite modest, with only 10 percent of federal receipts in 1914 garnered from this new revenue source and barely 1 percent of reported net incomes and profits appropriated. Already they feared mass persecution of business. Theodore Roosevelt, for example, wrote to his cousin in 1915 that "my withers are unwrung" and that he concurred with the assault upon this income tax law.[3] Potential splits within the pro-tax movement, however, did not prove historically significant. Under the pressure of military preparedness and war, the income tax was raised to levels entirely unforeseen by even its strongest advocates. In the postwar return to normalcy, the debate over fiscal obligations resumed but it was recast in a structurally different, non-zero-sum form.

With the decline in tariff revenues caused by the outbreak of World War I in Europe and with the need for funds to finance rearmament at home, an emergency income tax increase was approved in 1914 and extended the following year. The agreement was that new legislation would be proposed shortly. In contrast to the Wilson administration's subsequent recommendation to lower the personal exemption, the 1916 act doubled the normal tax rate and raised the surtax to 13 percent, while leaving exemptions untouched. It further imposed a graduated inheritance tax and levied a special tax on the profits of munitions manufacturers.

Paradoxically, it was the insurgents opposed to foreign intervention who were the most emphatic proponents of the revenue measure designed to pay for war preparedness. In addition to the customary justifications based upon distributional equity, agrarian Democrats believed that northeastern manufacturers would take a less aggressive stand on foreign policy if the cost of such a stand were greater. As Warren Bailey (Democrat, Pennsylvania) declared, "if the forces of big business are to plunge this country into a saturnalia of extravagance for war purposes at a time of peace, it is my notion that the forces of big business should put up the money."[4] The principal Republican complaint was that the 1916 act represented a new and dangerous direction in fiscal policy. Employment of the income tax had not been reserved for dire national emergency, nor merely to compensate for downward revisions of the tariff. The tax could no longer be seen just as a secondary fiscal tool to be used when traditional sources of revenue proved inadequate. Critics claimed, with much prescience, that income taxation was attaining an autonomous development that increased the possibility of its use for redistributive ends.

America's entry into the war placed great strains upon the nation's economy and supplied the pretext for an enormous expansion of the income tax as virtually the only elastic source of federal funds. Two sizable war revenue bills were enacted, in October 1917 and in December 1918, both of which were approved by overwhelming majorities and endorsed by the leaderships of both parties. Treasury Secretary McAdoo, determined not to follow the example of Chase during the Civil War, organized the broad distribution of Liberty Bonds and resolved to finance at least one-third of government expenditures out of current receipts. An economically rational fiscal policy would have been far more regressive, since it would have reduced consumer spending to encourage a shift to war production and to help curb demand inflation. Such a policy, however, would not have been acceptable to the dominant political coalition in the Congress, which was concerned primarily with preventing war profiteering and with forcing the wealthy to bear a just share of expenses.

As a result of the war revenue acts, income and profits taxes in 1918 generated 63.1 percent of total federal receipts, customs duties only 4.9 percent, and miscellaneous excises 23.8 percent. The maximum personal income tax rate of 77 percent (12 percent plus a 65 percent surtax) was five times the prewar level and eleven times the 7 percent maximum rate originally imposed just six years before. As for corporations, 37.2 percent of net reported profits went to the government, as compared to merely 2.0 percent in 1916.[5] Part of this increased corporate burden came from an excess profits tax on surplus business income, termed by one newspaper "the first attempt in a country whose industries are organized under capitalist leadership to limit profits as part of its economic system."[6] Ways and Means Chairman Claude Kitchen had wanted to follow the Canadian model, which was based on profits as a percentage of invested capital, rather than the British model, which was based on prewar average returns. Kitchen hoped that the former approach would permit the tax to become a permanent feature of the campaign for revenue equity. The Wilson administration and Senate Democrats disagreed, claiming that the Canadian system demanded a complex and hazy definition of capital, encouraged overinvestment, and discriminated against growing and risky enterprises. The final provision embodied a compromise combining bits of both principles in an ad hoc fashion.

Among the problems confronted by the Congress was an unavoidable ignorance regarding the amount of taxation the nation would willingly bear. Never before had so much been taken, both directly and indirectly, from incomes and profits. Given the highly progressive rate structure, concern was for the first time expressed that a level might be reached where business would lose its incentive to invest. Academic moderates began to remind their radical colleagues demanding the conscription of wealth as well as soldiers that some profits were necessary if industry was to carry out the expansion required for war production. The Congressional opinion was that, with net profits more than double the prewar average, it was unreasonable to assert that business could not stand increased taxes. Yet a few conservatives in debate registered their dissent from the Republican strategy of cooperation. "Unnecessary taxation," said Warren Harding, "only halts and hampers the needed activity of capital."[7] An indication of the new attention to the possible economic consequences of heavy taxation can be seen in the Finance Committee minority report in 1918. Already knowing that they would control the next Congress, Republicans objected that it would be wrong to fix rates as far ahead as 1920, not merely because of the difficulty of estimating government needs, but especially because it was impossible to forecast postwar business conditions and because an inflexible policy might "disarrange our industrial system."[8]

Spokesmen for private industry were surprisingly restrained in their remonstrations that very high taxes were destructive of the capitalized energy necessary to keep the war machine functioning. Business was being extremely careful to avoid all action that might cast aspersions on corporate motives. There was still considerable feeling in the country that this was a rich man's war, entered into for imperialistic gain and windfall profits. The example of the Russian Revolution was a caution for those who wished that mass attitudes could be ignored and the cost of the war shifted downward. The business campaign against progressive taxation was thus reserved for after the close of hostilities, when it emerged with vehemence. For example, the National Industrial Conference Board and the National Tax Association arranged educational seminars on high taxes as they contributed to rising prices and fettered industrial expansion; a movement was launched on behalf of a national sales tax, sponsored by organizations such as the Business Men's National Tax Committee and the Tax League of America, and a United States Chamber of Commerce referendum resulted in a 1718-to-44 vote against the retention of the excess profits tax.[9] The outgoing Wilson administration gave some support to the campaign for tax reduction, but no legislation was advanced. Tax relief for the wealthy had to wait until after the inauguration of Harding.

Thus the first public consideration of taxation's economic effects on the private market, and therefore the initial shift away from taxation as a narrow zero-sum struggle solely over the immediate allocation of government burdens, occurred at the end of World War I. Business agitation for reductions in tax rates entailed far more than a reactionary dream of returning to normalcy. Finding its best spokesman in the incoming Secretary of the Treasury, Andrew Mellon, a new conservatism arose that accepted the principle of graduated taxation but proclaimed that rates on profits and high incomes ought not be set so as to restrict economic expansion. There had always been complaints that the income tax penalized thrift and discouraged industriousness. But the thrust of these objections was that the tax violated normative values fundamental to American life. Now, however, the very existence of the income tax was not in question, and certain political actors began to evaluate the marginal effects of tax changes on such critical economic variables as growth, prices, and unemployment. The fiscal tools were rudimentary, economic understanding limited, and it was more assumed than proved that tax reduction for the wealthy would have the desired stimulative effects. Nevertheless, the application of a non-zero-sum logic to internal revenues gave conservatives a new, more sophisticated position from which to resist the possible redistributive uses of income taxation.

The most comprehensive statement of the new tax ideology is to be found in

Mellon's book, *Taxation: The People's Business,* published in 1924. According to Mellon, "the principle that a man should pay tax in accordance with his 'ability to pay' is sound, but like other general statements, has its practical limitations and qualifications, and when, as a result of an excessive or unsound basis of taxation, it becomes evident that the source of taxation is drying up and wealth is being diverted into unproductive channels, yielding neither revenue to the Government nor profit to the people, then it is time to readjust our basis of taxation upon sound principles."[10] In contrast to the situation just a few years before, the income tax was no longer seen as confiscation and progressive rates were not indicative of encroaching communism. The problem with the tax system was merely that it contained inefficient provisions that required readjustment. The existing high levels of taxation, an inheritance from the war, were said to violate sound principles in three ways: they drove investment funds away from gainful employment and into such unproductive sources as tax-exempt securities; they hampered incentives and quashed the spirit of enterprise; and they reduced the total amount of private investment capital. In order to unleash economic growth, the secretary recommended, the maximum level of taxation must never diminish after-tax profits on investment to a lower point than can be obtained from speculation or from tax-free bonds. Thus he proposed a complete repeal of the excess profits tax, a reduction in the top-bracket personal surtax to 25 percent on incomes over $100,000, and a major slash in the estate tax. By encouraging private capital to contribute more fully to the nation's well being, government policy could generate long-run economic prosperity that would permit sufficient government receipts under low nominal rates, a gradual reduction in the public debt, ample profits, and full employment.

According to Mellon, what had been missing from earlier fiscal theories, which focused entirely upon zero-sum struggles over public contributions, was the recognition that the consequences of taxation extended beyond the individual called upon to pay, affecting the economic development of the nation as a whole. Even workers, he contended, would be better off supporting the kind of regressive tax cuts sought by the Harding administration. "The hardship of suffering resulting from business depressions and unemployment inevitably falls most seriously not upon those paying high income taxes, but upon the great body of the people of small incomes. Under our form of government there is, and very rightly so, little danger of any undue burden from the taxes imposed directly upon those of small means, but there is danger of serious hardship and suffering to them because of high prices, unemployment, and high living costs, resulting from unjust or unwise tax laws."[11] Mellon's conclusion is a full statement of the integrative, cooperative aspect of business-stimulative tax policy arising from the new conservative fiscal ideology. "The prosperity of each individual," he wrote, "is, after all, dependent upon the prosperity of the whole country; and anything that endangers or retards the country's normal development also jeopardizes to that extent the prosperity of each individual taxpayer."[12]

While explanations for this rapid shift in basic ideology must be tentative, four interrelated causes emerge from the account given above. First, the state of economic knowledge changed considerably over these thirty years, and politicians became more sensitive to academic teachings during the war. Nevertheless, there is certainly no automatic correlation between economic pedagogy and political practice, and one should always look for concrete inducements when politicians adopt the categories of professionals.

Second, the huge increases during the war in the size of the state and the amount of taxation meant both that a greater percentage of the income of the wealthy was publicly appropriated and that, for the first time, progressive taxation could have substantial effects on the social distribution of income. As one Washington attorney euphemistically stated, "In 1917 and 1918, when the rates very suddenly went way up, we realized with equal suddenness the importance of fundamental, sound, right principles both in the provisions and in the administration of the income tax."[13]

Third, the very concept of an excess profits tax presented a challenge to the assumed right of a firm to whatever it receives, demanding a clear ideological response from capital. As James Emery of the National Association of Manufacturers said, "I think the excess profits tax carries, first of all, a false social implication. It insidiously insinuates, in the phrase that qualifies the tax, that the amount which is exempted from the operation of the tax comprises a fair, normal return, all above which is in its nature an excessive and socially improper return. In this hour, in this day, we cannot be too careful about the social implications of the phraseology of our taxation, for that carries a dangerous and incorrect idea into the public mind.[14] In replying to the connotation that earnings above a certain base are illegitimate, it was logical to claim that profits, even very high profits, serve a necessary and useful social function. The direct attack upon unlimited returns brought forth an answer based upon economics rather than equity, that the accumulation of surplus corporate income was a precondition to the investment needed initially for war production and later for national economic growth and progress.

Fourth, the new emphasis upon the effect taxation can have on industry came not merely from an awareness of the greater percentage of the national income now taken and from a business reaction and protest. It also came from a recognition that government policies can have an impact upon social relations. If subordinate classes could be convinced that the private market gains secured by means of tax-stimulated increases in productivity were greater than those possible through tax redistribution, they would be more likely to accept and participate in the emerging system of corporate capitalism. Thus the changes in the pattern of tax politics beginning during the 1920s can be seen as part of the movement toward the integration rather than the repression of organizations representing workers' material interests. This also found expression in, for example, Herbert Hoover's corporatist vision of a voluntarily self-regulating society.

It had taken thirty years, from the origin of the redistributive threat posed by income taxation, for hegemonic, capital-dependent considerations to emerge as a defense used by dominant groups in society. Under capitalism, savings and investment out of profits are necessary preconditions for generating future income streams to all social classes. To the extent that the manipulation of taxation influences capital decisions, through adjustments in the level and allocation of burdens, it provides a useful technique for any state seeking ways to affect private economic performance. Yet given the explicit prewar denials of such a broad impact, it was not at all obvious that this functional tax logic would appear. Moreover, once admitted into the revenue discourse, its acceptance was not immediate and it became an object of controversy during the inter-war era. Hegemonic taxation theory did quickly become a central tenet of mainstream Republicanism, but the positions adopted by others were inconsistent. For the coming period, the enactment of fiscal policies based upon hegemonic principle would depend upon the number of moderate and conservative Republicans in Congress and upon the responses of Democrats, insurgent Progressives, and the leaders of labor and agrarian interest organizations. . . .

Conclusion

The issues relevant to taxation politics have become much more complex since the time of Andrew Mellon. Yet the non-zero-sum logic basic to his program and the hegemonic concerns that he articulated remain essential to any analysis of the contemporary federal revenue system. They exercise significant influence over non-decisions restricting demands for greater effective tax progressivity and limiting the sorts of distributive claims responsible groups can make. Correspondingly, hegemonic, class-cooperative yet capital-dependent arguments also provide the principal defense for a number of the most well-entrenched and expensive of current tax preferences. Special tax stimulants to business investment have been proposed and passed by every single American president since Eisenhower, a surprising record of bipartisanship. Ability to pay has thus been substantially eroded, and the equitable apportionment of burdens has virtually ceased to be a politically potent doctrine. In other words, the federal income tax has gradually been tamed. It has lost its initial radical potential, has failed to reapportion incomes, and is now even being used to support capitalist accumulation.

Conventional zero-sum models of tax politics would explain this taming of the federal income tax by saying that a preponderance of legislative resources are held by business elites and that, while workers persistently oppose the awarding of fiscal advantages to the wealthy, they lack the political power to prevent it. Such a zero-sum game would certainly be very risky for dominant classes, for with any appreciable shift in class capacities, especially in a democracy where representatives responsible to the voting populace have an institutionalized say, they might lose all privileges. Historically, in fact, American income taxation did once portend real redistribution, and elites responded by taking the matter to the least democratic branch of government, the Supreme Court, to proscribe changes in the revenue base.

The important point, however, is that our story did not stop there. The 1895 tactic of legal prohibition was defeated by the passage of the Sixteenth Amendment, and a graduated tax was eventually levied. Yet income and wealth have not been expropriated. Instead, federal taxation politics has been slowly transformed. Strictly allocative concerns have been supplemented by, even subordinated to, a market philosophy that gives priority to capital investment and that emphasizes the cooperative national benefits to be derived from business stimulants for expanded productive potential. As a result, a relatively steep nominal tax progressivity is counterbalanced by numerous targeted erosions and inducements, many of which are intended to promote allegedly desirable social ends and have sometimes been approved with a degree of consensus inconsistent with traditional theory.

Actors do not appear sui generis in the political arena, and moreover, the institutional and ideological constitution of that arena affects the capacity of those actors to define and satisfy their interests. In this sense, the structured mode of insertion becomes an essential element in understanding political practice. Using terms of analogy to alternative types of rational games, this paper has argued that between 1921 and 1963 the ideological insertion of classes into tax politics was reformulated, which affected the pattern of conflict and the expected range of outcomes. After 1913, it was not the formal rules governing the aggregation of citizen preferences that constrained popular egalitarianism. Participation was left open through the normal channels of access and influence. However, a change gradually occurred in how classes viewed fiscal issues, affecting the objectives sought through taxation, the factors relevant to the calculation of net advantage and the possible appeal of class conciliation.

From the strictly zero-sum perspective, distributional struggles appear merely as private matters. Particularistic factions seek their own benefit at the expense of others, and no inherent merit resides in any group. The only restriction is that outcomes remain within relatively wide boundaries so that none can foresee such striking and persistent losses that they withdraw support from the prevailing social system. For example, during the late nineteenth and early twentieth centuries, certain reformers believed we had drifted sufficiently close to one boundary as to advocate state redistribution for purposes of public safety. Heeding the protests of farmers and workers about the inequity of revenue burdens, an income tax was urged, in the words of Benton McMillin, to "diminish the antipathies that now exist between the classes," by removing the basis of that "iconoclastic complaint which finds expression in violence and threatens the very foundations upon which our whole institutions rest."[15]

The situation is substantially altered, however, once dynamic, non-zero-sum market ramifications are introduced. Under the rules of a taxation game played by actors seeking to maximize revenues stemming from interconnected public and private spheres, those who control the mechanism that determines the size of the economic pie are the privileged ones. To protect after-tax profits and to insure their use in productive investment, the distributive interests of the capitalist minority can become the interest of all. Thus the terrain inside the boundaries gets structured, and effective tax progressivity disappears not simply because of the extraordinary power of an economic elite, nor because of any abstract purpose given to the state apparatus, but because of the organization of competitive tax politics in a capitalist democracy.

Nevertheless, and this has been fundamental to my narrative, there is no *a priori* reason for federal taxation to have become dominated by the goal of insuring stable growth for the American corporate economy. The restructuring of tax politics away from zero-sum redistribution was not unilaterally imposed upon an unwilling mass populace. Rather, the institutionalization of a revised fiscal outlook occurred over four decades, was itself an object of struggle among social forces, and was the culmination of a series of reasonable strategic choices. Only in retrospect does it appear inevitable that taxation would become the primary location for aggregate state macroeconomic interventions within which an asymmetric class coalition dependent upon capitalist investment would emerge as fundamental in patterning policy outcomes. . . .

Notes

1. Pollock vs. Farmers' Loan and Trust Co., 157 U.S. 429 (1895), p. 607.

2. Phrases used by William Guthrie and William Choate, counsels for the appellants, in Pollock vs. Farmers' Loan and Trust Co., *The Records and Briefs of the Supreme Court of the United States, 1782–1896,* microfilm edition (Wilmington, Del.: Scholarly Resources, Inc.), vol. 939, roll 427.

3. Theodore Roosevelt, Letter to William Emlen Roosevelt, January 24, 1915, *The Letters of Theodore Roosevelt,* ed. Elting Morrison (Cambridge: Harvard University Press, 1952), 8: 884.

4. Bailey quoted in Arthur S. Link, *Woodrow Wilson and the Progressive Era, 1910–1917* (New York: Harper and Row, 1954), p. 194.

5. Calculated from the historical tables found in U.S. Treasury Department, *Statistical Appendix to the Report of the Secretary of the Treasury on the State of the Finances,* fiscal year 1979 (Washington, D.C.: U.S. Government Printing Office, 1980), p. 8; and in U.S. Treasury Department, Bureau of Internal Revenue, *Statistics of Income for 1932* (Washington, D.C.: U.S. Government Printing Office, 1934), pp. 38, 47.

6. *New York Globe,* in *Literary Digest,* 54, no. 4 (January 27, 1917): 176.

7. *Congressional Record,* August 31, 1917; 55: 6471.

8. U.S. Congress, Senate, Committee on Finance, *Senate Report* no. 617, December 6, 1918, 65th Cong., 3rd sess., pt. 3, p. 2.

9. Chamber of Commerce of the United States, *Annual Report of the Board of Directors,* 9th Annual Meeting, April 1921, Report on the Results of Referendum no. 34 (Washington, D.C.: Chamber of Commerce, 1921), pp. 26–7. For a review of the sales

tax debate, see K.M. Williamson, "The Literature on the Sales Tax," *Quarterly Journal of Economics* 35, no. 4 (August 1921): 618–33.

10. Andrew Mellon, *Taxation: The People's Business* (New York: Macmillan, 1924), pp. 15–16.

11. Andrew Mellon, U.S. Treasury Department, *Annual Report of the Secretary of the Treasury on the State of the Finances,* fiscal year ending June 30, 1921, transmitted November 28, 1921 (Washington, D.C.: U.S. Government Printing Office, 1922), p. 13.

12. Andrew Mellon, *Taxation: The People's Business,* p. 138.

13. J.C. Peacock, "Revision of the Income Tax to Promote Equity and Develop Sources of Taxable Income," *Proceedings, Second National Industrial Conference,* New York City, October 22, 1920, Special Report no. 17 (New York: National Industrial Conference Board, 1920), p. 14.

14. James A. Emery, "Address," *Proceedings, National Industrial Tax Conference,* Chicago, April 16, 1920, Special Report no. 9 (Boston: National Industrial Conference Board, 1920), pp. 8–9.

15. *Congressional Record,* January 29, 1894; 26: appendix 415.

3C. The Politics of Deficits

Viewed from the standpoint of Keynesian theory, national deficits are sometimes good and sometimes bad. Deficits are good in recessionary periods when lower taxes and increased expenditures stimulate the economy, but they are bad in boom periods, when they overstimulate the economy. Deficits that exist only in recessionary periods are called cyclical deficits. Deficits that persist in good times are called structural deficits.

Most economists agree that cyclical deficits are a good thing but structural deficits are not. In theory, structural deficits can cause inflation, crowd out private investment, weaken the competitive position of export industries, and pass the tax burden forward to future generations. However, in practice, there is not a great deal of evidence that the deficits of the past fifteen years have resulted in the expected negative effects. Factors such as tight monetary policy, international financing of the deficit, the fact that most other developed countries have much larger deficits, and people's expectation that current tax cuts will lead to future tax increases appear to have weakened or eliminated most of the possible negative effects. Even those who find evidence that structural deficits slow growth generally find the effects small in the United States. Deficits do tax future generations to pay for current expenditures, but, given that federal expenditures include capital spending, that is partly appropriate. Indeed there are disputes over the size of the deficit, with Eisner and others claiming that the way it is calculated greatly overstates the size of the problem.

Despite the weak evidence that the deficit is a major problem, both politicians and the public have elevated it into the major economic problem facing America. The deficit has been at or near the top of the Gallup Poll's frequently asked question, "What is the major problem facing America today," for most of the last two decades. Its persistence has led to major changes in the policies of the Democratic Party and appeared to propel third-party candidate Ross Perot into serious presidential contention. It can be blamed for President Bush's reversal of his pledge of "no new taxes" and for changing the priorities of President Clinton.

It has led to almost two decades of tight money policies from the Federal Reserve.

The readings in this section give two rather different views of the political dynamics of deficit spending. Buchanan and Wagner see deficits as caused by a combination of democracy and Keynsian ideology. They feel that citizens are always prone to push for more spending and less taxes, and are resistant to cutting back spending or increasing taxes in expansionary periods. Keynsian ideas legitimate cyclical deficits and these are transformed into structural deficits when the public refuses to accept tax increases or spending decreases in good times. They feel that the only way to deal with this in the long term is to embed balanced budgets in the Constitution. Schneider, on the other hand, feels that calls to deal with the deficit often disguise conservative policies that lack popular support. He also feels that a balanced-budget amendment would be difficult to execute and would be likely to reduce support for the Constitution.

The Readings

Richard Cebula's *The Deficit Problem in Perspective* is a good summary of the literature on the effects of the deficit on growth. Stephen Maris's *Deficits and the Dollar: The World Economy at Risk* is a good analysis of the international financing problem. Robert Eisner's classic *How Real Is the Federal Deficit?* shows why the size of the deficit may be far less than it appears. Buchanan and Wagner's *Democracy in Deficit: The Political Legacy of Lord Keynes* gives a more extended version of the argument in our reading. Donald Kettl's *Deficit Politics: Public Budgeting in Its Institutional and Historical Context* and Joseph White and Aaron Wildavsky's *The Deficit and the Public Interest: The Search for Responsible Budgeting in the 1980s* give good accounts of the struggle for deficit reduction in the 1980s; and Bob Woodward's *The Agenda* updates the struggle to the middle of the Clinton administration.

References

Buchanan, James M., and Richard E. Wagner. 1977. *Democracy in Deficit: The Political Legacy of Lord Keynes.* New York: Academic Press.

Cebula, Richard. 1987. *The Deficit Problem in Perspective.* Lexington, Mass.: D.C. Heath.

Eisner, Robert. 1986. *How Real Is the Federal Deficit?* New York: Free Press.

Kettl, Donald F. 1992. *Deficit Politics: Public Budgeting in its Institutional and Historical Context.* New York: Macmillan.

Maris, Stephen. 1985. *Deficits and the Dollar: The World Economy at Risk.* Washington D.C.: Institute for International Economics.

White, Joseph, and Aaron Wildavsky. 1989. *The Deficit and the Public Interest: The Search for Responsible Budgeting in the 1980s.* Berkeley, Calif.: University of California Press.

Woodward, Bob. 1995. *The Agenda: Inside the Clinton White House.* New York: Pocket Books.

3C.1. Democracy and Keynesian Constitutions: Political Biases and Economic Consequences

JAMES M. BUCHANAN and
RICHARD E. WAGNER

For most of the period since the end of World War II, American economic policy has been guided by the economic theories of John Maynard Keynes. Keynes, possibly the most influential economist of this century, held that capitalist economies were not self-correcting but needed constant government guidance to avoid the twin perils of depression and hyperinflation. Keynes held that it was important for governments to run deficits in recessionary periods to accelerate the economy and to have surpluses in boom times to slow the economy down.

In this extremely influential work, Richard Wagner and Nobel Prize winner James Buchanan argue that Keynes's prescription was likely to do more harm than good in a democratic society. They hold that the tax decreases and spending increases that Keynes prescribes during recessions are politically popular and likely to be enacted. But they feel that the spending decreases and tax increases that Keynes recommends during good times are highly unpopular and unlikely to be passed. The result should be a steadily increasing structural deficit.

This analysis underlies much of the current movement for a constitutional

Reprinted with permission from *The Consequences of Mr. Keynes* by James M. Buchanan, John Burton, and R. E. Wagner (London: Institute of Economic Affairs, 1978), pp. 13–27.

amendment to balance the budget, an amendment that the authors were among the first to propose.

A. Visions of the Economic Order: Classical and Keynesian

The Classical or pre-Keynesian notions of prudent fiscal conduct were reasonably summarized by drawing an analogy between the state and the family. It was another British intellectual 'export', Adam Smith, who noted that 'What is prudence in the conduct of every private family, can scarce be folly in that of a great kingdom.' Prudent financial conduct by the state was conceived in basically the same image as that for the family. Frugality, not profligacy, was the cardinal virtue, and this norm assumed practical shape in the widely shared principle that public budgets should be in balance, if not in surplus, and that deficits were to be tolerated only in extraordinary circumstances. Substantial and continuing deficits were interpreted as the mark of fiscal folly. Principles of sound family and business practice were deemed equally relevant to the fiscal affairs of the state.

During this period, a free-enterprise economy was generally held as being characterized by 'Say's Equality'.[1] While fluctuations in economic activity would occur in such an economy, they would set in motion self-correcting forces that would operate to restore prosperity. Within this economic framework, the best action for government was simply to avoid injecting additional sources of instability into the economy. The profligacy of government was one latent source of disturbance, and it was considered important that this governmental proclivity should be restrained. Avoiding such sources of instability, along with keeping debt and taxes low so as to promote thrift and saving, was the way to achieve prosperity. A balanced or surplus budget was one of the practical rules that reflected such constraints and beliefs. Such siren songs as the 'paradox of thrift' were yet to come.[2]

From Classical Stability to Keynesian Instability

The idea that the spontaneous co-ordination of economic activities within a system of markets would generally produce economic stability was replaced in the Keynesian vision by the idea of an inherently unstable economy. Say's Equality was deemed inapplicable. The Keynesian paradigm was one of an economy alternately haunted by gluts and secular stagnation.[3] The prosperous co-ordination of economic activities was a razor's edge. The economic order is as likely to be saddled with substantial unemployment as it is to provide full employment. An important element in the Keynesian paradigm was the absence of an equilibrating process by which inconsistencies among the plans of the participants in the economic process became self-correcting. Prosperity, accordingly, could be assured only through deliberate efforts of government to help the economy avoid the buffeting forces of inflation and recession. 'Fine tuning' became the ideal of Keynesian economic policy.

The Keynesian message, in other words, contained two central features. One was the image of an inherently unstable economy, ungoverned by some 'natural law' of a generally smooth co-ordination of economic activities. The other was of government as having both the obligation and the ability to offset this instability so as to bring about a more smoothly functioning economic order. The notion of an unstable economy whose performance could be improved through the manipulation of public budgets produced a general principle that budgets *need not* be in balance: indeed, they *should not* be in balance, since that would mean government was failing in its duty. Some years of deficit and others of surplus were both necessary to, and evidence of, corrective macroeconomic management. A stable relation between revenues and expenditures, say a relatively constant rate of surplus, would indicate a failure of government to carry out its managerial duties.

B. The Idealized Environment for Keynesian Economic Policy

While Lord Keynes published his *General Theory* in 1936, his presuppositions did not infuse themselves into generally held understandings or beliefs for about a generation in America, though sooner in Britain, much as he anticipated in a famous passage on the time-lag between the articulation of an idea and its influence on policy.[4] While the Keynesian vision of the nature of our economic order and the proper pattern of budgetary policy gained dominance in academia in the 1940s and 1950s, it did not filter into the general climate of American opinion until the 1960s. With this conversion or shift in generally-held perspectives or beliefs, macroeconomic engineering became the province of government.[5]

As developed by the economists who advocated macroeconomic engineering, fiscal policy would be devoted to smoothing out cycles in private economic activity. Fiscal policy would be guided by the same principle during both recession and inflation. Deficits would be created during recession and surpluses during inflation, with the object of smoothing out peaks and troughs. The policy precepts of Keynesian economics were alleged to be wholly symmetrical. In depressed economic conditions, budget deficits would be required to restore full employment and prosperity. When inflation threatened, budget surpluses would be appropriate. The time-honored norm of budget balance was thus jettisoned, but, in the pure logic Keynesian policy, there was no one-way departure. It might even be said that Keynesian economics did not destroy the principle of a balanced budget, but only lengthened the time-period over which it applied, from a calendar year to the period of a business cycle. In this way, rational public policy would operate to promote a more prosperous and stable economy during both recession and inflation.

While the idealized setting for the symmetrical application of Keynesian economic policy is familiar, the political setting within which the policy is to be formulated and implemented is much less familiar. We have now learned that mere exhortations to politicians to promote prosperity do not guarantee they will do so: they may lack the knowledge required to promote such an outcome, or the incentive to act in the required manner, or both. In other words, the actions of politicians on budgetary policy as well as on other types of policy depend upon both the knowledge politicians have and the incentives they confront.

Keynes's Defective Assumptions

Keynes largely begged questions pertaining to knowledge. Central to his approach was the presumption that economists could possess knowledge sufficient to enable them to give advice which, if acted upon, would facilitate the co-ordination of human activities within the economic order. This extremely questionable assumption about knowledge melded nicely with his normative assumptions about political conduct. Keynes was an élitist, and he operated under what his biographer called the 'presuppositions of Harvey Road'—that governmental policy, and economic policy in particular, would be made by a relatively small group of wise and enlightened people.[6] Keynes did not consider the application of his policy prescriptions in a contemporary democratic setting—in which government is tempted to yield to group pressures to retain or return to power. Rather, the small group of enlightened men who made economic policy would, he assumed, subconsciously—even if in defiance of historical experience—always tend to act in accordance with the 'public interest', even when this might run foul of constituency, sectional or other organized pressures.

In the unreal economic and political environment envisaged by Keynes, there could be little or no question raised about the application of the Keynesian policy instruments. To secure a stable, prosperous economy, expenditures would be expanded and contracted symmetrically. Budget deficits would be created during periods of sluggish economic activity, and surpluses as the pace of economic activity became too quick. There would be no political pressures, he implicitly supposed, operating to render the surpluses fictional and the deficits disproportionately large or ill-timed. The ruling elite would be guided by the presuppositions of Harvey Road; they would not act as competitors for electoral favor in a democratic political environment.

There was little awareness that the dictates of political survival might run contrary to the requirements of macroeconomic engineering (assuming for now that the economic order is aptly described by the Keynesian paradigm). It was tacitly assumed either that the political survival of politicians was automatically strengthened as they came to follow more fully the appropriate fiscal policies, or that the ruling elite would act without regard to their political fortunes. But what happens when we make non-Keynesian assumptions about politics? What if we commence from the assumption that elected politicians respond to pressures emanating from constituents and the state bureaucracy? When this shift of perspective is made in the political setting for analysis, the possibilities that policy precepts may unleash political biases cannot be ignored. On this score, it should be noted that Keynes's own biographer seemed prescient, for in continuing his discussion of the presuppositions of Harvey Road, he mused:

> If, owing to the needs of planning, the functions of government became very far-reaching and multifarious, would it be possible for the intellectual aristocracy to remain in essential control? Keynes tended till the end to think of the really important decisions being reached by a small group of intelligent people, like the group that fashioned the Bretton Woods plan. But would not a democratic government having a wide multiplicity of duties tend to get out of control and act in a way of which the intelligent would not approve?
>
> This is another dilemma—how to reconcile the functioning of a planning and interfering democracy with the requirement that in the last resort the best considered judgment should prevail. It may be that the presuppositions of Harvey Road were so much of a second nature to Keynes that he did not give this dilemma the full consideration which it deserves.[7]

C. Keynesian Presuppositions, Democratic Politics, and Economic Policy

Anyone, citizens no less than politicians, would typically like to live beyond his means. Individual citizens generally face a personal or household budget constraint which prevents them from acting on this desire, although some counterfeit and others go bankrupt. In the century before the shift in belief wrought by the Keynesian revolution, politicians acted as if they sensed a similar constraint when making the nation's budgetary choices.

Contemporary political institutions, however, are constrained differently because of the general belief in the Keynesian vision. This shift in constraints due to the shift in general beliefs alters the character of governmental budgetary policy. While there is little political resistance to budget deficits, there is substantial resistance to budget surpluses. Hence, fiscal policy will tend to be applied asymmetrically: deficits will be created frequently, but surpluses will materialize only rarely. This bias results from the shift in the general, public impression or understanding of the Western economic order, and of the related rules of thumb held generally by the citizenry as to what constitutes prudent, reasonable, or efficacious conduct by government in running its budget. Old-fashioned beliefs about the virtue of the balanced budget rule and of redeeming public debt during periods of prosperity became undermined by Keynesian ideas, and lost their hold upon the public. In consequence, debt reduction lost its claim as a guiding rule. Budget surpluses lost their *raison d'etre*. Deficits allow politicians to increase spending without having directly and openly to raise taxes. There is little obstacle to such a policy. Surpluses, on the other hand, require government to raise taxes without increasing spending—a program far more capable of stimulating political opposition than budget deficits, especially once the constraining norm of debt retirement had receded from public consciousness.

Market and Political Competition:
Similarities and Essential Differences

In a democracy, political competition bears certain resemblances to market competition. Private firms compete among themselves in numerous, complex ways to secure the patronage of customers. Politicians compete among themselves for the support of the electorate by offering and promising policies and programs which they hope will get them elected or re-elected. A politician in a democratic society, in other words, can be viewed as proposing and attempting to enact a combination of expenditure programs and financing schemes that will secure him the support of a majority of the electorate. This realistic view of the formulation of economic policy in a political democracy found no place in Keynes's *General Theory*. Its absence made his policy proposals unsound, because unrealistic.

There are also, it is worth noting, important differences between market and political competition. Market competition is continuous; at each purchase, a buyer is able to select among competing sellers. Political competition is intermittent; a decision is binding generally (as in the USA) for a fixed number of years. Market competition allows several competitors to survive simultaneously; the capture by one seller of a majority of the market does not deny the ability of the minority to choose their preferred supplier. Political competition leads to an all-or-nothing outcome: the capture of a majority of a market gives the entire market to that supplier. Again, in market competition, the buyer can be reasonably certain as to just what it is that he will receive from his purchase. In political competition, the buyer is in effect purchasing the services of an agent, whom he cannot bind in matters of specific compliance, and to whom he is forced to grant wide latitude in the use of discretionary judgment. Politicians are simply not held liable for their promises and pledges as are private sellers. Moreover, because a politician needs to secure the co-operation of a majority of politicians, the meaning of a vote for a politician is less clear than that of a 'vote' for a private firm. For these reasons, among others, political competition is different from, and inferior to, market competition, even though there is a fundamental similarity.[8] This was generally overlooked in economic analysis until recent years, and entirely ignored by Keynes and the Keynesians who followed him.

Budgets: Political Gains and Losses

The essential feature of democratic budgetary choice may be illustrated by considering the gains and losses to politicians of supporting various-sized budgets, and the taxes and expenditures they entail. It is the expectation of political gains and losses from alternative taxing and spending programs which shapes the budgetary outcomes that emerge within a democratic system of political competition. The size and composition of public budgets in such a system of competitive democracy can thus be viewed as a result of the preferences of a politician's constituents and the constitutional-institutional rules that constrain the political system.

With a balanced-budget rule, any proposal for expenditure must be coupled with a proposal for taxation. The elimination of the balanced-budget rule as a result of the advent of the Keynesian revolution altered the institutional constraints within which democratic politics operates. The nature of the pressures of political competition consequently would differ in this revised, Keynesian constitutional setting from what they were in the Classical constitutional setting. What we must do now is consider the respective survival prospects of budget surpluses and budget deficits, showing in the process that deficits have stronger political survival value than surpluses once the Keynesian vision and its concomitant beliefs replaced the Classical vision.

(i) Budget Surpluses and Democratic Politics

Assuming an initial situation of budget balance, the creation of a budget surplus requires an increase in real rates of tax, a decrease in real rates of public spending, or some combination of the two. In any event, budget surpluses will impose direct and immediate costs on some or all of the citizenry. If taxes are increased, some persons will have their disposable incomes reduced. If public spending is reduced, some beneficiaries of public services will suffer. In terms of *direct* consequences, a policy of budget surpluses will create losers among the citizenry, but no gainers.

Gainers must be sought for in the *indirect* consequences of budget surpluses. There may be some general acceptance of the notion that the prevention of inflation is a desirable objective for national economic policy. It could be argued that people should be able to see beyond the direct consequences of budget surpluses to the *indirect* consequences. They should understand that a budget surplus was required to prevent inflation, and that this was beneficial. The dissipation of a surplus through public spending or tax cuts, therefore, would not be costless, for it would destroy the benefits that would result from the control of inflation.

These direct and indirect consequences act quite differently on the choices of typical citizens. The direct consequences of the surplus take the form of reductions in *presently enjoyed consumption.* If taxes are raised, the consumption of private services is reduced. If government spending is lowered, the consumption of government services is reduced. In either case, a budget surplus requires citizens to sacrifice services they are consuming.

The indirect consequences, on the other hand, are of an altogether different nature. The benefit side of a budget surplus is not directly experienced, but rather must be *imagined*. It takes the form of the hypothetical or imagined gains from *avoiding* what would otherwise have been an inflationary experience.[9]

A variety of evidence suggests that these two types of choices are psychologically quite different. Moreover, appreciation of the benefits from a budget surplus would require a good deal of information and understanding. The task is not a simple matter of choosing whether to bear $100 more in taxes this year in exchange for $100 of benefits in two years, and then somehow comparing the two, historically distinct, situations. The imagining process requires an additional step. The person must form some judgment of how he, *personally,* will be affected by the surplus; he must reduce his estimate of the total ('macroeconomic') impact of the surplus to a personal ('microeconomic') level. As such future gains become more remote and less subject to personal control, however, there is strong evidence to suggest that such future circumstances tend to be neglected. 'Out of sight, out of mind' is the commonsense statement of this effect.[10]

Budget surpluses clearly have weaker survival prospects in a political democracy than in a social order controlled by a set of Keynesian wise men following the presuppositions of Harvey Road. Budget surpluses may emerge in a democratic political system, but democratic political processes possess institutional biases against them. Viewed in this light, there really should be no difficulty in understanding why we have never observed the explicit creation of budget surpluses during the post-Keynesian years.

(ii) Budget Deficits and Democratic Politics

In a democratic society, there would be no obstacles to budget deficits in a Keynesian economic setting. Budget deficits make it possible to spend without taxing. Whether the deficit is created through reduced taxes or increased expenditures, the form each takes will, of course, determine the distribution of gains among citizens. The key difference from a budget surplus, however, is that there are only direct gainers from such deficits and no losers.

Deficits will also create losers indirectly, due to the resulting inflation. Such indirect consequences are, however, dimensionally different, as we have seen. The direct consequences of debt creation take the form of increased consumption of currently enjoyed services; these would be privately-provided services if the deficit took place through a tax reduction, and government-provided services if through an increase in government expenditure. The indirect consequences, however, relate not to present experience, but to future conjecture. The benefit of deficit finance resides in the increase in currently enjoyed services, whereas the cost resides in the inflationary impact upon the future, in the creatively-imagined reduction in well-being at some future date. The analysis of these indirect consequences is essentially the same as that of the indirect consequences of the budget surplus.

A democratic society, therefore, will tend to resort to an excessive use of deficit finance once acceptance of the Keynesian paradigm has led to a revision of the fiscal constitution. For this reason, the post-Keynesian record in fiscal policy is not difficult to understand. The removal of the balanced-budget principle of constitutional rule generated an asymmetry in the conduct of budgetary policy in our form of competitive democracy. Deficits are created, but to a larger extent than justified by the Keynesian principles; surpluses sometimes result, but they occur less frequently than required by Keynesian prescriptions. When plausible assumptions are made about the institutions of decision-making in political democracy, the effect is to increase the biases against the use of budgetary adjustments to prevent and control inflation, as well as to increase the bias toward budgetary adjustments aimed at stimulating spending.

(iii) Keynesian Economics in Political Democracy

The grafting of Keynesian economics onto the fabric of a political democracy has wrought a significant revision in the underlying fiscal constitution. The result has been a tendency toward budget deficits and, consequently, once the workings of democratic political institutions are taken into account, inflation. Democratic governments will generally respond more vigorously in correcting for unemployment than in correcting for inflation. Budgetary adjustments aimed at the prevention or control of inflation will rarely be observed as the result of deliberate policy. Budget deficits will come to be the general rule, even when inflation is severe. In slack years, when deficits might seem warranted by strict application of the Keynesian precepts, the size of these deficits will become disproportionately large. Moreover, the perceived cost of government will generally be lower than the real cost because of the deficit financing. As a consequence, there will also be a relative increase in the size of the government sector in the economy. Budget deficits, inflation, and the growth of government—all are intensified by the Keynesian destruction of former constitutional principles of sound finance.

D. The Destructive, Self-Fulfilling Character of the Keynesian Political Biases

These political biases towards budget deficits also become a bias towards inflation, because monetary institutions as they are currently constituted operate, to some extent, to increase the stock of money in response to budget deficits. The one-sided application of Keynesian policy precepts which emerges from a democratic political setting may itself create economic instability in the process.

While inflation is usually thought of as a proportionate rise in all prices, as a rise in the absolute level of prices, in practice the structure of *relative* prices changes as well.[11] Indeed, what are commonly referred to as macroeconomic policies are not instruments intended to influence all prices proportionately, but rather are instruments intended to influence the structure of *relative* prices. The dictates of political survival operate in this direction because it is only through policies designed to act on relative prices that the vote-buying activities of politicians and parties can take place. A macroeconomic policy aimed only at the general price level would be typified by an indiscriminate dropping of money from a helicopter.[12] But any such nondiscriminatory policy would be defeated politically by a policy designed to benefit specific recipients, such as a spending program in marginal constituencies. In other words, the primary phenomenon to be considered in examining the inflationary bias of Keynesian economics is not the level of absolute prices, but rather the change in the structure of relative prices. Macroeconomic consequences are simply the sum of these microeconomic consequences.[13]

Once it is recognized that the important consequence of inflation is its impact on relative prices, and particularly once it is recognized that rational political action would aim at selective shifts in relative prices rather than at non-selective shifts in absolute prices, a new perspective on the destructive character of the Keynesian political biases emerges.[14] This is particularly true once it is also recognized that the essential nature of the economic order is vastly different from that implied by the standard treatments of inflation and macroeconomic policy. In these standard treatments the economy is viewed much like a balloon. Blow and the economy expands; suck and it contracts. This vision of the economy inherent in most macroeconomic models makes it appear to be a simple matter to achieve both the desired *degree* of inflation or contraction and the desired *timing* of those expansions and contractions.

Such a view of the economic order, while making life easy for economists, hardly conforms to economic experience. Rather, an economy is a complex web of contractual relations that reflect the anticipations and plans of the various participants. Metaphorically, it is far more like a gigantic erector set running throughout a 200-room mansion, with each piece connected to pieces in many different rooms. Changes made at one point will exert effects throughout the system, and will do so with varying time delays. *And no one person will be able to apprehend the entire apparatus,* quite unlike the case of the balloon. Moreover, shifts taking place at one point can be the consequence of earlier shifts elsewhere, and there is no assurance about the consequences of additional changes made at that point.

Today's economic occurrences and disturbances are a complex, only partially-apprehendable result of previous changes in many places at many different times in the past. Thus, the injection of new changes in budgetary policy is quite unlike inflating or deflating a balloon.[15] It is rather like readjusting some of the particular links in the erector set, only the metaphor should be even more complicated because the individual nodes have a will, so, therefore, they can think, create, and act.[16]

These readjustments will disturb a whole set of anticipations and plans, with the consequences of these readjustments extending over various periods.

Hayek's Analysis of the Impact of Inflation

There are several facets to the story about how the shifts in relative prices, induced by inflation, can have discoordinating impacts upon our economic order. One was articulated by Professor F. A. Hayek in the 1930s.[17] The initial impact of the inflation in Hayek's analysis was to shift the structure of relative prices in favor of capital goods of long gestation periods. The resultant lengthening of the structure of production, however, is inconsistent with the underlying data of wants, resources and knowledge. Such a pattern of employment and output cannot be maintained without an acceleration of the inflation. But a continually accelerating inflation is not sustainable as a long-run feature of an economic order. In the absence of such acceleration, the structure of production will revert to its former state. This process of readjustment leads to unemployment and recession. A recession becomes a necessary price of the *political* activities that produced the inflation in the first place, unless some movement toward an incomes policy to repress the inflation takes place, in which event the distortions would simply manifest themselves somewhat differently. Reallocations of labor must take place before the economy's structure of production will once again reflect the underlying data to which the economy adapts. Thus people respond to non-sustainable price signals generated by the inflation and the resulting mistakes must be worked out before the economy can return to normalcy. Recession is an inherent part of the recovery process.

In Hayek's framework, the excessive expansion occurred in the capital goods industries. In these days of massive government spending, however, the story is more complex, for it is the activities on which politicians increase spending that generate an excessive absorption of resources. This attraction of resources due to the shift in relative prices need not be confined to the capital goods industries, because there can be other industries that will be differentially favored by the government spending policies. Nonetheless, the central consequence remains: a pattern of resource allocation will be brought about that is not sustainable without still further efforts at distorting the structure of relative prices through inflationary finance. The Keynesian inflationary biases can be considerably more destructive than a simple increase in the general price level, because the changes in relative prices lead to further distortions as people act on the basis of price signals that are inconsistent with the underlying structure of preferences and technology. As a result of these mistakes, decisions will be made on investment and the employment of resources that are not sustainable by the economy. Unemployment and capital waste will then result as people readjust their plans and actions to correct mistakes based on erroneous signals in the economy.

E. Conclusion

Why does Camelot[18] lie in ruins? Intellectual error of monumental proportion has been made, and not exclusively by the politicians. Error also lies squarely with the economists. The 'academic scribbler' who must bear substantial responsibility is Lord Keynes, whose thinking was uncritically accepted by establishment economists in both America and Britain. The mounting historical evidence of the ill-effects of Keynes's ideas cannot continue to be ignored. Keynesian economics has turned the politicians loose; it has destroyed the effective constraint on politicians' ordinary appetites to spend and spend without the apparent necessity to tax.

Sober assessment suggests that, politically, Keynesianism represents a substantial disease that over the long run can prove fatal for the survival of democracy.

Notes

1. A recent restatement of this perspective is in W. H. Hutt, *A Rehabilitation of Say's Law,* Ohio University Press, Athens, Ohio, 1974. 'Say's Equality' (after J. B. Say, the French 19th-century classical economist) is usually summarized as the proposition that 'supply creates its own demand', provided that markets operate in a competitive manner.

2. The 'paradox of thrift' is the Keynesian proposition that a reduction in thriftiness (an increase in private or governmental spending propensities) will boost the economy.

3. A specific discussion of these two economic cosmologies is in Axel Leijonhufvud, 'Effective Demand Failures', *Swedish Journal of Economics,* 75, March 1973, pp. 31–33.

4. 'I am sure that the power of vested interests is vastly exaggerated compared with the gradual encroachment of ideas. Not, indeed, immediately, but after a certain interval; for in the field of economic and political philosophy there are not many who are influenced by new theories after they are twenty-five or thirty years of age, so that the ideas which civil servants and politicians and even agitators apply to current events are not likely to be the newest. But, soon or late, it is ideas, not vested interests, which are dangerous for good or evil.' (J. M. Keynes, *The General Theory of Employment Interest and Money,* Macmillan 1936, pp. 383–84.)

5. A thorough survey of this shift in paradigm toward fiscal policy in the United States is in Herbert Stein, *The Fiscal Revolution in America,* University of Chicago Press, Chicago, 1969.

6. 'We have seen that he [Keynes] was strongly imbued with what I have called the presuppositions of Harvey Road. One of these presuppositions may perhaps be summarized in the idea that the government of Britain was and would continue to be in the hands of an intellectual aristocracy using the method of persuasion.' (The late Sir Roy Harrod, *The Life of John Maynard Keynes,* Macmillan, 1951, pp. 192–93.) Harvey Road was the location of the Keynes family residence in Cambridge.

7. Ibid., p. 193.

8. A fuller examination of the similarities and differences is in James M. Buchanan, 'Individual Choice in Voting and the Market', *Journal of Political Economy,* 62, August 1954, pp. 334–43; reprinted in *idem, Fiscal Theory and Political Economy,* University of North Carolina Press, Chapel Hill, 1960, pp. 90–104.

9. This point about the categorical difference between present and future has been a

theme of many of the writings of G. L. S. Shackle. A terse statement appears in his *Epistemics and Economics,* Cambridge University Press, 1972, p. 245: 'We cannot have experience of actuality at two distinct "moments." The moment of actuality, the moment in being, "the present," *is solitary.* Extended time, beyond "the moment," appears in this light as a figment, a product of thought' (Shackle's italics).

10. And even to the extent that citizens do creatively imagine such alternative, conjectural futures, democratic budgetary processes may produce a different form of bias against the surplus. To the extent that budgetary institutions permit fragmented appropriations, for instance, a 'prisoner's dilemma' (in which choices made by each person individually will produce undesirable results compared with what would result if all made a common choice) will tend to operate to dissipate revenues that might produce a budget surplus. Suppose, for instance, that a potential $10 billion budget surplus is prevented from arising due to the presentation of 10 separate spending proposals of $1 billion each, as opposed to the presentation of a single expenditure proposal of $10 billion. In the first case, although each participant may recognize that he would be better off if none of the spending proposals carry, institutions that allow separate, fragmented budgetary consideration may operate to create a result that is mutually undesirable akin to the prisoner's dilemma. An analysis of this possibility is in James M. Buchanan and Gordon Tullock, *The Calculus of Consent,* University of Michigan Press, Ann Arbor, 1962, especially Ch. 10.

11. Discussed, for instance, by Daniel R. Vining and Thomas C. Elwertowski, 'The Relationship between Relative Prices and the General Price Level', *American Economic Review* 66, September 1976, pp. 699–708.

12. A popular, textbook abstraction of the nature of macroeconomic policy originated by Professor Don Patinkin.

13. For example, Friedrich A. Hayek, *Monetary Theory and the Trade Cycle,* Harcourt Brace, New York, 1932; and *idem, Prices and Production,* 2nd Edn., Routledge and Kegan Paul, 1935.

14. Much of this is discussed in Richard E. Wagner, 'Economic Manipulation for Political Profit: Macroeconomic Consequences and Constitutional Implications', *Kyklos,* 30, No. 3, 1977, pp. 395–410.

15. Further discussion of the neglect of the real world of complex micro-relations in orthodox macroeconomic analysis is in L. M. Lachmann, *Macro-economic Thinking and the Market Economy,* Hobart Paper 56, IEA, 1973.

16. See particularly such works by Henri Bergson as *Essai sur les données immédiates de la conscience,* F. Alcan, Paris, 1899; and *idem, L'Evolution créatrice,* F. Alcan, Paris, 1907. A related treatment within the context of economic analysis is in G. L. S. Shackle, *Decision, Order, and Time in Human Affairs,* Cambridge University Press, 1961.

17. *Prices and Production,* Routledge & Kegan Paul, 1931.

18. [Camelot was the capital of King Arthur's ideal society of chivalric literature from the 10th to the 13th centuries. It proved unfeasible because good intentions belied human nature.—Ed.]

3C.2. A Clear and Present Danger: The Politicization of the Constitution

WILLIAM SCHNEIDER

For the last ten years or so, the public has consistently rated the federal deficit as one of the major problems facing the country. But most economists who have looked closely at deficits have been less persuaded. While all concede that, other things being equal, it would be better if we did not have a structural deficit, many think that at current levels the deficit poses few immediate dangers.

In this interesting article William Schneider, generally a supporter of balanced budgets, attacks the idea of a constitutional amendment to balance the budget. He argues that such an amendment would make it more difficult to fight recessions, and could result in the dismantling of the welfare state. He sees the movement to pass such an amendment as an attempt to enshrine the current Republican agenda of low taxes and low government spending in the Constitution. He is worried that inserting one side of a major current debate into the Constitution might erode the consensus supporting the Constitution.

The reader might wish to note the resemblance between this argument and King's view that conservatives often disguise the less popular parts of their agenda by making them seem necessary to some other aim that benefits the entire country.

If you win the game, it doesn't give you the right to change the rules. But that's what Republicans are trying to do with the balanced-budget amendment. They won the 1994 election. Now they're trying to change the rules to make sure the game is rigged in their favor.

Reprinted with permission of the author from *Los Angeles Times*, Section M (February 26, 1995).

The balanced-budget amendment would declare the federal budget deficit unconstitutional. So what's the big deal? There's a near-universal consensus that the deficit is a bad thing. Why not codify that consensus into constitutional law?

Because deficit reduction isn't what the debate is really about. It's about changing the role of the federal government. The GOP's not-so-hidden agenda is to dismantle the welfare state and limit federal intervention in the economy.

Nothing wrong with those goals. They are perfectly respectable conservative objectives. Ronald Reagan made them explicit when he offered his economic program to Congress in 1981, saying, "Taxes should not be used to regulate the economy or bring about social change." That conservative agenda is quite properly treated by Republicans as their mandate coming out of the 1994 elections.

But that's just the point. It's a *political* agenda. In fact, it's the defining issue for Democrats and Republicans. Democrats believe in activist government—whether it's the old Democratic version (protecting and providing) or the new Democratic version (solving problems). Republicans believe in limited government of the boardroom (for traditional conservatives) and out of the bedroom (for libertarian conservatives).

A political agenda should be advanced through the political process, through legislation, policy initiatives, campaigns. It should not be enshrined in the Constitution. The most likely consequence will not be to put the issue "above politics." The most likely consequence will be to politicize the Constitution.

The Constitution is not a liberal document or a conservative document. It can't be. It's the repository of sovereignty in this country, the ultimate source of legal and political authority. The British vest sovereignty in a monarch. The United States vests sovereignty in a document. But the same rule applies: The sovereign must never be identified with a political cause other than the nation's preservation.

The agency assigned to interpret the Constitution is the U.S. Supreme Court. Is the court above politics? Absolutely not. "The Supreme Court follows th' iliction returns," as Finley Peter Dunne's Mr. Dooley once said. And when it comes to political blunders, the court has made some beauts—like the Dred Scott decision that hastened the Civil War and the Plessy vs. Ferguson decision that endorsed the racial doctrine of "separate but equal."

But only one political blunder was ever written into the Constitution—Prohibition. It took 14 years to get it out, tumultuous years when every politician had to be either a "wet" or a "dry." The point is that given a few "iliction returns," the Supreme Court can change its mind. The Constitution is more permanent.

That's exactly why Republicans are rushing to get the balanced-budget amendment into the Constitution. It will make permanent the results of the 1994 election and change the role of the federal government, presumably forever. Conservatives expect that, once the amendment is in place, it will become extremely difficult—literally unconstitutional—for the federal government to increase spending.

In fact, the amendment will mandate spending cuts. The kinds of cuts so politically controversial that supporters of the amendment are unwilling to spell them out in advance for fear of undermining passage of the amendment. Once it is ratified, however, politicians will presumably be able to argue that they have no choice but to cut Medicare and veterans' benefits and farm subsidies. Angry constituents will, of course, understand and forgive. The Constitution must be obeyed!

Some liberals, like Sen. Paul Simon (D-Ill.), support the balanced-budget amendment for similar reasons. They know Congress lacks the political will to raise taxes. But the amendment will force them to do it. Angry taxpayers will, of course, understand and forgive. The budget must be balanced!

In the immortal words of the late Sen. Everett McKinley Dirksen (R-Ill.), "Ha, ha, ha. And I might add, ho, ho, ho."

For most politicians, reducing the deficit isn't a cause. It's a pretext. Reagan's real cause was to reduce the size of government. The deficit was a convenient device for institutionalizing that goal.

That's not to say the Reagan Administration deliberately created the deficit. Perish the thought—though Reagan's budget director, David A. Stockman, did eventually reveal that the idea occurred to him. Instead, the Reaganites allowed themselves to believe a cockamamie theory called supply-side economics— which held that if they cut taxes and increased defense spending, government revenues would go up. Congress did its part by refusing to carry out its promise to cut domestic spending.

Anyway, it worked. For 14 years now, the federal government has been under constant and intense pressure from the deficit to keep spending down. It has been impossible to pass any major new domestic programs—even when Democrats were in control of both the White House and Congress. President Bill Clinton's national-service program is little more than a pilot project. The crime bill was mutilated. Health-care reform was DOA.

Democrats have been no less guilty of using the deficit as a pretext. As soon as he got into the White House, Clinton declared himself a born-again convert to deficit reduction. The deficit justified his initial program of tax hikes and defense cuts—two things Democrats had been dreaming of ever since Walter F. Mondale ran for President. In Clinton's budget proposal, two-thirds of the new revenues were earmarked for deficit reduction and one-third for public investments—i.e., new domestic spending.

It didn't work. Congress got wise to Clinton and cut out most of the new investment spending. That was the end of Clintonomics. The result was still a sizable amount of deficit reduction: about $100 billion a year, for which the voters showed themselves to be supremely ungrateful in last year's election.

This year, Clinton returned the favor by dropping any plans to expand deficit reduction. Why should he? If the Republicans pass their balanced-budget amendment, that will take care of the problem.

But isn't there a consensus for deficit reduction? Yes, and it's probably strong enough to get a balanced-budget amendment passed. But the amendment would have two intended consequences for which there is no strong consensus.

One would be to curtail the federal government's ability to stabilize the economy during a recession. In a recession, tax revenues fall and government outlays rise. That instantly throws the budget out of balance.

That couldn't happen under a balanced-budget amendment, unless three-fifths of both houses of Congress voted to allow emergency spending. Otherwise, the federal government would be forced to raise taxes or cut spending to balance the budget. Either would deepen the recession.

The amendment would also help dismantle the welfare state. The welfare state has meant the gradual expansion of social rights—like the right to free school lunches or unemployment compensation or veterans' benefits.

These days, they're called entitlements. Some, like welfare, are unpopular. Others, like Social Security and Medicare, are entrenched. The Republican agenda is to change most of these programs—from entitlements to discretionary spending. No one will be "entitled" to assistance.

House Speaker Newt Gingrich (R-Ga.) is clear about his objective. "It doesn't say anywhere in the Declaration of Independence or the Constitution that anyone is entitled to anything except the right to pursue happiness," he said.

That's why Congress is proposing to replace welfare and food stamps and school-lunch programs with block grants. Instead of paying benefits to people directly, the federal government would turn over the money to the states and let them decide what to do with it.

Notice Congress wouldn't have to cut individual benefits. It could just cut grants to states and let them figure out how to divide up the money. "We can't give you any more money for food stamps," Congress could say. "We have to balance the budget. It's in the Constitution."

OK, but what happens if the government runs short of money for Social Security or Medicare? The Republicans have promised not to touch Social Security. But they rejected a proposal to write that promise into the balanced-budget amendment. Gingrich has also promised a thorough reexamination of Medicare to figure out how to make it cheaper. Maybe by requiring Medicare recipients to join health maintenance organizations.

These are enormous changes. They are properly the subject of political debate. Putting the GOP agenda into the Constitution will not mandate a consensus on these issues. But it will endanger the consensus that puts the Constitution above politics.

3D. Monetary Policy

In the heyday of Keynsianism there was a tendency to rely heavily on fiscal policy to control the economy and to relegate monetary policy to a supporting role. While all acknowledged that monetary policy would eventually change consumer behavior, the length of time it would take was thought to be long and uncertain and the size of the effect on the economy difficult to predict. The rise of the Chicago school and neoclassical economics has led to a complete re-evaluation of the role of monetary policy. There is now a range of views, with monetarists generally holding that monetary policy is the major determinant of inflation and the most reliable tool for controlling the economy, and neo-Keynesians assigning it a more or less equal role with fiscal policy. There is, however, general agreement that controlling the quantity of money is of first importance and that, under most circumstances, monetary policy can severely limit what fiscal policy can achieve.

Monetary policies determine the amount of money and credit that is available in a society. When the amount of money and credit is reduced, the price borrowers have to pay for money (the interest rate) goes up. When the money supply is increased, the interest rate is driven down. People borrow more when the interest rate is lower; they use the borrowed money to purchase goods, such as cars and houses, and invest in machinery and factories. Thus, increasing the money supply stimulates the economy. Of course, beyond some point the economy can be overstimulated. With more money in their pockets, people bid up the prices of goods and the result is inflation. Reducing the amount of money available to borrowers tends to depress the economy and reduce inflation. Many analysts think it was the rapid money growth during the Carter administration that led to the high inflation of the 1979-to-1982 period, while it was the restrictive monetary policies pursued by Federal Reserve Board Chair Paul Volcker that led to the lower inflation and the major recession of the first Reagan term.

The political aspects of monetary policy, long neglected by political scientists, have in recent years attracted considerable interest. Most of the new work has revolved around two topics: who controls monetary policy and why we get the kind of monetary policy that we do. Interest in the first topic was sparked by the fact that the United States, like many other democracies, has chosen to take formal responsibility for this vital policy out of the hands of elected officials, lodging it instead in the Federal Reserve Board, a small body appointed by the president for thirteen-year terms. This naturally leads to the related questions of whether, and why, this important policy has been left in the control of an undemocratic body. Actually, as we shall see, there is general agreement that the president and the Congress are more powerful monetary policy actors than might at first appear to be the case, but there is considerable disagreement over the extent of their power (Weintraub 1978; Kane 1982; Beck 1982).

The literature on the determinants of monetary policy has also focused on two primary questions. The larger body of research looks at the short-term determinants of monetary policy, seeking to determine why the Federal Reserve Board chooses to switch from stimulative to restrictive policies and vice versa. This inquiry has been prompted by the observation that both stimulation and restriction have often taken place much later than they were justified on economic grounds. There is also some research that asks why the policies pursued by the Federal Reserve Board are in general more restrictive and anti-inflationary than the fiscal policies undertaken by the president and the Congress.

The article below by Michael Reagan outlines the structure of power within the Federal Reserve and shows that it is an extremely undemocratic body. He argues that in the world's premier democracy it is undesirable to hand over control of the economy to a group with no accountability to voters. He feels that it would be better if control were in the hands of the White House. The article by Alan Greenspan takes strong exception to this view. In an argument that reminds one of Buchanan's, he contends that all the incentives in a democracy are for continual expansion and that the natural result of this is high rates of inflation. To avoid this it is necessary to delegate authority over monetary policy to a group that is insulated from the voters' continual pressures for expansion. The selection by Edward Kane sees the argument between Reagan and Greenspan as resting on a misunderstanding. Despite surface appearances, he argues, real power over monetary policy lies with the president and the Congress. However, because it is often necessary to pursue deflationary policies, which are unpopular, elected officials have preferred to assign formal responsibility to the Federal Reserve Board, permitting elected officials to control policy while evading the blame for recessions.

For Further Reading

The best introduction to this field is John T. Woolley's well-written book *Monetary Politics: The Federal Reserve and the Politics of Monetary Policy*. Donald Kettl's *Leadership at the Fed* covers some of the same ground. A brief introduction to the area can be found in Nathaniel Beck's article "Domestic Politics and Monetary Policy." Milton Friedman and Anna J. Schwartz's *A Monetary History of the United States, 1867–1960* is a classic history of monetary policy formation. A still useful book on monetary policy in the 1950–1970 period is George L. Bach's *Making Monetary and Fiscal Policy*. Robert Weintraub's article "Congressional Supervision of Monetary Policy" offers a good account of Congress's role in the 1980s. James Alt's "Leaning into the Wind or Ducking Out of the Storm" provides a nice integration of major theories with recent events.

References

Alt, James E. 1991. "Leaning into the Wind or Ducking Out of the Storm: U.S. Monetary Policy in the 1980s," in Alberto Alesina and Geoffrey Carliner, eds., *Politics and Economics in the Eighties*. Chicago: University of Chicago Press.

Bach, George L. 1971. *Making Monetary and Fiscal Policy*. Washington D.C.: The Brookings Institution.

Beck, Nathaniel. 1982. "Presidential Influence on the Federal Reserve in the 1970s." *American Journal of Political Science* 26 (August): 415–45.

Beck, Nathaniel. 1987. "Domestic Politics and Monetary Policy," in Thomas D. Willett, ed., *Political Business Cycles: The Economics and Politics of Stagflation*. San Francisco: Pacific Institute for Public Policy Research.

Friedman, Milton, and Anna J. Schwartz. 1963. *A Monetary History of the United States, 1867–1960*. Princeton N.J.: Princeton University Press.

Kane, Edward. 1982. "External Pressures and the Operation of the Fed," in Raymond E. Lombra and Willard E. Witte, eds., *Political Economy of International and Domestic Monetary Relations*. Ames, Iowa: Iowa State University Press.

Kettl, Donald. 1986. *Leadership at the Fed*. New Haven: Yale University Press.

Meltzer, Alan. 1982. "Politics and Economics in the Federal Reserve," in Raymond E. Lombra and Willard E. Witte, eds., *Political Economy of International and Domestic Monetary Relations*. Ames, Iowa: Iowa State University Press.

Weintraub, Robert. 1978. "Congressional Supervision of Monetary Policy." *Journal of Monetary Economics* 4 (April): 341–62.

Woolley, John T. 1984. *Monetary Politics: The Federal Reserve and the Politics of Monetary Policy*. New York: Cambridge University Press.

3D.1. The Political Structure of the Federal Reserve System

MICHAEL D. REAGAN

Monetary policy is unique among the major areas of public policy, in that formal authority over the policy lies with two bodies—the Federal Reserve Board and the Federal Open Market Committee—neither of which includes any members directly elected by the public at large. This means that there is no direct accountability to the public for monetary policy outcomes.

In this article Michael D. Reagan briefly outlines how this peculiar governmental arrangement came about, who exercises power within the Federal Reserve system, and the interests those people represent. He argues that the mixed public-private nature of the policy-making system arose in an era when the importance of monetary policy for the national economy was not understood. He then looks at the arguments for continuing this arrangement, paying particular attention to the notion that the independence of the system must be maintained if it is to keep inflation in check. Reagan concludes that, despite the danger that elected officials would not make the hard choices that are required in monetary policy, there is a strong argument for bringing it more directly under the control of the president.

Public policy is not self-generating; it emerges from institutions. Foremost among the institutions charged with monetary and credit policy formation—an area, like fiscal policy, that has not received from political scientists the attention accorded to micro-economic regulation of particular firms or industries—is the Federal Reserve System. The purpose of this paper is to examine the "fit" of the

Reprinted with permission of the author and *The American Political Science Review* 55, *1* (September 1966), pp. 64–76 (with deletions).

system's formal structure to (1) the policy functions and the informal policy-forming mechanisms of the "Fed," and (2) the pattern of interests and values affected by monetary policy. Its thesis is that a substantial gap has developed between these elements.

A brief sketch of the formal structure of authority and the historical development of system functions is needed to begin with; this is followed by analysis of the formal and the effective roles of each component of the System along with the internalized interest representation at each level. Then the linkage between the Federal Reserve System and general economic policy is explored. Finally, the conclusion summarizes the findings and suggests briefly how formal structure and policy functions might be brought into closer, more effective alignment.

I. Structural and Functional Development

The Pyramid

The Federal Reserve System[1] can be described as a pyramid having a private base, a mixed middle level and a public apex. At the apex stands the Board of Governors (frequently referred to as the Federal Reserve Board or FRB). Its seven members are appointed by the president, with the consent of the Senate, for fourteen-year, overlapping terms, one term expiring at the end of January in each even-numbered year. Members are removable for cause, but the removal power has not been exercised. In making appointments, the president must give due regard to "fair representation of financial, agricultural, industrial, and commercial interests, and geographical divisions of the country," and not more than one member can be appointed from a single Federal Reserve District. The Chairman is selected by the president for a renewable four-year term. The board is independent of the appropriations process, for its operating funds come from semi-annual assessments upon the twelve Reserve Banks.

At a level of equivalent authority to the Board itself, but in the "middle" of the public-private pyramid, stands the statutory Federal Open Market Committee. It is composed of all FRB Members plus five of the twelve Reserve Bank Presidents, with the president of the New York Reserve Bank always one of the five and the others serving in rotation. The Chairman of the Board of Governors is, by custom, the Chairman of the Committee. . . .

The Reserve Bank Presidents are not government appointees; they are elected by the boards of directors of their respective Banks, subject to FRB veto; and their compensation—far above civil service levels—is fixed in the same way. Thus their selection is initially private, but with public supervision. The Board of Directors of each Reserve Bank consists of nine persons, six of whom are elected by the member commercial banks of that District (these banks, the "owners" of the Reserve Banks, constituting the private base of the pyramid), while three (including the Chairman and Deputy Chairman) are appointed by the FRB in Washington.

Off to the side stands the final element of statutory organization, the Federal Advisory Council (FAC). This group of twelve men is composed of one commercial-banker representative from each District, annually elected by the respective regional Boards. The FAC meets quarterly with the FRB to discuss general business conditions and may make recommendations to the Board on matters of policy. The twelve Reserve Bank Presidents constitute a non-statutory Conference of Presidents that meets three times a year; a Conference of Reserve Bank Chairmen meets annually with the FRB.

The Location of Policy Powers

The three major tools of monetary policy are the rediscount rate charged by Reserve Banks to member bank borrowers on their loans from the System; the setting of reserve requirement levels for the member banks; and—most important today—open market operations in securities of the federal government. Decisions regarding each of these instruments is formally located in a different organ of the System, although (as will be developed below) channels for advice and influence cause a mingling of the decisional powers in fact. The levels of reserve requirements are set by the FRB; open market policy is a function of the Open Market Committee (OMC), thus providing the regional and quasi-private elements of the System with formal access to the heart of monetary policy formation; and the Reserve Bank Boards of Directors share with the FRB formal authority over the discount rate. The rate is "established" every fourteen days by each regional Bank, but "subject to the review and determination" of the Board of Governors. In addition the FRB shares with the Comptroller of the Currency, the FDIC and state authorities a very considerable list of regulatory and supervisory powers over member banks and their officers.

Functional Change Since 1913

When established, the Federal Reserve System was thought of as exercising only the technical function of quasi-automatic adjustment of an elastic currency supply to the fluctuating needs of commerce and industry. The System was pictured as a "cooperative enterprise" among bankers for the purpose of increasing the security of banks and providing them with a reservoir of emergency resources.[2] To this day the Federal Reserve Act mandate reflects this view: it instructs that the discount rate and open market policy shall be operated with "a view of accommodating commerce and business," and that reserve requirements shall be handled so as to prevent "excessive use of credit for the purchase or carrying of securities." Nothing in the Act relates the monetary authority to the function of national economic stabilization; yet this is its prime task today.

In 1913, it was not foreseen that the techniques of monetary policy would become instruments of economic stabilization with their consequences for employment, growth and price stability overtaking their specific banking objectives in importance. Yet this is what has happened, beginning in the Twenties but more strongly and with more explicit recognition in the policy process since the Great Crash. With this shift, the operation of the Federal Reserve System necessarily moved into the political mainstream, for the goal of stabilization requires making choices among alternatives that have important and visible consequences for substantial interests and community values. Once macro-economic policy had become the primary *raison d'être* of the System, the breadth of interests involved became coterminous with the nation, not just with the bankers; and monetary policy, as well as depositors' safety, became a public concern rather than a private convenience.

A corollary of the rise of stabilization to stage center is that the scope of FRB action has become essentially national, belying the assumption of relative regional independence that underlay the original legislation. Divergent policies for each region become undesirable—even impossible—if national stabilization is to be achieved in an increasingly interdependent national economy.

II. Roles and Interests of the Components

We turn now to a comparison of formal roles and interest composition with the informal roles and interest-impact of each level of the System's structure.

The Commercial Bank Base

The formal role of the member banks is that of an electoral constituency in the selection of six of the nine directors for each Reserve Bank. While the member banks have no direct policy voice, this electoral role originally gave them an indirect one, on the assumption that the regional boards would be policy-making bodies through their authority over the discount rate. That authority is negligible today. Furthermore, the "ownership" of the Reserve Banks by the commercial banks is symbolic; they do not exercise the proprietary control associated with the concept of ownership nor share beyond the statutory dividend, in Reserve Bank "profits." . . .

Bank ownership and election at the base are therefore devoid of substantive significance, despite the superficial appearance of private bank control that the formal arrangement creates.

Reserve Bank Boards of Directors

The Reserve Bank Boards' authority to set rediscount rates, subject to "review and determination" by the FRB, is considerably diminished by the ultimate formal authority of the latter, for "determination" includes final decision and even initiation of rate changes. It is further reduced by informal practice: to avoid the embarrassments of public disputes, discount rate policy is discussed at OMC meetings and the determinations settled upon therein are usually followed through uniformly at the next meetings of the respective regional Boards of Directors.[3] The special formalities are "of little significance: rediscount policy is made in much the same way and on essentially the same considerations as is reserve and open-market policy."[4] The nationalization of function has thus removed the basis for the assumption of regional autonomy that underlay the original grant of authority to the Reserve Banks. The major tasks of the Directors now are to provide information on regional conditions for OMC and the FRB to take into account, and to serve as a communications and public relations link between the System and local communities—both the general community and the specific "communities" of commercial banking, industry, merchants and other financial institutions. They do not exercise important substantive authority.

This may be fortunate in view of the structure of interests that prevails at this level. For the range of interests, reflecting the banker-business orientation of 1913, is narrow by legal specification and narrower still in fact. By statute, each regional Board has three classes of membership: Class A consists of three commercial bankers; Class B of three men active in commerce, agriculture or "some other industrial pursuit"; and Class C, without occupational restriction. Class C members are appointed by the FRB; the others are elected by the member banks of each region. . . .

The Reserve Bank Presidents

The presidents, by virtue of the membership of five of their number on the OMC (and the participation of all twelve in OMC discussions) are more significantly related to the policy process than are their nominal superiors, the regional Boards.

Selection of the presidents is by the respective Boards, but subject to FRB veto: initially private but finally public. Increasingly, they are men with substantial Reserve System experience. Two-thirds of the incumbents have had such experience; one-third have come to their posts from careers in commercial banking. Their daily contacts are with private bankers and one observer suggests that they have been "inclined to favor more cautious, mild policies that would be less disturbing to the normal courses of banking and the money markets" than has the FRB.[5] Yet another writer, granting a "commercial banker mentality" in the early days of the System, argues that a public, central banking view is coming to prevail as a majority come up through the System.[6] In one respect the presidents have clearly differed from the FRB: in their support of a change urged by commercial bankers that would place authority for all monetary actions in the OMC—a change the FRB has opposed.

As a statutory minority on the OMC, the views of the presidents cannot be controlling in themselves. In the apparently unlikely event of a split within the

FRB segment of the Committee, however, a solid front by the five President-members would enable them to determine public policy. Since they are not appointed by the president, nor removable for policy differences with either the president or the FRB within their five-year terms, the present structure allows the possibility that policy with a highly-charged political potential may be made by men who lack even indirect accountability to the national public affected. Former FRB Chairman Marriner Eccles has pointed out the uniqueness of the arrangement in these words: "there is no other major governmental power entrusted to a Federal agency composed in part of representatives of the organizations which are the subject of regulation by that agency."[7]

The situation of the Reserve Presidents reverses that of the regional Boards: while the latter's structurally important place has been downgraded by loss of function, the former's structurally inferior position has been upgraded by increased authority.

The Board of Governors and the Board Chairman

The gap between formal and informal roles in the Federal Reserve is readily apparent at the FRB level. By statute, it controls by itself only one of the major monetary instruments, the setting of reserve requirements. In fact, it is in a position to, and does, exercise authority in varying degrees over all three instruments of policy—and is popularly recognized as *the* monetary policy authority. Further, the effective voice within the Board is that of the Chairman, despite the formal equality of all seven members—and this too is popularly recognized. William McChesney Martin's name may not be a household word, but it is far better known than those of his colleagues. Over the years, the Board has seldom contained, besides the Chairman, more than one or two members at a time whose stature commanded independent respect.

The Board has final authority over discount rates through its power to "review and determine" the decisions of the Reserve Directors. The Members of the FRB constitute a seven-to-five majority in the OMC and thus—barring defections—control the most important of monetary tools. In fact, decisions on all three instruments of policy are taken on the basis of discussion within OMC. Since 1955 the Committee has been used as a "forum, a clearinghouse for all of the aspects of policy determination in the System."[8] Thus the formal distribution of authority is belied in practice by unified consideration. Unified control seems inevitable, since the types of decision are logically related and it would be unthinkable to have them operating in contradictory directions. Because of the political importance of monetary policy, however, and the desirability of fiscal-monetary coordination, it is questionable whether a twelve-man, quasi-private body provides an adequate or appropriate locus for policy determination; of this, more presently.

The size, length of term and interest composition of the FRB have been the subject of considerable Congressional attention and have undergone some change over the years. The Board began with five appointed Members with staggered ten-year terms and two *ex officio*—the Secretary of the Treasury and the Comptroller of the Currency. Both the latter were removed in the 1935 revision of the Banking Act, at the insistence of Senator Carter Glass, then chairman of the Banking and Currency Committee. Now there are seven Presidential appointees, and the term is fourteen years. No Member, incidentally, has yet served a full fourteen-year term, but a few have served *more* than fourteen years through successive appointments to unexpired terms.

The Chairman is selected by the president for a four-year, renewable term. This definite term was adopted in 1935, apparently with the intent that an incoming President should have a free hand. Resignations and new appointments have not coincided with presidential inaugurations, however, with the result that the incumbent's appointment, for example, expires in 1963.

The Federal Reserve Act has from the beginning stipulated group-interest qualifications for FRB Members. Originally, two had to be experienced in banking or finance, and the total membership had to provide "fair representation" of industrial, commercial and financial interests—as well as a regional balance designed to avoid eastern "domination." In 1922 the requirement of financial experience was dropped and agriculture was added to the list of represented interests. The actual composition for the 1914–50 period was as follows: thirteen from banking, five each from business and agriculture, and four from law.[9] Those appointed since 1950 have included one from private banking, two from business, two from agriculture and one each from the deanship of a business school and from a government career. Two of the post-1950 group also had experience of several years each on a Reserve Bank Board and one appointee's major experience had been as a Reserve Bank officer. "Promotion from within" is the trend. Among the major organized interests, labor is conspicuous by its absence. Business has been represented, but by substantial independents (ranchers, lumbermen, realtors) rather than by executives of large industrial corporations.

The size, length of term, interest composition and geographic distribution are all of questionable value to the System's policy functions and administrative effectiveness. It has been argued that fourteen-year terms provide an opportunity for Members to develop a knowledge of monetary economics and that they insulate the Board from partisan considerations. But many posts of equal technical complexity in other agencies are adequately staffed on a much shorter basis and, more importantly, insulation from politics is as impossible as it is democratically undesirable for an agency functioning so near the center of national economic policy. I shall return to this point later.

Although replacement of the Board by a single executive has been suggested only rarely, many observers, including Chairman Martin, are on record as favoring a smaller group than seven, on the ground that more capable men might then be attracted to the Board.[10] Clearly a seven-man board cannot collectively negotiate effectively with the president, the Secretary of the Treasury, the Chairman of the Council of Economic Advisers, or the lending agencies whose programs impinge on economic stability; yet coherent policy requires negotiation, consultation and program coordination constantly. Nor would a five-man board be notably better in this respect.

As it is now, the Chairman *is* the Federal Reserve Board for purposes of negotiation. In recent years he has lunched with the Secretary of the Treasury weekly,[11] and has sat in with the president's informal inner council on economic policy.[12] Congressional committees rely upon the Chairman to speak for the Board and rarely bother to interrogate other Board members. These arrangements apparently work because none of the other members is strong enough, personally or politically, to challenge the Chairman; and also, it seems reasonable to suggest, because there is no alternative save chaos. It is supported too by the tradition of secrecy that attends the actions of central banks, and that is defended as necessary to prevent the exploitation of leaks to private advantage: the fewer the negotiators, the less the likelihood of leaks. The gap between formal structure and the necessities of action reflected in the informal but decisive accretion of power to the Chairman (not only to the incumbent, but to McCabe and Eccles before him) is too great to be bridged by a minor adjustment in the size of the group.

Because of the importance of the Chairmanship, and the necessity for cordial relations between the head of the FRB and the president, Martin and McCabe have both suggested that the four-year term of the Chairman should end on March 31 of the year in which a President begins his term of office. Simpler still is the suggestion that the Chairman's term should be at the president's pleasure, as with most other national regulatory commissions. Whichever way the matter is handled, the need is for a relationship of mutual trust between President and Chairman, both for the sake of consistent economic policy and for democratic accountability through the president as chief elected representative of the public.[13] The present system of a fixed four-year term that (accidentally) does not coincide with Presidential inaugurations is unfortunate on both counts. Moreover, since the staggered 14-year terms of members expire in January of even-numbered years, a new President—even if the Chairman stepped aside—would be confined to the membership he inherits, in choosing a new Chairman, unless some member resigned to create a vacancy.

The policy suitability of geographic and interest qualifications for membership on the Board is a question that would become moot if the Board were replaced by a single head. If not, the answer must be that such qualifications are unsuitable because they are irrelevant and, in their present form, inequitable as well. They are irrelevant because the function of the Board is no longer simply to accommodate business, but to stabilize the national economy. The Board is not engaged in mediating group conflicts where the direct representation of parties-in-interest may be an irresistible political demand, but in a task of economic analysis and political judgment affecting the interests and values of *all* groups and individuals. Given the agency's function, independence of mind and familiarity with government finance and money markets, and with macro-economic analysis, are far more desirable qualifications than group representation.[14] Sensitivity to basic political currents—a quite different kind of "expertise"—is also pertinent, but not sensitivity only to the needs of a few special segments of the economy.

The inequity of existing group representation requirements lies in the exclusion of interests as much affected by monetary policy as those that are included by statute. The present range reflects the original, restricted concept of the system. Today, if groups are to be represented as such, labor has as strong a claim as the farmers or industrialists, because employment levels are dependent on monetary policy to a significant extent; fixed-income receivers, whether corporate bond-clippers or Social Security pensioners, are directly and adversely affected if the tools of the FRB are not used with sufficient vigor to combat inflationary tendencies. Chairman Martin has even defined the objectives of monetary policy as providing job opportunities for wage earners and protection of those who depend upon savings or fixed incomes.[15]

Even if labor and pensioner representation were added, however, the list of affected interests would be far from exhausted. As Emmette Redford has written of interest representation in regulatory agencies generally, "It is difficult, if not impossible, to include representation of all the interests which might legitimately make a claim for some representation."[16] A non-interest or "general interest" criterion for appointments would be the simplest way to avoid the problem entirely if a multi-member Board is retained. A statement expressing the views of the House Committee on Banking and Currency in 1935 sums up the matter nicely:

> It is important to emphasize in the law that Board Action should reflect, not the opinion of a majority of special interests, but rather the well considered judgment of a body that takes into consideration all phases of the national economic life.[17]

The Open Market Committee and Policy Unification

In origin and development, the OMC represents the leading structural response of the Federal Reserve System to its change in function. But the response has not been entirely adequate and further modifications in the structure and scope of authority of the Committee have been advanced from a number of quarters.

When the System began operations, the discount rate and the levels of reserves were thought to be the major tools of policy. As the public debt grew, and as the macro-economic function of stabilization developed, open market operations by the Reserve Banks increased in importance. The initial structural re-

sponse came in 1922 when an Open Market Committee was established informally, more under the leadership of President Benjamin Strong of the New York
Reserve Bank than of the FRB. The Banking Act of 1933 gave the OMC statutory recognition as a twelve-man group, selected by the Reserve Banks, to carry
on open market operations under rules laid down by the FRB, thus substantially
increasing the power of the national, public component. The Banking Act of
1935, largely written by then-Chairman Eccles as an effort to enhance the centralized, public character of the monetary authority, reorganized the Committee
into its present form: the seven FRB members and five Reserve Presidents.[18]
(The House version—not enacted—of the 1935 Act would have gone further
with the centralizing process by transferring authority for open market operations
to the Board alone, with a requirement of consultation with an advisory committee of the regional Banks.) In short, change in economic circumstance, i.e., the
growth of a large federal debt as an inescapable component of the nation's
financial structure, and the development of a new function led to an institutional
addition to the System. Informally, the change has gone one step further: as
mentioned earlier, the OMC is used as a forum for discussion of the entire range
of monetary actions, not just for decisions regarding the tool that lies formally
within its jurisdiction.

There is widespread agreement among participants and observers that unified
handling of the three major techniques is essential for coherence; but there is
sharp disagreement over the appropriate composition of the OMC and over the
division of labor between OMC and FRB. The disagreements involve in a politically sensitive way the central-regional and public-private balances in the policy
process. The range of specific proposals is as follows:

(1) Consolidate all instruments in a publicly appointed Board, either the present FRB or a smaller one, abolishing the OMC but requiring consultation with
the Reserve Bank Presidents. Variants of this have been suggested by the Hoover
Commission Task Force, Eccles, and Bach, who see this approach as the proper
way to secure the advantages of both public responsibility and "grass roots"
information.[19]

(2) Consolidate by merging the OMC and FRB into a single Board constituted of three Members appointed by the president and two Reserve Bank Presidents, each of the latter group serving full time for a year on a rotating basis.
This was proposed by former Chairman McCabe in 1949 as the proper change if
any were to be made at all;[20] it would have the effect of displacing the New York
Bank President from his present permanent seat on the OMC.

(3) Consolidate in the OMC as presently constituted. This is the position
once favored by the regional Presidents.[21]

(4) Consolidate reserve requirements and open market policy in a reconsti-
tuted OMC consisting of the present five Reserve Bank representatives and a
smaller FRB of five Members—thus creating an even balance between central
and regional, publicly and semi-privately appointed elements. This proposal was

advanced by the New York Clearing House Association, which also urged that in case of a disagreement between a Reserve Bank and the FRB over the rediscount rate, either party should be allowed to refer the question to the OMC for final decision.[22] The Association apparently felt that commercial bank influence was greater with the presidents than with the national Board.

Those preferring no change at all include Martin, who has defended the existing arrangement as consistent with the "basic concept of a regional" System and as a way of promoting close relations between the presidents and the Board.[23] The Patman subcommittee saw no reason, as of 1952, to disturb the status quo, but Representative Patman has more recently proposed consolidation in an enlarged FRB of twelve Presidential appointees.[24]

The rationale underlying the all-powers-to-the-Board approach can be summarized in the principle that public functions should be lodged in public bodies, and the assertion that open market operations are in no sense regional in character. Eccles has pointed out that the Reserve Presidents are not appointed by or accountable to either the president or Congress, and for this reason argues that their participation in national, public policy formation is inappropriate.[25] Bach has emphasized the national character of open market policy,[26] and he is joined in this view by Jacob Viner, who has said that:

> The regional emphasis in central banking is an obsolete relic of the past. No country, not even Canada, which is much more a collection of distinct economic regions than is the United States, has thought it expedient to follow our initial example of introducing regionalism into central banking.[27]

The argument for OMC as the top body derives from the importance attributed to regionalism and (inferentially at least) from a belief in the financial community that the Committee is more sympathetic than the FRB to the felt needs of bankers. The regional case has been most strongly stated by President Delos C. Johns of the St. Louis Reserve Bank:

> Each Reserve bank president is in a position to judge possible alternatives of national monetary policy with due regard to the particular characteristics of his region. This makes for adoption of national monetary policy that squares realistically with actual conditions in the regions. . . .[28]

Macro-stabilization as the major function of the System clearly forecloses regional devolution in the making of policy, yet regional circumstances should be considered. The valid claims of regionalism, however, require only a consultative voice, not a decisional one. And public policy, I would agree with Eccles, should not be made by a body containing men who are not accountable to the national public whose welfare is affected by the decisions made.

In *operations,* as distinct from policy determination, regionalism may well possess continued utility; and centralization of policy is entirely compatible with a considerable degree of regional diversification in operations. The point of greatest overlap between national policy and Reserve Bank operations appears to be in the handling of the "discount window," that is, the ease or difficulty with which a member bank may avail itself of the rediscount privilege. A uniform national policy could, for example, suggest "easier" loan conditions in any District whose area rate of unemployment was "x" percentage points above the national average, and thus provide for regional differentiation while maintaining central policy control.

Federal Advisory Council

The Federal Advisory Council began as a compensation to the commercial bankers for their failure to obtain direct representation on the FRB.[29] Its function today has been described as providing "firsthand advice and counsel from people who are closely in touch with the banking activities of their particular districts,"[30] although available information does not explain how these bank representatives are able to contribute something that the Reserve Bank Presidents, with their extensive staff aids, could not supply as well or better. Assuming that their advice is not redundant, however, it is questionable whether the FRB should accord *statutory* advisory status to commercial bankers only, now that the System's policy may affect many other social groups just as significantly as the bankers; e.g., non-bank financial institutions, home builders, state and local governments, Golden Age Clubs, wage-earners, and so on. The board has at times used formal consultants from outside the commercial banking sphere, as when consumer credit regulations were being formulated;[31] but this is apparently infrequent. Once again, we see that the System's structure has become outmoded by the change in scope of function.

III. The Federal Reserve and National Economic Policy

The analysis to this point has focused upon internal factors. We come now to the questions: What is the source of the Federal Reserve's policy goals? Does the existing structure adequately relate the monetary authority to the president and to the monetary management operations of the Treasury, to lending agency decisions, and to the Council of Economic Advisers? Does an adequate mechanism exist for resolving disputes that threaten the coherence of an Administration's overall economic policy? These can only be answered by going beyond the internal organization of the Fed to a consideration of its external relationships.

The first place to look for the mandate of an agency is in its organic statute; but the Federal Reserve Act deals sparsely with the matter of goals, and has in any case, as already noted, been outpaced by events. Since the law does not provide a mandate fitted to the modern concerns of the System, it is to the Employment Act of 1946 that one must look for goals written in macro-economic language: "it is the continuing policy and responsibility of the Federal Government to use all practicable means . . . to promote maximum employment, production, and purchasing power." This declaration applies to the Federal Reserve as to all other agencies of the national government, and is often mentioned in FRB descriptions of the system's role. But as a policy guide it is less than complete. For one thing, it does not mention price stability, although it has been widely interpreted as including this goal by logical extrapolation from those explicitly specified. For another, it leaves open such questions as, should employment be maximized today by measures that may bring on unemployment tomorrow by over-stimulating a "boom," or conversely, contribute to unemployment today lest inflation come tomorrow?

Thus the Employment Act mandate shares the imprecision of most such statements. While it could perhaps be sharpened, a need for interpretive subsidiary definition probably cannot be eliminated because any language tight enough to do this would inevitably place too inflexible a straightjacket on agency operation. Elaboration of goals at later stages of the policy process may be expected to continue. The president, who enters office with a vague mandate that is partly personal, partly party doctrine, commonly sets at least the tone for the specific interpretation of statutory directives, by the nature of his appointees. But the president's authority over the Federal Reserve is restricted, unless vacancies occur, to one appointment of a member (for fourteen years) every other year starting a year after his own term begins; and to appointment of the Chairman for a fixed four-year term. The independence of the agency conflicts with the president's responsibilities for overall economic policy.

In support of the position that independence should prevail—i.e., that the FRB should not take its mandate from the president—the argument is advanced that anti-inflationary measures are unpopular though necessary; that "hard" decisions are more acceptable "if they are decided by public officials who, like the members of the judiciary, are removed from immediate pressures";[32] and that the accountability of the system to the electorate is adequately achieved through its responsibility to Congress.[33] On the other side, the president is required by the Employment Act to submit a program for achieving the Act's goals; such a program must include recommendations on monetary policy to be meaningful; and thus the president must be "the coordinating agent for the whole national economic program."[34] Men on both sides agree on one point: there should be a strong advocate within the government for the monetary stability viewpoint, and the central bank is the logical home for such advocacy. The major disagreements are whether a substantial degree of insulation from other agencies engaged in economic policy determination helps or hinders the expression of that viewpoint, and whether a clear locus of authority is required for settlement of disputes between the institutions variously responsible for monetary and fiscal policies.

The issue of FRB accountability to Congress is a false one and should be exposed as such. Contrary to a myth strongly held by System spokesmen—and many Congressmen—the FRB, even more than the other regulatory commissions, is *less* accountable to Congress than are the line departments in the presidential hierarchy. The Federal Reserve does not depend on appropriations and thus is freed from the most frequently used tool of Congressional administrative supervision. And Congress has exercised an unusual degree of restraint in even suggesting its policy views to the Board. All executive agencies that have statutory bases may be said to be "creatures of Congress," and those with single heads are more easily held accountable than those with boards that diffuse responsibility.[35] For agencies with substantive powers, the price of accountability to Congress is accountability to the president.

On the need for a coordinating authority, Martin's position has been to grant the need for coordination but to argue that it can be achieved adequately through informal consultation.[36] The Advisory Board on Economic Growth and Stability established by President Eisenhower in 1953 would appear to be in line with his thinking: ABEGS (under leadership of the then CEA Chairman Arthur Burns) could bring about full exchange of information and full discussion, but could not *commit* the participating agencies to a unified course, even before it fell into desuetude after Burns' departure. The same was true of the Treasury Secretary–FRB Chairman luncheons and the president's informal economic policy discussions with agency heads during the Eisenhower Administration. Thus the problem of a possible stalemate or contradiction between Presidential and FRB policy is not resolved by these consultative arrangements.[37] . . . Only if the FRB Chairman served at the will of the president, and a centralized authority directed the use of all credit instruments, would a formal basis for cohesion and accountability be laid.

Would a proposal of this kind mean the subordination of monetary stability to a frequently assumed low-interest, easy money predilection in the Treasury Department and the White House? While an unambiguous "No" cannot be given in reply, the weight of argument is in the negative direction. Independence may mean isolation rather than strength, for independent agencies lack the power of Presidential protection and Presidential involvement. Paradoxically, the real ability of the Fed to influence national economic policy might very well be increased if its formal independence were diminished. Have not the informal steps taken in the past seven or eight years toward closer liaison between the FRB and Presidential policy makers already made the Board (*i.e.,* the Chairman) somewhat stronger than was the case during the Truman Administration?

In addition to Presidential elaboration of Congressional policy statements, further interpretation is invariably made at the agency level. When the FRB or OMC decides to change, or not to change, the degree of restraint or ease in credit policy it is deciding—*necessarily*—whether to place emphasis for the short-run on the price stability or the maximum-employment-and-growth side of its imprecise mandate. The question of internal interpretation, therefore, is whether the policy preferences of the monetary authority are likely to coincide with those of the politically accountable originators and interpreters of the mandate. The probability is that the central banking agency will be to some extent more conscious of the monetary than of the employment-and-growth aspects of stabilization, the major reasons being (1) the role of the institution, (2) the inevitably close relationships of the policy makers to their commercial banking "clientele" as the focal point of immediate policy impact, and (3) the social backgrounds of the policy makers. The Administration (of whichever party) and Congress, however, are likely to give greater weight to employment than are the central bankers, simply because the political consequences of unemployment are likely to be—and are even more likely to be perceived as—more unfortunate for elected office holders than those of price inflation. This difference may be pronounced or slight, depending on the personal emphasis and understandings of the men involved; but that they will continue to exist even when the general orientation of both sides is similar was shown by the occasional disputes between the president's economic advisers and the FRB during the Eisenhower Administrations.[38] . . .

In the absence of any but the traditional instruments the FRB is faced with a cruel choice: its own rationale calls for it to fight inflation, but doing so would create rising unemployment. If it refrains from acting, in order to preserve high employment, it may fail to stop inflation. Does it have a mandate to make such a choice? One could be extrapolated from the general stabilization directive, but not with any clear political sanction. As economist Gardiner C. Means has said, "there is a good deal of question whether such a momentous decision should rest with the Federal Reserve Board."[39]

IV. Conclusion

The basic finding of the analysis presented above is that the formal structure of the Federal Reserve System is inappropriate to its functions and out of line with informal arrangements that have the logic of necessity behind them. These gaps flow from changes in the monetary authority's function and in the structure of the economy. Devised as a service agency for banking and commerce—to achieve a semi-automatic adjustment of the money supply—the Federal Reserve has become as well a policy-making institution with major responsibility for national economic stabilization. Ancillary arrangements for interest representation based on an assumption that monetary actions were of important concern only to bankers and businessmen now have the appearance of unjustified special access because the range of affected interests and values is seen to be as broad as the nation itself.

Informal developments—most notably the unified handling of major monetary techniques and the preeminence of the Chairman's position—and the formal changes of 1935 that in a degree publicized and nationalized the Open Market Committee did something to improve the fit of form to function. But these alterations have not been sufficient to ensure adequate accountability for what is today an authority of first rank political importance; they have not brought the quasi-private "face" of the System into line with its public responsibilities; and they do not provide a sufficient organizational base for coherent integration of the fiscal and monetary components of national economic policy. A more complete face-lifting is in order.

The Chairmanship is the key both to accountability and to effective performance. The four-year fixed term, having produced a result contradictory to the one intended, should be repealed in favor of service at the pleasure of the president. The informal preeminence of the Chairman should be recognized formally by abolishing the Board and the OMC and centralizing authority over the discount rate, reserve requirements and open market operations in the hands of the Chairman, who might be retitled the Governor of the Federal Reserve System. The need for information from below could be handled through regularized reporting from the Reserve Bank Presidents on regional conditions, and by strengthened staff analysis in the Office of the Governor. By these alterations, the public, i.e., political, quality of monetary policy would be accorded appropriate recognition; responsibility would be clearly located; a means of settling possible disputes between fiscal policy under the president and monetary under the Fed would be created; and the process of consultation and negotiation by the Fed with the Treasury, the CEA and the lending agencies would be made more effective. In short, a single head, enjoying the confidence of the president, would be able to speak with vigor for the central banking viewpoint in the formation of economic policy; yet once the deliberations had been completed an assurance would exist that the Fed would be at one with the rest of the government in executing the policy determined upon.

A second, lesser category of structural change would have the object of revising the Fed's appearance to fit the public nature of its responsibilities. Election of two-thirds of the Reserve Bank Directors by commercial banks, and "ownership" of the Reserve Banks by commercial banks, are admittedly matters of no great substantive importance today. But since they are functionless elements, and their appearance of special interest access is harmful to the legitimacy of monetary actions, the Reserve Boards should be eliminated (or, at least, all of their members should be publicly appointed) and the commercial banks' shares in the Reserve Banks should be bought out by the government—thus making the Reserve Banks in form what they largely are in fact: field offices of the national, public monetary authority.

Adoption of this series of proposals—or others, perhaps milder in form but having the same essential consequences—would significantly improve the economic policy machinery of the national government. These changes represent a logical extension of the premises of the Employment Act:

In no major country of the world today, except in the United States, is there a central bank that can legally, if it wishes, tell the head of its own Government to go fly a kite. It seems to me that if we are to hold Government responsible for carrying out the new doctrine of economic stabilization, there must be a chain of responsibility reaching through the Presidency to all the instrumentalities that do the stabilizing.[40]

Notes

1. For more detailed description of the formal organization, see Board of Governors, *The Federal Reserve System* (Washington, D.C., 1961) and G.L. Bach, *Federal Reserve Policy-Making* (New York, 1950).

2. E.A. Goldenweiser, *American Monetary Policy* (New York, 1951), p. 295.

3. Joint (Patman) Committee on the Economic Report, *Monetary Policy and the Management of the Public Debt, Replies to Questions,* Sen. Doc. 123, 82d Cong., 2d sess., 1952, pp. 278–79. Cited hereafter as Sen. Doc. 123.

4. Bach, pp. 81–82.

5. Bach, pp. 57–58.

6. Goldenweiser, p. 296.

7. Joint (Douglas) Committee on the Economic Report, *Hearings, Monetary, Credit and Fiscal Policies,* 81st Cong., 1st sess., 1949, p. 221.

8. Chairman Martin in Senate Committee on Finance, *Hearings, Investigation of the Financial Condition of the United States,* 85th Cong., 1st sess., 1957, p. 1260. Cited hereafter as Senate Finance Committee Hearings.

9. Bach, p. 119.

10. Sen. Doc. 123, p. 30.

11. Senate Finance Committee Hearings, 1959, p. 2180.

12. Conversation with staff members, Council of Economic Advisers.

13. Bach, pp. 227–28.

14. See Chairman Martin's remarks, Sen. Doc. 123, p. 300, and Bach, p. 121.

15. Senate Finance Committee *Hearings,* p. 1262.

16. *Administration of National Economic Control* (New York, 1952), p. 270; and see ch. 9 generally.

17. House Report No. 742, 74th Cong., 1st sess. (April 19, 1935), p. 6.

18. Marriner S. Eccles, *Beckoning Frontiers* (New York, 1951), pp. 167–71. These pages contain an excellent capsule summary of OMC development.

19. Commission on Organization of the Executive Branch of the Government, *Task Force Report on Regulatory Commissions,* Appendix N., January 1949, pp. 113–14; Eccles, pp. 224–26; Bach, pp. 234–35.

20. Joint Committee on the Economic Report, *Monetary, Credit, and Fiscal Policies, A Collection of Statements,* 81st Cong., 1st sess., 1949, pp. 68–69.

21. Ibid., p. 162. By 1952, the presidents were less enthusiastic for change (see Sen. Doc. 123, p. 673). They perhaps feared that the unified control might go to the FRB rather than to the OMC if the subject were opened up at all.

22. New York Clearing House Association, *The Federal Reserve Reexamined* (New York, 1953), pp. 138–39.

23. Sen. Doc. 123, p. 294.

24. Subcommittee on General Credit Control and Debt Management, Joint Committee on the Economic Report, *Monetary Policy and the Management of the Public Debt,* Sen. Doc. 163, 82d Cong., 2d sess. (1952), p. 54; H. R. 2790, 86th Cong., 1st sess. (1959).

25. Joint Committee on the Economic Report, *Hearings, Monetary, Credit and Fiscal Policies,* 81st Cong., 1st sess. (1949), p. 221.

26. Bach, p. 234.

27. Subcommittee on General Credit Control and Debt Management, Joint Committee on the Economic Report, *Hearings, Monetary Policy and the Management of the Public Debt,* 82d Cong., 2d sess. (1952), p. 756, cited hereafter as General Credit Control Subcommittee *Hearings,* 1952. Regionalism in the Federal Reserve—or at least its modern defense—perhaps owes more to an unexamined bias in favor of "federalism" as a matter of political ideology than to an empirical examination of the national economic structure.

28. Sen. Doc. 123, pp. 677–79.

29. Robert E. Cushman, *The Independent Regulatory Commissions* (New York, 1941), p. 160.

30. Martin, in Senate Finance Committee *Hearings,* 1957, p. 1261.

31. Letter, Kenneth A. Kenyon, Assistant Secretary, Board of Governors, to the author, August 17, 1960.

32. Martin, in Sen. Doc. 123, p. 242.

33. See, for example, FRB Research Director Ralph A. Young's remarks, Antitrust Subcommittee, Senate Committee on the Judiciary, *Hearings, Administered Prices,* 86th Cong., 1st sess. (1959), Part 10, pp. 4887–91.

34. See H. Christian Sonne's comments, from which the quotation is taken, in General Credit Control Subcommittee *Hearings,* 1952, pp. 848–50.

35. For discussion of this and other pertinent administrative myths, see Harold Stein's remarks in General Credit Control Subcommittee *Hearings,* 1952, pp. 758–59.

36. Sen. Doc. 123, pp. 263–73.

37. See the remarks of Leon H. Keyserling and Roy Blough in Sen. Doc. 123, pp. 848–51.

38. E.g., in the spring of 1956: see discussion in Senate Finance Committee *Hearings,* 1957, pp. 1361–63.

39. Antitrust Subcommittee, Senate Committee on the Judiciary, *Hearings, Administered Prices,* 86th Cong., 1st sess. (1959), Part 10, p. 4917.

40. Elliott V. Bell. "Who Should Manage Our Managed Money?" An address before the American Bankers Association Convention, Los Angeles, California, October 22, 1956.

3D.2. In Defense of the Federal Reserve

ALAN GREENSPAN

Few people have had as much experience of economic policy making as Alan Greenspan, who has headed a consulting firm, been chair of the Council of Economic Advisors, and served two terms as chair of the Federal Reserve Board. This reading gives his testimony before the Committee on Banking, Finance and Urban Affairs of the U.S. House of Rerresentatives, responding to proposals that the structure of the Federal Reserve System be altered to make it slightly more democratic.

Greenspan here gives what has come to be the conventional defense of the current structure of the Federal Reserve System. In essence he argues that leaving monetary policy in the control of elected officials is likely to result in high rates of inflation. To prevent inflation it is necessary sometimes to tighten the money supply in order to slow down the economy. But such slowdowns are always unpopular with voters, so politicians tend to delay decisions until inflation is obvious, by which time it is much harder to control. It is therefore in the interests of the nation that monetary policy be left in the hands of responsible experts who cannot be overruled by irresponsible politicians. Increasing democratic control, as Reagan advocates, would therefore result in harmful levels of inflation.

I appreciate this opportunity to discuss the important issues raised by recent legislative initiatives to alter the structure of the Federal Reserve System. I will begin my remarks this morning by placing these issues in some historical perspective before commenting specifically on provisions that would change the status of Reserve Bank presidents, broaden the authority of the General Accounting Office (GAO) to audit the Federal Reserve, and mandate additional disclosure of monetary policy decisions and discussions.

The appropriate role of a central bank in a democratic society is an important and controversial issue. The performance of such an institution has profound implications for the nation's economy and the people's standard of living. Americans have pondered the question of the appropriate role and structure for the central bank at length, beginning with the debate over the First Bank of the United States, which George Washington signed into existence in 1791.

Echoing the earlier discussions surrounding the chartering of the First and Second Banks of the United States, extended debate and compromise preceded the establishment of the Federal Reserve System. Much of the focus of the debate was on the balance that should be struck between public and private authorities in governing the central bank.

In 1908, in response to the periodic financial crises that had plagued the country in the latter part of the nineteenth century and in the early years of the twentieth century, a National Monetary Commission, consisting entirely of members of the Congress, was established by legislation. Four years later, the commission, in submitting its report to the Congress, called for the creation of a National Reserve Association to provide stability to our financial system. Both the commission's plan and an alternative, proposed by President Woodrow Wilson, envisioned the central bank as containing public and private elements. President Wilson's plan won the approval of the Congress and established the Federal Reserve System as our nation's central bank. Over the intervening years, the Congress has initiated many reviews of the System's structure but with rare exceptions has chosen to leave the basic structure intact.

The major piece of legislation affecting the Federal Reserve's organization since its inception in 1913 was the Banking Act of 1935, which established the Federal Open Market Committee (FOMC) in its current form as the central decision-making body for monetary policy. When it was clear by the 1930s that the buying and selling of securities by the Federal Reserve was a crucial monetary policy instrument, there was again debate in the Congress over whether it should be carried out entirely by government appointees or whether the Reserve Bank presidents, who were not politically appointed, should share in that policymaking role. In the 1935 act, the Congress reaffirmed that the Reserve Bank presidents should have a substantive voice in policy. They were granted five of the twelve positions on the FOMC, while the seven members of the Board constituted the majority.

The wisdom of the Congress in setting up the structure of the System has stood the test of time. Federal District Court Judge Harold Greene, in commenting in 1986 on the constitutionality of the FOMC, noted, "The current system[,] ... the product of an unusual degree of debate and reflection[,] ... represents an exquisitely balanced approach to an extremely difficult problem."

The role of a central bank in a democratic society requires a very subtle balancing of priorities between the need for sound, farsighted monetary policy and the imperative of effective accountability by policymakers. Accountability and control by the electorate are vital; the nation cannot allow any instrument of government to operate unchecked. The central bank, just like other governmental institutions in a democracy, must ultimately be subject to the will of the people.

In this regard, the Federal Reserve's activities are constantly scrutinized by this committee and others in the Congress. The Federal Reserve Board reports semiannually both to the House of Representatives and to the Senate pursuant to the Humphrey-Hawkins Act, and we regularly respond to other congressional requests for testimony. We recognize our obligation to do so and appreciate the importance of maintaining open communication with the nation's elected representatives. We also provide a great deal of information about our operations directly to the public. And we consult frequently with those responsible for economic and financial policy in the Administration.

We have to be sensitive to the appropriate degree of accountability accorded a central bank in a democratic society. If accountability is achieved by putting the conduct of monetary policy under the close influence of politicians subject to short-term election-cycle pressures, the resulting policy would likely prove disappointing over time. That is the conclusion of financial analysts, of economists, and of others who have studied the experiences of central banks around the globe, and of the legislators who built the Federal Reserve.

The lure of short-run gains from gunning the economy can loom large in the context of an election cycle, but the process of reaching for such gains can have costly consequences for the nation's economic performance and standards of living over the longer term. The temptation is to step on the monetary accelerator, or at least to avoid the monetary brake, until after the next election. Giving in to such temptations is likely to impart an inflationary bias to the economy and could lead to instability, recession, and economic stagnation. Interest rates would be higher, and productivity and living standards lower, than if monetary policy were freer to approach the nation's economic goals with a longer-term perspective.

The recognition that monetary policies that are in the best long-run interest of the nation may not always be popular in the short run has led not only the United States but also most other developed nations to limit the degree of immediate control that legislatures and administrations have over their central banks. More and more countries have been taking actions to increase the amount of separation between monetary policy and the political sphere.

In this nation, several aspects of the current setup promote the central bank's distance from the political fray. The fourteen-year terms of the governors on the Federal Reserve Board are one of those elements, with only two vacancies scheduled to occur during the four years of any single presidential term. Once in office, those governors cannot be removed by the President over a policy dispute. In addition, regional Reserve Bank presidents—who are selected at some remove from political channels—are included on the FOMC. To prevent political pressure from being applied on monetary policymakers via the power of the purse, the Federal Reserve is not required to depend upon appropriated funds to meet its expenses.

H.R. 28, The Federal Reserve System Accountability Act of 1993, would remove some of that insulation. I would view the enactment of legislation of this type as a major mistake. Provisions that, in effect, increase political leverage on Federal Reserve decision-making amount to assaults on the defenses that Congress has consciously put in place to ensure the appropriate degree of central bank independence. Weaken those defenses, and, I firmly believe, the economy is at risk. The Federal Reserve must be free to focus on advancing the nation's ultimate economic goals.

In an amendment to the Federal Reserve Act, the Congress has charged the central bank with furthering the goals of "maximum employment, stable prices, and moderate long-term interest rates." To promote those objectives, the Federal Reserve must take a long-run perspective.

In that vein, as I have indicated to this committee on previous occasions, the determination of the effectiveness of a federal agency has to be based, in the end, on whether it has carried out the objectives the Congress has set for it. In discharging its tasks over the years, the Federal Reserve has faced a variety of challenges; our economy has been buffeted by swings in fiscal policy and by strong external forces, including oil price shocks and wars. In often difficult economic circumstances, the Federal Reserve has implemented policies aimed at promoting the nation's economic health. We have not always been entirely successful, but we have learned from experience what monetary policy can do and what it cannot do.

In my view, current Federal Reserve policy is promoting conditions vital to maximizing the productive potential of the U.S. economy. Monetary policy is, and will continue to be, directed toward fostering sustained growth in economic output and employment.

As the nation's central bank, the Federal Reserve stands at the nexus of monetary policy, supervisory policy, and the payments system. Part of our task is to minimize the risk of systemic crises while endeavoring to implement a macroeconomic policy that supports maximum sustainable economic growth. When, for example, threats to the nation's financial system loomed large in the wake of the 1987 stock market crash, the Federal Reserve effectively contained the secondary consequences of the crash with prompt but prudent injections of liquidity and with constant consultations with depository institutions during the crisis. The bulk of our efforts in this area, however, of necessity garners considerably less publicity, as it is directed at ongoing efforts to fend off financial sector problems before those problems emerge as full-blown crises that could threaten American jobs and living standards. Much of our success over the years, therefore, reflects crises that did *not* happen. In working with other regulatory agencies, the Federal Reserve has also brought its broad perspective to bear on supervisory actions that could have had macroeconomic or monetary policy implications.

In practice, the central bank of the United States works, and it works well. On paper, however, its structure can appear unwieldy—an amalgam of regional and centralized authority and of public and private interests. If we were constructing a central bank for the United States now, starting from scratch, would it be identical to the Federal Reserve System described in current law? Perhaps not. But the Federal Reserve has evolved to be well suited to today's policy tasks.

One of the reasons why the Federal Reserve is effective is that its basic structure has been in place for a long time. The institution has been able to take that framework as a given and to adapt and build on it during decades of invaluable experience in the financial and economic setting of this country.

As the Federal Reserve has evolved over the years, it has been permeated by a culture of competence and dedication to public service. As a consequence, the Federal Reserve has attracted highly skilled analysts, technicians, and policymakers. Although we might imagine a different initial structure for our central bank, implementing a major change at this stage could, for all intents and purposes, destroy the exceptionally valuable culture that has evolved over time and that continues to serve this nation well. And there is always the risk that changing a complex organization, even with the laudable goal of improving one or more parts of it, may well have unforeseen and unfortunate consequences elsewhere in the structure.

Nonetheless, the Federal Reserve recognizes that an organization that does not appropriately respond to changes in the environment in which it functions will soon become ineffectual. Accordingly, the Federal Reserve has suggested, initiated, and instituted several measured changes over the years. When confronted with a new development requiring change, we advocate change. For example, not long ago we recognized, as did this committee, an apparent weakness in the way the discount window could be used in the case of insured failing institutions, a condition that we had rarely before experienced. We saw change as a constructive response, and, while we were prepared to implement the change by adapting our regulations, we cooperated with this committee, which chose to amend our discount window procedures as part of the Federal Deposit Insurance Corporation Improvement Act of 1991.

I hope, and I expect, that the Federal Reserve will continue to change but always prudently—in response to clearly identified problems—and only for the better. One area in which I see major need for change is the inadequate pace at which women and minorities have moved into the top echelons of the Federal Reserve. We share your concerns in this regard and are working diligently to improve opportunities for women and minorities throughout the System.

In the remainder of my remarks this morning, I would like to address three specific issues, under the more general topic of Federal Reserve accountability. These issues are, first, the status of the Reserve Bank presidents on the FOMC, second, the General Accounting Office's purview in auditing the Federal Reserve System, and, third, the disclosure of FOMC deliberations and decisions.

The Status of Reserve Bank Presidents

The Federal Reserve Banks represent a unique blend of the public and private sectors. I believe that those who label the Reserve Bank presidents as representatives of the banking interests, as opposed to the public interest, misunderstand the position of the presidents—and the Reserve Banks—in the Federal Reserve System.

The Federal Reserve Banks are instrumentalities of the U.S. government organized on a regional basis. They are in a tangible sense "owned" by the federal government. The bulk of their net income is handed over to the government each year. Their accumulated surplus, were they to be liquidated, would revert to the U.S. Treasury. And although a portion of the capital of the Reserve Banks represents contributions by member commercial banks, those member banks are not free to withdraw the capital, their dividends are fixed by statute, and their capital stake in no way affords them the usual attributes of control and financial interest.

The member commercial banks do select the majority of the directors of their local Reserve Bank. But the Federal Reserve Board chooses the remaining directors and, among those directors, designates a chairman and a deputy chairman. The directors, in turn, select the Reserve Bank's president, but their selection is subject to the Board's approval.

Those Reserve Bank presidents then receive top-secret clearances from our government and are subject to the federal conflict-of-interest statute. They can be removed by the Federal Reserve Board, and it is the Board that sets their pay. Upon joining the FOMC, they take an oath of office to uphold the Constitution of the United States, and—uniformly in my experience—they are dedicated to the service of our country.

However, regardless of whether the presidents of the Reserve Banks are viewed as more public than private or more private than public, the real question remains, Does their participation on the FOMC make for better monetary policy? I can assure you that it does.

The input of Reserve Bank presidents who reside in and represent the various regions of the country has been an extremely useful element in the deliberations of the FOMC. By virtue of their day-to-day location and their ongoing ties to regions and communities outside of the nation's capital, the presidents see and understand developments that we in Washington can overlook. They consult routinely with a wide variety of sources within their districts, drawing information from manufacturing concerns, retail establishments, agricultural interests, financial institutions, consumer groups, labor and community leaders, and others. Moreover, because their selection is apolitical, they tend to bring different skills and perspectives to the policymaking process.

The public and private and the regional makeup of the Federal Reserve System was chosen by the Congress, in preference to a unitary public central bank, only after long and careful debate. The system was designed to avoid an excessive concentration of authority in federal hands and to ensure responsiveness to local needs. Nonetheless, then as now, the operations of the Reserve Banks were placed under the general supervision of the Board of Governors. When the FOMC was given its current form in 1935, five Reserve Bank presidents were placed on that committee, but their presence was outweighed by the seven presidentially appointed members of the Board.

This blending of public and quasi-public institutions has a long history in this country and has been reaffirmed repeatedly in the Congress. Nonetheless, the presence of Reserve Bank presidents on the FOMC periodically resurfaces as an issue. This occurs despite the long and successful history of the presidents' membership on the FOMC, which counters a similarly lengthy history of claims that their participation would be detrimental to our nation. The involvement of quasi-government officials in monetary policy-making has survived a series of challenges over the years. It has survived the test of time. One must wonder why we would wish to tinker with a unique partnership of the public and the private that has worked well for more than half a century.

Some who agree that the Reserve Bank presidents provide a unique perspective would nonetheless argue that such input could still be obtained by reducing the Reserve Bank presidents' role to an advisory one. I doubt that, for two reasons. First, let us not delude ourselves: Anyone permanently denied a vote sees his or her influence diminish markedly. Not only would the presidents' varied experiences and regional perspectives likely become less well reflected in policy decisions, but their ability to solicit real-time information from their communities would be diminished as well. Second, I believe that a fair number of my colleagues who serve as presidents of the Reserve Banks would have declined that office had voting rights on the FOMC not attached to it. These people do not lack for opportunities. If the Reserve Bank presidents were denied votes, we could not attract individuals of the same caliber to these jobs that we do today. As a result, the advice received would be adversely affected, and FOMC deliberations would be less productive.

A different proposal would retain the Reserve Bank presidents on the FOMC but would have them appointed by the President of the United States. Such a proposal is not new: it was considered and rejected by this committee as recently as 1976. The clearest drawback to this suggestion is one that I have already mentioned, that is, the potential for increased partisanship that would erode the quality of policy, as the central bank was drawn more closely into the ambit of daily political concerns. In addition, however, such an arrangement would create significant managerial problems for the Federal Reserve System as an organization.

Under current law, Reserve Bank presidents are directly accountable to the Board for their performance in carrying out System-wide policies in such areas as bank supervision, payments systems responsibilities, and discount window administration. The Board's ultimate defense against a Bank president who is either incompetent or purposely obstructing the effective implementation of System policy is its power to remove that person from office.

If the heads of the Reserve Banks were instead presidentially appointed, we presume that they could be constitutionally removed only by the President. In that circumstance, System-wide coordination of policies and interbank cooperation could be seriously impaired.

In sum, if the sole duty of Reserve Bank presidents were to vote on the FOMC, granting the President of the United States the power to appoint and remove them would be unwise on only one count—that of adversely affecting the conduct of the nation's monetary policy. However, Reserve Bank presidents also run large organizations charged with such tasks as collecting data, processing currency, operating the book entry system, and auctioning Treasury bills. The twelve Banks must operate as one in these various areas, and the Congress has given the Board general oversight of the Banks to ensure that they do. A proposal that divested the Board of the power to remove a Reserve Bank president from office would subtly but significantly undermine the ability of the Board to manage the Federal Reserve System.

Scope of GAO Audits

As you know, the passage in 1978 of the Federal Banking Agency Audit Act made most of the operations of both the Federal Reserve Board and the Federal Reserve Banks subject to review by the General Accounting Office. Since then, the GAO has completed more than 100 reports on various aspects of System operations, as well as numerous others that involved us less directly. At present, the GAO has roughly twenty-five audits of the Federal Reserve under way and maintains several of its staff in residence at the Board and at selected Reserve Banks.

The GAO has free rein to audit the System, with the explicit exemption of only three functions: Those are deliberations, decisions, or actions on monetary policy matters; transactions made under the direction of the FOMC; and transactions with, or for, foreign official entities. By excluding these areas, the 1978 act represented another effort to balance, on the one hand, the public accountability of the Federal Reserve with, on the other hand, its ability to perform its policy functions most effectively.

The benefits, if any, of broadening the GAO's authority into the monetary policy and FOMC areas would be small, in part because a GAO audit would tend to duplicate functions that are already performed. With regard to purely financial audits, the Federal Reserve Act already requires that the Board conduct an annual financial examination of each Reserve Bank, including open market and international operations. And these exams are complemented by other Board reviews of Reserve Bank effectiveness and efficiency, as well as by comprehensive audits conducted by each Reserve Bank's independent internal audit function. To provide the Board with additional assurance of the quality and comprehensiveness of the Board's audit process, complete financial audits are currently being conducted by nationally recognized independent accounting firms at Reserve Banks. Two such audits were conducted this year. The results of these audits to date have confirmed the integrity and quality of the System's audit process. In addition, the Board itself is audited annually by an independent public accounting firm, and the results of those audits are furnished regularly to the Congress.

More broadly, the Congress has, in effect, mandated its own review of monetary policy by requiring semi-annual monetary policy reports and by holding hearings. In addition, a vast and continuously updated literature of expert evaluations of U.S. monetary policy exists. In this environment, the contribution that a GAO audit would make to the active public discussion of the conduct of monetary policy is not likely to outweigh the negatives.

Those negatives would include a potential compromising of Federal Reserve effectiveness, in part, because the change could peel away a layer of the central bank's insulation from day-to-day political pressures. Even what appears to be a very limited audit of the efficiency of our operations could, in fact, turn into pressure for a change in monetary policy itself as the 1978 act understood. For example, the question being posed to Comptroller Bowsher in these hearings of whether the magnitude of our open market operations reflects unnecessary buying and selling of government securities is a monetary policy question, not an efficiency question. The volume of transactions that the Open Market Desk completes in carrying out the FOMC's directive correlates directly with the substance of the policy in place.

GAO scrutiny of policy deliberations, discussions, and actions could also impede the process of formulating policy. A free discussion of alternative policies and possible outcomes is essential to minimize the chance of policy errors. The prospect of GAO review of formative discussions, background documents, and preliminary conclusions could have an adverse effect on the free interchange and consensus building that leads to good policy.

Transactions made under the direction of the FOMC primarily involve domestic monetary policy operations but also include foreign exchange operations. Expanding GAO audit authority into this latter area would risk impairing our sensitive working relations with foreign central banks and governments. Important daily contacts and exchanges of information with foreign monetary authorities now take place in a candid and constructive atmosphere. The possibility of a GAO audit of our foreign exchange operations would reduce the willingness of foreign authorities to share information with us and thereby would reduce the effectiveness and efficiency of our operations. This caution also applies to the third exempted area—transactions with or for foreign entities; however, there the principal issue is one of sensitive proprietary information about foreign governments, foreign central banks, and international organizations.

In sum, I believe that the current structure of internal controls and audits and congressional review strikes the right balance between public accountability and policy effectiveness.

FOMC Disclosure

The issue of fuller or more immediate disclosure of FOMC discussions and decisions has been a controversial one historically. In the Congress, the financial markets, and academia, this topic has been debated repeatedly over the years. The FOMC itself has frequently reviewed policies and procedures in this area and has revised its practices several times. At the heart of this issue is, again, balance. The appropriate degree of openness comes from striking the right balance between the public's right to know and the need for effective policymaking and implementation.

In a democratic society, all public policymaking should be in the open, except when such a forum impedes the primary function assigned to an institution by law. Accordingly, the Federal Reserve makes its decisions public immediately, except when doing so could undercut the efficacy of policy or compromise the integrity of the policy process. When we change the discount rate or reserve requirements, those decisions are announced at once. When we establish new ranges for money and credit growth, those ranges are set forth promptly in our reports to the Congress. And when the Congress requests our views, we come before this committee and others to testify. Moreover, we publish our balance sheet every week with just a one-day lag, enabling analysts to review our operations in considerable detail.

What we do not disclose immediately are the implementing decisions with respect to our open market operations. However, any changes in our objectives in reserve markets are quickly and publicly signalled by our open market operations. We publish a lengthy record of the policy deliberations and decisions from each FOMC meeting shortly after the next regular meeting has taken place.

Nevertheless, the Federal Reserve has a reputation, along with other central banks, of being secretive. I suspect this is largely a result of the nature of a central bank's mission. The operations of central banks have a direct impact on financial and exchange markets; therefore, these institutions often find themselves in the position in which premature openness and disclosure could inhibit or even thwart the implementation of their public purpose.

Suppose, for example, a central bank that operated by targeting the foreign exchange rate decided that it might be appropriate to change the target rate at a given point in the future. Or, to bring the discussion closer to home, say that the central bank phrased its policies in terms of contingency plans—that is, if a given economic or financial event occurs, a particular policy action would ensue. If those decisions were made public, markets would tend to incorporate the changes immediately, preventing the policies from being effectively carried out as planned.

More broadly, immediate disclosure of these types of contingencies would tend to produce increased volatility in financial markets, as market participants reacted not only *to actual* Federal Reserve actions but also to *possible* Federal Reserve actions. It is often the case that the FOMC places a bias toward change into its directive to the Open Market Desk, without any change in instrument settings in fact resulting. In such circumstances, the release of those directives during the period in which they are in force would only add to fluctuations in financial markets, moving rates when no immediate change was intended.

As a consequence, a disclosure requirement would impair the usefulness of the directives, as Committee members, concerned about the announcement effect of a directive biased either toward ease or tightening, would tend to shy away from anything but a vote of immediate change or of no change at the meeting. An important element of flexibility in the current procedures would be lost, which can scarcely serve the public interest. Immediate disclosure of the directive would change the nature of monetary policymaking, and it would not be a change for the better.

Of course, our current policies on information release are grounded on an assumption of confidentiality. Any unauthorized, premature release of FOMC decisions is a very serious matter, and it undermines our policies. Such leaks are abhorrent. As I noted in my recent letter to you, leaks of FOMC proceedings are clearly unfair to the public, potentially disruptive of the policymaking process, and undoubtedly destructive of public confidence in the Federal Reserve. We have taken steps that we believe will be effective to curb any further unauthorized release of information.

To repeat, as a general matter, public institutions are obliged to conduct their business in open forums. The Federal Reserve endorses this principle and adheres to it, except when doing so would prevent us from fulfilling our fundamental mission of producing sound public policy.

Holding open meetings of the FOMC or releasing a videotape, audiotape, or transcript of them would so seriously constrain the process of formulating policy as to render those meetings nearly unproductive. The candid airing of views, the forthright give and take, and the tentative posing of new ideas would likely disappear. Monetary policy would suffer, and the economy with it.

In open forum, several important items currently discussed at FOMC meetings simply could not be mentioned. We would no longer have the benefit of sensitive information from foreign central banks and other official institutions or of proprietary information from private sector sources, as we could not risk the publication of information given us in confidence.

Moreover, to avoid creating unnecessary volatility in financial and exchange markets, the FOMC might have to forgo explorations of the full range of policy options. Our discussions would, in effect, become self-censored to prevent the voicing of any views that might prove unsettling to the markets. Even a lag in releasing a verbatim record of the meetings would not eliminate this problem but only attenuate it. Unconventional policy prescriptions and ruminations about the longer-term outlook for economic and financial market developments might never be surfaced at meetings, for fear of igniting a speculative reaction when the discussion was disclosed.

It has been averred that because the minutes we release do not indicate which individuals voiced which views at the meetings, the FOMC members themselves escape accountability for their actions. This is contrary to fact. The vote of each FOMC member is recorded, by name, and the reasons for that vote are also recorded. In the case of a dissent from the majority, the reasoning behind the vote is generally explained separately. In the case of a vote cast with the majority, the members assure themselves that the minutes accurately reflect their views and the reasons for voting as they did.

In both the Freedom of Information Act (FOIA) and the Government in the Sunshine Act, the Congress explicitly recognized that types of information and kinds of meetings should be protected from dissemination to the public. Certain exemptions have been provided in the FOIA for information that, for example, is of a confidential financial nature and in the Sunshine Act for meetings that would prompt speculation in financial markets. In the exempted areas, it was determined that information release would not be in the public interest. As I have indicated, I believe that the consequences of requiring the prompt release of a verbatim record of FOMC meetings would most certainly not be in the nation's best interest.

Conclusion

You have made it clear that, in your view, this legislation does not represent an attempt to politicize the Federal Reserve or to infringe on its independence. I feel I must respond that, whatever its intent, legislation of this type would have precisely that deleterious effect.

I take this legislative initiative seriously not only because it would emanate from this committee but also because of monetary policy's key position in the nation's overall economic policy. At the flashpoint of financial crisis, monetary policy, if mishandled, can pose a threat to our economic system. And in this century we have witnessed inflation—a monetary phenomenon—turn virulent in too many nations around the world. To a considerable degree, then, both the earnestness with which we approach our task and the unique position accorded the Federal Reserve in our governmental structure derive from the potential for just such dire consequences of monetary policy mismanagement.

In imposing significant change on the Federal Reserve System, we would run the risk of real damage to the institution's effectiveness from unintended, adverse consequences. The Federal Reserve is not a flawless institution. It is, however, a very good one. In my view, it would be a mistake to legislate structural reform when, as in this case, compelling evidence of the need for change is lacking.

3D.3. External Pressure and the Operations of the Fed

EDWARD J. KANE

As Michael Reagan notes, there is something extraordinary about the fact that, in one of the world's oldest democracies, something as important as monetary policy should be formally under the control of a non-elected body.

In this paper Edward Kane argues that the arrangement is retained in order to protect members of Congress and the President from having to bear the responsibility for taking unavoidable but unpopular decisions. It is often necessary, in order to cool inflation, to pursue a tight *monetary policy—which will drive up interest rates, slow business expansion, and increase unemployment. Such outcomes are unpopular with the electorate; if they were thought to have been brought about by a particular politician, he might have trouble getting reelected. Thus, it is in the interest of elected officials to have a scapegoat that can be blamed for these unpopular consequences of necessary policies.*

Scapegoats can, of course, have real power, but Kane does not think the Federal Reserve has the predominant influence on monetary policy. Rather, he argues, the real power over policy is largely retained by the president and Congress, with the Federal Reserve having little independent power and serving largely to deflect blame from the real policy makers.

The reader should note that while others have supported the idea that the president has more power over monetary policy than he appears to (Beck 1987, Wooley 1984), Kane attributes more power to Congress than do most other observers and he has been criticized for underestimating the degree to which

Adapted from *Political Economy of International and Domestic Relations*, edited by Raymond E. Lombra and Willard E. Witte, pp. 211–232 (with deletions). Copyright © 1982 by Iowa State University Press.

formal institutional arrangements can result in real power shifts (Meltzer 1982). Nonetheless, even Kane's critics find his thesis insightful and thought-provoking.

Introduction

Fed goals do not hatch full formed like Athena from the brow of Zeus. They are hammered and shaped on the anvil of national politics by artisans who never cease to reheat and touch up their work.

Nor is any particular macroeconomic goal absolutely good. Reputed macroeconomic public enemies such as unemployment, inflation, stagnation, and payments imbalance are neither entirely bad for the national economy nor bad at all for every sector. Unemployment probably retards inflation and strengthens the balance of payments; inflation reduces repayment burdens borne by debtors and encourages many types of investment; economic stagnation makes it easier to preserve the quality of the physical environment; and international payments imbalances lower the cost of living, reduce shortages, and generate profits for importers.

No logically coherent strategy exists for promoting every macroeconomic goal at the same time. Policies meant to promote one goal tend to interfere—either in the short or the long run—with efforts to achieve at least one other. Typically, the difference between macroeconomic good and macroeconomic level depends principally on how political power is distributed. Macroeconomic goal formation is inevitably a political process of trade-offs, in which the economic interests and political clout of different groups of citizens are, along with the timing of the next election, carefully weighed and balanced.

Elected and appointed politicians use constitutionally granted market power to resolve, to their personal and professional satisfaction, sectoral conflicts over the distribution of economic resources. Fiscally under-restrained sectoral demands on government resources combine with cyclically shifting electoral payoffs to incumbent politicians to induce accommodative monetary policies that squeeze private-sector real incomes and impose a politically induced overlay on the ordinary business cycle. In the United States, the trade-offs made in formulating monetary policy are seldom openly admitted either by elected politicians or by Federal Reserve officials. Surreptitious politics clouds the process of central-bank goal formation and encourages Fed officials to describe their decisions in a ludicrously sanctimonious kind of code. To understand the workings of the Federal Reserve System one must learn both to sort out political events affecting Fed policy decisions and to crack the several codes in which political communication takes place.

This paper develops the hypothesis that political events—not economic events—are the proximate determinants of Fed actions. It focuses on the elaborate system of contacts, threats, rewards, and punishments by which incumbent politicians in Congress and in the executive branch transmit monetary policy instructions to the Fed. Four main classes of relevant political events can be discerned: impacts of individual sectors on incumbent politicians; incumbents' impacts on Fed officials; Fed dealings with incumbent officials and individual sectors, including those that comprise the operative constituency against inflation; and internal Fed dealings: transactions among Fed officials and among component staffs. The analysis offered here concentrates on events of the second and third type.

To maintain the unfavorable trends in inflation and in the foreign exchange value of the dollar that the United States has experienced during the last fifteen years, U.S. politicians had to revise institutional arrangements for selecting monetary policy priorities. Incumbent federal politicians and political appointees preferred to ratify excessive sectoral demands on government fiscal resources in the short run, relying on taxation levied covertly by inflation to rebalance sectoral demands over the longer run. Moreover, incumbents found that they could at least occasionally curry votes by pursuing slight preelection improvements in macroeconomic indices at the expense of substantial postelection deterioration (Gordon 1975; Nordhaus 1975; Tufte 1978). To carry out these policies, incumbents had to persuade Fed officials to monetize a succession of federal deficits. Political pressure on the Fed fostered monetary policies that allowed incumbents to take credit for distributing current sectoral benefits and for bringing about short-run decreases in unemployment without requiring them to accept consonant blame for the inflationary consequences that these policies generated over the longer haul.

Analysis of the political economy of Fed decision making suggests that the Fed's role in this process of blame displacement is carefully scripted. Underlying this hypothesis is the principle that adjustments in Fed procedures and structural arrangements must be politically optimal at the time they are made. By revealed preference, authorities with jurisdiction (i.e., incumbent politicians or top Fed officials) have rejected other feasible approaches as less desirable than those chosen. Over time, legislation amending the Federal Reserve Act and extending the Fed's stabilization responsibilities via the Employment Act (and amendments thereto) have produced a U.S. central bank very different from the one originally conceived. This legislation, while undermining the Fed's ability to carry out its primordial assignment of acting as a roadblock to short-sighted economic policies, has left the Fed just enough apparent autonomy to provide incumbent politicians with a plausible scapegoat for all untoward macroeconomic events. By accommodating, year after year, a cumulative fiscal deficit, the Fed has come to function like a chaperone at a fraternity party. It legitimizes the process without changing it very much. Time after time, Fed officials accept the contradictory policy assignment of singlehandedly bringing inflation and unemployment down to satisfactory levels, stoically accepting the blame when these impossible goals fail to materialize. That intelligent observers continue to be swayed by Fed promises is a phenomenon for which (in contrast to P.T. Barnum) modern theories of expectations formation have no good answer.

Fed Appearances Versus Fed Reality

The place that the Federal Reserve System holds today in the macroeconomic policy formation process calls to mind Chesterton's conception of politics as the art of not telling the truth without actually lying. To decipher the Federal Reserve Act and most official Fed statements, one needs to recognize that key words have come to mean almost precisely the opposite of what they would mean in ordinary discourse. For example, Fed independence is now a code word for Fed political subservience and a Fed stock certificate no longer represents anything more than a nonmarketable, fixed-coupon bond of indefinite maturity.

In all too many cases, disguised politics transform the appearances of contemporary Fed practices, processes, and reasoning into the opposite of underlying realities. Fed fiction begins with its legal form of organization as a quasi-private corporation. Formal ownership of Federal Reserve stock certificates by so-called "member" banks makes the Fed look suspiciously like a bank-owned corporation. In reality, the Fed operates as an agency of the federal government. Fed staff members see themselves as government employees, and members of the Fed's Board of Governors are appointed by the president of the United States subject to the consent of the Senate. Fed stockholders have no proxy decisions to make and no beneficial interest in Fed earnings. . . .

Federal Reserve "Independence" Is Greatly Exaggerated

Although the Federal Reserve is generically just another federal agency, it is a species unto itself. Bureaucratically, the Fed enjoys a set of formal privileges that in the short run insulate its budget from partisan incursion and its highest officials from the threat of dismissal.

Federal Reserve governors are granted a degree of autonomy surpassed only by the Supreme Court, in the form of long terms of appointment and an independent source of operating funds (Burns 1978). The seven members of the Federal Reserve Board enjoy 14-year terms in office, staggered to make it hard—at least in theory—for a president (in his maximum eight years in office) to dominate the board by threats of non-reappointment. Moreover, neither the president's Office of Management and Budget nor the Congress can influence Federal Reserve decisions through the conventional discipline of the budgetary process. The Federal Reserve is chartered as a quasi-private corporation with first call on the interest that accrues on its portfolio of over $125 billion in U.S. Treasury and agency securities.

At best, this special bureaucratic shielding works *only* in the short run. Unlike Supreme Court justices who are appointed for life, Federal Reserve governors must concern themselves with post-separation career planning. Unless they are appointed at an advanced age, they must regularly review alternative job opportunities. This need to consider their future career profiles increases the separation rate and the number of partial-term appointments available over time. Governors appointed to unexpired partial terms are particularly susceptible to reappointment pressure.

Moreover, in the long run, successive presidents and Congresses must be persuaded to maintain the statutory armorplate. Fed officials possess a narrow political base. What political strength they have is drawn from the Fed's client banks, backed up by constituencies against inflation and for bank regulation. On the issue of inflation, popular allegiance has been weak and becomes even weaker when and as a recession develops. This is when the Fed—whose previous anti-inflationary policies inevitably take the blame for surging unemployment—is most vulnerable. In boom and recession, Fed officials must struggle in Congress to turn aside or to soften bills (such as H.R. 7001 in the 1980 Congressional session) that threaten to chip away at various pieces of the Fed's suit of armor. The necessity to campaign continually for the preservation of Fed autonomy makes Fed officials far more submissive to the short-run political interests of incumbent presidents and congressmen than they care to admit.

Debate about the desirability of an independent Federal Reserve system proceeds from a dangerously false premise. The Fed is approximately as independent as a college student whose room and board is financed by a parentally revocable trust fund. Some conflict will be tolerated, but the limits of the benefactors' patience must always be kept in mind.

Just as other federal agencies, the Fed is fully accountable to representatives elected by people (Board of Governors of Federal Reserve System 1974, p. 3). The difference lies in the intricate pattern of accountability and in the precise rewards and punishments elected officials are able to manipulate. Although dissatisfied politicians can't discipline recalcitrant Fed officials by forcing their dismissal or even by cutting next year's budget, they can and do restrain them by threatening to make unfriendly new appointments and to take back various elements of the Fed's vaunted independence.

Therefore, in addition to coping with the System's nominal responsibilities for economic policy and for facilitating the flow of domestic payments, Federal Reserve officials worry about avoiding public confrontations and preserving the System's structural autonomy. Each regime wants to bequeath to its successors an agency at least as strong in structure as the one they inherited. No regime wants to be recorded as gaining a string of Pyrrhic policy victories for which the System itself is made to pay dearly in the long run.

Political Events and Forces Influencing Fed Decisions

As scientists, economists are interested in observable phenomena. Unfortunately, external influences on the Fed and Fed reactions to these influences leave a deliberately muddled trail behind them. How to read this trail is the focus of this paper.

Political action for and against the Fed emanates from many sources and occurs along a broad spectrum of events. Presidential scoldings, special-interest attacks or pleas for help, and formal votes to approve or to reject legislative proposals are merely the most visible of these events. Private interests and elected officials work at the day to day task of influencing Fed officials by subtle means. These less dramatic tools include promises of jobs, public praise, use of rumors and trial balloons, informal meetings, hearings on legislative recommendations of various kinds, and redistribution of bureaucratic privileges.

Congress and the president impact on Fed officials formally and informally through the link of their shared responsibility for macroeconomic and financial events. Private interests act through governmental agencies sensitized to their needs, through the press, and through channels of social and economic contact.

A Framework for Assessing Incumbent Self-Interest

In the tradition of Anthony Downs (1957), we may conceive of elected officials as managing a production process, whose inputs consist of their own time, wealth, and office budgets and whose output is the probability of reelection. For a congressional incumbent, at least four intermediate products enter the reelection-probability production functions:

1. A record of individual achievement in office, as perceived by constituents. This record may be decomposed into different elements of constituent service (broadly considered).

    a. Service to the constituent business community in sponsoring important legislation or in shepherding it toward enactment

    b. Positions and votes taken on important issues, as reflected in favorable ratings by special interest groups, including so-called public interest groups

    c. Casework for individual constituents in dealing with the federal bureaucracy, e.g., in clearing claims for lost veterans' pensions or social security checks and following up constituent appeals against denials of benefits

    d. Providing responsive answers to opinionated mail from irate constituents

    e. Name recognition—keeping his or her name before constituents in as many ways as possible

2. The prestige which the office and particular mix of committee assignments currently enjoys

3. The size of the campaign budget

4. The short-term performance of the national economy, as represented (say) in Okun's "discomfort index," which sums the current rates of inflation and unemployment.

Holding hearings on legislation threatening to impose new congressional controls on Fed procedures enhances incumbents' ability to influence Fed thinking about what adjustments in the monetary aggregates would prove desirable.[1] It also elevates the status of service on a banking committee and, if legislation is enacted, raises the chairman's and committee members' record of achievement (Woolley 1980). In addition, raising manifold possibilities for restructuring Fed regulatory powers triggers greater involvement by bank and savings and loan lobbies, increasing the flow and selectivity of campaign contributions from these institutions' political action committees (PACs).[2]

Statutory Framework Within Which the Fed Operates

Fed officials' legal authority to make macroeconomic policy decisions on their own is contained in two frequently amended pieces of legislation: the Federal Reserve Act (1913) and the Employment Act of 1946. Proposed readjustments in the scope of Fed autonomy and responsibilities under these acts can be manipulated as a system of rewards and punishments, to increase or to diminish the prestige and quality of life enjoyed by Fed bureaucrats.

The President

As the hub of the executive branch, the office of the presidency provides numerous points of contact with Fed officials. Presidents can steer Fed decision makers in the direction they desire by holding out carrots of accommodation or by beating them with administrative sticks.

Appeals for policy coordination serve as tasty carrots. The ideal of assisting in the design of unified macroeconomic policies plays directly upon the ego of Fed officials by promising to enlarge their scope of activity. Governors and staff representatives may be invited to participate in policy formation over a broad field of economic issues with top officials from the Treasury, State Department, Commerce Department, Council of Economic Advisers, and Office of Management and Budget. Given that governors are drawn from a pool of predominantly idealistic and public spirited persons who see their service as a personal sacrifice made for the greater good, such appeals and opportunities are hard to resist.

The president appoints members of the Federal Reserve Board (FRB) and designates one member to serve as chairman. Economists widely regard the FRB chairmanship as the single most powerful economic policy post in the federal government. However, because a chairman's power is predicated on the cooperation of a majority of other board members, a president can punish an FRB chairman by appointing "difficult" but loyal persons to the board when and as vacancies arise. Less formally, he can make life in Washington uncomfortable in many ways for any set of government officials who stubbornly refuse to bend toward his view of the common good. Since such pressure should increase board turnover, it can reinforce the president's appointment power precisely when it promises to be most useful.

Every chairman is anxious to influence new appointments to the board. In the 1970s, when accelerating inflation drove levels of compensation for competitive positions in the private economy far above board salaries, board turnover soared. President Carter's first three and a half years saw six resignations. This turnover magnified the president's leverage on his FRB chairman and, early in Volcker's chairmanship, may have been used to make appointments specifically intended to blunt a politically uncomfortable policy thrust.

During the 1950s and 1960s, Fed officials were publicly called on the carpet by two different sitting presidents (Truman and Johnson) for resisting broad macroeconomic policy recommendations. The first such incident (in early 1951) cost Chairman McCabe his job, although two months later (see Clifford 1965) it led to an accord with the Treasury that strengthened the Fed. On the other hand, the second incident marked the high-water mark of Fed power, after which Chairman Martin never publicly challenged a president's economic policies again. In 1972, Chairman Burns permitted an election-year spurt in the monetary aggregates that assisted President Nixon's reelection campaign (Kane 1974a). In July 1975, President Ford pointedly celebrated his birthday with the board. Under Carter, beginning with the presidential press conference of November 1, 1978, the Federal Reserve Board chairman began to appear at the president's side to pledge in advance Fed support for the latest changes in Presidential economic policy strategy.

This increased receptiveness to shows of presidential attention reflected in part the Fed's increasing need for presidential support both to stop the inflation-accelerated exodus of member banks from the System and to fend off the accelerating congressional criticisms of its policies. As Fed problems became embodied in the concrete form of individual bills that would either extend or limit the Fed's powers, it became important to have the ability to call on a presidential veto in the clutch.[3]

Congress

Congressional power over the Fed also resides in ability to grant or to withhold rewards (legislative changes that Fed officials want) and to impose punishments (legislative changes that they don't want). Besides simple praise, the class of congressional rewards consists principally of two items. First, Congress could allow the salaries of Fed governors (which are currently constrained by those of Cabinet officers) to move as freely as those of the Reserve Bank presidents (which are tied instead to salaries received by local commercial-bank presidents). More competitive salaries for members of the Board of Governors would strengthen the Fed politically. It would increase the board's prestige and reduce its turnover. It would permit top staff salaries to be more competitive as well.

Second, Congress could increase the degree of Fed authority over nonmember banks and savings institutions. Through the 1970s, Fed officials were especially anxious to gain the power to set reserve requirements for nonmember depository institutions.

Congressional restraints on governor salaries strongly limit the population of individuals for whom FRB service poses an attractive career opportunity. For individuals of a given age, salary levels for FRB governors are more adequate for academics and career bureaucrats than for lawyers and bank executives. Similarly, low current salaries are less unattractive for youngish individuals, who can extract substantial implicit income by planning to parlay board service either into the name recognition required to campaign for elective office or into many years of higher-paying jobs in the private sector. Recently, Congress has taken action to reduce the present value of even this implicit or steppingstone income. The Ethics in Government Act of 1978 (as amended in May 1980) applies specifically to FRB members and serves to restrict their post-separation employment even more than the stringent "Boy Scout rules" the Fed adopted in 1973. Post-employment conflict-of-interest restrictions are especially severe for board members who fail to serve out the (possibly partial) term to which they were appointed. They are prohibited for two years from taking a wide class of jobs in the financial industry. Moreover, since the early 1960s, the board's own rules have prevented sitting governors from earning outside income from speaking fees. Taken together, congressional and in-house restrictions on FRB members' ability to earn explicit and implicit income make it hard to recruit competent governors with broad experience and make it uneconomic for all but a narrow class of FRB members to plan to serve more than a fraction of a full fourteen-year term.

Accelerating inflation tends to reduce the after-tax real value of governors' salaries and to increase the differential burden of reserve requirements on member banks. By letting the membership problem fester through the 1970s, Congress kept Fed officials under constant pressure. The Fed's fundamental membership problem was that declining membership (which for economic reasons was concentrated among small- to medium-sized banks) simultaneously reduced and narrowed its political base. This undermined Fed clout with Congress by impairing its ability to rally widespread bank lobbying activity in support of its policies. To close the Fed's longstanding political wound, in March 1980, Congress extended Fed-imposed reserve requirements to nonmember institutions, but permitted reserve balances to be held in the form of correspondent balances at member banks. This legislation denies the correspondent-balance option to all banks that were members on July 1, 1979. To establish incentives to restore the blood the system lost in the years prior to July 1, 1979, the Fed proposes to administer the statute by requiring a 100 percent pass-through of correspondent-held reserve balances to Fed accounts.

Although the class of congressional deprivations is virtually unbounded, recent threats have focused on the following issues:

1. Expanded Congressional oversight of decisions made by the Federal Open Market Committee, FOMC. Starting in 1975, the Fed was required to report quarterly (now semiannually) to the congressional banking committees on interim FOMC policy targets for the next twelve months and, since February 1979 (under the Humphrey-Hawkins amendment to the Employment Act), to square these targets verbally with administration plans. Related controversy has centered on the number and identity of the targets reported, on the desirability of simultaneously reporting interim targets, on whether the Fed should adopt a monetarist strategy, and on the contents and timely release of FOMC minutes, including the possibility of opening FOMC meetings under the Government in the Sunshine Act.

2. Reducing Fed budgetary autonomy. Congressman Wright Patman's overarching objective was to force the Fed to obtain its operating funds from annual appropriations from Congress. He urged retirement of Fed stock and regular audits of Federal Reserve accounts and policies by the Government Accounting Office, GAO. In 1977, a GAO audit was finally established, but the scope of the audit was limited to the Fed's bank supervisory functions. H.R. 7001 sought to redeem Fed stock and to end Federal Reserve bank presidents' membership in the FOMC.

3. Full-cost pricing for Fed banking services. This is now required by 1980 legislation. Although intended nominally to help private banks compete more effectively with Federal Reserve banks in the market for correspondent services, it affects the Fed's ability to tailor offers of implicit interest to the advantage or disadvantage of individual banks.

4. The propriety of having Federal Reserve bank directors and Board Chairmen lobby members of Congress. Although lobbying expense is legal for the Fed, government agencies that are restricted to congressionally appropriated funds are disallowed from spending funds in this way. This issue is designed to restrain the political activity of Fed officials.

5. Realigning the four-year term of FRB chairman to coincide with that of incoming presidents. This would ensure each new president a chance to place his own person in this top policymaking post. Although it incorporated a one-year delay, such a bill passed the House in 1980.

6. Extending the need for Senate confirmation to cover Reserve Bank presidents (because they are potential members of the FOMC) and to require new confirmation for an FRB chairman who had been confirmed previously as a board member. The first part of this proposal (which has not been enacted) would reduce the FRB's power to select Reserve Bank presidents and would allow Congress to screen all members of the FOMC. The second part addressed a loophole that could have allowed the president and the FRB to make an end run around the process of congressional screening. Since 1977, it has been necessary for all FRB chairmen and vice-chairmen to be explicitly confirmed in their posts.

7. Broader representation of women, minorities, and regional nonfinancial

interests on F.R. bank boards and on the Board of Governors itself. For example, in May, 1980, before granting approval of Lyle Gramley's appointment to the FRB, the Senate passed a resolution decrying "Eastern" domination of recent board appointments. Except that this issue impinges slightly on presidential and Fed officials' freedom of appointment, it is essentially symbolic.

8. Transferring the Fed's supervisory authority over member banks and bank holding companies (BHCs) to a new agency, which would consolidate in a single office all federal bank regulatory functions, including those currently exercised by the U.S. Comptroller of the Currency and the Federal Deposit Insurance Corporation (FDIC). By segregating the locus of monetary control from that of bank and BHC regulation, this change would deprive the Fed of a major element of leverage over credit policy at individual banks (Kane 1973).

9. Pressures to allocate credit in favor of specific sectors. These range from proposed bailouts of troubled industries, cities, and firms to proposals meant to provide better access to credit for small businesses and would-be homeowners. These pressures for sectoral relief constrain the Fed's ability to impose sharp or sustained increases in nominal interest rates on the macroeconomy.

One consequence of the assault in 1975 by post-Watergate freshman legislators on executive branch autonomy and on the congressional seniority system was an intensification of interest in reassessing Fed officials' rights and duties (Kane 1975; Weintraub 1978). Prior to Wright Patman's being stripped in 1975 of the House Banking Committee chairmanship, he had perennially pushed these same issues without effect. In the rush to build can-do records, his successor Henry Reuss, and his Senate counterpart William Proxmire (who succeeded John Sparkman in the same year), transformed what had been widely perceived as Patman's personal vendetta against the Fed into a careful reevaluation of congressional oversight responsibilities.

Since 1975, Fed officials have found themselves besieged simultaneously on many fronts. Month after month, House and Senate banking committees and subcommittees have held hearings to consider a series of bills that would either strengthen the Fed by relieving its membership problem or weaken it by chipping away at one or another of the Fed's special bureaucratic privileges. Few weeks pass in which a contemporary Fed chairman does not spend time preparing or delivering testimony for committee hearings. Legislation passed during this era has reduced the Fed's ability to keep internal procedures and debates from public scrutiny.

Beyond the Statutory Framework:
The Scapegoat Hypothesis

As a matter of legislative formula, the Fed is "merely a creature of Congress" in the same sense that Mary Shelley's fictional green monster was a "creature of

Frankenstein." In both cases, the issue is whether the "creator" can ever truly bring the creature back under control.

Although a few congressmen and senators work very hard for this result, one can legitimately question whether the Congress as a whole has any taste for the task (Kane 1975; Roberts 1978; Weintraub 1978; Woolley 1980). In practice, the ponderous multilayered structure of congressional decision making and the economic naivete of the great preponderance of elected officials provide effective limitations on congressional ability to dominate a reluctant Fed. Members who cannot to any great extent interpret current macroeconomic information fear the possibility that a Fed chairman's election-year counterattack might tar them with the label of "inflationists," while the slowness and unwieldiness of Congress itself virtually ensure that its influence even on quarter-to-quarter decisions by the Fed will prove more apparent than real.

At election time, incumbent congressmen find it extremely convenient to be free to blame the economic ills of the country on the "misguided" policies of an "independent" Federal Reserve system. A skeptic would say that the knowledgeable congressional leaders consent to small adjustments in Fed powers and responsibilities just often enough to keep the activist reformers among them hard at their job of reminding Fed officials of their accountability to Congress.

As this suggests, congressional dealings with the Fed have levels of meaning quite different from their surface appearance. Many of the most important transactions occur away from the public eye. The most palpable transactions take place when Fed witnesses testify at open hearings of congressional committees. A closely related type of encounter takes the form of sparring in the press and on TV over the severity and causes of alleged macroeconomic problems and the workability of reputed "solutions." Such public transactions are theatrically disputatious. They involve a great deal of posing and game playing, some of which is carefully rehearsed. Harsh exchanges are sometimes initiated solely for symbolic effect, to assure some troubled Fed or party constituency that its plight (which in most cases will continue to be neglected) has not been forgotten.

Private meetings occur frequently at the staff level. When necessary, congressional and Fed staff members negotiate legislative compromises for their principals, but in most cases they meet merely to exchange analysis and information about matters of "mutual interest." These meetings are generally friendly ones, but reluctance, resistance, and hostility are not unknown. In top-level contacts, persuasion is applied and deals are sealed. Fed officials lobby key congressmen and senators much as other special interests do, except that they are severely limited in the kind of inducements they can offer. Still, with what they have to work with Fed officials try—just as private contractors and other federal agencies do—to build up a coterie of friendly congressmen and senators.

In open forums, congressional criticisms of Fed policy vary predictably over the business and electoral cycles. At the top of a boom when unemployment first begins to increase, legislators focus on the Fed's "inhumane" willingness to sacrifice unemployed workers to the cause of slowing inflation and on the tendency of monetary restraint to reduce the flow of credit to small businesses and participants in housing markets (builders, construction workers, and would-be homeowners). Although these sectors tend to lobby for low interest rates at all times, a guilty suspicion exists that the social costs of using tight money to fight inflation falls disproportionately on them, and on the automobile industry as well. Reinforcing this view is a perennial complaint that, no matter how tight money becomes, loans of "low social value" somehow get made. In times of recession when unemployment is high and inflation begins to relent, congressional critics tend to accuse Fed officials of aggravating and then aborting the previous boom instead of keeping the economy moving along on a smooth path of "sustainable growth." They demand that the Fed relent in its "pathological" concern with fighting inflation and assist troubled firms or cities and fight single-mindedly the now-pressing problem of unemployment. Especially in election years, congressmen tend to continue this pressure until long after the recovery has begun and strong inflationary pressure has built up once more. As the recovery solidifies and turns into an inflationary boom, the foreign exchange and gold value of the dollar weakens and monetary policy is discovered to have been too easy for too long. At this stage, Fed officials are ceremonially urged to tighten up monetary discipline. The intertwining cycles run on and on, but this brings the analysis full circle.[4]

Although at each point of the cycle Fed officials offer ritualistic defenses against each charge, they cannot fail to recognize that political benefits accrue to them from allowing incumbents to use the Fed as a scapegoat. Bearing such criticism patiently contributes to the stereotype of Fed decisions as a continuing series of policy errors, but Fed officials are compensated by the survival of the unique bureaucratic privileges the Fed enjoys.

Lesser Sources of External Pressure on the Fed Officials

Almost everyone has an opinion about the state of the national economy and what could be done to improve it. Some opinions are better informed and less self-serving than others, but all of them are affected by the owner's perspective as an interested member of various political and economic groups. Perspectives on many macroeconomic issues differ markedly between creditors and debtors, between workers and employers, between jobholders and the unemployed, between landlords and tenants, between a product's producers and its consumers, between bureaucrats and the public that pays their salaries, between Fed staff economists and their counterparts in academe, and between incumbent politicians and those seeking to unseat them. The best- articulated opinions come from the business, financial, and foreign central-banking communities and from various elements of the economics profession.

Central Bankers in Other Countries

As the events of October 6, 1979, and Fed documents (e.g., Board of Governors of Federal Reserve System, 1974) testify, Fed officials maintain important points of regular contact with the international central-banking community. The detailed features of these connections adapt to the flow of political and economic events, with structural changes becoming clear only after the passage of time (Coombs 1976; Solomon 1977). The Board of Governors and New York Reserve Bank are linked formally to counterparts in Europe, Canada, and Japan through a network of daily telephone calls and through face-to-face meetings held under the aegis of various international organizations. The principal organizations are the Bank for International Settlements (which except in August, conducts monthly meetings in Basel), the International Monetary Fund (which holds a high-level meeting once a year in one or another major world capital), and the Organization for Economic Cooperation and Development (headquartered in Paris).

Since the tribe of central bankers is genetically encoded to resist inflation, they operate as an explicit part of the constituency against inflation. Just as any domestic interest group, the central-banking community seeks to impact politically on incumbent U.S. politicians. They do this primarily through their powers of persuasion and their power to improve or to worsen the dollar's standing on foreign exchange markets.

As the world's major reserve and vehicle currency, the dollar is inherently vulnerable to speculative attack. Fed officials labor long and hard to maintain an assured capacity to coordinate central-bank intervention against any large scale flight from dollars. For this reason, as the dollar has weakened secularly, the foreign central-banking community has gained more and more leverage over Fed officials and, through them (at least on occasions—such as October 6, 1979— when the dollar is highly vulnerable), over U.S. politicians as well.

Domestic Business and Financial Community

Because monetary policy affects the income statements and balance sheets of every kind of business firm, managers and stockholders strive energetically to communicate their policy perspectives to Fed officials. Whereas most members of Congress openly confess their inability to make sense of macroeconomic developments, spokespersons for the domestic and international business and financial communities profess to understand economic events and policies perhaps too well. On the symbolic level, businessmen regard the Fed as a restraining force in federal policymaking and the chairman as a spokesperson for their view of the public interest. Many lobby simultaneously against inflation and big government and for measures to strengthen the dollar and to grant relief to their own troubled industries. They firmly expect the Fed to value these same goals. In return, they support the Fed in its struggles with Congress to maintain its "independence" and urge the retention of "proven" Fed leaders when an unsympathetic president has a chance to make a change.

This mutuality develops partly because Fed officials and executives are of the same social class. Top and middle managers at the Fed are alumni of the same schools, live in the same types of neighborhoods, and float in the same executive labor pool as those in the private economy. Between this pool and the Federal Reserve, regular interchange occurs in both directions. In particular, stints of employment at the Fed add gloss to a career as a securities dealer or commercial banker. For this and the following list of other reasons, dealers and bankers influence Fed policies more than any other industry groups.

1. They serve as sources of information about the distribution of policy burdens that may help guide open-market policy in the short run. First, banks and dealers bear the initial impact of open-market policy. Their impressions of how that policy is working and their observable reaction to Federal Reserve actions are important pieces of distributional information. Monitoring these responses provides feedback that can be used to guide short-run policy adjustments and to evaluate long-run issues concerning the appropriate institutional framework of monetary control.

Officials that manage the Fed's open-market account in New York describe the ease or difficulty with which banks and dealers can adjust to policy actions as the "tone" or "feel" of the money market. For years, this subjective tone or feel occupied an untoward and politically sensitive central place in the FOMC's assessment of whether or not its policies were realizing its intentions.

2. Banker and dealer interpretations of events can contribute to the system's understanding of its own policies. One element of Fed stabilization policy is to discover more about how its policy instruments actually work. To produce better effects, Fed officials need better theories of how its instruments link up with intermediate targets and goals. Although one may debate how well Fed officials learn from experience, evolutionary changes in FOMC strategy have developed as pragmatic adaptions to lessons taught by past mistakes.

From a research perspective, each business-cycle turning point begins a fresh scientific experiment from which to learn something new about how monetary policy works. Bankers' and dealers' self-interest makes them keen (if biased) observers of these experiments. By publicizing their developing forecasts and critical insights, bank and securities-industry analysts (such as Henry Kaufman) can put a great deal of pressure on the FOMC.

3. Regulator-regulatee symbiosis. To some extent, regulators tend to think of regulatees as customers or clients whose approval needs to be cultivated. Prior to the 1980 extension of Fed reserve requirements to nonmember banks, this tendency exemplified itself in Fed discussions of its membership problem. Membership in the system is wholly voluntary for state-chartered banks. Even though national banks are required to join the system, their ability to convert to a state charter made even their continued membership a quasi-voluntary decision. This "exit option" gave member banks leverage they could use to soften Fed supervisory and regulatory policies. Persistent failure to respond to widespread banker criticisms could embarrass Fed officials by reducing the very reach of the system. To keep at least a semblance of an exit option open, commercial banks lobbied successfully against instituting compulsory membership *per se*.

This clientele orientation explains a parallel tendency for regulatees and regulators to view themselves as victims of a common enemy: the unreasoned demands of well-intentioned but naive legislators. Far more often than not, U.S. banking firms and their federal regulators stand together for or against proposed reforms in banking regulation.

Such solidarity is useful to both parties. In backroom legislative showdowns, bankers have considerable political power. They pointedly contribute funds to the election campaigns of state, local, and national candidates, giving special attention to the needs of candidates who serve on banking committees. More subtly, some congressmen and senators have been induced to make investments in bank stock. Such holdings create an unavoidable conflict of interest, by linking industry profits with the legislators' personal financial welfare.

On the other hand, in dealing with issues that capture the public's imagination, bankers' grasping (if not villainous) image in American folklore puts them at a severe disadvantage. With the general public, the media, and most politicians easily confused about how financial markets and monetary policy work, it is hard for bankers to argue the economic merits of their own case. Their obvious self-interest makes observers skeptical of their motives and arguments.

A political fire storm develops whenever bankers make cumulative increases in their *prime rate*,[5] even when anticipated inflation is accelerating very quickly and prime rate increases merely defend banks' real incomes. In times of tight credit, borrowers whose loan requests are turned down tend to band together to blame refusals on bankers' greedy disregard for the national interest. The event of raising the rate on bank loans and reducing availability is taken as prima facie evidence of a banker conspiracy to exploit monopoly power. In the popular press, bankers' fiduciary responsibilities to stockholders and the risks and returns available on alternative assets are seen as pretexts for tightening credit terms rather than as causes.

Bankers' need for assistance in media politics and the Fed's inability to offer financial incentives impart a symbiotic character to their mutual relationships with Congress. When legislation is introduced to hold down bank interest rates or to channel bank loan funds toward or away from favored or disfavored classes of borrowers, sponsors inevitably seek to involve the Fed in administering the program.

When called to testify on the subject, Fed officials underscore the administrative difficulties and long-run economic problems that would almost certainly attend such control programs. Fed officials' willingness to help bankers resist gross regulatory incursions creates a political debt on which the Fed sometimes calls to resist attacks (often from the same regulatory activists) on its bureaucratic autonomy. On issues of Fed reform, bankers' solid lines of communication and influence into Congress and the administration can be used more openly. Bankers' less direct interest makes it easier for them to lay out the Fed's case. To argue convincingly that "good intentions" will produce bad effects, it is nice to possess hands that appear relatively clean.

4. *Points of formal contact.* Although of minor practical significance, business and financial interest have three points of formal contact with Fed officials. These occur in the Reserve Bank Directorates, the Federal Advisory Council, and the Consumer Advisory Council.

Reserve Bank boards of directors consist of six persons (three bankers and three other persons actively engaged in commerce, agricultural, or industrial pursuits) elected by the member banks in that district (usually after considerable prior screening by Fed officials) and three "class C directors" appointed from the public at large by the Board of Governors in Washington. These regional boards meet regularly to "supervise and control" Reserve Bank operations. This gives a director many opportunities to exchange views on Fed policies with the Reserve Bank president, who represents the district in the FOMC.

Directors also elect each district's member of the Federal Advisory Council. This council meets at least four times a year with the Board of Governors in Washington, to confer about the economic outlook and any elements of Fed policies and operations its members wish to discuss. The council is specifically empowered to make oral and written representations on these matters and to collect information and issue policy recommendations as well. It (and a larger counterpart Consumer Advisory Council that focuses on consumer-related banking issues) is widely thought not to exercise important influence.

Economists

In policy debates, an economist's role depends both on the nature of the issues and on where he or she is employed. Labor and business economists function principally as advisors and advocates. After advising their clients of the advantages and disadvantages of current and prospective policies, they help their clients to state their side of an issue as clearly and as forcefully as they can. They may or may not have much role in deciding what stand their employer takes on a given issue. They may not even agree with the position they are called upon to represent.

On issues where political pressure or ideological bias predetermines their employer's stand, presidential, congressional, and Fed staff economists function in much the same way—the major difference being that they are expected to gather and process statistically a great many numbers to support their principals' case. Still, government economists feel a responsibility to their craft (nurtured by their academic colleagues) to represent their professional perceptions of the public interest to some degree as well.

On some issues and under some chairmen, Fed staff economists play a leading role in policy formation (Wallich 1982). As a matter of tradition, even on controversial issues Fed staff economists play an active and politically nonpartisan role in system decision making (Maisel 1973; Pierce 1979; Lombra and Moran 1980). Fed economists are jealous of this role and of their reputation for preparing for internal consumption an objective analysis of even the most controversial problems facing the Fed. When a chairman resists what staff members firmly believe to be the public interest (as, for example, when a chairman thinks of himself as the "best economist in the system"), the more adventurous among them may supply helpful arguments and data to dissident governors or district bank presidents. When board and FOMC decisions run seriously counter to their conception of the public interest, at least a few individual staff members will regard it as their right (if not their duty) to explain matters to their colleagues in the academic or banking communities. On rare occasions (and usually only after another job has been lined up), some have gone so far as to "leak" their independent analysis of a given issue to the press.

In most bureaucracies, habitual violation of administrative secrecy is tantamount to mortal sin. During the Burns era, a siege mentality, featuring a narrow view of proper staff lines of communication, took root at the Fed. But, though impaired, a more open, public-interest tradition survives among the professional staff. Many staff members remain eager to debate Fed policies informally with outside observers.

By fostering this tradition and engaging in such debates, academic economists pose an indirect influence on Fed decision making. Formally, the governors and their senior staff meet several times a year with a panel of distinguished academic consultants to discuss Fed policies and the national economic outlook. Informally, staff members exchange views with academic economists in professional assemblies and during looser contacts of a diverse sort. A particularly interesting forum is the Shadow Open Market Committee (SOMC) formed in 1973 by academic economists Karl Brunner and Allan Meltzer. The SOMC is a group of prominent monetarist economists who gather twice a year to evaluate Fed open market policy in the light of contemporaneous monetary policy recommendations of their own. Their goal is to produce academic criticism in which elements of "Monday morning quarterbacking" play a minimal role.

The Media and Main Street

Because of what may be described as the "gross economic illiteracy" of the American journalistic establishment, the Fed and its political, business, and academic critics set the tone and dimensions of journalistic discussions of macroeconomic goal formation. For the most part, the press concentrates on what financial and governmental *celebrities* have to say. The space allocated to items of monetary policy news tends to be proportional to the public standing of the celebrity newsmaker and to bear little relation to the intellectual quality of the case developed. Journalists act as a channel for disseminating and explaining the positions of the contending parties rather than as agents for skeptically investigating and reconciling competing claims.

Contemporary economic journalism is almost completely an exercise initiated by—and focusing on—a media event or press release of some kind. This concentration on reportable events rather than on evidence and logical argument reinforces politicians' tendency to focus on the quick-to-develop effects of policies rather than on their long-run implications. To enhance their effect, distributors of official handouts often support their documents with individual background interviews. These are offered both to guard against embarrassing misunderstandings and to reward individual journalists for friendly reports in the past.

The Fed's Internal Workings Are Adapted to Its Scapegoat Role

The Federal Reserve System is a political institution designed by politicians to serve politicians. Framers of the Federal Reserve Act deliberately dispersed jurisdiction over Fed actions among twelve regional (district) banks and a coordinating Board of Governors in Washington, D.C. Precise control over the Fed's various policy instruments is statutorily fractionated among 127 individuals: the nine-member boards of directors at each Reserve Bank, the twelve regional bank presidents, and the seven governors. Intricate legislative formulas differentiate among bodies that may initiate policy actions and bodies that must review these initiatives. By these formulas, the chairman of the Federal Reserve Board appears as a governor only to be "first among equals" and not obviously more powerful than the president of the Federal Reserve Bank of New York, who also has a permanent place on the FOMC and whose salary (usually a reliable index of organizational authority) runs about twice that of the chairman.

Such contrived structural confusion must serve a political purpose. Government institutions evolve by natural selection, albeit without a genetic overlay. In bureaucracies, although change is often painfully slow, structural innovations occur principally as creative ways of relieving external and internal pressure on top management. Form follows function in the sense that organizational changes that serve continuing agency purposes survive while those that do not are eventually eliminated.

Elements of the Fed's bureaucratic structure are best seen as rational adaptations to ongoing and sporadic political pressures on the Fed's management team. As their principal functions, these adaptations serve to establish a cautious posture vis-à-vis incumbent politicians, to blur internal responsibility for controversial decisions, and to diffuse external blame for policy mistakes widely among system personnel.

Although the office of Federal Reserve Board chairman has come to occupy—in practice and over time—the predominant position in the hierarchy of the Fed, formally all Fed policy decisions are made jointly. Reinforced by the ambiguous formal dispersal of jurisdiction over the Fed's major policy instruments, the jointness makes it easier for Fed chairmen to let congressmen and senators blame them unfairly after the fact for whatever financial or macroeconomic developments their constituents dislike. The Fed's internal structure rolls the blame displaced from elected politicians into a thin film that spreads smoothly across a host of internal committees, councils, and boards.

The duality and ambiguity enshrined in the language of the Federal Reserve Act erect a uniquely confusing bureaucratic structure that makes the Fed appear both independent of short-run political influence and decentralized in its internal organization. The Employment Act of 1946, as amended by the Humphrey-Hawkins Act of 1978, enlarges the Fed's statutory mission while providing no specific guidance as to how Fed officials should execute politically sensitive trade-offs among conflicting goals. In accepting a series of impossible economic policy tasks, Fed officials set themselves up as shields for elected politicians, institutionally absorbing and distributing the blame for repeatedly choosing shortsighted policies. When the Fed fails to achieve its contradictory goals, how sharply these politicians and their successors attack (and whether or not they try to impose punitive damages) depends on the quality of Fed efforts to get along.

Being programmed to fail repeatedly at their policy assignments, Fed officials find it useful to express their intentions in a code that makes it hard for hindsighted critics to score cleanly. Fed officials consistently refuse congressional requests to identify their implicit short-term targets for inflation and unemployment. They won't even commit themselves as to which combination of the many values reported in their ranges of tolerable monetary aggregate growth rates they would most prefer. This obfuscation masks the Fed's openness to political influence and facilitates the formulation of quasi-contradictory explanations both of the mechanics of their policies and of the rationale behind them. To protect the system from criticism and bureaucratic punishment, Fed chairmen are systematically led to employ their bully pulpit to miseducate the U.S. public about the macroeconomic consequences of alternative economic policies.

Why Does the Fed End Up Having a Procyclical Impact?

Despite the FOMC's progressive adoption since 1970 of counter-cyclical targets for monetary growth rates, U.S. monetary aggregates continue to move procyclically (Kaminow 1979). In fact, in the presence of accelerating inflation, deposit-rate ceilings and the structure of bank reserve requirements and FDIC insurance premiums make observed movements in monetary aggregates understate the procyclical thrust of Fed monetary policy (Kane 1978). These regulations make the stock of money substitutes expand rapidly whenever interest rates rise.

In a now-classic piece, Brunner and Meltzer (1964) show that the Fed's procyclical impact can be traced to "money-market myopia," i.e., to the Fed's obsessive concern with damping the size of short-run increases in nominal interest rates. What I wish to add to their analysis is the hypothesis that Federal Reserve officials aren't fooled into thinking that focusing on short-term interest rates is sound policy. I maintain that the political response system, driven by sectors that are ill-served by rising interest rates (including firms and individuals that consciously or unconsciously speculate against interest rate increases), makes it necessary for the Fed to follow nominal interest rates closely and to increase them less rapidly in the face of accelerating inflation than farsighted, independent policymaking would require (Kane 1980a). It is merely convenient internally and externally for Fed officials to rationalize their interest rate focus as they have.

Experience teaches that when the inflation rate varies over time, the policy effects of changes in the level of nominal interest rates become hard to interpret. Nominal interest rates treat loan repayments of future dollars as the equivalent in value of *current* dollars. But with inflation, future dollars have increasingly less purchasing power. To account for this, it is better to focus on real interest rates. These are nominal interest rates minus the anticipated rate of price inflation. For example, with 10 percent of anticipated inflation, a 12 percent Treasury bond rate would pay only 2 percent real.

Although real and inflation-adjusted interest rates would measure the thrust of monetary policy more accurately, in the popular mind and in the popular press the Fed's chief task is to act as the arbiter of nominal interest rates. During times of monetary restraint, this adversary perception subjects the Fed to political pressures from sectors that are hurt by rising interest rates. These sectors' political action leads elected officials to resist increases in nominal interest rates.

Fed efforts to reassure its anti-inflation constituency focus attention on observed changes in nominal interest rates and reinforce the mistaken popular notion that changes in the level of nominal interest rates are reliable indicators of the macroeconomic thrust of monetary policy. In times of gathering inflation, to placate the Fed's natural constituency in the business and financial communities, Fed officials tend to emphasize that they are fighting inflation with high and rising nominal rates of interest. However, unexpectedly accelerating inflation would push up nominal rates anyway. The issue is how hard the Congress and the administration are simultaneously pushing Fed officials to fight unemployment by expanding the money stock.

Money market myopia is rooted in an underlying political and societal myopia with respect to the long-run and short-run consequences of economic policy. To end money market myopia, the fundamental need is not just to change Fed operating procedures and to disentangle the Federal Reserve System from excessively short-term political influences, but also to help the American public to understand who is responsible for bad monetary policy performance. Accountability for our economic policies, and for monetary policy in particular, should flow through to elected officials. What I find offensive in the current U.S. situation is that the Federal Reserve tries to convince people that it is independent. Every senator and congressman knows that the Fed responds to political pressures, as indeed every agency should under our system of government. Why should the Fed take the blame institutionally for mistakes of policy that are forced on it? The problem is not so much that the Federal Reserve fails to flatten out business cycles, but that it acts in ways that aggravate the cycle in economic activity. As a minimum, voters should insist that the Fed not be made to serve as a mechanism for injecting politically induced, procyclical influences that make business cycle swings wider.

Despite their efforts to do the best job humanly possible, given the political constraints they accept, Fed officials end up adopting policies that reinforce rather than offset cyclical influences. An important part of the difficulty is the emphasis Fed officials place on nourishing the false image of "the independence of the monetary authority within the structure of government" (Burns 1978, p. 381). In the 1970s, the desire to preserve this independence locked Fed officials into a "Caesar's wife" syndrome, in which they became more sensitive to political pressure than even a less "independent" central bank would need to be. They sought to avoid the controversy that would attend their making hard decisions about the sectoral distribution of income precisely in order to maintain a latent capacity to make such decisions at some unspecified future date. If Fed officials could accept openly either in their charter or in their hearts that they are fundamentally servants of the elected representatives of the people no different from any other bureaucrats, the electorate would have a fairer chance to punish inflationists and to reward farsighted economic statesmanship.

Because recurring sectoral and election-year pressures lead policymakers to adopt an inappropriately short-run horizon, somewhat longer terms of elected office might prove helpful. But frequent elections are not the major source of stop and go monetary policy. The ultimate sources are the exaggerated expectations that voters (as pressure groups) have as to what government can do for them economically and the lack of constraints on the ability of special interests to beg benefits from the federal government. In the final analysis, lawmakers register and balance the distribution and intensity of voter opinion. Inflation will not slow appreciably until the constituency against inflation becomes a political majority. For this to occur, interest groups must learn, as parts of a "constituency of the whole," that society's relying habitually and permanently on the government to improve on demand the lot of any individual sector produces in the long run not more wealth for some sectors but less for everybody. . . .

Summary Statement

External pressure is to politics what arbitrage is to economics and finance. It is a force that explains how individuals and groups of individuals manage their affairs. As applied to the operations of the Fed, external pressure is a stress that helps the Fed officials to decide what priorities to assign to conflicting macroeconomic goals.

In resolving any of the dilemmas of monetary policymaking, the key pressure points are Congress and the president. Every other group is subsidiary. To have a genuine effect, arguments for changing the operative set of monetary policy priorities must first impact politically on elected or appointed politicians.

Conceiving of the Fed as a willing scapegoat, whose task is to absorb guilt efficiently, explains very well the complicated, arbitrary-looking structure of the Federal Reserve system. Most of the Fed's special bureaucratic features (its independence, its acceptance of contradictory policy assignments, and its murky lines of internal authority) and its incomplete policy strategies serve definite political ends. If one accepts the hypothesis that the Fed's main function is to serve as a policy scapegoat for elected officials, these apparent anomalies may be seen to be intelligible adaptations to recurring political pressures.

Fed officials desire good monetary policy performance even more than anyone else. With the best of intentions, they revise the structure of Fed decision making and modify procedures for conducting their operations and for monitoring their effects. However, as long as these changes have no perceptible impact on the relevant political forces, they can have precious little effect on the short-run compromises Fed leaders find it prudent to make among alternative policy goals.

On the other hand, the Depository Institution Deregulation and Monetary Control Act of 1980 does affect the balance of political forces. Because it removes an important source of external pressure on Fed officials, it is potentially far more important than the largely cosmetic past pledges of Fed allegiance to monetary aggregate targets. Extending Fed-administered reserve requirements to nonmember deposit institutions lessens the value of member banks' exit option and increases the Fed's ability to command their political support. This enhanced political muscle makes it politically feasible for the Fed to take more effective action against secular inflation in the 1980s than it has at any time during the last two decades.

Notes

This paper brings together in a single source analysis developed earlier in Kane (1973, 1974a, 1974b, 1975, 1978, 1979a, 1979b, 1980a, 1980b). The author wishes to thank Benjamin Friedman, Benson Hart, George Kaufman, Allan Meltzer, Thomas Mayer, Anna Schwartz, and the editors of this volume for valuable comments on an earlier draft and to acknowledge the impact on his thinking of repeated conversations with Richard C. Aspinwall, Robert Eisenbeis, Raymond Lombra, and Edward J. McCarthy. All opinions expressed are those of the author and not those of the National Bureau of Economic Research.

1. Consider this statement about election year monetary policy by House Banking Committee Chairman Henry Reuss: "I think a build-up in the money supply during the

Presidential election is a good thing. It would have helped in 1970, actually; but when you continued it into 1973 and made it worse, and continued in 1974, I and others did protest" (Committee *Hearings,* February 19, 1975, p. 21).

2. The great spurt in the number of bills introduced in the last two Congresses (which approached 20,000 pieces of legislation in the 1979–80 Congress) suggests a larger strategy of shaking down PACs of all kinds.

3. In private correspondence, Stephen V. O. Clarke has emphasized that the importance to the Fed of maintaining friendly relations with the White House was appreciated even in the early 1920s. In a 1922 letter to Montagu Norman, Benjamin Strong wrote:

> In the face of a powerfully organized antagonism in Congress, the Federal Reserve System must, to a considerable extent, rely for its protection against political attack and interference upon the present administration. . . . We cannot afford, practically or politically, to embark upon a course which ignores the policy of the administration, which would possibly antagonize the administration and place us in the position where we would be quite helpless to resist the repeated efforts which have been made in Congress to effect important and possibly vital modifications in the underlying principles of the Federal Reserve System (Clarke 1967, p. 30).

4. It is instructive to compare the cyclical shifts in banking committee members' evaluations of current monetary policies with contemporaneous *Policy Statements* put out semiannually by the nonpolitical Shadow Open Market Committee led by Karl Brunner and Allan Meltzer.

5. This is the lowest rate of interest that banks *admit* collecting on funds lent to their best business customers.

References

Beck, Nathaniel. 1987. "Domestic politics and monetary policy." In Thomas D. Willett, ed. *Political Business Cycles: The Economics and Politics of Stagflation*. San Francisco: Pacific Institute for Public Policy Research.

Board of Governors of Federal Reserve System. 1974. *The Federal Reserve System: Purposes and Functions*. 6th ed. Washington, D.C.: Board of Governors, Federal Reserve System.

Brunner, K., and A. H. Meltzer. 1963. "Predicting velocity: Implications for theory and policy." *Journal of Finance* (May): 319–54.

———. 1964. The Federal Reserve's attachment to the free reserve concept. U.S. House of Representatives, Committee on Banking and Currency, Subcommittee on Domestic Finance, May 7. Washington, D.C.: Government Printing Office.

Burns, Arthur R. 1978. *Reflections of an Economic Policy Maker: Speeches and Congressional Statements, 1969–1978*. Washington, D.C.: American Enterprise Institute.

Clarke, Stephen V. O. 1967. *Central Bank Cooperation: 1924–31*. New York: Federal Reserve Bank of New York.

Clifford, Jerome A. 1965. *The Independence of the Federal Reserve System*. Philadelphia: University of Pennsylvania Press.

Coombs, Charles A. 1976. *The Arena of International Finance*. New York: Wiley.

Downs, Anthony. 1957. *An Economic Theory of Democracy*. New York: Harper and Row.

Gordon, Robert J. 1975. "The demand and supply of inflation." *Journal of Law and Economics* (December): 807–36.

Kaminow, Ira P. 1979. "Fed policy under resolution 133 (1975–1978): Is what they said what they did?" Government Research Corporation, Working Paper.

Kane, Edward J. 1973. "The central bank as big brother." *Journal of Money, Credit and Banking* 5 (November): 979–81.

———. 1974a. "The re-politicization of the Fed." *Journal of Financial and Quantitative Analysis 9* (November): 743–52.

———. 1974b. "All for the best: The Federal Reserve Board's 60th Annual Report." *American Economic Review* 64 (December): 835–50.

———. 1975. "New congressional restraints and Federal Reserve independence." *Challenge* 18 (November-December): 37–44.

———. 1978. "EFT and monetary policy." *Journal of Contemporary Business* 7 (Spring): 29–50.

———. 1979a. Statement. In U.S. Senate, Committee on Banking, Housing and Urban Affairs, *Hearings, Federal Reserve's First Monetary Policy Report for 1979,* February 20 and 23, 1979, pp. 154–60.

———. 1979b. "The three faces of commercial-bank liability management." In M. P. Dooley, H. M. Kaufman, and R. E. Lombra, eds. *The Political Economy of Policy Making.* Beverly Hills: Sage, pp. 149–74.

———. 1980a. "Politics and Fed policymaking: The more things change, the more they remain the same." *Journal of Monetary Economics* 6 (April): 199–211.

———. 1980b. Accelerating inflation and the distribution of savings incentives. Mimeograph. Columbus: Ohio State University.

Lombra, Raymond E., and Michael Moran. 1980. "Policy advice and policymaking at the Federal Reserve." In K. Brunner and A. Meltzer, eds. *Monetary Institutions and the Policy Process.* Carnegie-Rochester Conference Series on Public Policy, vol. 13, pp. 9–68.

Maisel, Sherman J. 1973. *Managing the Dollar.* New York: W. W. Norton.

Meltzer, Allen. 1982. "Politics and Economics at the Federal Reserve." In Raymond E. Lombra and Willard E. Witte, *Political Economy of International and Domestic Monetary Relations.* Ames, Iowa: Iowa State University Press.

Nordhaus, William D. 1975. "The political business cycle." *Review of Economic Studies* 42 (April): 169–90.

Pierce, James. 1979. "The political economy of Arthur Burns." *Journal of Finance* 34 (June): 485–96.

Roberts, Steven M. 1978. "Congressional oversight of monetary policy." *Journal of Monetary Economics* 4 (August): 543–56.

Solomon, Robert. 1977. *The International Monetary System 1946–1976: An Insider's View.* New York: Harper and Row.

Tufte, Edward. 1978. *Political Control of the Economy.* Princeton: Princeton University Press.

Wallich, Henry C. 1982. "Policy research, policy advice and policy making." In Raymond E. Lombra and Willard E. Witte, *Political Economy of International and Domestic Monetary Relations.* Ames, Iowa: Iowa State University Press.

Weintraub, Robert E. 1978. "Congressional supervision of monetary policy." *Journal of Monetary Economics* 4 (August): 341–62.

Woolley, John T. 1980. "Congress and the conduct of monetary policy in the 1970s." Political Science Paper, no. 52, April. St. Louis: Washington University.

———. 1984. *Monetary Politics.* New York: Cambridge University Press.

Recent Changes in Monetary and Fiscal Policy

Fiscal Policy During the Last Decade

During the past fifteen years there has been a change in the political balance in the United States. As the South has moved from being solidly Democratic to being primarily Republican, the balance of power between the two major parties has shifted. Before this era the Republican Party was more or less resigned to being the minority party in Congress and expected to share the presidency if it could come up with moderate and attractive candidates. But starting around 1980 the parties moved into a more competitive stance. The Republicans held the Senate from 1980 to 1986 and took control of both houses of Congress in 1994.

As this happened, the balance of power within the two parties also shifted. The Democrats lost many of the conservative legislators from the South, leaving it more liberal in composition. The Republicans, cognizant of the need to appeal to a more fundamentalist constituency, moved to the right, especially on social policies.

The shift also had an effect on economic policy. Parties always balance the policy positions that they would prefer against the ones necessary to get elected. Usually this is a good thing, as it shifts parties toward the center where most citizens actually are. But sometimes it can be negative. There are some policies that, while politically popular and beneficial in the short term, are unwise in the long term. So long as the governing party is sure that party loyalty will give it a majority, it can resist such policies. But as the political scene becomes more competitive, both the challenging and the governing parties are tempted to adopt such policies to gain electoral advantage.

The specific form that this has taken in the past fifteen years is for the challenging party to propose a tax cut and an increase in spending (in defense for Republicans; in domestic spending for Democrats) while also promising to reduce the deficit. In 1980 Reagan promised a massive income tax cut, a big increase in defense spending, no decrease in social security spending, and a decrease in the deficit. President Clinton in 1992 promised a middle-class tax cut, more spending on roads and bridges, more spending retraining workers, and a decrease in the deficit. The Republicans elected to Congress in 1994 promised a variety of tax cuts, an increase in defense spending, no reductions in social security, and the elimination of the deficit within seven years. These promises were impossible to carry out without the cooperation of the other party, as they required big cuts in programs close the hearts of those in that party. But the interest of the other party was in protecting "its" programs and refusing cooperation. As a result, the only real question was which of these preelection promises would be broken once the candidate was in power.

The worst choice was made by President Reagan in 1980 to 1982. He decreased the income tax by about 30 percent, gave business a number of tax breaks, and increased defense spending considerably. While he did make a number of cuts in domestic programs, these were kept down by the Democratic House. The result was a tremendous increase in the deficit. The deficit which had stood at $74 billion in 1980 ballooned to $208 billion by 1983. Putting it another way, the budget deficit accounted for 2.7 percent of gross domestic product in 1980, but increased to 6.1 percent in 1983. As we have seen, it is possible to argue for a *cyclical deficit* which turns into a surplus in boom times. But once the deficit became this large, it was clear that America had a *structural deficit,* which would remain in good times as well as bad.

The effects of this expansion of the deficit live on to this day. Ever since 1982 the budgetary process has been dominated by the question of how to reduce and/or eliminate the structural deficit. In principle it is not that difficult to reduce the deficit. One can reduce social security spending, reduce other domestic spending, reduce defense spending, and/or increase taxes. Or, if one is prepared to look at the long term, one can wait for long-term growth to raise revenues, thereby cutting the deficit. And in the period since 1982, all of these things have been done. But to eliminate a huge deficit in a politically significant time frame, massive cuts in spending or massive increases in taxes are necessary. Whereas small changes were possible, big changes spelled political suicide for whichever party was blamed for them. As a result, there has been a political stalemate, with each party trying to goad the other into taking responsibility for politically unpopular spending cuts or tax increases.

The Process

It is characteristic of Americans, when faced with a substantively difficult problem, to devise a process that will eventually take care of the problem. It is characteristic of politicians to delay any pain to the future. Faced with the deficit problem, our political leaders have tried to devise processes that would solve the deficit problem while delaying most of the pain into the future. To date they have not succeeded.

The first attempt to change the process to solve the deficit problem was the so-called Gramm-Rudman-Hollings Bill of 1985. This was an attempt by Congress to discipline its own tendencies toward deficit spending. It set mandatory deficit targets for the next five years with the most severe cuts toward the end of the period. If Congress and the president could not agree on cuts to reach the deficit targets, mandatory cuts would be imposed, half on defense spending and half on a selected list of domestic programs. In the first version of the bill these cuts were to be imposed by the General Accounting Office, a subsidiary of Congress. When the Supreme Court ruled in 1987, as most had expected, that the General Accounting Office could not make such cuts because it was not an executive agency, a new bill was passed, Gramm-Rudman-Hollings II, which passed the responsibility to the Office of Management and Budget, and stretched out the mandatory targets.

In 1990, faced with the difficulty of meeting the totals, President Bush and Congress reached a new agreement that essentially replaced Gramm-Rudman-Hollings II. This agreement combined a substantive package of spending cuts and tax increases to reduce the deficit with yet another new process. This imposed separate mandatory caps on discretionary spending for domestic, defense, and international programs, but was more flexible on entitlements, revenues, and what to do in emergency situations. It also contained the useful provision that any new spending proposal had to be accompanied by a source of funds that would provide as much as the spending proposal needed. While this process has been more successful than the Gramm-Rudman-Hollings process, it has not resulted in the expected amount of deficit reduction.

While whole books have been written about these changes in the budgetary process the bottom line is that they have been more flash than substance. At best one can argue that they resulted in the deficit being a little lower than it would otherwise have been. At worst one can argue that failure to spend money when it was needed exacerbated problems like the Savings and Loan crisis, costing taxpayers more than would otherwise have been the case.

Table 1 shows the degree to which the three attempts to reduce the budget through changing the process were successful. The table is misleading in that in a formal sense the targets were always met at the beginning of the fiscal year. However, they were met essentially by making optimistic assumptions about likely revenues and spending needs and by a variety of accounting tricks. But during the fiscal year, "unexpected" increases in spending or decreases in spending took place. Hence, at the end of the fiscal year, more had always been spent than was "intended." When accounting tricks and optimistic assumptions no longer worked it was time for a new process with new targets that were easier to meet.

The table is also misleading in another direction. The deficit figures after 1990 are billions lower than they would have been had the substantive Bush-Congress deficit reduction plan not been passed, and the deficit figures after 1993 were reduced by a similar amount by the Clinton deficit reduction package. This makes the process changes seem *more* effective than they actually were,

Table 1

Gramm-Rudman Targets, Bush Deficit Expectations, and Actual Deficits

Fiscal Year	1985 Law Target	1987 Law Target	1990 Law Expectation	Budget Deficit	Total Deficit	Deficit as a Percent of GNP
1986	174.9			238	212.3	5.3
1987	144			169.3	149.8	3.5
1988	108	144		194	155.2	3.5
1989	72	136		205.2	152.5	3.2
1990	36	100		278	221.4	4.2
1991	0	64	327	321.4	269.2	4.9
1992		28	317	340.5	290.4	5.1
1993		0	236	300.5	255.1	4
1994			102	258.8	203.2	3.1
1995			83	251.8	192.5*	2.7
1996				262	196.7*	2.7

Note: Data from Albert Hyde, *Government Budgeting*, 2d ed., p. 470, and from Council of Economic Advisors, *Economic Report of the President 1995*, p. 365.

although as can be seen, even without correcting for this bias, the process changes do not appear to have achieved their intended result.

The Substance

While on the surface it looked like politics as usual, behind the scenes important changes were taking place. Although in the past Republicans had believed in avoiding deficit spending, Democrats had generally been less concerned about deficits. Now the roles began to change. Republicans became more divided. Republicans like Newt Gingrich began to view tax cuts as a means of making themselves the new majority party. While they did not want deficits, the insurgents were prepared to accept them to get tax cuts if their preferred option, massive spending cuts, were to prove impossible. Other, more traditional Republicans, like Pete Domenici, chair of the Senate Finance Committee, continued to view deficits as abhorrent and were prepared to sacrifice tax cuts on the altar of fiscal balance.

Just as interesting was the change taking place on the Democratic side of the aisle. Years of large deficits had left Congressional Democrats feeling boxed in. Every time they tried to start some new program, it was cut off at the knees by the existence of the deficit. The leaders of the House and Senate economic committees felt that they had been put in a position where they could never offer tax cuts or new programs without being blamed for worsening the deficit. The result was that over time they began to feel that solving the deficit problem was a precondition to pursuing a Democratic program. Solving the deficit became a concern in its own right. Three of the most important of these Congressional leaders—Lloyd Bentsen, Leon Panetta, and Alice Rivlin—were appointed by Clinton to the key positions in the Treasury and the Office of Management and Budget, bringing their concern with solving the budget deficit with them.

There were also pressures from outside government. The problem of the deficit was often assuming first place in the regular Gallup Poll survey on what Americans saw as the most important problem facing the country. Even more impressive to politicians was the ability of Ross Perot, an eccentric billionaire running as the candidate most opposed to the deficit, to pick up 20 percent of the vote in the 1992 Presidential election.

This general environment led to a series of massive compromise deficit-reduction packages which bypassed the normal budgetary process, and were essentially negotiated by the congressional leadership on one side and the president and his major economic advisors on the other. The first and least important of these was negotiated between President Bush and the Democratic leadership in Congress in 1990. In addition to the process changes already mentioned, there was agreement to cut $500 billion from the deficit over the next five years. Forty percent of this was to come from reductions in discretionary spending, primarily in the defense area; around 25 percent was to come from income tax increases; and the rest from somewhat vaguely defined reductions in future entitlement spending and interest payments. While the real savings were less than advertized, the agreement did in fact inflict pain on both sides. The Democrats had to accept reductions in many of their prized domestic spending programs. The president was forced to repudiate his 1988 election pledge of no new taxes and to accept real limits on defense spending.

In 1993 a similar, albeit somewhat more solid, budget reduction package was put together in negotiations between President Clinton and his economic advisors, the House and Senate leadership, and the heads of the key economic committees. Both Clinton and the Democrats in Congress had been spooked by the Perot phenomenon and Clinton's initial proposal to shave $475 billion over five years was actually increased by Congress to a $500 billion package. But unlike the Bush package where most of the savings were to come from spending cuts, in the Clinton package almost three-quarters of the savings came from tax increases.

As part of his strategy to win Republican control of the House of Representatives, Newt Gingrich and his advisors came up with a series of promises called the "Contract with America." One of these was a promise to abolish the deficit in seven years. When the Republicans unexpectedly assumed control of both the House and the Senate in 1995, they felt it necessary to produce a third deficit-reduction package. Whereas the Bush package had focused primarily on discretionary spending and the Clinton package had focused primarily on taxes, this package primarily targeted entitlement spending, with over half the proposed savings coming from the future growth in Medicare and Medicaid spending.

Somewhat surprisingly, Clinton responded by producing another budget reduction plan of his own, setting the stage for what is currently expected to be a compromise plan that will reduce the budget deficit to the point where it will cease to be a significant political problem. However, one should note that, in the past, such expectations have not been met, and as the deficit decreases it will become harder for politicians to resist the temptation to decrease taxes or institute new programs. As Robert Reischauer, the respected former head of the Congressional Budget Office, said after looking at the Republican compromise proposal, "I'll sell you my youngest child if the number in 2002 is zero" (Gleckman 1995).

In part because of this standing temptation, there have been a number of attempts recently to pass a constitutional amendment making a balanced budget mandatory except in variously specified special circumstances. The most recent attempt, in 1995, passed the House and failed to pass the Senate by only one vote. Most economists and Washington politicians think that enshrining balanced budgets in the Constitution is unwise, as it limits the ability of fiscal policy to deal with recessions. However, it is enormously popular with the public, which has little understanding of the differences between personal and public budgeting and, as the Buchanan reading makes clear, has serious advocates among both politicians and economists.

The Outcomes

The decade-long struggle over the deficit has had important effects, some of them directly related to the deficit and others that are side effects of the struggle. Starting with the budget deficit itself, it is clear that despite the public perception that the problem is at an all-time high, the deficit problem in the United States is currently fairly mild. While it is true that the absolute size of the deficit appears to be in the same range as it was for most the 1980s, we must remember that because of inflation, dollars are worth less than they once were and the economy has expanded. When we look at the deficit as a percent of GNP, it has dropped from over 6 percent of GNP at the height of the Reagan era to 2.7 percent of GNP in 1995. But the size of the deficit is determined by two things. One is the underlying structural deficit. The other is the effect of the business cycle. Figure 1, taken from the *Economic Report of the President 1995*, attempts to remove the effects of the business cycle and show the underlying structural deficit. As can be seen, the structural deficit is now in a range more typical of the pre-Reagan than the post-Reagan years.

Further, it is clear that by international standards, the United States has done rather well. If we look at countries such as Germany, Japan, and France, which are prone to lecture the United States on its failure to control the deficit, we find that their own deficits are all higher than ours. Other developed nations such as Italy appear to do reasonably well with deficits three times as large as our own.

Figure 1. **Structural Budget Deficit after 1993 Deficit Reduction and Initial 1996 Budget**

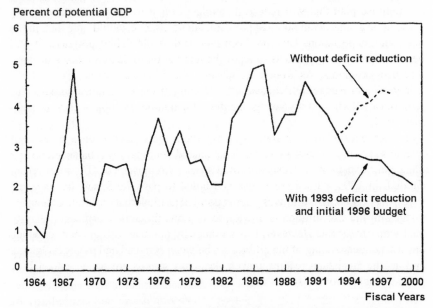

Percent of potential GDP

Source: Council of Economic Advisors, *Economic Report of the President 1995* (Washington, D.C.: Government Print Office, 1995), p. 67.

Note: Structural deficit excludes cyclical revenues and outlays.

But this relative success in dealing with the deficit has not been costless. The 1990 and 1993 budget accords both contained reasonably large tax increases, especially for the upper middle classes and the wealthy. The Clinton election promise of a middle-class tax cut was sacrificed to deficit reduction (Woodward 1995), and all indications are that the Republicans in 1995 will achieve much less in tax reduction than they promised, for the same reason.

The impact on spending has also been important. The federal government provides much less aid to states and localities in areas such as roads, bridges, education, and economic development. Aid to Families with Dependent Children (AFDC), the major cash welfare program, has become steadily less generous over the last fifteen years. Defense spending has declined and military bases are being closed all over the country, though this is due at least as much to the end of the cold war as to the deficit problem. Regulatory agencies are short of inspectors. Alternative energy programs are being cut back. While not all of these changes are bad, most of the cutbacks have real costs.

Less obvious are the spending increases that have not taken place. President Bush, who came in promising to help education and the environment, was not able to spend very much on either. President Clinton, who came into office with big plans for investing in work training and infrastructure, ended up with small programs in both areas. But the most important casualty of the deficit process was national health care. Because the deficit problem made it impossible for the public sector to bear the real costs of covering the uninsured, Clinton was forced to try to unload the costs onto small business and other private parties. Resistance from these parties was in turn responsible for dooming a program that initially had overwhelming public support.

Examination of these effects reminds us that the large deficit-reduction packages have enabled politicians to do things that they wanted to do for other reasons. The most notable of these hidden agendas are Clinton's ability to impose large tax hikes on the rich under the umbrella of deficit reduction and House Republicans' ability to slash medical and welfare programs under the same rubric. But they also have had political costs. Most obvious is the Bush administration's failure to stimulate the economy the year before the election, which may well have cost him his presidency (Risen 1992).

Finally, the deficit reduction struggle had effects on the budgeting process. While the 1974 Budget Control and Impoundment Act formally changed the process to a more centralized system, the heart of the process remained a series of individualized deals controlled from the subcommittees of the Appropriations Committees in the Senate and House. But the recent trend toward budget-reduction packages in which pain for one set of interests has to be balanced against pain for other interests has necessarily moved much real power to the center. There can be little doubt that the budget committees and the House and Senate leadership play a larger role than they used to within Congress and that the role of the Office of Management and Budget and central groupings such as Clinton's National Economic Council has grown at the expense of the individual agencies.

The Theories

To what degree do the events of the last decade illuminate the theories put forward in the articles in this book? Wildavsky argues that the budgetary process is basically incrementalist. Natchez and Bupp argue that it is more pluralist in character. Niskanen sees a budgetary process in which better informed bureaucrats push politicians into overexpanding the budget.

It should be clear that the events of the last ten years are not consistent with incrementalist theory as we normally understand it. Under the Reagan administration, large increases in defense spending accompanied large decreases in some categories of domestic spending. Under the Bush and Clinton administrations, we have seen uneven cutbacks that are dictated by the current political balance rather than the small, even increases or decreases that incrementalism would lead us to expect.

Niskanen's view of a bureaucracy driving the budget for its own advantage also does not seem to fit the events of the last decade very well. The number of bureaucrats has actually decreased in recent years, and the heavy cutbacks in discretionary spending that have taken place under all three administrations clearly do not fit the model. Further, it is clear that the implementation of these cutbacks also does not fit the model, with the dominant pattern being one of political appointees and congresspersons forcing cuts on unwilling bureaucrats.

On the other hand, pluralism fits much better. When one looks at the fights over which programs get cut and by how much, one sees exactly the kind of battle between interest groups and parties mediated by congressmen seeking advantage for their constituencies that pluralists talk about.

On the tax side, all of our articles have some applicability. Looking first at Peters's article, it is clear that while not all of the actors he describes have been crucial, many have played an important part. The extraordinary number of tax bills in the last fifteen years primarily echo the larger clashes of party politics. Interest groups have played their customary part in altering tax bills in Congress to better fit their needs, although the 1986 bill showed that there are limits to their power (Birnbaum and Murray 1987).

The influence of supply-side economics has come primarily at the beginning and end of our period. Supply-side economics provided the primary economic justification for the massive Reagan tax cut of 1981, and the various tax-cut proposals put forward by House Republicans in 1995 also embody some of their assumptions. However, it is hard to find evidence to show that supply-side changes have had the anticipated effects. In particular, savings rates actually fell after the big Reagan tax cuts and it is hard to find any of the anticipated labor supply effects in the 1980s.

King's theory that changes in taxes that benefit the wealthy are often justified by reference to supposed benefits to all citizens through increased economic growth certainly seems to fit the early Reagan cuts, the capital gains tax cuts proposed by the Bush administration, and the continual Republican advocacy of either a flat tax or a consumption tax to replace the progressive income tax. However, one should note that, contrary to King, it matters a lot which political party is in power. In both the 1990 and 1993 tax increases, congressional Democrats were able to make the income tax substantially more progressive.

The events of the last decade provide fodder for both of our deficit articles. Buchanan's article, written in 1977, appears to predict fairly well the big American and European deficits of the next twenty years. It should be clear that in the largest sense the reasons behind the deficit are indeed rooted in the kinds of short-sighted demands from the general public that Buchanan had in mind, and it is clear that efforts to reduce the deficit in good times have been resisted by the public. However, in a more detailed sense the Buchanan model fits less exactly. The Reagan tax cuts, the proximate cause of the large deficits, were not really undertaken for Keynesian reasons, and the public's emphasis on deficit reduction does not fit with Buchanan's image of a public unwilling to bear pain to solve deficits.

Finally, Schneider's point that the deficit can be used as cover for party political agendas certainly seems to fit what has happened in the last ten years, with each party choosing deficit-reduction targets that advanced its long-term platform.

Monetary Policy During the Last Decade

The last decade has marked a high-water point for the power and prestige of the Federal Reserve Bank. Every public utterance of the chairman is scrutinized in the media for hints as to the future course of the economy. Bond and stock prices rise and fall on comments from individual board members. Presidents rail against board decisions while changing their policies to meet the board's approval. All this has happened at a time when most observers think that the board has an ever decreasing power to move the economy.

The high prestige and power of the board has not come about through changes in the formal political powers of either the Federal Reserve System or its opponents. The formal system described by Reagan in 1971 remains much the same as it did then. As the reading by Greenspan makes clear, there have been proposals to alter the formal system slightly in this period but none of these proposals have been accepted by Congress.

Changes in Powers

One can reasonably make a case that this should have been a period of declining, not increasing, power for the Federal Reserve System. A number of changes made the tools at the disposal of the Fed less useful. The most general change was the effects of the internationalization of world financial markets. The Federal Reserve has no direct powers over banks in other countries, over currency speculators, and over other central banks, but all of these can now affect the success of Fed policies. To give one example, when the German Bundesbank kept its interest rates extraordinarily high in order to attract capital to rebuild the former East Germany, people who might otherwise have invested in Treasury bonds sent their money to Germany, keeping long-term interest rates higher than they would otherwise have been.

In addition, there were a series of less obvious changes that served to reduce the power of the Fed. There has been an expansion in foreign banking within the United States, reducing the part of the banking system subject to regulation. More important has been the growth of near-money options such as money market funds, which are not controlled by the Fed. This meant that most of the monetary tools available to the Fed directly affected a smaller and smaller percentage of the nation's financial resources. In addition, the erratic flows between different financial resources made indicators of the money supply such as M1, M2, and M3 less reliable indicators of the state of inflation, complicating an already complicated forecasting problem.

The Growth in Influence

Despite these technical problems, monetary policy became the chief tool for controlling the economy in our period. A number of factors led to this result. One is that what was once a theory—that when monetary policy and fiscal policy conflict, monetary policy dominates—now seems more like fact. The high deficits of the last fifteen years mean that fiscal policy has been inflationary for all of the period. But by keeping real interest rates above their historic average for this period, the Federal Reserve has more than offset this stimulus, keeping inflation low.

Further, the fact that inflation has been kept in check in and of itself has increased the prestige of the Fed. Most view the primary job of the Fed as inflation fighting, and assume that the low and generally declining rates of the last decade are a tribute to its effectiveness.

Another factor has been the lack of a real alternative. Wage-price policy is now generally seen as ineffective. The deficit has made it extraordinarily difficult to use fiscal policy to control the economy. Monetary policy is all that is left.

Finally, the presidents over the last fifteen years have enhanced the prestige of the Federal Reserve System. For most of the period, the country has had Republican presidents, who normally lean toward monetary policy and feel that the independence of the Federal Reserve is a good thing. Even George Bush, whose chances of reelection were clearly harmed by Federal Reserve policies, found it hard to attack the institution, as opposed to its policies. Clinton, the only Democratic president in our period, is a pragmatist, who after concluding that the Federal Reserve's slow-growth policies were likely to benefit him, formed an alliance with Greenspan. Greenspan supported his deficit-reduction policies and Clinton opposed efforts to make the Federal Reserve System more democratic.

The Politics

The key political questions with regard to monetary policy are what the balance of power is within the Federal Reserve, to what degree the actions of the Fed are constrained by other political actors, and the trade-off the Fed makes between lowering inflation and its other economic aims such as growth and employment.

In this period the balance of power within the Federal Reserve swung to the right. Both Reagan and Bush appointed very conservative people to the board, and the Open Market Committee members from the regional Feds proved if anything even more conservative. Alan Greenspan, the chair of the Federal Reserve for most of the last ten years, is also a long-time conservative, albeit a little less so that some other board members. This meant that the Fed was composed of people who believed that it should be as independent as possible and who thought that fighting inflation was the Fed's dominant responsibility.

There is nothing harder to measure than the relative political influence of two political entities over a given policy. However, there is general agreement that during the last ten years the power of the president and Congress over the Federal Reserve has been even lower than normal. This has been particularly apparent during the Bush and Clinton administrations. The Bush administration made heroic efforts a number of times to persuade the Federal Reserve to ease up on the monetary brake, but there is little evidence that these efforts had much success (Woodward 1992, Greenhouse 1992). And while the Clinton administration did not have problems with the monetary policies of the Fed, much of its early emphasis on deficit reduction rather than investment can be traced to Greenspan's position that there would be no interest-rate reductions without deficit reduction (Woodward 1995). Congressional influence is even harder to measure, but it can reasonably noted that congressional efforts to reform the Fed were not successful. Much of this increased independence is probably due to the deficit. With a self-induced deficit constraining the efficacy of fiscal policy, it was hard to make the argument that Congress and the president should have more authority over monetary policy.

What did the Federal Reserve System do with this increased power and independence? The primary changes were to lay even more emphasis than usual on the goal of reducing inflation, to make more explicit attempts to move fiscal policy in a more deflationary direction, and to show even less sympathy than usual for the plight of presidents whose popularity was declining because of a poor economy.

These trends are best exemplified by monetary policy in the Bush era. Normally the Federal Reserve is fairly cozy with Republican presidents. But in the Bush era this coziness did not exist. In the first year of the Bush presidency, the Federal Reserve saw an opportunity to push inflation down to near zero (Berry 1989). In pursuit of this aim, it increased the discount rate (the rate at which they lend to banks) and decreased the money supply. The lagged effects of this move, together with the oil price shock in the first few months of the Gulf War, were the immediate causes of the 1990 recession. While the Federal Reserve had expected a slowdown, its hope had been to engineer a "soft landing," a small downturn followed by a rapid rebound. But this was not to be.

Once the recession had started, the Federal Reserve was slow to reduce rates. This was not entirely due to its obsession with lowering inflation. It was also because it had to walk a narrow tightrope between overstimulation and understimulation. The Fed could only affect short-term rates. If these were reduced too rapidly, investors might come to fear future inflation, with the result that the crucially important long-term rates might actually increase. Thus the Federal Reserve needed to increase the money supply enough to lower interest rates in the short term, but not enough to make people expect that long-term inflation would increase.

However, most observers felt that the Federal Reserve was overly cautious in its interest-rate reductions, seeing a danger of inflation where none existed and making many small changes rather than a few big ones (Merrifield 1992). Partly as a result, the economic recovery was slow in coming and growth in the recovery period was less than half the postwar average.

The Outcomes

Monetary policy during the last fifteen years has been driven largely by the need to contain inflation. Helping the economy grow, lowering unemployment, and aiding incumbent politicians have clearly taken a secondary position. Has the Federal Reserve succeeded in its aim?

On the whole, it is clear that it has been successful in its primary goal. In 1980 inflation was running at 12.5 percent annually. During the 1985 to 1995 period it has ranged between 1.1 percent and 6.1 percent. Even more notably, it stayed below 3 percent in 1993, 1994, and 1995, despite the fact that the economy had been expanding for a number of years. These lower rates were not entirely due to American monetary policy. Other factors such as demographic shifts and the declining power of labor also played a part. But it nonetheless seems fair to credit much of the result to the actions of the Federal Reserve System.

However, in economics every plus has its minus. Critics think that in its determination to drive inflation downward, the Federal Reserve may have prolonged the 1991 recession and reduced growth. The high real-interest rates over most of our period have also been seen as benefiting the rich at the expense of the poor and reducing investment.

Our Readings

To what degree do the changes of the past ten to fifteen years bear upon the points made in the readings in this section? It is clear to begin with that there is little support for the view, advocated by Kane, that the Federal Reserve acts as Congress and the president desire, and serves as a scapegoat for the more unpopular of these decisions. It is clear that both Congress and the president have wanted changes in our period that the Federal Reserve was unwilling to make and, far from being a scapegoat, one can reasonably argue that the Fed has been more popular in this period than its "sponsors." There are two possible ways of interpreting this. One is that the Fed has always been independent and that those arguing the opposite are wrong. The other is that it is the sort of creation that Kane envisages, but that, like Frankenstein, it has escaped from the control of its creators.

The events of the last decade do much to illustrate the argument between Reagan and Greenspan, but little to resolve it. Greenspan claims that central bank independence will make the goal of dealing with inflation easier. The events of the last ten years support this. Reagan thinks that an independent central bank will be inclined to emphasize inflation at the expense of other worthy aims. This too seems consistent with the events of the last decade. The argument about legitimacy and the desirability of democratic control, even when there are costs, clearly goes beyond the scope of this book and is ultimately a question of values.

Conclusion

The last fifteen years have seen considerable change in the way that tax and expenditure policies are conducted and relatively minor change in the way that monetary policy is formed. What can we learn from the changes?

On the fiscal side, two lessons stand out. One is that when there is divided government and no agreement on substantive changes, changes in the process through which budgets are made do not make a good substitute. As we have seen, changes in the budgetary process did not appear to achieve their chief aim of deficit reduction (although they may have achieved their secondary aim of making it appear as though something was being done), and it was only when there was some agreement between the two parties on the necessity of deficit reduction that the deficit began to diminish.

The other, less obvious lesson is the two-edged nature of centralization of authority. We have seen that before 1974 many blamed the problems of fiscal policy on the fragmented nature of the policy process both within the executive branch and in Congress. As we have seen, the period since the Budget Control and Impoundment Act of 1974 has seen much more centralized authority within the executive branch and somewhat more centralization of authority in Congress. But it is hard to claim that this has led to the anticipated improvements. While we have sometimes seen the added coordination and weighing of options that was anticipated, centralization has also made it easier to pass unwise policies such as the early Reagan budgets and has often led to cuts in programs by people with only a weak understanding of what they were cutting.

For monetary policy, what is most noticeable is the lack of change in the process through which monetary policy is made. The process as it stands appears to do what it was intended to do. When fiscal policy became overly stimulative, inflation was prevented through tight monetary controls, at least after 1979. And the Fed has learned from its critics, making real efforts to tighten and loosen the money supply before it was too late. Because of this, there has been little pressure for changes in the process. However, a cynic might argue that if Congress and the president had not been able to rely on an independent Fed to prevent inflation that would have otherwise resulted from their fiscal policies, it might have been less stimulative and more responsible. In politics, where appearance is often more important than reality, all is not always what it seems.

References

Berry, James. 1989. "Fed Chief Supports Zero-Inflation Resolution." *Washington Post* (October 26).

Birnbaum, Jeffery, and Alan Murray. 1987. *Showdown at Gucci Gulch: Lawmakers, Lobbyists and the Unlikely Triumph of Tax Reform.* New York: Basic Books.

Gleckman, Howard. 1995. "You Can't Balance Tomorrow's Budget Today." *Business Week* (July 10): 35.

Greenhouse, Steven. 1992. "Bush Calls on Fed for Another Drop in Interest Rates." *New York Times* (June 24).

Merrifield, Bruce D. 1992. "Was This Recession Really Necessary?" *World Monitor* (September).

Reich, Robert. 1992. *The Work of Nations: Preparing Ourselves for 21st Century Capitalism.* New York: Random House.

Risen, James. 1992. "Bush Bypassed Last Chance to Spur Economy." *Los Angeles Times* (November 2).

Woodward, Bob. 1992. "The Anatomy of a Decision: Six Words That Shaped—and May Sink—the Bush Presidency." *Washington Post,* National Edition (October 12).

———. 1995. *The Agenda: Inside the Clinton White House.* New York: Pocket Books.

4. Politics and Economic Outcomes

Introduction

In the previous two sections we looked at the process through which economic policy is determined in the United States. In this section we will pay more attention to the consequences of those policies. There is no ideal way to divide up the literature in this area. I have chosen to roughly separate it into international and domestic causes of economic outcomes. However, I would stress that this is primarily for convenience. Many of the outcomes that we examine could have either international or domestic causes and in some cases both are plausible partial explanations.

International Causes

The period since 1945 has seen ever increasing amounts of trade liberalization. The most visible way in which this has taken place is through the formation of trade blocs such as the European Economic Community and the North American Free Trade Area. Less visible but probably more important has been a series of multilateral trade agreements under the aegis of the General Agreement on Tariffs and Trade (GATT), which have lowered trade barriers between industrialized and nonindustrialized nations. These tariff reductions, largely invisible to the average citizen, have had important consequences for all.

Most obviously they have made all industrialized countries more dependent on exports for their prosperity. As nations specialize in the goods that they have a *comparative advantage* in producing, these form a larger percentage of their output. In turn, countries are more likely to import goods that other nations can produce more efficiently. This tends to make nations more interdependent. Countries rely on other countries for needed products and raw materials.

Companies farm out some of their production to plants in other countries that can do that particular job more efficiently. Money flows across international borders seeking higher rates of return or safer investments.

These changes in turn complicate economic management. A given amount of fiscal stimulus has less effect. Monetary policy moves can be offset by developments overseas. Recessions in other countries can spill over to the United States as export demand dries up. These changes have led to increasing attempts by industrial countries to coordinate their policies. The attempt to form a single European currency, the increasing regular meetings of the so-called group of seven industrial nations, the increasing importance of GATT and the IMF, and increasing coordination between the central banks of the major industrial nations are all road signs on the road to an integrated international economic policy.

The readings in this section attempt to show some of the effects of this international economic integration on the United States. The reading by Reich is a precis of the argument in his well known book *The Work of Nations* (1992). He argues that the new conditions have made money and capital mobile. What is distinctive about countries is the quality of their workers (often called *human capital*) and their *infrastructure* (roads, communications, etc.). The higher the quality of these, the wealthier the country. Within the United States, money increasingly flows toward those with skills unavailable elsewhere, while unskilled manufacturing workers, forced to compete with those in poorer countries, see their wages drop. The solution, argues Reich, is for the government to improve the infrastructure and invest in the education and training of its workers.

The reading by Jeff Frieden looks at the effects of capital mobility on American economic policy and on the balance of power between labor and capital and different types of industry. He argues that, in the long term, capital mobility strengthens the political position of capital at the expense of labor, but in the short term, the more important effect may well be the increase in the influence of multinational firms and export industries.

Finally, the reading by Cameron looks at the long-term growth of government and, after examining a number of possible domestic political reasons for that growth, attributes it instead to the degree to which nations are exposed to international competition. He argues that increasing exposure to international competition forces governments to expand expenditures to compensate for the changes that such exposure entails.

Domestic Causes

Turning from the effects of changes at the international level to the effects of changes at the national level, most of the literature has focused on two political phenomena likely to affect the economy. A large literature looks at whether politicians successfully change the economy to improve their reelection chances.

A smaller, but significant literature looks at whether economic policy outcomes are different under the two major political parties.

Since Roman times it has been the conventional wisdom that people are more likely to reelect an incumbent when economic times are good. Beginning around 1970, a huge quantitative literature has refined this simple concept. In its original form, the *political business cycle* literature held that voters base their vote on economic conditions during the last year. Knowing that their reelection is dependent on the economy, politicians seek to make sure the economy is booming in the year leading up to the election. Because the economy cannot boom all the time, politicians have an incentive to depress the economy right after their election and reflate it in time for the next election.

Over the past twenty-five years this simple message has been complicated. Authors have argued over whether people pay more attention to unemployment, personal income, or inflation. Some have argued that both the president and Congress are punished while others argue that only the president is. Some argue that politicians are successful in changing the economy through fiscal and monetary policy, others that they are successful only in altering fiscal policy, and still others that they have had little success in changing the economic cycle to fit their reelection needs. Some feel that people are driven by their own economic fortunes, while others feel that they are more likely to vote based on the effect of the economy on the country as a whole. On balance the trend has been to weaken the message, with the more sophisticated works generally playing down the size of the effects and the number of things explained by the theory.

In this section we have three articles that show the growth of this literature over time. The first, by Edward Tufte, gives the political business cycle theory in its full glory. The more recent articles, by Fiorina and Alesina, Londregen, and Rosenthal, are more modest in their claims. Both are skeptical about the applicability of the theory to Congress, and the Alesina et al. article also supports others who have found it hard to demonstrate that presidents have been successful in manipulating the economy to secure reelection.

The articles by Fiorina and Alesina et al. also look at the relation between which party is in power and economic outcomes. Fiorina is interested in the effects of economic success on party power. He explores the idea, taken as a given by many politicians, that success at managing the economy can translate into long-term support for the party that has been successful. Alesina et al. look at the other side of the coin. They ask whether one gets more or less economic growth if one elects the Democratic or Republican candidate to the presidency. As in earlier articles in this tradition, they find that one gets more economic growth from Democratic presidents, but unlike the earlier work, they find that this effect is confined to the first two years of the president's term.

Economic growth is something that both parties seek. But there are real differences on the question of redistribution, with Democrats seeing themselves as much more sympathetic to the poor. One would therefore expect systematic differences in redistribution when the different parties are in power. These differences are not always easy to demonstrate, as other factors such as those discussed by Reich can affect distribution. The article from the Congressional Budget Office looks at the effect on the distribution of income of the major tax bills passed in the last fifteen years, thus abstracting from other influences. Looking at it, one cannot help but be struck by the extent to which the political power of the two major parties is reflected in tax redistribution. It is especially interesting to contrast the 1981 tax bill, passed when Republicans controlled both the Senate and the presidency, with the 1993 tax bill when the Democrats controlled all three branches of government.

For Further Reading

International Political Economy

Interesting general theories of international politics are Robert Keohane and Joseph Nye's *Power and Interdependence* and Mancur Olson's *The Rise and Decline of Nations.* Solid texts on international trade theory are Richard Caves et al.'s *World Trade and Payments* and Paul Krugman and Maurice Oldfeld's *International Economics.* Good textbooks on international political economy are Joan Spero's *The Politics of International Economic Relations* and Robert Walters and David Blake's *The Politics of Global Economic Relations.* Robert Gilpin's *The Political Economy of International Relations* applies various theories to recent economic history. Robert Reich's *The Work of Nations* gives a more extended version of the theory in this book.

Government Growth

The seminal book in this area is Adolph Wagner's *Finanzwissenschaft,* which lays out the theories of the effects of rising income and industrialization on government growth usually known as Wagner's Law. Good early reviews of the literature are Daniel Tarschys's article "The Growth of Public Expenditures: Nine Modes of Explanation," and the last few chapters of James Alt and Alec Crystal's *Political Economics.* A good recent review of the literature in economics on this topic is Cheryl Holsey and Thomas Borcherding's "Why Does Government's Share of National Income Grow?" A test between different theories of government growth in the United States can be found in David Lowery and William Berry's article "The Growth of Government in the United States: An Empirical Assessment of Competing Explanations." There are also explanations of the growth of individual parts of government such as Martha Derthick's classic work *Policymaking for Social Security* and Frances Fox Piven and Richard Cloward's *Regulating the Poor.*

The Political Business Cycle

The seminal books are Edward Tufte's *Political Control of the Economy*, and Rod Kiewit's *Macroeconomics and Micropolitics*. Douglas Hibbs's "The Dynamics of Political Support for American Presidents Among Occupational and Partisan Groups," and Bruno Frey's "An Empirical Study of Politico-Economic Interaction in the U.S.," argue that poorer Americans worry more about unemployment and richer ones about inflation. Donald Kinder and Roderick Kiewit's "Economic Discontent and Political Behavior" shows that voters worry more about the economy as a whole than their own personal finances.

Parties and Economic Outcomes

Douglas Hibbs's *American Political Economy* summarizes much of his pioneering work demonstrating a relation between which party is in power and macroeconomic outcomes. Alberto Alesina and Jeffrey Sachs's "Political Parties and the Business Cycle in the United States" gives an alternative view of the relation, based upon different assumptions. My own *The Political Economy of Inflation in the United States* shows how interest groups and parties attempt to forge economic policy and the connection with the views of their supporters. Ian Budge and Richard I. Hofferbert's "Mandates and Policy Outputs" and Henry Chappell and William R. Keech's "Party Differences in Macroeconomic Policies and Outcomes" outline effects of party on macroeconomic policy and expenditures. Benjamin Page's *Who Gets What from Government*, Thomas Edsal's *The New Politics of Inequality*, and Sidney Verba's *Inequality in America* give different perspectives on politics and inequality. A good reader on economic policy making is Alberto Alesina and Geoffrey Carliner's *Politics and Economics in the Eighties*.

References

Alesina, Alberto, and Geoffrey Carliner. 1991. *Politics and Economics in the Eighties.* Chicago: University of Chicago Press.

Alesina, Alberto, and Jeffrey Sachs. 1988. "Political Parties and the Business Cycle in the United States." *Journal of Money Credit and Banking* 20, 1: 63–82.

Alt, James E., and K. Alec Crystal. 1983. *Political Economics.* Berkeley, Calif.: University of California Press.

Budge, Ian, and Richard I. Hofferbert. 1990. "Mandates and Policy Outputs: U.S. Party Platforms and Federal Expenditures." *American Political Science Review* 84, 1: 111–131.

Caves, Richard E., Jeffrey A. Fankel, and Ronald W. Jones. 1993. *World Trade and Payments: An Introduction.* 6th ed.. New York: HarperCollins.

Chappell, Henry W., Jr., and William R. Keech. 1986. "Party Differences in Macroeconomic Policies and Outcomes." *American Economic Review* 76, 2: 71–74.

Derthick, Martha. 1979. *Policymaking for Social Security*. Washington D.C.: The Brookings Institution.

Edsal, Thomas. 1984. *The New Politics of Inequality*. New York: W.W. Norton.

Fischer, Gregory W., and Mark S. Kamlet. 1984. "Explaining Presidential Priorities: The Competing Aspiration Levels Model of Macrobudgetary Decision Making." *American Political Science Review* 78 , 2: 356–71.

Frey, Bruno S. 1978. "An Empirical Study of Politico-Economic Interaction in the U.S." *Review of Economics and Statistics* 60 (May): 174–83.

Gilpin, Robert. 1987. *The Political Economy of International Relations*. Princeton, N.J.: Princeton University Press.

Hibbs, Douglas. 1982. "The Dynamics of Political Support for American Presidents Among Occupational and Partisan Groups." *American Journal of Political Science* 26 (May): 312–333.

———. 1989. *American Political Economy*. Cambridge, Mass.: Harvard University Press.

Holsey, Cheryl, and Thomas Borcherding. 1996. "Why Does Government's Share of National Income Grow?: An Assessment of the Recent Literature on the U.S. Experience," in Dennis Mueller, ed., *Perspectives on Public Choice*. New York: Cambridge University Press (forthcoming).

Keohane, Robert, and Joseph Nye. 1977. *Power and Interdependence: World Politics in Transition*. Boston: Little Brown.

Kiewit, D. Roderick. 1983. *Macroeconomics and Micropolitics*. Chicago: University of Chicago Press.

Kinder, Donald, and Roderick Kiewit. 1979. "Economic Discontent and Political Behavior: The Role of Collective Economic Judgements in Congressional Voting." *American Journal of Political Science* 31 (August): 495–527.

Krugman, Paul R., And Maurice Oldfeld. 1991. *International Economics: Theory and Practice*. 2d ed. New York: HarperCollins.

Lowery, David, and William D. Berry. 1983. "The Growth of Government in the United States: An Empirical Assessment of Competing Explanations." *American Journal of Political Science* 27 (November): 665–94.

Olson, Mancur. 1982. *The Rise and Decline of Nations: Economic Growth Stagflation and Social Rigidities*. New Haven: Yale University Press.

Page, Benjamin. 1983. *Who Gets What from Government*. Berkeley: University of California Press.

Peretz, Paul. 1983. *The Political Economy of Inflation in the United States*. Chicago: University of Chicago Press.

Piven, Frances Fox, and Richard Cloward. *Regulating the Poor*. New York: Vintage, 1971.

Spero, Joan Edelman. 1981. *The Politics of International Economic Relations*. 2d ed. New York: St. Martin's Press.

Tarschys, Daniel. 1975. "The Growth of Public Expenditures: Nine Modes of Explanation." *Scandinavian Political Studies* 10: 9–31.

Tufte, Edward. 1978. *Political Control of the Economy*. Princeton, N.J.: Princeton University Press.

Verba, Sidney. 1985. *Inequality in America*. Cambridge, Mass.: Harvard University Press.

Wagner, Adolph. 1962 (1883). *Finanzwissenschaft*. Portions of this work have been translated and reprinted as "Three Extracts on Public Finance," in R. A. Musgrave and Alan T. Peacock, eds., *Classics in the Theory of Public Finance*. London: Macmillan.

Walters, Robert S., and David H. Blake. 1992. *The Politics of Global Economic Relations*. 4th ed. Englewood Cliffs, N.J.: Prentice Hall.

4.1. The REAL Economy

ROBERT B. REICH

In this reading Robert Reich argues that the United States needs to train American workers to fit into an increasingly global economy.

He argues that as trade barriers fall, unskilled manufacturing jobs will increasingly be performed by poorly paid workers in underdeveloped countries. He argues that the comparative advantage of United States workers lies in performing jobs that require skills and education. Less skilled Americans will increasingly compete with unskilled workers in developing countries who can be hired for very low wages. He feels that this competition is driving down the wages of unskilled American workers, and reducing returns to traditional manufacturing plants in the United States.

To solve this problem, he thinks that the United States must specialize in industry and services that require a high level of skill and must insure that workers have the skills to fit into this new work environment. He therefore recommends state support of research and development spending, education, and job training.

The central tenet of Republican economics is that everyone benefits when the rich are allowed to keep more of their income for themselves. Ronald Reagan believed that the benefits of the 1981 tax cut for wealthy Americans would "trickle down" to everyone else. For most of his presidency thus far, George Bush has claimed that a lower tax on capital gains (which would benefit the wealthy, who own most of the nation's capital assets) would give a surge of momentum to the economy, and thus help all of us. In contrast, the central tenet of Democratic economics is that this allocation of the tax burden isn't fair. Taxes on the wealthy should be raised, and government should spread the wealth directly, through a myriad of social programs.

From *The Atlantic* (February 1991), pp. 35–52. Reprinted with the permission of Robert Reich.

The two sides were at a stalemate throughout the 1980s. Taxes on the wealthy stayed low and entitlements stayed high (while military expenditures grew), with the result that the federal budget ballooned. In last year's budget agreement both sides conceded a bit: taxes on the rich will rise somewhat (but not anywhere near as high as they were in the late 1970s), and entitlement programs will grow when there is money to finance them. But underlying the compromise—which is more like a truce in an ongoing war—the same choice remains: growth or fairness, private investment or public spending, tax cuts for the rich or entitlements for everyone else. In this contest Republicans continue to represent the brute force of American capitalism, Democrats the softer and more generous side of our natures.

But this isn't the real choice facing Americans as we approach the twenty-first century, and it creates a false picture of where the economy is heading and what must be done. Republican economics is wrong: The success of American capitalism no longer depends on the private investments of highly motivated American capitalists. Our nation's future economic success depends instead on our unique attributes—the skills and insights of our work force, and how well we link those skills and insights to the world economy. The Democratic rejoinder is equally wrong-headed: The government's role is not just to spread the wealth. It is to build our human capital and infrastructure, and to bargain with global capital on our behalf. To prepare us for twenty-first-century capitalism, American economic policy must be adapted to the new realities of the world economy.

Global Capital

Again, Republicans have it wrong. The investments of wealthier Americans (who have the wherewithal to save and invest) no longer trickle down to the rest of the American population. Instead, they trickle out to wherever on the globe the best returns can be had. The savings of foreigners, meanwhile, trickle in to find promising projects within the United States. Foreign investments in America rose to a record $2 trillion in 1989, up 12 percent from the year before. Since 1980 foreign capital investment in the United States has increased fourfold. Capital—in the form of loans, shares of stock, and corporate factories, equipment, and research laboratories—moves around the world with scant respect for national boundaries.

Global stock trading is now commonplace. In 1989 Americans poured $13.7 billion into foreign stocks, up 813 percent from 1988. All told, net cross-border equity investments soared to a record $92.3 billion—nearly triple the previous high of $31.7 billion, set in 1986. Such cross-border investments are undertaken quietly; the American investor, assigning his or her savings to a mutual fund, an insurance fund, or a pension plan, may often be unaware of lending to or buying into companies with foreign-sounding names, headquartered in exotic places. But the people who manage the funds, and who compete furiously to achieve higher returns than other fund managers, now scour the globe for investment prospects. . . .

American capital also leaves the United States in the form of factories, equip-ment, and laboratories placed in foreign lands by American-owned corporations. Here, too, the reason is that higher profits are often available abroad. Europe is booming in anticipation of 1992's integrated European market. Many East Asian economies continue to expand at a breakneck rate (although not quite so fast as they did). Thus, although profits earned in the United States by American multi-national corporations dropped by 19 percent in 1989, the overseas profits of these firms surged by 14 percent. Small wonder that American firms, having increased their capital investments abroad by 13 percent in 1989, expected to increase them still more—by a whopping 17 percent—last year, while increasing their American investments by slightly more than six percent. Hewlett-Packard now designs and makes personal computers in France; Texas Instruments makes a large percentage of its semiconductor chips in Japan; more and more of the automobiles produced by the Big Three are designed and engineered in Ger-many, Italy, or Japan.

Wealthy Americans may reap high returns from their worldwide investments, but the rest of us enjoy few of the beneficial consequences. With the connections between American capitalists and the American economy thus unraveling, all that remains rooted within our borders is the American *people*.

National Assets

The answer isn't simply to take money from the wealthy and spread it around, however, as Democrats often want to do. Even though the investments of indi-vidual Americans are becoming disconnected from the American economy, there is a growing connection between the amount and kind of investments we make together as a nation and the capacity of America to attract global capital. Herein the new logic of economic nationalism: the skills and insights of a nation's work force, and the quality of its transportation and communication links to the world (its infrastructure), are what make it unique, and uniquely attractive, in the new world economy. Increasingly, educated brainpower—along with roads, airports, computers, and fiber-optic cables connecting it up—determines a nation's stan-dard of living.

To understand why, it's first necessary to grasp what is happening to the global economy. The highest earnings in most worldwide industries are to be found in locations where specialized knowledge is brought to bear on problems whose solutions define new horizons of possibility. Whether the industry is old or new, mature or high-tech, specialized knowledge is accounting for a larger and larger portion of its revenues. The hottest sector of the tool-and-die-casting industry, for example, produces precision castings out of aluminum and zinc for computer parts. The leading textile businesses depend on the knowledge needed to produce specially coated and finished fabrics for automobiles, office furniture, rain gear, and wall coverings, among a great many other products. The fastest-growing semiconductor firms make microprocessors and customized chips that are tailored to the particular needs of buyers. As computers with standard operating systems become virtually identical, the high profits come from devising software to meet particular user needs. . . .

These businesses are highly profitable both because customers are willing to pay a premium for goods and services that exactly meet their needs and, more important, because they are knowledge-intensive businesses that cannot easily be duplicated by low-cost competitors elsewhere in the world. Worldwide competition continues to compress profits on anything that is uniform, routine, and standard—that is, on anything that can be made, reproduced, or extracted in volume almost anywhere on the globe. The evidence shows that successful businesses in advanced nations respond to this dynamic by moving toward the higher ground of specialized products and services.

To be sure, successful companies have not entirely jettisoned high-volume, standardized production. Japanese companies, for example, continue to improve their synchronized systems for mass-producing automobiles, video-cassette recorders, and semiconductor chips. And there will always be a lucrative worldwide market for Coca-Cola, blue jeans, and other staples of modern society. But to maintain competitiveness even in mass-produced commodities requires continuous improvement. Japanese cars, VCRs, and computer chips appear in ever greater variety and at ever higher quality; Coca-Cola develops new formulas and products and marketing techniques. Here, as elsewhere, the barrier to entry is not volume or price; it is skill in finding new and ever-more-valuable connections between particular ideas and particular markets.

The Core Skills

Look closely at these high-value businesses and you see three different but related skills that drive them forward. First are the *problem-solving* skills required to put things together in unique ways (be they alloys, molecules, semiconductor chips, software codes, movie scripts, or pension portfolios). Next are the *problem-identifying* skills required to help customers understand their needs and how those needs can best be met by customized products. In contrast to marketing and selling standard commodities—which requires persuading many customers of the virtues of one particular product, taking lots of orders for it, and meeting sales quotas—the key here is to identify new problems to which customized products might be applicable. The art of persuasion is replaced by the identification of opportunity.

Third are the skills needed to link problem-solvers and problem-identifiers. Those with such skills must understand enough about specific technologies and markets to see the potential for a new product, raise whatever money is necessary to launch the project, and assemble the right personnel to solve and identify problems. They play the role of *strategic brokers*.

In the high-value businesses, profits derive not from scale and volume but from an ongoing discovery of connections between the solutions to problems and the identification of new needs. The idea of "goods" as something distinct from "services" has become meaningless, because so much of the value provided by a successful enterprise—in fact, the only value that cannot be easily replicated worldwide—entails services: the specialized research, engineering, design, and production services necessary to solve problems; the specialized sales, marketing, and consulting services necessary to identify problems; and the specialized strategic, financial, and management services necessary to broker the first two. High-value enterprises are in the business of providing such services.

Steelmaking, for example, is becoming a service business. When alloys are molded to a specific weight and tolerance, services account for a significant part of the value of the resulting product. Steel service centers help customers choose the steels and alloys they need, and then inspect, slit, coat, store, and deliver the materials. . . .

Ninety-one percent of the increase in the number of jobs since the 1982 recession was in services, and, remarkably, 73 percent of private-sector employees now work in service businesses. But as the line between services and goods blurs, such numbers are increasingly meaningless—they do not tell us what is actually going on in the economy, and where the real value lies. . . .

Why Ownership Matters Less

The key industrial struggle of the late nineteenth and the first half of the twentieth century was between those who owned the machines and those who ran them. Each side wanted a larger share of the resulting revenues. American politics reflected this tug-of-war: the Republican Party emerged as the voice of the American industrialist, the Democratic Party as that of the American blue-collar worker. The dominant images of the two parties even today owe much to this struggle.

In the emerging global economy, however, the interests both of laborers and of investors are increasingly subordinated to the interests of those who solve, identify, and broker new problems. This trend has been gathering momentum for several decades. Through the postwar era the wages of U.S. workers engaged in routine production have steadily declined as a percentage of the gross national product, from 11.6 percent in 1949 to approximately 4.6 percent in 1990. During the same interval corporate profits have also diminished as a percentage of the gross national product. In the mid-1960s corporate profits reached 10.98 percent of GNP, and then fell, to 7.48 percent in 1970. Subsequent percentages have been lower at both expansionary heights and recessionary lows. By the end of the 1980s profits claimed only 6.29 percent of GNP.

As the portions of GNP going to routine laborers and to investors have steadily dwindled, the portion going to those who solve or identify problems and those who broker solutions has steadily grown. In 1915 the wages of routine production workers in the typical American manufacturing firm accounted for about 45 percent of the cost of making the product. By 1975 they made up only 25 percent, with most of the remainder going to designers, technicians, researchers, manufacturing engineers, industrial engineers, planners, strategists, financial specialists, accountants, executive officers, lawyers, advertisers, and marketers. Almost 80 percent of the cost of a high technology item such as a computer is attributable to conceptualizers like these. . . .

The steady subordination of financial capital to intellectual capital has confused Americans who worry that foreigners are "buying up" the nation's technological assets. Such worries are usually unfounded. In fact it is often the case that without the foreign money, the intellectual capital that has already accumulated in the United States would not develop further.

Consider two typical American firms that were acquired by foreigners in 1989: Materials Research, a semiconductor-equipment manufacturer whose American owners sold it to Sony after the firm found it impossible to raise money from American investors or to borrow it from American banks; and Arco Solar, sold to Germany's Siemens by Atlantic Richfield, the giant American oil company, which was no longer willing to finance Arco's effort to become the world leader in photovoltaic technology. Superficially it appears that foreigners are running off with two of America's leading-edge technology companies. But look closely at these two firms and you find groups of American problem-solvers and problem-identifiers who have accumulated potentially valuable insights about how to produce highly efficient semiconductor equipment and solar energy, respectively. In acquiring them, the foreign firms have not destroyed this cumulative learning, nor have they enslaved these Americans and shipped them back to Japan and Germany; the American problem-solvers and problem-identifiers have no intention of leaving the United States. That some of the profits now go to investors outside the United States is no cause for great alarm; the assets with the greatest value, commanding the highest return, remain within our borders.

Such cumulative skills and insights, upon which future innovations are based, make up the nation's key technological assets. They will be lost only if insufficiently nurtured and developed, as they might have been in these cases had foreign capital not come to the rescue.

The Virtuous Cycle

In the emerging economy of the twenty-first century only one asset is growing more valuable as it is used: the problem-solving, problem-identifying, and strategic-brokering skills of a nation's citizens. Unlike machinery that gradually wears out, raw materials that become depleted, and patents and copyrights that grow obsolete, the skills and insights that come from discovering new linkages between technologies and needs increase with practice.

The more complex the task, the better preparation it provides for the next, even more complex task. One puzzle leads to another. Assembling just the right combination of technical and marketing skills to develop software for assisting mechanical engineers can help strategic brokers gain insight into what's needed to develop more complex software for aerospace engineers. Developing and marketing specialty chemicals can lead to developing and marketing high-performance ceramics and single crystal silicon. And so forth.

Conventional economic theory assumes that a resource gets used up when it is put to work. As it becomes scarce, its price increases; the price rise in turn encourages buyers to conserve the resource and find cheaper substitutes, which ultimately brings the price down again. One of the great advantages of a price system, as all economists will quickly attest, is that it tends to balance itself automatically. But human capital operates according to a different principle. Because people learn through practice, the value of what they do tends to increase as they gain experience. This system is not self-correcting, in the sense that workers who first gain knowledge and insights do not eventually lose whatever premium in price they have commanded in world markets when others catch up with them. Rather, a work force can become steadily more valuable over time as insights lead to other insights.

Thus a virtuous cycle can be set in motion: A work force possessing a good basic education, which can efficiently bring the fruits of its labors to the global economy, can attract global capital for its performance of moderately complex tasks. The experience gained by performing these tasks generates additional on-the-job training and experience, which serve to lure global capital for more complex activities. As skills build and experience accumulates, the nation's citizens receive more and more from the rest of the world in exchange for their services—which permits them to invest in better schools, transportation, research, and communications systems. As their problem-solving, problem-identifying, and brokering skills grow, and their links with the world steadily improve, their income rises.

But without adequate skills and infrastructure, the relationship can be the opposite—a vicious cycle in which global money and technology are lured only by low wages and low taxes. These enticements in turn make it more difficult to finance adequate education and infrastructure; the jobs available under these conditions provide little on-the-job training or experience pertinent to more complex jobs in the future. Such a vicious cycle has no natural stopping place. Theoretically it can continue to push wages downward until the citizens of the nation (or region, or city) have a standard of living like that typical of the Third World. . . .

In virtuous cycles low wages are not the central attraction. The average worker in the former West Germany earns a higher hourly wage than the average American, but global capital is nonetheless attracted to Germany by the nation's pool of skilled workers and its first-class transportation and communications facilities. There, most non-college-bound young people enter apprenticeship programs, in which they learn technical skills. Germany is already on the way to transforming its modern system of autobahns into "smart" superhighways that can regulate traffic flow by computer. France, another high-wage nation, has provided a videotext system free of charge to all telephone subscribers, has recently launched a computerized library and information bank designed to be accessible from every home, and is aggressively training scientists and engineers. Japan is building a $250 billion fiber-optic network that by the year 2000 will carry video, voice, and data around the nation up to 1,000 times faster than existing networks can. All three of these nations are spending significant sums of money on education, training, and research and development.

The National Bargain

It is easier to form a virtuous relationship with global capital if you are a nation strongly committed to economic development—ruled by a benevolent dictator like Singapore's Lee Kuan Yew, dominated by a single political party and an "old boy" oligarchy, as in Japan, or habituated to a form of corporatist planning orchestrated by big banks and major industrial firms, as in Germany. In such countries political power is sufficiently concentrated that substantial resources can be mobilized for education, training, research, and infrastructure—and sacrifices can be elicited from the public in order to make these investments. Moreover, deals can be cut with global corporations—offering subsidies, tax breaks, or access to the national market in exchange for good jobs.

But what of a decentralized and contentious democracy like the United States, which deeply distrusts concentrated power? Apart from war emergencies, are we able to make large public investments and demand sacrifices of ourselves in order to pay for them? Are we capable of bargaining with global corporations?

Much of the responsibility for America's national economic development has fallen by default to states and cities. America bids for global capital through fifty state governments that compete against one another, and thousands of cities and townships, which also compete. Who successfully lures the jobs becomes a matter of state and local pride as well as employment; it may also bear significantly on the future careers of politicians who have pledged to win them. The possibility of establishing a factory in the region sets off a furious auction; a threat to remove one initiates equally impassioned negotiations. All too often these jurisdictions bargain for routine jobs that will be automated out of existence in years to come or else will drift to the Third World. . . . As the bidding has intensified during the past fifteen years, the incentives have become more generous. In 1977 the state of Ohio induced Honda to build an auto plant there by promising $22 million in subsidies and tax breaks; by 1986 it took a $100 million package from Kentucky for Toyota to create about the same number of jobs there.

The total amount of subsidies and tax breaks flowing to global firms of

Table 1

Federal Government Investment Spending as a Percentage of GNP

	1970	1975	1980	1985	1990
Physical Investment	.97	1.03	1.14	.91	.75
Education	.43	.43	.51	.4	.37
Nondefense R & D (excluding space)	.36	.39	.42	.37	.31

Source: "The Federal Budget and the Nation's Economic Health," by Charles L. Schultze, in *Setting National Priorities* (The Brookings Institution, 1990).

whatever nationality is much higher than it would be if the United States did its bargaining as a whole, through the federal government. Nations whose constituent parts refrain from internecine battles end up paying far less to lure jobs their way. Although direct comparisons between the United States and other nations are hard to come by, an analogous situation suggests the magnitude of the difference. In seeking the rights to televise the 1988 Olympic Games in Calgary, the Western European nations bid as a whole. In the United States, in contrast, each television network made its own separate bid. The Western European market contains even more people than the U.S. market, with buying power that is at least as great. Nevertheless, because Western Europe negotiated as a whole, it got the rights to televise the Olympics in Europe for $5.7 million. The winning network in the United States paid $309 million to televise the Olympics here.

Disinvestment

Even if America bargained for global capital as a nation, it would still have difficulty attracting good jobs unless it could offer an educated work force and first-class transportation and communications systems. And here lies a more serious problem. For even as other nations have been increasing their public investments in people and infrastructure, the United States as a *nation* has been cutting back. As Table 1 shows, federal spending on infrastructure, nondefense research and development, and education has steadily dropped as a proportion of the gross national product from 1980 onward. By 1990 federal investment as a proportion of GNP was lower in each of these categories than it was in 1970. States and cities with large populations of poorer Americans have been hard pressed to make up the difference.

Consider infrastructure. David Aschauer, an economist at Bates College and formerly a researcher at the Federal Reserve Bank of Chicago, has shown a direct link between America's investments in infrastructure and the productivity of the nation's work force: a one-dollar increase in the stock of public infrastructure adds as much to the productivity of Americans as a four-dollar increase in the stock of business capital. His calculations imply that a one-time increase of $10 billion in the stock of public infrastructure would result in a *permanent* increase of $7 billion in the annual GNP. Aschauer's study has been criticized for being too optimistic; after all, he demonstrates only that public investment and national productivity growth have increased and decreased together, over the same interval of time—not that the one necessarily caused the other. But even accepting the possibility of other explanations for why American productivity growth has slowed, the correlation is striking. The United States began to cut back on public investments just when public investments became uniquely important in the new global economy.

In the early 1960s the United States began building a modern transportation system. Spending on infrastructure at all levels of government then absorbed almost four percent of the nation's GNP; it held that position through the 1960s. That's when we began to build the interstate highway system, for example. The productivity of the American work force soared. But the growth of public spending on the nation's transportation system declined throughout the 1970s, just as our productivity growth declined. Infrastructure spending declined even more sharply in the 1980s, to the point where the nation was spending only two percent of GNP on building and maintaining infrastructure. Hence the specter of collapsing bridges, crumbling highways, and rush-hour traffic jams extending for miles.

Although part of the decline in spending represents a failure to maintain existing infrastructure, spending on new infrastructure has fallen even more dramatically, from 2.3 percent of GNP in 1963 to only one percent in 1989. As Western Europe and Japan lay plans for "smart" roads, high-speed trains, and national information networks, America lies dormant; the nation has not even built a new airport since 1974. As of the beginning of last year Washington was annually investing about the same amount of money in infrastructure (in constant dollars) as it had invested thirty years before, although the gross national product had grown 144 percent in the interim. It is projected that physical capital investment, which accounted for 24 percent of total federal outlays in 1960, will account for less than 11 percent in 1991.

Expenditures on public elementary and secondary education have shown a similarly perverse pattern—falling short just as intellectual capital has become a uniquely important national asset. Many politicians and business leaders (and many ordinary citizens) are quick to claim that the current crisis in public education is unrelated to a lack of public funding. One premise of their argument—that there are many means of improving American schools that do not require large public outlays—is surely correct. Yes, responsibility for teaching needs to be transferred from educational bureaucracies to classroom teachers; and yes, the inculcation of basic skills must be the primary mission of the schools.

Researchers have, however, found that schools with smaller classes and better-paid teachers produce young people who command higher salaries once they join the work force. David Card and Alan Krueger, researchers at Princeton University, studied the education and incomes of a million men born from 1920 to 1949 who attended public schools. They found that even within the same socioeconomic group, higher lifetime earnings correlate with smaller class size and better-paid teachers (for every year of schooling above eighth grade, students' subsequent earnings increased 0.4 percent for every five fewer students per teacher, and for every 10 percent hike in teacher salaries, subsequent earnings increased 0.1 percent). The extra tax revenues generated by these higher lifetime incomes alone would finance the smaller classes and better-paid teachers.

Controlled for inflation, public spending on primary and secondary education per student increased during the 1980s, when the nation began to fret openly about the quality of its public schools, but not appreciably faster than it did during the 1970s. From 1970 to 1980 annual spending per student grew 36 percent in real terms; since 1980 it has grown 38 percent.

Yet there are several reasons for believing that the more recent increases have been inadequate. First is the comparative measure of what other nations are spending. By the late 1980s America's per-pupil expenditures were below per-pupil expenditures (converted to dollars using 1988 exchange rates) in eight other nations—namely Sweden, Norway, Japan, Denmark, Austria, West Germany, Canada, and Switzerland. (Even using the exchange rate from 1985, when the dollar was at its height relative to other currencies, the United States is still behind—but in fourth place rather than ninth.)

International comparisons aside, it is true that the demands on public education in the United States have grown significantly during the past fifteen years. Increasing numbers of broken homes, single-parent households, and immigrants (both legal and illegal) have placed great strains on our schools, particularly in poor inner-city and rural areas. And with one out of five American children now falling below the poverty line, a significantly higher proportion than obtained fifteen years ago, challenges are magnified. As for today's teachers, their wages have barely risen in real terms since the early 1970s—and yet talented women today have many more lucrative career options than teaching, and we also want to attract talented men to the profession.

Ironically, the schools facing the biggest social problems have been getting the least help. The averaging of figures on per-pupil expenditures in the United States disguises growing disparities among states and school districts. As federal support for elementary and secondary education has waned and states and localities have been forced to pick up the bill, the burden has fallen especially heavily on the poorest jurisdictions with the most limited tax bases. New Trier High School, in one of Chicago's most affluent suburbs, pays its teachers 34 percent more than the average teacher in Chicago's public high schools, whose pedagogic challenges are substantially greater. Public schools in White Plains and Great Neck, two of the richest suburbs of New York, spend twice as much per pupil as schools in the Bronx. (The first set of students in each of these comparisons is on the way to a virtuous relationship with global capital, the second set to a vicious one.)

In 1965 the nation decided that all students who qualified to attend college should have access to higher education. Here again, public investment ranked high on the nation's agenda. The resulting Higher Education Act established a system of grants and loan guarantees for low-income students, thus increasing their proportion even at private universities, from 22 to 26 percent by the mid-1970s. But by 1988, with grants and loan guarantees drying up, the proportion of low-income students at private universities had fallen below 20 percent. The high costs of higher education have helped to push them out and set them on their way toward a vicious relationship with global capital. (In the compromise 1991 budget federal funds for student aid will increase 10 percent for the academic year 1991–1992, but the prospect for the following year looks grim.) Meanwhile, in an equally ominous development, the federal retreat from higher education is being replicated at the state level. The rate of increase in state support for higher education dropped to a thirty-year low in 1990, representing the smallest increment since data on this subject have been collected. State universities have long promoted mobility among children of less affluent families. These data suggest that in future there will be less mobility. Even high schoolers safely in the middle class are being squeezed out of college. From 1982 to 1989, while the proportion of American middle-income families ($40,000 to $60,000) dropped five percent, the proportion of middle-income students in public universities dropped 10 percent.

Federal support for research and development (excluding defense and space) has also languished; it now accounts for 0.31 percent of GNP, the smallest proportion in twenty years. Corporate America hasn't filled the gap. All told, nondefense R&D accounts for two percent of GNP in the United States, compared with almost three percent in Japan and 2.6 percent in the former West Germany. We have sacrificed, as a consequence, not breakthrough discoveries (which, after all, are almost immediately shared in by the scientific community and corporations worldwide) but the know-how and experience that come from *doing* current research.

While Western Europe, Japan, and many developing nations are ensuring that their scientists and engineers are ready to embrace the microelectronic and molecular technologies of the future, America is squandering its scientific and engineering brainpower. Federal funding of university research dropped 18 percent in real terms from 1967 to 1990. The National Science Foundation's 1990 budget for most small research projects in mathematics, physics, chemistry, engineering, biology, and computer science—the seed corn of science—fell below even that for 1988. Steven Younger, of the Los Alamos National Laboratory, told *The New York Times,* "The foundation of university science is dying."

Federal funding to train and retrain workers, meanwhile, dropped by more than 50 percent during the 1980s, from $13.2 billion to $5.6 billion. Most other industrialized nations—including Germany, France, Britain, and Japan—devote much higher percentage of their GNP to workplace training. Private training, the costs of which corporations deduct from their taxable incomes, has hardly made up the difference. American companies claim to spend some $30 billion a year training their employees, but most of these funds have been used on what is euphemistically termed "executive training." College graduates are 50 percent more likely to be trained by their corporations than are high school graduates, and employees with postgraduate degrees are 30 percent more likely than college graduates. Those who lack a rudimentary educational background receive little compensatory training from the private sector.

Can We Afford It?

The official reason given for why America cannot invest more money in infrastructure, education, research, and training is that we cannot afford it. In his inaugural address George Bush noted regretfully, "We have more will than wallet." It has become a frequent lament. But only excessive politeness constrains one from inquiring, Whose will? Whose wallet?

The claim that America cannot afford to invest any more money than it does in the future productivity of its citizens is a curious one, to say the least. Americans are not overtaxed. In 1989 we paid less in taxes as a percentage of GNP (about 30 percent) than the citizens of any other industrialized country. Wealthy Americans, in particular, are not overtaxed. Their marginal income-tax rate is the lowest top tax rate in any industrialized nation. Nor does the government overspend. If defense is excluded from the calculation, the combined spending of state, local, and federal government accounts for a smaller share of GNP in America than in any other industrialized country, including Japan.

This nation was willing to dig deep into its wallet to rebuild Western Europe and Japan after the Second World War. Now, with an economy four times as large as it was then, we should be able to rebuild America. Bush has it backward: We have the wallet. What we lack is the will.

Republicans do not want taxes on the wealthy raised; Democrats do not want entitlement programs diminished for the middle class. As a result, less and less is left over for public investment.

The current debate between Republicans and Democrats over economic growth or fairness obscures the real issue, which is how much we are willing to invest in the future productivity of Americans. Each year the American economy generates about $5 trillion worth of goods and services. If we dedicated only four percent of this sum—about $200 billion a year—to public investment during the 1990s, the nation could get ready for the twenty-first century.

Where would the money come from? First: a more progressive income tax.

During each of the past few years American citizens have had about $3,500 billion to spend, after taxes. About half this sum has gone to the lower four fifths of wage earners, the other half to the top fifth. Were the personal income tax as progressive as it was even as late as 1977, in 1989 the top tenth would have paid $93 billion more in taxes than they did. At that rate, from 1991 to 2000 they would contribute close to a trillion dollars more, even if their incomes failed to rise.

Second: limiting entitlements to those who need them. If there were no cap on the income on which the pension and disability portions of Social Security payroll taxes are levied, and if all Social Security benefits were treated as taxable income, another $600 billion would be freed during the decade.

Third: defense cuts. If defense spending were to fall during the decade by 15 percent (a fairly modest, and by most accounts realistic, decrease, even considering the cost of policing regional conflicts in the Middle East and elsewhere), we would have an additional $450 billion. A strong national economy is more important to our national security than troops and weapons.

The grand total: more than $2 trillion for the 1990s—to say nothing of all the savings that could be achieved by bargaining with global capital through the federal government instead of the states and cities. This sum would constitute a significant down payment on the future productivity of *all* Americans. The $2 trillion should be spent on education (at all levels), training, research, and infrastructure. It should *not* be used to reduce the budget deficit. Contrary to what many in government and much of the public assumes, there is nothing wrong with being indebted so long as the borrowings are invested in means of enhancing our future wealth. In fact, taking on debt for this purpose is preferable to maintaining a balanced budget by deferring or cutting back on such investments. Debt is a problem only if the borrowings are squandered on consumption. Any competent business person understands the soundness of this principle: If necessary, you borrow in order to invest in the greater future productivity of your enterprise. Once the new levels of productivity are achieved, they enable you to pay back the debt and enjoy higher returns thereafter. . . .

Yet the national wealth no longer depends, as it once did, on the accumulation of financial capital in American hands. It depends on the development of the skills and insights of our citizens, and on the infrastructure necessary to link them to the new world economy. The Democrats have displayed almost as little insight on this point as have the Republicans. In the final budget compromise of last October the Democrats carefully insulated Social Security benefits from future cuts by removing the entire program from budget calculations, and barely touched Medicare. As a result, these programs for the elderly will account for the only real growth in domestic spending to occur between now and the year 2000. But what about the nation's future productivity? As part of the same compromise, the total of public investments in education, training, research and development, and infrastructure will be frozen at the 1991 level, adjusted for inflation. (Slight increases for several of these programs in 1991 will be offset by cuts in 1992.) It was further agreed that any additional revenues from tax increases would be used only to expand entitlements or to reduce the budget deficit.

A message for Republicans and Democrats alike: Stop fighting over how much money government is taking from the wealthy and redistributing to everyone else. Start worrying about the capacity of Americans to add value to the emerging global economy. What we own is coming to be far less important than what we are able to do.

4.2. Invested Interests: The Politics of National Economic Policies in a World of Global Finance

JEFFRY A. FRIEDEN

In the past few decades, changes in technology, the increasing importance of international trade, and the increasing coordination of monetary policies have led to a significant increase in the flow of money across international borders. Like the changes in international trade discussed in the previous reading, this has led to important changes in both the United States' economy and in the political sphere.

In this reading Jeff Frieden shows that increased capital flows have significant effects on the welfare of major domestic actors. As was the case with increased international trade, these changes tend to benefit capitalists but weaken the position of labor. They also tend to benefit some firms while harming others. In addition the increased mobility of capital makes monetary policy a much less effective tool. The more flexible the exchange rate, the harder it becomes to stem currency surges which can weaken national control of the money supply. Frieden argues this can result in political coalitions in which firms that trade across national frontiers push for stable currency levels at the expense of monetary control, while domestically oriented firms thrust for flexible rates but greater control of the money supply.

A striking characteristic of the contemporary international economy is the great mobility of capital across national borders. Technological innovations, economic trends, and government policies have brought international investment to extremely high levels. Many business executives, politicians, and observers believe that capital now moves so freely that the financial markets of industrialized countries are essentially subsets of one global market. This is widely regarded as a fundamental change in the international economy—something new or at least not seen since the classic gold standard. It is also widely believed to have generated such prominent developments as European Community (EC) movement toward a single currency, harmonization of taxes across national borders, and international convergence of macroeconomic policies.

Economists have devoted a great deal of time and energy to analyzing the economic implications of the movement of capital across national borders. Other social scientists have also analyzed the political implications of international investment. The studies of this latter group have tended to focus on one or another subset of the issue, such as multinational corporations in developed and developing countries, foreign borrowing by developing nations, and the politics of international banking.[1] Despite the quantity and quality of work on specific aspects of the politics of cross-border investment, this literature remains disjointed and short on general analytic principles.

This article proposes a framework for analyzing the politics of international capital mobility. It focuses on the distributional implications of cross-border capital movements and on the distributional implications of various economic policies in light of the high degree of international capital mobility.

The first section describes just how mobile capital is today and discusses the implications of existing levels of financial integration for national economic policy autonomy. It argues that while financial capital is extremely mobile across borders, other types of investment (especially in equities and sector-specific capital) are far less mobile. In this context, foreseeable levels of international capital mobility restrict but do not eliminate the possibility for national economic policies. Sectoral policies remain feasible, as do policies whose goals directly or indirectly involve the exchange rate.

The second section of the article examines the policy preferences of various socioeconomic groups toward financial integration. It emphasizes the differential effects of the increase in capital mobility and focuses on questions concerning which actors are better (or worse) off after financial integration than before and how the various actors can be expected to respond politically to this change in the economic environment. The conclusion here is twofold. Over the long run, international financial integration tends to favor capital over labor, especially in developed countries. But in the shorter run, which is more relevant to politics and policies, the issue is more complex: in the developed world, financial integration favors capitalists with mobile or diversified assets and disfavors those with assets tied to specific locations and activities such as manufacturing or farming.

The third section of the article explores what high levels of financial integration imply for the policy preferences of economic interest groups in regard to such other issues as macroeconomic policy and the exchange rate. The section takes a high level of capital mobility as given, to see how various interest groups are expected to behave in this environment. It argues that international capital mobility tends to remake political coalitions by way of its impact on the effects of national policies. The political division between producers of tradable goods and producers of nontradable goods and services is likely to become more important, as are distinctions between internationally diversified and undiversified investors. All of these factors have significant implications for the analysis of politics and economic policy in the advanced industrialized nations.

The relationship between international capital mobility and national policies is a prominent example of the much-discussed impact of external conditions on domestic politics.[2] Elucidating this specific relationship thus also serves the broader purpose of clarifying the domestic effects of international trends. The article, then, both develops an integrated approach to the politics of international capital movements and addresses more general conceptual issues about the interaction of the domestic and international political economies. In so doing, it presents a summary and empirical illustrations not only of the direct impact of international capital mobility on the effectiveness of national economic policy but also of the distributional effects of capital mobility on the social groups whose demands themselves affect national economic policy.

Capital Mobility and National Economic Policies

It would be foolish to inquire about the effects of integrated international capital markets on interest group competition over national economic policy if such policy could not be implemented in a financially integrated world or if contemporary international capital markets were not in fact highly integrated. The initial question therefore concerns the degree to which national economic policy autonomy is compromised by existing levels of international capital mobility.

The events of the 1970s and the 1980s have led many to conclude that capital mobility severely limits or contravenes national policy. Between 1978 and 1982, for example, private financial inflows swamped Chile's conservative policies even as private financial outflows thwarted Mexico's free-spending policies. In mid-1981, the economic expansion attempted by the new French Socialist government rapidly confronted a large capital outflow and a run on the franc, leading to a reversal of the policies soon after their adoption.[3] Parallel stories about government efforts hampered by capital and currency movements could be told about many other developing and developed countries in the past two decades. Some observers have drawn dire conclusions, such as that of John Freeman, who observed that in the context of the globalization of finance "the nation state has become at best immobilized and at worst obsolete."[4]

The first step in evaluating the effects of contemporary levels of international capital mobility is to get a clear picture of where the levels stand in relation to the past. Long-term capital movements across borders were relatively limited for the first twenty-five years after World War II and took place primarily in the form of direct investment. Today, long-term international investment flows are extraordinarily large, and direct investment has been dwarfed by other, more arms-length, forms of cross-border capital movements.

According to one source, net international bond and bank lending was $440 billion in 1989, up from $180 billion just five years earlier. Capital outflows from the thirteen leading industrialized countries averaged $444 billion in 1989, with almost two-thirds of the amount consisting of portfolio investment, in contrast to $52 billion in the late 1970s, with two-thirds consisting of foreign direct investment. Capital outflows were equivalent to 15 percent of world merchandise trade in 1989, in contrast to 7 percent in the late 1970s.[5] According to another source, the outstanding stock of international bank and bond lending was $3.6 trillion in 1989, equivalent to 25 percent of the aggregate gross national product (GNP) of the industrialized countries, in contrast to under $200 billion and 5 percent of aggregate GNP in 1973.[6]

Recent changes in regulations and technology have made it possible for money to travel across borders almost instantly, giving rise to massive short-term international financial transactions. In April 1989, foreign exchange trading in the world's financial centers averaged about $650 billion *a day,* equivalent to nearly $500 million a minute and to forty times the amount of world trade a day. Markets for short-term international financial instruments are comparably large, although exact figures are not available.[7]

Impressive as these numbers are, they do not amount to full international capital mobility. In fact, economic studies have consistently shown that borders and *currencies* are still substantial barriers to investment flows.[8] Although these barriers have been and are still being reduced, there are a number of reasons why international investment is by no means yet a seamless web. First, movement of capital across borders still involves country and currency risks. Investors must take into account the possibility that assets in one country may be riskier than those in another country and that movements in exchange rates may affect the return on their investments. Of course, both of these problems are addressed by adjustments to asset prices and returns and by forward markets, but they imply that capital movements among industrialized countries are more difficult than capital movements within them.[9]

Second, while some forms of capital do move quite easily across borders, others remain more geographically specific. Most assertions of full international capital mobility refer to international transfers of financial assets, especially bonds and bank claims. Equity markets appear to be far less integrated,[10] and other forms of capital still less so. In most interpretations, this is because many forms of capital, such as technological and managerial knowledge, skills, and networks, are specific to their current use and cannot easily be transferred from place to place.[11] Although detailed analyses do not exist, most observers would probably agree that financial capital is most mobile across borders, followed by equities and then by firm- or sector-specific capital assets.[12]

The greater international mobility of financial assets, the more modest international mobility of other assets, and the continued importance of unexpected exchange rate movements must all be taken into account in assessments of national policy autonomy in the contemporary international economy. The appraisal can be divided into policy targeted at well-defined segments of the economy (industries, sectors, and regions) and policy of macroeconomic import. The baseline is the assertion that asset markets are internationally linked to varying degrees: financial markets are closely linked, equity markets are less connected, and markets for firm- and sector-specific capital are quite nationally segmented. In other words, among industrialized countries, financial capital flows freely but other assets flow relatively less freely or very little.

Inasmuch as capital is specific to location, increased financial integration has only limited effects on policies targeted at particular industries. Whether or not a sector-specific policy is effective depends greatly on how easily firms can enter the sector. Financial markets can affect the ease of entry by extending funds to new firms. The easier it is for new firms to enter the sector, the more quickly the benefits of the policy to preexisting firms will dissipate and thus the less effective the policy will be. This is a general feature of sector-specific policies and holds as long as financial capital is mobile domestically; it would be true even if capital were not mobile internationally.

Where cross-border financial flows reduce entry barriers to a favored sector, they contravene sector-specific policy. International capital mobility may have increased the ability of foreign producers to respond to trade protection by locating in the protected market; inasmuch as the purpose of protection was to support locally owned firms, this objective may be frustrated. The proliferation of Japanese-owned automobile factories in the United States in response to automobile import controls may have been made easier by the integration of financial markets and may have reduced some of the benefits of the controls to shareholders and employees of American-owned automobile manufacturers.[13]

All in all, however, increased financial capital mobility probably has little effect on most sector-specific policies. Supporters of such policies can generally design them to avoid their frustration by financial flows, domestic or international. Financial capital mobility, within or across borders, is not likely to affect the impact of cash transfers to farmers on their incomes. Nor can financial flows significantly impede government health and safety standards. Financial integration may make it more difficult to design some sector-specific policies to avoid undesirable side effects (namely, benefits accruing to untargeted firms), but it rarely makes them unsustainable.

On the other hand, integration of financial markets has significant effects on the effectiveness and the differential distributional impact of national macroeconomic policies. To get a handle on the issue, it is useful to start with what might be called the Mundell-Fleming conditions, taken from the most influential approach to payments balance developed in the early 1960s.[14] These conditions include the possibility that financial assets may be fully mobile across borders. (In what follows, I use "capital mobility" to mean the mobility of financial capital, as does the literature in question.)

Simply put, the Mundell-Fleming approach indicates that a country can have at most two of the following three conditions: a fixed exchange rate, monetary policy autonomy, and capital mobility. Without capital mobility, national authorities can adopt and sustain a monetary policy that differs from the policies of the rest of the world and can hold their exchange rate constant; however, with mobile capital, the attempt will be contravened by financial flows. Assume the authorities want an expansionary monetary policy. Without capital mobility, a fall in interest rates will lead to a rise in demand, and the economy will be stimulated (we ignore longer-term effects on the payments balance). With capital mobility, reduced domestic interest rates will lead to an outflow of capital in search of higher interest rates abroad, and long before monetary policy has a real effect, interest rates will be bid back up to world levels.[15]

The reason for the result is straightforward: if capital is fully mobile across borders, interest rates are constrained to be the same in all countries and national monetary policy can have no effect on national interest rates. However, to go back to the original conditions, if capital mobility is given (or imposed), monetary policy can be effective if the value of the currency is allowed to vary. Monetary policy operates, in other words, via exchange rates rather than via interest rates as in a typical closed-economy model. With capital mobility, monetary expansion greater than that in the rest of the world causes a financial outflow in which investors sell the currency; the result is currency depreciation. Depreciation in most cases stimulates the economy as prices of foreign goods rise relative to prices of domestically produced goods, thereby increasing local and foreign demand for locally produced goods.[16]

A parallel story can be told about fiscal policy. If capital is not mobile and the exchange rate is fixed, expansionary fiscal policy raises national interest rates as the government finances increased spending by floating more bonds. The resultant "crowding out" of private investment dampens the expansion. However, if capital moves freely across borders, bonds floated to finance increased government spending are bought by international investors, and there is no effect on interest rates, which are set globally.[17] The fixed exchange rate constraint has different effects with fiscal policy than with monetary policy. If the exchange rate varies, as foreigners buy more government bonds the resultant capital inflow causes a currency appreciation that tends to reduce domestic demand for domestically produced goods and thus to dampen the fiscal expansion.[18]

The general point is that in a world of fully mobile capital, national policy cannot affect the national interest rate;[19] it can, however, affect the exchange rate. The above discussion of open-economy macroeconomics is meant simply to highlight this result.

It may seem unimportant that the world has changed from one in which national macroeconomic policy operated primarily via interest rates to one in which policy operates primarily via exchange rates, but several points to defend the significance of this observation can be made. First, the distributional effects of interest rate changes are different from those of exchange rate changes. If monetary expansion in a stylized world before capital mobility (BCM) meant lower interest rates, then monetary expansion in a stylized world after capital mobility (ACM) means depreciation. To take one distributional example, lower interest rates are good for the residential construction industry, while depreciation is bad for it inasmuch as it tends to switch domestic demand away from nontradable goods and services. By the same token, manufacturers might have been more sympathetic to a tight money stance in the past, when the principal effect of this stance was to raise interest rates, than they are now, when the principal effect is a currency appreciation that tends to increase import penetration. This means that policy preferences of economic interest groups, and therefore political coalitions, are likely to differ between the BCM and ACM worlds. I later return to this point and discuss it in detail.

Second, although by definition there is an international component to exchange rate changes, there is not necessarily an international component to interest rate changes. If monetary expansion simply reduces national interest rates, chances are that most foreigners will be indifferent. If, however, it leads to currency depreciation in the expansionary country, foreigners are likely to be concerned about their resultant loss of competitiveness.[20]

Third, the focus on how macroeconomic policy takes effect through the exchange rate helps clarify some observed anomalies of the ACM world. If an American administration in the BCM world had pursued fiscal expansion and monetary stringency, the result might well have been that the policies canceled each other out: tight money would have reinforced the "crowding out" effects of the fiscal expansion. As it was, however, in the ACM world, the Reagan-Volcker fiscal expansion and monetary stringency of the early 1980s had a markedly different impact. Fiscal policy was largely financed by foreign borrowing, which reduced or eliminated the effects of crowding out and contributed to appreciation of the dollar. At the same time, tight money reinforced the rise of the dollar by strengthening the international investment attractiveness of dollar-denominated securities. The result was striking both on macroeconomic grounds, as the dollar soared and the United States became a major net debtor to the rest of the world, and on distributional grounds, as the dollar appreciation devastated U.S. producers of tradable goods (manufacturing and agriculture) and favored producers of nontradable goods and services (real estate, health care, leisure activities, and education).

To summarize this section, financial capital moves across the borders of developed countries with great ease, while other asset markets are less integrated and some capital remains quite fixed. In this context, while global financial integration may reduce the efficacy of some sector-specific policies, it does not impede most of them. And while international financial integration does not make national macroeconomic policy obsolete, it does shift the effect of macroeconomic policy from the interest rate to the exchange rate. These features of the ACM world are expected to have a significant impact on the interests of various domestic economic interest groups. I return to ACM interest group competition over economic policy after first looking at the expected effects of the shift from BCM to ACM itself.

The Distributional Effects of Capital Mobility

The distinction I draw here is nuanced but important. On the one hand, I am interested in how economic agents are expected to act in a world characterized by capital mobility: What sorts of policies will be pursued by what sorts of groups and coalitions? On the other hand, I am interested in how the shift from a pre-1970 world of limited capital mobility to a post-1980 world of relatively high capital mobility affected the interests and influence of economic agents: Who gained and who lost as we went from capital immobility to capital mobility? And what are the political implications of these gains and losses? In other words, in one context I analyze the dynamics of the ACM world; in another context, I compare conditions in the BCM world with those in the ACM world.

The first set of questions addressed in this section pertains to the overall impact of international financial integration on major economic interest groups in advanced industrialized societies. Once again, I have recourse to rudimentary tools of economic analysis. There are, however, several different (albeit potentially complementary) approaches that contend for attention. Many analyses focus implicitly or explicitly on the portfolio choice approach or on an application of the Heckscher-Ohlin model of international trade. While these give interesting insights, I believe that they are not directly relevant to our political a policy questions. After reviewing them, then, I summarize and discuss th cific-factors" model, which I believe is best suited to assessing the d effects of increased capital mobility and to determining the distributional effects on lobbying for policy.

Perhaps the most common and simplest possible c look at increased capital mobility from the standp lio decisions, whom it must help. It can hardly investment options than before, which is v the same token, increasing the options of r by making it less costly for capital to mo

This surmise captures important effec wider menu of investments open to asset governments, labor, and others. The 1980s n in response to increased capital mobility, in which governments all over the world were forced to provide more attractive conditions for capitalists. Such conditions include everything from lower wealth and capital gains taxes to relaxed regulation of financial activities and labor relations. In a world in which financial capital moves freely across borders, it is difficult for one country to insist on stiff capital taxation when other countries are removing or reducing it. Inasmuch as this effect holds, increased financial integration implies an across-the-board, lasting increase in the social and political power of capital.[21]

But this picture is incomplete, for it ignores the dynamic effects of aggregate portfolio choices on asset-holders. The ability of capital to move freely across borders can in fact be bad for capitalists in a given country or good for labor in it. The result depends on the country's underlying endowment of capital and other resources, and this leads some to believe that the Heckscher-Ohlin approach is the appropriate analytic tool.

According to the Heckscher-Ohlin trade model, the effects of goods movements on returns to factors will vary according to whether the factors are locally scarce or abundant. Perhaps the best-known extension is the Stolper-Samuelson theorem, which posits that protection (that is, decreased trade) benefits the locally scarce factor: protection is good for labor in a labor-poor country and is good for capital in a capital-poor country. The intuition is straightforward. With trade, demand for the product in which the country has a comparative advantage will rise, and this comparative advantage is a function of how well endowed the country is with various factors. A labor-rich country tends to export products that use labor intensively; the more the country trades, the more labor is used, and the more wages rise. Trade and factor movements are substitutes: exporting labor and labor-intensive products have the same effect, as do exporting capital and capital-intensive products.

In the Heckscher-Ohlin view, then, increased capital mobility (like increased world trade) benefits capital where it is abundant and hurts capital where it is scarce. Capital flows out of capital-rich countries, raising the return to local capital, and flows toward capital-poor countries, lowering the return to local capital. The effect is analogous to that examined by Ronald Rogowski, who assessed periods in which there was an exogenous increase or decrease in world trade to explore the Heckscher-Ohlin effects on national politics.[22]

To illustrate the above points, we can compare two countries with opposite sets of endowments. In the BCM world, the first country is rich in capital and poor in labor, so its local interest rates are relatively low and its local wages relatively high. In the ACM world, capital is free to move to countries in which the rate of return is higher; the local interest rates rise to the world level, and wages fall. In this case, the result favors capital and disfavors labor, but this is a function of the beginning endowments—which are characteristic of developed countries. Now take the opposite case. In the BCM world, the country is poor in capital and rich in labor, so its local interest rates are relatively high and its local wages relatively low. In the ACM world, capital will flow in, reducing the local interest rates and tending to raise wages. In this case, since the local rate of return on capital is constrained to fall to the (lower) world level, local capitalists are harmed while local workers benefit.

This may capture some of what has happened as capital mobility has advanced. Capitalists in the developed world (in countries relatively rich in capital) have probably benefited from international capital mobility. It might be argued that the developing countries' access to international financial markets tended to strengthen labor (perhaps by increasing investment in labor-intensive activities), but this seems far from clear-cut.

In fact, while the Heckscher-Ohlin approach may be useful in predicting long-term economic trends, it is probably not a very good way to analyze the distributional effects of international factor movements, for several reasons. First, it is extremely sensitive to the number of factors involved. The predictions are straightforward with two factors, but they become ambiguous at best with more than two. Second, it assumes that capital, labor, and other factors can move costlessly from one activity to another within a country, even if they are internationally immobile. This is certainly untrue, since an automobile factory cannot costlessly be converted into a brewery, nor can a seamstress costlessly become an aerospace engineer. Although factors of production may move from one use to another over the long run, they cannot do so in the short and medium run, which is the time frame more relevant to political analysis. And, third, empirical evidence suggests that political behavior, especially with regard to economic policy, is less commonly factoral (laborers as a class, capitalists as a class) than sectoral (the steel industry, the dairy farming industry).[23]

As useful as the Heckscher-Ohlin approach may be for long-term economic analysis, it is more appropriate to investigate the political economy of international trade and capital movements with an approach which assumes that at least some factors of production are specific to a particular use for at least the short run. In this "specific-factors" model, changes in the relative prices of goods have their principal effect on the sector-specific producers of the goods, rather than on a whole class of factor-owners. Thus, an increase in milk prices is good for dairy farmers rather than landowners as a whole; a decline in clothing prices is bad for owners and workers in the garment industry rather than for capitalists or workers as a class.[24]

In the specific-factors approach, which I regard as most useful to the task at hand, the economy is organized into activities (or sectors) to which factors are specific, along with factors that can move freely from activity to activity. The classic setup is an economy in which capital is specific either to the production of clothing or to the production of housing, while labor is an input for both sectors and can move freely from the garment industry to the construction industry. The result, as mentioned above, is that changes in the prices of goods have their principal effects on the specific factors, with collateral (and generally ambiguous) effects on the mobile factor. In the above example, an increase in the relative price of clothing, perhaps due to a tariff, is good for capital in the garment industry and bad for capital in the housing industry; its effect on labor depends on the mix of clothing and housing that workers consume. If, however, the supply (thus, the price) of the mobile factor changes, the interests of the specific factors are opposed to those of the mobile factor. In the above example, if the supply of labor shrinks and wages rise, this is unambiguously good for workers and bad for capital in the garment and construction industries, since the price of their labor input rises.[25]

The application of the specific-factors approach to our problem is straightforward. I clarify again that with capital mobility I mean the mobility of financial capital rather than sector-specific capital. A secular increase in international capital mobility implies movement of financial assets from capital-rich to capital-poor countries (from low to high interest rates) and therefore an increase in the supply of finance to countries poor in capital and a reduction in the supply of finance to countries rich in capital. Specific factors in capital-poor countries do well, since they can now borrow at lower interest rates; specific factors in capital-rich countries do badly, since they must now pay higher interest rates; and owners of liquid financial assets in capital-rich countries do well, while those in capital-poor countries do badly.

I should note that the distinction made here between capital-rich and capital-poor countries may be somewhat misleading, or at least incomplete. Capital flows in response to differences in rates of return, and interest rates can vary for reasons other than underlying endowments of capital. The United States was a net capital importer in the 1980s not because it had suddenly become capital-poor but, rather, because national savings were insufficient to finance domestic investment; foreign savings were especially needed to help fund the government budget deficit. By the same token, many developing countries became net capital exporters during the 1980s, as they lost access to overseas finance and had to service their existing debts. Countries can import or export capital for reasons that have little to do with their endowments, especially over the short and medium run. Nonetheless and over the longer run, developed countries tend to be net capital exporters, while developing countries tend to be net capital importers. The point is simply that actual applications require attention to specific national circumstances.

In any case, I believe that the specific-factors model has three important features which make it useful for the analysis of the political economy of international finance. First, it emphasizes the political relevance of short-term fluctuations in the returns to different sorts of economic activity, rather than longer-term changes in the conditions of workers or capitalists as a class. Second, it assumes that most people and investments are "caught" in their current activity to one degree or another. To be sure, some are more caught than others, but there is no recourse to the highly unrealistic assumption common in other models that, for example, automobile workers faced with import penetration will have no trouble finding jobs at the same wage in another industry. Third, it recognizes that some factors may be mobile, while others are specific. For example, it is consonant with the specific-factors approach to assume that unskilled labor is quite mobile among industries, while skilled labor is industry-specific, or to assume that financial capital is mobile among industries, while physical capital is industry-specific. This feature allows for variations in the degree to which people or investments are "stuck" in one place. These three interrelated emphases—on the political significance of the short run, on the relative specificity of most people and investments to their current activity, and on the possibility that some factors are more mobile than others—seem both realistic and analytically useful.

For those unfamiliar with the method, it may be helpful to identify it as a sectoral approach to political economy as opposed to a class-based approach.[26] In the class-based approach, differences among workers are less important than differences between workers and capitalists; the same is held to be true of capitalists and landowners. Politics is competition among these classes, not within them. In the sectoral approach, steelworkers have cross-cutting interests. On the one hand, they are workers, and their interests in the long run are similar to those of other workers. On the other hand, they produce steel, and their interests in the short run are similar to those of managers and shareholders in the steel industry. Politics, in this view, is primarily competition among various sectors of the economy, although long-term class interests sometimes play a role.

The specific-factors or sectoral view of the world tells us a great deal about the distributional implications of capital mobility. As indicated above, as we move from a BCM to an ACM world, financial capital leaves areas where rates of return are lower and enters areas where they are higher. Interest rates go up in capital-exporting regions and down in capital-importing regions; interest rate variations affect not only owners of financial assets but also borrowers, for whom they are a cost of production. In comparison with the BCM world, in the ACM world things are better for owners of financial assets in capital-exporting countries and for owners of sector-specific assets (capital, skills, and land) in capital-importing countries, and vice versa.

We can also introduce another important set of economic actors: internationally diversified (multinational) corporations. In the specific-factors view of the world, a crucial dimension of variation is the mobility or specificity of an asset, be it an investment, skill, or plot of land. In many ways, the dimension of diversification parallels that of specificity. An investor who holds an asset that can easily be moved from use to use is in a parallel position to an investor whose asset portfolio includes a large number of different economic activities. The most vulnerable position is to hold an asset that is completely specific to one industry; it is analogously vulnerable to have an asset portfolio that includes firms in only one industry.[27] In this sense, firms with operations that are diversified with respect to activity and location can be regarded as less specific and more mobile than firms whose operations are "stuck" in one activity and one place. The preferences of multinational corporations, with operations in many countries facing different conditions, thus parallel the preferences of investors with more mobile assets and diverge from those of nationally and sectorally specific corporations.[28]

A simple "map" of sectoral interests can thus be drawn in line with the specific-factors approach. On this map, increased capital mobility is generally good for financial asset-holders in the developed world and bad for those in the developing world; it is good for multinational corporations; and it is bad for (nonmultinational) specific factors in the developed world and good for those in the developing world.[29]

A few examples indicate the plausibility of this sectoral map. The opening of global financial markets to the less developed countries (LDCs) was good for industries in the Third World, which were suddenly able to borrow at reduced rates of interest. Industrial production in the LDCs grew rapidly as foreign finance flowed in, benefiting owners and managers (and usually workers) in these industries.[30] By the same token, overseas lending from developed countries almost certainly raised the cost of capital to industries at home, contributing to the problems of industrial sectors in Western Europe and North America. More generally, the increased financial integration of the advanced industrialized countries strengthened competitive pressures on specific industries and contributed to the industrial restructuring taking place in them.[31]

In line with the approach, the interests of two groups—the owners and managers of financial assets and the multinational corporations—are opposed to those of the specific factors, so that financial and multinational interests in the developed countries are expected to diverge from the interests of specific nationally based industrial sectors. This would appear a fair generalization from the experience of the 1970s and 1980s. The principal beneficiaries of the broad economic trends of the last two decades have been internationally oriented firms and the financial services industries; the principal losers have been nationally based industrial firms.[32]

These conclusions about the distributional effects of increased financial integration can be turned around to predict expected patterns of political support and opposition to policies that will increase international capital mobility. Perhaps the most obvious policies in this regard concern the removal of barriers to capital movements across borders, but they also include efforts to strengthen organizations that police international financial markets, especially the International Monetary Fund (IMF).

In the developed world, I expect support for increased financial integration from owners and managers of financial assets and from multinational firms with internationally diversified investments.[33] I expect opposition to increased financial integration from specific industries, especially those tied to a particular national market. It is my opinion that this accurately, albeit in the broadest terms, describes patterns of political activity on these issues. In the United States, support for financial deregulation, including deregulation of international financial relations, has come primarily from the country's financial centers and its internationally oriented nonfinancial corporations; domestic manufacturing and farm groups have been ambivalent or hostile.[34] By the same token, support for American backing of the IMF has been strongest in these sectors, while again opposition to government commitments to the international financial order have been concentrated in the industrial and agricultural heartlands.[35]

Europe's leading financial and multinational firms have been the stronghold of support for breaking down remaining barriers to EC financial and monetary integration.[36] Although systematic evidence is not available, indications are that the strongest backers of financial deregulation are in the EC's leading financial centers.[37] The chief Japanese promoters of international financial deregulation have been, again, financial and multinational firms. In Japan, the issue is complex, with major battles within the financial community over the contours of the regulatory changes. Nonetheless, the general patterns appear consonant with the approach set forth here.[38]

To summarize this section, the distributional effects of increased cross-border capital mobility can be striking. In a general and long-term sense, it may be that international financial integration increases the influence of capital by making it easier for owners of financial assets to take them abroad in response to national policies they do not like. The more immediate results in the developed world have been to drive a wedge between two camps, the first consisting of the financial sector, owners of financial assets, and integrated multinational firms, all of which have gained with financial integration, and the second consisting of firms specific to a particular industry and location, all of which have been harmed by the generally increased competition for scarce loanable funds. The clear prediction is for conflict between these "integrationist" forces and "anti-integrationist" forces. But political debate has not been and will not be restricted to policies directly concerned with increasing or retarding international capital mobility, and it is to the distributional and political implications of financial integration itself for these other debates that we now turn.

The Distributional Effects of Economic Policies in a Financially Integrated World

While the political divisions likely to emerge over the desired degree of international financial integration are important, the general increase in international capital mobility is also likely to change interest group activity on a wide range of other economic policy problems. Global financial integration has already shifted much political activity directly or indirectly toward the exchange rate in ways that imply new socioeconomic and political divisions. It raises problems of international policy cooperation that may be too new to analyze in detail. And, in some ways, financial integration may have an impact on the strength of sectoral lobbying. This section surveys these expected effects. Again, the problem here is not to do with the level of financial integration itself; I take as given a high level of international capital mobility in order to see how this level affects political behavior and policy in other realms.

One preliminary observation has to do with the potential effects of increased international capital mobility on the intensity of sectoral interests of owners of capital. The starting point is that the more specific the asset is to its current use—that is, the more substantial is the cost attached to moving the asset from its current use to its best alternative use—the more incentive the owner of the asset will have to lobby for supportive government policies.[39] Agents in a sector to which exit and entry are costless have little or no incentive to spend time, energy, and money to get government support, since this support will be dissipated by new entrants into the sector.

To pick up from the previous discussion of the effects of financial capital mobility on sectoral policies, inasmuch as global financial integration makes it easier for investors to get into or out of a particular sector, it reduces the incentive for sectoral lobbying. Although there is little evidence that this effect has been large, it is theoretically plausible. An integrated worldwide financial market of enormous size, compared with many segmented national markets, might indeed allow for the development of instruments and mechanisms that would facilitate the redeployment of capital from one use to another. These could include broader and deeper futures markets and insurance schemes, better information to potential borrowers and lenders, and more readily available venture finance.[40]

If indeed international financial integration does reduce barriers to entry and exit of investors to and from specific economic activities, it could reduce the sectoral orientation of lobbying by investors.[41] If financial integration makes it easier for firms to exit and enter many different sectors, their attachment to a particular sector may be reduced. Inasmuch as this takes place, we might expect more political action by owners of capital as a class and less participation of capitalists in sectoral lobbying.

However, as argued above, even if this trend exists, it is embryonic and its impact has yet to be felt: the sector specificity of capital has not been measurably reduced by international financial integration. The most prominent effect of increased capital mobility is not on the level of sectoral lobbying but, rather, on the character of sectoral lobbying and the policy preferences arising when the sectors are thrown together in pursuit of government support.

The impact of capital mobility on the expected political lineup over macroeconomic policy is in fact striking. Two interrelated dimensions of policy choice are especially important: the degree of exchange rate flexibility and the level of the exchange rate itself. With regard to the first dimension, the Mundell-Fleming conditions serve as a point of reference.[42] Recall that, with capital mobility, a

Figure 1. **Synopsis of the Policy Preferences of the Various Socioeconomic Actors in a World of Mobile Capital**

		Preferred degree of exchange rate flexibility and national monetary policy autonomy	
		High	Low
Preferred level of the exchange rate	Low	Import-competing producers of tradable goods for the domestic market	Export-oriented producers of tradable goods
	High	Producers of nontradable goods and services	International traders and investors

country faces something of a trade-off between exchange rate stability and monetary policy autonomy: the more the country's exchange rate is held constant, the less its monetary policy can deviate from that of the rest of the world. While some actors will favor a low degree of exchange rate flexibility (a fixed rate such as the gold standard) despite the loss of monetary policy autonomy, others will be willing to accept a high degree of exchange rate flexibility (freely floating rates) in exchange for policymaking autonomy. With regard to the second dimension, which is the preferred level of the exchange rate itself, some fixing of exchange rates is assumed. While some actors will prefer a high (more appreciated) exchange rate, others will prefer a low (more depreciated) exchange rate. The two dimensions and the expected policy preferences of socioeconomic actors along them are presented in Figure 1 and discussed in detail below. We should keep in mind that the figure provides only rough approximations; variation is, of course, along a continuum rather than dichotomous.

The first dimension involves the desired degree of exchange rate flexibility, which can be presented most starkly as whether the rate should be fixed or flexible. Fixing the rate in a world of mobile capital implies forgoing national monetary policy autonomy in favor of greater certainty about the value of the currency; in other words, it gives priority to a stable exchange rate over the ability of national policy to affect domestic prices. This is especially attractive to two groups of actors whose economic activities directly involve international trade and payments and who therefore are highly sensitive to currency fluctuations. International traders and investors and the producers of export oriented tradable goods tend to suffer from exchange market volatility, since it makes their business riskier.[43] By the same token, these actors are relatively unconcerned about domestic macroeconomic conditions, since they can respond to depressed local demand by shifting their business to other countries.

In contrast, two other groups of actors tend to be highly concerned about domestic macroeconomic conditions and thus favor the national monetary policy autonomy made possible by a flexible exchange rate. The first of these groups consists of producers of nontradable goods and services. Since their business does not involve the use of foreign exchange and since currency volatility has only indirect effects at best on them, they tend to have no clear preference for stable exchange rates.[44] The second group consists of producers of import-competing tradable goods for the domestic market, who tend to be relatively indifferent about exchange rate volatility (which may even reduce import pressure inasmuch as it makes importing riskier) and primarily concerned about policymaking autonomy.

The preferences of the various groups are relevant, most prominently, to policy debates about stabilizing exchange rates. Based on the above arguments, we can expect multinational firms, international investors more generally, and internationally oriented producers of tradable goods to be more sympathetic to currency stability, while we can expect producers in the nontradables sector and producers of import-competing tradable goods to be most interested in national monetary policy autonomy.

In policy debates about the level of the exchange rate, which is the second dimension noted in Figure 1, we can expect the interests of various economic sectors to track the relative price changes involved in depreciation or appreciation of the currency. From a differential distributional standpoint, the lower (more depreciated) the exchange rate, the higher is the price of tradable goods relative to nontradable goods. This, of course, tends to help producers of tradable goods—whose output prices rise more than the prices of the nontradable inputs they use—and to hurt producers of nontradable goods. Producers in the tradables sector therefore favor a weaker currency that makes their products more competitive in home and foreign markets. In contrast, producers in the nontradables sector generally benefit from currency appreciation, which raises the domestic relative price of their products and lowers the domestic relative price of tradable goods.[45] Similarly, international traders and investors, who are interested in purchasing assets overseas, favor a strong currency.[46]

Preliminary evidence seems to bear out these expectations both on the dimension of exchange rate flexibility and on that of the level of the exchange rate itself.[47] Perhaps the arena in which the choice between monetary policy autonomy and currency stability has been posed most directly is in the development of the exchange rate mechanism of the European Monetary System (EMS) and the subsequent movement toward a single EC currency.[48]

The above discussion has systematic predictions about private-sector attitudes toward the exchange rate mechanism (ERM) of the EMS.[49] I expect the ERM to be most favorable for, and to evince the most enthusiasm from, firms in the financial sector, major exporters, and diversified multinational corporations with major investments or customers in the EC. Evidence is scanty, but some can be presented. One study of potential British winners and losers from Britain's affiliation with the ERM essentially tracks my expectations. Internationally oriented manufacturing and finance and related services were expected to do well, while the domestically oriented manufacturing and services sectors were expected to be weaker.[50] Of Britain's twelve corporate members in the Association for Monetary Union in Europe, a private-sector lobbying organization for rapid currency union, eight are from firms in the financial and related services sectors, two are from diversified multinational corporations, and two are major exporters.[51] In the absence of systematic empirical work, few serious assessments can be made, but the patterns are suggestive.[52]

The second dimension, the level of the exchange rate, is a familiar topic of debate in many countries, especially those for which international trade is very important and those which have a history of exchange rate volatility (characteristics that apply primarily to developing and small developed countries). Political conflict over the exchange rate has become important in larger nations as well. One striking example is the United States, where between 1981 and 1986 much of the political activity that might otherwise have taken the form of pressure for trade protection instead focused on trying to get the authorities or other actors to force the dollar to depreciate relative to the currencies of the country's major trading partners.[53] The evidence, especially from the United States in the 1980s, appears consonant with the expectations presented above.[54]

These varying exchange rate preferences in turn affect preferences toward different macroeconomic policies. With capital mobility, an expansionary monetary policy leads to depreciation of the currency, while an expansionary fiscal policy leads to appreciation. Producers of tradable goods should thus prefer monetary expansion, and producers of nontradable goods and services should prefer fiscal expansion. This will especially be the case if the fiscal expansion takes the form of a direct or indirect increase in spending on nontradable goods, which is quite likely where government spending is involved (defense, infrastructure, and social spending are generally nontradables). This may help explain the peculiar pattern of U.S. economic policy during the Reagan years. With the administration's principal bases of support in the defense community, in real estate and related sectors, and in the international investors group, pressures were for increased spending on nontradables. The resultant appreciation might have been countered by monetary expansion, as was in fact demanded by the tradable goods producers hurt by the import surge, but the nontradables constituencies wanted it reinforced by tight money, not dissipated. In other words, the mix of loose fiscal and tight monetary policies may have been less a mistake, as most economists and observers concluded at the time, than it was a reflection of the dominance of political pressures from nontradable goods producers and other supporters of a strong dollar over tradable goods producers who wanted a weaker dollar.

Another issue that has gained in importance in a world of great capital mobility is international policy coordination. Because financial integration can make it difficult for national authorities to pursue macroeconomic policies that differ from those of their financial "neighbors," it may make sense to coordinate such policies. This would, for example, avoid competitive currency depreciations, in which a country pursuing an expansionary monetary policy and thus currency depreciation against its trading partners finds itself foiled as its partners match the monetary expansion and depreciation, leaving the currencies' relative levels unchanged. Alternatively, countries trying to prevent their currencies from depreciating might unnecessarily bid up interest rates in a competitive attempt to avoid a capital outflow. The obvious solution to such problems is for the relevant policymakers to cooperate in targeting exchange rates and other macroeconomic indicators.[55]

There are many potential problems with international macroeconomic policy coordination. Some believe that such government intervention is less desirable than letting the markets take their course; others believe that the difficulties of coordination are nearly insurmountable.[56] Among the coordination problems is that slight divergences in views among national policymakers may make welfare-improving cooperation extremely difficult.[57] It is indeed likely that the domestic political underpinnings of the potential cooperating governments will differ, leading to different preferences or interpretations about the gains from cooperation and how they might best be achieved.

In this light, once again the differential domestic distributional effects of such policy coordination are relevant. Not surprisingly, I expect those whose economic activities are most sensitive to foreign financial and exchange market conditions to be most favorable to the sacrifice of national policy autonomy implied by policy coordination. International investors, traders, and the like are apt to be well disposed, while those in the nontradables sector—whose businesses may be harmed by the sacrifice of autonomy with little or no corresponding benefit from coordination—are prone to be opposed. A related set of issues has to do with the coordination of other national policies, such as taxation.[58] On this subject, there is so little analytic work and indeed so little experience in the real world that coordination is mostly speculation. However, both the trends within the EC and the discussions among other developed countries indicate that it will likely be a topic of great importance in the 1990s.

These observations have to do with the interests in play, not necessarily with the outcome of political conflict among them. Political and policy outcomes will of course depend on how intense preferences are, how concentrated and organized the various interests are, and how political and other social institutions influence their interaction. How successful the various interest groups will be at obtaining their objectives will vary from case to case and from country to country. Nonetheless, a clear understanding of the economic interests involved is a crucial starting point for analysis.

This section can be summarized quite simply. Financial integration has implications for the distributional effects—and therefore the politics—of national policies. Over the long run, access to broader and deeper financial markets may tend to reduce the sectoral specificity of capital and thereby dampen some sectoral demands—but this gradual process is unlikely ever to eliminate such demands. The more immediate implication is that political lineups over macroeconomic policies are likely to change quite significantly.

A trade-off between national macroeconomic policy autonomy and exchange rate stability has developed, with international investors and traders more willing to give up autonomy for stability and with the nontradables and domestically oriented sectors more interested in autonomy than in fluctuations in the exchange rate. Conflict has intensified not only over the flexibility but also over the level of the exchange rate. While support for monetary expansion and depreciation has tended to come from producers of tradable goods, support for monetary contraction and appreciation has come from international investors and producers of nontradable goods and services. At the same time, the coordination of national macroeconomic policies has become an important political problem at both the international and the domestic level. Not surprisingly, those for whom overseas economic conditions are more relevant (international investors and traders and producers of tradable goods) will favor more coordinated policies—and thus a surrender of more national policy autonomy—than will those for whom domestic conditions are determinant.

Conclusions

Without repeating the points made in the article, I can emphasize a few conclusions. Hampered as national governments may be or appear to be in the face of an internationally integrated financial system, they continue to have weapons in their policy arsenal. These weapons may not be as sharp or numerous as before, but they exist. Many sectoral policies can be effective, as can macroeconomic policies if policymakers allow the exchange rate to vary.

However, the distributional implications of international capital mobility are striking. In the long run, owners of capital have probably gained relative to other groups. In the shorter run, owners and workers in specific sectors in the developed world face serious costs in adjusting to increased capital mobility.

International capital mobility also changes the pattern of lobbying over national policies. It may, over the long run, dampen some sectoral demands from owners of capital. More specifically, and in the shorter run, it tends to shift debate toward the exchange rate as an intermediate or ultimate policy instrument, thereby driving a wedge between those more sensitive and those less sensitive to exchange rate fluctuations and between those who favor currency appreciation and those who favor depreciation. To some extent, this tracks a division of the economy between producers of tradable goods on the one hand and international investors and producers of nontradable goods and services on the other.

This article sets forth a series of propositions that can be brought to bear on a wide variety of problems having to do with the politics of the international movement of capital. Such problems, it is safe to project, will be of great analytic and policy importance in years to come. The possibility for the empirical evaluation of the approach presented here and for further theoretical and empirical elaboration is clear. As we approach 1992 and as parallel developments evolve elsewhere in the world, the opportunity for and necessity of such work will be enormous, and a better understanding of what is at stake will be of great importance.

Notes

1. For prominent examples from each of these issue-areas, see Helen V. Milner, *Resisting Protectionism: Global Industries and the Politics of International Trade* (Princeton, N.J.: Princeton University Press, 1988); Peter Evans, *Dependent Development: The Alliance of Multinational, State, and Local Capital in Brazil* (Princeton, N.J.: Princeton University Press, 1979); David G. Becker et al., *Postimperialism: International Capitalism and Development in the Late Twentieth Century* (Boulder, Colo.: Lynne Rienner, 1987); Robert Kaufman and Barbara Stallings, eds., *Debt and Development in Latin America* (Boulder, Colo.: Westview Press, 1989); Benjamin J. Cohen, *In Whose Interest? International Banking and American Foreign Policy* (New Haven, Conn.: Yale University Press, 1987); and Charles Lipson, *Standing Guard: Protecting Foreign Capital in the Nineteenth and Twentieth Centuries* (Berkeley: University of California Press, 1985). The bodies of literature, of course, are far too large to cite or discuss here.

2. The two quintessential works on this subject are Peter Gourevitch's *Politics in Hard Times: Comparative Responses to International Economic Crises* (Ithaca, N.Y.: Cornell University Press, 1986) and Ronald Rogowski's *Commerce and Coalitions: How Trade Affects Domestic Political Alignments* (Princeton, N.J.: Princeton University Press, 1989).

3. Jeffrey Sachs and Charles Wyplosz, "The Economic Consequences of President Mitterand," *Economic Policy* 2 (April 1986), pp. 262–322.

4. See John Freeman, "Banking on Democracy? International Finance and the Possibilities for Popular Sovereignty," mimeograph, University of Minnesota, 1990. From a politically different quarter, former Citibank chief executive officer Walter Wriston has said similar things about the impact of financial internationalization—but approvingly: "It's a new world and the concept of sovereignty is going to change. . . . The idea of fifteenth-century international law is gone. It hasn't laid down yet, but it's dead. It's like the three-mile limit in a world of Inter-Continental Ballistic Missiles." Wriston is cited in my *Banking on the World: The Politics of American International Finance* (New York: Harper & Row, 1987), p. 115. See also Walter Wriston, *Risk and Other Four-Letter Words* (New York: Harper & Row, 1986).

5. Bank for International Settlements (BIS), *Sixtieth Annual Report* (BIS: Basle, 1990), pp. 63, 82, and 125.

6. See Morris Goldstein, Donald Mathieson, and Timothy Lane, "Determinants and Systemic Consequences of International Capital Flows," in *Determinants and Systemic Consequences of International Capital Flows* (Washington, D.C.: International Monetary Fund, 1991), p. 5. This assumes a low level of international bond lending in 1973, which is almost certainly the case. Exact figures are not available.

7. See BIS, *Sixtieth Annual Report,* pp. 208–9. See also pp. 146–52, which offer data regarding some short-term instruments and indicate that open positions in interest rate futures and options totaled about $1.6 trillion at the end of 1989.

8. The early classic work was M. Feldstein and C. Horioka's "Domestic Savings and International Capital Flows," *Economic Journal* 90 (June 1989), pp. 314–29. For more on the issue and debates over it, see Ralph Bryant, *International Financial Intermediation* (Washington D.C.: Brookings Institution, 1987), pp. 82–86. For a recent test see Tamim Bayoumi "Saving-Investment Correlations: Immobile Capital, Government Policy, or Endogenous Behavior?" *IMF Staff Papers* 37 (June 1990), pp. 360–87.

9. The most careful assessment of the Feldstein-Horioka findings, updated through the late 1980s, emphasizes the great increase in capital mobility and the continued importance of currency premiums. See Jeffrey A. Frankel, "Quantifying International Capital Mobility in the 1980s," in Douglas Bernheim and John Shoven, eds., *National Saving and Economic Performance* (Chicago: University of Chicago Press, 1991), pp. 227–60.

10. For rough evidence on intranational and international stock price differentials, see Barry Eichengreen, "Is Europe an Optimum Currency Area?" mimeograph, University of California at Berkeley, 1990, pp. 69. The differentials may have to do with nontransferable advantages accruing to national owners, such as greater access to information or to monitoring and enforcement mechanisms.

11. The modern theory of foreign direct investment is based on the proposition that multinational firms exist precisely because they facilitate (but do not make costless) the international transmission of such specific assets. The classic statement by Caves is still probably the most appropriate here. See Richard E. Caves, "International Corporations: The Industrial Economics of Foreign Investment," *Economics* 38 (February 1971), pp. 1–27.

12. This is a conclusion made by Frankel in "Quantifying International Capital Mobility in the 1980s." One indication of the high degree to which markets for financial assets are integrated is the virtual disappearance of significant spreads between domestic and offshore interest rates in most currency instruments of members of the Organization for Economic Cooperation and Development (OECD). Regarding this subject, see Goldstein, Mathieson, and Lane, "Determinants and Systemic Consequences of International Capital Flows," pp. 7–11.

13. Although I am unaware of any studies of this phenomenon, arguments to this effect are frequently heard among American competitors of the Japanese transplants, often in the context of complaints over the Japanese firms' access to low-cost Japanese funds. There are reasons to doubt the accuracy of the argument, however. First, most foreign direct investment is funded in the host country. Second, if Japanese firms have privileged access to Japanese finance, then financial markets are not fully integrated. The result might be due to preferential ties among Japanese financial and nonfinancial firms, which would constitute a "natural" barrier to financial capital mobility. Further study in this regard is required. A related issue is the effect of foreign-owned branch plants on political lineups in the host country. For anecdotal evidence that Japanese investment in the United States has created or reinforced domestic interest groups that favor freer trade, see "Influx of Foreign Capital Mutes Debate on Trade," *The New York Times,* 8 February 1987, p. 113.

14. See the following works of Robert A. Mundell: "The Appropriate Use of Monetary and Fiscal Policy Under Fixed Exchange Rates," *IMF Staff Papers* 9 (March 1962), pp. 70–77; "Capital Mobility and Stabilization Policy Under Fixed and Flexible Exchange Rates," *Canadian Journal of Economics and Political Science* 29 (November 1963),

pp. 475–85; and "A Reply: Capital Mobility and Size," *Canadian Journal of Economics and Political Science* 30 (August 1964), pp. 421–31. The basic model can be found in any good textbook discussion of open-economy macroeconomics; a useful survey is W.M. Corden's *Inflation, Exchange Rates, and the World Economy,* 3rd ed. (Chicago: University of Chicago Press, 1986).

15. The argument presented here is in simplified form. Variation in monetary autonomy is actually along a continuum, not dichotomous: the choice is not starkly between full monetary independence and none at all; it is instead among different degrees of autonomy.

16. This ignores the potential contravening effects of the depreciation on national income; that is, it assumes that substitution effects dominate income effects or that expenditure switching dominates expenditure reduction.

17. The point is not that foreigners buy all the government bonds but, rather, that the increased domestic demand for credit is met by an increased supply of credit as capital flows in, with the result that the price of credit remains unchanged. This of course assumes that the deficit country is not large enough to affect world interest rates, which may not always be the case. It also assumes that the government does not engage in monetary policies that accommodate the fiscal expansion.

18. For a good survey and evaluation, see Michael M. Hutchison and Charles A. Pigott, "Real and Financial Linkages in the Macroeconomic Response to Budget Deficits: An Empirical Investigation," in Sven Arndt and J. David Richardson, eds., *Real Financial Linkages Among Open Economies* (Cambridge, Mass.: MIT Press, 1987), pp. 139–66.

19. More accurately, it does not affect the *covered* interest rate—that is, the interest rate minus (or plus) the market's expectation of currency movements. Obviously, if investors expect a currency to fall, they demand a higher interest rate for securities denominated in it, and vice versa. Covered interest parity appears to have held well from the mid-1970s onward among almost all major currencies.

20. For an illuminating discussion of cross-border effects, see Michael Mussa, "Macroeconomic Interdependence and the Exchange Rate Regime," in Rudiger Dornbusch and Jacob Frenkel, eds., *International Economic Policy: Theory and Evidence* (Baltimore, Md.: Johns Hopkins University Press, 1979), pp. 160–204.

21. American tax reform in 1986, for example, was followed by widespread OECD movement toward the new American corporate tax rates. By 1989, direct corporate tax rates in the principal EC member countries were all in the 35 to 42 percent range. See Price Waterhouse, *Tax: Strategic Corporate Tax Planning* (London: Mercury Books, 1989). Across industries, there is evidence that such footloose sectors as finance face lower effective tax rates. In the United States in 1983, for example, while twenty-four nonfinancial industries paid an average effective federal income tax rate of 17.5 percent, the three financial sectors (insurance, investment, and financial services companies) paid an average of 8.5 percent. See "New Threat to Smokestack America," *The New York Times,* 26 May 1985, p. 3:1.

22. Rogowski, *Commerce and Coalitions.*

23. The classic statement is Stephen Magee's "Three Simple Tests of the Stolper-Samuelson Theorem," in Peter Oppenheimer, ed., *Issues in International Economics* (London: Oriel, 1980), pp. 138–53. In *Commerce and Coalitions,* pp. 16–20, Rogowski addresses these objections and more; needless to say, I am unconvinced by his treatment. Benjamin J. Cohen has pointed out to me that this simple transfer of the Heckscher-Ohlin approach from trade to capital movements ignores the inherent differences between the two realms and especially the importance of expectations in determining asset prices (and therefore capital movements). This may be another reason to avoid a straightforward application of the approach to capital movements.

24. The seminal modern statement is Ronald W. Jones's "A Three-Factor Model in Theory, Trade, and History," in Jagdish Bhagwati et al., eds., *Trade, Balance of Payments, and Growth* (Amsterdam: North-Holland, 1971), pp. 3–21. Two other important articles, which essentially argue for combining specific factors in the short run with the Heckscher-Ohlin approach in the long run, are Wolfgang Mayer's "Short-Run and Long-Run Equilibrium for a Small Open Economy," *Journal of Political Economy* 82 (September 1974), pp. 955–68, and Michael Mussa's "Tariffs and the Distribution of Income: The Importance of Factor Specificity, Substitutability, and Intensity in the Short and Long Run," *Journal of Political Economy* 82 (November 1974), pp. 1191–1204. Based on these two articles, the approach is sometimes known as the Mayer-Mussa framework. For a useful summary and geometric representation of the short-term and long-term adjustment processes, along with a critique of the Heckscher-Ohlin assumption of intersectoral capital mobility, see J. Peter Neary, "Short-Run Capital Specificity and the Pure Theory of International Trade," *The Economic Journal* 88 (September 1978), pp. 488–510.

25. In a slight variation on the usual specific-factors or Ricardo-Viner model, the one presented here implies that there are both mobile and specific forms of both labor and capital. The effect of relative price movements and changes in endowments thus depends in part on the potential substitutability of the forms of factors or the factors themselves— for example, substitutability of mobile for specific labor or of mobile labor for mobile capital. For our purposes, it is sufficient to stop with the simpler version. Adding complexity to the model does not fundamentally change the analytic points; it only changes the details of their empirical application.

26. I refer here to those Marxist (and non-Marxist) views that assume labor-capital contradictions to be the principal axis of political conflict. Many other Marxists focus on intraclass differences or blocs; for a good example of relevance to the issue at hand, see Stephen R. Gill and David Law, "Global Hegemony and the Structural Power of Capital," *International Studies Quarterly* 33 (December 1989), pp. 475–99.

27. The point is not that portfolio diversification is the same as asset mobility but, rather, that the policy implications are parallel. A more sophisticated but somewhat more controversial version of this argument might focus on multinational corporations as combinations of intangible assets within a vertically integrated firm; the relevant literature is surveyed by Martin Perry in "Vertical Integration: Determinants and Effects," in R. Schmalensee and R. D. Willig, eds., *Handbook of Industrial Organization*, vol. I (Amsterdam: North-Holland, 1989), pp. 183–255. Inasmuch as such assets can more easily be moved within multinational corporations, this does in fact make the assets of these corporations more geographically mobile than those of other firms in similar industries. See, for example, Daniel M. Shapiro, "Entry, Exit, and the Theory of the Multinational Corporation," in Charles P. Kindleberger and David B. Audretsch, eds., *The Multinational Corporation in the 1980s* (Cambridge, Mass.: MIT Press, 1983), pp. 103–22.

28. For an application of similar ideas to the cases of U.S. and French trade policies in the 1920s and the 1970s, see Milner, *Resisting Protectionism.*

29. It is worth emphasizing again that these conclusions abstract from many specifics that may indeed override them. For example, in the early 1980s, financial asset-holders in many Latin American countries benefited strongly from capital mobility. In the context of political instability and strong and unsustainable currency appreciations, they were able to get their money out of Latin America and to overseas bank accounts. On the process, see Donald Lessard and John Williamson, eds., *Capital Flight and Third World Debt* (Washington, D.C.: Institute for International Economics, 1987). Clearly, other characteristics of these political economies outweighed the tendencies discussed here.

30. For a more detailed argument to this effect, see Jeffry A. Frieden, "Third World Indebted Industrialization: State Capitalism and International Finance in Mexico, Brazil,

Algeria, and South Korea," *International Organization* 35 (Summer 1981), pp. 407–31. The degree to which workers and others benefited from the capital inflow would depend, in this framework, on how specific their assets were.

31. For an elaboration of this argument, see Frieden, *Banking on the World,* especially pp. 196–246.

32. Much of this discussion abstracts to an extent from the effects of specific policy episodes, such as those involving the United States in the 1980s. I return to this problem in the following section of the article. My discussion here also does not take into account such significant national variations as different rates of productivity growth on the part of domestically based firms.

33. This must be qualified on the basis of the institutional and industrial structure of the various sectors. For example, in cases in which the domestic financial services industry or subsections of it are local cartels, financial integration may serve to undermine the cartel. Such nuances are of course important, but so broad a sweep as in this article cannot do them justice.

34. See David Dollar and Jeffry Frieden, "The Political Economy of Financial Deregulation in the United States and Japan," in Giacomo Luciani, ed., *Structural Change in the American Financial System* (Rome: Fondazione Olivetti, 1990), pp. 72–102. Again, this generalization ignores specific national policy episodes, such as that involving American capital imports in the 1980s. In my own defense, however, I can note that those involved in political debates over the regulation of international financial flows to and from the United States do appear to have longer-term considerations in mind.

35. For details on the 1983 IMF quota increase debate, see Frieden, *Banking on the World,* pp. 179–90.

36. Again, as mentioned above, this should be qualified with careful attention to national institutional differences. In such countries as Spain and Italy, the national banking system tended to function as a protected cartel, so that the removal of capital controls and financial regulations may have harmed segments of the financial community. The issue is not clear-cut; banks might support the removal of capital controls but oppose the entry of foreign banks, and the stronger local banks might welcome deregulation if this would allow them to begin building relations with banks abroad. This is, of course, a topic on which further research must be done.

37. See Benjamin J. Cohen, "European Financial Integration and National Banking Interests," in Pier Carlo Padoan and Paolo Guerrieri, eds., *The Political Economy of European Integration* (London: Harvester Wheatsheaf, 1989), pp. 145–70. For an interesting perspective on the implications of financial deregulation, see the following works of Vittorio Grilli: "Financial Markets and 1992," Brookings Papers on Economic Activity, no. 2, 1989, pp. 301–24; and "Europe 1992: Issues and Prospects for the Financial Markets," *Economic Policy* 9 (October 1989), pp. 388–421. Regarding the important issue of the U.S. response to European and Japanese policies, see Thomas Bayard and Kimberly Ann Elliot, "Reciprocity in Financial Services: The Schumer Amendment and the Second Banking Directive," mimeograph, 1990.

38. Two excellent studies are Louis W. Pauly's *Opening Financial Markets: Banking Politics on the Pacific Rim* (Ithaca, N.Y.: Cornell University Press, 1988) and Frances McCall Rosenbluth's *Financial Politics in Contemporary Japan* (Ithaca, N.Y.: Cornell University Press, 1989). In Japan, as in some European nations, members of the banking community were reluctant to see international competition threaten their domestic cartel, but the rapid globalization of financial markets appears to have led them to regard deregulation as the better of two evils. For a more detailed elaboration of this argument, see Dollar and Frieden, "The Political Economy of Financial Deregulation in the United States and Japan." For an argument that is complementary in many ways to the one

presented here, see John Goodman and Louis Pauly, "The New Politics of International Capital Mobility," mimeograph, Harvard University Business School and University of Toronto, 1990.

39. There are a number of ways of thinking about this. In one, the result obtains because difficulty of exit from a sector constitutes a barrier to entry to it: the knowledge that investment in the sector contains an important irreversible component will reduce the likelihood of new investors entering in response to relative price changes that may not be permanent. In this sense, barriers to exit are barriers to entry; since entry barriers increase the effectiveness of sector-specific policies in aiding existing agents in the sector, they increase the returns to political lobbying.

40. Possibilities such as these tend to imply imperfect competition—increasing returns and learning-by-doing—in the financial sector, which is almost certainly the case. For a representative theoretical approach along these lines, see Stephen D. Williamson, "Increasing Returns to Scale in Financial Intermediation and the Non-Neutrality of Government Policy," *Review of Economic Studies* 53 (October 1986), pp. 863–75.

41. This is just a restatement of the general notion that the capital markets and political lobbying are in some sense substitutes (albeit imperfect ones). This idea sounds absurd to most political scientists, but perform the following thought experiment: if import-competing automobile manufacturers could sell all of their equipment to the Japanese at a price that would allow them to make a market profit, their incentive to engage in costly and time-consuming lobbying for protection would be much lower. Or, alternatively, if autoworkers could in some way sell their skills and their seniority to Japanese autoworkers for an amount equal to what they might have hoped to earn with these skills and seniority, their incentive to lobby would be lower. The fact that markets for these assets are incomplete or nonexistent simply serves to point out that the politicization of the issue is expected. While there are not markets for these assets, there are good markets for other assets—and we expect owners of such assets to be less politically active.

42. Some complications may result from this melding of the Mundell-Fleming and specific-factors models. The Mundell-Fleming model generally assumes some unutilized resources and some wage stickiness, while the specific-factors model does not. The contradiction may be relevant for the analysis of effects on national welfare, but it does not appear to matter much for the short- and medium-term distributional effects, which are the focus here. For a discussion, see Corden, *Inflation, Exchange Rates, and the World Economy*, pp. 22–34.

43. There are exceptions: producers of tradable goods in which competition is not primarily on price (and is instead, for example, on quality) will be less sensitive to exchange rate movements.

44. Inasmuch as a devaluation changes the price of tradable goods relative to that of nontradable goods, it affects producers in the nontradables sector. However, such price volatility affects all national nontradables producers more or less equally and is therefore far less significant to them than it is to tradables producers, who see their output change in price relative to that of their competitors.

45. For those unfamiliar with the approach, the real exchange rate can be expressed as the relationship between the price of nontradable goods and that of tradable goods. By assumption, the price of tradables is set on world markets and cannot be changed (in foreign currency terms) by national policy. In other words, the foreign currency price of tradables is an anchor around which domestic prices move. Depreciation makes tradables relatively more expensive in domestic currency terms, while nontradables become relatively cheaper. Appreciation has the opposite effects. In the real world, these effects can be offset, for example by characteristics of product markets, but there is little doubt that the general pattern holds. When the dollar was strong, the dollar prices of television sets

and clothing were low. while the price of housing soared. As the dollar fell, the dollar price of hard goods rose, while the price of housing stagnated or declined. Despite some controversy about the approach, it is close enough to consensual to warrant its use.

One important consideration to keep in mind is the extent to which the relative price effect (say of an appreciation on raising demand for nontradable goods) may be counteracted by the macroeconomic effect (say of reduced aggregate demand more generally): this is, so to speak, the contest between the income and substitution effects or between expenditure reduction and expenditure switching. For a useful survey and application to the LDCs, see Sebastian Edwards, *Real Exchange Rates, Devaluation and Adjustment* (Cambridge, Mass.: MIT Press, 1989). For more technical essays, see John Bilson and Richard Marston, eds., *Exchange Rate Theory and Practice* (Chicago: University of Chicago Press, 1984). Another point to keep in mind is that the nontradable goods and services sector includes those who operate behind prohibitive barriers to trade (especially quotas).

46. Of course, from the standpoint of an overseas investor, the desire for a strong home currency to allow greater purchases of overseas assets is balanced by the desire to maximize home currency earnings from these assets, which demands a weak home currency. The best possible scenario, as usual, is to buy cheap and sell dear—that is, to buy foreign currency when the home currency is strong and sell it when the home currency is weak. There are a number of defensible theoretical reasons why international investors might favor strong home currencies; it is probably enough to note here that empirically they tend to do so. On the relationship between foreign direct investment and the exchange rate, see Steven W. Kohlhagen, "Exchange Rate Changes, Profitability, and Direct Foreign Investment," *Southern Economic Journal* 44 (July 1977), pp. 43–52.

47. Practically the only systematic empirical study on these issues in recent years is I. M. Destler and C. Randall Henning's *Dollar Politics: Exchange Rate Policymaking in the United States* (Washington, D.C.: Institute for International Economics, 1989), which appears to bear out some of these observations. The issue is somewhat clouded by the difficulty, which Destler and Henning recognize, of separating debates over the level of the exchange rate from debates over its volatility; in the early 1980s in the United States, the former tended to dominate the latter. The authors note that international financial institutions benefit from exchange market volatility, which can make their trading desks extremely profitable. However, they should—and many do—weigh this benefit against the cost of international business foregone because of uncertainty about currency values. At least some portion of the international business of American money-center banks is due to the widespread belief in the reliability of the dollar and the American macroeconomic environment more generally.

48. The literature on the EMS is now enormous, and almost all of it is purely economic in content. For an excellent survey along these lines, see Francesco Giavazzi and Alberto Giovannini, *Limiting Exchange Rate Flexibility: The European Monetary System* (Cambridge, Mass.: MIT Press, 1989). For a good study that discusses many of the domestic and international political aspects of the EMS, see Peter Ludlow, *The Making of the European Monetary System* (London: Butterworth, 1982); unfortunately, events have moved far beyond what Ludlow described in 1982.

49. I avoid three issues that are more closely associated with a single currency per se: the potential welfare costs of reduced seignorage opportunities, the welfare gains associated with reduced transactions costs, and the potentially differential impact of these reduced transactions costs on various economic agents. I focus entirely on the more immediate issue of the differential effects of fixed but adjustable exchange rates within the EMS. For a discussion of some of these other issues, see Barry Eichengreen, "One Money for Europe?" *Economic Policy* 5 (April 1990), pp. 118–87.

50. See S.G. Warburg Securities, *Into the ERM: The Outlook for the UK Economy and Equity Market,* London, August 1990. A summary table is on p. 31, but more useful sectoral summaries are on pp. 32–52. The projections are complicated a bit (for our purposes) by the study's conflation of greater exchange rate stability with a firmer pound sterling, both of which it expects to ensue but which may operate in slightly different directions distributionally, as I discuss below. The study also notes that while 45 percent of profits from firms in the Financial Times stock exchange index are from overseas activities (exports and profits of foreign affiliates), only 13 percent come from the EC and 17 percent from North America. This may help explain some of the British reluctance to tie sterling to the ERM, especially at a time when the European currencies were appreciating strongly against the dollar.

51. The twelve corporate members are Barclays, British Aerospace, British American Tobacco, British Petroleum, Citibank, Ernst and Young, Goldman Sachs, Imperial Chemical Industries, Midland Montagu, Salomon International, Shearson Brothers, and S.G. Warburg. The Association of Corporate Treasurers is also a member.

52. For an evaluation of many of these developments, see Jeffrey Frankel, "The Making of Exchange Rate Policy in the 1980s," mimeograph, University of California at Berkeley, 1990. Again, the political economy component of Frankel's discussion focuses, as did most of the debates, on the level of the exchange rate rather than on its volatility.

53. In *Dollar Politics,* pp. 17–80, Destler and Henning provide an excellent interpretive survey of the course of dollar politics and policies over the 1980s.

54. For descriptions of the interplay of the various interest groups, see Destler and Henning, *Dollar Politics;* Frankel, "The Making of Exchange Rate Policy in the 1980s"; and C. Randall Henning, "International Monetary Policymaking Within the Countries of the Group of Five," mimeograph, 1990.

55. One influential and controversial proposal was offered by John Williamson and Marcus Miller in *Targets and Indicators: A Blueprint for the International Coordination of Economic Policy* (Washington, D.C.: Institute for International Economics, 1987).

56. For some representative surveys of this rapidly growing literature, see Martin Feldstein, ed., *International Policy Coordination* (Chicago: University of Chicago Press, 1988); and Jeffrey Frankel, *Obstacles to International Macroeconomic Policy Coordination,* Princeton Studies in International Finance no. 64 (Princeton, N.J.: Department of Economics, International Finance Section, 1988).

57. For a demonstration of this point, see Jeffrey Frankel and Katharine Rockett, "International Macroeconomic Policy Coordination When Policy-Makers Do Not Agree on the True Model," *American Economic Review* 78 (June 1988), pp. 318–40. The argument is controversial; among other things, it assumes that policymakers try to maximize national welfare, ignores the potential costs of not cooperating (or not appearing to cooperate), and makes it difficult to explain circumstances in which coordination has apparently been achieved.

58. See, for example Alberto Giovannini, "National Tax Systems Versus the European Capital Market," *Economic Policy* 9 (October 1989), pp. 346–86.

4.3. The Expansion of the Public Economy: A Comparative Analysis

DAVID R. CAMERON

A host of competing explanations for government growth have grown up in the last thirty years. In this article David Cameron summarizes much of the previous literature and then attempts to test five different types of explanation. Economic explanations, such as Adolph Wagner's, hold that economic growth is an important determinant of government growth. Fiscal explanations hold that government growth depends on the degree to which the tax burden is visible to the voter. Political explanations hold that the degree of electoral competition, and/or the parties that hold power, are key determinants. Institutional explanations argue that bureaucratic empire-building or fiscal decentralization can increase spending. International explanations hold that the openness of the domestic economy to international competition is of central importance.

Having outlined the explanations, Cameron runs some simple statistical tests using cross-national data in order to see which type of explanation is most useful. In general, he finds that the international explanation is best supported by his data, that there is some evidence for political factors having some effect, and that there is very little evidence to support the other possible explanations.

Cameron's critics have generally focused on whether he fully controls for other important variables and whether the particular period he examined is typical. The reader should also note that Cameron leaves many important theories untested. Nonetheless, this is a useful and provocative essay.

Reprinted with permission of the author and *The American Political Science Review* 72 (December 1978), pp. 1243–61. Copyright © 1978 by the American Political Science Association.

During the three decades following World War II, the role of government in most advanced capitalist economies increased dramatically. With the maturation of the "welfare state," governments increased their provision of social services and income transfers for the unemployed, the sick, the elderly, and the poor. Furthermore, governments have become important producers of goods, and in several European nations publicly owned corporations dominate the petroleum, automotive, and transportation industries. In addition, by using a variety of fiscal and monetary instruments such as public spending programs, taxes, and discount rates, governments have attempted to manipulate the levels of unemployment and inflation and dampen the effects of business cycles. They have also sought to guide the long-term development of the economy through the creation of planning institutions and, occasionally, through their control of the assets of financial institutions. And in order to finance their activities in each of these domains, governments have instituted new taxes and raised the levels of old taxes. Indeed, the growth of the extractive role of public authorities has been so great that Schumpeter's words, written half a century ago and pertaining to the historical development of Europe, seem even more appropriate today: "Tax bill in hand, the state penetrated the private economies and won increasing dominion over them" (1918, p. 19).

This article explores the causes of the expansion of the extractive role of government during the recent past in 18 relatively developed capitalist nations. The first section presents several alternative explanations of that expansion. Following the argument developed, rather imprecisely, by Wagner (1883) in the late nineteenth century, most economists have concentrated on the impact of economic growth in accounting for the inexorable increase in government activity. In addition to outlining the Wagnerian argument, I will discuss several alternative causes of the expansion of public revenues. In particular, the analysis examines the impact on taxation of two aspects of the policy-making environment whose effects have been frequently disputed or neglected in many comparative studies of public policy: (1) the electoral politics of a nation—for example, the existence of electoral competition and the partisan composition of government; and (2) the institutional structure of government—for example, the existence of unitary or federal government, and the extent of fiscal centralization. The analysis also considers the extent to which the scope of government activity within a nation is influenced by the position of the domestic economy vis-à-vis the world economy. In this regard, the analysis investigates whether the openness, or exposure, of a nation's economy to the international marketplace stimulates an expansion in the role of government.

The several explanations of the expansion of the public economy[1] will be evaluated by analyzing the experience of 18 nations since 1960. All 18 have capitalist economies; this criterion allows the inclusion of nations for which the expansion of the public economy might represent a source of tension and conflict with the traditional reliance on, and legitimation of, the market economy for the allocation of goods. The nations are: the United States, Canada, Britain, Ireland, Australia, Japan, the Federal Republic of Germany, France, Italy, Spain, the Netherlands, Austria, Belgium, Switzerland, Sweden, Norway, Denmark, and Finland.

Measuring the Scope of the Public Economy

The scope of activity of public authorities can be described by enumerating the programs and types of expenditures carried out by government (King, 1973). However, in the contemporary era in the nations considered here, the increase in the level of expenditure and the multiple uses of funds have been accompanied by an expansion of the revenue-generating capacity of government. Although imbalances occasionally occur between the aggregate totals of all government revenues and expenditures, the two have usually moved in tandem. Thus, the scope of the public economy can be compared as well by considering the revenues of governments rather than their expenditures—that is, by considering the extractive aspect of government.[2] The public economy is defined in terms of the total of all revenues obtained by all levels of government in a nation. Included are all direct taxes, e.g., those on personal and corporate incomes and property; all indirect taxes, e.g., those on sales and value added; all social insurance contributions by employers and employees; and all other fees, taxes, rents, and withdrawals from enterprises which flow into governmental treasuries. To convey the relative importance of the funds which are appropriated (and subsequently distributed) by public authorities, and to control for the obvious differences among nations in the size of the economy, I have calculated the ratio of all governmental revenues to Gross Domestic Product (GDP). This ratio, calculated for all years between 1960 and 1975 (the latest for which data are available), is treated as a measure of the scope of the public economy.[3] In order to measure and compare across nations the degree of expansion in the scope of the public economy, I have calculated the first-order difference in this ratio for the earliest and latest years.[4]

There has been significant variation in both the level and rate of change in the scope of the public economy among these 18 nations. In 1960, for example, the scope of the public economy, which averaged 28.5 percent of GDP, varied from 18 percent in Spain to 35.4 in Germany. By 1975, the average scope of the public economy increased to 38.5 percent of GDP and the variation among the nations also increased, ranging from 23.5 percent in Japan to 53.5 percent in the Netherlands. Thus, while there was a general trend of expansion of the public economy at work in all the nations, there were also great differences among them in the rate of expansion. Why that rate of expansion varied as much as it did is the question to which we now turn.

Five Explanations of the Expansion
of the Public Economy

Several distinct explanations of why the scope of the public economy changes over time can be identified. This section elaborates five types of explanation— one economic, the second fiscal, the third political, the fourth institutional, and the fifth international in character—and derives predictions to account for the considerable differences in the rate of expansion of the public economy in the 18 nations.

The Economic Explanation

The most frequently mentioned explanation of the increase in the scope of the public economy is that derived from Wagner's "law of expanding state activity" (1883, pp. 1–8). The "law" holds that, among European nations, the "pressure for social progress" leads inevitably to the growth of the public sector. Writing in the midst of a period of rapid urbanization and industrialization, and just as Bismarck was developing the first programs of the welfare state, Wagner recognized the growing role of the state as a provider of social overhead investments in such areas as transportation and education and the need, even in an authoritarian state, for the state to retain legitimacy by providing public funds to compensate for the human costs of economic development.

As elaborated by numerous scholars of public finance,[5] Wagner's "law" suggests that citizens' demands for services and willingness to pay taxes are income-elastic, and therefore bound to increase with the increase in economic affluence. If this "law" is correct, one would expect that, in comparing the experiences of a number of nations, the greater the increment in economic affluence of a nation during a given period, the greater the expansion of the public economy.

Several scholars have rejected the logic and evidence in support of Wagner's "law." Bird (1971, p. 19), Musgrave (1969, pp. 112–13), and Gupta (1968) find that any positive cross-national relationship between economic growth and government share in the economic product disappears when analysis is confined to the wealthier nations of the world. Apparently there exists an upper threshold to the scope of public economy; beyond certain levels of income, international demonstration effects and internally derived perceptions of marginal benefit are less likely to generate increases in spending. Peacock and Wiseman (1967) also reject the "historical determinism" implicit in Wagner's "law" and in their discussion of the "displacement effect" emphasize the importance of crises such as war and depression in inducing infrequent but large changes in the tolerable burden of taxation. This provides little assistance in explaining a secular upward trend during periods of prosperity and peace (both of which existed in most of the 18 nations during most of the period between 1960 and 1975). However, the Peacock and Wiseman argument, taken with the findings of Bird, Musgrave, and Gupta, might lead one to expect a negligible relationship between economic growth and state expansion.

Wildavsky (1975, pp. 232–35) provides a third perspective on the economic sources of public sector expansion. In what might be termed a "counter-Wagner" law, Wildavsky suggests that the degree of expansion in the scope of the public economy varies inversely, rather than directly, with economic growth. Where national affluence increases very rapidly, as in Japan, any increased demand for public funds can be met by the added revenues obtained by applying a constant public share to a larger economic product. But where economic growth is so modest that it generates insufficient revenues to meet demands for additional public goods, as in Britain, those demands must be met through an expansion of the public share of the economic product. In short, Wildavsky's argument would predict that the relationship between growth and public sector expansion would be negative, indicating the greatest expansion of the public economy in low-growth nations.[6]

The Fiscal Explanation

The second type of explanation of public sector growth is fiscal in nature. As elaborated by Downs (1960) and Buchanan and Wagner (1977), this perspective emphasizes the structure of the system of revenue generation as a determinant of how much revenue can be raised. Downs argues that because public goods are inherently nondivisible, costs and benefits are not directly linked. Benefits frequently are uncertain (as in preventive or long-term policies). In addition, public goods are, when taken as a whole, inevitably suboptimal, since each citizen will pay for some programs that provide no individual benefit. As a result, the costs, i.e., taxes, are perceived to exceed the benefits of public goods. Therefore, it is only when public officials can conceal the costs of policies in a "fiscal illusion" that they can spend large amounts without incurring the wrath of the electorate. As Buchanan and Wagner (1977) argue, "complex and indirect payment structures create a fiscal illusion that will systematically produce higher levels of public outlay than those that would be observed under simple payments structures" (p. 129).

The major form of tax concealment, according to Downs (1960, p. 558), Wildavsky (1975, pp. 235–39), and Wilensky (1975, p. 52), is indirect taxation. In addition to taxes on value added or sales, relatively invisible forms of revenue generation might include taxes which are paid before individuals receive income, e.g., social insurance contributions by employees, and taxes which can be passed on to third parties, e.g., the social insurance contributions of employers. Applying this "fiscal illusion" argument to the present analysis, one might expect that the nations with the largest increase in the scope of the public economy would be ones in which there is a large and increasing reliance on indirect taxes and social insurance contributions.[7]

The Political Explanation

A third type of explanation of the expansion of the public economy involves politics. The impact of politics on the scope of the public sector has seldom been recognized, in spite of Downs' assertion (1960, p. 541) that "in a democratic society, the division of resources between the public and private sector is roughly determined by the desires of the electorate." Recently, however, studies by Kramer (1971), Nordhaus (1975), Tufte (1975, 1978), and Hibbs (1978) have suggested that politics—especially electoral politics—exerts a significant influence on the public economy. Two aspects of politics may influence the magnitude of expansion of the public economy: (1) the effect of electoral competition in "bidding up" the scope of expenditure programs; and (2) the effect of variations in the partisan composition, and presumably the ideological preferences, of government.

In his revision of the classical doctrine of democracy, Schumpeter (1950, p. 269) defined democracy in terms of electoral competition: "the democratic method is that institutional arrangement for arriving at political decisions in which individuals acquire the power to decide by means of a competitive struggle for the people's vote." As elaborated by Downs (1957), this theory of democracy implies that the contenders for political office alter their programs in order to enhance their electoral appeal. An important weapon in this competitive struggle is the public economy: some political contenders will attempt to garner votes by promising cuts in taxes; others will promise increases in spending; and others will promise both (see Downs, 1960; Buchanan and Wagner, 1977).

Ever since Key (1949) noted the propensity of political opponents to appeal to the "have-not" voters by promising more spending, scholars have been virtually unanimous in attributing to electoral competition an expansionist impulse (see Brittan, 1975, pp. 139–40). Empirical studies of the American electorate by Kramer (1971) and Tufte (1975) have demonstrated that voters have tended to provide short-term electoral rewards to incumbents who can effect, through their tax, fiscal, and monetary policies, increases in real personal income. And as Tufte (1978, Ch. 2) demonstrates, because incumbents are aware of this relationship, most adopt policies in anticipation of elections which stimulate the economy and increase personal income by pumping funds into the economy. As a result, periodic electoral competition frequently produces a long-term cyclical effect on the economy. The most important consequence, for our concerns here, is that this "political business cycle" is marked by increased spending and other reflationary policies in the period immediately before and after an election (Nordhaus, 1975; Lindbeck, 1976).

The existence of a "political business cycle," the likelihood that incumbents will attempt to use spending policies to enhance their support in anticipation of elections, as well as the tendency of opposition parties to build electoral support by promising more spending on particular government policies, all tend to suggest that public spending increases at an unusually rapid rate immediately before elections (and immediately afterward, if the opposition takes control of government). One application of this argument to the cross-national perspective is to consider the impact of variations among nations in the frequency of national elections. Since the measure of the scope of the public economy relies on revenues (i.e., taxes) rather than expenditures, frequent electoral competition might be expected to dampen the growth of the public economy. However, because revenues and expenditures moved in tandem in most, if not all, of the nations during the period under consideration, the effects of electoral competition on public spending tended to be reflected in tax increases (often in the post-election period). Therefore, one might expect that nations with frequent elections during 1960–75 experienced larger increases in the public economy than nations without frequent elections, since there were more opportunities for government and opposition elites to indulge in "competitive bidding."[8]

One of the most contested issues in political science is whether or not partisanship influences public policy, and if so, how. Many scholars conclude that parties do not differ significantly in their positions on major issues. Proponents of the "decline of ideology" thesis argue, for example, that parties—particularly those on the left—have forsaken traditional ideologies in order to assemble larger electorates.[9] Even if parties resist the temptation of assembling socially and ideologically heterogeneous electorates and retain some measure of ideological distinctiveness, they may be unable to implement their preferences when in office. The complexities of the internal processes of revenue and spending decisions (Klein, 1976), the vagueness of campaign proposals and the frequent lack of experience, and turnover, of ministers (Gordon, 1971), the importance of policy professionals in the civil service (Heclo, 1974, p. 301), the impulse of incrementalism and the tendency to follow established routines (Wildavsky, 1974), as well as the occasional movement by governments in directions not consistent with their traditional ideologies (King, 1969, p. 136) all do much to circumscribe the impact of party. Largely for these reasons, King concludes that the policy role of parties is "sharply restricted. . . . While organized party generally remains one of the forces . . . in the formation of public policy . . . it has never been the only one, and there is reason to suppose that in many countries in the late 1960s it is not even a major one" (pp. 136–37).

In spite of the support which can be mustered for the skeptical view of the importance of parties in the policy process, some evidence suggests that parties may be relevant in defining the scope of the public economy. For example, Hibbs (1978) contends that strike activity decreased in European nations where Social Democratic and Labor parties increased their representation in cabinets in the 1930s and 1940s. This decrease occurred, says Hibbs (p. 165), because of the propensity of leftist parties to provide funding for new and expanded welfare programs. This caused a much larger portion of the national income to flow through the public sector, thereby shifting the focus of the distributional struggle from the private sector, where labor and capital compete through industrial conflict, to the public sector, where these economic actors compete through electoral mobilization and political bargaining with each other and with government.[10]

The budgetary studies of Davis, Dempster, and Wildavsky (1966, 1974) provide additional evidence that the partisanship of government may influence public policy. In their first study, the authors found "shift points" in the incremental drift of spending which coincided with changes in the control of the White House. Wildavsky's analysis (1975, p. 371) of British budgets during 1964–74 found that the direction of the trend line of public spending shifted when the Conservatives replaced the Labour party in government in 1970.[11] Also, Davis, Dempster, and Wildavsky (1974) found that the magnitude of the increments granted to American federal agencies was influenced by such partisan variables as the strength of the liberal wing of the Democrats in Congress and Democratic control of the presidency. The Hibbs and Wildavsky studies suggest that as the partisan composition of government varies over time, within a nation, and among nations, so too the priorities and substance of policy vary, including the definition by governments of the "proper" scope of the public economy. One might expect, therefore, that the considerable variation among nations in the rate of expansion of the public economy reflects differences in the frequency of control of national governments over a period of years by parties which, in general, favor that expansion. Following Downs (1957, p. 116), who viewed leftist parties as more favorable than others to the extension of governmental intervention in the economy, one might expect that the rate of expansion of the public economy was positively associated with the extent to which governments relied for their support on leftist parties during 1960–75.[12]

The Institutional Explanation

A fourth type of explanation of the expansion of the public economy involves the institutional structure of government. Two aspects of that structure are considered here: (1) the formal relationship among levels of government within a nation—in particular, the existence of multiple, independent centers of public authority; and (2) the degree of fiscal centralization. Downs (1964), Niskanen (1971), Wildavsky (1974), and Tarschys (1975) argue that government bureaucracies develop internal pressures for self-aggrandizement and expansion. If that is true, then a multiplicity of autonomous governmental bureaucracies would enhance this tendency. Thus, in nations where no single authority controls the bulk of public spending—where, in other words, spending authority is fragmented—and where the institutional structure guarantees that some units and levels spend funds that were raised by other units or levels (Tarschys, 1975, p.

25), the rate of increase in spending should be unusually high. The institutional arrangement of government which most closely approximates this situation is federalism: that arrangement provides considerable autonomy for subnational and local governments, fragments the control of public spending, allows some levels or units the luxury of spending funds which have been raised by other levels or units, and multiplies the number of self-aggrandizing bureaucracies. Therefore, one might expect that the nations with a federal structure of government experienced larger increases in the scope of the public economy than those with a unitary structure.

A second aspect of the institutional structure of government that may influence the expansion of the public economy is the degree of fiscal centralization. Centralization, defined here as the proportion of all governments' revenues generated by the central government, reflects, to some extent, the formal institutional structure of government; nations with unitary government tend to be more centralized than federal nations. Nevertheless, the degree of centralization varies widely among both the federal and the nonfederal nations considered here, and it is plausible to think that it exerts an impact on the scope of the public economy that is independent of the formal structure of government.[13]

Several studies conclude that government spending tends to increase most rapidly at subnational and local levels of government. Wagner (1883, p. 8) was perhaps the first to note that local authorities' requirements for funds were most likely to expand when administration was decentralized. Recent studies of the United States (Freeman, 1975, p. 208), Britain (Bacon and Eltis, 1976), and Sweden (Tarschys, 1975, p. 25) have found that increases in public spending were greater at the subnational and local, rather than at the national, levels of government. Heidenheimer (1975, p. 28) suggests a reason for these findings in his comparison of the difference in spending for health care in Britain and Sweden: "The monopolistic control of the national Treasury and the Health Ministry over financing sources enabled Britain, much better than Sweden [where health financing is decentralized and the responsibility of the counties], to hold down the proportion of national income allocated to the health sector." In other words, the ability of central government decision makers to oversee spending and, presumably, their awareness of the cost-benefit tradeoffs among policy sectors serve to limit aggregate spending. These studies support a contention that, for the same reasons mentioned in regard to the impact of federalism, relatively decentralized nations experienced larger increases in the scope of the public economy than did highly centralized nations.

The International Explanation

The four alternative explanations of the expansion of the public economy presented thus far share a common element. The rate of economic growth, the degree of "invisibility" in the revenue-generating mechanism of the state, electoral politics, and the institutional structure of government all involve internal aspects of nations. However, nations are not wholly autonomous and entirely independent of the external world. In fact, certain nations are highly dependent on their external environments as markets for export goods or sources of capital.[14] To the extent that there is a high degree of substitution of foreign and domestic goods, with domestic prices of commodities, labor, and capital established by supply and demand in the international rather than the domestic market, these economies are "open" (see Lindbeck, 1976, p. 2). They are, in other words, exposed to pressures on markets and prices which are transmitted from other nations via international exchange.

The concept of the open economy is applicable, in varying degrees, to almost all of the advanced capitalist societies considered here, but it is especially relevant for the smaller nations. As Dahl and Tufte (1973) note, trade dependence— one aspect of openness—is strongly, and inversely, related to the size of a nation:

> By free trade, small political systems can achieve the same economies of scale as large systems. . . . [Thus] a partial solution to the problem for small systems [is] to engage in foreign trade. . . . In general, the smaller a political system the higher the proportion of foreign trade to total trade. . . . Few relationships with size hold up more uniformly than this one (p. 115).

In several of the smaller nations considered here, such as Belgium and the Netherlands, the value of imports and exports is almost as large as the Gross Domestic Product. In fact, the value of trade exceeded 50 percent of GDP in 12 of the 18 nations in 1975.[15] Even in the larger nations, such as the United States and Japan, however, the economies are not impervious to the international economy. Like the smaller nations, they depend on external producers for important commodities such as oil and other raw materials, and they depend on external consumers to provide the markets for export goods.

The most important political consequence of an "open" economy is the constraint it imposes on the effectiveness of a variety of macroeconomic policies (see Krasner, 1976, p. 319). To quote Dahl and Tufte again (1973, pp. 116, 130):

> economies of scale tend to erode the independence and autonomy of the smaller democracy, making it dependent—officially or not—on the actions of people outside the country. . . . In order to develop and maintain a relatively high standard of living, the small country must go beyond its own boundaries in search of markets, and often in search of raw materials, labor, and capital investment as well. As a consequence, the small country is highly dependent on the behavior of foreign actors not subject to its authority.

Lindbeck (1975, 1977) and Aukrust (1977) have noted the several ways in which the trade dependence of the Scandinavian economies has limited the ability of national officials to manage aggregate demand and control inflation. Aggregate demand in small, open economies is, in part, a function of the demand in the world market for domestically produced export goods; thus, unemployment, which is a function of demand relative to operating capacity in the economy, is somewhat uncontrollable. And since price levels in export industries are set in the world market, they may not move in accordance with changes in domestic costs, causing either low profitability (if external demand, and prices, do not increase with increases in domestic costs) or high profitability (if external demand, and prices, increase more than domestic costs). Whether export profits are small or large, they may destabilize the economy: a lack of profits in the export sector may cause a reduction in the funds available for capital investment and, ultimately, a reduction in the rate of growth; a high level of export profits may, on the other hand, contribute to inflation, since they may be used to justify higher wages in the export industries and these wage increases may, in turn, be generalized to the nonexport sector through centralized collective bargaining.[16]

Just as a high degree of dependence on the international economy for markets for export industries may limit a government's ability to manage aggregate demand and control levels of unemployment and capital formation, a high degree of penetration of the domestic market by external producers also limits the control by the national government over the economy. High levels of imports tend to remove decisions regarding the production, and pricing, of goods for domestic consumption to external actors. In addition, import penetration may transmit inflationary pressures from the rest of the world—particularly if the domestic demand for particular commodities is relatively inelastic with regard to price, as, for example, oil (see Aukrust, 1977; Lindbeck, 1975). Furthermore, high levels of imports may contribute to balance of payments deficits, the solution of which usually requires the funding of deficits with foreign borrowings, devaluation, and the institution of deflationary "austerity" programs—all of which may be unattractive to national policy makers.

Several scholars have suggested that the vulnerability of the open economy can be lessened by an assertion of the role of the state. Gilpin (1975, p. 45) concludes, for example, that a likely result of the national anxieties and insecurities produced by economic interdependence will be a resurgence of mercantilism—that is, of states intervening between the domestic and international economy on behalf of national economic objectives. Myrdal (1960) suggested a similar development nearly two decades ago when noting that in order to protect national objectives of internal stability, employment of workers, and undisturbed domestic production and consumption in a world of more chaotic economic relations, "all states have felt themselves compelled to undertake new, radical intervention, not only in the sphere of their foreign trade and exchange relations, but also in other sectors of the national economy" (pp. 70–72). More recently, Lehmbruch (1977) reached a similar conclusion, arguing that

> in a national economy subject to strong interpenetration with international markets, monetary policies often are of rather limited effectiveness. The same

is more and more true of "Keynesian" techniques of macroeconomic budgetary and fiscal demand management. . . . Faced with "control deficits" of this sort, governments increasingly turn to more direct attempts at influencing the economic behavior of business and/or labor (p. 98).

Lindbeck (1975, p. 56) argues that governments can dampen the effects of the open economy on production, employment, and consumption by increasing the scope of the public economy. He notes that the growth of social insurance and tax systems represent "built-in stabilizers" which allow policy makers to "smooth out" the peaks and valleys of business cycles. And through extensive labor market policies which include not only unemployment compensation but also subsidies to firms to retain and retrain workers who might otherwise be laid off, as well as through large increases in public employment, governments can maintain near-full employment in spite of the uncertainties of demand inherent in an open economy. In addition, through the provision of capital funds to the private sector (Lindbeck, 1974, pp. 9, 214–27), governments may be able to dampen the effect on capital accumulation of volatile profits in export industries as well as stimulate the development of import substitution industries.[17]

It may not always be the case that an expansion of the role of the state provides a sufficient means by which governments can enhance their control over open economies. Indeed, Vernon (1974) suggests that the efforts by European states to formally "plan" their economies failed because of increasing openness produced by the creation of the EEC and EFTA and the maturation of multinational enterprises: "None of these efforts to shore up the idea of the independent comprehensive national plan had much chance of succeeding; the contradiction between independent national plans of that sort and open national boundaries was simply too strong" (p. 16). In spite of this caveat, it is reasonable to expect that the arguments of Myrdal, Lehmbruch, and Lindbeck may be reflected in the experience of the 18 nations during the last two decades. Applying their arguments about the response of governments to a condition of external economic dependence, one might expect that the expansion of the public economy was most pronounced in nations in which the economy is relatively "open," in the sense of being exposed to the vagaries of the international economy. Using the ratio of imports and exports as a proportion of GDP as a measure of "openness," this argument would predict a strong positive association between the level, and the rate of increase, of "openness" and the expansion of the public economy.

Findings: Why the Public Economy Expanded in 1960–75

Table 1 presents the result of an analysis of the five plausible explanations of the expansion of the public economy. That analysis, based on data for the 18 nations, supports the following conclusions:

Table 1

The Expansion of the Public Economy: Fiscal

Variable	Level and rate of increase in economic output		Reliance on indirect and Social Security taxes		Partisanship of government and the frequency of elections		Inter-governmental structure and the degree of centralization		Openness of the economy	
	r	beta	r	beta	r	beta	r	beta	r	beta
Governments' revenues as a percent of GDP, 1960	0.28 (0.91)[a]	.25	0.42 (1.49)	.36	0.09 (0.34)	.08	0.52 (1.78)	.46	0.09 (0.45)	.08
GDP per capita	−0.002 (0.77)	−.22								
Average annual increase 1960–75 in real GDP	−1.34 (1.16)	−.35								
Percent of all governments' revenues from indirect taxes and Social Security contributions, 1960			−.15 (1.10)	−.27						
Increase in percent of all governments' revenues from indirect taxes and Social Security contributions, 1960–75			−0.17 (0.75)	−.18						

Independent variable	(1)	(2)	(3) b (t)	(3) β	(4) b (t)	(4) β	(5) b (t)	(5) β
Percent of governments' electoral base composed of Social Democratic or Labor parties, 1960–75			0.10 (2.15)	.54				
Number of national legislative elections, 1960–75			0.21 (0.29)	.07				
Federal structure of government					−2.56 (0.82)	−.23		
Percent of all governments' revenues recieved by central government, 1960					0.13 (0.92)	.28		
Exports and imports as a percent of GDP, 1960							0.19 (4.86)	.79
Increases in percent of GDP represented by exports and imports, 1960–75							0.00 (0.00)	.00
Coefficient of determination (R^2)	.19	.20	.37		.31		.67	
	(.02)[b]	(.03)	(.24)		(.16)		(.60)	

[a] Parentheses contain the regression coefficient divided by its standard error.

[b] Parentheses contain the R^2 adjusted for degrees of freedom ($\bar{R}^2$).

(a) Contrary to Wagner's "law," the rate of growth in the economic affluence of a nation does not contribute to the expansion of the public economy. Apparently citizens' demands for services and their willingness to accept higher levels of taxes, or both, are not income-elastic. Instead, the analysis supports Wildavsky's argument that the public economy grows, in relative terms, when economic growth is modest ($B = -.35$). In high-growth nations such as Japan and France, the demands of government for funds can be met with the "dividend" produced by applying a constant share to an expanding economic product. In low-growth nations, where governments do not enjoy that dividend, however, the almost inevitable increase in funding required for "uncontrollable" costs associated with mandated programs, as well as discretionary increments and new programs, absorbs a larger share of the economic product.

(b) Contrary to Downs and to Buchanan and Wagner, budgets do not expand most easily when taxes are concealed in a "fiscal illusion." A high and increasing reliance on "hidden" taxes exerted a significant dampening effect on the degree of expansion of the public economy, as indicated by the strong negative coefficients in Table 1. Instead, the public economy expanded most rapidly after 1960 in nations which relied heavily, and to an increasing degree, on wealth-elastic taxes, such as those on personal and corporate incomes.

(c) Contrary to the skeptics' view, politics is important in influencing the scope of the public economy. The partisanship of government is associated with the rate of expansion, and whether a nation's government was generally controlled by Social Democrats (and their leftist allies), or by non-leftist parties, provides a strong clue to the relative degree of change in the scope of the public economy ($B = .54$). Thus, nations such as Sweden, Norway, and Denmark, in which leftist parties tended, on average, to possess a majority of the government's electoral base, experienced increases in public revenues which were much larger, as a proportion of GDP, than those in nations such as Japan, Italy, or France, where the Left either participated in government only as the minority partner of non-leftist parties or was excluded from government altogether.

The frequency of electoral competition displays a modest positive correlation with the increase in the public economy, indicating that competition may indeed exert an inflationary impact on budgets. However, after we control for the effects associated with the partisan composition of government, the impact of the frequency of electoral competition is negligible ($B = .07$).

(d) Contrary to our predictions, federalism tends to dampen the degree of expansion of the public economy and centralization tends to facilitate that expansion. Any inherent tendency for aggregate revenues to increase in federal systems because of the fragmentation of spending authority among several quasi-autonomous levels of government is apparently more than offset by other effects. Among these may be the larger number of access points which federalism provides for those who wish to intervene in public policy making in order to oppose the extension of government activity (Heidenheimer, 1975, pp. 20–29,

48–65). Also, the fragmentation of authority which characterizes federalism may contribute to an aggregate pattern of offsetting policy developments among the subnational units that lessens the magnitude of change in the nation taken as a whole. A high degree of centralization, on the other hand, seems to facilitate the expansion of the public economy ($B = .28$). Thus, it appears that expansion was greatest in unitary, highly centralized nations. We might speculate that institutional arrangement minimizes the effects of fragmentation and provides the means by which national elites can insure uniformity in existing policies and can most easily avoid the institutional obstacles to policy innovation.

(e) As the discussion of the concept of the open economy suggested, a high degree of trade dependence is conducive to a relatively large expansion of the public economy. Nations with open economies were far more likely to experience an increase in the scope of public funding than were nations with relatively closed economies ($B = .79$). Apparently, governments in nations with open economies have sought to counter the effects of external dependence by expanding their control over the domestic economy through the "nationalization" of a large portion of consumption (Lindbeck, 1974, p. 9).[18]

In order to ascertain the importance of each of the explanations presented in Table 1, I performed a regression analysis which included the six variables most closely associated with the expansion of the public economy. Table 2 presents the results of that analysis. The analysis suggests that about 75 percent of the variation among the nations in the degree of expansion can be accounted for by the six variables. The analysis also suggests that two variables are far more important to the explanation than the others; the two are the partisanship of government ($B = .34$) and the openness of the economy ($B = .58$).

Figure 1 arrays the measure of the expansion of the public economy with that for the partisanship of government. The array provides a clue as to why the strong bivariate relationship between the two (r = .60) is reduced in the regression analysis. It suggests that the dominance in government of leftist parties was a sufficient condition for a relatively large increase in the scope of public activity; there was no nation in which the Left had a large share of the government's electoral base which did not also experience a relatively large increase in the public economy. However, leftist domination was not a necessary condition, since several nations experienced large increases in spite of the absence of a strong leftist representation in government. Included in this latter group are the Netherlands, Belgium, Ireland, and Canada. All share at least one common trait: their economies are relatively open. To some extent, then, the impact of partisanship on the scope of the "tax state" is more pronounced in larger nations with more closed economies than in the smaller nations with more open economies. In the latter, apparently, all governments—whether formed by leftist or nonleftist parties—have been impelled by the exigencies of the open economy to expand the role of the state. To illustrate this, Table 3 presents the year-by-year change in the measure of the public economy in four nations in which the partisan

Table 2

The Relative Importance of the Economic, Fiscal, Political, Institutional, and International Explanations of the Public Economy

	Increase 1960–75 All Governments' Revenues as a Percent of GDP		
	Simple correlation	Regression coefficient	Beta coefficient[a]
Levels of public economy, 1960 (governments' revenues as percent of GDP)	.35	0.11 (0.46)	0.10
Average annual percentage increase, 1960–75, in real GDP	−.31	0.06 (0.09)	0.02
Percent of governments' revenues obtained from indirect taxes and Social Security contributions, 1960	−.23	−0.06 (0.68)	−0.12
Percent of government's electoral base composed of Social Democratic or Labor parties, 1960–75	.60	0.07 (1.75)	0.34
Percent of all governments' revenues received by central governments, 1960	.21	0.08 (0.97)	0.17
Exports and imports of goods and services as percent of GDP, 1960	.78	0.13 (3.22)	0.58

Coefficient of determination ($R^2 = .75$. $\bar{R}^2 = .61$).
[a]Beta coefficient is the standardized regression coefficient.

control of government alternated between leftist and nonleftist parties. In the two larger nations, Britain and Germany, a clear partisan effect is noted. In Britain, for example, the change was positive in every year in which the Labour party was in power (1964–70, 1974–75), and was negative in five of the seven years during which the Conservatives governed. Similarly, in Germany, the years of Christian Democratic government, particularly when Ludwig Erhard, the former minister of economics and proponent of the neoliberal "social market policy," was chancellor (1963–66), were marked by modest increases or decreases, while the period of Social Democratic control was marked by a cumulative increase in the scope of the public economy. In contrast, in Denmark and Norway, nonleftist governments were no less inclined than those dominated by the Social Democratic and the Labor parties to increase the public revenues at a rapid rate, relative to the rate of economic growth. Thus, while the size of the public economy grew considerably in Denmark during the Social Democratic minority government and subsequent "red coalition" of 1964–67, the largest increase

Figure 1. **The Partisan Composition of Government and the Expansion of the Public Economy**

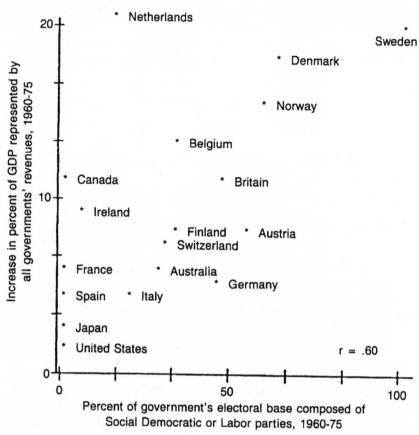

Percent of government's electoral base composed of
Social Democratic or Labor parties, 1960-75

occurred during the nonleftist coalition government of 1968–71. Likewise, in Norway, the bourgeois coalition which governed during 1966–71 and again during 1972–73 expanded the scope of state activity at a rate which in some years approached that achieved by Labor governments.

The regression analysis presented in Table 2 suggests that the openness of the economy is the best single predictor of the growth of public revenues relative to the economic product of a nation. In Figure 2, the measure of openness is displayed with that of the change in the scope of the public economy. A strong relationship is observed and no major exceptions appear to the pattern of co-variation: larger nations with more closed economies experienced relatively modest increases in the scope of the public economy compared to the smaller nations with open economies.[19] Within the latter group, one finds some distinction between the Scandinavian nations, where the Left frequently governed, and Belgium and

Table 3

The Partisan Composition of Government and Change in the Scope of the the Public Economy in Four Nations[a]

Year	Britain[b]	Germany	Denmark	Norway
1961	0.5	0.8	−0.5	**1.1**
1962	1.7	0.6	**1.5**	**1.4**
1963	−0.5	−0.1	**1.5**	−0.1
1964	−0.2	−0.4	0.1	−0.5
1965	1.7	−0.8	**1.3**	**1.2**
1966	**1.0**	*0.5*	**2.2**	1.1
1967	**1.8**	*0.6*	0.6	1.6
1968	**1.6**	*−0.5*	2.9	0.4
1969	**2.1**	*1.8*	0.2	2.1
1970	**1.3**	−0.8	4.5	0.5
1971	−1.9	0.9	3.4	**3.1**
1972	−1.7	0.3	0.2	**2.1**
1973	−0.8	**2.4**	0.1	**1.2**
1974	**3.3**	0.3	**2.1**	**−1.2**
1975	**0.6**	−0.4	**−3.1**	**1.5**

[a]Entries are the first order changes between sucessive years in the percent of GDP recieved by all governments.

[b]Boldface entries indicate that the Social Democratic or Labor parties controlled government for at least six months during the year. The British entry for 1970 is credited to Labour, in spite of its defeat in the June election. Italicized entries for Germany denote the period of the Grand Coalition between the SPD and the CDU/CSU (1966–69).

Ireland, where centrists or conservatives usually dominated government. But the overall message is clear: the best explanation of why public authorities in some nations have expanded their control over the appropriation and allocation of resources while those in other nations have not is international in character. Among the nations considered here, the expansion of the public economy was most closely associated with a relatively high exposure to, and dependence upon, external producers and consumers.[20]

Discussion

The Domestic Consequences of the Open Economy

Why is the degree of trade dependence the best predictor of the extent of expansion of the public economy? Is it simply the force of the exigencies posed by exposure to the international economy that causes government to extract and allocate a large share of the economic product? Or does openness generate certain structural characteristics in advanced capitalist economies which are conducive to an expansion of the scope of the public economy? We shall attempt to

Figure 2. **The Openness of the Economy and the Expansion of the Public Economy**

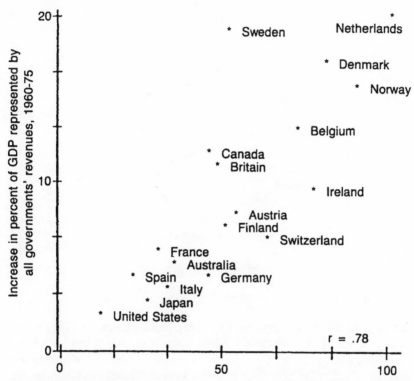

Exports and imports as a percent of Gross Domestic Product, 1960

provide an answer to these questions by identifying a sequence of economic, sociological, and political characteristics that derive, ultimately, from the openness of the economy. This sequence, presented in Figure 3, includes the following: (a) the degree of industrial concentration; (b) the density of unionization; (c) the scope of collective bargaining; and (d) the strength of labor confederations.

One of the structural attributes that frequently characterizes small, open economies is a high degree of industrial concentration—that is, an unusually large share of production and employment in a few large firms. According to Ingham (1974, pp. 40–41), "those societies in which industrialization was based upon exports because of too small a domestic market have tended to develop highly concentrated industries. Sharp competition in the export field has, in these countries, tended to force out the smaller and less efficient companies which were less able to contend with fluctuations in world markets."

High levels of industrial concentration appear, in turn, to facilitate the formation of employers' associations and labor confederations which include a rela-

Figure 3. **The Domestic Consequences of an Open Economy**

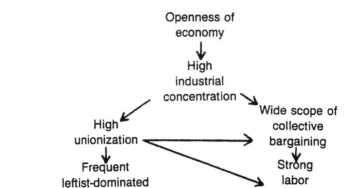

tively large portion of all firms and employees. Ingham notes, for example, that small, open, and highly concentrated economies tend to have "a small number of oligopolistic and non-competitive sectors . . . which facilitates collective organization" (p. 42). And the labor force in such economies tends to be somewhat less differentiated in terms of occupation and skill levels and, as a result, less fragmented (p. 43). The existence of such a labor force—relatively homogeneous and relatively concentrated in large firms in a small number of non-competitive sectors—is conducive to the growth of union organization. The existence of a relatively high level of unionization is, in turn, an important prerequisite for enduring leftist government, since unionized workers provide the core of the electoral base of most Social Democratic and Labor parties (see Stephens, 1978). Thus, in following the left-hand branch in Figure 3, we see that the openness of the economy contributes to an expansion of the public economy by facilitating the development of the social infrastructure upon which Social Democratic and Labor party electoral support rests.[21]

In addition to its effects on unionization and, ultimately, the structure of the party system, industrial concentration influences the scope of collective bargaining. The existence of "a small number of oligopolistic and non-competitive sectors," composed of a relatively small number of large firms, coupled with the proliferation of labor and employer organizations, widens the scope of collective bargaining. In some nations considered here, bargaining is decentralized and usually conducted at the level of the enterprise, either by enterprise unions as in Japan, or by national unions as in the United States. In most European nations, on the other hand, bargaining is conducted at the industry level with important additional negotiations at the enterprise level, as in Britain and Italy, or the regional level, as in Germany. But in the smaller open economies, industry bargaining often follows guidelines established in national negotiations (see Mouly, 1967; Schregle, 1974; Elvander, 1974; Lehmbruch, 1977; Hibbs, 1976). Thus, in Norway, Sweden, and Denmark, economy-wide "framework" agreements are formally negotiated between labor and employer confederations. And in Austria, Belgium, and the Netherlands, institutions exist in which representatives of the major confederations consult about, and occasionally negotiate, collective bargaining guidelines.[22]

One of the more important consequences of industrial and economy-wide collective bargaining is the power it bestows on labor confederations. Since they are the representatives of organized labor in economy-wide consultations and negotiations, they have tended to acquire formal powers over their affiliates in regard to collective bargaining. In Norway, Sweden, Finland, Austria, Belgium, and the Netherlands, for example, the major confederations can withhold strike funds from affiliates, thereby weakening the latter's ability to use the threat of strike action. In Austria, Norway, and the Netherlands, confederations can veto wage settlements obtained by their affiliates, and in these and most of the other open economies in Europe confederations have, *de jure* or *de facto,* the right to consult with affiliates prior to negotiations (Headey, 1970, pp. 421–25).[23]

The ability of labor confederations to intervene in collective bargaining makes them major actors in the political economy. This is especially true in nations where the domain of macroeconomic issues about which confederations consult with employers and/or government has been extended beyond collective bargaining in recent decades. This occurred in some nations through the creation of consultative institutions, such as the Austrian Parity Commission and the Dutch Foundation of Labor and the Social and Economic Council; in other nations, consultation is less institutionalized but equally important, as in Norway and Sweden where the confederation and the Labor party have traditionally represented the two arms of the labor movement (see Lehmbruch, 1977). This access to government can be used by labor confederations in many ways, but two are of special relevance here. Acting as representatives of the labor movement, confederations may advocate policies that will enhance the economic condition of their members by supporting programs that provide income supplements. On the other hand, confederations may act as allies of government—particularly when it is informed by Social Democratic or Labor parties—to moderate wage demands in the export sector in order to maintain international competitiveness. For example, they may voluntarily participate in programs of wage restraint negotiated between themselves, employer federations, and government (see Rall, 1975; Ulman and Flanagan, 1971; Galenson, 1973; Headey, 1970; and

Lehmbruch, 1977). More frequently than not, labor confederations involved in such cooperative programs of wage restraint have felt compelled to use their access to government to obtain increments to the disposable income of their members, thereby compensating them for wage sacrifices. Whether they act as the representatives of organized labor or as allies of government, then, the existence of strong labor confederations tends to produce the same effect—an unusually large increase in publicly funded income supplements. And this, in turn, requires a comparable expansion in the scope of the public economy.[24]

The Consequences of the Expansion of the Public Economy

Does it matter that in some nations the public economy expanded to the range of 50 percent of GDP, while in others it increased only slightly in the years since 1960?[25] Thus far, this article has examined the reasons for the large cross-national variation in the degree of expansion of the public economy. It is appropriate to conclude, however, by shifting our attention from cause to consequence and examining the impact of changes in the scope of the public economy. A variety of effects might be considered, ranging from macroeconomic policy to electoral behavior; we have chosen two related effects which demonstrate the magnitude of the impact of different rates of cumulative change and the value dilemmas that accompany policy choices in this domain. The two involve economic equality and private capital accumulation.

In Figure 4 we illustrate the relationship among 12 of the 18 nations between the cumulative expansion of the public economy and measures of economic equality and private capital accumulation. A strong positive correlation ($r = .83$) exists between the size of the increase in the public economy and a measure of economic equality involving the difference in the proportion of all national income received, after taxes, by the top and bottom 20 percent of households. A strong negative correlation ($r = -.89$) exists between the size of the cumulative increase in the public economy and the change in the proportion of GDP represented by private capital accumulation.[26]

The data in Figure 4 suggest the existence of a trade-off between relatively high degrees of economic equality and increasing rates of private capital accumulation.[27] And they suggest that the collective choice of a nation in regard to this tradeoff is strongly influenced by choices made in regard to taxation policy. Nations such as the United States, Japan, Spain, and Italy, where the extractive capacity of government did not significantly increase, relative to the economic product, have, in a sense, opted for a relatively inegalitarian distribution of income and an increasing rate of private capital accumulation.[28] Other nations, however, have, in the cumulative effect of their policies, made a different choice and have attained a relatively greater degree of economic equality at the cost of lower rates of private capital accumulation. Given the structural features that tend to accompany economic openness—a high degree of unionization, rela-

Figure 4. **The Tax Tradeoff: The Expansion of the Public Economy, Economic Equality, and Capital Accumulation**

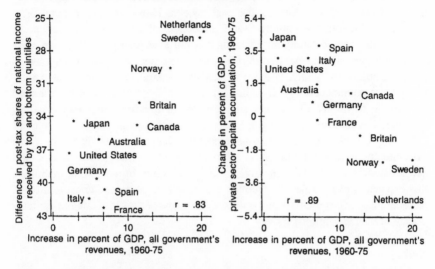

tively frequent government by Social Democratic and Labor parties, strong labor confederations, and, ultimately, a large increase in taxation—it is perhaps not surprising that the nations which tended to favor distributional equity rather than private accumulation were those with open economies.

Conclusion

Most studies of public policy in advanced industrial society confine themselves to an analysis of internal, or domestic, causes and consequences. Only rarely, and only recently, have students of public policy examined the linkage between the international economy and domestic policy (Katzenstein, 1976, 1977). The predominant image implicit in most policy studies is that of political autarky—of autonomous states whose policy processes are wholly insulated from external influences. Yet in a world marked by "complex interdependence" (Keohane and Nye, 1977) such an image is increasingly anachronistic; because, as Cooper argues, "increased economic interdependence . . . erodes the effectiveness of national economic policies and hence threatens national autonomy in the determination and pursuit of economic objectives," governing elites are likely to feel compelled to use public policy to confront the challenges posed by the international economy (1972, p. 164).

Governments use a variety of policy instruments to shelter their economics from the competitive risks of the international economy. Some states adopt explicitly neo-mercantilist policies (Katzenstein, 1978, pp. 879–920); others favor certain enterprises, whether in the private or public sector, as "national champions" (Vernon, 1974, Ch. 1); still others adopt a variety of industry-specific protectionist measures. Each type of policy has occurred in one or more of the nations considered here during the past decade. However, neo-mercantilism, support of "national champions," and protectionism are often ineffective for nations with open economies, given their small size relative to some of their most important trading partners. For such nations, another type of response is more feasible—one which is more defensive in character and involves a relatively large public economy. Governments in small open economies have tended to provide a variety of income supplements in the form of social security schemes, health insurance, unemployment benefits, job training, employment subsidies to firms, and even investment capital. Prompted in part by the incentive to maintain price competitiveness of export goods in the world market and accentuated by the social structural features generated by economic openness, this expansion of the role of government in the distribution and consumption of national income has dramatically enlarged the scope of the "tax state" in contemporary advanced capitalist society.

Notes

1. The term "public economy" refers here to that portion of a nation's economic product which is consumed or distributed by all public authorities.

2. In most nations, during most years, the total of all governments' revenues exceeds the total of all governments' expenditures. During the world recession of 1975, the aggregate of all governments' expenditures exceeded all revenues in six nations—the United States, Belgium, Germany, Ireland, Italy, and Britain. In the prior half-decade (1970–74), however, only two nations (the United States in 1971 and Italy in 1971–74) experienced an aggregate deficit. Thus, a measure of the public economy based on revenues is less likely to understate the fiscal scope of governmental activity than one based on expenditures. See Organization for Economic Cooperation and Development (OECD) (1977a).

3. The data were obtained from OECD (1973, 1977a). The measure includes withdrawals from, but not operating revenues of, public enterprises, which in some nations (for example, Austria, Finland, Britain, and Italy) are among the largest industrial firms.

4. First-order differences, rather than percentage changes, are used in order to avoid artificially deflating the magnitude of change in nations with a relatively *high* value in the initial year. To control for the tendency of first-order differences to deflate the magnitude of change in nations with relatively *low* initial values, regression analyses will include both the value in the initial year and the measure of change.

5. See Bird (1970, p. 70; 1971), Musgrave (1969, p. 74), and Gupta (1968).

6. The data for the level of per capita Gross Domestic Product are reported in United Nations (1976, pp. 701–02). The data for the average annual increase in real GDP were obtained from OECD (1977b, Technical Annex).

7. Data pertaining to the structure of governments' revenues, and the portion that was generated through indirect taxes and social security contributions, are reported in OECD (1977b, Technical Annex).

8. During 1960–75, the number of national legislative elections ranged from zero in Spain to seven in Australia and Denmark. During this period, of course, Spain was nondemocratic; thus our arguments concerning the impact of electoral competition on

fiscal policy are irrelevant for that case. For purposes of comparability with the other nations, we treat only the four American presidential elections rather than all eight congressional elections. It is, of course, true that the argument regarding the effect of electoral competition on fiscal policy is relevant to the latter elections; see Kramer (1971) and Tufte (1975).

9. See Lipset (1960, pp. 439–56) and Bell (1960). For rejoinders, see LaPalombara (1966) and Putnam (1973).

10. The most dramatic instances of reduced industrial conflict after World War II are found in Scandinavia. For discussions of the institutionalization of industrial conflict in those nations, see Elvander (1974) and Ingham (1974).

11. The effect is less pronounced when one considers the trend in British expenditures in part because the government of Edward Heath ran down the surplus of funds allocated to capital formation. The result was a marked increase in borrowings from abroad, beginning in 1972, and actual deficits beginning in 1975. See Klein (1976, p. 418) and Brittan (1975).

12. Leftist parties are defined as those which are Social Democratic, Labor, or Communist. Thus, the American Democratic party is not considered to be leftist; it is, of course, true that the party is to the left of the Republican party and that it does matter whether Republicans or Democrats control the executive and legislative branches. (In this regard, see Tufte [1978, pp. 71–83].) Nevertheless, it is also true that it differs considerably from most European Socialist and Social Democratic-Labor parties—for example, in its electoral support among middle-class voters and in its unusually large body of self-declared "middle-of-the-roaders" and "conservatives." See, on the former point, Hamilton (1972, pp. 190–93). In regard to the latter point, Flanigan and Zingale (1975, p. 114) find that 66 percent of 1972 Democratic identifiers called themselves "conservative" or "middle-of-the-road" rather than "liberal." The measure of the partisan composition of government was calculated as follows: in each year, I summed the votes received in the previous national legislative election by all parties participating in government (i.e., holding cabinet positions) and divided the total into the number of votes received by all Social Democratic, Socialist, Labor, Communist, and smaller leftist parties (such as the Dutch Radicals and the Danish Socialist Peoples' parties) that were participants in government. This proportion ranges from 0 (when no leftist parties were in government) to 100 (when the government was composed entirely of leftist parties). I then summed the values for the 16 years between 1960–75 and calculated the average. That average represents the average proportion of the government's electoral base that was accounted for by leftist parties. It is highly correlated (on the order of $r = .99$) with a measure of the proportion of Cabinet portfolios held by leftist parties. The electoral data were obtained from Mackie and Rose (1974, 1975, 1976).

13. The measure of the formal structure of government is binary: 0 for unitary nations; 1 for federal nations. The measure of centralization was obtained from OECD (1973). The degree of centralization in 1960 for the federal nations varied between 38.2 percent (Germany) and 79.7 percent (Australia). Among the unitary nations, the measure of centralization varied from 59 percent (Italy) to 85.8 percent (Ireland). The correlation between the measure of federalism and that of centralization is $r = -.53$.

14. See Lindbeck (1975, 1976, 1977); Aukrust (1977); Cooper (1972); and Keohane and Nye (1977).

15. The figures refer to exports and imports of all goods and services, and are derived from data reported in OECD (1973, 1977a).

16. Recent Swedish experience confirms the argument here. Capitalizing on the rise in prices in several of the nations to which it exports goods, Swedish exports enjoyed high profits in 1973–74. Subsequent wage negotiations in late 1974 provided unusually large

increments. As a result, prices for Swedish goods rose in the world market and, even with slender profit margins, firms lost markets. The result has been large balance of trade deficits, three devaluations since 1976, and negative growth in 1977.

17. More recently, Lindbeck (1977, pp. 13, 42) notes that the increased international-ization of the economy has caused an upsurge in international coordination of economic policy. Two recent examples are the development of protectionist limitations on imports and domestic capacity restrictions in the European steel industry (the Davignon plan), and the institution of annual economic summit conferences of western heads of state (Ram-bouillet, 1975; Puerto Rico, 1976; London, 1977; Bonn, 1978).

18. Lindbeck notes here the distinction—relevant to Sweden and several other small open economies—between the nationalization of the consumption of income, which impl-ies a large "tax state," and the nationalization of the production of income, which implies, instead, a large number of publicly owned enterprises.

19. As Dahl and Tufte (1973, p. 130) suggest, there is a strong inverse correlation between the population of a nation and the degree of economic openness ($r = -.65$).

20. Contrary to our expectation, the extent of increase in openness during 1960–75 is not related to the extent of increase in the public economy. While all 18 nations became increasingly open during this period (in terms of exports and imports as a percent of GDP), the wide variation among the 18 nations was unaltered and the ordering of the nations remained, in 1975, almost as it was in 1960 ($r = .95$ between the measures of openness in 1960 and 1975). The findings reported here imply that it is the extent of openness, rather than the rate of change, that stimulates an expansion of the public economy.

21. This argument is supported by the existence of a positive correlation between the measure of the openness of the economy and the proportion of the work force that belong to labor unions ($r = .41$), and the positive correlation ($r = .56$) between the extent of unionization and the extent of government by leftist parties. Unfortunately, no satisfactory data exist with which cross-nationally comparable measures of concentration might be constructed. Data on unionization were obtained from Europa Publications (1977). We might note that our argument here implies a more complex relationship·between the openness of the economy and the partisanship of government than is suggested by the assumption of independence in the regression analysis reported in Table 2. In fact, there is a positive, albeit modest, correlation between the two measures ($r = .37$).

22. The argument in this paragraph is supported by the very strong correlation be-tween the measure of openness and a measure of the scope of collective bargaining derived from Mouly (1967), Schregle (1974), Lehmbruch (1977), and Hibbs (1976). The correlation is $r = .74$.

23. The argument that labor confederations are stronger, in terms of their ability to intervene in collective bargaining, in nations in which the scope of collective bargaining is relatively broad is supported by the strong correlation of $r = .65$ between the measure of the scope of collective bargaining (which ranges from 1 for Japan where collective bar-gaining often involves enterprise unions, to 6 for Austria, Ireland, Denmark, Norway, and Sweden, where economy-wide "framework" agreements, or similar consultations, take place) and a measure of the formal right of labor confederations to intervene in collective bargaining through prior consultation, post-negotiation approval, and/or control of strike funds.

24. This argument is supported by the high correlation between the measure of the right of labor confederations to intervene in collective bargaining and a measure of the increase in the proportion of GNP spent on social security schemes (as defined by the International Labour Organisation) between 1960 and 1971. The correlation is $r = .74$. That increase in spend-ing effort for social security schemes is, in turn, highly correlated with the measure of the

expansion of the public economy ($r = .72$). The data on the increase in Social Security spending are reported in I.L.O (1964, 1976).

25. By 1975, the public economy absorbed 53.5 percent of the Dutch GDP, 50.2 percent of the Norwegian GDP, 52.2 percent of the Swedish GDP, and 45.0 percent of the Danish GDP. To a very large extent the scope of the public economy in 1975 was determined by the magnitude of the increase between 1960 and 1975. Thus the correlation between the measure of expansion in 1960–75 and the scope of the public economy in 1975 was $r = .89$, compared to a correlation of $r = .35$ between the 1960 and 1975 measures.

26. The data on the size distribution of income are reported in OECD (1976). The data used here represent the first-order difference between the proportion of all after-tax income received by the top 20 percent and the bottom 20 percent of households. To control for national differences in the size of households and enhance the cross-national comparability of the data, the OECD reports standardized figures. These are the data used here. The measure of the change in the proportion of GDP that represents all private capital accumulation (i.e., savings and consumption of fixed capital) is the first-order difference of the proportions in 1960 and 1975. The data are reported in OECD (1973, 1977a).

27. That a trade-off exists between equality and accumulation is further suggested by the high negative correlation between the two measures ($r = -.74$).

28. In spite of the increase in the rate of capital accumulation in the private sector, the low rate of governmental savings—and indeed aggregate government deficits in several years—caused the proportion of gross capital accumulation in GDP to drop in Italy and the United States between 1960 and 1975. See OECD (1977a).

References

Aukrust, Odd (1977). "Inflation in the Open Economy." In Lawrence B. Krause and Walter S. Salant (eds.), *Worldwide Inflation: Theory and Recent Experience.* Washington, D.C.: Brookings, pp. 107–53.

Bacon, Robert, and Walter Eltis (1976). *Britain as Economic Problem: Too Few Producers.* London: MacMillan.

Bell, Daniel (1960). *The End of Ideology.* Glencoe: Free Press.

Bird, Richard M. (1970). *The Growth of Government Spending in Canada.* Toronto: Canadian Tax Foundation.

———. (1971). "Wagner's 'Law' of Expanding State Activity." *Public Finances/Finances Publiques* 26:1–26.

Brittan, Samuel (1975). "The Economic Contradictions of Democracy." *British Journal of Political Science* 5:129–59.

Buchanan, James M., and Richard E. Wagner (1977). *Democracy in Deficit: The Political Legacy of Lord Keynes.* New York: Academic Press.

Collier, David, and Richard E. Messick (1975). "Prerequisites vs. Diffusion: Testing Alternative Explanations of Social Security Adoption." *American Political Science Review* 69:1299–1315.

Cooper, Richard N. (1972). "Economic Interdependence and Foreign Policy in the Seventies." *World Politics* 24:159–81.

Dahl, Robert, and Edward Tufte (1973). *Size and Democracy.* Stanford: Stanford University Press.

Davis, Otto A., M. A. H. Dempster, and Aaron Wildavsky (1966). "A Theory of the Budgetary Process." *American Political Science Review* 60:529–47.

———. (1974). "Toward a Predictive Theory of the Federal Budgetary Process." *British Journal of Political Science* 4:419–52.

Downs, Anthony (1957). *An Economic Theory of Democracy.* New York: Harper and Row.
———. (1960). "Why the Government Budget is Too Small in a Democracy." *World Politics* 12:541–63.
———. (1964). *Inside Bureaucracy.* Boston: Little, Brown.
Elvander, Nils (1974). "The Role of the State in Settlement of Labor Disputes in the Nordic Countries: A Comparative Analysis." *European Journal of Political Research* 2:363–83.
Europa Publications (1977). *Europa Yearbook 1977.* London: Europa.
Flanigan, William H., and Nancy Zingale (1975). *Political Behavior of the American Electorate,* 3rd ed. Boston: Allyn and Bacon.
Freeman, Roger A. (1975). *The Growth of American Government.* Stanford: Hoover Institute.
Galenson, Walter, ed. (1973). *Incomes Policy: What Can We Learn from Europe?* Ithaca: Cornell University Press.
Gilpin, Robert (1975). "Three Models of the Future" in C. Fred Bergsten and Lawrence B. Krause (eds.), *World Politics and International Finance.* Washington, D.C.: Brookings, pp. 37–60.
Gordon, Michael (1971). "Civil Servants, Politicians, and Parties." *Comparative Politics* 4:29–58.
Gupta, Shibshankar P. (1968). "Public Expenditure and Economic Development." *Finanzarchiv* 28:26–41.
Hamilton, Richard (1972). *Class and Politics in the United States.* New York: Wiley.
Headey, Bruce W. (1970). "Trade Unions and National Wages Policies." *Journal of Politics* 32:407–39.
Heclo, Hugh (1974). *Modern Social Politics in Britain and Sweden.* New Haven: Yale University Press.
Heidenheimer, Arnold J., et al. (1975). *Comparative Public Policy.* New York: St. Martin's.
Hibbs, Douglas A., Jr. (1976). "Industrial Conflict in Advanced Industrial Societies." *American Political Science Review* 70:1033–58.
———. (1977). "Political Parties and Macroeconomic Policy." *American Political Science Review* 71:467–87.
———. (1978). "On the Political Economy of Long-Run Trends in Strike Activity." *British Journal of Political Science* 8:153–75.
Ingham, Geoffrey K. (1974). *Strikes and Industrial Conflict.* London: Macmillan.
International Labour Organisation (1964). *The Cost of Social Security 1958–60.* Geneva: I.L.O.
———. (1976). *The Cost of Social Security 1966–71.* Geneva: I.L.O.
Katzenstein, Peter J. (1976). "International Relations and Domestic Structure: Foreign Economic Policies of Advanced Industrial States." *International Organization* 30:4–13.
———, ed. (1977). "Between Power and Plenty: Foreign Economic Policies of Advanced Industrial States." *International Organization* 31:587–920.
Keohane, Robert O., and Joseph S. Nye (1977). *Power and Interdependence: World Politics in Transition.* Boston: Little, Brown.
Key, V. O. (1949). *Southern Politics.* New York: Knopf.
King, Anthony (1969). "Political Parties in Western Democracies: Some Skeptical Reflections." *Polity* 2:111 41.
———. (1973). "Ideas, Institutions and the Policies of Governments: A Comparative Analysis: 1, 11." *British Journal of Political Science* 3:291–313.
Klein, Rudolf (1976). "The Politics of Public Expenditure: American Theory and British Practice." *British Journal of Political Science* 6:401–32.

Kramer, Gerald H. (1971). "Short-Term Fluctuations in U.S. Voting Behavior, 1896–1964." *American Political Science Review* 65:131–43.

Krasner, Stephen D. (1976). "State Power and the Structure of International Trade." *World Politics* 28:317–47.

LaPalombara, Joseph (1966). "Decline of Ideology: A Dissent and an Interpretation." *American Political Science Review* 60:5–16.

Lehmbruch, Gerhard (1977). "Liberal Corporatism and Party Government." *Comparative Political Studies* 10:91–126.

Lindbeck, Assar (1974). *Swedish Economic Policy.* Berkeley: University of California Press.

———. (1975). "Business Cycles, Politics and International Economic Dependence." *Skandinaviska Enskilden Bank Quarterly Review* 2:53–68.

———. (1976). "Stabilization Policy in Open Economies with Endogenous Politicians." *American Economic Review* 66:1–19.

———. (1977). "Economic Dependence and Interdependence in the Industrialized World." Stockholm: Institute for International Economic Studies, University of Stockholm.

Lipset, Seymour Martin (1960). *Political Man.* Garden City: Doubleday.

Mackie, Thomas T., and Richard Rose (1974). *International Almanac of Election Statistics.* London: Macmillan.

———. (1975). "General Elections in Western Nations During 1974." *European Journal of Political Research* 3:319–28.

———. (1976). "Election Data: General Elections in Western Nations During 1975." *European Journal of Political Research* 4:329–32.

Mouly, Jean (1967). "Wage Determination: Institutional Aspects." *International Labour Review* 96:497–526.

Musgrave, Richard A. (1969). *Fiscal Systems.* New Haven: Yale University Press.

Myrdal, Gunnar (1960). *Beyond the Welfare State.* New Haven: Yale University Press.

Niskanen, William A. (1971). *Bureaucracy and Representative Government.* Chicago: Aldine.

Nordhaus, William D. (1975). "The Political Business Cycle." *Review of Economic Studies* 42:160–90.

Organisation for Economic Cooperation and Development (1973). *National Accounts of OECD Countries: 1960–71.* Paris: OECD.

———. (1976). *Occasional Studies: Income Distribution in OECD Countries.* Paris: OECD.

———. (1977a). *National Accounts of OECD Countries: 1975,* Vol. 2. Paris: OECD.

———. (1977b). *Economic Outlook,* Vol. 22. Paris: OECD.

Peacock, Alan R., and Jack Wiseman (1967). *The Growth of Public Expenditure in the United Kingdom,* 2nd ed. London: Allen and Unwin.

Putnam, Robert D. (1973). *The Beliefs of Politicians.* New Haven. Yale University Press.

Rall, Wilhelm (1975). *Zur Wirksamkeit der Einkommenspolitik.* Tubingen: Mohr.

Schregle, Johannes (1974). "Labour Relations in Western Europe: Some Topical Issues." *International Labour Review* 109: 1–22.

Schumpeter, Joseph (1918). "The Crisis of the Tax State." *International Economic Papers* 4:5–38.

———. (1950). *Capitalism, Socialism and Democracy.* New York: Harper and Row.

Shonfield, Andrew. (1969). *Modern Capitalism.* New York: Oxford University Press.

———. (1976). *International Economic Relations of the Western World, 1959–1971,* 2 Vols. London: Oxford University Press.

Stephens, John D. (1978). *The Transition from Capitalism to Socialism.* London: Macmillan.

Tarschys, Daniel (1975). "The Growth of Public Expenditures: Nine Modes of Explanation." *Scandinavian Political Studies* 10:9–31.

Tufte, Edward (1975). "Determinants of the Outcome of Midterm Congressional Elections." *American Political Science Review* 69:812–26.

———. (1978). *Political Control of the Economy.* Princeton: Princeton University.

United Nations (1976). *Statistical Yearbook 1975.* New York: United Nations.

Vernon, Raymond, ed. (1974). *Big Business and the State.* Cambridge: Harvard University.

Wagner, Adolf (1883). "The Nature of the Fiscal Economy." In Richard A. Musgrave and Alan R. Peacock, eds., *Classics in the Theory of Public Finance.* London: Macmillan.

Wildavsky, Aaron (1974). *The Politics of the Budgetary Process,* 2nd ed. Boston: Little, Brown.

———. (1975). *Budgeting: A Comparative Theory of Budgetary Processes.* Boston: Little, Brown.

Wilensky, Harold (1975). *The Welfare State and Equality.* Berkeley: University of California Press.

4.4. The Electoral-Economic Cycle

EDWARD R. TUFTE

Edward Tufte was one of the earliest and strongest proponents of the view that there is a political business cycle. In this excerpt from his book Political Control of the Economy, *Tufte outlines his idea of the electoral-economic cycle and provides evidence to support it.*

He begins by showing, with judicious use of quotations, that some American political actors have claimed to act in ways that fit the theory. He then looks at some comparative evidence from twenty-seven democracies that appears to support the idea that the cyclical economy predicted by the theory occurred more often than could be expected by chance. Then Tufte looks more closely at the United States, in an effort to show that people's real incomes increase more, and unemployment decreases more, in election years, and that the so-called "prosperity index," which adds the rate of inflation to the rate of unemployment, has been lower in election than nonelection years. He also tries to demonstrate that the effects of the political business cycle will be greatest in elections in which the president has the greatest stake.

The evidence contained in this excerpt has been attacked on a variety of grounds (many of them outlined in the next reading). Most of the criticisms concern Tufte's selective choice of data and his exclusion of data from years that do not fit the theory. However, while one can object to much of his evidence, the reader should note that Tufte has been careful to provide a range of evidence, precisely to allow for possible weaknesses in individual indicators.

> A Government is not supported a hundredth part so much by the constant,
> uniform, quiet prosperity of the country as by those damned spurts which
> Pitt used to have just in the nick of time.
>
> *Brougham, 1814*

> The year 1972 ended with considerable forward momentum in economic
> activity. According to preliminary fourth quarter data, GNP rose by $32 billion,
> or at a seasonally adjusted rate of 11½ percent. . . . Judging from
> monthly indicators such as industrial production, the course of output was
> strongly upward through the quarter.
>
> *Annual Report of the Council of Economic Advisers, 1973*

> Some circumstantial evidence is very strong, as when you find a trout in the
> milk.
>
> *Henry David Thoreau*

The government of a modern democratic country exerts very substantial control
over the pace of national economic life and the distribution of economic benefits.
While it cannot always dilute the consequences of exogenous shocks, reduce
unemployment or inflation below certain levels, or protect its citizens from the
vicissitudes of world markets, the government's control over spending, taxes,
transfers, money stock, and the like enables it to direct the short-run course of
the economy to a significant degree. We need not, therefore, be as agnostic as the
Council of Economic Advisers' 1973 Report with respect to the causes of "considerable forward momentum in economic activity"—in this case, an 11.5 percent growth rate—occurring in the fourth quarter of a presidential election year.
It is hardly a novel hypothesis that an incumbent administration, while operating
within political and economic constraints and limited by the usual uncertainties
in successfully implementing economic policy, may manipulate the short-run
course of the national economy in order to improve its party's standing in up-
coming elections and to repay past political debts. In particular, incumbents may
seek to determine the location and the timing of economic benefits in promoting
the fortunes of their party and friends.

The hypothesis of an electoral-economic cycle is nearly integrated into the
folklore of capitalist democracies; political motives are regularly attributed to
economic policies in election years. Furthermore, the formal possibilities for
such a cycle have been developed in some technical detail in economic analysis.[1]
As is often the case with folklore and with economic theory, however, little
empirical evidence bearing on the question is available. A few case studies of a
single country over a short period of time have found some evidence for the
acceleration of the national economy in an election year, but these studies leave
one wondering if other times or places would testify differently. After all, no
investigators have sought to find the lack of a link between economic policy and
elections. The only analysis comparing a number of countries, after a casual
review of unemployment data, yielded very mixed findings: "The overall results

indicate that for the entire period a political cycle seems to be implausible as a description for Australia, Canada, Japan, and the UK. Some modest indications of a political cycle appear for France and Sweden. For three countries—Germany, New Zealand and the United States—the coincidence of business and political cycles is very marked."[2] In short, virtually no evidence confirming even the existence of an electoral-economic cycle is at hand, let alone considerations on its measurement, causes, and consequences. The absence of evidence, however, is not convincing evidence of absence.

Let us begin by seeking a motive, an initiating cause for an electoral-economic cycle. It is obvious enough: incumbent politicians desire reelection and they believe that a booming pre-election economy will help to achieve it.

The Economic Theory of Elections Held by Politicians and Their Economic Advisers

It has been a political commonplace since the massive political realignment growing out of the Great Depression that the performance of the economy affects the electoral fate of the dominant incumbent party. Ample evidence confirms that politicians and high-level economic advisers appreciate what they see as an economic fact of political life. At hand is the rueful testimony of politicians and the more self-important pronouncements of their economic advisers that short-run economic fluctuations are very important politically. Walter Heller, the chairman of the Council of Economic Advisers from 1961 to 1964, wrote:

> As a political leader, President Johnson has found in modern economic policy an instrument that serves him well in giving form and substance to the stuff of which his dreams for America are made, in molding and holding a democratic consensus, and in giving that consensus a capital "D" in national elections. That the chill of recession may have tipped the Presidential election in 1960, and that the bloom of prosperity boosted the margin of victory in 1964, is widely acknowledged, especially by the defeated candidates.[3]

Richard Nixon expressed a similar view in *Six Crises:*

> I knew from bitter experience how, in both 1954 and 1958, slumps which hit bottom early in October contributed to substantial Republican losses in the House and Senate. The power of the "pocketbook" issue was shown more clearly perhaps in 1958 than in any off-year election in history. On the international front, the Administration had had one of its best years. . . . Yet, the economic dip in October was obviously uppermost in the people's minds when they went to the polls. They completely rejected the President's appeal for the election of Republicans to the House and Senate.[4]

And, with regard to the 1960 presidential contest, Nixon wrote:

Unfortunately, Arthur Burns turned out to be a good prophet. The bottom of the 1960 dip did come in October and the economy started to move up in November—after it was too late to affect the election returns. In October, usually a month of rising employment, the jobless rolls increased by 452,000. All the speeches, television broadcasts, and precinct work in the world could not counteract that one hard fact.[5]

The matter was put most bluntly in a memorandum that Paul Samuelson wrote to President Kennedy and the Council of Economic Advisers:

> When my grandchildren ask me: "Daddy, what did you do for the New Frontier?," I shall sadly reply: "I kept telling them down at the office, in December, January, and April that, WHAT THIS COUNTRY NEEDS IS AN ACROSS THE BOARD RISE IN DISPOSABLE INCOME TO LOWER THE LEVEL OF UNEMPLOYMENT, SPEED UP THE RECOVERY AND THE RETURN TO HEALTHY GROWTH, PROMOTE CAPITAL FORMATION AND THE GENERAL WELFARE, INSURE DOMESTIC TRANQUILITY AND THE TRIUMPH OF THE DEMOCRATIC PARTY AT THE POLLS.[6]

A month before the 1976 presidential election, L. William Seidman, a top economic adviser and confidant of President Ford, commented on the slight downturn in the leading economic indicators for September: ". . . the economic issue could be important. It had been one of the strongest things we had going for us. When things turn sluggish, we lose some of the advantage."[7] A week before the election, Seidman again expressed his concern about the fall pause in the economy: "I think Mr. Ford's chances for re-election are very good. As for the economic lull, we considered the use of stimulus to make sure we didn't have a low third quarter, but the President didn't want anything to do with a short-term view."[8]

News reports, memoirs, and internal political documents abound with similar analyses by politicians, their economic advisers, and journalists.[9] In fact, since the 1930s only one administration has seemingly taken exception to the hypothesis that economic growth and stimulative fiscal policy are the important things politically. President Eisenhower and most of his cabinet officers (other than Richard Nixon), perhaps projecting their own ideological views on the electorate, felt that what voters wanted was a balanced federal budget—or, even better, a budget in surplus—and protection against inflation. But the belief in the political value of big budget surpluses and muted economic growth never took hold among politicians and economic policy-makers, particularly since they attributed the Republican losses of 1954, 1958, and 1960 to economic declines during those election years.[10]

The main propositions, in summary, of the politicians' theory of the impact of economic conditions on election outcomes emphasize short-run economic shifts:

1. Economic movements in the months immediately preceding an election can tip the balance and decide the outcome of an election.

2. The electorate rewards incumbents for prosperity and punishes them for recession.

3. Short-run spurts in economic growth in the months immediately preceding an election benefit incumbents.

What are the consequences of the politicians' economic theory of elections? Do incumbent administrations act on the theory and attempt to engineer election-year economic accelerations? Do macroeconomic fluctuations ride the electoral cycle? If so, what instruments of economic policy are deployed in election years?

My first concern [here will be] to show that electoral-economic cycles actually do exist.

Electoral-Economic Cycles in 27 Democracies

How is an electoral-economic cycle to be detected and measured? A whole range of economic indicators might be matched up with election dates in a shotgun search for correlations. Instead of cycle-searching through economic time-series, however, let us try to obtain some theoretical guidance to the electoral-economic cycle by considering the perspective of the incumbent administration on election-year economics. If the administration seeks a pre-election economic stimulation, it seems likely that the economic policy instruments involved must be easy to start up quickly and must yield clear and immediate economic benefits to a large number of voters—or at least to some specific large groups of voters if the benefits are targeted as well as timed. Increased transfer payments, tax cuts, and postponements in tax increases—all of which have a widespread impact and can be legislated and implemented quickly—are the policy instruments that come to mind. Election-year economics is probably not often a matter of sophisticated macroeconomic policy. The politicians' economic theory of election outcomes gives great weight to economic events in the months before the election; thus the politicians' strategy is to turn on the spigot surely and swiftly and fill the trough so that it counts with the electorate.

These considerations suggest that short-run fluctuations in real disposable income might be a good aggregate signal of the pre-election stimulation of the economy. Real disposable income, unlike other major aspects of aggregate economic performance (such as unemployment, inflation, or real growth), can be immediately and directly influenced by short-run government action through taxes and transfers with little uncertainty about the time lag between activation of the policy instruments and the resulting change in real disposable income. For example, a few days after increased social security or veterans checks are in the mail, real disposable personal income has increased. In fact, in normal economic times, taxes and transfers have more to do with determining real disposable income than whether the economy goes faster or slower. Changes in real disposable income, furthermore, have special political relevance: several studies have found that upswings in real disposable income per capita are highly correlated with greater electoral support for incumbents.[11]

It is appropriate to look at the rate of change in real disposable income in relation to elections in all the world's democratic countries. Earlier we saw evidence that U.S. politicians believed that pre-election prosperity would help them retain office when they sought re-election. No doubt similar beliefs—as well as the desire to be re-elected—animate members of the political elite in almost any democracy. Consequently, I assembled electoral and economic time-series (election dates, disposable income, price changes, and population) for all 29 countries classified as "democracies" circa 1969—those nations with both widespread participation in free elections and an effective political opposition.[12] For 27 of the 29 (missing were Lebanon and Trinidad-Tobago), data sufficient to compute changes in real disposable income per capita for each year from 1961 to 1972 were found. Then the yearly acceleration-deceleration in real disposable income per capita was compared with the timing of elections in each of the 27 democracies.

The findings are clear. Evidence for an electoral-economic cycle was found in 19 of the 27 countries; in those 19, short-run accelerations in real disposable income per capita were more likely to occur in election years than in years without elections. Table 1 shows the results. Combining all the experience of the 27 countries over the period 1961–1972 reveals that real disposable income growth accelerated in 64 percent of all elections years (N = 90) compared to 49 percent of all the years without elections (N = 205). Furthermore, for those 19 countries whose economies ran faster than usual in election years, the effect was substantial: real disposable income growth accelerated in 77 percent of election years compared with 46 percent of years without elections.

The data in Table 1 provide only aggregate testimony; to convince ourselves that in each of the 19 individual countries a political-economic cycle occurs would require considerably more evidence—a longer data series, more detail about the structure of the cycle, and a deeper understanding of the politics of economic policy in the various democracies. The fundamental point of the aggregate evidence is that 70 percent of the countries showed some signs of a political business cycle.[13]

A few countries have been studied more systematically. For Israel, Ben-Porath reports:

> In following the timing of discrete policy decisions, one can observe a fairly consistent pattern. Thus, for example, of the seven devaluations that took place in the period [1952–1973], the closest that one ever came to preceding an election was eighteen months. (The eighth devaluation took place in November 1974 approximately three years before the next scheduled elections.) When a public committee recommended reducing income tax rates and imposing a value added tax the government proceeded to implement the first in April 1973, expecting elections in November 1973, but waited with the second.[14]

For the six parliamentary elections from 1952 to 1973, per capita annual

Table 1

Elections and Economic Acceleration, 27 Democracies, 1961–1972

	Percentage of years in which rate of growth of real disposable income increased				Did acceleration in real income growth occur more often in election years compared to years without an election?
	election years	N	years without elections	N	
Australia	75%	4	29%	7	yes
Austria	25%	4	86%	7	no
Belgium	67%	3	63%	8	yes
Canada	100%	5	57%	7	yes
Chile	50%	2	44%	9	yes
Costa Rica	100%	2	50%	8	yes
Denmark	25%	4	43%	7	no
Finland	67%	3	50%	8	yes
France	60%	5	33%	6	yes
Germany	33%	3	38%	8	no
Iceland	33%	3	75%	8	no
India	50%	2	43%	7	yes
Ireland	67%	3	63%	8	yes
Israel	67%	3	50%	8	yes
Italy	33%	3	50%	8	no
Jamaica	100%	2	44%	9	yes
Japan	100%	4	29%	7	yes
Luxembourg	100%	2	56%	9	yes
Netherlands	50%	4	57%	7	no
New Zealand	75%	4	43%	7	yes
Norway	100%	2	33%	9	yes
Philippines	60%	5	67%	6	no
Sweden	67%	3	50%	8	yes
Switzerland	67%	3	50%	8	yes
United Kingdom	67%	3	38%	8	yes
United States	83%	6	40%	5	yes
Uruguay	33%	3	50%	8	no

consumption accelerated during the year before the election five out of six times; the average pre-election increase in consumption was 7.4 percent compared to 2.0 percent in the post-election periods. Similarly, per capita GNP increased a pre-election average of 7.9 percent as against a post-election 3.7 percent.

In the Philippines, the economy moved with the electoral cycle in a "biennial lurch" from 1957 to 1966 according to Averch, Koehler, and Denton. They sketch out a fairly complete pattern of political economies:

Although it is growing rapidly, the Philippine economy also appears to be rather unstable. At least until 1966, the reported rate of growth of real GNP

alternately rose and fell in a two-year cycle. . . . The survey data . . . suggest
that both politicians and voters perceive election strategy in terms of allocating
public works, jobs, and various other payoffs to maximize votes . . . the un-
evenness we observe is in part the consequence of fiscal and monetary policies
that work together to destabilize the economy. The instability does not reflect
the impact of uncontrollable events but is built into the Philippine political
system. As Philippine policymakers pursue and *achieve* their goals, they generate the cycles we have observed.[15]

The policy instrument implicated was the government budget: deficits were
run in six straight election years and surpluses in the five intervening years.

The studies of Israel and the Philippines help shore up the wishy-washy
results for these two countries recorded in Table 1. All the available material
combined—the case studies of Israel and the Philippines, Nordhaus's report on
the coincidence of unemployment and electoral cycles in Germany, New Zealand, and the United States, and, most importantly, the results of Table 1—yields
evidence of electoral-economic cycles in 21 of the world's 27 democracies.[16]

The Political History of Real Disposable Income
in the United States

Incumbent administrations in postwar America have generally enjoyed quite a
perky electoral-economic cycle. Figure 1 displays the path of yearly changes in
real disposable income per capita in the United States since 1947. During the
Truman, Kennedy, Johnson, Nixon, and Ford administrations, the short-run
growth in real disposable income per capita tended to swing up in election years
and drop down in odd-numbered years. The tie between elections and a quicken-
ing economy is a strong one: in those five administrations, real income growth
accelerated in eight of eleven election years (73 percent) compared to only two
of ten years (20 percent) without elections.

Things were different during the Eisenhower administration. Real income
growth declined in every election year (1954, 1956, 1958, and 1960), but rose in
three of the four intervening years without elections. Things were different because the economic goals and the evaluations of what was politically sound
economic policy were different. The dominant political-economic goals of the
Eisenhower presidency, unlike those of other postwar administrations, were the
reduction of inflation and a balanced (and small) federal budget. These economic
beliefs were initially reinforced by the election returns: Eisenhower read his
landslide victory in 1952 as the voters' express approval of these goals and as the
rejection of the Democratic focus on governmental intervention to reduce unemployment. The Eisenhower administration memoirs, fiscal histories, and dia-
ries—unlike those of any other postwar administration—bristle with determined
statements on the need to avoid inflation and reduce the federal budget. Stimulative interventionist policies by the government were to be avoided because they

Figure 1. **Yearly Changes in Real Disposable Income Per Capita, 1946–1976**

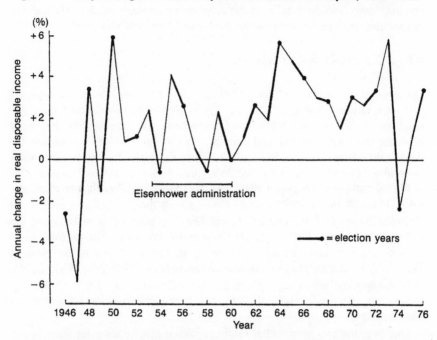

ultimately stifled creative business initiative and because they served little purpose, since economic downturns and unemployment were seen as self-curing.[17] These doctrines held firm even in the face of the deep pre-election economic slump of 1958 and the Burns-Nixon proposal to the cabinet to stimulate the economy in the months before the 1960 election.[18] In fact, going into the elections of 1954, 1956, and 1960, the federal budget was less stimulative than in the previous odd-numbered years; for two of those election years, moreover, the federal budget was in surplus. Perhaps there was a political budget cycle.[19] That policy, if it was a policy, may have grown out of a conviction that voters cared as strongly about a balanced federal budget as those who shaped economic policy. Certainly the economic outcomes differed; the results for all 15 election years from 1948 to 1976 were:[20]

	Number of years in which growth in real disposable income	
	accelerated	decelerated
Eisenhower administration	0	4
Other administrations	8	3

The Eisenhower years demonstrated that when the administration's views on political economy changed the political-economic cycle also changed. Once a new administration came into office in 1961 with a contrary doctrine about what was politically important as far as the economy was concerned, the match of the ups and downs of real income growth to election years was restored.[21]

A Four-Year Cycle in Unemployment

Let us examine another indicator of economic well-being, the unemployment rate, in relation to the U.S. electoral cycle. Nordhaus found that unemployment has tended to reach a low point around election time in Germany, New Zealand, the United States, and perhaps France and Sweden.[22] Evidence for the United States is shown in Figure 2, where the path of monthly unemployment is centered around the schedule of presidential elections from 1948 to 1976. In the main, unemployment has bottomed out every fourth November.[23] Unemployment levels twelve to eighteen months before presidential elections have exceeded unemployment levels at election time in six of the last eight presidential elections. (If the planned economic targets from 1977 to 1980 are achieved, the score will be up to seven out of nine by 1980.[24]) The elections during the Eisenhower administration, 1956 and 1960, are the only exceptions: while unemployment dipped slightly in 1956, everything was wrong, politically, with the pre- and post-election shifts in unemployment in 1960.

Omitting the two presidential elections taking place during the Eisenhower administration, the pre-election downturn in the unemployment rate in all the other postwar presidential elections is quite phenomenal:

—The unemployment rate in November 1948 was lower than in *all but five* of the preceding twenty-four months.
—The unemployment rate in November 1952 was lower than in *all but one* of the preceding twenty-four months.
—The unemployment rate in November 1964 was lower than in *all but two* of the preceding twenty-four months.
—The unemployment rate in November 1968 was lower than in *all* of the preceding twenty-four months.
—The unemployment rate in November 1972 was lower than in *all* of the preceding twenty-four months.
—The unemployment rate in November 1976 was lower than in *eleven* of the preceding twenty-four months.

Except in the Eisenhower years, the election-day unemployment rate has averaged about one percentage point below the rate twelve to eighteen months before the election and nearly two percentage points below the post-election unemployment rate twelve to eighteen months after the presidential election.

Figure 2. **Unemployment Rates and the Cycle of Presidential Elections, 1946–1976**

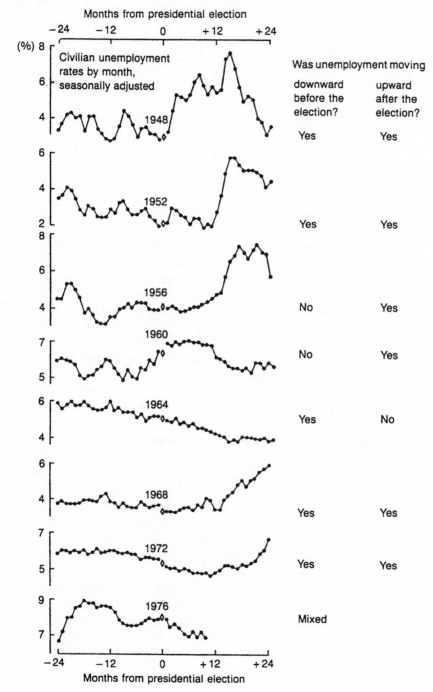

Table 2

Inflation, Unemployment, and Presidential Elections, 1946–1976

Yearly change in unemployment rate and inflation (real GNP deflator):	Presidential election years	All other years
less unemployment and less inflation	50%	9%
less unemployment, but more inflation	13	30
less inflation, but more unemployment	38	43
more inflation and more unemployment	0	17
	101%	99%
	(8)	(23)

Presidential Elections in Relation to the Trade-off Between Inflation and Unemployment

Since 1946, the American economy has beaten the putative trade-off between inflation and unemployment—by having less of both—in only six years. Four of these six great economic successes were delivered in presidential election years. The trade-off broke down in four other years when both inflation and unemployment increased. None of these failures took place in a presidential election, although three of them—in 1946, 1970, and 1974—did occur at the time of off-year congressional elections.

Table 2 shows the joint inflation-unemployment movements in relation to presidential elections for all thirty-one years from 1946 to 1976. It is apparent that the way to defeat the trade-off between inflation and unemployment in the short-run is to hold a presidential election.

The Electoral Stakes and the Electoral-Economic Cycle

Elections differ in how much is at stake. An election year in which an incumbent president seeks reelection is far more important, from the perspective of the incumbent administration, than a midterm congressional election. The incentives for producing a booming pre-election economy are greater in some election years than others. Is it true, then, that the greater the electoral stakes, the greater the likelihood and the greater the magnitude of pre-election economic acceleration?

The short-run stimulation of the economy for electoral purposes involves several possible costs to an administration: inflationary pressures, destabilization, political attacks on deficit spending or the other policy instruments used to stimulate the economy, disruption of governmental programs due to shifts in the rate of government spending, political attacks on the fact of the stimulation itself, having to forgo stimulation at other times when it might be useful for long-run economic management. Such costs are more tolerable, of course, when the potential electoral benefits are greater.

From the vantage point of the incumbent administration—particularly the incumbent president—years can be ordered from maximum to minimum electoral importance:

1. On-years, incumbent president seeking re-election
2. Midterm congressional elections
3. On-years, incumbent president not seeking re-election
4. Odd-numbered years

There are surely special incentives to the administration in those on-years when the incumbent president seeks re-election; his direct personal interest in political survival coincides with what must be a particularly tempting opportunity to hit the economic accelerator. In those on-years when the incumbent president is not seeking re-election, his interest is not so clear. While his political party would inevitably consider more important all on-year over all off-year elections, a president might quite reasonably consider the congressional elections in the middle of his term as more important than an election at the conclusion of his political career. Success at midterm—or at least curbing the losses of his congressional allies, which is about the best the president can expect in an off-year—may allow him to maintain the force and continuity of his program, and may also serve as the beginnings of a drive for re-election. The downgrading of the electoral importance (from the president's point of view) of the on-year when he is retiring is reinforced by the apparent ambivalence that presidents seem to have felt toward their party's nomination of a successor (consider Truman-Stevenson in 1952, Eisenhower-Nixon in 1960, and Johnson-Humphrey in 1968—the only relevant cases in many years). Finally on our list, there is no doubt that odd-numbered years are the least important electorally.

Having ranked the electoral importance of each year of a president's term, we can test the prediction that the greater the political importance of the year, the greater the efforts that an administration will make to accelerate the economy. Table 3 shows the clear link between the extent of economic well-being and the electoral importance of the year: *the greater the electoral stakes, the greater the economic improvement.* Real disposable income increased an average of 3.4 percent in years when the incumbent president sought re-election, 2.6 percent in midterm election years, 2.0 percent in those on-years when the incumbent president did not seek re-election, and a dismal 1.5 percent in odd-numbered years.[25]

The most important finding here—the difference between presidential elections when an incumbent seeks re-election and other years—holds over the entire set of elections from 1946 to 1976, *including* the Eisenhower years. During those thirty-one years the median rate of growth in real disposable income per capita was 3.3 percent in years when the incumbent president sought re-election compared to 1.7 percent in all other years.

Table 3

Annual Change in Real Disposable Income per Capita in Relation to the Political Complexion of the Years, all Postwar Administrations Except Eisenhower's

	No election	On-year incumbent president not seeking re-election	Midterm election	On-year incumbent president seeking re-election
1946			−2.6%	
1947	−5.9%			
1948				3.4%
1949	−1.5%			
1950			5.9%	
1951	0.9%			
1952		1.1%		
1961	1.0%			
1962			2.6%	
1963	1.9%			
1964				5.6%
1965	4.8%			
1966			3.9%	
1967	3.0%			
1968		2.8%		
1969	1.5%			
1970			3.0%	
1971	2.6%			
1972				3.3%
1973	5.9%			
1974			−2.3%	
1975	1.0%			
1976				3.3%
Median amount	1.5%	2.0%	2.8%	3.4%

The rhetoric of policy initiatives matches the reality of the electoral-economic cycle. A content analysis of presidential State of the Union messages from 1946 to 1969 revealed that the most important topic after international relations was social welfare and allocative policy, and that its importance varied with the presidential election cycle and the term of the president:

> ... the modal activity in this policy area is for the president to respond to the claim of a single segment of American society by asking Congress to pass legislation to confer some benefit on them.
>
> The temporal pattern in this policy area is almost the opposite to that characteristic of international involvement. The distribution of social benefits is primarily a first term phenomenon. It rises gradually, but does not over-

shadow the more important international policy area until the president's fourth year in office. When faced with re-election needs, he is likely to be bountiful. But during a president's second term, the loadings on this factor fall sharply. One might argue that a second term president does not have much influence with Congress and hence is less likely to urge them to undertake new activities. Whether or no, it does seem clear that there are political gains accruing from giving population groupings benefits they want: health, welfare assistance, housing, consumer protection, and so forth. Presidents attempt to distribute this largess when they have the greatest need to increase their political support.[26]

Conclusion

There is, then, an electoral rhythm to the national economic performance of many capitalist democracies. The electoral cycle causes substantial macroeconomic fluctuations.

In the United States, the electoral-economic cycle from 1948 to 1976 (other than the Eisenhower years) has consisted of:

—A two-year cycle in the growth of real disposable income per capita, with accelerations in even-numbered years and decelerations in odd-numbered years.

—A four-year presidential cycle in the unemployment rate, with downturns in unemployment in the months before the presidential election and upturns in the unemployment rate usually beginning from twelve to eighteen months after the election.

These patterns are consistent with the character of the economic tools available to control real disposable income and unemployment. Real disposable income—which is directly and immediately affected by taxes and transfer payments—can be manipulated in the short run. The unemployment rate, by contrast, is affected by fiscal and monetary policies that act more slowly and with more uncertain time lags on unemployment than do taxes and transfers on real disposable income.

Further, the greater the electoral stakes, the greater the economic stimulation. In particular, those years when incumbent presidents sought re-election enjoyed the most favorable short-run economic conditions. It comes as no surprise, however, to discover that upon re-election several of those incumbent presidents had to undertake, as their first economic priority, deflationary policies.

Like a detective in a murder mystery, I have tried so far to establish a motive and to find a pattern. The questions that remain are those of means and opportunity: How is the electoral-economic cycle produced? What specific instruments of economic policy are involved?

Notes

1. The three fundamental papers, each with a very different perspective on political economics, are M. Kalecki, "Political Aspects of Full Employment," *Political Quarterly,*

14 (October-December 1943), 322–331; William D. Nordhaus, "The Political Business Cycle," *Review of Economic Studies*, 42 (April 1975), 169–190; and Assar Lindbeck, Stabilization Policy in Open Economies with Endogenous Politicians," *American Economic Review*, 66 (May 1976), 1–19. Other major developments are found in C.A.E. Goodhart and R.J. Bhansali, "Political Economy," *Political Studies*, 18 (March 1970), 43–106; W. Miller and M. Mackie, "The Electoral Cycle and the Asymmetry of Government and Opposition Popularity," *Political Studies*, 21 (September 1973), 263–279; C.O. Duncan MacRae, "A Political Model of the Business Cycle," working paper, December 1971, The Urban Institute, Washington, D.C.; Raford Boddy and James Crotty, "Class Conflict and Macro-Policy: The Political Business Cycle," *Review of Radical Political Economics*, 7 (Spring 1975), 1–19; and the many papers of Frey and his co-workers, including Bruno S. Frey and Friedrich Schneider, "On the Modelling of Politico-Economic Interdependence," *European Journal of Political Research*, 3 (1975), 339–360. Suggestions for further research are developed in Ryan C. Amacher, William J. Boyes, Thomas Deaton, and Robert D. Tollison, "The Political Business Cycle: A Review of Theoretical and Empirical Evidence," manuscript, 1977.

2. Nordhaus, "Political Business Cycle," p. 186. Similar mixed results are reported in Martin Paldam, "Is There an Electional Cycle? A Comparative Study of National Accounts," Institute of Economics, University of Aarhus, Denmark, 1977, no. 8.

3. Walter W. Heller, *New Dimensions of Political Economy* (Cambridge, Mass.: Harvard University Press, 1966), p. 12.

4. Richard M. Nixon, *Six Crises* (Garden City, N.Y.: Doubleday, 1962), p. 309.

5. Ibid., pp. 310–311.

6. Paul Samuelson, "Memorandum for the President and the Council of Economic Advisers: That 'April Second Look' at the Economy," March 21, 1961 (John F. Kennedy Presidential Library).

7. Hobart Rowen, "Ford Aide Sees Lag in GNP Aiding Carter," *Washington Post*, October 6, 1976, p. A17.

8. Vartanig G. Vartan, "Seidman Expects Leveling in Leading Economic Index: Ford Adviser Says Pause Is Now Lull," *New York Times*, October 26, 1976, p. 51.

9. The best guides are Herbert Stein, *The Fiscal Revolution in America* (Chicago: University of Chicago Press, 1969) and James L. Sundquist, *Politics and Policy: The Eisenhower, Kennedy, and Johnson Years* (Washington, D.C.: The Brookings Institution, 1968). For Britain, David Butler and Donald Stokes report: ". . . how deeply rooted in British politics is the idea that the Government is accountable for good and bad times. Popular acceptance of this idea means that the state of the economy has loomed large in the minds of all modern Prime Ministers as they pondered on the timing of a dissolution. And in the post-Keynesian era more than one government has been tempted to seek a favorable context for an election by expanding the economy, although dissolutions are more easily timed to coincide with expansion than the other way round" (*Political Change in Britain*, 2nd ed. [New York: St. Martin's Press, 1974], p. 369).

10. Nixon pointed to economic downturns in the few months before the elections of 1954, 1958, and 1960 (*Six Crises*, pp. 309–312). Sundquist makes a similar point: "Three elections [1954, 1958, and 1960] had taught the politicians that they *must* respond to the issue of unemployment whenever it appears. In a more positive sense, experience since 1964 had also taught them that a full employment economy provides the greater revenues from which the politicians' dreams are realized" (*Politics and Policy*, p. 56). And James Tobin sharpens the observation: "Recessions of course are politically dangerous, as Republican defeats in 1932, 1954, 1958, 1960—we might add 1970—indicate. But a first-derivative mentality is strong in American politics. Provided economic indicators are moving up, their level is secondary. Incidentally, politico-econometric studies of the

influence of economic variables on elections confirm this instinctive feeling of politicians: the current growth rate of GNP counts for votes, but not the level of unemployment" (*The New Economics One Decade Older* [Princeton: Princeton University Press, 1974], p. 20).

11. Gerald Kramer, "Short-Term Fluctuations in U.S. Voting Behavior, 1896–1964," *American Political Science Review,* 65 (March 1971), 131–143; and Edward R. Tufte, "Determinants of the Outcomes of Midterm Congressional Elections," *American Political Science Review,* 69 (September 1975), 812–826. Further evidence is discussed in Chapters 4 and 5 below.

12. The list is from Robert A. Dahl, *Polyarchy: Participation and Opposition* (New Haven: Yale University Press, 1971), pp. 231–248. The data sources for each table and figure are described in the Appendix, "Data Sources," p. 155.

13. Since election dates in these democracies are scattered over the years, the observed relationship between the occurrence of elections and short-run economic stimulation is not the artifactual product of common worldwide changes in economic conditions. At least such was the case in the 1960s. In Chapter 3, however, I shall present evidence for the increasing synchronization since 1970 of election timing in the major capitalist democracies.

14. Yoram Ben-Porath, "The Years of Plenty and the Years of Famine—A Political Business Cycle?" *Kyklos,* 28 (1975), 400.

15. Harvey A. Averch, John E. Koehler, and Frank H. Denton, *The Matrix of Policy in the Philippines* (Princeton: Princeton University Press, 1971), pp. 95–96. The capital-intensive character of Philippine elections, election-stimulated inflation, and post-election retrenchment appear to have combined to produce both an unstable economy and unstable ruling coalitions. On this, see the excellent analysis in Thomas C. Nowak, "The Philippines before Martial Law: A Study in Politics and Administration," *American Political Science Review,* 71 (June 1977), 522–539.

16. I investigated the possibility that electoral-economic cycles might be more likely to occur in countries having irregular election schedules, where the date of the election is set by the incumbent government. The cycle, however, appeared with nearly equal frequency in countries with flexible election dates and in countries with fixed dates. A more subtle possibility is that countries with non-periodic election dates have elections called at economic extremes, with the incumbent government seizing the opportunity for electoral gains in prosperous times and crumbling in times of economic crisis. The hypothesis is too subtle to test with the data of Table 1. For countries with non-periodic elections, the direction of the causal arrow must remain ambiguous: does a buoyant economy produce elections or does the prospect of elections produce stimulative economic policies? Such questions, which depend among other things on the time horizons of politicians and how politicians perceive the time horizons of voters, pose difficult problems of model specification and estimation.

17. Full details are in Stein, *Fiscal Revolution,* chapters 11–14, and Sundquist, *Politics and Policy.* See also Edward S. Flash, Jr., *Economic Advice and Presidential Leadership* (New York: Columbia University Press, 1965) and Eisenhower's memoirs *Mandate for Change* (Garden City, N.Y.: Doubleday, 1963) and *Waging Peace* (Garden City, N.Y.: Doubleday, 1965).

18. See Eisenhower, *Waging Peace,* pp. 307–310; and Nixon, *Six Crises,* pp. 309–311.

19. Evidence on this point is found in a letter from the Secretary of the Treasury, George M. Humphrey, to President Eisenhower on December 6, 1956 (Eisenhower Presidential Library):

> These are a few thoughts I hope you may have in mind as you think of the problem of the budget. The matter of timing is of very great importance as to both politics and economics.
>
> *As to politics:* I believe we can resist any major tax reductions this coming year provided there is a real prospect of an important reduction to be effective in 1958. . . .

Barring a war, I think there will have to be a substantial general tax reduction sometime during the next four years and, politically, the best time to have it will be in 1958. If this occurs, we will be in approximately the same situation as in the past four years and the voters will actually have the benefit of a tax cut for a couple of years before the next Presidential election.

20. The exact probability (via the hypergeometric distribution) of observing an outcome as extreme as that shown in the two-by-two table in the text, under the null hypothesis that there is no difference between the Eisenhower and the other administrations, is only 1/39 or about 0.026 (under the assumptions of fixed marginals and independence of observations). Consequently we reject either the null hypothesis or the assumptions. The Eisenhower case is bothersome, naturally raising questions about the selective use of evidence. It appears that the Eisenhower administration did make electoral cycle calculations in formulating its economic policies, but that other priorities—preventing inflation, limiting government intervention in the economy, seeking a budget surplus—were far more important than the all-out stimulation of the economy in election years. Given Eisenhower's assured re-election in 1956 and his quite limited devotion to the 1960 Nixon campaign, it is not surprising that ideological priorities in economic policy substituted for heating up the pre-election economy. Finally, in this chapter as well as the next two we shall see a great deal of additional evidence (mostly not dependent on the Eisenhower exclusion) that details the structure and content of the electoral-economic cycle.

21. A sharp contrast between the two administrations is provided in Paul Samuelson, "Economic Policy for 1962," *Review of Economics and Statistics,* 44 (1962), 3–6; and in Seymour E. Harris, *The Economics of the Two Political Parties* (New York: MacMillan, 1962). See also Tobin, *The New Economics One Decade Older.*

22. Nordhaus, "Political Business Cycle," p. 186. I have borrowed the arrangement for my Figure 2 from an unpublished draft of Nordhaus's paper.

23. The unemployment rates reported here are seasonally adjusted, thereby removing (among other things) the normal downturn in unemployment (unadjusted) occurring in the fall of each year. Thus the actual, unadjusted unemployment rates would show a sharper pre-election improvement. This becomes an interesting issue in understanding how the electorate responds to pre-election economic changes: Do voters seasonally adjust? If not, then the normal autumn economic upswing benefits incumbents in those countries holding elections late in the year.

24. In his press conference on November 16, 1976, President-elect Carter said: "We believe that we can get the unemployment rate down over a fairly long period of time— two, three or perhaps four years—to the 4 to 4½ percent figure before excessive inflation will be felt. But I will reveal my plans as they are evolved. They are not final enough now to discuss further" (*New York Times,* November 16, 1976, p. 32). Later, the 1980 unemployment goal became 4.75 percent. See James T. Wooten, "Carter Delay on Endorsing Bill Linked to 4% Unemployment Provision," *New York Times,* October 20, 1977, p. A12.

25. Let E_i = real disposable income per capita in year i. The annual change (in percentage terms) in real disposable income per capita is simply

$$\Delta E = \frac{E_i - E_{i-1}}{E_{i-1}} \times 100.$$

In Chapter 5 [of *Political Control of the Economy]* ΔE [is] related to the national vote for members of the incumbent (White House) party.

26. John H. Kessel, "The Parameters of Presidential Politics," *Social Science Quarterly* (June 1974), 8–24, at pp. 11–14.

4.5. Elections and the Economy in the 1980s: Short- and Long-Term Effects

MORRIS P. FIORINA

The early work on the relation between economic conditions and electoral success, like that of Tufte above, focused on the short-term effects of economic conditions on the vote for the president and Congress. The early work tended to confirm Tufte's result that the state of the economy helped determine who became president, but was more mixed on the effects on Congress.

The later work in this tradition has sought to extend these early results. Fiorina represents one direction in which this more recent research has gone. Even those who held that economic conditions were an important determinant of electoral success held that other factors, such as the popularity of the candidate and the popularity of his party, were also important. In this work, Fiorina asks whether in the longer term voters' identification with a party is partly determined by that party's success in managing the economy. This is an important question both because it makes economic management even more important than the short-term models would lead us to believe and because it would provide politicians with an incentive to avoid political business cycles such as those Tufte discusses.

In 1980 Ronald Reagan led the Republican party into the Promised Land. That the Reagan-Bush ticket carried 49 states was noteworthy enough, but the party also scored unanticipated victories in numerous Senate races, giving it control of that body for the first time since 1954, and a respectable gain of 33 seats in the House of Representatives gave the president a "working conservative majority" in that Democratic stronghold. All of this set off talk of a "turn to the right," a "Reagan Revolution," and a(nother) new Republican majority. After the rhetoric cleared, however, research pronounced a less sweeping verdict. The 1980 elections were just another example of the rejection of failed leadership. In particular, Americans found the Carter administration wanting in two major respects (Schneider 1981). First, there was national frustration with the course of international affairs, especially with America's apparent helplessness in the face of terrorism. Second, there was deep dissatisfaction with the course of economic affairs. A Democratic president with comfortable Democratic majorities in Congress had presided over a "stagflation" culminating in double-digit inflation and interest rates combined with moderate unemployment and low growth.

The succeeding elections of the 1980s confirmed the view that traditional, off-the-shelf explanations still applied. In 1982, coming out of the worst recession since the Great Depression, the Republicans lost 26 House seats. But with inflation crushed and the economy growing, Republican fortunes rebounded and in 1984 Reagan enjoyed a sweeping reelection victory. To the surprise of many economists and the consternation of many Democrats, the recovery continued, and in 1988 George Bush profited by leading the Republican party to its third straight presidential victory and fifth out of the past six.[1]

Some commentators argue that the story of the Reagan elections is little more than the story of the economy (Kiewiet and Rivers 1985). Others argue that the story is more complicated, but no one denies that the economy was a major element of the story. This paper briefly recounts that story. Part of it is as straightforward as these introductory sentences suggest: the economy had the expected effects on presidential approval, the presidential vote, and the distribution of congressional seats. What political scientists refer to as the "short-term" effects of the economy operated much as models and methods developed with data from the 1960s and 1970s predicted inflation and rising incomes are political goods, while the opposites are "bads." From this standpoint the 1980s simply gave us more observations and a bit more variance. But the economy had a deeper, more subtle effect as well. During the 1980s the balance of partisan affiliations shifted toward the Republicans. This shift involves what political scientists refer to as long-term effects, the basis of statements about the "majority party," the "emerging Republican majority," and the end of the "New Deal party system." The two major sections of this paper describe the short- and long-term effects of the economy in the 1980s. In the next section I will survey the short-term effects. Then, in the more original part of the paper, I will report some preliminary analyses that suggest deeper, more lasting effects that will be felt in elections yet to come.

1.1 Economic Conditions, Public Opinion, and Voting

In the past two decades few topics have received more scholarly attention than the relationship between economic conditions on the one hand and public opinion and voting on the other. First, political scientists attempted to match fluctuations in economic time series with fluctuations in the congressional vote (Kramer 1971; Tufte 1975) and presidential approval (Mueller 1970; Kernell 1978; Monroe 1978). Then, seeing easy pickings, economists improved on our methods and models (Fair 1978; Frey and Schneider 1978; Golden and Poterba 1980) and even endogenized economic conditions themselves via models of the "political business cycle" (Nordhaus 1975). The literature is too vast to even attempt to review here.[2] I will simply survey its principal findings by taking a closer look at the electoral politics of the 1980s.

1.1.2 Economic Conditions and Reagan Approval

Studies of presidential approval have a standard design though they differ in numerous details. Gallup presidential approval figures (often quarterly averages) are regressed on measures of economic conditions (typically variations in unemployment, inflation, and real income), variables designed to capture the effects of wars (Korea, Vietnam), dummy variables representing important events (Watergate, the Iranian hostage crisis), and variables that capture changes in presidential administrations. Analysts have reached no firm consensus about the lagged effects of economic variables (Golden and Poterba 1980; Hibbs 1982; Norpoth 1985) and whether approval follows well-defined cycles or trends (Stimson 1976). Within administrations, however, recent economic conditions have clear and reasonably precise effects on presidential approval.

Casual consumers of 1980s political commentary will be surprised by the thrust of research findings in this area. From the standpoint of approval models, there was no "teflon" president, at least in the economic realm. When economic dirt hit, it stuck. The Reagan administration took harsh action to halt the inflation of the previous decade. As an economic result, the country entered into a serious recession. As a political result, Reagan's approval figures plummeted more than 30 points to a low of 35 percent (as a benchmark consider that Richard Nixon's ratings bottomed out at 23 percent just before resigning). As the economy recovered Reagan's approval ratings recovered with it. By the 1984 election he had gained 20 points. After careful analysis Kiewiet and Rivers conclude that "differences between Carter's and Reagan's levels of popularity are satisfactorily explained by the differences between the respective economic records and rally points of the two administrations. . . . Reagan's popularity at reelection was almost solely a function of the performance of the economy after the 1982 midterm elections" (1985, 81–82).

The most recent analyses using data extending to 1987 agree. The pattern of

Reagan's popularity—not just one but two recoveries after declines—may have been unprecedented, but the underlying causes were not.[3] Ostrom and Simon (1989) make a heroic effort to augment the standard analyses with measures of the Reaganauts' purported flair for the dramatic—the heart-tugging prime-time speech and the well-covered presidential trip. They conclude that such public relations efforts had little effect. When the economy faltered, Reagan's approval figures weakened; when the economy gathered steam, Reagan's figures perked up.[4] He left office the most popular president since Eisenhower because he left office with a strong economy.

1.1.3 Economic Conditions and the Presidential Vote

The frequency with which pollsters inquire about presidential approval makes time-series analysis a natural choice for students of presidential popularity. The infrequency with which presidential elections actually occur has the opposite effect on students of the presidential vote. Only Niskanen (1975) and Fair (1982) have carried out analyses and votes analogous to those for approval.

Niskanen examined the 20 elections between 1896 and 1972, regressing the log of the incumbent party's vote on economic variables, the previous party vote, and incumbency. A noteworthy feature of his analysis is that changes in the economy were measured across the *four-year* interval between elections. While there is some disagreement in the literature, the modal analysis supports a shorter frame of reference (i.e., myopic voters). Nonetheless, Niskanen's estimates indicate that voter support for presidents is significantly related to real per capita net national product since the previous election.

Fair develops a general model that includes Kramer's backward-looking voters as a special case, but with so few observations—the 22 elections between 1892 and 1976—he is not able to analyze the full model. Constrained analyses indicate that the presidential vote responds to the growth rate of real per capita GNP, change in unemployment, and perhaps to change in the price level. Developments in the election year appear to be most important, except in the case of prices where a two-year change is better.

The 1980s provided Fair (1982, 1988) the opportunity to update the basic model. With the 1980 and 1984 elections included in the estimation the negative electoral effect of inflation becomes more apparent. And the evidence of voter myopia grows stronger, as the growth rate of GNP during the second and third quarters of the election year is more important than change measured over a longer interval. For purposes of this discussion the most interesting question is how well the original Fair model predicts the elections of the 1980s. Coefficient estimates based on the 1892–1976 elections predict that Reagan would get about 53 percent of the vote in 1980, an underestimate of 2 percent, and 55 percent of the vote in 1984, an underestimate of about 4 percent. Bush was predicted to get only 49 percent of the vote in 1988, an underestimate of 5 percent.[5] Do the underestimates for the 1980s elections reflect the vaunted Reagan personality factor? Probably not. Fair's equations do not take account of foreign relations, which were working against the Democrats in all three elections.[6] Thus, these underestimates are perfectly comprehensible.

In view of the data limitations and theoretical difficulties encountered by analyses like Niskanen's and Fair's,[7] and given the existence of high-quality election year surveys, political scientists have concentrated on cross-sectional analysis of the effects of the economy and economic issues on the presidential vote. The existence and importance of economic influences has never been much in question; rather, the variety of such effects and the manner in which they operate have been the concerns of political scientists. Numerous analyses demonstrate that voting reflects individual perceptions of both one's own economic circumstances (Fiorina 1978), and of the broader economic climate (Kinder and Kiewiet 1979). Judgments of the economic performance of the government are most important of all, but such judgments reflect factors such as partisanship and candidate attractiveness as well as pure economic performance (Fiorina 1981b). To some extent perceptions of the condition of their *group* (e.g., blacks, farmers) shape how people react to real economic conditions (Kinder, Adams, and Gronke 1989). In general, the political science cross-sectional studies suggest that the individual behavior underlying aggregate election results is more heterogeneous (Rivers 1988) and more complicated than might appear from an examination of aggregate time-series analyses. Voters do not simply look at their wallets and vote accordingly; rather, they make a more complex judgment that reflects individual, sectoral, and national conditions, both those already realized and others only expected.[8]

Complications aside, however, it was these cross-sectional studies that established that 1980 was largely a rejection of Jimmy Carter's performance rather than an endorsement of supply-side economics (Markus 1982; Miller and Wattenberg 1985). Similarly, cross-sectional studies established that in 1984 voters chose Reagan despite closer agreement with Mondale on issues such as defense spending, Central America, and abortion. They chose Reagan because they thought he had performed well as president, and one of the reasons they thought he had performed well was because the economy was thought to be strong (Abramson, Aldrich, and Rohde 1986). At the time of this writing, cross-sectional studies are establishing that George Bush's victory in 1988 was not just an artifact of the diabolical cleverness of Republican media wizards. Rather, he won because the economy continued strong and people who approved of Reagan's performance transferred their approval to Bush (Shanks and Miller 1990; Weisberg 1989).

1.1.4 Economic Conditions and the Congressional Vote

Kramer's 1971 article is clearly the seminal piece in the modern study of economics and elections. Taking the House elections between 1896 and 1964, Kramer regressed the aggregate Republican vote on a series of economic variables including unemployment, inflation, and real income. The estimates indicate that variations in real income carried the explanatory weight in the equation, with a 1 percent decline in real income producing a .5 percent decline in the House vote share of the administration.

Kramer's model assumed identical economic effects in presidential and off-year elections. Noting that, with the exception of 1934, the incumbent administration had lost House seats in every midterm election since the Civil War, Tufte (1975) argued that off-year elections should be treated separately as referenda on the performance of the incumbent President. Taking the eight elections between 1946 and 1974, Tufte regressed (the logit of) the aggregate congressional vote on the rate of change in real per capita disposable income during the election year, presidential approval at the time of the election, and a measure of the "baseline" vote. His estimate of the vote consequence of real income change (.35 percent) is smaller than Kramer's but this estimate is net of changes in presidential popularity that, as noted above, also varies with changes in real income.

Forecasting the results of congressional elections quickly developed into a cottage industry, with producers such as Jacobson and Kernell (1983), Lewis-Beck and Rice (1984), and Campbell (1985). Like the Tufte model, all of these refinements include measures of presidential approval and economic conditions and in some way or another take account of differences between midterm and presidential-year elections.[9] The models differ in their assumptions about the lags with which presidential approval and economic conditions affect the election results. Oppenheimer, Stimson, and Waterman (1986) add an "exposure" variable that represents the number of seats held by a party in excess of its "normal" holding. A party that is highly exposed (the 1966 Democrats) is in greater danger than one that is minimally exposed (the 1986 Republicans). In a sense the exposure variable provides a substantive explanation for an observed regression to the mean.

How well did such models perform in the 1980s? Each election tends to yield a new winner, but as a group they do quite well.[10] The Marra-Ostrom model (1989) misses the 1984 outcome by one seat.[11] The 1986 case was particularly instructive. Early in the election year journalists speculated about the "six-year itch." Since 1932 the average midterm seat loss for the party of a reelected president was more than 50 (Cook 1985). So, in a classic case of naive forecasting some pundits anticipated a Republican disaster. In actual fact the Republicans lost only five seats, one of the smallest midterm losses ever, but exactly as predicted by Marra and Ostrom and very close to the prediction of Oppenheimer et al. (1986) (seven) for a minimally exposed party. There have been some disastrous sixth year showings, but they reflect conditions (the 1938 and 1958 recessions, the 1966 city and campus riots, and the 1974 recession and Watergate crisis) that were not present in 1986.

Although the accuracy of the congressional models is impressive, their forecasting performance again exceeds our capacity to describe the underlying behavioral processes. For one thing, the early studies of Kramer (1971) and Tufte (1975) sought to predict the House *vote,* whereas the later generation models focus directly on House *seats.* The justification for the shift is that the analyst is interested in a system-level response (control of Congress) to a system-level condition (state of the economy). This is obviously a specious argument. Seats are not affected directly by economic conditions; seats do not experience employment or inflation; seats do not vote. The United States has a single-member simple plurality (SMSP) electoral system, not a proportional representation (PR) system, and, as is well known, SMSP systems translate seats into votes in a nonproportional and variable manner (Gudgin and Taylor 1979). Moreover, there is evidence that the translation of votes into seats underwent a structural change in the 1960s, a regime shift not incorporated in existing midterm models (Ansolabehere, Brady, and Fiorina 1988). Nevertheless, such models forecast rather accurately. Apparently aggregation saves the forecasting models from the consequences of their logically questionable specifications.

A second area of uncertainty again involves the microbehavior that underlies the effects of aggregate economic conditions. Cross-sectional studies using survey data have found no effect of individual financial condition on the congressional voting, at least after 1960 (Fiorina 1978). This has stimulated two alternative theories. First, Kinder and Kiewiet (1979, 1981) argue that voting behavior is based less on individual economic circumstances than on individual perceptions of collective circumstances, that voters are "sociotropic" rather than individually self-interested. Second, Jacobson and Kernell (1983) maintain that the effect of economic conditions on elections is partially a self-fulfilling prophecy, as strong candidates decline to run and contributors decline to give in "bad" years for their party. For this reason the Jacobson and Kernell forecasts utilize presidential approval and economic conditions in the *spring* of the election year, since that is when the deadlines for candidate filing occur.

Kramer (1983) mounted a vigorous attack on these lines of work, arguing that cross-sectional variation in real income does not much reflect government policies or actions, whereas a substantial portion of temporal variation does. Thus, cross-sectional studies of economic conditions and voting are essentially useless. Markus (1988) and Rivers (1990) utilize pooled time-series cross-sectional designs to refute Kramer partially and to identify some individual basis for the aggregate results. At this time, scholarly guns are quiet, but the matter is still open.

Finally, several scholars recently have questioned the very existence of a direct link between aggregate economic conditions and midterm election results. They argue that although economic conditions affect the *presidential* vote two years prior, the midterm loss reflects a "presidential penalty" (Erikson 1988, 1990) or "moderation" of the president (Alesina and Rosenthal 1989) that is not a direct effect of the economic circumstances prevailing between the presidential and midterm elections. Jacobson (1990) rebuts these analyses, questioning their specifications, and suggesting alternative specifications under which recent economic conditions do affect the congressional outcome. For present purposes, the answer to this question is not important. Even if Erikson, Alesina, and Rosenthal are correct, they do not suggest that the 1980s are in any way different; rather, the implication of their work is that analysts misinterpreted the data all along.

In sum, whatever the resolution of the remaining puzzles and controversies about the effects of the economy on public opinion and national voting, it is clear that they derive from the normal progress of a research program. Nothing about the politics of the 1980s called into question models first developed in the 1970s. From the standpoint of the short-term effects of the economy, the 1980s have been politics as usual.

1.2 Economic Conditions and the Party Balance

The work discussed in the preceding section focuses on the short-term effects of the economy, that is, the impact of economic conditions on particular decisions, like whom to support in presidential and congressional contests. Such analyses implicitly view elections as determined by the particular circumstances surrounding them. The apparent statistical evidence for voter myopia further reinforces that presumption. But while the particular circumstances surrounding elections obviously are important, political scientists have long been aware that election outcomes also reflect long-term factors that are *relatively* constant from election to election. One such long-term factor is *party image,* the popular view of a party based on a history of policy and performance extending considerably beyond the previous two quarters. For more than a generation Americans viewed the Democratic party as the party of prosperity.[12] From the time Gallup began asking the question in the early 1940s until 1981, the Democrats trailed the Republicans only three times.[13] The Republicans pulled ahead in 1981, fell back in 1982–83, and pulled ahead for good in 1984. Most students of elections considered this development as important as the actual election results of the 1980s, for the simple reason that many voters are innocent of the particular candidates and issues in an election and vote on the basis of these general, long-standing party images.

For election analysts the quintessential long-term force is party identification, called partisanship or party ID for short. Gallup has *never* taken a poll in which more respondents identified themselves as Republicans than as Democrats. The same is true for the American National Election Studies (NES). Every postelection survey, including those in which Republicans embarrassed the Democratic opposition (1956, 1972, 1980, 1984, 1988), has found a plurality of citizens classifying themselves as Democrats. In panel studies (interviews with the same respondents at two or more times) no survey item shows greater stability, and movements in aggregate party ID typically are described as "glacial" (Table 1 and Figure 1).

So impressed by its stability were the first students of party identification that

Figure 1. **Party Identification in the United States, 1952–88**

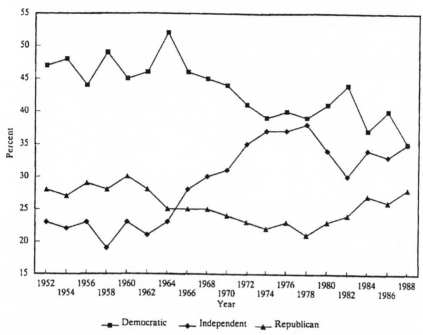

they likened it to popular religious affiliations—learned in childhood, devoid of doctrinal underpinnings, and impervious to change in later life (Campbell, Converse, Miller, and Stokes 1960). Not only was it a preexisting "bias" that most voters carried into the voting booth, but it also served as a "perceptual screen" through which voters selectively perceived the candidates, issues, and conditions of the time. Election analyses of the 1960s pronounced party ID to be the single most important factor in American elections.

Developments of the late 1960s and early 1970s led to revisions in the prevailing view. First, there was the much-discussed rise in self-identified independents. By the late 1970s pundits regularly referred to independents as the second largest "party," ahead of the Republicans.[14] Second, there was an erosion of "strong" partisans, as fewer respondents admitted to an unconditional affiliation with either party. Third, there was a weakening of the link between professed party identification and the presidential vote, as self-identified Democrats blithely chose Republican presidential candidates. Stimulated by such anomalies younger researchers began to contemplate the possibility that party ID was not an unmoved mover and took the heretical step of putting it on the left-hand side in their analyses. Jackson (1975) showed that party ID was partly a function of the issue positions held by voters. Fiorina (1981a) demonstrated that party ID moved with judgments of party performance. Such analyses did not deny that

Table 1

Party Identification, 1952–88 (in %)

Year	Strong DEM	Weak DEM	Leaning DEM	INDEP	Leaning REP	Weak REP	Strong REP
1952	22	25	10	6	7	14	14
1954	22	26	9	7	6	14	13
1956	21	23	6	9	8	14	15
1958	27	22	7	7	5	17	11
1960	20	25	6	10	7	14	16
1962	23	23	7	8	9	16	12
1964	27	25	9	8	6	14	11
1966	18	28	9	12	7	15	10
1968	20	25	10	11	9	15	10
1970	20	24	10	13	8	15	9
1972	15	26	11	13	11	13	10
1974	18	21	13	15	9	14	8
1976	15	25	12	15	10	14	9
1978	15	24	14	14	10	13	8
1980	18	23	11	13	10	14	9
1982	20	24	11	11	8	14	10
1984	17	20	11	11	12	15	12
1986	18	22	10	12	11	15	11
1988	17	18	12	10	13	14	14

Source: National Election Studies.
Note: DEM = Democrat; INDEP = independent; REP = Republican.

party ID was "sticky"—it clearly has a strong inertial component. But these analyses did establish that aggregate stability masked politically explicable individual movement. Today, the prevailing view is that partisanship continues to be one of the most important factors in how people vote. No cross-sectional analysis of voting could be published without including it.[15] But partisanship responds, albeit slowly, to evaluations of party positions and judgments of government performance.

Thus, when electoral analysts search for a Reagan "legacy," they look beyond his personal victories to shifts in the underlying distribution of party ID that would indicate the end of the New Deal Democratic majority and the emergence of a new Republican majority. Nothing so grand appears to have occurred, but change on a smaller scale has become increasingly apparent. Between the mid-1960s and mid-1970s the Democrats lost ground among white Southerners and blue-collar workers, losses that surely owe much to the party's stands on racial and social issues (Petrocik 1987; 1989). But Republican ID showed no commensurate gain during this period. In the mid-1980s however, Republican ID did move upward especially among the young (Norpoth 1987; Norpoth and Kagay 1989).[16]

Given the erosion of the Democratic party-of-prosperity image and the attribution of recent Republican electoral successes to economic good times, it is somewhat surprising that few analysts have focused on economic developments as the basis for recent changes in party ID. The inflation set in motion by Lyndon Johnson and uncontrolled by Carter ate away at nominal wage gains and pushed workers into higher tax brackets. Meanwhile, Democratic identification eroded from its 1964 high. Then, an electorate that yelled "No!" when queried whether they were better off today than four years ago elected Ronald Reagan, who stopped inflation and presided over a sustained recovery. Meanwhile, Republican identification strengthened. Coincidence?

Probably not. In an important recent contribution MacKuen, Erikson, and Stimson (1989) analyze a Gallup party ID series (1953–87). They find that, like presidential popularity, fluctuations in quarterly party ID averages are significantly associated with fluctuations in the economy, in this case consumer confidence as measured by the University of Michigan Surveys of Consumer Attitudes.

The remainder of this paper extends and refines the MacKuen-Erickson-Stimson analysis. Using National Election Studies (NES) data, losses in Democratic identification and gains in Republican identification can be located in the 33rd to 95th percentiles of the income distribution, with somewhat offsetting gains in Democratic identification in the bottom sixth of the distribution. At all income levels expressed party identification varies with economic conditions, though the poor and the better-off show differential sensitivity to unemployment and growth.

1.2.1 Data

The NES surveys have been carried out after each national election since 1952.[17] Their national samples range from a low of 1,139 in 1954 to a high of 1,705 in 1972, with the number being a joint function of available resources and the larger intellectual themes underlying each survey. The common content in these surveys is available in a major collection called the Cumulative Data File (CDF) that reorganizes the data so that variable numbers, codes, and so on, are identical from year to year. The CDF now contains 19 observations on national party identification.[18]

The CDF classifies respondents very roughly into five income categories. These are not quintiles, however, but represent instead a more sociological interpretation of income.[19] The lowest category, whom I will call the "poor," runs through the 16th percentile of the income distribution. The next category, the "lower-middle," runs through the 33rd percentile. The "middle" category includes the *third* of the distribution from the 34th to 67th percentiles. The upper-middle" category runs from the 68th to 95th percentiles. Finally, the "rich" are the top five percent (noneconomists will be surprised and sobered to learn that in 1988 the 96th percentile was a bit less than $90,000.)[20]

Table 2 reports a preliminary examination of trends in party ID within the income categories. Because of the controversy surrounding the classification of independent leaners, I have examined both ways: "broad" Democrats and Re-

Table 2

Trends in Party ID by Income Category

	Narrow DEM	Broad DEM	Narrow REP	Broad REP
Lower	−.02	.24	−.41	−.23
	(.23)	(2.38)	(4.37)	(2.48)
Lower-middle	−.16	.03	−.08	−.04
	(2.38)	(.35)	(.88)	(.43)
Middle	−.38	−.22	−.05	.09
	(5.71)	(3.40)	(.78)	(1.25)
Upper-middle	−.42	−.36	.01	.26
	(8.29)	(6.37)	(.24)	(3.58)
Upper	−.11	−.07	−.16	.05
	(.78)	(.43)	(.97)	(.26)

Note: Entries are regression coefficients of Party ID (% in each category) on time (1952–88) and dummy variables for 1964 and 1974. Absolute values of t-statistics are in parentheses. DEM = Democrat; REP = Republican.

publicans include the Democratic and Republican leaning independents as partisans, while "narrow" Democrats and Republicans exclude Democrat and Republican leaners. Within each income category I have regressed the measures of partisanship on a constant on the election year (1952–88), and on dummy variables for Goldwater (1964) and Watergate (1974), both of which were thought to have "shocked" partisanship. To summarize:

1. The poorest segment of the population shows a clear loss in Republican partisanship, narrowly and broadly defined, and a gain in Democratic partisanship, broadly defined (i.e. independent, but leaning Democratic).
2. The lower-middle category has the most stable party affiliations of all the categories, showing only a slight decline in narrowly defined Democratic ID.
3. The middle third of the distribution shows a significant decline in Democratic partisanship, but no commensurate gain in Republican partisanship.
4. The upper-middle sixth shows a clear decline in Democratic ID along with a clear rise in Republican ID, broadly defined (i.e., independent, but leaning Republican).
5. Because of the small number of rich respondents, partisanship figures fluctuate greatly. None of the coefficients are significant in the four regressions.

These preliminary regressions are unimpressive, with low R2s and unsatisfactory Durbin-Watson (D-W) statistics, but they suggest that the party loyalties of the population have not moved in unison during the past generation. Rather, different parts of the income distribution show different movements. The question now arises as to whether the addition of suitable economic variables can improve on the statistical qualities of the regressions and add to our substantive understanding of the observed movements in party identification. The answer is a clear yes.

Table 3 reports regressions that augment those just reported in two ways. First, previous party ID was added to the equations in order to capture the notion of party ID as a running tally of party performance that is continuously updated as the world unfolds (Fiorina 1981a). Second, various economic variables were added to the equations. With only 19 observations, collinearity often precluded including more than one or two economic variables in an equation; in such cases I kept the variable that produced the best overall equation.[21] Usually such decisions were not difficult, but in a few cases two alternative specifications were so close in their performance that I present both in table 3. In the interest of efficiency I omitted the Goldwater, Watergate, lagged partisanship, and trend terms when they fell far short of significance, except in a few cases where their omission greatly detracted from the quality of the overall regression or the performance of other variables.[22] Table 3 provides the details. Again, I will summarize the findings rather than proceeding seriatim through 25 regressions.

1. *Poor.* Within the lowest income category there continues to be a trend away from the Republicans and toward the Democrats, broadly defined. Goldwater's candidacy added about 10 points to Democratic ID and detracted at least that much from Republican ID. Of most interest, movements in party ID, however measured, are associated with changes in the level of unemployment. Democratic ID responds most strongly to unemployment change since the last election, while changes in Republican ID are predicted equally well by one-year or two-year changes. Looking at the two-year change equations, a one-point rise in unemployment goes along with a two-point net swing in narrowly defined ID and a three- or four-point net swing in broadly defined ID.

2. *Lower-middle.* Within the lower-middle income category the trend away from narrowly defined Democratic ID becomes clearer. Goldwater's candidacy had roughly a 10 point impact on all categories; Watergate affected broadly defined Republicanism only. While the estimates are more tenuous than those for the poor, movements in all four measures of party ID show some responsiveness to two-year changes in unemployment, with estimated magnitudes about three-fourths as large as in the lowest income category.

3. *Middle.* Within the large middle-income category the previously identified trend away from the Democrats remains intact. The Goldwater candidacy gave the Democrats almost 10 points and Watergate took half as much away from the Republicans. The economic impacts on partisanship are different from those in lower income categories. Democratic ID shows a highly significant relationship to the growth rate of GNP and to the unemployment *level* during the election

Table 3

Economic Conditions and Party ID Change

Category and Variable	NDEM	BDEM	NREP	NREP	BREP	BREP
A. Low income:						
Constant	47.66	22.89	20.93	19.66	35.22	33.13
	(48.78)	(2.24)	(1.98)	(1.89)	(3.19)	(2.97)
EY		.30	−.20	−.21	−.24	−.28
	. . .	(2.97)	(2.02)	(2.09)	(2.60)	(2.92)
Lag ID		.20	.74	.84	.38	.59
	. . .	(2.97)	(4.01)	(4.53)	(1.74)	(2.50)
GW	10.78	11.91	−13.90	−16.49	−10.44	−15.16
	(2.62)	(2.93)	(4.25)	(4.81)	(2.78)	(3.65)
ΔUE1	. . .	. . .	. . .	−1.38	. . .	−2.53
				(2.32)		(3.34)
ΔUE2	1.37	1.71	−.98	. . .	−1.75	. . .
	(2.19)	(2.78)	(2.30)		(3.43)	
$\bar{R}^2$	0.35	0.54	0.82	0.83	0.60	.59
D-W	1.99	. . .	. . .	. . .	. . .	. . .

Category and Variable	NDEM	BDEM	NREP	BREP
B. Lower-middle income:				
Constant	56.72	56.75	7.26	13.71
	(12.31)	(66.79)	(1.28)	(2.00)
EY	−.14	. . .	. . .	. . .
	(2.12)			
Lag ID	. . .	. . .	.72	.60
			(2.84)	2.48
GW	11.69	9.94	−9.06	−12.03
	(3.83)	(2.79)	(2.11)	(2.66)
	. . .	. . .	. . .	
W				−10.15
ΔUE2	.69	.98	−.92	−1.34
	(1.45)	(1.82)	(1.76)	(2.51)
$\bar{R}^2$	.56	.33	.35	.47
D-W	1.83	1.58	. . .	. . .

Category and Variable	NDEM	BDEM	BDEM	NREP	BREP
C. Middle income:					
Constant	64.80	63.50	64.71	12.29	25.45
	(17.94)	(18.78)	(21.24)	(2.36)	(4.49)
EY	−.31	−.14	−.15	. . .	. . .
	(6.24)	(2.99)	(3.71)		
Lag ID	. . .	. . .	. . .	.49	.26
				(2.21)	(1.51)

Table 3 continued

Category and Variable	NDEM	BDEM	BDEM	NREP	BREP
GW	9.33 (3.98)	9.41 (4.16)	9.68 (4.89)	. . .	−7.69 (2.96)
W	. . .	. . .	. . .	−4.02 (1.50)	−6.24 (2.39)
ΔGNP1	−.77 (3.99)	−.81 (4.35)	. . .	. . .	. . .
ΔGNP2	. . .	. . .	−.09 (1.40)	. . .	. . .
UE	.44 (3.50)	.39 (3.22)	. . .	. . .	. . .
ΔUE2	. . .	. . .	1.39 (4.50)	. . .	−1.51 (3.84)
$\bar{R}^2$	0.86	0.79	0.84	0.32	0.64
D-W	2.14	1.91	2.02	. . .	. . .

Category and Variable	NDEM	BDEM	BDEM	NREP	BREP
D. Upper-middle income:					
Constant	65.84 (19.50)	46.28 (3.80)	47.78 (4.11)	20.74 (3.55)	27.24 (7.57)
EY	−.38 (7.93)	−.17 (2.49)	−.19 (2.95)	. . .	.17 (3.38)
Lag ID	. . .	.30 (1.95)	.31 (2.09)	.27 (1.28)	. . .
W	−5.08 (2.40)	. . .	. . .	. . .	. . .
ΔGNP1	−.33 (2.44)	−4.0 (3.71)	. . .	. . .	.33 (2.14)
ΔGNP2	. . .	. . .	−.22 (4.09)	.12 (1.42)	. . .
ΔUE2	. . .	.90 (3.12)	.91 (3.35)	−.84 (2.33)	−1.25 (3.34)
$\bar{R}^2$	0.86	0.90	.91	0.41	0.75
D-W	2.44	. . .	. . .	. . .	1.94

Category and Variable	NDEM	BDEM	NREP	NREP	BREP
E. Upper income:					
Constant	24.68 (5.28)	33.25 (5.05)	66.29 (5.87)	64.09 (5.98)	50.36 (3.86)
EY	. . .	(2.97)	−.31 (2.02)	−.28 (2.09)	. . . (2.60)
Lag ID	−.07 .43	−.02 (.13)	. . .	. . .	.12 (.74)
W	−14.16 (2.96)	−5.85 (1.12)	9.29 (1.31)	5.99 (.85)	5.67 (.85)

(continued)

Table 3 continued

Category and Variable	NDEM	BDEM	NREP	NREP	BREP
ΔGNP1	−1.04	−1.40	1.13		
	(3.61)	(4.56)	(2.52)	. . .	. . .
ΔGNP2	. . .	. . .		.58	.80
				(2.65)	(3.61)
$\bar{R}^2$	0.54	0.53	0.24	0.26	0.44
D-W	. . .	. . .	1.93	1.88	. . .

Note: EY = election year; GW = Goldwater (1964 = 1); W = Watergate (1974 = 1); Lag ID = percentage in party ID category 2 years earlier; ΔUE1 = change in unemployment during last election year; ΔUE2 = change in unemployment since last election year; ΔGNP1 = growth rate of GNP during election year; ΔGNP2 = growth rate of GNP since last election year; UE = unemployment level in election year. Absolute values of t-statistics are in parentheses.

year. Thus, the 1982 unemployment level of almost 10 percent added about 4 points to Democratic ID, and the 6.75 percent growth in GNP in 1984 took away 5 points of Democratic ID. In contrast, movements in narrowly defined Republican ID show no relation to economic variables, and movements in broadly defined Republican ID correspond only to movements in two-year changes in unemployment.[23]

4. *Upper-middle.* Within the upper-middle income category the Democrats have clearly been losing and the Republicans less clearly gaining. Although all categories except narrow Republicans show a significant relationship with growth of GNP, the relationship is only half as strong as in the middle category. Moreover, narrowly defined Democrats and broadly defined Republicans show a response to one-year changes, while narrowly defined Republicans show a response to two-year changes, and broadly defined Democrats show a response to both. All categories except narrow Democrat show a significant relation to two-year changes in unemployment, with each one-point increase in unemployment taking away one point of narrow Republican ID and creating a net swing of two points in broad ID. In this group Watergate *took away* a few points of narrow Democratic ID.

5. *Rich.* Among the rich, Democratic ID rises and falls with the growth rate of GNP, though Democrats show more of a response to the short term and Republicans to the longer term. Each one-point increase is associated with a two-point net shift in the narrow ID balance. Only in this blessed category does party ID show no sensitivity at all to unemployment. Watergate was costly to the *Democrats* within this category with a particularly strong impact on narrowly defined Democratic ID.

Overall, these simple analyses support two arguments. First, party identification responds *not only to perceived* economic conditions as established by

MacKuen et al. (1989). The finding is stronger: party ID shows a clear relationship to fluctuations in *actual* economic conditions. Second, the party loyalties of the population do not move in unison as the economy moves; different income levels respond in different ways. Not surprisingly, the less affluent show a greater sensitivity to changes in unemployment, whereas general economic expansion has greater importance among those who enjoy higher income levels.

Finally, I emphasize that nothing in the foregoing analyses conflicts with the extensive political science literature on the subject. The adjustment of previous party ID as new performance information becomes available is consistent with micromodels already supported by cross-sectional data (Fiorina 1981a).[24] And the economic effects that we have found do not detract from the discussions of race and social issues as sources of the Democratic party's current disarray. Most of the regressions for the lower-middle, middle, and upper-middle income groups show a significant anti-Democratic trend that may well reflect the party's estrangement from middle America on issues of race and culture. But whatever other issues are at work, the economy continues to influence the underlying balance of party affiliations just as it did during the New Deal and as it will undoubtedly continue to do in the future.

1.3 Conclusion

The economic developments of the 1980s had an impact on the electoral politics of the decade, an impact not only on the outcomes of the elections held between 1980 and 1988, but also on the elections that will occur in the 1990s and possibly beyond. Economic conditions affected the immediate election outcomes to the Democrats' dismay in 1980, 1984, and 1988, and to their joy in 1982. But beyond those short-term impacts, economic conditions left an imprint on the distribution of party identification among the citizenry. Whatever the economic conditions that existed in 1988, the conditions that existed in 1984 and earlier had been incorporated in voter partisanship to the general good fortune of George Bush. Of course, economic bad times under Bush would have the reverse effects. The hard-won gains in Republican ID during the 1980s could be dissipated by economic misfortunes in the years ahead. Fortunately for the Republicans they have been profiting from Democratic policies and performance in other issue domains such as racial/cultural issues and foreign policy; economic success was the third ace in their hand. Thus, less-than-stellar economic performance need not cost them presidential elections, nor even all their gains in party identification. But continued economic success would buttress the gains they already have made. And attention to employment, in particular, would enable them to continue to make inroads in the lower ranges of the income distribution that are traditionally viewed as "natural" Democratic territory.

Notes

1. Of course, the Republicans did lose control of the Senate in 1986. Economic distress in farm states was often cited as a partial explanation. But the 1980 Senate victories that were reversed in 1986 were something of a fluke to begin with (Fiorina 1984).

2. A number of excellent reviews are available. On the effects of economic conditions on voting and presidential approval see Monroe (1979) and Kiewiet and Rivers (1984). For an excellent general review that deals with sociological as well as economic aspects of the topic see Weatherford (1986). And for a review of the recent political business cycle literature see Alesina (1988).

3. Generally, when a president's ratings plummet, they never fully recover. Reagan's, however, dropped from 67 percent in the flush of his 1981 legislative victories to 35 percent after the 1982 elections. But by late 1983 he was back over 50 percent and, following his reelection, hovered near 65 percent through most of 1985–86. While analysts were studying this unusual recovery, the Iran-Contra scandal dropped him back to 40 percent, but again he recovered and left office with approval ratings over 60 percent.

4. Ostrom and Simon (1989) attribute more than three-fourths of the 1981–82 decline and the 1983–84 resurgence to economic factors. Particular events (Lebanon bombings, Grenada, etc.) also were important. Speeches had no significant impact, presidential trips were of minor import.

5. For the 1980 and 1984 elections I utilized eq. 4 and the data reported in Fair (1982). (This is the original 1892–1976 equation reestimated with national accounts data revised in 1980.) For the 1988 prediction I substituted NBER data generously provided by Gerald Cohen.

6. According to numerous survey studies, the Iranian hostage crisis severely damaged Carter in 1980. Conversely, in 1984 the Grenada invasion, destruction of the Libyan MIGs, and the capture of the hijackers of the Achille-Lauro buttressed Reagan's image as a no-nonsense leader. The administration had a major arms control treaty by 1988. A recent update of Fair's model (1988) adds a variable that measures change in the size of the armed forces relative to the population. While this captures major wars, it will not pick up incidents and developments such as those just mentioned.

7. To get enough data, time-series analysts must venture across what political scientists and historians refer to as different party systems (where structural changes are hypothesized). For example Fair (1978) observes that the model performs badly before 1916, though that is not a date ordinarily identified with a change in party system. He also cautions (1988) that the positive-trend term for the Democrats appears questionable in light of 1980s political developments. Political historians would argue that the Democratic base was higher in the New Deal party system (1932–64, approximately) than either before or since. While Fair could dummy in such considerations, he naturally worries about being accused of "mining" his data.

8. These findings do not necessarily contradict the time-series finding that voters are myopic. If voters are heterogeneous, with varying time horizons, different foci (national vs. local), differential sensitivities to growth, unemployment, and inflation, etc., it may be difficult to find evidence of nonmyopic behavior inasmuch as different voters will incorporate different information in different ways. For a discussion of voter rationality that touches on time horizons among other things, see Nordhaus (1989).

9. Some, like Jacobson and Kernell (1983) and Campbell (1985), use only midterms for their estimations. Others, like Lewis-Beck and Rice (1984) use a dummy variable for midterms.

10. The one exception was 1982 when all the models overestimated the Republican

losses. Jacobson and Kernell (1983) argue that in the euphoria following Reagan's 1980 victory, the Republicans were able to recruit good candidates and raise considerable money, which cushioned their losses when the economy turned sour in late 1981.

11. This model incorporates all the others. It predicts across presidential and mid-term years, includes the exposure variable, and also includes measures of major events (as in approval models) and party identification.

12. With somewhat less regularity the Republicans were viewed as the party of peace.

13. April 1943, December 1955, and September 1972.

14. This turns out to be a highly controversial matter. Unlike Gallup, academic surveys ask self-identified independents whether they lean toward either party. The rise in independents occurred almost entirely among these "leaners," whose presidential votes are often more loyal than those of weak partisans of the same party. See Keith et al. (1987).

15. Assuming no interactions with other variables, time-series analyses will pick up the average level of party ID in the constant term.

16. There is some disagreement on this point, with some subscribing to the "young Republican" thesis (Norpoth 1987; Miller 1990), while others argue that Republican gains are more evenly scattered across the age distribution (Petrocik 1989). The CBS/NYT data appears to give somewhat different answers than NES data, and classifying independent leaners as partisans gives somewhat different answers than classifying them as independents (see n. 14 above).

17. Since 1952 election year surveys have been carried out under the auspices of the Institute for Survey Research at the University of Michigan. Since 1978 these surveys have been funded by the National Science Foundation and carried out under the supervision of an academic governing board.

18. Although the Gallup series is longer, the NES series has two advantages. The first is simple convenience. Take the income variable, for instance. The NES staff codes each respondent according to national income percentile. To use Gallup data, one would have to take each Gallup survey and do the calculations and recoding oneself. Even if bountiful research assistance were available, however, the NES collection would still be preferable for present purposes. Gallup makes only a simple three-category classification of party ID, whereas the NES differentiates between strong and weak partisans and pure and learning independents. As noted in n. 14 above, these finer differences are consequential.

19. Personal conversation with Warren Miller, principal investigator of the NES surveys, April 13, 1990.

20. Since respondents are not asked their exact incomes, but only a range, these proportions are only approximate. In 1988 the upper boundaries of the first four categories were $9,999, $14,999, $34,999, and $89,999.

21. In all cases the economic variables are multiplied by a binary variable for control of the Presidency (Democrat = -1, Republican = 1). Good economic conditions under Republican presidents are expected to enhance Republican partisanship while detracting from Democratic partisanship, and poor economic performance should have the opposite effect. I did consider the alternative hypotheses that the parties "own" different issues, so that inflation always helps Republicans and unemployment Democrats even if they are in office when it occurs. Fortunately (in view of the perverse incentives posited by these hypotheses) I found no support for them. Keech and Swain (1990) argue, however, that particularly sensitive subpopulations—e.g., blacks—behave somewhat in line with the alternative hypotheses. At this level of aggregation I can not take account of their argument.

22. One might object that the dummy variables for 1964 and 1974 act as proxies for the economic conditions (quite good in 1964, quite poor in 1974) that prevailed in those years and thus detract from the impact of the economic variables in the regressions. On

the contrary, eliminating the Goldwater and Watergate dummies when significant generally detracts greatly from the overall regressions and produces weaker impacts for the economic variables. In short, there was more to the 1964 and 1974 experiences than good and bad economic times, respectively.

23. Note that an alternative specification for broadly defined Democrats also suggests the importance of two-year changes in unemployment.

24. Some readers have asked why few of the lagged party ID terms attain significance when they are invariably highly significant in cross-sectional analyses. The answer appears to be the aggregate level of analysis. In the absence of a time trend, aggregate ID levels fluctuate around the constant baseline in accord with variations in economic variables.

References

Abramson, Paul R., John H. Aldrich, and David Rohde. 1986. *Change and Continuity in the 1984 Elections.* Washington, D.C.: *Congressional Quarterly* Press.

Alesina, Alberto. 1988. Macroeconomics and Politics. *NBER Macroeconomics Annual,* edited by Stanley Fischer, 3:13–51. Cambridge, Mass.: MIT Press.

Alesina, Alberto, and Howard Rosenthal. 1989. Partisan Cycles in Congressional Elections and the Macroeconomy. *American Political Science Review* 83:375–98.

Ansolabehere, Stephen, David Brady, and Morris P. Fiorina. 1988. The Marginals Never Vanished. Research Paper no. 970. Stanford University, Graduate School of Business.

Campbell, Angus, Philip E. Converse, Warren E. Miller, and Donald E. Stokes. 1960. *The American Voter.* New York: Wiley.

Campbell, James E. 1985. Explaining Presidential Losses in Midterm Congressional Elections. *Journal of Politics* 47: 1140–57.

Cook, Rhodes. 1985. Will the "Six-Year Itch" Strike Again in 1986? *Congressional Quarterly Weekly Report* 43: 1284–86.

Erikson, Robert S. 1988. The Puzzle of Midterm Loss. *Journal of Politics* 50: 1011–29.

———. 1990. Economic Conditions and the Congressional Vote: A Review of the Macrolevel Evidence. *American Journal of Political Science* 34: 168–79.

Fair, Ray C. 1978. The Effect of Economic Events on Votes for President. *Review of Economics and Statistics* 60:159–73.

———. 1982. The Effect of Economic Events on Votes for President: 1980 Results. *Review of Economics and Statistics* 64:322–25.

———. 1988. The Effects of Economic Events on Votes for President: A 1984 Update. *Political Behavior* 10:168–79.

Fiorina, Morris P. 1978. Economic Retrospective Voting in American National Elections: A Micro-Analysis. *American Journal of Political Science* 22:426–43.

———. 1981a. *Retrospective Voting in American National Elections.* New Haven, Conn.: Yale University Press.

———. 1981b. Short- and Long-Term Effects of Economic Conditions on Individual Voting Decisions. In *Contemporary Political Economy,* edited by Douglas Hibbs, Heino Fassbender, and R. Douglas Rivers. Amsterdam: North Holland.

———. 1984. The Presidency and the Contemporary Electoral System. In *The Presidency and the Political System,* edited by Michael Nelson. Washington, D.C.: Congressional Quarterly Press.

Frey, Bruno S., and Friedrich Schneider. 1978. An Empirical Study of Politico-Economic Interaction in the United States. *Review of Economics and Statistics* 60:174–83.

Golden, David G., and James M. Poterba. 1980. The Price of Popularity: The Political Business Cycle Reexamined. *American Journal of Political Science* 24:696–714.

Gudgin, Graham, and Peter Taylor. 1979. *Seats, Votes, and the Spatial Organization of Elections.* London: Pion Press.

Hibbs, Douglas A., with R. Douglas Rivers and Nicholas Vasilatos. 1982. On the Demand for Economic Outcomes: Macroeconomic Performance and Mass Political Support in the United States, Great Britain, and Germany. *Journal of Politics* 43:426–62.

Jackson, John E. 1975. Issues, Party Choices, and Presidential Votes. *American Journal of Political Science* 19:161–85.

Jacobson, Gary C. 1990. Does the Economy Matter in Midterm Elections? *American Journal of Political Science* 34:400–404.

Jacobson, Gary C., and Samuel Kernell. 1983. *Strategy and Choice in Congressional Elections.* 2d ed. New Haven, Conn.: Yale University Press.

Keech, William R., and Carol M. Swain. 1990. Party, Race and Electoral Decision Rules Regarding Economic Performance. Paper presented at the meetings of the Public Choice Society, March 16–18, 1990, Tucson.

Keith, Bruce E., David B. Magleby, Candice J. Nelson, et al. 1987. The Myth of the Independent Voter. Typescript. University of California, Berkeley.

Kernell, Samuel, 1978. Explaining Presidential Popularity. *American Political Science Review* 72:506–22.

Kiewiet, D. Roderick, and Douglas Rivers. 1984. A Retrospective on Retrospective Voting. *Political Behavior* 6:369–92.

———. 1985. The Economic Basis of Reagan's Appeal. In *New Directions in American Politics,* edited by John E. Chubb and Paul E. Peterson. Washington, D.C.: Brookings.

Kinder, Donald R., Gordon S. Adams, and Paul W. Gronke. 1989. Economics and Politics in the 1984 American Presidential Election. *American Journal of Political Science* 33:491–515.

Kinder, Donald R., and D. Roderick Kiewiet. 1979. Economic Discontent and Political Behavior: The Role of Personal Grievances and Collective Economic Judgments in Congressional Voting. *American Journal of Political Science* 23:495–517.

———. 1981. Sociotropic Politics: The American Case. *British Journal of Political Science* 11:129–61.

Kramer, Gerald H. 1971. Short-Term Fluctuations in U.S. Voting Behavior, 1896–1964. *American Political Science Review* 5:131–43.

Kramer, Gerald H. 1983. The Ecological Fallacy Revisited: Aggregate- versus Individual-Level Findings on Economics and Elections and Sociotropic Voting. *American Political Science Review* 77:92–111.

Lewis-Beck, Michael S., and Tom W. Rice. 1984. Forecasting U.S. House Elections. *Legislative Studies Quarterly* 9:475–86.

MacKuen, Michael B., Robert S. Erikson, and James A. Stimson. 1989. Macropartisanship. *American Political Science Review* 83:1125–42.

Marra, Robin F., and Charles W. Ostrom, Jr. 1989. Explaining Seat Change in the U.S. House of Representatives, 1950–86. *American Journal of Political Science* 33:541–69.

Markus, Gregory B. 1982. Political Attitudes during an Election Year: A Report on the 1980 NES Panel Study. *American Political Science Review* 76:538–60.

———. 1988. The Impact of Personal and National Economic Conditions on the Presidential Vote: A Pooled Cross-sectional Analysis. *American Journal of Political Science* 32:137–54.

Miller, Arthur H., and Martin P. Wattenberg. 1985. Throwing the Rascals Out: Policy and Performance Evaluations of Presidential Candidates, 1952–1980. *American Political Science Review* 79:359–72.

Miller, Warren E. 1990. The Electorate's View of the Parties. In *The Parties Respond,* edited by L. Sandy Maisel. Boulder, Colo.: Westview Press.

Monroe, Kristen R. 1978. Economic Influences on Presidential Popularity. *Public Opinion Quarterly* 42:360–69.

———. 1979. Economic Analyses of Electoral Behavior: A Critical Review. *Political Behavior* 1:137–73.

Mueller, John E. 1970. Presidential Popularity from Truman to Johnson. *American Political Science Review* 64:18–34.

Niskanen, William A. 1975. Economic and Fiscal Effects on the Popular Vote for the President. Graduate School of Public Policy Working Paper no. 25. University of California, Berkeley, May.

Nordhaus, William D. 1975. The Political Business Cycle. *Review of Economic Studies* 42:169–90.

———. 1989. Alternative Approaches to the Political Business Cycle. In *Brookings Papers on Economic Activity,* edited by William C. Brainard and George L. Perry, 1–68. Washington, D.C.: Brookings Institution.

Norpoth, Helmut. 1987. Under Way and Here to Stay: Party Realignment in the 1980s? *Public Opinion Quarterly* 51:376–91.

Norpoth, Helmut, and Michael R. Kagay. 1989. Another Eight Years of Republican Rule and Still No Partisan Realignment? Paper presented at APSA annual meeting, Atlanta, GA.

Oppenheimer, Bruce I., James A. Stimson, and Richard W. Waterman. 1986. Interpreting U.S. Congressional Elections: The Exposure Thesis. *Legislative Studies Quarterly* 11: 227–47.

Ostrom, Charles W., Jr., and Dennis M. Simon. 1989. The Man in the Teflon Suit: The Environmental Connection, Political Drama, and Popular Support in the Reagan Presidency. *Public Opinion Quarterly* 53:353–87.

Petrocik, John R. 1987. Realignment: New Party Coalitions and the Nationalization of the South. *Journal of Politics* 49:347–75.

———. 1989. Issues and Agenda: Electoral Coalitions in the 1988 Election. Paper presented at APSA annual meeting, 1989.

Rivers, Douglas. 1988. Heterogeneity in Models of Electoral Choice. *American Opinion Quarterly* 42:360–69.

———. 1990. Microeconomics and Macropolitics: A Solution to the Kramer Problem. Caltech Social Science Working Paper 602, March 1986.

Schneider, William. 1981. The November 4 Vote for President: What Did It Mean? In *The American Elections of 1980,* edited by Austin Ranney. Washington, D.C.: American Enterprise Institute.

Shanks, J. Merrill, and Warren E. Miller. 1990. Policy Direction and Performance Evaluation: Complementary Explanations of the Reagan Elections. *British Journal of Political Science* 20:143–235.

Stimson, James A. 1976. Public Support for American Presidents: A Cyclical Model. *Public Opinion Quarterly* 40:1–21.

Tufte, Edward R. 1975. Determinants of the Outcomes of Midterm Congressional Elections. *American Political Science Review* 69:812–26.

Weatherford, M. Stephen. 1986. Economic Determinants of Voting. *Research in Micropolitics* 1:219–69.

Weisberg, Herbert F. 1989. Some Perspectives on the 1988 Presidential Election: The Roles of Turnout and Ronald Reagan. Presented at APSA annual meeting, Atlanta, GA.

4.6. A Model of the Political Economy of the United States

ALBERTO ALESINA, JOHN LONDREGAN, and HOWARD ROSENTHAL

This article may be the most difficult in this book and uses state-of-the-art quantitative techniques. I have included it to give you an idea of what current cutting-edge research looks like. In it the authors try to use recent data to test three hypotheses. One is the familiar one that lies at the heart of the political business cycle literature, the degree to which the state of the economy determines the electoral success of incumbent presidents and congressmen. The second, also familiar from the political business cycle literature, is the degree to which politicians successfully manipulate the economy to ensure their reelection. The third is the question of whether unemployment, inflation, and growth differ when Republicans and Democrats hold the presidency. Because both the party and the political business cycle effects should affect the economy simultaneously, the authors use a single model to test all three hypotheses.

It is instructive to contrast their results with the earlier work of Tufte. They confirm his argument that the economy affects presidential elections but, like others, they are skeptical of effects on Congressional elections. They find little evidence that politicians have changed the business cycle to ensure reelection. They show that, other things being equal, economic growth in the second year of a Democratic administration is about 3 percent higher than in the second year of a Republican administration.

We develop and test a model of joint determination of economic growth and national election results in the United States. The formal model, which combines developments in the rational choice analysis of the behavior of economic agents and voters, leads to a system of equations in which the dependent variables are the growth rate and the vote shares in presidential and congressional elections. Our estimates support the theoretical claims that growth responds to unanticipated policy shifts and that voters use both on-year and midterm elections to balance the two parties. On the other hand, we find no support for "rational" retrospective voting. We do reconfirm, in a fully simultaneous framework, the "naive" retrospective voting literature's finding that the economy has a strong effect on presidential voting. We find congressional elections unaffected by the economy, except as transmitted by presidential coattails.

The literature on macroeconomic fluctuations and general elections divides into three branches. One studies the impact of economic conditions on voting: economic fluctuations are viewed as predetermined, while electoral results are the endogenous variables (see, e.g., Chappell and Suzuki 1990; Erikson 1989, 1990; Fair 1978, 1982, 1988; Fiorina 1981; Kiewiet 1983; Kramer 1971). A second emphasizes that political parties pursue different policies that result in "partisan effects" on the economy.[1] A third line of research emphasizes the "opportunistic" behavior of politicians who try to manipulate the economy in order to increase their chances of remaining in office (see Alesina, Cohen, and Roubini 1992; Haynes and Stone 1987; Nordhaus 1975, 1989; Tufte 1978).

For the United States in the twentieth century, this literature discloses several regularities:

1. Presidential elections are strongly influenced by the business cycle. The vote share of the incumbent president's party's presidential candidate increases with the rate of gross national product (GNP) growth in the election year; other economic variables (e.g., unemployment, inflation) are less significant in explaining presidential results.[2]

2. Congressional vote shares are less sensitive to economic conditions (Alesina and Rosenthal 1989; Chappel and Suzuki 1990; Erikson 1990; Lepper 1974).[3]

3. There is a midterm electoral cycle where the party holding the White House loses plurality in midterm congressional elections (Alesina and Rosenthal 1989; Erikson 1988).

4. Since World War II, in the first half of Republican administrations, economic growth tends to decelerate, reaching its minimum during the second year of each term, while the economy grows more rapidly than average during the first half of Democratic administrations. In the last two years of each term, there are no significant differences between growth rates for Democratic and Republican administrations (Alesina 1988; Alesina and Sachs 1988).[4]

5. The rate of economic growth is not systematically higher than average

in election years (see Alesina 1988; Alesina and Roubini 1992; Beck 1992; Golden and Poterba 1980; Hibbs 1987; McCallum 1978).

We construct and test a model consistent with the aforementioned regularities. In this model economic and electoral outcomes are jointly endogenous. The model, which posits rational choice by both voters and economic agents, is based upon four key ideas:

1. The two political parties are "partisan" and polarized. The Republicans, *relative* to the Democrats, are more concerned with containing inflation than with stimulating growth (Hibbs 1977, 1987). The Democrats also favor expansionary monetary and fiscal policies in order to support relatively large government programs.

2. Economic agents form "rational expectations," but wage "stickiness" prevents an immediate adjustment of wages to economic shocks or "news." Because the two parties follow different policies, uncertainty about the outcome of elections engenders uncertainty about postelection policies. Agents are forced to hedge this uncertainty in nominal wage contracts concluded prior to elections remaining in effect after the elections.[5] The actual postelection policies then produce real effects on economic growth. In particular, growth will be relatively high following the election of a Democrat, whereas recessions are most likely after a Republican victory (Alesina 1987).

3. Policy outcomes depend both upon which party holds the presidency and the relative share of seats in Congress. For instance, Democratic control of Congress "pulls" policy outcomes with a Republican president to the left. Voters take advantage of this institutional structure of "checks and balances" to bring about middle-of-the-road, moderate policies (Alesina and Rosenthal 1989, 1991; Fiorina 1988, 1992). The midterm cycle is an instance of this type of moderating behavior.

4. Administrations vary in their degree of "administrative competence." For a given rate of inflation (expected or unexpected), a more competent administration is likely to produce more growth than a less competent one (Persson and Tabellini 1990). Since voters prefer more competence to less, elections will turn on not only partisan preferences but also efficiency arguments. However, a voter cannot observe "competence" directly but only its effect on the economy. Since the economy is also affected by technological innovations, oil price changes, wars, and other matters that have little to do with administrative competence, voters cannot immediately distinguish competence from "luck." A "rational" retrospective voter can only use available information to make a forecast of the incumbent's postelectoral competence. This forecast, as we shall show, leads economic growth to affect electoral results in a manner distinct from "naive" retrospective voting, where no attempt is made to distinguish good luck from good government.[6]

Figure 1. **Schematic Overview of the Model**

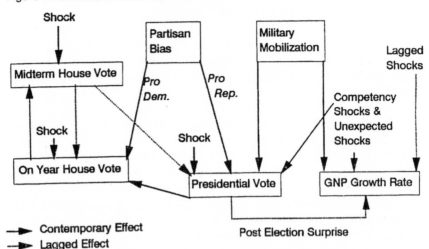

We shall integrate these ideas in a single theoretical model that encompasses both political and economic outcomes. The theory is followed by econometric estimation. Our theoretical model fares well in these tests, which support the theory on several key points including (1) institutional "balancing," manifest in the midterm cycle (the party controlling the White House loses vote share in the midterm elections); (2) the economy has a much greater impact on presidential elections than on congressional elections; and (3) the "partisan" effects on growth appear in the wake of presidential elections. On the other hand, we do not find support for "rational" retrospective voting, a result we shall later discuss at length.

Before embarking on a formal presentation of the model, we use the schematic shown in Figure 1 to provide the reader with a brief overview. The theoretical model leads to four equations in the empirical estimation: the GNP growth rate, the presidential vote, the on-year House vote, and the midterm House vote. Each of these equations has, as is common practice, independent random shocks. The GNP equation reflects the two aforementioned channels of government influence on economic growth. The first is "partisan" politics coupled with electoral uncertainty and nominal wage contracting. The second arises from variations in the competence of different administrations.

The partisan effect, present only at the beginning of each four-year term, arises because agents have to take into account that there are two possible inflation policies that will be pursued *after* the elections: high inflation if a Democrat wins the presidency or low inflation if a Republican wins. Wage contracts signed *before* the elections will be based on the *expected* postelection rate, which, since there is electoral uncertainty, lies in between the high Democratic rate and the low Republican rate. After the election, there is "unexpected" inflation represented by the difference between this *expected* rate and the *actual* rate implemented by the winner. If the Democrats win, for example, this unexpected "surprise" generates an upsurge in growth. The upsurge lasts, however, only for a couple of years, until new wage contracts have incorporated the higher, now expected, inflation policy. Subsequently, the economy returns to its "normal" rate of growth, implying that there is not a "partisan" influence on the rate of growth in the second half of each term.

The partisan growth model thus implies that the effects of macroeconomic policy on growth are short-lived. In contrast, Hibbs's (1977, 1987) model has persistent partisan effects on the economy. Moreover, in our model, an administration cannot use unexpected inflation to generate an upsurge in growth before elections. In fact, "rational" economic agents would predict such maneuvers and, in so doing, render them ineffective. Therefore, we do not predict a systematic preelectoral burst of growth, as in the Nordhaus (1975) "political business cycle."

In contrast to the partisan effect, the second, competence effect is present in election years and is the key to "rational" retrospective voting. Although we cannot measure "competence" directly, we can test a direct implication of the model. The model predicts that the intertemporal covariation in growth should be *higher* when there is no change in the party holding the White House than when there is one.

This is because a change in control leads to a completely new level of competence while with no change the previous level persists. Therefore, the growth equation will be used to provide a very direct test of whether there is a basis for "rational retrospective voting." Indeed, preelectoral economic performance should matter to voters only if there is evidence that the government, as well as outside forces, has an important influence on performance. We will conclude against "rational" retrospective voting: the American electorate pays "too much attention" to the rate of GNP growth in election years.

We estimate both the partisan surprise and competence effects by using an autoregressive moving average representation of GNP growth similar to the unemployment equation in the seminal work of Hibbs (1977). Since we use only a first-order moving average, our representation is simpler than his. On the one hand, this simple representation renders the theoretical model tractable; on the other, statistical tests reject the need for more complexity in the empirical model. The estimation also includes a military mobilization variable as an exogenous measure for the effect of wars.

The presidential vote reflects both the electorate's partisan preferences *and* their evaluation of the incumbent's competence in managing the economy. In a standard "naive" retrospective voting model (e.g., Fair 1988), one would simply enter election-year economic performance as a predictor. But the rational "competency" model says that the voters should focus only on that portion of growth likely to persist after the election. This portion is represented by the shocks directed at growth in Figure 1. In addition to the test for growth, we also test, in the presidential equation, for a "rally 'round the flag" effect from military mobilizations.

The presidential equation and the on-year House equation jointly test the basic idea of institutional balancing. Balancing implies that if one party is advantaged in one institution, its opponent should be stronger in the other. We allow for partisan bias in both on-year voting equations. The on-year House vote further reflects our theoretical framework in allowing for "coattails" from the presidential vote. In contrast, the off-year House elections reflect only the balancing of the midterm cycle, which, as we shall show, is embedded in the lagged effect of the on-year House vote.

Recognizing the overbearing importance of incumbency in American politics, we include the lagged House vote in every voting equation. Indeed, these lagged variables greatly improve the fit. The incumbency advantage is not handled within our formal model for reasons of tractability. To some extent, the lags may proxy for serial correlation in the preferences of the electorate (such as an alleged liberal mood in the 1960s). But the lags have an additional, important role. Being strong in Congress currently facilitates retaining future control of Congress and, to a lesser extent, the presidency. This advantage is offset by the midterm effect, where winning the presidency today causes losses in Congress two years later. In fact, if all exogenous shocks were absent, our estimates show that the lags and the midterm effect would combine to produce a governmental cycle with divided government prevailing over most of the cycle.

The Theoretical Model

We simplify the discussion here by treating a "period" as two calendar years. We use t to index periods.

The Economy

We consider a model in which nominal wage contracts are signed at the end of period t and cannot be revised until the end of period $t + 1$ (Fischer 1977). Thus, the rate of nominal wage growth equals ex ante expected inflation, since we assume that expected productivity growth is zero. Disregarding capital, a supply function for this economy can be written as follows:

$$g_t = \bar{g} + \gamma(\pi_t - \pi_t^e) + \varepsilon_t,\qquad(1)$$

where g_t is the output growth, $\bar{g}$ is the "natural" rate of growth, π_t is the inflation rate, and ($\pi_t^e = E(\pi_t \mid I_{t-1})$) is the rational expectation of inflation based upon the information available in period $t - 1$.[7]

The error ε_t consists of two components, which cannot be separately observed by the voters (nor by econometricians):

$$\varepsilon_t = \zeta_t + \eta_t. \tag{2}$$

The transitory shock ζ_t (independently and identically distributed with mean 0 and variance σ_ζ^2) represents unanticipated economic events beyond the scope of government control (e.g., oil price shocks, some technological innovations). The term η_t captures administrative "competence." In fact, *given inflation,* growth is higher, the higher η_t. In this context, competence can be interpreted as the administration's ability to avoid inefficiency and, generally speaking, to create an environment conducive to growth without inflation.

Competence does not disappear overnight. *Within parties,* the competency level exhibits inertia, evolving according to a first-order moving average, or MA(1), process:

$$\eta_t = \mu_t^R + \rho\mu_{t-1}^R \quad \text{if } R \text{ president at } t. \tag{3}$$
$$\eta_t = \mu_t^D + \rho\mu_{t-1}^D \quad \text{if } D \text{ president at } t.$$

The disturbances are independently and identically distributed and satisfy

$$E(\mu_t^R) = E(\mu_t^D) = 0$$
$$\text{Var }(\mu_t^R) = \text{Var }(\mu_t^D) = \sigma_\mu^2 .$$

This specification implies that we regard parties as ongoing organizations with competence that persists to the same degree whether the incumbent is reelected or a new president from the same party is chosen. The validity of the assumption can be argued by noting the relatively slow turnover of the cadre that forms cabinets. Note also that competence is given, not chosen by an administration. In fact, our model does not even require that the government knows its own competency level!

While for tractability, we do not consider congressional competence, it is reasonable to assume that variations of competence are more important to the presidency, since individual variations in competence are likely to cancel out in a legislative setting with large numbers of decision makers.

In our model, competence shocks persist for one period only, which (as we shall show), suffices to induce rational retrospective voting. Higher-order moving average (MA) processes could be introduced without changing our qualitative results as long as the shocks that precede a presidential election do not influence the competency level of the incumbent's party beyond a single presidential term.

The Two Political Parties

Two parties, D and R, compete for office, with no entry of third parties. All presidential and legislative candidates of a party have identical preferences. These preferences and those of voters are represented by utility functions that are, for tractability quadratic in the inflation rate and linear[8] in output growth:

$$W^i = \sum_{t=0}^{\infty} \beta^t \left[-\frac{1}{2} (\pi_t - \bar{\pi}^i)^2 + b^i g_t \right] 0 < \beta < 1, \tag{4}$$

where the index i takes on the values D, R for the political parties and generic value i for an individual voter. The parties and voters have a common discount factor β. The following inequalities capture the "partisan" nature of our model:

$$\bar{\pi}^D > \bar{\pi}^R \geq 0; b^D > b^R > 0 .$$

While the parties agree that output growth is desirable, they differ both in terms of their most preferred inflation rates ($\bar{\pi}$) and in the trade-off between output and deviations of inflation from its most preferred level (b). Party D is relatively more concerned with growth than with inflation. That the parties prefer positive rates of inflation to zero inflation is motivated by three features of the economy. First, inflation is a tax on nominally denominated assets. To finance public spending, it is optimal to distribute the burden of taxation as widely as possible, including the implicit tax represented by inflation. Second, empirical evidence suggests a negative correlation between *real* interest rates and the inflation rate. Third, Tobin (1972) and many others have argued that moderate inflation facilitates smooth adjustments of prices and wages, particularly (as appears to be the case) if the latter are rigid downward. Thus, the preferences on inflation can be interpreted as a reduced form of underlying preferences on public spending and real interest rates. We assume that the policymakers control the inflation rate directly.[9]

Institutions

The president is elected for two periods by majority rule. The entire legislature is elected each period by strict proportionality.[10] These institutional characteristics, combined with the assumption that the growth shock persists for only one period, greatly facilitate the development of the formal model. Since presidents serve two periods, expectations about the results of midterm elections are relevant to on-year decisions; but voters never need to anticipate the effects of their decisions on the next presidential election. We can thus characterize the voting equilibrium in terms of a game with two moves, the simultaneous election of a president and Congress in on-years and the election of Congress at midterm. Split tickets are permitted on the first move. There is no abstention.

While economic and electoral outcomes will vary as a consequence of the random variables in the model, the equilibrium voting strategies used in each two-move game will be repeated indefinitely. Consequently, we use subscripts 0, 1, and 2 to denote elections occurring at the end of periods 0 and 1 and economic outcomes occurring in periods 1 and 2.

The Voters

There is a continuum of voters whose preferences are parameterized by $(\bar{\pi}^i, b^i)$. We assume that the distribution of voter preferences is not fully known, by anyone. This realistic feature of the model leaves electoral results uncertain even if the two parties' preferences and policies are common knowledge. Specifically, the inflation ideal points $\bar{\pi}^i$ are uniformly distributed, without loss of generality, on an interval of length 1. Now,

$$\bar{\pi}^i \sim U[\, \mathbf{a}, 1 + \mathbf{a}\,], \tag{5}$$

where $\mathbf{a}$ is a random variable, drawn independently[11] in every period from a uniform distribution on the temporally constant interval $[-w, w]$:[12]

$$\mathbf{a} \sim U[-w, w]. \tag{6}$$

We adopt the simplifying assumption that all voters have the same weight on growth b ($b^i = b$ for all i).

Rational Retrospective Voting and the Competency Model

Since voters benefit from growth (via b), they are inclined to retain in office an incumbent whom they believe to have greater-than-average competence. The key to the Persson and Tabellini (1990) model is that while the voters fully know the model of equations 1–3, they are missing one key piece of information, which is μ_t, the current period's contribution to the MA(1) competence process. They are assumed to know not only g_t, π_t, and π_t^e but also μ_{t-1}, the competency innovation of the previous period. With this information, their optimal forecast of the incumbent's competence in the period after the election is[13]

$$\hat{\eta}_{t+1} = [\, g_t - \bar{g} - \gamma (\pi_t - \pi_t^e) - \rho\mu_{t-1}\,] \, \rho \, \frac{\sigma_\mu^2}{\sigma_\zeta^2 + \sigma_\mu^2} \, ; \tag{7}$$

that is, a rational retrospective voter's decision will be influenced only by growth net of the terms subtracted (average growth, $\bar{g}$, growth from unexpected inflation, $\gamma(\pi_t - \pi_t^e)$ and the portion of competence that does not carry over to the next term, $\rho\mu_{t-1}$). The term in square brackets is multiplied by ρ, the fraction of μ_t that gets carried over to the next period, and by a term that includes the variances. This last term allows the voter to reduce a forecast of future competence if the role of "luck" (ζ) in the economy is large relative to the role of "competence" (μ). In contrast to the rational retrospective voter, the naive retrospective voter keys on all of g_t.

The Timing of the Model

Schematically, the timing of events in our model is as follows:

Periods t $= 0, 2, 4, \ldots$

Inflation (π_t) is determined by the government; shocks ζ_t, μ_t are assigned by "nature."

Output growth (g_t) is realized.

Binding economic plans (wage contracts) for period $t + 1$ are made by uncoordinated private agents.

The president (who serves in $t + 1$ and $t + 2$) and Congress (which serves in $t + 1$) are elected.

Periods t $= 1, 3, 5 \ldots$

[Identical except that president remains in office and only Congress (which serves in $t + 1$) is elected.]

The Time-Consistent Inflation Policies of the Two Parties

A time consistency problem (Barro and Gordon 1983; Kydland and Prescott 1977) arises in this model. Each party would be better off if it could credibly commit to implementing, whenever it had control over policy, its inflation bliss point ($\bar{\pi}^D$ or $\bar{\pi}^R$). But a party in power, unable to resist the temptation to stimulate short-run growth through an inflation surprise, inflates up to the point at which the disutility of a surprise increment of inflation just offsets the resulting short-run output stimulation. Substituting equation 1 into equation 4 and taking first-order conditions yields the time-consistent inflation policies:

$$\pi_t^{D^*} = \bar{\pi}^D + \gamma b^D > \pi_t^{R^*} = \bar{\pi}^R + \gamma b^R \quad \forall \quad t. \tag{8}$$

These inflation rates are higher than the corresponding party bliss points. But absent credible commitments to lower inflation rates, economic agents and voters anticipate the time-consistent rates, and parties implement them. Note that if voter i were dictator, his or her time-consistent policy would be

$$\pi_t^{i^*} = \bar{\pi}^i + \gamma b \quad \forall \quad t.$$

The Executive-Legislative Policy Interaction

Postelectoral inflation reflects the time-consistent policies of both parties, since policy is a function of which party holds the presidency and of the composition of Congress. The nature of the policy interaction between the legislature and the executive in practice is, of course, a complex question. We capture this interaction by the following expressions for the actual inflation rate when parties R and D hold the presidency, respectively:

$$\pi_t^R = \alpha \pi^{R^*} + (1-\alpha)[\ \pi^{D^*}(1 - V_{t-1}^R) + \pi^{R^*} V_{t-1}^R\ ] \tag{9a}$$

and

$$\pi_t^D = \alpha \pi^{D^*} + (1-\alpha)[\ \pi^{D^*}(1 - V_{t-1}^R) + \pi^{R^*} V_{t-1}^R\ ] \tag{9b}$$

where $0 < \alpha < 1$ and V_{t-1}^R is the Republican vote share in the congressional election at the end of period $t - 1$. These equations imply that the actual policy outcomes (π_t^D and π_t^R) are linear combinations of the president's policy (π^{D^*} or π^{R^*}) and the policy that would be pursued by an all-powerful Congress. The latter (given by the term in square brackets in the equations) is itself a linear combination where each party's time-consistent policy is weighted by its congressional vote share. The parameter α captures the relative weight of the president in policy formation.

Given that both parties are represented in Congress, the actual inflation rate will exceed the time-consistent policy of party R, π^{R^*}, and fall short of that of party D, π^{D^*}. Conditional on the party of the president, the rate of inflation is increasing in the vote share for party D. Likewise, holding congressional vote shares constant, inflation is higher with a party D president than with a party R president:

$$\pi_t^D > \pi_t^R\ .$$

Analysis of the Electoral Model

In standard two-candidate voting models, since voters have only a binary choice, there is a unique voter equilibrium once weakly dominated strategies have been cast aside. In our model, only "extreme" voter types with indirect bliss points less than π^{R^*} (greater than π^{D^*}) have a weakly dominant strategy of always voting for party R (D).[14] More moderate voters do not have weakly dominant strategies. How they vote depends upon their conjectures about the behavior of other voters. Thus, there is a fundamental problem of coordination of voter strategies.

A plausible unique equilibrium can be characterized, however, by adapting the concept of coalition-proof Nash equilibria to this macroeconomic policy context (Bernheim, Peleg, and Whinston 1987).[15] The basic idea is that equilibrium strategies should be robust to "credible" defections of coalitions, as well as of individuals; that is, no "credible" coalition of voters would want to modify the electoral outcome by changing their votes.

Midterm Elections

At midterm, each voter has a single binary choice—vote D or R for Congress. This makes the equilibrium analysis very simple. With party R holding the presidency, there is a unique pivotal voter ideal point, $\bar{\pi}^{CR}$. Any voter with $\bar{\pi}^i < \bar{\pi}^{CR}$ votes for party R, and those with $\bar{\pi}^i > \bar{\pi}^{CR}$ prefer D. The expected R congressional vote is

$$E(V_1^R) = \bar{\pi}^{CR}. \tag{10}$$

The equilibrium-expected inflation level represents the indirect bliss point of the pivotal voter (Alesina and Rosenthal 1989):

$$E(\bar{\pi}_2^R) = \bar{\pi}^{CR} + \gamma b. \tag{11}$$

Suppose, to the contrary, that $E(\pi_2^R) < \bar{\pi}^{CR} + \gamma b$. By continuity, voters with ideal points slightly less than $\bar{\pi}^{CR} + \gamma b$ would also find that inflation was too low, and vote D to increase inflation, implying that $\bar{\pi}^{CR}$ did not specify an equilibrium. A similar argument precludes $E(\pi_2^R) > \bar{\pi}^{CR} + \gamma b$. Using equations 9–11, we find

$$\bar{\pi}^{CR} = \frac{\pi^{R^*} - b\gamma + (1-\alpha)(\pi^{D^*} - \pi^{R^*})}{1 + (1-\alpha)(\pi^{D^*} - \pi^{R^*})}. \tag{12}$$

Analogous arguments show that when there is a D president at $t + 1$, there exists another cut-point, $\bar{\pi}^{CD}$, given by

$$\bar{\pi}^{CD} = \frac{\pi^{D^*} - b\gamma}{1 + (1-\alpha)(\pi^{D^*} - \pi^{R^*})}. \tag{13}$$

Equations 12 and 13 imply that the midterm vote for party D is increasing in b (which captures voters' tolerance for higher inflation in exchange for higher growth) regardless of the president's party. However, expected output is unaffected, since at higher values for b, economic agents correctly anticipate the higher inflation that ensues from D's higher congressional vote.

The Two-Period Model: President Unconstrained in Period 1

In the two-period model, each voter simultaneously makes two choices in on-years. Insight into the analysis is provided by decoupling these two choices and assuming, first, that a president unconstrained by Congress is elected in the first period.

For period 1, we now require an additional cutpoint $\bar{\pi}^P$. Individuals with indirect bliss points lower than $\bar{\pi}^P$ will vote R for president, while those with higher bliss points will vote D. Thus, the expected vote for the Republican presidential candidate will be

$$E\left(V_0^{RP}\right) = \bar{\pi}^P. \tag{14}$$

For an equilibrium to hold, a voter with ideal point $\bar{\pi}^P$ must obtain the same expected utility from an R victory as from a D victory. This means that a voter at $\bar{\pi}^P$ must be indifferent as between the two-period bundle of inflation and growth associated with the election of an R president and the bundle represented by a D president.

We have already computed the inflation outcomes in the bundles, namely

If a D president $\qquad\Big\}\quad \pi_1^D = \pi^{D^*}$ $\qquad\qquad\qquad\qquad$ (15)
(unconstrained in period 1) $\qquad E\left(\pi_2^D\right) = \bar{\pi}^{CD} + \gamma b$ $\qquad\qquad$ (16)

If an R president $\qquad\Big\}\quad \pi_1^R = \pi^{R^*}$ $\qquad\qquad\qquad\qquad$ (17)
(unconstrained in period 1) $\qquad E\left(\pi_2^R\right) = \bar{\pi}^{CR} + \gamma b$ $\qquad\qquad$ (18)

We also need to compute the expected growth outcomes in the bundles; in order to do so, we need to evaluate the period 0 rational expectation of inflation in period 1. This requires knowledge of the probability of a D presidential victory, given $\bar{\pi}^P$. This probability, denoted $Q\left(\bar{\pi}^P\right)$, can be easily computed, given the uniform distribution of **a.** The inflation expectation is then evaluated as

$$\pi_1^e + Q\left(\bar{\pi}^P\right)\pi^{D^*} + \left(1 - Q\left(\bar{\pi}^P\right)\right)\pi^{R^*} \tag{19}$$

Equation 19 is central to both wage contracting and voting. It underlines that before presidential elections, electoral uncertainty forces agents to "hedge their bets" in forming expectations about future policies. Using 19, we can now compute growth in the two periods. We assume a D president in period 0, the R case being symmetric. Expected growth is[16]

if a D $\qquad\Big\}\quad E\left(g_2^D\right) = E\left(g_2^R\right) = \bar{g}$ $\qquad\qquad\qquad\qquad\qquad$ (20)
president $\qquad\Big\}\quad E\left(g_1^R\right) = \bar{g} - Q\left(\bar{\pi}^{D^*} - \bar{\pi}^{R^*}\right)$ $\qquad\qquad$ (21)
at $t = 0$ $\qquad\Big\}\quad E\left(g_1^D\right) = \bar{g} + (1-Q)\left(\bar{\pi}^{D^*} - \bar{\pi}^{R^*}\right) + \hat{\eta}_1.$ $\qquad$ (22)

Equation 20 implies that control of the White House will not affect growth in period 2. This result follows because even before the presidential election takes place, the voters know that new wage contracts will be signed at the end of period 1. At that time, there will be no uncertainty about the identity of the president.

Equation 21 gives the expected growth in the first period of an R administration. It is obtained by substituting equations 17 and 19 into equation 1 and by noting that expected competence is at its "normal" value of 0, as R is the challenging party, and so there is no information about its competence. Equation 21 shows that *below*-normal growth is expected at the outset of an R administration. This does not imply that R likes recessions. On the contrary, since $b^R > 0$, party R prefers higher growth to lower growth. The problem is that the possibility of a D electoral victory keeps inflation expectations (see equation 19) *higher* than the low-inflation policy of party R.

Equation 22 represents expected growth in period 1 when party D retains control of the White House. The equation is symmetric to equation 21 in that there is *above*-normal growth from surprise inflation. The additional term, $\hat{\eta}_1$, is the expected value of the incumbent party's competence in period 1, from equation 7. (The expectation at $t = 0$ for period 2 is 0 because competence is MA(1).) This is the key to "rational" retrospective voting. Voters will tilt to incumbents with large $\hat{\eta}$s.

With equations 14–22, we have all the necessary information to compute $\bar{\pi}^P$ and $Q(\bar{\pi}^P)$. It should be clear now that there are two influences on presidential voting. The first is how the parties are located relative to the distribution of voter preferences. If R's time-consistent policies are closer to the median indirect bliss point than are D's, R will be favored ($Q < \frac{1}{2}$). The second is the rate of economic growth in the preelection period, via g's influence on $\hat{\eta}$. We emphasize that the relevant portion of growth reflects only "competence" and "luck" and not the "partisan" inflation policies of the two parties (see equation 7).

The Two-Period Model with Congress Elected in Both Periods

Now we must find one more cut-point, $\bar{\pi}^C$, which applies to the on-year congressional elections. Again voters with indirect bliss points below the cutpoint will vote for R, and those above will vote for D. As in the midterm case, first-period inflation equals, in expectation, the bliss point of the pivotal voter. Applying results from Alesina and Rosenthal (1991), we have

$$\bar{\pi}^C = Q(\bar{\pi}^P)\bar{\pi}^{CD} + (1 - Q(\bar{\pi}^P))\bar{\pi}^{CR}. \tag{23}$$

The first-period congressional cutpoint is a weighted average of the second-period cut-points, with the weights given by the probability of the presidential election outcome. This equation implies that on-year congressional voting responds directly to future partisan effects on economic policy, via $\bar{\pi}^{CD}$ and $\bar{\pi}^{CR}$, but only indirectly to the current state of the economy, via the linkage to presidential voting provided by $Q(\bar{\pi}^P)$. There is no direct response because voters evaluate competence only for the executive.

A "midterm cycle" occurs if and only if $0 < Q(\bar{\pi}^P) < 1$, so that, from equation 23:

$$\bar{\pi}^{CR} < \bar{\pi}^C < \bar{\pi}^{CD}; \tag{24}$$

that is, a midterm cycle results when there is uncertainty about the outcome of the presidential election, leading voters to hedge their bets in on-years. With presidential uncertainty resolved, voters in midterm elections "fully" moderate the presidential winner. For example, consider a voter who desires moderately high inflation, with $\bar{\pi}^i \in (\bar{\pi}^C, \bar{\pi}^{CD})$. If the R presidential candidate were to win, a strong R congressional vote would result in inflation far below the rate favored by voter i. Accordingly, in the on-year, this voter protects against a possible R presidential win by supporting the D congressional delegation. But if party D captures the White House, the risk of a party R win evaporates and at the ensuing midterm election, voter i supports the party R delegation to moderate the D president.

Equation 24 implies that the less unexpected the outcome of presidential elections, the smaller the size of the midterm effect. The amount of uncertainty depends upon $\bar{\pi}^P$, which, in turn, is a function of the parameters of the model. The value of this cut-point can again be obtained by equating the expected utility from an R presidential victory to that from a D victory, this time taking into account the presence of a legislative vote in the first period. One can then compute expectations over growth and, after substitution, the presidential cut-point. The expressions for the presidential and congressional cutpoints generate two equations in two unknowns that are otherwise functions only of the parameters of the model (π^D, π^R, γ, β, ρ, b, w, σ_ζ^2, and σ_μ^2).

Alesina and Rosenthal (1991) show how to solve this problem and demonstrate, for a large set of parameter values, the existence of a unique equilibrium (in a different parameterization) characterized by uncertain presidential elections ($0 < Q < 1$) and thus a midterm cycle.

Estimation

The Sample

Our empirical analysis of the joint determination of economic growth and the results of national elections covers 1915–88. We began with 1915 because the previous year, 1914, was the beginning of a new financial regime, marked by the inception of

Table 1

Descriptive Statistics, 1915–88

Variable	Mean	S.D.	N
Growth rate of real GNP (g)	3.062	5.981	74
Nonelection year growth rate	3.610	4.967	37
Midterm year growth rate	1.528	8.192	18
Presidential year growth rate	3.447	5.404	19
Party ($D = 0, R = 1$) of president (r)	.486	.503	74
Presidential vote for incumbent's party (V^p)	53.053	7.805	19
On-year House vote for incumbent's party (V^{hp})	49.907	5.610	19
Lagged House vote (at midterm)	49.279	4.790	19
Midterm House vote for Incumbent's Party (V^{hm})	49.220	4.922	18
Lagged House vote (at midterm)	53.320	4.551	18
Partisan effect (pe) in 2d year of term	.000	1.029	18
Military mobilization (mm)	.010	1.007	74

Sources: Voting data from U.S. Bureau of the Census, *Historical Statistics of the United States, Colonial Times to 1970 Bicentennial Edition, part 2* (Washington: GPO, 1975); *idem, Statistical Abstract of the United States 1990*, 110 ed. (Washington: GPO, 1990). Erikson 1989, 1990; Real GNP data from Balke and Gordon 1989 and Citibase. The Balke and Gordon series is similar to that of Romer (1989).

the Federal Reserve and the collapse of the gold standard.[17] Furthermore, economic data before this date are of dubious quality, and the three-party presidential race of 1912 would pose estimation problems. Descriptive statistics and data sources are given in Table 1. In the theoretical model, each period represents two calendar years, mimicking the intervals between national elections.

The Growth Equation

The growth equation of our theoretical model reflects two potential channels of political influence on the economy. First, there is "surprise inflation" in the wake of every presidential election. To capture this effect empirically, we construct a "partisan effect" variable, pe_t, set equal to 1 during the second year of a Republican administration, -1 during the second year of a Democratic administration, and 0 otherwise. The coefficient on this variable should be negative. The second channel from politics to growth is the executive branch's competence at promoting economic performance. In the theoretical model, executive competence, which is not directly observable, evolves according to an MA(1) process. This model implies that successive residuals from the growth equation will be less highly correlated when there is a change of administration.

The specification of pe_t has three features deserving explanation. First, the variable is nonzero only in the *second* year of presidential terms. This reflects the view that real effects of monetary policy do not show up in output before 2–4 quarters.[18] Using quarterly data, Alesina (1988) shows that the postelectoral effects on the economy appear no sooner than 2 quarters after a presidential election, peak in about 5–6 quarters, and disappear by 10 quarters. Analogous results for several other countries are reported by Alesina and Roubini (1992). Second, with pe_t, the magnitude of the inflation surprise is equal across parties, whereas in the theory, the surprise (see equations 21–22) is greater for the party with the lower probability of winning.[19] Third, in addition to the presidential inflation surprise captured by pe_t, our theoretical model also allows for surprise inflation from the outcome of congressional elections. However, whereas the presidential outcome is discrete, the impact of congressional elections depends on deviations of V^R from its expected value. These deviations should be roughly of the magnitude of the small forecast errors from our House equations. In addition, presidential influence on policy is likely to exceed that of Congress (Hibbs 1987); that is, α is likely to be large, implying that the impact of congressional surprises is sufficiently small that we can simplify the empirical model by excluding them.

With the term ζ_t in equation 2, we modeled transitory effects on growth as random events. But military activities, especially wars, represent an obvious source of transitory effects that can be included in the analysis.[20] Define m_t to be the number of individuals in military service as of 30 June of year t and POP_t to be the population of the United States for the same year. Then the rate of military mobilization is given by

$$mm_t = (m_t - m_{t-1})/\mathrm{POP}_t.$$

This variable highlights the beginnings and endings of wars, and it scales conflicts relative to one another. Including pe_t and mm_t and substituting into equation 1 from equations 2 and 3, our growth equation is

$$g_t = \gamma_0 + \gamma_1 pe_t + \gamma_2 mm_t + \zeta_t + \mu_t^R + \rho\mu_{t-1}^R \qquad \text{if an } R \text{ president}$$

$$g_t = \gamma_0 + \gamma_1 pe_t + \gamma_2 mm_t + \zeta_t + \mu_t^D + \rho\mu_{t-1}^D \qquad \text{if a } D \text{ president.} \qquad (25)$$

Let θ denote the covariance between the two parties' competency shocks:

$$\theta = \mathrm{Cov}(\mu_t^R, \mu_t^D).$$

In our model, $\theta = 0$, while $\theta = \sigma_\mu^2$ in the standard MA(1) model. The two models are nested in a generalized growth equation with parameters γ_0, γ_1, γ_2, σ_ζ^2, σ_μ^2, ρ, and θ.

Nelson and Plosser (1982) show that the standard MA(1) model where $\theta = \sigma_\mu^2$, and $\sigma_\zeta^2 = 0$ is not rejected in favor of more complicated autoregressive moving average (ARMA) process models.[21] Thus, the standard MA(1) model adequately describes the annual growth series.[22] In contrast, our model implies $\theta = 0$ and does not restrict σ_ζ^2. The model implied by equation 25 is underidentified: we cannot recover ρ, σ_μ^2, σ_ζ^2, and θ without further structure. However, we can estimate $c_0 = \rho\sigma_\mu^2$, and $c_1 = \rho\theta$, enabling us to test both the competency-based model, which implies H_0: $c_0 > c_1 = 0$, and the standard MA(1) model, which implies H_1: $c_0 = c_1$.

Our estimate of c_1 is 10.51, with a standard error of 3.98, leading to rejection of H_0 at all standard levels of significance. Is there evidence that $c_0 > c_1$—as we might see if the competency shocks for the two parties were positively (but imperfectly) correlated? The estimated value of c_0 is 7.85, *less* than c_1, providing no evidence against H_1 in favor of the alternative that $c_1 < c_0$. We thus *reject* the competence model. This implies that rational voters should not be retrospective—the rate of GNP growth in election years should not affect presidential elections. We return to this point when we discuss the presidential vote results.[23]

Our test of H_1 against the unrestricted model is more favorable, indicating acceptance at all standard significance levels.[24] We thus adopt the standard MA(1) model:

$$g_t = \gamma_0 + \gamma_1 pe_t + \gamma_2 mm_t + \rho\mu_{t-1} + \mu_t. \tag{26}$$

Purely to facilitate estimation of the full model, we allow for heteroscedasticity with separate variances for nonelection years, midterm election years, and years in which there is a presidential election: $\sigma_{\mu\mathcal{N}}^2$, $\sigma_{\mu\mathcal{M}}^2$, and $\sigma_{\mu\mathcal{P}}^2$ respectively.[25] Our estimates do not lead to rejection of the null hypothesis that these variances are equal.

Presidential Elections

For convenience in estimation, we specify, for both presidential and congressional elections, the dependent variables as *shares of the two-party vote for the party of the incumbent president.*

In our theoretical model, voters evaluate both party policies and presidential competence. But since the tests of the growth model provided no evidence that variations in competence are an important factor in growth, any evidence of retrospective voting on the economy will, within the context of our model, constitute a rejection of voter rationality.

Our theoretical model of presidential voting implies a cut-point $\bar{\pi}_p$ that may not be at the expected median. Consequently, one party may have an expected vote share greater than one-half. We capture the embodiment of policy preferences in the cut-point via r_t, which takes on a value of 1 if the incumbent is a Republican, and 0 otherwise.

However, we allow the cut-point implicit in r_t to be "adjusted" via v_{t-2}^{hm}, the share of the popular vote cast for the incumbent president's House delegation during the preceding midterm election. This variable can be proxying for several effects. First, the locations of the parties *relative* to the distribution of the voters may adjust slowly in time, whereas they are assumed to be constant in the theoretical model. Second, the independent preference shocks in the theoretical model are likely to be serially correlated in practice. Third, incumbency advantage in the House may directly improve chances of winning the presidency. None of these mechanisms is included (for reasons of tractability) in our theoretical model, but our results suggest they are empirically relevant.

The presidential voting equation also contains an additional disturbance φ_t^P that is orthogonal to the growth shocks and measures. This incorporates **a** in the theoretical model. "Rally 'round the flag" effects from wars perhaps represent a systematic short-run shift in the distribution of preferences. Consequently, we also include mm_t in the equation.

Last—and certainly not least—is retrospective voting on the economy. We test for this effect by including g_t in the regression. But to pursue our investigation of "rational" versus "naive" voting further, we break g_t into two components: μ_t, the contemporaneous shock, and $\hat{g}_t$, which is the expected growth rate based on the parameters of equation 26 and lagged shock (recall that $pe = 0$ in an election year):

$$\hat{g}_t = \gamma_0 + \gamma_2 mm_t + \rho\mu_{t-1}.$$

Our voting equation is, then,

$$v_t^p = \psi_0 + \psi_1 r_t + \psi_2 v_{t-2}^{hm} + \psi_3 mm_t + \psi_4 \hat{g}_t + \psi_5 \mu_t + \varphi_t^p. \tag{27}$$

Since we rejected the competence model, voter rationality would imply, in this model, that $\psi_4 = \psi_5 = 0$. Purely naive retrospective voting implies $\psi_4 = \psi_5 > 0$; that is, the electorate votes on the basis of GNP growth and does not even attempt to make any distinction between shocks to growth and predictable growth. For a naive voter, growth is growth: its pedigree does not matter.

Note that φ_t^p does not appear in equation 26. Consequently, equations 26–27 represent a recursive system. The recursive structure is preserved when we add congressional voting.[26] We also estimate a restricted presidential equation in which there is no direct "rally 'round the flag" effect:

$$v_t^p = \psi_0 + \psi_1 r_t + \psi_2 v_{t-2}^{hm} + \psi_4 \hat{g}_t + \psi_5 \mu_t + \varphi_t^p. \tag{28}$$

House Elections

For House elections, we distinguish between presidential election years and midterm contests. In both cases we include military mobilization, the lagged House vote, and the incumbent's party affiliation, the latter to allow congressional cut-points to differ from the median.

In presidential years, we allow for coattails (Calvert and Ferejohn 1983; Erikson 1990). Two avenues for coattails need to be considered.[27] First, our formal model includes a random preference shock, **a**, which affects both races and induces positive correlation between the presidential vote and the congressional vote. Following Kramer (1971), we allow for this effect by making the House vote dependent on the presidential vote shock φ_t^p. We expect a coefficient on this variable of less than 1, since the presidential shock may contain candidate-specific effects that are "outside" our formal model. Second, naive retrospective voting may induce positive coattails in congressional elections due to a "feel good" effect: some of the effect of economic performance on the presidential vote carries over to the benefit of the party's congressional delegation (Erikson 1990).

We test for positive or negative coattails based on economic performance by estimating two versions of the presidential year house voting equation. In the first specification, there is no direct effect from the presidential vote. The instrumented growth rate and contemporaneous growth shock enter directly. Coattails arise solely from the shock to presidential voting:

$$v_t^{hp} = \lambda_0 + \lambda_1 r_t + \lambda_2 v_{t-2}^{hm} + \lambda_3 mm_t + \lambda_4 \hat{g}_t + \lambda_5 \mu_t + \lambda_6 \varphi_t^p + \varphi_t^{hp} . \qquad (29)$$

In a second specification, neither the economy nor military mobilization nor the president's party affiliation matter once the effects of the shock to presidential preferences have been accounted for:

$$v_t^{hp} = \lambda_0 + \lambda_2 v_{t-2}^{hm} + \lambda_6 \varphi_t^p + \varphi_t^{hp} . \qquad (30)$$

As for midterm elections, our theory predicts a consistent midterm backlash against the incumbent president's party as voters seek to moderate the policy impact of the incumbent president; formally, $v_t^{hm} < v_{t-2}^{hp}$. Two specifications are used. In the first, the midterm House vote depends on all variables that appear in the other equations (save for pe_t is perfectly collinear with r_t during midterm years):

$$v_t^{hm} = \kappa_0 + \kappa_1 r_t + \kappa_2 v_{t-2}^{hp} + \kappa_3 mm_t + \kappa_4 \hat{g}_t + \kappa_5 \mu_t + \varphi_t^{hm} . \qquad (31)$$

A more extreme specification of the midterm cycle is that the seat loss is unaffected by anything other than the previous election's winning margin. This is embodied in our second specification of midterm voting:

$$v_t^{hm} = \kappa_0 + \kappa_2 v_{t-2}^{hp} + \varphi_t^{hm} . \qquad (32)$$

Table 2

Equation for Annual Growth Rate: Percentage of Real Gross National Product, 1915–1988

Variable	Coefficient	Unrestricted[a]	System Restricted[b]
Constant	γ_0	3.254	3.214
		(.728)	(.726)
Partisan effect	γ_1	−1.700	−1.698
		(.902)	(.887)
Military mobilization	γ_2	3.027	3.087
		(.516)	(.447)
Lagged growth shock	ρ	.518	.484
		(.101)	(.122)
Type of year			
Nonelection year[c]	$\sigma^2_{\mu \mathcal{N}}$	13.503	—
		(3.254)	
Midterm election year[d]	$\sigma^2_{\mu \mathcal{M}}$	21.704	—
		(7.453)	
Presidential election year[e]	$\sigma^2_{\mu \mathcal{P}}$	19.377	—
		(6.336)	

Note: The restricted estimates are computed using Rothemberg's (1973) optimum minimum distance technique, which does not produce fresh σ^2 estimates. Standard errors are in parentheses.

[a]Equation 26, estimated jointly with equations 27, 29, and 31.
[b]Equation 26, estimated jointly with equations 28, 30, and 32.
[c]$R^2 = .438$.
[d]$R^2 = .658$.
[e]$R^2 = .300$.

Estimation Results

For each of the three voting equations in our model, we have just presented two versions, restricted and unrestricted. First, we jointly estimated the three unrestricted equations and the growth equation via maximum likelihood. The results appear in the first columns of Tables 2–5. We then estimated the restricted version of each voting equation, with the other equations unrestricted. These results are in the second columns of Tables 3–5. Finally, our preferred model, dubbed "system restricted," simultaneously restricts all three equations, with results in the last columns of Tables 2–5.

The estimates of the growth equation appear in Table 2. The partisan effect, the lagged growth shock and military mobilization are all significant at the 5% level. There are no statistically significant differences in the estimated variances, although the estimate for nonelection years is somewhat lower than the estimates for presidential and midterm years.

The estimated partisan effects parameter, γ_1, is of the same magnitude re-

Table 3

Equation for Midterm Popular Vote for House of Representatives: Percentage of Two Party Vote for Incumbent President's Party, 1918–1986

Variable	Coefficient	Unrestricted[a]	Parameter Estimates Equation Restricted[b]	System Restricted[c]
Constant	κ_0	−1.398 (6.771)	−1.422 (6.230)	−1.418 (6.230)
Republican incumbent	κ_1	.240 (1.096)	—	—
Previous House vote	κ_2	.939 (.123)	.950 (.116)	.950 (.116)
Military mobilization	κ_3	−.369 (1.079)	—	—
Expected growth, $\hat{g}_t$	κ_4	.090 (.115)	—	
Current growth shock	κ_5	.181 (.299)	—	—
Residual variance[d]	σ^2_{hm}	4.753 (1.586)	—	—

Note: The restricted estimates are computed using Rothemberg's (1973) optimum minumum distance technique, which does not produce fresh σ^2 estimates. Standard errors are in parentheses.

[a]Equation 31, estimated jointly with equations 26, 27, and 29.
[b]Equation 32, estimated jointly with equations 26, 27, and 29.
[c]Equation 32, estimated jointly with equations 26, 28, and 30.
[d]$R^2 = .853$.

ported by Alesina and Sachs (1988) for a single-equation estimation covering 1948–84. It indicates that growth rates during the second year of Republican administrations with no changes in the level of the armed forces will average under 2%, while during the corresponding year of a Democratic administration, the economy will typically grow by almost 5%.

As expected, the beginnings and endings of wars overshadow other economic events. We estimate that the economy expands by about 3% for each 1% of the population that is mobilized into military service. When the same 1% are demobilized, the economy contracts, again by approximately 3%.[28]

Our estimate of ρ indicates that the effect of the lagged shock, μ_{t-1}, is approximately half the effect of the current shock, μ_t. This estimate is very similar to Nelson and Plosser's (1982) results.

Estimates for the unrestricted midterm House election equation (equation 31) appear in the first column of Table 3. This equation has an R-squared of

.85. However, the predictive power of this equation stems almost entirely from the presence of the lagged House vote among the regressors. While no other explanatory variable is significant at the 10% level, the lagged House vote coefficients "t-ratio" is over 7. Equation 32 therefore imposes the restriction that the midterm House vote is influenced only by the preceding on-year vote. This results in a test statistic of $\chi_4^2 = 1.824$, corresponding to a p-value of .768, a "success" for our theoretical model in which the state of the economy does not affect House elections.

Estimates of equation 32 appear in the second column of Table 3. Routine calculations show that the predicted vote loss is 3.73% when the president's party won 46% (the sample minimum for victorious presidents) of the on-year House vote and increases to 4.54% at 62% (the sample maximum). Although the estimated intercept is insignificantly different from 0 and the coefficient of the lagged vote is insignificantly different from 1, the predicted vote loss is significant for the range of sample observations. For example, the party of an incumbent president that received 50% of the House vote in the preceding presidential election year is expected to lose 3.93%. The estimated standard deviation of this expected loss is only .65%. This result echoes Erikson (1990), who imposed $\kappa_2 = 1$ and used only postwar data.

To summarize our midterm House estimates, the systematic midterm effect is consistent with our theoretical prediction of a moderation of the president's party. Moreover, the fact that the midterm effect is increasing in the lagged vote for the president's party is consistent with regression to the mean induced by the random shock to preferences, **a**.

The first column of Table 4 displays the unrestricted presidential vote shares equation (equation 27). The economy has a pronounced effect on presidential voting. Both instrumented growth (ψ_4) and the current growth shock (ψ_5) have statistically significant coefficients. As we have discussed, the naive retrospective voting hypothesis has $\psi_4 = \psi_5$. Tests of this hypothesis indicate acceptance, whether one uses the unrestricted or system restricted estimates. In the former case, the asymptotic t-ratio is $-.96$, while in the latter it is 1.32. Both results are consistent with the hypothesis of naive retrospective voting. In fact, since the results show that voters do not treat components of growth differentially (though they might be expected to under rational retrospection), these results provide stronger support for naive retrospection than is available in previous single equation estimates. The effect of growth is substantial; in the system restricted estimation, a 1% increase in the election-year growth rate increases the vote for the incumbent president's party by .795%.[29] Even larger impacts arise in the other specifications.

The insignificant coefficient on the military mobilization variable in equation 27 shows that "rally 'round the flag" effects are manifest only through growth. The beginning and ending of wars, except insofar as they stimulate growth, are neutral for the incumbents' electoral fortunes. Estimates of the other coefficients change little when mm_t is deleted.

Table 4

Equation for Popular Vote for President: Percentage of Two Party Vote for Incumbent President's Party, 1916–1988

Variable	Coefficient	Parameter Estimates		
		Unrestricted[a]	Equation Restricted[b]	System Restricted[c]
Constant	ψ_0	5.622	5.981	12.209
		(10.410)	(10.147)	(9.470)
Republican incumbent	ψ_1	10.365	10.362	8.842
		(1.929)	(1.919)	(1.223)
Previous House vote	ψ_2	.743	.739	.692
		(.194)	(.193)	(.187)
Military mobilization	ψ_3	−.406	—	—
		(2.358)		
Expected growth, $\hat{g}_t$	ψ_4	1.636	1.590	.795
		(.509)	(.405)	(.216)
Current growth shock	ψ_5	1.139	1.140	1.174
		(.208)	(.208)	(.201)
Residual variance[d]	σ_p^2	13.601	—	—
		(4.425)		

Note: The restricted estimates are computed using Rothemberg's (1973) optimum minimum distance technique, which does not produce fresh σ^2 estimates. Standard errors are in parentheses.

[a]Equation 27, estimated jointly with equations 26, 29, and 31.
[b]Equation 28, estimated jointly with equations 26, 29, and 31.
[c]Equation 28, estimated jointly with equations 26, 30, and 32.
[d]$R^2 = .764$.

The estimated pro-Republican bias of 10% (ψ_1) is only partly counteracted by the effect of the lagged House vote, which favors the Democrats. Ceteris paribus, for a Democratic incumbent president to be more favored than a Republican, the Democrats would have to have done exceptionally well in the preceding midterm election, obtaining almost 57% of the House vote.

While our theoretical model allows for a partisan bias by voters, it requires that there be no bias to the incumbent party in presidential voting. This hypothesis is testable: the predicted Republican presidential vote in an election year with a Republican incumbent and the predicted Democratic presidential vote given a Democratic incumbent—in both cases with the explanatory variables at the sample mean—should sum to 100% of the two-party vote. If the sum is significantly greater, then there is a bias toward incumbents in addition to the pro-Republican bias. We test this in the context of the unrestricted model. The sum of the predicted incumbent totals is 105.59. With respect to the null hypothesis of 100, the t-ratio is 2.12, indicating rejection of the null hypothesis of no bias toward incumbents at the 5% level.

Table 5

Equation for Popular Vote for House of Representatives in Presidential Election Years: Percentage of Two Party Vote for Incumbent President's Party, 1916–1988

Variable	Coefficient	Parameter Estimates		
		Unrestricted[a]	Equation restricted[b]	System restricted[c]
Constant	λ_0	3.637 (7.424)	7.855 (6.492)	7.809 (6.497)
Republican incumbent	λ_1	1.345 (1.366)	—	—
Previous House vote	λ_2	.886 (.138)	.860 (.131)	.860 (.131)
Military mobilization	λ_3	1.567 (1.688)	—	—
Expected growth, $\hat{g}_t$	λ_4	.554 (.370)	—	—
Current growth shock	λ_5	−.032 (.153)	—	—
Presidential vote shock	λ_6	.547 (.105)	.534 (.065)	.531 (.065)
Residual variance[d]	σ^2_{hp}	2.841 (.937)	—	—

Note: The restricted estimates are computed using Rothemberg's (1973) optimum minimum distance technique, which does not produce fresh σ^2 estimates. Standard errors are in parentheses.

[a]Equation 29, estimated jointly with equations 26, 27, and 31.
[b]Equation 30, estimated jointly with equations 26, 27, and 31.
[c]Equation 30, estimated jointly with equations 26, 28, and 32.
[d]$R^2 = .905$.

The presidential year House voting results appear in Table 5. As with midterm voting, the party affiliation of the president, military mobilization, and the growth variables have individually insignificant effects. The absence of a significant partisan bias in the congressional races coupled with the significant pro-Republican bias for the presidency shows that the Democrats are relatively more favored in the House than in presidential races, leading, other effects aside, to split-ticket voting.

The absence of a significant effect for growth is consistent with recent work by Erikson (1990), who included both the current presidential vote and the current growth rate on the right-hand side of a House voting equation and found that the coefficient of growth was insignificant. Our analysis confirms this result in a context that is free from the possible simultaneity bias of Erikson's estimator.

The presidential vote shock does have a highly significant effect on the on-year House vote, with a one-percentage-point shock to the presidential vote translating into approximately half an extra percentage point in the popular vote for the president's House delegation. This is consistent with the view that observed coattails result from a shock to preferences that shifts more voters to the same side of both the presidential and House voting cut-points.

When the insignificant variables from the on-year House voting equation are simultaneously dropped, the resulting χ_4^2 statistic of 6.63 indicates acceptance at all standard significance levels. The restricted presidential-year and midterm-year House voting equations have very similar structures, save for the effects of the presidential vote shock in the on-year equation. However, while the midterm voting equation reflects a systematic bias against the president's House delegation, we find no evidence of such bias in the on-year House elections. Holding the presidential vote shock equal to zero, and setting all other variables at their sample means, routine calculations reveal a statistically insignificant expected vote gain of about 1 percentage point for the president's party in a presidential year House election. The estimates do reveal a slight—but statistically insignificant—tendency toward mean reversion, with an expected vote gain of 2.08 percentage points with the lagged House vote at the sample minimum of 41% and a loss of .29 percentage points with a lagged House vote of 58%, the sample maximum for presidential election years.

Our preferred model consists of the system restricted set of equations—equations 26, 28, 30, and 32—whose jointly estimated values appear in the right-hand columns of Tables 2–5. To explore the dynamics of the system, we use our coefficient estimates to simulate the system in the absence of any random shocks to either growth or voting behavior and with military mobilization set to zero. Regardless of the starting value for the previous House vote, the system converges to an 36-year cycle, with the White House changing hands at regular intervals (see Table 6).

The cycling results from the cumulative effect of midterm losses. Each midterm loss costs the party of the incumbent a larger share of the vote than it wins back through mean reversion in the ensuing presidential election two years later. Indeed, when the president's House delegation is sufficiently large, small additional losses through mean reversion are expected in the on-year election. The longer a party retains control of the White House, the greater the cumulative erosion of its congressional delegation. Because the presidential vote is an increasing function of the lagged House vote, erosion of support for the incumbent's House delegation reduces its presidential vote. This process eventually costs the incumbent's party the White House.

The marked partisan bias toward Republican presidential candidates (which we have discussed) results in the Republican party's retaining control of the White House for 24 of the 36 years of the cycle. However, Republican control of the White House typically occurs with a divided government. There is unified Republican control of the executive and legislative branches for only 2 of the 36

Table 6

Long-Run Stable Cycle for the System

Year	Growth Rate	Vote for Inc. Pres. Party		Election Winner	
		President	House	President	House
1	3.214				
2	4.912		55.08		D
3	3.214				
4	3.214	52.88	55.18	D	D
5	3.214				
6	4.912		51.00		D
7	3.214				
8	3.214	50.06	51.67	D	D
9	3.214				
10	4.912		47.67		R
11	3.214				
12	3.214	47.75	48.81	R	R
13	3.214				
14	1.516		47.22		D
15	3.214				
16	3.214	56.28	48.41	R	D
17	3.214				
18	1.516		44.58		D
19	3.214				
20	3.214	54.45	46.14	R	D
21	3.214				
22	1.516		42.42		D
23	3.214				
24	3.214	52.96	44.29	R	D
25	3.214				
26	1.516		40.66		D
27	3.214				
28	3.214	51.74	42.77	R	D
29	3.214				
30	1.516		39.22		D
31	3.214				
32	3.214	50.74	41.54	R	D
33	3.214				
34	1.516		38.04		D
35	3.214				
36	3.214	49.93	40.52	D	D

Note: The system simulated is

$$g_t = 3.214 - 1.698 pe_t \qquad t = 0, 1, 2, 3, 4 \ldots$$
$$V_t^p = 12.209 + 8.842 r_t + .642 V_{t-2}^{hm} + .795 g_t \qquad t = 2, 6, 10, 14 \ldots$$
$$V_t^{hp} = 7.809 + .860 V_{t-2}^{hm} \qquad t = 2, 6, 10, 14 \ldots$$
$$V_t^{hm} = -1.418 + .950 V_{t-2}^{hm} \qquad t = 0, 4, 8, 12 \ldots$$

Starting values must be assigned to r_t and V_{t-2}^{hp}. The steady state is reached from all starting values assigned. See Table 1 and text for definitions of variables.

years. Although the Democratic party only controls the White House for 12 years of the cycle, it receives a majority of the House vote during 10 of these years. Thus, to the extent that unified government is important to policy initiatives, the Democrats may actually have more opportunities to implement new policies than the Republicans.

The pattern of divided government, with Republicans occupying the White House and Democrats entrenched in Congress, is similar to actual post–World War II experience. However, it does not resemble the political climate of the 1930s, which was dominated by the "shock" of the Great Depression.

Conclusion

We have tested, in a fully simultaneous estimation, a macro model of economic growth and national elections. This model incorporates (1–2) the "rational partisan model" of growth; (3) voters' moderating behavior, which counterbalances the president via the congressional vote both in on-years via split tickets and in midterm elections; and (4) the "competency" model of rational retrospective voting. We found strong support for features 1–2 and 3 and rejected feature 4. Rather than summarizing these results in detail, we conclude by highlighting some open issues.

There are two inherent limitations to our enterprise. On the theoretical side, formulating a tractable model has forced us to limit dynamic considerations to the anticipation of midterm elections in years when the presidency is at stake; that is, with respect to the strategies pursued by political and economic agents, "the world starts over" every four years. Our finding of a bias in favor of presidential incumbents suggests an interest in developing a model with a longer time horizon, where voters are risk-averse with regard to the growth rate. On the empirical side, data are thin. In the model, only presidential elections have an important impact on the economy; and they occur only every four years. While output is produced continuously, persistence in the time series limits the information available for testing. In addition, the presence of only seven shifts in party control of the presidency since 1915 makes it difficult to distinguish persistence in administrative competence from other forms of persistence in the economy.

Even with these limitations in mind, our results are not good news for the attempt to explain retrospective voting on the economy via rational choice models. Shocks to the economy appear to be short-lived and unlinked to changes in partisan control of the White House. The analysis of growth gives no evidence that voters should use information about aggregate growth to learn about competence. Nevertheless, the effects of the economy on voting are consistent with naive retrospective voting.

A further challenge to rational choice models might result if we were to include measures of the probability of victory in our econometric model. While elections that are several months distant may always appear uncertain to economic agents, many postwar elections were known landslides on election eve. In such cases, we should not, according to our theoretical model, observe a midterm effect. But the midterm cycle is uniformly present. Discriminating true failures of the model from changes in preferences is, of course, difficult. While Nixon's 1972 election may have been "certain," Watergate intervened to produce a pro-Democratic shift at midterm. Even if it were possible to measure either probabilities or preference shifts, an expansion of the econometric model would further tax degrees of freedom. Nonetheless, the pervasiveness of the midterm cycle may attest to voters treating probabilities differently than in standard rational choice models.[30] Consequently, an explicit treatment of voter expectations just prior to voting is a strong candidate for future research.

In short, we have presented a unified rational choice model of national elections and the macroeconomy. The empirical tests of the model led to rejection of rational retrospective voting but to strengthened support for rational responses to electoral uncertainty via both the midterm electoral cycle and the partisan business cycle. To reconcile these contrasting results on rationality would be an excellent aim for future theoretical and empirical research.

Notes

1. The seminal work in this area is by Hibbs (1977, 1987). See also Alesina 1988; Alesina and Roubini 1992; Alesina and Sachs 1988; Chappell and Keech 1988. Beck (1982) suggests that in addition to partisan effects, there are important administration specific effects, as well.

2. But Kiewiet and Udell (1991) find that Kramer's (1971) initial results change when recently improved historical data series are used in place of his original data.

3. See Jacobson 1990 for a contrasting view.

4. Similar partisan effects are observed in many other industrial democracies; see Alesina and Roubini 1992 and the references cited therein.

5. Most wage contracts last one to three years (Taylor 1980).

6. Our formulation of the competence model closely follows Persson and Tabellini 1990. This model, applied to a different economic problem, was originally proposed by Rogoff and Sibert (1988). Related results are in Cukierman and Meltzer 1986.

7. Allowing for persistence in output growth in equation 1 would not change our qualitative conclusions, given the functional forms used in the model.

8. Results would go through even if utility were also quadratic in growth. See Alesina and Sachs 1988.

9. The model can easily be generalized, without changes in the results, to one in which the government controls the money supply, rather than inflation. See Alesina 1988.

10. This is a very rough characterization of the American electoral system. We ignore the electoral college, the bicameral legislature based on geographic constituencies, and the presence of staggered terms in the Senate.

11. The qualitative results of the model would be preserved if there were serial dependence in **a.**

12. It is natural to think of the inflation rate, π, as a percentage. In this context, it may seem strained to think of the desired rate as having a range of only 1% and, for **a** < 0, to include desired deflation. Equations 5 and 6, however, are arbitrary scaling used to sim-

plify the algebra. The analysis would not be changed by allowing for a wider uniform support limited to positive ideal points.

13. Equation 7 uses standard results in signal extraction theory presented in Cukierman 1984.

14. To guarantee that the pivotal voter's own ideal point is uninformative about the realization of the random variable **a**, we further assume that $0 < w < \min |\bar{\pi}^{R^*} - \gamma b, 1 - \bar{\pi}^{D^*} + \gamma b|$. This guarantees that the fraction of the electorate without weakly dominant strategies of voting is uniformly distributed over the interval $(\bar{\pi}^{D^*}, \bar{\pi}^{R^*})$ for *any* realization of **a**.

15. See Alesina and Rosenthal 1991 for technical derivations. Since we have a continuum of voters, the coalition-proof Nash concept is implemented by using recent results of Greenberg 1989.

16. Note that voter expectations depend upon the election forecasts, represented by Q, of the agents in the economy. Say that the agents in the economy had some forecast $\hat{Q}$. It might be thought that $\bar{\pi}^P$ depended on $\hat{Q}$ so we would require $\bar{\pi}^P(\hat{Q})$; and at the wage-setting stage, wages would be set taking into account the "reaction function" of the electorate. However, the functional forms in our model imply that $\bar{\pi}^P$ is independent of the electoral forecasts of the agents in the economy. The basic intuition is that increasing $\hat{Q}$ makes for a larger recession in the case of an R victory but at the same time results in a smaller expansion if D wins. The *difference* in growth rates offered by the parties remains constant as $\hat{Q}$ varies. Thus, there is a single value of $\bar{\pi}^P$.

17. Mankiw, Miron, and Weil (1987) provide empirical evidence of an important regime shift in 1914.

18. For a recent discussion and survey, see Romer and Romer 1989.

19. We did experiment with a specification that allowed for a constant Q different from ½. This entailed estimating separate impacts for Democrats and Republicans. We were not able to reject the null hypothesis of equal coefficients ($Q = $ ½), a not-surprising result given our small sample size.

20. The price of oil represents an additional source of transitory shocks. As adding a measure of oil prices to our growth equation leaves results (available on request) virtually unchanged and uses degrees of freedom, we have chosen not to use this variable.

21. Note however that the GNP growth series can be well described by either an MA(1) or an AR(1) process. Our choice of the MA(1) representation was driven by the tractability of the theoretical model in this case. See Christiano and Eichenbaum 1989 and Campbell and Mankiw 1987 on the difficulty of discriminating among ARMA models of GNP growth.

22. This model, in which growth is MA(1), implies that transitory shocks to growth have permanent effects on the level of output. The alternative hypothesis that the economy reverts to its long-term trend level is tested and rejected by Campbell and Mankiw (1987), in favor of the hypothesis that growth shocks have permanent effects. See also Christiano and Eichenbaum 1989.

23. Note that we assume that the impact of competence is immediate, whereas the inflationary surprise occurs only in the second year of each administration. If there were a similar gestation lag between the implementation of policies related to the competency dimension of the executive and their effects, retrospection would be of no use in assisting rational voters' inferences about an incumbent candidate's postelection effectiveness. Moreover, we found that the standard MA(1) model could not be rejected in favor of a model of growth with lagged competency. Results are available on request.

24. Under H_1, the likelihood ratio test statistic of .402 is drawn from a χ_1^2 distribution, yielding a *p*-value of .53.

25. We also make the simplifying assumption that $\mu_{1914} = 0$.

26. Many analysts (see Erikson 1989) include a direct measure of the incumbent president's popularity on "noneconomic" dimensions. This is typically constructed from opinion poll data collected a few months prior to the election or immediately after the election. In our model "personality" effects are incorporated in the error term φ_t^p, while the lagged House vote tracks evolving differences between the parties' ideal points and those of the voters. While measures of individual candidate effects would be desirable, the standard measures are subject, as Fair (1978) pointed out, to simultaneity bias (leaving aside questions of data availability prior to 1948). Consequently, we do not include survey-based measures in our specification.

27. If, following our formal model, there were competency-based voting in presidential, but not congressional, elections, it would be possible to have a negative coattails effect, also. The probability of reelecting the incumbent would increase with greater competence, reducing, via equation 24, the vote for the incumbent's congressional party.

28. It is important to control for demobilization, as well as mobilization, in evaluating the partisan surprise to the economy. In particular, the massive demobilization following World War II picks up the recession of 1946, the second year of a Democratic watch.

29. This estimate is within one standard deviation of Fair's (1988) estimate that an extra 1% of growth corresponds to an additional 1.01% of the incumbent growth share.

30. See Popkin 1991, pp. 91–92, for discussion of this point.

References

Alesina, Alberto. 1987. "Macroeconomic Policy in a Two Party System as a Repeated Game." *Quarterly Journal of Economics* 102:651–78.

Alesina, Alberto. 1988. "Macroeconomics and Politics." *National Bureau of Economic Research Macroeconomic Annual* 1988:11–55.

Alesina, Alberto, Gerald Cohen, and Nouriel Roubini. 1992. "Macroeconomic Policy and Elections in OECD Democracies." *Economics and Politics* 5:1–30.

Alesina, Alberto, and Howard Rosenthal. 1989. "Partisan Cycles in Congressional Elections and the Macroeconomy." *American Political Science Review* 83:373–98.

Alesina, Alberto, and Howard Rosenthal. 1991. "A Theory of Divided Government." Economics Department Working Paper No. 537. Massachusetts Institute of Technology.

Alesina, Alberto, and Nouriel Roubini. 1992. "Political Cycles in OECD Economies." *Review of Economic Studies* 59:663–88.

Alesina, Alberto, and Jeffrey Sachs. 1988. "Political Parties and the Business Cycle in the United States, 1948–1984." *Journal of Money, Credit, and Banking* 20:63–82.

Balke, Nathan S., and Robert J. Gordon. 1989. "The Estimation of Prewar Gross National Product: Methodology and New Evidence." *Journal of Political Economy* 97:38–92.

Barro, Robert, and David Gordon. 1983. "Rules, Discretion, and Reputation in a Model of Monetary Policy." *Journal of Monetary Economics* 12:101–22.

Beck, Nathaniel. 1982. "Parties, Administrations, and American Macroeconomic Outcomes." *American Political Science Review* 76:83–94.

Beck, Nathaniel. 1992. "Political Business Cycles, What Have We Learned?" University of California, Irvine. Mimeo.

Bernheim, Douglas, Bezael Peleg, and Michael Whinston. 1987. "Coalition Proof Nash Equilibria." *Journal of Economic Theory* 42:1–12.

Calvert, Randall L., and John A. Ferejohn. 1983. "Coattail Voting in Recent Presidential Elections." *American Political Science Review* 77:407–16.

Campbell, John Y., and N. Gregory Mankiw. 1987. "Are Output Fluctuations Transitory?" *Quarterly Journal of Economics* 102:857–79.

Chappell, Henry W., and William R. Keech. 1988. "The Unemployment Consequences of Partisan Monetary Policy." *Southern Economic Journal* 55:107–22.

Chappell, Henry W., and Mototshi Suzuki. 1990. "Aggregate Fluctuations for the U.S. Presidency, Senate, and House." University of South Carolina. Mimeo.

Christiano, Larry, and Martin Eichenbaum. 1989. "Unit Roots in GNP: Do We Know and Do We Care?" Federal Reserve Bank of Minneapolis. Mimeo.

Cukierman, Alex. 1984. *Inflation, Stagflation, Relative Prices, and Imperfect Information.* Cambridge: Cambridge University Press.

Cukierman, Alex, and Alan Meltzer. 1986. "A Positive Theory of Discretionary Policy, the Cost of Democratic Government, and the Benefits of a Constitution." *Economic Inquiry* 24:367–88.

Enelow, James, and Melvin Hinich. 1984. *The Spatial Theory of Voting.* Cambridge: Cambridge University Press.

Erikson, Robert. 1988. "The Puzzle of Midterm Loss." *Journal of Politics* 50:1012–29.

Erikson, Robert. 1989. "Economic Conditions and the Presidential Vote." *American Political Science Review* 83:67–76.

Erikson, Robert. 1990. "Economic Conditions and the Congressional Vote: A Review of the Macrolevel Evidence." *American Journal of Political Science* 34:373–99.

Fair, Ray. 1978. "The Effects of Economic Events on Votes for Presidents." *Review of Economics and Statistics* 60:159–72.

Fair, Ray. 1982. "The Effect of Economic Events on Votes for President: 1980 Results." *Review of Economic and Statistics* 64:322–25.

Fair, Ray. 1988. "The Effect of Economic Events on Votes for President: 1984 Update." *Political Behavior* 10:168–79.

Fiorina, Morris. 1981. *Retrospective Voting in American National Elections.* New Haven: Yale University Press.

Fiorina, Morris. 1988. "The Reagan Years: Turning Point to the Right or Creeping Towards the Middle." In *The Resurgence of Conservatism in Anglo-American Democracies,* ed. Barry Cooper et al. Durham: Duke University Press.

Fiorina, Morris. 1992. *Divided Government.* New York: Macmillan.

Fischer, Stanley. 1977. "Long Term Contracts, Rational Expectations, and the Optimal Money Supply Rule." *Journal of Political Economy* 85:191–206.

Golden, David, and James Poterba. 1980. "The Price of Popularity: The Political Business Cycle Reexamined." *American Journal of Political Science* 24:696–714.

Greenberg, Joseph. 1989. "Deriving Strong and Coalition-Proof Nash Equilibria from an Abstract System." *Journal of Economic Theory* 49:195–202.

Haynes, Stephen, and Joe Stone. 1987. "Should Political Models of the Business Cycle Be Revived?" Working Paper No. 8716. University of Oregon.

Hibbs, Douglas. 1977. "Political Parties and Macroeconomic Policy." *American Political Science Review* 71:1467–87.

Hibbs, Douglas. 1987. *The American Political Economy: Electoral Policy and Macroeconomics in Contemporary America.* Cambridge: Harvard University Press.

Jacobson, Gary. 1990. "Does the Economy Matter in Midterm Elections?" *American Journal of Political Science* 34:400–404.

Kiewiet, D. Roderick. 1983. *Macroeconomics and Micropolitics.* Chicago: University of Chicago Press.

Kiewiet, D. Roderick, and Michael Udell. 1991. "Back to the Beginning: A Reconsideration of the Electoral Effects of Short-Term Economic Fluctuations." Presented at the annual meeting of the Midwestern Political Science Association, Chicago.

Kramer, Gerald. 1971. "Short Term Fluctuations in U.S. Voting Behavior, 1896–1964." *American Political Science Review* 65:131–43.

Kydland, Finn, and Edward Prescott. 1977. "Rules Rather than Discretion: The Inconsistency of Optimal Plans." *Journal of Political Economy* 85:473–90.

Lepper, Susan. 1974. "Voting Behavior and Aggregate Policy Targets." *Public Choice* 18:67–82.

McCallum, Bennett. 1978. "The Political Business Cycle: An Empirical Test." *Southern Economic Journal* 44:504–15.

Mankiw, N. Gregory, Jeffrey A. Miron, and David N. Weil. 1987. "The Adjustment of Expectations to a Change in Regime: A Study of the Founding of the Federal Reserve." *American Economic Review* 77:358–74.

Nelson, Charles R., and Charles T. Plosser. 1982. "Trends and Random Walks in Macroeconomic Time Series." *Journal of Monetary Economics* 10:139–62.

Nordhaus, William. 1975. "The Political Business Cycle." *Review of Economic Studies* 42:169–90.

Nordhaus, William. 1989. "Alternative Approaches to Political Business Cycles." Paper on Economic Activity No. 2. Brookings Institution.

Persson, Torsten, and Guido Tabellini. 1990. *Macroeconomic Policy, Credibility, and Politics.* New York: Harwood Academic.

Popkin, Samuel. 1991. *The Reasoning Voter: Communication and Persuasion in Presidential Campaigns.* Chicago: University of Chicago Press.

Rogoff, Kenneth, and Anne Sibert. 1988. "Elections and Macroeconomic Policy Cycles." *Review of Economic Studies* 55:1–16.

Romer, Christina D. 1989. "The Prewar Business Cycle Reconsidered: New Estimates of Gross National Product 1869–1908." *Journal of Political Economy* 97:1–37.

Romer, Christina, and David Romer. 1989. "Does Monetary Policy Matter—a New Test in the Spirit of Friedman and Schwartz." *Macroeconomic Annual.* Cambridge: National Bureau of Economic Research.

Rothemberg, Thomas J. 1973. "Efficient Estimations with A Priori Information." Cowles Foundation Monograph No. 23. New Haven: Yale University Press.

Taylor, John B. 1980. "Aggregate Dynamics and Staggered Contracts." *Journal of Political Economy* 88:1–23.

Tobin, James. 1972. "Inflation and Unemployment." *American Economic Review* 62:1–18.

Tufte, Edward B. 1978. *Political Control of the Economy.* Princeton: Princeton University Press.

4.7. Recent Trends in Tax Progressivity

Congress of the United States, Congressional Budget Office

The last two decades have seen unprecedented changes in tax policy. Major changes were made in 1981, 1986, 1989, and 1993, and smaller but significant changes were enacted in 1978, 1982, 1984, and 1990. These various changes were usually justified in terms of their effects on economic efficiency. But they also had significant effects on equality.

This reading from the Congressional Budget Office outlines the effects of the major changes in tax policy. Two separate stories emerge from this account. We see an extraordinary number of changes in the income tax. The changes in the early part of the Reagan administration benefited the wealthy and made the tax more regressive. Most of the other changes, especially the changes made by the Clinton administration in 1993, made the tax more progressive. By 1994 the tax was more progressive than it had been at the beginning of the period. There was very little legislative activity affecting the Social Security tax, the other major source of federal tax revenue. But over the period the overall share of this regressive tax increased relative to the income tax.

Major tax changes seem likely to continue. Most of the tax changes proposed by the Republican congressional majority elected in 1994 would have the effect of making the income tax significantly more regressive.

On August 10, 1993, the President signed into law the Omnibus Budget Reconciliation Act of 1993. That act was the latest in a series of major changes in the federal tax laws. Since 1977, the Congress has enacted no fewer than eight major tax bills: the Revenue Act of 1978, the Economic Recovery Tax Act of 1981 (ERTA), the Tax Equity and Fiscal Responsibility Act of 1982 (TEFRA), the Deficit Reduction Act of 1984 (DEFRA), the Tax Reform Act of 1986 (TRA), the Omnibus Budget Reconciliation Act of 1989 (OBRA–89), the Omnibus Budget Reconciliation Act of 1990 (OBRA–90), and, most recently, OBRA–93. The Congress also passed the Social Security Amendments of 1977, which scheduled a series of increases in payroll tax rates that took place over the following decade, and the Social Security Amendments of 1983, which accelerated the effective dates of those increases and, for the first time, made a portion of Social Security benefits subject to the individual income tax.

These changes in the law have resulted in a very different tax structure today than before 1980. The income tax rate schedule is lower and flatter, and many tax preferences under the individual income tax have been tightened or eliminated. The top corporate tax rate is lower, but the investment tax credit has been repealed, and other business investment incentives, which were expanded in ERTA, were scaled back or eliminated by subsequent legislation. The base for payroll taxes is wider, and rates are higher. Some excise tax rates are higher today than they were a decade ago, partly offsetting the tendency of revenues from excise taxes to decline in real terms with inflation.

Despite these major changes, the distribution of federal taxes among income groups was nearly the same by the end of the 1980s as it was in 1977. When the latest changes from OBRA–90 and OBRA–93 are fully in place, however, the distribution of federal taxes will be more progressive than it was in 1977. This overall pattern is explained by two developments that tug in opposite directions. The individual income tax will be significantly more progressive, but the government has also come to rely more on social insurance taxes, a relatively regressive source.

Greater Progressivity in Total Effective Tax Rates

One way to gauge tax progressivity is to compare the ratio of taxes paid to before-tax income for different family groups. This ratio is called the effective tax rate. A tax is progressive if the effective tax rate for groups with higher income is greater than the effective rate for groups with lower income.

To analyze the progressivity of the tax structure, CBO divides families into five groups by family income, with equal numbers of people in each group. In 1994, the effective tax rate—the combination of income, payroll, and excise taxes—is projected to range from 5.1 percent for the 20 percent of the population with the lowest income (the bottom quintile) to 27.7 percent for the 20 percent of families with the highest income (the top quintile).

The sweeping revisions in tax laws that were enacted between 1977 and 1993 actually resulted in little change in either the overall levels or the distribution of effective tax rates by income groups between the beginning and the end of that 16-year span (see Figure 1). The major exception is the lowest income group. Once the changes enacted in OBRA–90 and OBRA–93 are fully in place, the effective tax rate for families in the lowest income quintile will be lower than in any year from 1977 to the present.

The level and distribution of effective tax rates did, however, shift in one

Table 1

Effect of Extending Tax Provisions That Have Recently Expired or Will Expire in 1994 Through 1999 (By fiscal year, in billions of dollars)

Tax Provision	Expiration Date	1994	1995	1996	1997	1998	1999
Expired Provision							
Health Insurance Deduction for Self-Employed	12/31/93	-0.2	-0.5	-0.5	-0.6	-0.6	-0.7
Provisions Expiring in 1994							
Generalized System of Preferences	9/30/94	n.a.	-0.5	-0.6	-0.6	-0.6	-0.7
Deductions for Contributions to Private Foundations	12/31/94	n.a.	a	a	a	a	a
Targeted Jobs Tax Credit	12/31/94	n.a.	-0.1	-0.2	-0.4	-0.4	-0.5
Exclusion for Employer-Provided Education Assistance	12/31/94	n.a.	-0.2	-0.5	-0.6	-0.6	-0.7
Orphan Drug Tax Credit	12/31/94	n.a.	a	a	a	a	a
Provisions Expiring in 1995							
Denial of Deduction for Certain Noncomplying Health Plans	5/12/95	n.a.	-0.1	-0.1	-0.2	-0.2	-0.2
Research and Experimentation Credit	6/30/95	n.a.	-0.3	-1.0	-1.7	-2.1	-2.6
Allocation Rules for Research and Experimentation Credit	7/31/95	n.a.	-0.3	-0.6	-0.6	-0.6	-0.7
Fees for IRS Letter Rulings	9/30/95	n.a.	n.a.	b	b	b	b
Commercial Aviation Exemption from Transportation Fuels Tax	9/30/95	n.a.	n.a.	-0.4	-0.4	-0.4	-0.5
Corporate Tax Dedicated to Superfund	12/31/95	n.a.	n.a.	0.4	0.7	0.7	0.7
Provision Expiring in 1996							
Nonconventional Fuels Credit for Fuel from Biomass and Coal	12/31/96	n.a.	n.a.	n.a.	a	a	a
Provision Expiring in 1998							
FUTA Surtax of 0.2 Percentage Points	12/31/98	n.a.	n.a.	n.a.	n.a.	n.a.	0.9

Source: Joint Committee on Taxation.

Notes: No provisions are scheduled to expire in 1997, and the provisions expiring in 1999 do not expire until the end of the fiscal year. The list does not include expiring excise taxes that are assumed to be extended.

a. Loss of less than $50 million.
b. Increase of less than $50 million.

Figure 1. **Effective Federal Tax Rates in Selected Years, 1977–1994, by Income Group**

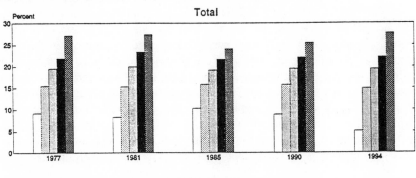

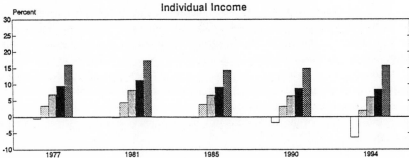

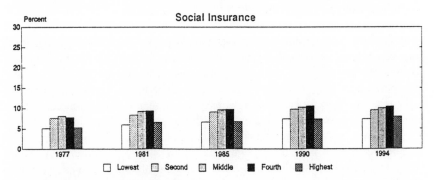

Source: Congressional Budget Office.

Note: Families are ranked by adjusted family income, with an equal number of people per quintile. Rates for 1994 are projected using the fully implemented rates for the earned income tax credit set in the Omnibus Budget Reconciliation Act of 1993.

direction and then back again during the intervening years. Federal taxes became less progressive between 1977 and 1985, as effective rates fell for high-income families and rose for low-income families. They then became more progressive, reversing the trend of the previous eight years.

For the most part, the pendulum had already swung back by 1990; in that year, effective tax rates for most family income groups were nearly the same as they had been for comparable families in 1977, except for families in the highest income group. Those families faced a total tax rate of 25.5 percent in 1990 versus 27.2 percent in 1977, with most of the decline concentrated in the top 1 percent of the income distribution. Several factors contributed to the fall in effective tax rates for these highest-income families. The top individual income marginal tax rate dropped from 70 percent in 1977 to 28 percent in 1990; the drop in the top marginal rate applicable to earned income and to capital gains, which had not been subject to the full 70 percent rate, was somewhat less. Effective corporate income tax rates (measured in relation to these families' total income) declined as taxable corporate profits grew more slowly than personal income.

But between 1990 and 1993, families at the top of the income scale were subjected to several tax increases. OBRA–90 set the top marginal income tax rate at 31 percent and limited the benefits from itemized deductions and personal exemptions for those families. Among other changes, OBRA–93 added new individual income tax rates of 36 percent and 39.6 percent and made all earnings subject to Medicare's Hospital Insurance (HI) payroll tax. (In 1993, earnings over $135,000 were shielded from that tax.) These changes will push the total effective tax rate for the highest income families back near the rate for comparable families in 1977.

Greater Progressivity in Individual Income Tax Rates

Total federal taxes became more progressive because of the trends in their leading component, individual income taxes. Nearly half of all federal revenues come from individual income taxes. Social insurance payroll taxes now account for more than one-third, corporate income taxes for about 10 percent, and excise taxes for less than 5 percent of revenues. The remaining revenues come from estate and gift taxes, customs duties, and other miscellaneous receipts.

Viewed in isolation, individual income taxes will be more progressive than they were in 1977 once the changes enacted in OBRA–90 and OBRA–93 are fully implemented, largely because of an expanded earned income tax credit. The EITC is a refundable credit available to low-income working families. Although the refundable portion of the credit is counted as an outlay in the federal budget, it nevertheless stems from provisions of the tax code and is thus treated in distributional analyses as a feature of the individual income tax system. OBRA–90 greatly increased the amount of the credit, as did OBRA–93; and the 1993 expansion for the first time made low-income workers without children eligible for a small credit.

Average effective individual income tax rates were lower for families in all income quintiles in 1990 than for comparable families in 1977. In fact, effective individual income tax rates became significantly less than zero for families in the lowest income quintile for the first time in 1990 because of the liberalizations in the EITC; that is, the average family in the lowest quintile received payments from the government under the individual income tax.

Once all of the changes from OBRA–90 and OBRA–93 are in place, effective individual income tax rates will still be lower for families in the four lower income quintiles than in 1977 but will have returned to 1977 levels for the top quintile. And the effective subsidy received by families in the lowest income quintile will be about 10 times as big as the subsidy received by comparable families in 1977.

Greater Reliance on Payroll Taxes

Total federal taxes might have become even more progressive if payroll taxes for social insurance had not grown in importance as a source of federal revenues. They will account for an estimated 37 percent of federal revenue in 1994, up from 30 percent in 1977. Payroll taxes are less progressive than federal income taxes; effective federal payroll tax rates are progressive only at the lowest end of the income distribution, virtually flat across the three middle income quintiles, and regressive at the top (see the bottom panel of Figure 1). Although payroll taxes did become more progressive between 1977 and 1994—mainly because the ceiling on wages subject to the Social Security and Medicare taxes was steadily lifted (and ultimately, in the case of Medicare, repealed)—payroll taxes remain much less progressive than income taxes. Hence, their increasing weight in the revenue totals has dampened the overall move toward greater progressivity.

Marginal Tax Rates After OBRA–93

With the enactment of OBRA–93, marginal tax rates on earnings—the fraction of the last dollar of earnings paid in taxes will range from a subsidy of 26 percent to a tax of 49 percent when both individual income taxes and payroll taxes are taken into account (see Figure 2).

Taxpayers with the highest income will face marginal tax rates of nearly 43 percent. This rate is lower than the 50 percent top rate on earnings in 1977. As recently as 1990, however, the highest income tax bracket was 28 percent, and high-income taxpayers were not subject to further payroll taxes as their income rose. OBRA–93 added a 39.6 percent bracket to the individual income tax. When the limitation on itemized deductions, which was made permanent by OBRA–93, is taken into account, the top income tax rate reaches 40.8 percent. Furthermore, all earnings are now subject to Medicare's HI payroll tax of 1.45 percent paid by both employers and employees. Because the employer share of the payroll tax is deductible, the extension of the HI tax to high-income workers adds another 2.1 percentage points to the top tax rate.

Figure 2. **Marginal Tax Rate on Earnings in 1994, Including Payroll and Income Taxes, for a One-Earner Couple with Two Children**

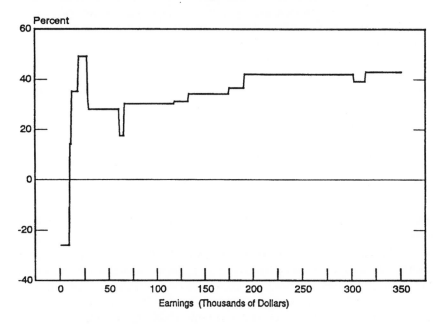

Source: Congressional Budget Office.

Note: All calculations use 1994 tax law except for the earned income tax credit, which is at 1996 levels. The estimates assume that all income is from self-employment and that the taxpayer has deductions equal to the greater of the standard deduction or 20 percent of earnings.

The workers facing the highest marginal tax rates are those whose earnings are in the range in which the EITC disappears—essentially, in the low $20,000 range for a couple with two children. Such families lose about 21 cents of EITC payments for every dollar of additional earnings. Added to the 15 percent individual income tax and the Social Security payroll tax of 7.65 percent on both employees and employers, the total marginal tax rate on these families is just over 49 percent when interactions between the taxes are taken into account.

Very low income workers with children are subsidized by the federal government. These workers are exempt from the regular income tax; and for workers with at least two children, the EITC is increased by 40 cents for each additional dollar of earnings up to $8,425. This subsidy more than offsets the additional payroll taxes they owe, and their marginal tax rate is negative.

Recent Trends in Economic Outcomes

The Effects of Changes in Tariffs

In the period since the Second World War, two developments have opened up world trade. One is the formation of regional trading blocs such as the European Economic Community (EEC). The other is a series of tariff reductions agreed to by most nations under the sponsorship of the General Agreement on Tariffs and Trade (GATT). These reductions have had the largest effect in Europe. But, as Figure 1 makes plain, they have also substantially increased both imports and exports in the United States. Since the mid-1970s, imports have tripled and exports have almost doubled as a percent of GDP. This was not just due to the GATT agreements, but they are an important reason.

Since 1967 trade liberalization has become more difficult, as interests hurt by previous cuts pushed for protection. But despite the greater pressure for protection, there has been a continuance of trade liberalization. In the last decade Presidents Reagan and Bush negotiated a free-trade agreement with Canada, our largest trading partner, and Presidents Bush and Clinton extended the agreement to our third-largest trading partner, Mexico, thereby creating the North American Free Trade Area. At least as significant was the so-called Uruguay Round of GATT negotiations ratified by the United States in 1994. This agreement among 158 nations lowered tariffs and nontariff barriers and included provisions on services and agricultural products as well as on manufactured goods. While less important than previous GATT agreements, the Uruguay Round extended free trade when there were many pressures to reduce it. Even in its more protectionist moods, the United States has often pushed for free trade. For example, in 1995 President Clinton threatened the Japanese with prohibitive 100 percent tariffs on its luxury cars, but he did it to try to open the Japanese automobile market to free trade, not to close off the American market to Japan.

As international trade and investment have expanded, so have international

501

Figure 1. **Imports and Exports as a Percentage of GDP, 1946–1993**

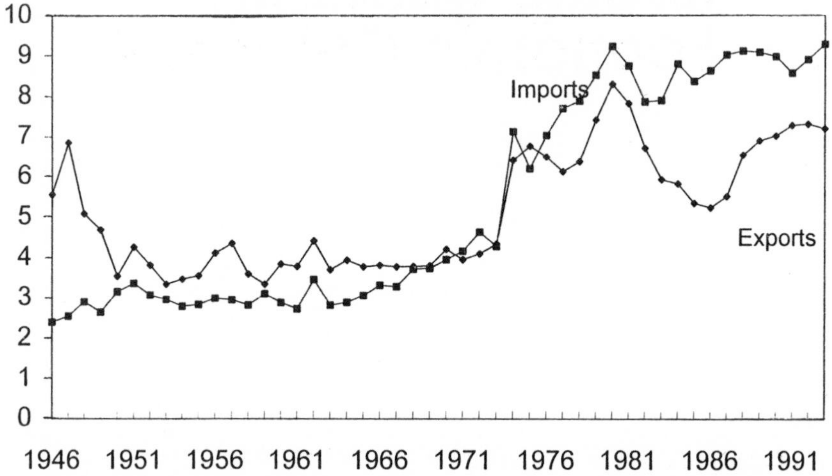

Source: Council of Economic Advisors, *Economic Report of the President 1995.*

currency markets. Over one trillion dollars worth of currencies are traded every day. It has become increasingly difficult for nations to manage the value of their currency or to control where their citizens invest their money. While there have been no major institutional changes in the last decade, cooperation between governments and central banks has increased in this period, partly in response to the increasing inability of individual countries to affect the currency markets. While the greatest attempts at coordination have taken place between European countries trying to move toward a unified currency, the United States has also increasingly coordinated its monetary policies with other countries; as, for example, when the United States and Japan both lowered interest rates in July 1995.

These recent changes generally reinforce the points made by Reich and Frieden. Both authors see the position of labor weakening relative to capital, and recent events support this. Union strength has continued to decline, with the major exceptions being in government and service employment, where jobs cannot easily be exported. Between 1983 and 1993 the percent of the workforce that was unionized fell from 20 percent to 16 percent (*Statistical Abstract 1994*, 439). As this happened, the share of gross domestic product going to wage earners fell. While GDP expanded 39 percent from 1980 to 1994, average hourly earnings actually *fell* by 5 percent in the same period even before one counts the erosion in wage and salary benefits (*Economic Report of the President* 1995, 276, 326). In the economic recovery from 1991 to 1995, profits increased at a rate of about 50 percent more than in previous recoveries, while hourly wages and benefits increased at around half the rate of previous recoveries. It is, however, worth noting that the effects of competition are not confined to unskilled and semi-skilled workers, as Reich implies. In recent years there has been some exporting

Figure 2. **Unemployment and Real Per Capita Disposable Income, 1987–1995**

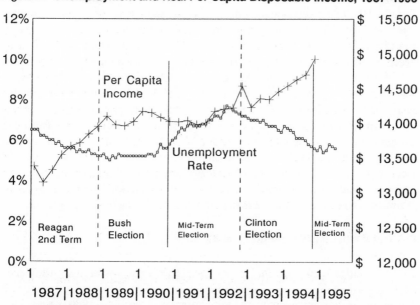

Sources: Council of Economic Advisors, *Economic Report of the President 1995*; *Los Angeles Times*, July 8, 1995, p. 17.

of skilled jobs, with consequent negative effects on professional and managerial pay (Bernstein 1995, 54–62).

There is also data to support Reich's contention that inequality is increasing. In 1989 the portion of market income going to the bottom 40 percent of the population was 8.6 percent. By 1992 it had fallen to 8.3 percent. However, this evidence should be taken cautiously, as most experts think the 1986 tax changes have affected income reporting (Feldstein 1995).

The Short-Term Political Business Cycle

Political business cycle theory says that, for political purposes, the timing of economic growth is more important than its extent. Growth in the year before an election secures reelection, while the earlier record is barely relevant. How has this theory performed in the last fifteen years? Figure 2 indicates that it has done reasonably well but has not always predicted accurately. In terms of presidential elections, it was consistent with the 1984 and 1988 elections where first Reagan, and then Bush, won after substantial economic growth in the preceding year. But it did less well in predicting the 1992 election. Before the election many of the most sophisticated proponents of the theory predicted a Bush victory, based on the fact that the economy had been growing the year before the election. The fact that Bush lost does not necessarily disprove that the economy affected the election, however. Bush, after all, had delivered anemic rates of growth for most of his term. But it does cast doubt on the notion that short-term movement is all that voters look at. The fit to recent congressional mid-term elections is even less impressive. The loss of Republican seats in 1990 fits the data, but the Republican sweep in 1994 should have been a Democratic sweep, according to the theory.

Finally, one should note that the part of the theory that says presidents manipulate the economy to secure reelection has run into the weak control actually exercised by presidents over the economy. While every president in our period tried to make sure that the economy was doing well at election time, Bush did not get the economy moving early enough. Further, the part of the theory that says presidents should depress the economy shortly after the election does not seem to accurately describe the behavior of any of the three presidents in our period. Overall, then, the results seem more consistent with the more skeptical positions of Fiorina and Alesina than with the stronger claims made by Tufte.

Political Parties and Economic Growth

Taken overall, the government has not been terribly successful in securing economic growth in this period. Unemployment in the 1981–1994 period averaged 7 percent of the workforce, compared to 5.2 percent in the 1947–1980 period. Real per capita GDP increased at a rate of 1.5 percent from 1981 to 1994, compared to 1.8 percent in the 1947–1980 period. However, inflation at 4.3 percent from 1980 to 1994 was a little better than the 4.5 percent averaged in the earlier period.

Table 1 shows economic outcomes under each president since 1947. On the face of it, it would appear that Reagan was successful in managing the economy, Clinton was about average, and Bush was a crashing failure, with the worst rate of economic growth since the Great Depression. In fact, the numbers are misleading. Most think that Bush's failure can be directly traced to the extravagant tax cuts and defense increases of his predecessor, and a look at the record shows that the economic policies undertaken under Bush and Clinton are more alike than different. Bush should be given credit for his willingness to break his no new taxes pledge when he thought that the state of the economy demanded it be broken, and Clinton should be given credit for understanding that deficit reduction would serve the country better than the tax cuts and investment spending that formed the bulk of his platform.

Political parties seek to deliver things that will improve their chances of reelection, while furthering their ideology. Both parties believe that it is good to have more economic growth, less inflation, and less unemployment. However, the Republicans historically have placed more weight on controlling inflation while the Democrats have worried more about unemployment. As Table 1 shows, economic growth has typically been greater and unemployment lower under Democratic presidents, while Republican presidents have typically reduced inflation from the high rates obtaining at the end of Democratic presiden-

Table 1

Economic Outcomes under Recent American Presidents

	Truman	Eisenhower	Kennedy/ Johnson	Nixon/ Ford	Carter	Reagan	Bush	Clinton
Unemployment Rate	4.1	4.9	4.9	5.8	6.5	7.5	6.2	6.5
Inflation	5.8	1.4	2.0	6.4	9.7	4.7	4.2	2.7
Per Capita Growth in GNP	2.2	0.6	3.2	1.5	1.3	2.1	0.1	1.8

Source: Council of Economic Advisors, *Economic Report of the President 1995*, U.S. Department of Commerce *Historical Statistics*.

Notes:

1. The Truman figures start in 1947 in order to exclude the atypical war and postwar years.
2. The change in per capita GNP figures starts six months after a president assumes office and ends six months afterward to allow for lagged effects on growth. The Clinton figures cover only the first three years.

Table 2

Government Redistribution of Family Income 1992

	Lowest fifth	Second fifth	Third fifth	Fourth fifth	Highest fifth
Market income	0.9	7.4	15.4	25.3	51
Less federal and state taxes	1.1	8.4	16.3	25.5	48.6
Plus Social Security and other non-means tested cash transfers	3.6	10.2	16.5	24.5	45.1
Plus Medicare	3.8	10.7	16.9	24.4	44.3
Plus means tested cash transfers	4.4	10.8	16.8	24.2	43.9
Plus Medicaid	4.5	10.9	16.8	24.2	43.7
Plus means tested non-cash transfers	4.9	11.0	16.7	24.0	43.3
Plus imputed income from home ownership	5.1	11.0	16.7	23.9	43.3

Source: U.S. Department of Commerce, *Statistical Abstract of the United States 1994*, p. 481.

cies. Events over the last fifteen years have been roughly in line with this tendency. The Federal Reserve was given free reign under the Reagan administration to reduce inflation, and growth under the two Republican presidents taken together has been below long-term averages. The first two years of the Clinton presidency also show declining unemployment and the increase in growth predicted by Alesina et al. But there also seems some tendency toward convergence. The tax cuts advocated by Reagan and House Republicans are reminiscent of previous Democratic presidents such as Kennedy, and the deficit reduction undertaken by Clinton reminds one of the policies of earlier Republican presidents.

Parties and Income Redistribution

Income redistribution is often seen as the defining difference between the two parties. Democrats typically seek to redistribute downwards and Republicans typically seek to redistribute upwards. Most Americans do not realize how dependent the less fortunate are on government programs. Table 2 shows the percent of all income going to each fifth of the population. Without government programs, the 13,600,000 families in the lowest fifth would earn 0.9 percent of all income, or around $1,500 a year. After government programs, this increases to around $8,500. For families in the second fifth, government intervention increases their average incomes from around $15,500 to around $23,000.

But is also clear that government programs leave a substantial amount of inequality in place. Even after government redistribution, the average person in the top quintile makes around $9 for every $1 made by someone in the bottom quintile.

A lot of the redistributional sound and fury between the two major parties has been concentrated on taxes, and it is clear from the CBO reading that the income tax has become more or less progressive depending largely on the political balance. But while taxes are important to the upper fifth of the population, the most important programs for the lower 40 percent of the population are Social Security, Medicare and Medicaid, and means-tested programs such as Aid to Families with Dependent Children and Food Stamps. For most of the postwar period, the pattern has been one where Democrats expanded all these programs when politically strong and Republicans left Social Security and Medicare alone and cut means-tested welfare programs a little when they were strong.

With the Democratic stranglehold on Congress finally broken, the Republicans are showing signs of wanting to change this pattern. As well as pushing for the standard tax changes to make the income tax more regressive, Congressional Republicans are currently pushing for reasonably heavy cuts in means-tested welfare programs and fairly heavy reductions in the future growth of Medicare and Medicaid. While President Clinton has vetoed some of these cuts, he has proven willing to make some cuts in all the programs, and a Republican victory in the 1996 presidential race could lead to substantial changes in government redistribution.

Government Growth

Perhaps the biggest change that has taken place in the last fifteen years has been in the area of government spending. Between 1950 and 1975 federal government spending rose from 16 percent of GDP to 22.1 percent of GDP. But since then, despite continual laments about runaway government spending, outlays have changed very little as a percent of GNP. Spending was 22.3 percent of GDP in 1980, 23.9 percent in 1985, 22.9 percent in 1990, and 22.3 percent in 1994. There was also a change in the composition of spending. In 1985 defense was 27 percent of outlays and social programs were 50 percent. By 1994 defense had fallen to 19 percent and human resources had risen to 59 percent (Council of Economic Advisors).

This slowdown is partly due to the increasing power of Republicans and particularly the limits placed on Congress by the Reagan-era deficits. But government spending was slowing worldwide in this period and other explanations are probably also important. Slower economic growth and the decline of communism were especially significant. The slowdown in spending growth would have been greater but for the maturing of expensive social programs and high rates of medical inflation. Finally, it is worth noting that whatever has caused the halt in the growth of government, it is very unlikely to be the factors cited by Cameron.

The reader will recall from Figure 1 that the exposure of the United States to international competition almost doubled in the 1974–1978 period. Yet far from sparking a big increase in spending, this increase coincided with the halt in government growth.

Conclusion

We saw at the beginning of this book that many think that the government bears primary responsibility for keeping the economy healthy, for ensuring proper distribution, and for securing the correct amount of public goods. How successful has the federal government been in securing these aims in the past fifteen years? Starting with stabilization, the key facts are that economic growth in this period has been lower than in the period preceding it and unemployment has been higher. Offsetting this to some degree are decreases in inflation and improvements in productivity, which may help future growth. It is also fair to note that the slowdown in growth has been even more pronounced in other countries. Nonetheless this has not been a good period for economic growth.

It has also been a bad period for redistribution. The most important factor was that changes in international trade and other factors have worsened the distribution of market income. As we have seen, the wages of working-class and middle-class families have declined while the income of the upper middle class and the wealthy has increased. While this was not the fault of government, it made its task harder. Looking at government attempts at redistribution this was a period of little change. The first half of the '80s saw changes in the tax code and cuts in expenditures that benefited the rich at the expense of the poor. But the period since then has reversed this trend, with the federal income tax becoming more progressive and social welfare expenditures increasing a little. However, these changes have not reversed the market changes, and poverty has generally grown in this period. The recent Republican victory in Congress should accelerate this trend.

The allocation between public and private goods has been moving in the direction of private goods. If one excludes transfer payments (which are not really public goods), the percent of GDP spent on public goods has declined during the last fifteen years. This is likely to continue for the next few years. Whether this is good or bad depends on what one values. Are the cuts in energy research, defense, highways, and Amtrak justified by the increased spending on computers, clothes, insurance, and drugs that they make possible? Would a national health system have been a good idea? Reasonable people can disagree on these questions.

Taken overall, the last fifteen years have not been a high point for economic growth, redistribution, or sensible policy making. It will be interesting to see if policy and outcomes improve in the future.

References

Bernstein, Aaron. 1995. "The Wage Squeeze." *Business Week*, July 17: 54–62.

Feldstein, Martin. 1995. "Behavioral Responses to Tax Rates: Evidence from the Tax Reform Act of 1986." *American Economic Review* 85 (May): 170–174.

U.S. Council of Economic Advisors. 1995. *Economic Report of the President 1995.* Washington D.C.: U.S. Government Printing Office.

U.S. Department of Commerce. 1975. *Historical Statistics of the United States.* Washington D.C.: U.S. Government Printing Office.

U.S. Department of Commerce. 1994. *Statistical Abstract of the United States 1994.* Washington D.C.: U.S. Government Printing Office.

About the Editor

Paul Peretz completed his B.A. in economics and political science at the Victoria University and earned a Ph.D. at the University of Chicago. He has taught at Columbia, the University of Washington, Brown, and Cornell and is currently professor of political science at the California State University, Fullerton. Peretz is the author of *The Political Economy of Inflation in the United States* and has written extensively on political-economic topics.